# The Polar World: A Popular Description of Man and Nature in the Arctic and Antarctic Regions of the Globe

## Georg Hartwig

THE 'EREBUS' AND THE 'TERROR' AMONG ICEBERGS.

# THE POLAR WORLD:

A POPULAR DESCRIPTION OF

## MAN AND NATURE

IN THE

ARCTIC AND ANTARCTIC REGIONS OF THE GLOBE.

BY

### DR. G. HARTWIG,

AUTHOR OF
'THE SEA AND ITS LIVING WONDERS,' 'THE HARMONIES OF NATURE,'
AND 'THE TROPICAL WORLD,'

*WITH EIGHT CHROMOXYLOGRAPHIC PLATES, THREE MAPS, AND*
*NUMEROUS WOODCUTS.*

LONDON:
LONGMANS, GREEN, AND CO.
1869.

# PREFACE.

THE OBJECT of the following pages is to describe the Polar World in its principal natural features, to point out the influence of its long winter-night and fleeting summer on the developement of vegetable and animal existence, and finally to picture man waging the battle of life against the dreadful climate of the high latitudes of our globe either as the inhabitant of their gloomy solitudes, or as the bold investigator of their mysteries.

The table of contents shows the great variety of interesting subjects embraced within a comparatively narrow compass; and as my constant aim has been to convey solid instruction under an entertaining form, I venture to hope that the public will grant this new work the favourable reception given to my previous writings.

G. HARTWIG.

HEIDELBERG: *January* 2, 1869.

# CONTENTS.

## PART I.

## THE ARCTIC REGIONS.

—◆◇◆—

### CHAPTER I.

#### THE ARCTIC LANDS.

### CHAPTER II.

#### ARCTIC LAND QUADRUPEDS AND BIRDS.

## CHAPTER VII.

### THE ICELANDERS.

## CHAPTER VIII.

### THE WESTMAN ISLANDS.

## CHAPTER IX.

### FROM DRONTHEIM TO THE NORTH CAPE.

## CHAPTER X.

### SPITZBERGEN—BEAR ISLAND—JAN MEYEN.

## CHAPTER XI.

### NOVAYA ZEMLYA.

## CHAPTER XII.

### THE LAPPS.

## CHAPTER XIII.

### MATTHIAS ALEXANDER CASTRÉN.

## CHAPTER XIV.

### THE SAMOJEDES.

## CHAPTER XV.

### THE OSTJAKS.

## CHAPTER XVI.

### CONQUEST OF SIBERIA BY THE RUSSIANS—THEIR VOYAGES OF DISCOVERY ALONG THE SHORES OF THE POLAR SEA.

## CHAPTER XVII.

### SIBERIA—FUR TRADE AND GOLD-DIGGINGS.

## CHAPTER XVIII.

### MIDDENDORFF'S ADVENTURES IN TAIMURLAND.

## CHAPTER XIX.

### THE JAKUTS.

## CHAPTER XX.

### WRANGEL.

## CHAPTER XXI.

### THE TUNGUSI.

## CHAPTER XXII.

### GEORGE WILLIAM STELLER.

## CHAPTER XXIII.

### KAMTSCHATKA.

## CHAPTER XXXIV.

### NEWFOUNDLAND.

## CHAPTER XXXV.

### GREENLAND.

# PART II.

# THE ANTARCTIC REGIONS.

## CHAPTER XXXVI.

### THE ANTARCTIC OCEAN.

## CHAPTER XXXVII.

### ANTARCTIC VOYAGES OF DISCOVERY.

## CHAPTER XXXVIII.

### THE STRAIT OF MAGELLAN.

## CHAPTER XXXIX.

### PATAGONIA AND THE PATAGONIANS.

## CHAPTER XL.

### THE FUEGIANS.

# LIST OF ILLUSTRATIONS.

## CHROMOXYLOGRAPHS.

## MAPS.

## WOODCUTS.

*The following Illustrations are taken, by permission of* Mr. MURRAY, *from* Sir John Ross' Voyage, *viz.* —

The Erebus and Terror among Icebergs.
Cape Crozier and Mount Terror.
Christmas Harbour, Kerguelen's Land.
Mount Minto.

# PART I.

————•————

# THE ARCTIC REGIONS.

Arctic Forest and Aurora.

# CHAPTER I.

### THE ARCTIC LANDS.

The Barren Grounds or Tundri—Abundance of Animal Life on the Tundri in Sum-
mer—Their Silence and Desolation in Winter—Protection afforded to Vegetation
by the Snow—Flower-growth in the highest Latitudes—Character of Tundra
Vegetation—Southern Boundary-line of the Barren Grounds—Their Extent—
The Forest Zone—Arctic Trees—Slowness of their Growth—Monotony of the
Northern Forests — Mosquitoes — The various Causes which determine the
Severity of an Arctic Climate—Insular and Continental Position—Currents—
Winds—Extremes of Cold observed by Sir E. Belcher and Dr. Kane—How is
Man able to support the Rigours of an Arctic Winter?—Proofs of a milder
Climate having once reigned in the Arctic Regions—Its Cause according to
Dr. Oswald Heer—Peculiar Beauties of the Arctic Regions—Sunset—Long Lunar
Nights—The Aurora.

A GLANCE at a map of the Arctic regions shows us that
many of the rivers belonging to the three continents—
Europe, Asia, America—discharge their waters into the Polar
Ocean or its tributary bays. The territories drained by these
streams, some of which (such as the Mackenzie, the Lena,
the Yenisei, and the Obi) rank among the giant rivers of
the earth, form, along with the islands within or near the

Arctic circle, the vast region over which the frost-king reigns supreme.

Man styles himself the lord of the earth, and may with some justice lay claim to the title in more genial lands where, armed with the plough, he compels the soil to yield him a variety of fruits; but in those desolate tracts which are winter-bound during the greater part of the year, he is generally a mere wanderer over its surface—a hunter, a fisherman, or a herdsman—and but few small settlements, separated from each other by immense deserts, give proof of his having made some weak attempts to establish a footing.

It is difficult to determine with precision the limits of the Arctic lands, since many countries situated as low as latitude 60° or even 50°, such as South Greenland, Labrador, Kamtschatka, or the country about Lake Baikal, have in their climate and productions a decidedly Arctic character, while others of a far more northern position, such as the coast of Norway, enjoy even in winter a remarkably mild temperature. But they are naturally divided into two principal and well-marked zones—that of the forests, and that of the treeless wastes.

The latter, comprising the islands within the Arctic circle, form a belt, more or less broad bounded by the continental shores of the North Polar seas, and gradually merging towards the south into the forest-region, which encircles them with a garland of evergreen coniferæ.

This treeless zone bears the name of the 'barren grounds,' or the 'barrens' in North America, and of 'tundri' in Siberia and European Russia. Its want of trees is caused not so much by its high northern latitude as by the cold sea-winds which sweep unchecked over the islands or the flat coast-lands of the Polar Ocean, and for miles and miles compel even the hardiest plant to cronch before the blast and creep along the ground.

Nothing can be more melancholy than the aspect of the boundless morasses or arid wastes of the tundri. Dingy mosses and grey lichens form the chief vegetation, and a few scanty grasses or dwarfish flowers that may have found a refuge in some more sheltered spot are unable to relieve the dull monotony of the scene.

In winter, when animal life has mostly retreated to the south or sought a refuge in burrows or in caves, an awful silence, interrupted only by the hooting of a snow-owl or the yelping of a fox, reigns over their vast expanse; but in spring, when the brown earth reappears from under the melted snow and the swamps begin to thaw, enormous flights of wild birds appear upon the scene and enliven it for a few months. An admirable instinct leads their winged legions from distant climes to the Arctic wildernesses, where in the morasses or lakes, on the banks of the rivers, on the flat strands, or along the fish-teeming coasts, they find an abundance of food, and where at the same time they can with greater security build their nests and rear their young. Some remain on the skirts of the forest-region; others, flying further northwards, lay their eggs upon the naked tundra.

Eagles and hawks follow the traces of the natatorial and strand birds; troops of ptarmigans roam among the stunted bushes; and when the sun shines, the finch or the snow-bunting warbles his merry note.

While thus the warmth of summer attracts hosts of migratory birds to the Arctic wildernesses, shoals of salmon and sturgeons enter the rivers in obedience to the instinct that forces them to quit the seas and to swim stream upwards, for the purpose of depositing their spawn in the tranquil sweet waters of the stream or lake. About this time also the reindeer leaves the forests to feed on the herbs and lichens of the tundra, and to seek along the shores fanned by the cooled sea-breeze some protection against the attacks of the stinging flies that rise in myriads from the swamps.

Thus during several months the tundra presents an animated scene, in which man also plays his part. The birds of the air, the fishes of the water, the beasts of the earth, are all obliged to pay their tribute to his various wants, to appease his hunger, to clothe his body, or to gratify his greed of gain.

But as soon as the first frosts of September announce the approach of winter, all animals, with but few exceptions, hasten to leave a region where the sources of life must soon fail. The geese, ducks, and swans return in dense flocks to the south; the strand-birds seek in some lower latitude a softer soil which allows their sharp beak to seize a burrowing prey ; the water-fowl forsake the bays and channels that will soon be blocked up with ice ; the reindeer once more return to the forest, and in a short time nothing is left that can induce man to prolong his stay in the treeless plain. Soon a thick mantle of snow covers the hardened earth, the frozen lake, the ice-bound river, and conceals them all—seven, eight, nine months long—under its monotonous pall, except where the furious north-east wind sweeps it away and lays bare the naked rock.

This snow, which after it has once fallen persists until the long summer's day has effectually thawed it, protects in an admirable manner the vegetation of the higher latitudes against the cold of the long winter season. For snow is so bad a conductor of heat, that in mid-winter in the high latitude of 78° 50′ (Rensselaer Bay), while the surface temperature was as low as −30°, Kane found at two feet deep a temperature of −8°, at four feet +2°, and at eight feet +26°, or no more than six degrees below the freezing-point of water. Thus covered by a warm crystal snow-mantle, the northern plants pass the long winter in a comparatively mild temperature, high enough to maintain their life, while, without, icy blasts—capable of converting mercury into a solid body—howl over the naked wilderness ; and as the first snow-falls are more cellular and less condensed than the nearly impalpable powder of winter, Kane justly observes that no " eiderdown in the cradle of an infant is tucked in more kindly than the sleeping-dress of winter about the feeble plant-life of the Arctic zone." Thanks to this protection, and to the influence of a sun which for months circles above the horizon, and in favourable localities calls forth the powers of vegetation in an incredibly short time, even Washington, Grinnell Land, and Spitzbergen are able to boast of flowers. Morton plucked a crucifer at Cape Constitution (80° 45′ N. lat.), and, on the banks of Mary Minturn River (78° 52′), Kane came across a flower-growth which, though drearily Arctic in its type, was rich in variety and colouring. Amid festuca and other tufted grasses twinkled the purple lychnis and the white star of the chickweed ; and, not without its pleasing associations, he recognised a solitary hesperis—the Arctic representative of the wallflowers of home.

Next to the lichens and mosses, which form the chief vegetation of the treeless zone, the cruciferæ, the grasses, the saxifragas, the caryophyllæ, and the compositæ are the families of plants most largely represented in the barren grounds or tundri. Though vegetation becomes more and more uniform on advancing to the north, yet the number of individual plants does not decrease. When the soil is moderately dry, the surface is covered by a dense carpet of lichens (*Cornicularieæ*), mixed in damper spots with Icelandic moss. In more tenacious soils, other plants flourish, not however to the exclusion of lichens, except in tracts of meadow ground, which occur in sheltered situations, or in the alluvial inundated flats where tall reed grasses or dwarf willows frequently grow as closely as they can stand.

It may easily be supposed that the boundary line which separates the tundri from the forest zone is both indistinct and irregular. In some parts where the cold sea-winds have a wider range, the barren grounds encroach considerably upon the limits of the forests; in others where the configuration of the land prevents their action, the woods advance farther to the north.

Thus the barren grounds attain their most southerly limit in Labrador, where they descend to latitude 57°, and this is sufficiently explained by the position of that bleak peninsula, bounded on three sides by icy seas, and washed by cold currents from the north. On the opposite coasts of Hudson's Bay they begin about 60°, and thence gradually rise towards the mouth of the Mackenzie, where the forests advance as high as 68°, or even still farther to the north along the low banks of that river. From the Mackenzie the barrens again descend until they reach Bering's Sea in 65° N. L. On the opposite or Asiatic shore, in the land of the Tchuktchi, they begin again, more to the south, in 63°, thence continually rise as far as the Lena, where Anjou found trees in 71° N. L., and then fall again towards the Obi, where the forests do not even reach the Arctic circle. From the Obi the tundri retreat further and further to the north, until finally, on the coasts of Norway, in latitude 70°, they terminate with the land itself.

Hence we see that the treeless zone of Europe, Asia, and America occupies a space larger than the whole of Europe.

Even the African Sahara, or the Pampas of South America,
are inferior in extent to the Siberian Tundri.  But the
possession of a few hundred square miles of fruitful territory
on the south-western frontiers of his vast empire would be of
greater value to the Czar than that of those boundless wastes,
which are tenanted only by a few wretched pastoral tribes,
or some equally wretched fishermen.

The Arctic forest-regions are of a still greater extent than
the vast treeless plains which they encircle.  When we consider that they form an almost continuous belt, stretching
through three parts of the world, in a breadth of from 15° to
20°, even the woods of the Amazon, which cover a surface
fifteen times greater than that of the United Kingdom,
shrink into comparative insignificance.  Unlike the tropical
forests which are characterised by an immense variety of
trees, these northern woods are almost entirely composed of
coniferæ, and one single kind of fir or pine often covers
an immense extent of ground.  The European and Asiatic
species differ, however, from those which grow in America.

Thus in the Russian empire and Scandinavia we find the
Scotch fir (*Pinus sylvestris*), the Siberian fir and larch (*Abies
sibirica, Larix sibirica*), the Picea obovata, and the Pinus
cembra; while in the Hudson's Bay territories the woods
principally consist of the white and black spruce (*Abies
alba et nigra*), the Canadian larch (*Larix canadensis*, and the
grey pine (*Pinus banksiana*).  In both continents birch trees
grow further to the north than the coniferæ, and the dwarf
willows form dense thickets on the shores of every river and
lake.  Various species of the service tree, the ash and the
elder are also met with in the Arctic forests; and both under
the shelter of the woods and beyond their limits, nature, as if
to compensate for the want of fruit trees, produces in favourable localities an abundance of bilberries, bogberries, cran-
berries, &c. (*Empetrum, Vaccinium*), whose fruit is a great
boon to man and beast.  When congealed by the autumnal
frosts, the berries frequently remain hanging on the bushes
until the snow melts in the following June, and are then a
considerable resource to the flocks of water-fowl migrating
to their northern breeding-places, or to the bear awakening
from his winter sleep.

Another distinctive character of the forests of the high latitudes is their apparent youth, so that generally the traveller would hardly suppose them to be more than fifty years, or at most a century old. Their juvenile appearance increases on advancing northwards, until suddenly their decrepid age is revealed by the thick bushes of lichens which clothe or hang down from their shrivelled boughs. Further to the south, large trees are found scattered here and there, but not so numerous as to modify the general appearance of the forest, and even these are mere dwarfs when compared with the gigantic firs of more temperate climates. This phenomenon is sufficiently explained by the shortness of the summer, which, though able to bring forth new shoots, does not last long enough for the formation of wood. Hence the growth of trees becomes slower and slower on advancing to the north; so that on the banks of the Great Bear Lake, for instance, 400 years are necessary for the formation of a trunk not thicker than a man's waist. Towards the confines of the tundra, the woods are reduced to stunted stems, covered with blighted buds that have been unable to develop themselves into branches, and which prove by their numbers how frequently and how vainly they have striven against the wind, until finally the last remnants of arboreal vegetation, vanquished by the blasts of winter, seek refuge under a carpet of lichens and mosses, from which their annual shoots hardly venture to peep forth.

A third peculiarity which distinguishes the forests of the north from those of the tropical world is what may be called their harmless character. There the traveller finds none of those noxious plants whose juices contain a deadly poison, and even thorns and prickles are of rare occurrence. No venomous snake glides through the thicket; no crocodile lurks in the swamp; and the northern beasts of prey—the bear, the lynx, the wolf—are far less dangerous and bloodthirsty than the large felidæ of the torrid zone.

The comparatively small number of animals living in the Arctic forests corresponds with the monotony of their vegetation. Here we should seek in vain for that immense variety of insects, or those troops of gaudy birds which in the Brazilian woods excite the admiration, and not unfrequently

cause the despair of the wanderer; here we should in vain
expect to hear the clamorous voices that resound in the
tropical thickets.   No noisy monkeys or quarrelsome parrots
settle on the branches of the trees; no shrill cicadæ or
melancholy goat-suckers interrupt the solemn stillness of the
night; the howl of the hungry wolf, or the hoarse screech of
some solitary bird of prey, are almost the only sounds that
ever disturb the repose of these awful solitudes.

When the tropical hurricane sweeps over the virgin forests,
it awakens a thousand voices of alarm; but the Arctic storm,
however furiously it may blow, scarcely calls forth an echo
from the dismal shades of the pinewoods of the north.

In one respect only the forests and swamps of the northern
regions vie in abundance of animal life with those of the
equatorial zone, for the legions of gnats which the short
polar summer calls forth from the arctic morasses are a no
less intolerable plague than the mosquitoes of the tropical
marshes.

Though agriculture encroaches but little upon the Arctic
woods, yet the agency of man is gradually working a change
in their aspect.   Large tracts of forest are continually wasted
by extensive fires, kindled accidentally or intentionally,
which spread with rapidity over a wide extent of country,
and continue to burn until they are extinguished by a heavy
rain.   Sooner or later a new growth of timber springs up,
but the soil being generally enriched and saturated with
alkali, now no longer brings forth its aboriginal firs, but gives
birth to a thicket of beeches (*Betula alba*) in Asia, or of
aspens in America.

The line of perpetual snow may naturally be expected to
descend lower and lower on advancing to the pole, and hence
many mountainous regions or elevated plateaux, such as the
interior of Spitzbergen, of Greenland, of Novaya Zemlya, &c.,
which in a more temperate clime would be verdant with
woods or meadows, are here covered with vast fields of ice,
from which frequently glaciers descend down to the verge of
the sea.   But even in the highest northern latitudes, no land
has yet been found covered as far as the water's edge with
eternal snow, or where winter has entirely subdued the powers
of vegetation.   The reindeer of Spitzbergen find near 80°

N. L. lichens or grasses to feed upon ; in favourable seasons
the snow melts by the end of June on the plains of Melville
Island, and numerous lemmings requiring vegetable food
for their subsistence inhabit the deserts of New Siberia. As
far as man has reached to the north, vegetation, when
fostered by a sheltered situation and the refraction of solar
heat from the rocks, has everywhere been found to rise to a
considerable altitude above the level of the sea; and should
there be land at the north pole, there is every reason to
believe that it is destitute neither of animal nor vegetable
life. It would be equally erroneous to suppose that the cold
of winter invariably increases as we near the pole, as the
temperature of a land is influenced by many other causes
besides its latitude. Even in the most northern regions
hitherto visited by man, the influence of the sea, particularly
when favoured by warm currents, is found to mitigate the
severity of the winter, while at the same time it diminishes
the warmth of summer. On the other hand, the large continental tracts of Asia or America that shelve towards the
pole have a more intense winter cold and a far greater
summer's heat than many coast lands or islands situated far
nearer to the pole. Thus, to cite but a few examples, the
western shores of Novaya Zemlya, fronting a wide expanse
of sea, have an average winter temperature of only $-4°$, and a
mean summer temperature but little above the freezing-point
of water ($+36\frac{1}{2}°$), while Jakutsk, situated in the heart of
Siberia and 20° nearer to the equator, has a winter of
$-36° 6'$, and a summer of $+66° 6'$.

The influence of the winds is likewise of considerable importance in determining the greater or lesser severity of an
Arctic climate. Thus the northerly winds which prevail in
Baffin's Bay and Davis's Straits during the summer months,
and fill the straits of the American north-eastern Archipelago
with ice, are probably the main cause of the abnormal depres-
sion of temperature in that quarter; while, on the contrary,
the southerly winds that prevail during summer in the valley
of the Mackenzie tend greatly to extend the forest of that
favoured region nearly down to the shores of the Arctic Sea.
Even in the depth of a Siberian winter, a sudden change of
wind is able to raise the thermometer from a mercury-con-

gealing cold to a temperature above the freezing-point of water, and a warm wind has been known to cause rain to fall in Spitzbergen in the month of January.

The voyages of Kane and Belcher have made us acquainted with the lowest temperatures ever felt by man. On Feb. 5, 1854, while the former was wintering in Smith's Sound (78° 37′ N. lat.), the mean of his best spirit-thermometer showed the unexampled temperature of −68° or 100° below the freezing-point of water. Then chloric ether became solid, and carefully prepared chloroform exhibited a granular pellicle on its surface. The exhalations from the skin invested the exposed or partially clad parts with a wreath of vapour. The air had a perceptible pungency upon inspiration, and everyone, as it were involuntarily, breathed guardedly with compressed lips. About the same time (February 9 and 10, 1854), Sir E. Belcher experienced a cold of −55° in Wellington Channel (75° 31′ N.), and the still lower temperature of −62° on January 13, 1853, in Northumberland Sound (76° 52′ N.).

Whether the temperature of the air descends still lower on advancing towards the pole, or whether these extreme degrees of cold are not sometimes surpassed in those mountainous regions of the north which, though seen, have never yet been explored, is of course an undecided question: so much is certain, that the observations hitherto made during the winter of the Arctic regions have been limited to too short a time, and are too few in number, to enable us to determine with any degree of certainty those points where the greatest cold prevails.

All we know is, that beyond the Arctic Circle, and eight or ten degrees further to the south in the interior of the continents of Asia and America, the average temperature of the winter generally ranges from −20° to −30° or even lower, and for a great part of the year is able to convert mercury into a solid body.

It may well be asked how man is able to bear the excessively low temperature of an Arctic winter, which must appear truly appalling to an inhabitant of the temperate zone. A thick fur clothing ; a hut small and low, where the warmth of a fire, or simply of a train-oil lamp, is husbanded in a narrow space, and above all, the wonderful power of the human constitution to accommodate itself to every change of climate, go far to counteract the rigour of the cold.

After a very few days the body developes an increasing warmth as the thermometer descends; for the air being condensed by the cold, the lungs inhale at every breath a greater quantity of oxygen, which of course accelerates the internal process of combustion, while at the same time an increasing appetite, gratified with a copious supply of animal food, of flesh and fat, enriches the blood and enables it to circulate more vigorously. Thus not only the hardy native of the north, but even the healthy traveller soon gets accustomed to bear without injury the rigours of an Arctic winter.

'The mysterious compensations,' says Kane, 'by which we adapt ourselves to climate are more striking here than in the tropics. In the Polar zone the assault is immediate and sudden, and, unlike the insidious fatality of hot countries, produces its results rapidly. It requires hardly a single winter to tell who are to be the heat-making and acclimatised men. Petersen, for instance, who has resided for two years at Upernavik, seldom enters a room with a fire. Another of our party, George Riley, with a vigorous constitution, established habits of free exposure, and active cheerful temperament, has so inured himself to the cold, that he sleeps on our sledge journeys without a blanket or any other covering than his walking suit, while the outside temperature is −30°.'

There are many proofs that a milder climate once reigned in the northern regions of the globe. Fossil pieces of wood, petrified acorns and fir-cones have been found in the interior of Banks' Land by M'Clure's sledging parties. At Anakerdluk in North Greenland. (70° N.) a large forest lies buried on a mountain surrounded by glaciers, 1080 feet above the level of the sea. Not only the trunks and branches, but even the leaves, fruit-cones, and seeds have been preserved in the soil, and enable the botanist to determine the species of the plants to which they belong. They show that, besides firs and sequoias, oaks, plantains, elms, magnolias, and even laurels, indicating a climate such as that of Lausanne or Geneva,

flourished during the miocene period in a country where
now even the willow is compelled to creep along the ground.
During the same epoch of the earth's history Spitzbergen
was likewise covered with stately forests.   The same poplars
and the same swamp-cypress (*Taxodium dubium*) which
then flourished in North Greenland have been found in a
fossilised state at Bell Sound (76° N.) by the Swedish naturalists, who also discovered a plantain and a linden as high as
78° and 79° in King's Bay—a proof that in those times the
climate of Spitzbergen cannot have been colder than that
which now reigns in southern Sweden and Norway, eighteen
degrees nearer to the line.

We know that at present the fir, the poplar, and the beech
grow fifteen degrees further to the north than the plantain
—and the miocene period no doubt exhibited the same proportion.   Thus the poplars and firs which then grew in
Spitzbergen along with plantains and lindens must have
ranged as far as the pole itself, supposing that point to be
dry land.

In the miocene times the Arctic zone evidently presented
a very different aspect from that which it wears at present.
Now, during the greater part of the year, an immense glacial
desert, which through its floating bergs and drift-ice depresses
the temperature of countries situated far to the south, it then
consisted of verdant lands covered with luxuriant forests and
bathed by an open sea.

What may have been the cause of these amazing changes
of climate?   The readiest answer seems to be—a different
distribution of sea and land ; but there is no reason to believe
that in the miocene times there was less land in the Arctic
zone than at present, nor can any possible combination of
water and dry land be imagined sufficient to account for the
growth of laurels in Greenland or of plantains in Spitzbergen.
Dr. Oswald Heer is inclined to seek for an explanation of the
phenomenon, not in mere local terrestrial changes, but in a
difference of the earth's position in the heavens.

We now know that our sun, with his attendant planets
and satellites, performs a vast circle, embracing perhaps
hundreds of thousands of years, round another star, and that
we are constantly entering new regions of space untravelled by

our earth before. We come from the unknown, and plunge into the unknown; but so much is certain that our solar system rolls at present through a space but thinly peopled with stars, and there is no reason to doubt that it may once have wandered through one of those celestial provinces where, as the telescope shows us, constellations are far more densely clustered. But, as every star is a blazing sun, the greater or lesser number of these heavenly bodies must evidently have a proportionate influence upon the temperature of space, and thus we may suppose that during the miocene period our earth, being at that time in a *populous* sidereal region, enjoyed the benefit of a higher temperature which clothed even its poles with verdure. In the course of ages the sun conducted his herd of planets into more solitary and colder regions, which caused the warm miocene times to be followed by the glacial period, during which the Swiss flat lands bore an Arctic character, and finally the sun emerged into a space of an intermediate character, which determines the present condition of the climates of our globe.

Though Nature generally wears a more stern and forbidding aspect on advancing towards the pole, yet the high latitudes have many beauties of their own. Nothing can exceed the magnificence of an Arctic sunset, clothing the snow-clad mountains and the skies with all the glories of colour; or be more serenely beautiful than the clear starlight night, illumined by the brilliant moon, which for days continually circles around the horizon, never setting until she has run her long course of brightness. The uniform whiteness of the landscape and the general transparency of the atmosphere add to the lustre of her beams, which serve the natives to guide their nomadic life, and to lead them to their hunting-grounds.

But of all the magnificent spectacles that relieve the monotonous gloom of the Arctic winter, there is none to equal the magical beauty of the Aurora. Night covers the snow-clad earth; the stars glimmer feebly through the haze which so frequently dims their brilliancy in the high latitudes, when suddenly a broad and clear bow of light spans the horizon in the direction where it is traversed by the magnetic meridian. This bow sometimes remains for several hours, heaving or waving to and fro, before it sends forth streams of light ascending to the zenith. Sometimes these flashes proceed from the bow of light alone; at others they simultaneously shoot forth from many opposite parts of the horizon, and form a vast sea of fire whose brilliant waves are continually changing their position. Finally they all unite in a magnificent crown or cupola of light, with the appearance of which the phenomenon attains its highest degree of splendour. The brilliancy of the streams, which are commonly red at their base, green in the middle, and light yellow towards the zenith, increases, while at the same time they dart with greater vivacity through the skies. The colours are wonderfully transparent, the red approaching to a clear blood-red, the green to a pale emerald tint. On turning from the flaming firmament to the earth, this also is seen to glow with a magical light. The dark sea, black as jet, forms a striking contrast to the white snow plain or the distant ice mountain; all the outlines tremble as if they belonged to the unreal world of dreams. The imposing silence of the night heightens the charms of the magnificent spectacle.

But gradually the crown fades, the bow of light dissolves, the streams become shorter, less frequent, and less vivid; and finally the gloom of winter once more descends upon the northern desert.

The Great Snowy Owl.

MUSK OXEN AND ELKS.

Reindeer Travelling in Lapland.

# CHAPTER II.

## ARCTIC LAND QUADRUPEDS AND BIRDS.

The Reindeer—Structure of its Foot—Clattering Noise when Walking—Antlers—
Extraordinary Olfactory Powers—The Icelandic Moss—Present and former
Range of the Reindeer—Its invaluable Qualities as an Arctic domestic Animal
—Revolts against Oppression—Enemies of the Reindeer—The Wolf—The
Glutton or Wolverine—Gad-flies—The Elk or Moose Deer—The Musk-ox—
The Wild Sheep of the Rocky Mountains—The Siberian Argali—The Arctic
Fox—Its Burrows—The Lemmings—Their Migrations and Enemies—Arctic
Anatidæ—The Snow-bunting — The Lapland Bunting — The Sea-eagle—
Drowned by a Dolphin.

THE reindeer may well be called the camel of the northern
wastes, for it is a no less valuable companion to the Laplander or to the Samojede than the 'ship of the desert' to
the wandering Bedouin. It is the only member of the
numerous deer family that has been domesticated by man;
but though undoubtedly the most useful, it is by no means
the most comely of its race. Its clear dark eye has, indeed,
a beautiful expression, but it has neither the noble proportions of the stag nor the grace of the roebuck, and its thick
square-formed body is far from being a model of elegance.

Its legs are short and thick, its feet broad but extremely well adapted for walking over the snow or on a swampy ground. The front hoofs, which are capable of great lateral expansion, curve upwards, while the two secondary ones behind (which are but slightly developed in the fallow deer and other members of the family) are considerably prolonged: a structure which, by giving the animal a broader base to stand upon, prevents it from sinking too deeply into the snow or the morass. Had the foot of the reindeer been formed like that of our stag, it would have been as unable to drag the Laplander's sledge with such velocity over the yielding snow-fields as the camel would be to perform his long marches through the desert without the broad elastic sole-pad on which he firmly paces the unstable sands.

The short legs and broad feet of the reindeer likewise enable it to swim with greater ease—a power of no small importance in countries abounding in rivers and lakes, and where the scarcity of food renders perpetual migrations necessary.

When the reindeer walks or merely moves, a remarkable clattering sound is heard to some distance, about the cause of which naturalists and travellers by no means agree. Most probably it results from the great length of the two digits of the cloven hoof, which when the animal sets its foot upon the ground separate widely, and when it again raises its hoof, suddenly clap against each other.

A long mane of a dirty white colour hangs from the neck of the reindeer. In summer the body is brown above and white beneath; in winter, long-haired and white.

Its antlers are very different from those of the stag, having broad palmated summits, and branching back to the length of three or four feet. Their weight is frequently very considerable—twenty or twenty-five pounds; and it is remarkable that both sexes have horns, while in all other members of the deer race the males alone are in possession of this ornament or weapon.

The female brings forth in May a single calf, rarely two. This is small and weak, but after a few days it follows the mother, who suckles her young but a short time, as it is soon able to seek and to find its food.

The reindeer gives very little milk—at the very utmost,

after the young has been weaned, a bottleful daily; but the quality is excellent, for it is uncommonly thick and nutritious. It consists almost entirely of cream, so that a great deal of water can be added before it becomes inferior to the best cow-milk. Its taste is excellent, but the butter made from it is rancid and hardly to be eaten, while the cheese is very good.

The only food of the reindeer during winter consists of moss, and the most surprising circumstance in his history is the instinct, or the extraordinary olfactory powers, whereby he is enabled to discover it when hidden beneath the snow. However deep the *Lichen rangiferinus* may be buried, the animal is aware of its presence the moment he comes to the spot, and this kind of food is never so agreeable to him as when he digs for it himself. In his manner of doing this he is remarkably adroit. Having first ascertained, by thrusting his muzzle into the snow, whether the moss lies below or not, he begins making a hole with his fore feet, and continues working until at length he uncovers the lichen. No instance has ever occurred of a reindeer making such a cavity without discovering the moss he seeks. In summer their food is of a different nature; they are then pastured upon green herbs or the leaves of trees. Judging from the lichen's appearance in the hot months, when it is dry and brittle, one might easily wonder that so large a quadruped as the reindeer should make it his favourite food and fatten upon it; but towards the month of September, the lichen becomes soft, tender, and damp, with a taste like wheat-bran. In this state its luxuriant and flowery ramifications somewhat resemble the leaves of endive, and are as white as snow.

Though domesticated since time immemorial, the reindeer has only partly been brought under the yoke of man, and wanders in large wild herds both in the North American wastes, where it has never yet been reduced to servitude, and in the forests and tundras of the Old World.

In America, where it is called 'caribou,' it extends from Labrador to Melville Island and Washington Land; in Europe and Asia, it is found from Lapland and Norway, and from the mountains of Mongolia and the banks of the Ufa as far as Novaja Zemlya and Spitzbergen. Many centuries ago —probably during the glacial period—its range was still more extensive, as reindeer bones are frequently found in French and German caves, and bear testimony to the severity of the climate which at that time reigned in Central Europe, for the reindeer is a cold-loving animal, and will not thrive under a milder sky. All attempts to prolong its life in our zoological gardens have failed, and even in the royal park at Stockholm Hogguer saw some of these animals, which were quite languid and emaciated during the summer, although care had been taken to provide them with a cool grotto to which they could retire during the warmer hours of the day. In summer the reindeer can enjoy health only in the fresh mountain air or along the bracing sea-shore, and has as great a longing for a low temperature as man for the genial warmth of his fireside in winter.

The reindeer is easily tamed, and soon gets accustomed to its master, whose society it loves, attracted as it were by a kind of innate sympathy; for, unlike all other domestic animals, it is by no means dependent on man for its subsistence, but finds its nourishment alone, and wanders about freely in summer and in winter without ever being enclosed in a stable. These qualities are inestimable in countries where it would be utterly impossible to keep any domestic animal requiring shelter and stores of provisions during the long winter months, and make the reindeer the fit companion of the northern nomad, whose simple wants it almost wholly supplies. During his wanderings, it carries his tent and scanty household furniture, or drags his sledge over the snow. On account of the weakness of its back-bone, it is less fit for riding, and requires to be mounted with care, as a violent shock easily dislocates its vertebral column. You would hardly suppose the reindeer to be the same animal when languidly creeping along under a rider's weight, as when, unencumbered by a load, it vaults with the lightness of a bird over the obstacles in its way to obey the call of its master. The reindeer can be easily trained to drag a sledge, but great care must be taken not to beat or otherwise illtreat it, as it then becomes obstinate and quite unmanageable. When forced to drag too heavy a load, or taxed in any way above its strength, it not seldom turns round upon its tyrant, and attacks him with its horns and fore feet. To save himself from its fury, he is then obliged to overturn his sledge, and to seek a refuge under its bottom until the rage of the animal has abated.

After the death of the reindeer, it may truly be said that every part of its body is put to some use. The flesh is very good, and the tongue and marrow are considered a great delicacy. The blood, of which not a drop is allowed to be lost, is either drank warm or made up into a kind of black-pudding. The skin furnishes not only clothing impervious to the cold, but tents and bedding; and spoons, knife-handles, and other household utensils are made out of the bones and horns; the latter serve also, like the claws, for the preparation of an excellent glue, which the Chinese, who buy them for this purpose of the Russians, use as a nutritious jelly. In Tornea the skins of new-born reindeer are prepared and sent to St. Petersburg to be manufactured into gloves, which are extremely soft, but very dear.

Thus the cocoa-nut palm, the tree of a hundred uses, hardly renders a greater variety of services to the islanders of the Indian Ocean than the reindeer to the Laplander or the Samojede; and, to the honour of these barbarians be it mentioned, they treat their invaluable friend and companion with a grateful affection which might serve as an example to far more civilised nations.

The reindeer attains an age of from twenty to twenty-five years, but in its domesticated state it is generally killed when from six to ten years old. Its most dangerous enemies are the wolf, and the glutton or wolverine (*Gulo borealis* or *arcticus*), which belongs to the bloodthirsty marten and weasel family, and is said to be of uncommon fierceness and strength. It is about the size of a large badger, between which animal and the pole-cat it seems to be intermediate, nearly resembling the former in its general figure and aspect, and agreeing with the latter as to its dentition. No dog is capable of mastering a glutton, and even the wolf is hardly able to scare it from its prey. Its feet are very short, so that it cannot run swiftly, but it climbs with great facility upon trees, or ascends even almost perpendicular rock-walls, where it also seeks a refuge when pursued.

When it perceives a herd of reindeer browsing near a

wood or a precipice, it generally lies in wait upon a branch
or some high cliff, and springs down upon the first animal
that comes within its reach.  Sometimes also it steals unawares upon its prey, and suddenly bounding upon its back,
kills it by a single bite in the neck.  Many fables worthy of
Münchhausen have been told about its voracity; for instance, that it is able to devour two reindeer at one meal,
and that, when its stomach is exorbitantly distended with
food, it will press itself between two trees or stones to make
room for a new repast.  It will, indeed, kill in one night six
or eight reindeer, but it contents itself with sucking their
blood, as the weasel does with fowls, and eats no more at one
meal than any other carnivorous animal of its own size.

Besides the attacks of its mightier enemies, the reindeer is
subject to the persecutions of two species of gad-fly, which
torment it exceedingly.  The one (*Œstrus tarandi*), called
Hurbma by the Laplanders, deposits its glutinous eggs upon
the animal's back.  The larvæ, on creeping out, immediately
bore themselves into the skin, where by their motion and
suction they cause so many small swellings or boils, which
gradually grow to the size of an inch or more in diameter,
with an opening at the top of each, through which the larva
may be seen imbedded in a purulent fluid.  Frequently
the whole back of the animal is covered with these boils,
which, by draining its fluids, produce emaciation and disease.
As if aware of this danger, the reindeer runs wild and
furious as soon as it hears the buzzing of the fly, and seeks a
refuge in the nearest water.

The other species of gad-fly (*Œstrus nasalis*) lays its eggs
in the nostrils of the reindeer; and the larvæ, boring themselves into the fauces and beneath the tongue of the poor
animal, are a great source of annoyance, as is shown by its
frequent sniffling and shaking of the head.

A pestilential disorder like the rinderpest will sometimes
sweep away whole herds.  Thus in a few weeks a rich Laplander or Samojede may be reduced to poverty, and the proud
possessor of several thousands of reindeer be compelled to
seek the precarious livelihood of the northern fisherman.

The elk or moose-deer (*Cervus alces*) is another member of
the cervine race peculiar to the forests of the north.  In size

it is far superior to the stag, but it cannot boast of an elegant shape, the head being disproportionately large, the neck short and thick, and its immense horns, which sometimes weigh near fifty pounds, each dilating almost immediately from the base into a broad palmated form; while its long legs, high shoulders, and heavy upper lip hanging very much over the lower, give it an uncouth appearance. The colour of the elk is a dark greyish brown, but much paler on the legs and beneath the tail.

We owe the first description of this gigantic deer to Julius Cæsar, in whose times it was still a common inhabitant of the German forests. But the conqueror of Gaul can hardly have seen it himself, or he would not have ascribed to it a single horn, placed in the middle of the forehead, or said that both sexes are perfectly alike, for the female is smaller and has no antlers.

At present the elk is still found in the swampy forests of East Prussia, Lithuania and Poland, but it chiefly resides in the more northern woods of Russia, Siberia, and America. It is a mild and harmless animal, principally supporting itself by browsing the boughs of willows, asps, service trees, and other soft species of wood. It does not, like the reindeer, seek a refuge against the attacks of the gad-flies, by wandering to the coasts of the sea, or retreating to the bare mountains, where it would soon perish for the want of adequate food, but plunges up to the nose into the next river, where it finds, moreover, a species of water-grass (*Festuca fluitans*) which it likes to feed upon. Though naturally mild and harmless, it displays a high degree of courage, and even ferocity when suddenly attacked; defending itself with great vigour, not only with its horns, but also by striking violently with its fore feet, in the use of which it is particularly dextrous. It is generally caught in traps, as it is extremely shy and watchful, and finds an easy retreat in the swamp or the forest. The only time of the year when it can be easily chased is in the spring, when the softened snow gets covered during the night with a thin crust of ice which is too weak to bear the animal's weight.

Though not ranging so far north as the reindeer or the elk, we find in the Old World the red-deer (*Cervus elaphus*), in the vicinity of Drontheim in Norway, and along with the roebuck beyond Lake Baikal in Siberia, while in America the large-eared deer (*Cervus macrotis*), and the Wapiti or Canada stag (*Cervus strongylo-ceras*), extend their excursions beyond 55° of northern latitude. The latter is much larger and of a stronger make than the European red-deer, frequently growing to the height of our tallest oxen, and possessing great activity as well as strength. The flesh is little prized, but the hide, when made into leather after the Indian fashion, is said not to turn hard in drying, after being wet—a quality which justly entitles it to a preference over almost every other kind of leather.

One of the most remarkable quadrupeds of the high northern regions is the musk-ox (*Ovibos moschatus*), which by some naturalists has been considered as intermediate between the sheep and the ox. It is about the height of a deer, but of much stouter proportions. The horns are very broad at the base, almost meeting on the forehead, and curving down-wards between the eye and ears until about the level of the mouth, when they turn upwards. Its long thick brown or black hair hanging down below the middle of the leg, and covering on all parts of the animal a fine kind of soft ash-coloured wool, which is of the finest description and capable of forming the most beautiful fabrics manufactured, enables it to remain even during the winter beyond 70° of northern latitude. In spring, it wanders over the ice as far as Melville Island, or even Smith's Sound, where a number of its bones were found by Dr. Kane. In September it with-draws more to the south, and spends the coldest months on the verge of the forest-region. Like the reindeer, it subsists chiefly on lichens and grasses. It runs nimbly, and climbs hills and rocks with great ease. Its fossil remains, or those of a very analogous species, have been discovered in Siberia: at present it is exclusively confined to the New World.

In the Rocky Mountains, from the Mexican Cordillera-plateaux as far as 68° N. lat., dwells the wild sheep (*Ovis montana*), distinguished by the almost circular bend of its large, triangular, transversely striped horns, from its relative the Siberian argali (*Ovis argali*), which is supposed to be the parent of our domestic sheep, and far surpasses it in size and delicacy of flesh. Both the American and the Asiatic wild sheep are in the highest degree active and vigorous, ascending abrupt precipices with great agility, and, like the wild goat, going over the narrowest and most dangerous passes with perfect safety.

Among the carnivorous quadrupeds of the northern regions, many, like the lynx, the wolf, the bear, the glutton, and other members of the weasel tribe, have their head-quarters in the forests, and only occasionally roam over the tundras; but the Arctic fox (*Canis lagopus*) almost exclusively inhabits the treeless wastes that fringe the Polar ocean, and is found on almost all the islands that lie buried in its bosom. This pretty little creature, which in winter grows perfectly white, knows how to protect itself against the most intense cold, either by seeking a refuge in the clefts of rocks, or by burrowing to a considerable depth in a sandy soil.

It principally preys upon lemmings, stoats, polar hares, as well as upon all kinds of water-fowl and their eggs; but, when pinched by hunger, it does not disdain the carcases of fish, or the molluscs and crustaceans it may chance to pick up on the shore. Its enemies are the glutton, the snowy owl, and man, who, from the equator to the poles, leaves no creature unmolested that can in any way satisfy his wants.

The lemmings, of which there are many species, are small rodents, peculiar to the Arctic regions, both in the New and in the Old World, where they are found as far to the north as vegetation extends. They live on grass, roots, the shoots of the willow, and the dwarf birch, but chiefly on lichens. They do not gather hoards of provisions for the winter, but live upon what they find beneath the snow. They seldom prove injurious to man, as the regions they inhabit are generally situated beyond the limits of agriculture. From the voles, to whom they are closely allied, they are distinguished by having the foot-sole covered with stiff hairs, and by the strong crooked claws with which their fore feet are armed. The best known species is the Norwegian lemming (*Lemmus norwegicus*), which is found on the high mountains of the Dovrefjeld, and further to the north on the dry parts of the tundra, where it inhabits small burrows under stones or in the moss. Its long and thick hair is of a tawny colour, and prettily marked with black spots. The migrations of the lemming have been grossly exaggerated by Olaus

Magnus and Pontoppidan, to whom the natural history of
the North owes so many fables. As they breed several times
in the year, producing five or six at a birth, they of course
multiply very fast under favourable circumstances, and are
then forced to leave the district which is no longer able to
afford them food. But this takes place very seldom, for
when Mr. Brehm* visited Scandinavia, the people on the Dovrefjeld knew nothing about the migrations of the lemming,
and his enquiries on the subject proved equally fruitless in
Lapland and in Finland. At all events it is a fortunate circumstance that the lemmings have so many enemies, as their
rapid multiplication might else endanger the balance of
existence in the northern regions. The inclemencies of the
climate are a chief means for keeping them in check. A
wet summer, an early cold and snowless autumn destroy
them by millions, and then of course years are necessary to
recruit their numbers. With the exception of the bear and
the hedgehog, they are pursued by all the northern carnivora.
The wolf, the fox, the glutton, the marten, the ermine,
devour them with avidity, and a good lemming season is a
time of unusual plenty for the hungry Laplander's dog. The
snowy owl, whose dense plumage enables it to be a constant
resident on the tundra, almost exclusively frequents those
places where lemmings, its favourite food, are to be found;
the buzzards are constantly active in their destruction; the
crow feeds its young with lemmings; and even the poor
Lap, when pressed by hunger, seizes a stick, and, for want
of better game, goes out lemming-hunting, and rejoices
when he can kill a sufficient number for his dinner.

Several birds, such as the snowy owl and the ptarmigan
(*Lagopus albus*), which can easily procure its food under the
snow, winter in the highest latitudes; but by far the greater
number are merely summer visitants of the Arctic regions.
After the little bunting, the first arrivals in spring are the
snow-geese, who likewise are the first to leave the dreary
regions of the north on their southerly migration. The
common and king eider duck, the Brent geese, the great
northern, black and red throated divers, are the next to make
their appearance, followed by the pintail and longtail ducks

* 'Illustrirtes Thierleben.' Hildburghausen, 1865.

(*Anas caudacuta et glacialis*), the latest visitors of the season. These birds generally take their departure in the same order as they arrive. The period of their stay is but short, but their presence imparts a wonderfully cheerful aspect to regions at other times so deserted and dreary. As soon as the young are sufficiently fledged, they again betake themselves to the southward; the character of the season much influencing the period of their departure.

As far as man has penetrated, on the most northern islets of Spitzbergen, or on the ice-blocked shores of Kennedy Channel, the eider duck and others of the Arctic anatidæ build their nests; and there is no reason to doubt that, if the pole has breeding-places for them, it re-echoes with their cries. Nor need they fear to plunge into the very heart of the Arctic zone, for the flight of a goose being forty or fifty miles an hour, these birds may breed in the remotest northern solitude, and in a few hours, on a fall of deep autumn snow, convey themselves by their swiftness of wing to better feeding grounds.

One of the most interesting of the Arctic birds is the snow-bunting (*Plectrophanes nivalis*), which may properly be called *the* polar singing bird, as it breeds in the most northern isles, such as Spitzbergen and Novaja Zemlya, or on the highest mountains of the Dovrefjeld in Scandinavia, where it enlivens the fugitive summer with its short but agreeable notes, sounding doubly sweet from the treeless wastes in which they are heard. It invariably builds its nest, which it lines with feathers and down, in the fissures of mountain rocks or under large stones, and the entrance is generally so narrow as merely to allow the parent birds to pass. The remarkably dense winter plumage of the snow-bunting especially qualifies it for a northern residence, and when in captivity it will rather bear the severest cold than even a moderate degree of warmth. In its breeding-places it lives almost exclusively on insects, particularly gnats: during the winter it feeds on all sorts of seeds, and then famine frequently compels it to wander to a less rigorous climate.

The Lapland bunting (*Centrophanes lapponicus*), whose white and black plumage is agreeably diversified with red, is likewise an inhabitant of the higher latitudes, where it is frequently seen in the barren grounds and tundras. Both these birds are distinguished by the very long claw of their hind toe, a structure which enables them to run about with ease upon the snow.

Among the raptorial birds of the Arctic regions, the sea-eagle (*Haliœtus albicilla*) holds a conspicuous rank. At his approach the gull and the auk conceal themselves in the fissures of the rocks, but are frequently dragged forth by their relentless enemy. The divers are, according to Wahlengren, more imperilled from his attacks than those sea-birds which do not plunge, for the latter rise into the air as soon as their piercing eye espies the universally dreaded tyrant, and thus escape ; while the former, blindly trusting to the element in which they are capable of finding a temporary refuge, allow him to approach, and then suddenly diving, fancy themselves in safety, while the eagle is only waiting for the moment of their reappearance to repeat his attack. Twice or thrice they may possibly escape his claws by a rapid plunge, but when for the fourth time they dive out of the water, and remain but one instant above the surface, that instant seals their doom. The sea-eagle is equally formidable to the denizens of the ocean, but sometimes too great a confidence in his strength leads to his destruction, for Kittlitz was informed by the inhabitants of Kamtschatka that, pouncing upon a dolphin, he is not seldom dragged down into the water by the diving cetacean in whose skin his talons remain fixed.

The Elk.

Vessel lifted out of the Water by Ice.

# CHAPTER III.

### THE ARCTIC SEAS.

Dangers peculiar to the Arctic Sea—Ice-fields—Hummocks—Collision of Ice-
fields—Ice-bergs—Their Origin—Their Size—The Glaciers which give them
Birth—Their Beauty—Sometimes useful Auxiliaries to the Mariner—Dangers of
Anchoring to a Berg—A crumbling Berg—The Ice-blink—Fogs—Transparency
of the Atmosphere—Phenomena of Reflection and Refraction—Causes which
prevent the Accumulation of Polar Ice—Tides—Currents—Ice a bad Conductor
of Heat—Wise Provisions of Nature.

THE heart of the first navigator, says Horace, must have
been shielded with threefold brass—and yet the poet knew
but the sunny Mediterranean, with its tepid floods and smiling
shores : how, then, would he have found words to express his
astonishment at the intrepid seamen who, to open new vistas
to science or new roads to commerce, first ventured to face
the unknown terrors of the Arctic main?

In every part of the ocean the mariner has to guard against
the perils of hidden shoals and sunken cliffs, but the high
northern waters are doubly and trebly dangerous ; for here,
besides those rocks which are firmly rooted to the ground,

there are others which, freely floating about, threaten to crush his vessel to pieces, or to force it along with them in helpless bondage.

The Arctic navigators have given various names to these movable shoals, which are the cause of so much delay and danger. They are *ice-bergs* when they tower to a considerable height above the waters, and *ice-fields* when they have a vast horizontal extension. A *floe* is a detached portion of a field; *pack-ice,* a large area of floes or smaller fragments closely driven together so as to oppose a firm barrier to the progress of a ship; and *drift-ice,* loose ice in motion, but not so firmly packed as to prevent a vessel from making her way through its yielding masses.

The large ice-fields which the whaler encounters in Baffin's Bay, or on the seas between Spitzbergen and Greenland, constitute one of the marvels of the deep. There is a solemn grandeur in the slow majestic motion with which they are drifted by the currents to the south; and their enormous masses, as mile after mile comes floating by, impress the spectator with the idea of a boundless extent and an irresistible power. But, vast and mighty as they are, they are unable to withstand the elements combined for their destruction, and their apparently triumphal march leads them only to their ruin.

When they first descend from their northern strongholds, the ice of which they are composed is of the average thickness of from ten to fifteen feet, and their surface is sometimes tolerably smooth and even, but in general it is covered with numberless ice-blocks or hummocks piled upon each other in wild confusion to a height of forty or fifty feet, the result of repeated collisions before flakes and floes were soldered into fields. Before the end of June they are covered with snow, sometimes six feet deep, which melting during the summer forms small ponds or lakes upon their surface.

Not seldom ice-fields are whirled about in rotatory motion, which causes their circumference to gyrate with a velocity of several miles per hour. When a field thus sweeping through the waters comes into collision with another which may possibly be revolving with equal rapidity in an opposite direction—when masses not seldom twenty or thirty miles in diameter, and each weighing many millions of tons, clash together, imagination can hardly conceive a more appalling scene. The whalers at all times require unremitting vigilance to secure their safety, but scarcely in any situation so much as when navigating amidst these fields, which are more particularly dangerous in foggy weather, as their motions cannot then be distinctly observed. No wonder that since the establishment of the fishery numbers of vessels have been crushed to pieces between two fields in motion, for the strongest ship ever built must needs be utterly unable to resist their power. Some have been uplifted and thrown upon the ice; some have had their hulls completely torn open; and others have been overrun by the ice, and buried beneath the fragments piled upon their wreck.

The ice-bergs, which, as their name indicates, rise above the water to a much more considerable height than the ice-fields, have a very different origin, as they are not formed in the sea itself, but by the glaciers of the northern highlands. As our rivers are continually pouring their streams into the ocean, so many of the glaciers or ice-rivers of the Arctic zone, descending to the water-edge, are slowly but constantly forcing themselves further and further into the sea. In the summer season, when the ice is particularly fragile, the force of cohesion is often overcome by the weight of the prodigious masses that overhang the sea or have been undermined by its waters; and in the winter, when the air is probably 40° or 50° below zero and the sea from 28° to 30° above, the unequal expansion of those parts of the mass exposed to so great a difference of temperature cannot fail to produce the separation of large portions.

Most of these swimming glacier-fragments, or ice-bergs, which are met with by the whaler in the Northern Atlantic, are formed on the mountainous west coast of Greenland by the large glaciers which discharge themselves into the fiords from Smith's Sound to Disco Bay, as here the sea is sufficiently deep to float them away, in spite of the enormous magnitude they frequently attain. As they drift along down Baffin's Bay and Davis's Strait, they not seldom run aground on some shallow shore, where, bidding defiance to the short summer, they frequently remain for many a year.

Dr. Hayes measured an immense ice-berg which had stranded off the little harbour of Tessuissak to the north of Melville Bay. The square wall which faced towards his base of measurement was 315 feet high and a fraction over three quarters of a mile long. Being almost square-sided above the sea, the same shape must have extended beneath it; and since, by measurements made two days before Hayes had discovered that fresh-water ice floating in salt water has above the surface to below it the proportion of one to seven, this crystallised mountain must have gone aground in a depth of nearly half-a-mile. A rude estimate of its size, made on the spot, gave in cubical contents about 27,000 millions of feet, and in weight something like 2,000 millions of tons!

Captain Ross in his first voyage mentions another of these wrecked bergs, which was found to be 4169 yards long, 3689 yards broad, and 51 feet high above the level of the sea. It was aground in 61 fathoms, and its weight was estimated by an officer of the 'Alexander' at 1,292,397,673 tons. On ascending the flat top of this ice-berg it was found occupied by a huge white bear, who justly deeming 'discretion the best part of valour,' sprang into the sea before he could be fired at.

The vast dimensions of the ice-bergs appear less astonishing when we consider that many of the glaciers or ice-rivers from which they are dislodged are equal in size or volume to the largest streams of continental Europe.

Thus one of the eight glaciers existing in the district of Omenak in Greenland is no less than an English mile broad, and forms an ice-wall rising 160 feet above the sea. Further to the north, Melville Bay and Whale Sound are the seat of vast ice-rivers. Here Tyndall glacier forms a coast line of ice over two miles long, almost burying its face in the sea, and carrying the eye along a broad and winding valley, up steps of ice of giant height, until at length the slope loses itself in the unknown ice-desert beyond. But grand above all is the magnificent Humboldt glacier, which, connecting Greenland and Washington Land, forms a solid glassy wall 300 feet above the water-level, with an unknown depth below it, while its curved face extends full sixty miles in length from Cape Agassiz to Cape Forbes. In the temperate zone it would be one of the mightiest rivers of the earth; here, in the frozen solitudes of the North, it slowly drops its vast fragments into the waters, making the solitudes around re-echo with their fall.

As the Polar shores of continental America and Siberia are generally flat and below the snow-line, they are consequently deprived both of glaciers and of the huge floating masses to which these give birth.

In a high sea the waves beat against an ice-berg as against a rock; and in calm weather where there is a swell, the noise made by their rising and falling is tremendous. Their usual form is that of a high vertical wall, gradually sloping down to the opposite side, which is very low; but frequently they exhibit the most fantastic shapes, particularly after they have been a long time exposed to the corroding power of the waves or of warm rains pelting them from above.

A number of ice-bergs floating in the sea is one of the most magnificent spectacles of nature, but the wonderful beauty of these crystal cliffs never appears to greater advantage than when clothed by the midnight sun with all the splendid colours of twilight.

'The bergs,' says Dr. Hayes, describing one of these enchanting nights, 'had wholly lost their chilly aspect, and glittering in the blaze of the brilliant heavens, seemed in the distance like masses of burnished metal or solid flame. Nearer at hand they were huge blocks of Parian marble inlaid with mammoth gems of pearl and opal. One in particular exhibited the perfection of the grand. Its form was not unlike that of the Colosseum, and it lay so far away that half its height was buried beneath the line of blood-red waters. The sun, slowly rolling along the horizon, passed behind it, and it seemed as if the old Roman ruins had suddenly taken fire. In the shadow of the bergs the water was a rich green, and nothing could be more soft and tender than the gradations of colour made by the sea shoaling on the sloping tongue of a berg close beside us. The tint increased in intensity where the ice overhung the water, and a deep cavern near by exhibited the solid colour of the malachite mingled with the transparency of the emerald, while in strange contrast a broad streak of cobalt blue ran diagonally through its body. The bewitching character of the scene was heightened by a thousand little cascades which leaped into the sea from these floating masses, the water being discharged from lakes of melted snow and ice which reposed in quietude far up in the valleys separating the high icy hills of their upper surface. From other bergs large pieces were now and then detached, plunging down into the water with deafening noise, while the slow moving swell of the ocean resounded through their broken archways.'

A similar gorgeous spectacle was witnessed by Dr. Kane in Melville Bay. The midnight sun came out over a great berg, kindling variously-coloured fires on every part of its surface, and making the ice around the ship one great resplendency of gemwork, blazing carbuncles and rubies, and molten gold.

In the night the ice-bergs are readily distinguished even at a distance by their natural effulgence, and in foggy weather by a peculiar blackness in the atmosphere. As they are not unfrequently drifted by the Greenland Stream considerably to the south of Newfoundland, sometimes even as far as the fortieth or thirty-ninth degree of latitude (May 1841, June 1842), ships sailing through the north-western Atlantic require to be always on their guard against them. The ill-fated 'President,' one of our first ocean-steamers, which was lost on its way to New York, without leaving a trace behind, is supposed to have been sunk by a collision with an ice-berg, and no doubt many a gallant bark has either foundered in the night, or been hurled by the storm against these floating rocks.

But though often dangerous neighbours, the bergs occasionally prove useful auxiliaries to the mariner. From their greater bulk lying below the water-line, they are either drifted along by the under-current against the wind, or from their vast dimensions are not perceptibly influenced even by the strongest gale, but, on the contrary, have the appearance of moving to windward, because every other kind of ice is drifted rapidly past them. Thus in strong adverse winds, their broad masses, fronting the storm like bulwarks, not seldom afford protection to ships mooring under their lee.

Anchoring to a berg is, however, not always unattended with danger, particularly when the summer is far advanced, or in a lower latitude, as all ice becomes exceedingly fragile when acted on by the sun or by a temperate atmosphere.

The blow of an axe then sometimes suffices to rend an ice-berg asunder, and to bury the careless seaman beneath its ruins, or to hurl him into the yawning chasm.

Thus Scoresby relates the adventure of two sailors who were attempting to fix an anchor to a berg. They began to hew a hole into the ice, but scarcely had the first blow been struck, when suddenly the immense mass split from top to bottom and fell asunder, the two halves falling in contrary directions with a prodigious crash. One of the sailors, who was possessed of great presence of mind, immediately scaled the huge fragment on which he was standing, and remained rocking to and fro on its summit until its equilibrium was restored; but his companion, falling between the masses, would most likely have been crushed to pieces if the current caused by their motion had not swept him within reach of the boat that was waiting for them.

Frequently large pieces detach themselves spontaneously from an ice-berg and fall into the sea with a tremendous noise. When this circumstance, called 'calving,' takes place, the ice-berg loses its equilibrium, sometimes turns on one side, and is occasionally inverted.

Dr. Hayes witnessed the crumbling of an immense berg, resembling in its general appearance the British House of Parliament. First one lofty tower came tumbling into the water, starting from its surface an immense flock of gulls; then another followed; and at length, after five hours of rolling and crashing, there remained of this splendid mass of congelation not a fragment that rose fifty feet above the water.

One of the most remarkable phenomena of the Polar Sea is the ice-blink, or reflection of the ice against the sky. A stripe of light, similar to the early dawn of morning, but without its redness, appears above the horizon, and traces a complete aërial map of the ice to a distance of many miles beyond the ordinary reach of vision. To the experienced navigator the 'blink' is frequently of the greatest use, as it not only points out the vicinity of the drift-ice, but indicates its nature, whether compact or loose, continuous or open. Thus Scoresby relates that on the 7th of June, 1821, he saw so distinct an ice-blink, that as far as twenty or thirty miles all round the horizon he was able to ascertain the figure and probable extent of each ice-field. The packed ice was distinguished from the larger fields by a more obscure and yellow colour; while each water-lane or open passage was indicated by a deep blue stripe or patch. By this means he was enabled to find his way out of the vast masses of ice in which he had been detained for several days, and to emerge into the open sea.

The tendency of the pack-ice to separate in calm weather, so that one might almost be tempted to believe in a mutual repulsive power of the individual blocks, is likewise favourable to the Arctic navigator. The perpetual daylight of summer is another advantage, but unfortunately the sun is too often veiled by dense mists which frequently obscure the air for weeks together, particularly in July. These fogs, which are a great impediment to the whaler's operations, have a very depressing influence upon the spirits; and as they are attended with a low temperature, which even at noon does not rise much above freezing-point, the damp cold is also physically extremely unpleasant.

At other times the sun sweeps two or three times round the Pole without being for a moment obscured by a cloud, and then the transparency of the air is such that objects the most remote may be seen perfectly distinct and clear. A ship's top-gallant mast, at the distance of five or six leagues, may be discerned when just appearing above the horizon with a common perspective-glass; and the summits of mountains are visible at the distance of from sixty to a hundred miles.

On such sunny days, the strong contrasts of light and shade between the glistening snow and the dark protruding rocks produce a remarkable deception in the apparent distance of the land, along a steep mountainous coast. When at the distance of twenty miles from Spitzbergen, for instance, it would be easy to induce even a judicious stranger to undertake a passage in a boat to the shore, from a belief that he was within a league of the land. At this distance the portions of rock and patches of snow, as well as the contour of the different hills, are as distinctly marked as similar objects in many other countries, not having snow about them, would be at a fourth or a fifth part of the distance.

Nothing can be more wonderful than the phenomena of the atmosphere dependent on reflection and refraction, which are frequently observed in the Arctic seas, particularly at the commencement or approach of easterly winds. They are probably occasioned by the commixture, near the surface of the land or sea, of two streams of air of different temperatures, so as to occasion an irregular deposition of imperfectly condensed vapour, which when passing the verge of the horizon apparently raises the objects there situated to a considerable distance above it, or extends their height beyond their natural dimensions. Ice, land, ships, boats, and other objects, when thus enlarged and elevated, are said to loom. The lower part of looming objects are sometimes connected with the horizon by an apparent fibrous or columnar extension of their parts; at other times they appear to be quite lifted into the air, a void space being seen between them and the horizon.

A most remarkable delusion of this kind was observed by Scoresby while sailing through the open ice, far from land. Suddenly an immense amphitheatre enclosed by high walls of basaltic ice, so like natural rock as to deceive one of his most experienced officers, rose around the ship. Sometimes the refraction produced on all sides a similar effect, but still more frequently remarkable contrasts. Single ice-blocks expanded into architectural figures of an extraordinary height, and sometimes the distant, deeply indented ice-border looked like a number of towers or minarets, or like a dense forest of naked trees. Scarcely had an object acquired a distinct form, when it began to dissolve into another.

It is well known that similar causes produce similar effects in the warmer regions of the earth. In the midst of the tropical ocean, the mariner sees verdant islands rise from the waters. and in the treeless desert fantastic palm-groves wave their fronds, as if in mockery of the thirsty caravan.

When we consider the intense cold which reigns during the greatest part of the year in the Arctic regions, we might naturally expect to find the whole of the Polar Sea covered, during the winter at least, with one solid unbroken sheet of ice. But experience teaches us that this is by no means the case; for the currents, the tides, the winds, and the swell of a turbulent ocean are mighty causes of disruption, or strong impediments to congelation. Both Lieutenant de Haven and Sir Francis M'Clintock* were helplessly carried along, in the depth of winter, by the pack-ice in Lancaster Sound and Baffin's Bay. A berg impelled by a strong under-current rips open an ice-field as if it were a thin sheet of glass; and in channels, or on coasts where the tides rise to a considerable height, their flux and reflux is continually opening crevices and lanes in the ice which covers the waters. That even in the highest latitudes the sea does not close except when at rest, was fully experienced by Dr. Hayes during his wintering at Port Foulke; for at all times, even when the temperature of the air was below the freezing-point of mercury, he could hear from the deck of his schooner the roar of the beating waves. From all these causes there has at no point within the Arctic circle been found a firm ice-belt extending, either in winter or in summer, more than from fifty to a hundred miles from land. And even in the narrow channels separating the islands of the Parry Archipelago, or at the mouth of Smith Sound, the waters will not freeze over, except when sheltered by the land, or when an ice-pack, accumulated by long continuance of winds from one quarter, affords the same protection.

But the constant motion of the Polar Sea, wherever it expands to a considerable breadth, would be insufficient to prevent its total congelation, if it were not assisted by other physical causes. A magnificent system of currents is continually displacing the waters of the ocean, and forcing the warm floods of the tropical regions to wander to the Pole, while the cold streams of the frigid zone are as constantly migrating towards the equator. Thus we see the Gulf Stream flowing through the broad gateway east of Spitzbergen, and forcing out a return current of cold water to the west of Spitzbergen, and through Davis' Strait.

The comparatively warm floods which, in consequence of this great law of circulation, come pouring into the Arctic Seas naturally require some time before they are sufficiently chilled to be converted into ice; and as sea-water has its maximum of density, or, in other words, is heaviest a few degrees above the freezing-point of water, and then

* See Chapter XXXII.

necessarily sinks, the whole depth of the sea must of course be cooled down to that temperature before freezing can take place. Ice being a bad conductor of heat, likewise limits the process of congelation; for after attaining a thickness of ten or fifteen feet, its growth is very slow, and probably even ceases altogether; for when floating fields, or floes, are found of a greater thickness, this increase is due to the snow that falls upon their surface, or to the accumulation of hummocks caused by their collision.

Thus, by the combined influence of these various physical agencies, bounds have been set to the congelation of the Polar waters. Were it otherwise the Arctic lands would have been mere uninhabitable wastes; for the existence of the seals, the walrus, and the whale depends upon their finding some open water at every season of the year; and deprived of this resource, all the Esquimaux, whose various tribes fringe the coasts in the highest latitudes hitherto discovered, would perish in a single winter.

If the Arctic glaciers did not discharge their bergs into the sea, or if no currents conveyed the ice-floes of the north into lower latitudes, ice would be constantly accumulating in the Polar world, and, destroying the balance of nature, would ultimately endanger the existence of man over the whole surface of the globe.

The Finback Whale.

Whalers among Ice-bergs.

# CHAPTER IV.

### ARCTIC MARINE ANIMALS.

THE vast multitudes of animated beings which people the
Polar Seas form a remarkable contrast to the nakedness
of their bleak and desolate shores. The colder surface-waters
almost perpetually exposed to a chilly air, and frequently
covered, even in summer, with floating ice, are indeed unfavourable to the development of organic life ; but this adverse
influence is modified by the higher temperature which constantly prevails at a greater depth; for, contrary to what
takes place in the equatorial seas, we find in the Polar Ocean
an increase of temperature from the surface downwards, in
consequence of the warmer under-currents, flowing from the
south northwards, and passing beneath the cold waters of
the superficial Arctic current.

POLAR BEARS AND SEALS.

Thus the severity of the Polar winter remains unfelt at a greater depth of the sea, where myriads of creatures find a secure retreat against the frost, and whence they emerge during the long summer's day, either to line the shores or to ascend the broad rivers of the Arctic world. Between the parallels of 74° and 80° Scoresby observed that the colour of the Greenland sea varies from the purest ultramarine to olive green, and from crystalline transparency to striking opacity—appearances which are not transitory, but permanent. This green semi-opaque water, whose position varies with the currents, often forming isolated stripes, and sometimes spreading over two or three degrees of latitude, mainly owes its singular aspect to small medusæ and nudibranchiate molluscs. It is calculated to form one-fourth part of the surface of the sea between the above-mentioned parallels, so that many thousands of square miles are absolutely teeming with life.

On the coast of Greenland, where the waters are so exceedingly clear that the bottom and every object upon it are plainly visible even at a depth of eighty fathoms, the ground is seen covered with gigantic tangles, which together with the animal world, circulating among their fronds, remind the spectator of the coral-reefs of the tropical ocean. Nullipores, mussels, alcyonians, sertularians, ascidians, and a variety of other sessile animals, incrust every stone or fill every hollow or crevice of the rocky ground. A dead seal or fish thrown into the sea is soon converted into a skeleton by the myriads of small crustaceans which infest these northern waters, and, like the ants in the equatorial forests, perform the part of scavengers of the deep.

Thus we find an exuberance of life, in its smaller and smallest forms, peopling the Arctic waters, and affording nourishment to a variety of strange and bulky creatures— cetaceans, walruses, and seals—which annually attract thousands of adventurous seamen to the Icy Ocean.

Of these sea-mammalians, the most important to civilised man is undoubtedly the Greenland whale (*Balæna mysticetus*), or smooth-back, thus called from its having no dorsal fin. Formerly these whales were harpooned in considerable numbers in the Icelandic waters, or in the fiords of Spitzbergen and Danish Greenland; then Davis' Straits became the favourite fishing-grounds; and more recently the inlets and various channels to the east of Baffin's Bay have been invaded; while, on the opposite side of America, several hundreds of whalers penetrate every year through Bering's Straits into the Icy Sea beyond, where previously they lived and multiplied, unmolested except by the Esquimaux.

More fortunate than the smooth-back, the rorquals or fin-whales (*Balænoptera boops, musculus, physalis,* and *rostratus*) still remain in their ancient seats, from which they are not likely to be dislodged, as the agility of their movements makes their capture more difficult and dangerous; while at the same time the small quantity of their fat and the shortness of their baleen render it far less remunerative. They are of a more slender form of body, and with a more pointed muzzle than the Greenland whale; and while the latter attains a length of only sixty feet, the *Balænoptera boops* grows to the vast length of 100 feet and more. There is also a difference in their food, for the Greenland whale chiefly feeds upon the minute animals that crowd the olive-coloured waters above described, or on the hosts of little pteropods that are found in many parts of the Arctic seas, while the rorquals frequently accompany the herring-shoals and carry death and destruction into their ranks.

The seas of Novaja Zemlya, Spitzbergen, and Greenland are the domain of the narwhal or sea-unicorn, a cetacean quite as strange, but not so fabulous as the terrestrial animal which figures in the arms of England. The use of the enormous spirally wound tusk projecting from its upper jaw, and from which it derives its popular name, has not yet been clearly ascertained, some holding it to be an instrument of defence, while others suppose it to be only an ornament or mark of the superior dignity of the sex to which it has been awarded.

Among the numerous dolphins which people the Arctic and Subarctic Seas, the beluga (*Delphinus leucas*), improperly called the white whale, is one of the most interesting. When young it has a brown colour, which gradually changes into a perfect white. It attains a length of from twelve to twenty feet, has no dorsal fin, a strong tail three feet broad, and a round head with a broad truncated snout. Beyond 56° of latitude it is frequently seen in large shoals, particularly near the estuaries of the large Siberian and North American rivers, which it often ascends to a considerable distance in pursuit of the salmon. A troop of belugas diving out of the dark waves of the Arctic Sea, is said to afford a magnificent spectacle. Their white colour appears dazzling, from the contrast of the sombre background, as they dart about with arrow-like velocity.

The black dolphin (*Globicephalus globiceps*) is likewise very common in the Arctic Seas, both beyond Bering's Straits and between Greenland and Spitzbergen, whence it frequently makes excursions to the south. It grows to the length of twenty-four feet, and is about ten feet in circumference. The skin, like that of the dolphin tribe in general, is smooth, resembling oiled silk; the colour a bluish black on the back, and generally whitish on the belly; the blubber is three or four inches thick.

The full-grown have generally twenty-two or twenty-four teeth in each jaw; and when the mouth is shut, the teeth lock between one another, like the teeth of a trap. The dorsal fin is about fifteen inches high, the tail five feet broad, the pectoral fins are as many, long and comparatively narrow; so that, armed with such excellent paddles, the black dolphin is inferior to none of his relatives in swiftness. Of an eminently social disposition, these dolphins sometimes congregate in herds of many hundreds, under the guidance of several old experienced males, whom the rest follow like a flock of sheep—a property from which the animal is called in Shetland the 'ca'ing whale.' No cetacean strands more frequently than the black dolphin, and occasionally large herds have been driven on the shores of Iceland, Norway, and the Orkney, Shetland and Faeroe islands, where their capture is hailed as a godsend. The intelligence that a shoal of ca'ing whales or grinds has been seen approaching the coast, creates great excitement among the otherwise phlegmatic inhabitants of the Faeroe Islands. The whole neighbourhood, old and young, is instantly in motion, and soon numerous boats shoot off from shore to intercept the retreat of the dolphins. Slowly and steadily they are driven towards the coast; the phalanx of their enemies draws closer and closer together; terrified by stones and blows, they run

ashore, and lie gasping as the flood recedes. Then begins
the work of death, amid the loud shouts of the executioners
and the furious splashings of the victims. In this manner
more than 800 grinds were massacred on August 16, 1776;
and during the four summer months that Langbye sojourned
on the islands in 1817, 623 were driven on shore, and served
to pay one-half of the imported corn. But, on the other
hand, many years frequently pass without yielding one single
black whale to the tender mercies of the islanders.

The ferocious orc or grampus (*Delphinus orca*) is the tiger
of the Arctic Seas. Black above, white beneath, it is distinguished by its large dorsal fin, which curves backwards
towards the tail, and rises to the height of two feet or more.
Measuring no less than twenty-five feet in length and twelve
or thirteen in girth, of a courage equal to its strength, and
armed with formidable teeth, thirty in each jaw, the grampus
is the dread of the seals, whom it overtakes in spite of their
rapid flight; and the whale himself would consider it as his
most formidable enemy, were it not for the persecutions of
man. The grampus generally ploughs the seas in small troops
of four or five, following each other in close single file, and
alternately disappearing and rising so as to resemble the
undulatory motions of one large serpentiform animal.

The family of the seals has also numerous and mighty
representatives in the Arctic waters. In the sea of Bering
we meet with the formidable sea-lion and the valuable sea-
bear, while the harp-seal, the bearded seal, and the hispid
seals (*Phoca grœnlandica, barbata, hispida*), spreading from
the Parry Islands to Novaja Zemlya, yield the tribute of their
flesh to numerous wild tribes, and that of their skins to the
European hunter.

Few Arctic animals are more valuable to man, or more frequently mentioned in Polar voyages than the walrus or morse
(*Trichechus rosmarus*), which, though allied to the seals, differs
greatly from them by the development of the canines of the
upper jaw, which form two enormous tusks projecting downwards to the length of two feet. The morse is one of the
largest quadrupeds existing, as it attains a length of twenty
feet, and a weight of from fifteen hundred to two thousand
pounds. In uncouthness of form it surpasses even the un-
gainly hippopotamus. It has a small head with a remarkably

thick upper lip, covered with large pellucid whiskers or bristles; the neck is thick and short; the naked grey or red-brown skin hangs loosely on the ponderous and elongated trunk; and the short feet terminate in broad fin-like paddles, resembling large ill-fashioned flaps of leather. Its movements on land are extremely slow and awkward, resembling those of a huge caterpillar, but in the water it has all the activity of the seals, or even surpasses them in speed.

Gregarious, like the seals and many of the dolphins, the walruses love to lie on the ice or on the sand-banks, closely huddled together. On the spot where a walrus lands, others are sure to follow; and when the first comers block the shore, those which arrive later, instead of landing on a free spot further on, prefer giving their friends who are in the way a gentle push with their tusks, so as to induce them to make room.

Timorous and almost helpless on land, where, in spite of its formidable tusks, it falls an easy prey to the attacks of man, the walrus evinces a greater degree of courage in the water, where it is able to make a better use of the strength and weapons bestowed upon it by nature. Many instances are known where walruses, which never attack but when provoked, have turned upon their assailants, or have even assembled from a distance to assist a wounded comrade.

Like the seals, the walrus is easily tamed, and of a most affectionate temper. This was shown in a remarkable manner by a young walrus brought alive from Archangel to St. Petersburg in 1829. Its keeper, Madame Dennebecq, having tended it with the greatest care, the grateful animal expressed its pleasure whenever she came near it by an affectionate grunt. It not only followed her with its eyes, but was never happier than when allowed to lay its head in her lap. The tenderness was reciprocal, and Madame Dennebecq used to talk of her walrus with the same warmth of affection as if it had been a pet lap-dog.

That parental love should be highly developed in animals thus susceptible of friendship may easily be imagined. Mr. Lamont, an English gentleman whom the love of sport led a few years since to Spitzbergen, relates the case of a wounded walrus who held a very young calf under her right arm. Whenever the harpoon was raised against it, the mother carefully shielded it with her own body. The countenance of this poor animal was never to be forgotten : that of the calf expressive of abject terror, and yet of such a boundless confidence in its mother's power of protecting it, as it swam along under her wing, and the old cow's face showing such reckless defiance for all that could be done to herself, and yet such terrible anxiety as to the safety of her calf. This parental affection is shamefully misused by man, for it is a common artifice of the walrus hunters to catch a young animal and make it grunt, in order to attract a herd.

The walrus is confined to the coasts of the Arctic regions, unless when drift-ice, or some other accident, carries it away into the open sea. Its chief resorts are Spitzbergen, Novaja Zemlya, North Greenland, the shores of Hudson's and Baffin's bays; and on the opposite side of the Polar Ocean, the coasts of Bering's Sea, and to the north of Bering's Straits the American and Asiatic shores from Point Barrow to Cape North. It has nowhere been found on the coasts of Siberia, from the mouth of the Jenisei to the last-mentioned promontory, and on those of America from Point Barrow to Lancaster Sound; so that it inhabits two distinct regions, separated from each other by vast extents of coast. Its food seems to consist principally of marine plants and shell-fish, though Scoresby relates that he found the remains of fishes, or even of seals, in its stomach.

As the Polar bear is frequently found above a hundred miles from the nearest land, upon loose ice steadily drifting into the sea, it seems but fair to assign him a place among the marine animals of the Arctic zone. He hunts by scent, and is constantly running across and against the wind which prevails from the northward, so that the same instinct which directs his search for prey also serves the important purpose of guiding him in the direction of the land and more solid ice. His favourite food is the seal, which he surprises crouching down with his fore paws doubled underneath, and pushing himself noiselessly forward with his hinder legs until within a few yards, when he springs upon his victim whether in the water or upon the ice. He can swim at the rate of three miles an hour, and can dive to a considerable distance. Though he attacks man when hungry, wounded, or provoked, he will not injure him when food more to his liking is at hand. Sir Francis M'Clintock relates an anecdote of a native of Upernavik who was out one dark winter's day visiting his seal-nets. He found a seal entangled, and whilst kneeling down over it upon the ice to get it clear, he received a slap on the back—from his companion as he supposed ; but a second and heavier blow made him look smartly round. He was horror-stricken to see a peculiarly grim old bear instead of his comrade. Without taking further notice of the man, Bruin tore the seal out of the net, and began his supper. He was not interrupted, nor did the man wait to see the meal finished, fearing no doubt that his uninvited and unceremonious guest might keep a corner for him.

Many instances have been observed of the peculiar sagacity of the Polar bear. Scoresby relates that the captain of a whaler, being anxious to procure a bear without wounding the skin, made trial of the stratagem of laying the noose of a rope in the snow, and placing a piece of *kreng*, or whale's carcase, within it. A bear, ranging the neighbouring ice, was soon enticed to the spot. Approaching the bait, he seized it in his mouth ; but his foot at the same moment, by a jerk of the rope, being entangled in the noose, he pushed it off with the adjoining paw, and deliberately retired. After having eaten the piece he carried away with him, he returned. The noose, with another piece of kreng, being then replaced, he pushed the rope aside, and again walked triumphantly off with the kreng. A third time the noose was laid, and this time the rope was buried in the snow, and the bait laid in a deep hole dug in the centre. But Bruin, after snuffing about the place for a few minutes, scraped the snow away with his paw, threw the rope aside, and escaped unhurt with his prize.

The she bear is taught by a wonderful instinct to shelter her young under the snow. Towards the month of December she retreats to the side of a rock, where, by dint of scraping and allowing the snow to fall upon her, she forms a cell in which to reside during the winter. There is no fear that she should be stifled for want of air, for the warmth of her breath always keeps a small passage open, and the snow, instead of forming a thick uniform sheet, is broken by a little hole round which is collected a mass of glittering hoar-frost, caused by the congelation of the breath. Within this strange nursery she produces her young, and remains with them beneath the snow until the month of March, when she emerges into the open air with her baby bears. As the time passes on, the breath of the family, together with the warmth exhaled from their bodies, serves to enlarge the cell, so that with their increasing dimensions the accommodation is increased to suit them. As the only use of the snow-burrow is to shelter the young, the male bears do not hibernate like the females, but roam freely about during the winter-months. Before retiring under the snow, the bear eats enormously, and, driven by an unfailing instinct, resorts to the most nutritious diet, so that she becomes prodigiously fat, thus laying in an internal store of alimentary matter which enables her not only to support her own life, but to suckle her young during her long seclusion, without taking a morsel of food. By an admirable provision of nature, the young are of wonderfully small dimensions when compared with the parent; and as their growth, as long as they remain confined in their crystal nursery, is remarkably slow, they consequently need but little food and space.

The Polar bear is armed with formidable weapons, and a proportionate power to use them. His claws are two inches in length, and his canine teeth, exclusive of the part in the jaw, about an inch and a half. Thus the hoards of provisions which are frequently deposited by Arctic voyagers to provide for some future want, have no greater enemy than the Polar bear. 'The final cache,' says Kane, 'which I relied so much upon, was entirely destroyed. It had been built with extreme care, of rocks which had been assembled by very heavy labour, and adjusted with much aid often from capstan-bars as levers. The entire construction was, so far as our means permitted, most effective and resisting. Yet these tigers of the ice seemed hardly to have encountered an obstacle. Not a morsel of pemmican remained, except in the iron cases, which being round, with conical ends, defied both claws and teeth. They had rolled and pawed them in every direction, tossing them about like footballs, although over eighty pounds in weight. An alcohol can, strongly iron-bound, was dashed into small fragments, and a tin can of liquor smashed and twisted almost into a ball. The claws of the beast had perforated the metal and torn it up as with a chisel. They were too dainty for salt-meats: ground coffee they had an evident relish for; old canvas was a favourite for some reason or other; even our flag, which had been reared "to take possession" of the waste, was gnawed down to the very staff. They had made a regular frolic of it; rolling our bread-barrels over the ice; and, unable to masticate our heavy india-rubber cloth, they had tied it up in unimaginable hard knots.'

Numbers of sea-birds are found breeding along the Arctic shores as far as man has hitherto penetrated; some even keep the sea in the high latitudes all the winter, wherever open water exists. On the most northern rocks the razor-bill rears its young, and the fulmar and Ross' gull have been seen in lanes of water beyond 82° lat. As the sun gains in power, enormous troops of puffins, looms, dovekies, rotges, skuas, burgermasters, Sabine's gulls, kittiwakes, ivory gulls, and Arctic terns, return to the north. There they enjoy the long summer day, and revel in the abundance of the fish-teeming waters, bringing life and animation into solitudes seldom or perhaps never disturbed by the presence of man, and mingling their wild screams with the hoarse-resounding surge or the howling of the storm. In many localities they breed in such abundance, that it may be said, almost without exaggeration, that they darken the sun when they fly, and hide the waters when they swim.

Grampus.

E

Oræfa Jökull, from Keymivebir.

# CHAPTER V.

## ICELAND.

ICELAND might as well be called Fireland, for all its 40,000
square miles have originally been upheaved from the depths
of the waters by volcanic power. First, at some immeasurably
distant period of the world's history, the small nucleus of the
future island began to struggle into existence against the
superincumbent weight of the ocean; then, in the course of
ages, cone rose after cone, crater was formed after crater,
eruption followed on eruption, and lava-stream on lava-stream,
until finally the Iceland of the present day was piled up with
her gigantic ' jökulls,' or ice-mountains, and her vast promontories, stretching like huge buttresses far out into the
sea.

In winter, when an almost perpetual night covers the wastes of this fire-born land, and the waves of a stormy ocean thunder against its shores, imagination can hardly picture a more desolate scene; but in summer the rugged nature of Iceland invests itself with many a charm. Then the eye reposes with delight on green valleys and crystal lakes, on the purple hills or snow-capped mountains rising in Alpine grandeur above the distant horizon, and the stranger might almost be tempted to exclaim with her patriotic sons, 'Iceland is the best land under the sun.' That it is one of the most interesting—through its history, its inhabitants, and above all its natural curiosities—no one can doubt. It has all that can please and fascinate the poet, the artist, the geologist, or the historian; the prosaic utilitarian alone, accustomed to value a country merely by its productions, might turn with some contempt from a land without corn, without forests, without mineral riches, and covered for about two-thirds of its surface with bogs, lava-wastes, and glaciers.

The curse of sterility rests chiefly on the south-eastern and central parts of the island. Here nothing is to be seen but deserts of volcanic stone or immense ice-fields, the largest of which—the Klofa jökull—alone extends over more than 4000 square miles. The interior of this vast region of névè and glacier is totally unknown. The highest peaks, the most dreadful volcanoes of the island, rise on the southern and south-western borders of this hitherto inaccessible waste; the Oraefa looking down from a height of 6000 feet upon all its rivals—the Skaptar, a name of dreadful significance in the annals of Iceland, and further on, like the advanced guards of this host of slumbering fires, the Katla, the Myrdal, the Eyjafjalla, and the Hecla, the most renowned, though not the most terrible, of all the volcanoes of Iceland.

As the ice-fields of this northern island far surpass in magnitude those of the Alps, so also the lava-streams of Ætna or Vesuvius are insignificant when compared with the enormous masses of molten stone which at various periods have issued from the craters of Iceland. From Mount Skjaldebreith, on both sides of the Lake of Thingvalla as far as Cape Reykjanes, the traveller sees an uninterrupted lava-field more than sixty miles long and frequently from twelve to fifteen broad; and lava-streams of still more gigantic proportions exist in many other parts of the island, particularly in the interior. In general these lava-streams have cooled down into the most fantastic forms imaginable. ' It is hardly possible,' says Mr. Holland, ' to give any idea of the general appearance of these once molten masses. Here a great crag has toppled over into some deep crevasse,—there a huge mass has been upheaved above the fiery stream which has seethed and boiled around its base. Here is every shape and figure that sculpture could design or imagination picture, jumbled together in grotesque confusion, whilst everywhere myriads of horrid spikes and sharp shapeless irregularities bristle amidst them.' *

Oræfa Jökull, the Monarch of Icelandic Mountains.

By the eruptions of the Icelandic volcanoes many a fair meadow-land has been converted into a stony wilderness; but if the subterranean fires have frequently brought ruin and desolation over the island, they have also endowed it with many natural wonders.

In the ' burning mountains ' of Krisuvik on the south-western coast, a whole hill-slope, with a deep narrow gorge at its foot, is covered with innumerable boiling springs and

* ' Peaks, Passes, and Glaciers.'

fumaroles, whose dense exhalations, spreading an intolerable stench, issue out of the earth with a hissing noise and completely hide the view.

The Námar, or boiling mud-caldrons of Reykjahlid, situated amongst a range of mountains near the Myvatn (gnat-lake), in one of the most solitary spots in the north of the island, on the border of enormous lava-fields and of a vast unknown wilderness, exhibit volcanic power on a still more gigantic scale. There are no less than twelve of these seething pits, all filled with a disgusting thick slimy grey or black liquid, boiling or simmering with greater or less vehemence, and emitting dense volumes of steam strongly impregnated with sulphurous gases. Some sputter furiously, scattering their contents on every side, while in others the muddy soup appears too thick to boil, and after remaining quiescent for about half a minute, rises up a few inches in the centre of the basin, emits a puff of steam, and then subsides into its former state. The diameter of the largest of all the pits cannot be less than fifteen feet; and it is a sort of mud Geysir, for at intervals a column of its black liquid contents, accompanied with a violent rush of steam, is thrown up to the height of six or eight feet. Professor Sartorius von Waltershausen, one of the few travellers who have visited this remarkable spot, says that the witches in *Macbeth* could not possibly have desired a more fitting place for the preparation of their infernal gruel than the mud-caldrons of Reykjahlid.

Among the hot or boiling springs of Iceland, which in hundreds of places gush forth at the foot of the mountains, some are of a gentle and even flow, and can be used for bathing, washing, or boiling, while others of an intermittent nature are mere objects of curiosity or wonder. One of the most remarkable of the latter is the Tungo-hver at Reikholt, in the ' valley of smoke,' thus named from the columns of vapour emitted by the thermal springs which are here scattered about with a lavish hand. It consists of two fountains within a yard of each other—the larger one vomiting a column of boiling water ten feet high for the space of about four minutes, when it entirely subsides, and then the smaller one operates for about three minutes, ejecting a column of about five feet. The alternation is perfectly

regular in time and force, and there are authentic accounts
of its unfailing exactitude for the last hundred years.

But of all the springs and fountains of Iceland there is
none to equal, either in grandeur or renown, the great Geysir,
which is not merely one of the curiosities of the country, but
one of the wonders of the earth, as there is nothing to compare to it in any other part of the world.

At the foot of the Laugafjall hill, in a green plain, through
which several rivers meander like threads of silver, and where
chains of dark-coloured mountains, overtopped here and there
by distant snow-peaks, form a grand but melancholy panorama, dense volumes of steam indicate from afar the site of a
whole system of thermal springs congregated on a small piece
of ground which does not exceed twelve acres. In any other
spot, the smallest of these boiling fountains would arrest the
traveller's attention, but here his whole mind is absorbed by
the great Geysir. In the course of countless ages this monarch
of springs has formed, out of the silica it deposits, a mound
which rises to about thirty feet above the general surface
of the plain, and slopes on all sides to the distance of a
hundred feet or thereabouts, from the border of a large circular
basin situated in its centre and measuring about fifty-six feet
in the greatest diameter and fifty-two feet in the narrowest.
In the middle of this basin, forming as it were a gigantic
funnel, there is a pipe or tube, which at its opening in the
basin is eighteen or sixteen feet in diameter, but narrows
considerably at a little distance from the mouth, and then
appears to be not more than ten or twelve feet in diameter.
It has been probed to a depth of seventy feet, but it is more
than probable that hidden channels ramify further into the
bowels of the earth. The sides of the tube are smoothly
polished, and so hard that it is not possible to strike off a
piece of it with a hammer.

Generally the whole basin is found filled up to the brim
with sea-green water as pure as crystal, and of a temperature
of from 180° to 190°. Astonished at the placid tranquillity
of the pool, the traveller can hardly believe that he is really
standing on the brink of the far-famed Geysir; but suddenly
a subterranean thunder is heard, the ground trembles under
his feet, the water in the basin begins to simmer, and large

bubbles of steam rise from the tube and burst on reaching the surface, throwing up small jets of spray to the height of several feet. Every instant he expects to witness the grand spectacle which has chiefly induced him to visit this northern land, but soon the basin becomes tranquil as before, and the dense vapours produced by the ebullition are wafted away by the breeze. These smaller eruptions are regularly repeated every eighty or ninety minutes, but frequently the traveller is obliged to wait a whole day or even longer before he sees the whole power of the Geysir. A detonation louder than usual precedes one of these grand eruptions; the water in the basin is violently agitated; the tube boils vehemently; and suddenly a magnificent column of water, clothed in vapour of a dazzling whiteness, shoots up into the air with immense impetuosity and noise to the height of seventy or eighty feet, and, radiating at its apex, showers water and steam in every direction. A second eruption and a third rapidly follow, and after a few minutes the fairy spectacle has passed away like a fantastic vision. The basin is now completely dried up, and on looking down into the shaft, one is astonished to see the water about six feet from the rim, and as tranquil as in an ordinary well. After about thirty or forty minutes it again begins to rise, and after a few hours reaches the brim of the basin, whence it flows down the slope of the mound into the Hvita or White-river.

Soon the subterraneous thunder, the shaking of the ground, the simmering above the tube, and the other phenomena which attend each minor eruption, begin again, to be followed by a new period of rest, and thus this wonderful play of nature goes on day after day, year after year, and century after century. The mound of the Geysir bears witness to its immense antiquity, as its water contains but a minute portion of silica.

After the Geysir the most remarkable fountain of these Phlegræan fields is the great Strokkr, situated about four hundred feet from the former. Its tube, the margin of which is almost even with the general surface, the small mound and basin being hardly discernible, is funnel-shaped or resembling the flower of a convolvulus, having a depth of forty-eight feet, and a diameter of six feet at the mouth, but contracting, at twenty-two feet from the bottom, to only eleven inches. The water stands from nine to twelve feet under the brim, and is generally in violent ebullition. A short time before the beginning of the eruptions, which are more frequent than those of the great Geysir, an enormous mass of steam rushes from the tube, and is followed by a rapid succession of jets, sometimes rising to the height of 120 or 150 feet, and dissolving into silvery mist. A peculiarity of the Strokkr is that it can at any time be provoked to an eruption by throwing into the orifice large masses of peat or turf; thus choking the shaft and preventing the free escape of the steam. After the lapse of about ten minutes, the boiling fluid, as if indignant at this attempt upon its liberty, heaves up a column of mud and water with fragments of peat as black as ink.

About 150 paces from the great Geysir are several pools of the most beautifully clear water, tinting with every shade of the purest green and blue the fantastical forms of the silicious travertin which clothes their sides. The slightest motion communicated to the surface quivers down to the bottom of these crystal grottoes, and imparts what might be called a sympathetic tremor of the water to every delicate incrustation and plant-like efflorescence. 'Aladdin's Cave could not be more beautiful,' says Preyer; and Mr. Holland remarks that neither description nor drawing is capable of giving a sufficient idea of the singularity and loveliness of this spot. In many places it is dangerous to approach within several feet of the margin, as the earth overhangs the water and is hollow underneath, supported only by incrustations scarcely a foot thick. A plunge into waters of about 200° would be paying rather too dearly for the contemplation of their fairy-like beauty.

The gigantic chasm of the Almannagja is another of the volcanic wonders of Iceland. After a long and tedious ride over the vast lava-plain which extends between the Skalafell and the lake of Thingvalla, the traveller suddenly finds himself arrested in his path by an apparently insurmountable obstacle, for the enormous Almannagja, or Allman's Rift, suddenly gapes beneath his feet—a colossal rent extending above a mile in length, and enclosed on both sides by abrupt walls of black lava, frequently upwards of a hundred feet high, and separated from about fifty to seventy feet from each other. A corresponding chasm, but of inferior dimensions, the Hrafna Gja, or Raven's Rift, opens its black rampart to the east, about eight miles further on; and both form the boundaries of the verdant plain of Thingvalla, which by a grand convulsion of nature has itself been shattered into innumerable small parallel crevices and fissures fifty or sixty feet deep. 'Ages ago,' says Lord Dufferin, 'some vast commotion shook the foundations of the island; and bubbling up from sources far away amid the inland hills, a fiery deluge must have rushed down between their ridges, until, escaping from the narrower gorges, it found space to spread itself into one broad sheet of molten stone over an entire district of country, reducing its varied surface to one vast blackened level. One of two things then occurred: either the vitrified mass, contracting as it cooled, the centre area of fifty square miles (the present plain of Thingvalla) burst asunder at either side from the adjoining plateau, and sinking down to its present level, left two parallel gjas or chasms, which form its lateral boundaries, to mark the limits of the disruption; or else, while the pith or marrow of the lava was still in a fluid state, its upper surface became solid, and formed a roof, beneath which the molten stream flowed on to lower levels, leaving a vast cavern into which the upper crust subsequently plumped down.' In the lapse of years, the bottom of the Almannagja has become gradually filled up to an even surface, covered with the most beautiful turf, except where the river Oxeraa, bounding in a magnificent cataract from the higher plateau over the precipice, flows for a certain distance between its walls. At the foot of the fall, the waters linger for a moment in a dark, deep, brimming pool, hemmed in by a circle of ruined rocks, in which anciently all women convicted of capital crimes were immediately drowned. Many a poor crone, accused of witchcraft, has thus ended her days in the Almannagja. As may easily be imagined, it is rather a nerve-trying task to descend into the chasm, over a rugged lava-slope, where the least false step may prove fatal; but the Icelandic horses are so sure-footed, that they can safely be trusted. From the bottom it is easy to distinguish on the

one face marks and formations exactly corresponding, though
at a different level, with those on the face opposite, and
evidently showing that they once had dovetailed into each
other, before the igneous mass was rent asunder.

Two leagues from Kalmanstunga, in an immense lava-
field, which probably originated in the Bald Jökull, are
situated the renowned Surts-hellir, or caves of Surtur, the

Surts-Hellir.

prince of darkness and fire of the ancient Scandinavian
mythology. The principal entrance to the caves is an extensive chasm formed by the falling in of a part of the lava-
roof; so that, on descending into it, the visitor finds himself
right in the mouth of the main cavern, which runs in an
almost straight line, and is nearly a mile in length. Its
average height is about forty, and its breadth fifty feet. The
lava-crust which forms its roof is about twelve feet thick,
and has the appearance of being stratified and columnar,
like basaltic pillars, in its formation. Many of the blocks of
lava thus formed have become detached and fallen into the
cavern, where they lie piled up in great heaps, and heavily
tax the patience of the traveller, who has to scramble over
the rugged stones, and can hardly avoid slipping and stum-

bling into the holes between them, varied by pools of water and masses of snow. But after having toiled and plodded to the extremity of this dismal cavern, his perseverance is amply rewarded by the sight of an ice-grotto, whose fairy beauty appears still more charming in contrast with its gloomy vestibule. From the crystal floor rises group after group of transparent pillars tapering to a point, while from the roof, brilliant icy pendants hang down to meet them. Columns and arches of ice are ranged along the crystalline walls, and the light of the candles is reflected back a hundredfold from every side, till the whole cavern shines with astonishing lustre. Mr. Holland, the latest visitor of the Surts-hellir, declares he never saw a more brilliant spectacle; and the German naturalist, Preyer, pronounces it one of the most magnificent sights in nature, reminding him of the fairy grottoes of the Arabian Nights' Tales.

From the mountains and the vast plateau which occupies the centre of the island, numerous rivers descend on all sides, which, fed in summer by the melting glaciers, pour enormous quantities of turbid water into the sea, or convert large alluvial flats into morasses. Though of a considerable breadth, their course is frequently very short, particularly along the southern coast, where the jokulls from which they derive their birth are only separated from the sea by a narrow foreland. In their impetuous flow, they not seldom bear huge blocks of stone along with them, and cut off all communication between the inhabitants of their opposite banks.

The chief rivers of Iceland are, in the south, the Thiorsa and the Hvita, which are not inferior in width to the Rhine in the middle part of its course; in the north, the Skjalfan-dafljot and the Jökulsa and the Jökulsa i Axarfirdi, large and rapid streams above a hundred miles long; and in the east the Lagarfliot. As may be expected in a mountainous country, containing many glacier-fed rivers, Iceland has numerous cascades, many of them rivalling or surpassing in beauty the far-famed falls of Switzerland.

One of the most celebrated of these gems of nature is the Goda-foss in the northern part of the island, formed by the deep and rapid Skjalfandafljot, as it rushes with a deafening roar over rocks fifty feet high into the caldron below; but it is far surpassed in magnificence by the Dettifoss, a fall of the Jökulsa i Axarfirdi.

'In some of old earth's convulsions,' says its *discoverer*, Mr. Gould,—for from its remote situation, deep in the northern wilds of Iceland, it had escaped the curious eye of previous travellers—' the crust of rock has been rent, and a frightful fissure formed in the basalt, about 200 feet deep, with the sides columnar and perpendicular. The gash terminates abruptly at an acute angle, and at this spot the great river rolls in. The wreaths of water sweeping down; the frenzy of the confined streams where they meet, shooting into each other from either side at the apex of an angle; the wild rebound when they strike a head of rock, lurching out half way down; the fitful gleam of battling torrents, obtained through a veil of eddying vapour; the Geysir-spouts which blow up about seventy feet from holes whence basaltic columns have been shot by the force of the descending water; the blasts of spray which rush upwards and burst into fierce showers on the brink, feeding rills which plunge over the edge as soon as they are born; the white writhing vortex below, with now and then an ice-green wave tearing through the foam to lash against the walls; the thunder and bellowing of the water, which make the rock shudder under foot, are all stamped on my mind with a vividness which it will take years to efface. The Almannagja is nothing to this chasm, and Schaffhausen is dwarfed by Dettifoss.' *

Of the many lakes or 'vatns' of Iceland, the Thingvalla, the My, and the Hvitar, are the most considerable.

The ocean currents which wash the coasts of Iceland from opposite directions have a considerable influence on its climate. The south and west coasts, fronting the Atlantic, and exposed to the Gulf Stream, remain ice-free even in winter, and enjoy a comparatively mild temperature, while the cold Polar current flowing in a south-western direction from Spitzbergen to Jan Mayen and Iceland, conveys almost every year to the eastern and northern shores of the island large masses of drift-ice, which sometimes do not disappear before July or even August. According to Dr.

* Iceland, its Scenes and Sagas, by Sabine Baring Gould, 1863.

Thorstensen, the mean annual temperature of the air at Reykjavik is +40°, and that of the sea +42°, while according to Herr von Scheele the mean annual temperature at Akreyre on the north coast is only +33°, though even this shows a comparatively mild climate in so high a latitude.

But if Iceland, thanks to its insular position and to the influence of the Gulf Stream, remains free from the excessive winter cold of the Arctic continents, its summer, on the other hand, is inferior in warmth to that which reigns in the interior of Siberia, or of the Hudson's Bay territories.

The mean summer temperature at Reykjavik is not above +54°; during many years the thermometer never rises a single time above +80°; sometimes even its maximum is not higher than +59°; and on the northern coast, snow not seldom falls even in the middle of summer. Under such circumstances, the cultivation of the cereals is of course impossible; and when the drift-ice remains longer than usual on the northern coasts, it prevents even the growth of the grass; and want and famine are the consequence.

The Icelandic summer is characterised by constant changes in the weather, rain continually alternating with sunshine, as with us in April. The air is but seldom tranquil, and storms of terrific violence are of frequent occurrence. Towards the end of September winter begins, preceded by mists, which finally descend in thick masses of snow. Travelling over the mountain tracks is at this time particularly dangerous, although cairns or piles of stone serve to point out the way, and here and there, as over the passes of the Alps, small huts have been erected to serve as a refuge for the traveller.

In former times, Iceland could boast of forests, so that houses and even ships used to be built of indigenous timber; at present it is almost entirely destitute of trees, for the dwarf-shrubberies here and there met with, where the birch hardly attains the height of twenty feet, are not to be dignified with the name of woods. A service tree (*Sorbus ancuparia*) fourteen feet high, and measuring three inches in diameter at the foot, is the boast of the governor's garden at Reykjavik; it is, however, surpassed by another at Akreyre, which spreads a full crown twenty feet from the ground, but never sees its clusters of berries ripen into scarlet.

The damp and cool Icelandic summer, though it prevents the successful cultivation of corn, is favourable to the growth of grasses, so that in some of the better farms the pasture grounds are hardly inferior to the finest meadows in England. About one-third of the surface of the country is covered with vegetation of some sort or other, fit for the nourishment of cattle; but, as yet, art has done little for its improvement —ploughing, sowing, drainage, and levelling being things undreamt of. With the exception of the grasses, which are of paramount importance, and the trees, which, in spite of their stunted proportions, are of great value, as they supply the islanders with the charcoal needed for shoeing their horses, few of the indigenous plants of Iceland are of any use to man. The *Angelica archangelica* is eaten raw with butter; the matted roots or stems of the *Menyanthes trifoliata* serve to protect the backs of the horses against the rubbing of the saddle; and the Icelandic moss, which is frequently boiled in milk, is likewise an article of exportation. The want of better grain frequently compels the poor islanders to bake a kind of bread from the seeds of the sand-reed (*Elymus arenarius*), which on our dunes are merely picked by the birds of passage; and the oarweed or tangle (*Laminaria saccharina*) is prized as a vegetable in a land where potatoes and turnips are but rarely cultivated.

When the first settlers came to Iceland, they found but two indigenous land-quadrupeds: a species of field-vole (*Arvicola œconomus*) and the Arctic fox; but the seas and shores were no doubt tenanted by a larger number of whales, dolphins, and seals than at the present day.

The ox, the sheep, and the horse which accompanied the Norse colonists to their new home, form the staple wealth of their descendants; for the number of those who live by breeding cattle is as three to one compared with those who chiefly depend on the sea for their subsistence. Milk and whey are almost the only beverages of the Icelanders. Without butter they will eat no fish; and curdled milk, which they eat fresh in summer and preserve in a sour state during the winter, is their favourite repast. Thus they set the highest value on their cattle, and tend them with the greatest care. In the preservation of their sheep they are much hampered by the badness of the climate, by the scantiness of winter food, and by the attacks of the eagles, the ravens, and the foxes, more particularly at the lambing season, when vast numbers of the young animals are carried off by all of them. The wool is not sheared off, but torn from the animal's back, and woven by the peasantry, during the long winter evenings, into a kind of coarse cloth, or knit into gloves and stockings, which form one of the chief articles of export.

'While at breakfast,' says Mr. Shepherd, 'we witnessed the Icelandic method of sheep-shearing. Three or four powerful young women seized, and easily threw on their backs, the struggling victims. The legs were then tied, and the wool pulled off by main force. It seemed, from the contortions of some of the wretched animals, to be a cruel method; but we were told that there is a period in the year when the young wool, beginning to grow, pushes the old out before it, so that the old coat is easily pulled out.' * The number of heads of cattle in the island is about 40,000, that of the sheep 500,000.

The horses, which number from 50,000 to 60,000, though small, are very robust and hardy. There being no wheel carriages on the island, they are merely used for riding and as beasts of burden. Their services are indispensable, as without them the Icelanders would not have the means of travelling and carrying their produce to the fishing villages or ports at which the annual supplies arrive from Copenhagen. In winter the poor animals must find their own food, and are consequently mere skeletons in spring; they, however, soon recover in summer, though even then they have nothing whatever but the grass and small plants which they can pick up on the hills.

The dogs are very similar to those of Lapland and Greenland. Like them they have long hair, forming a kind of collar round the neck, a pointed nose, pointed ears, and an elevated curled tail, with a temper which may be characterised as restless and irritable. Their general colour is white.

* The North-Western Peninsula of Iceland, 1862.

In the year 1770, thirteen reindeer were brought from
Norway. Ten of them died during the passage, but the three
that survived have multiplied so fast that large herds now
roam over the uninhabited wastes. During the winter, when
hunger drives them into the lower districts, they are frequently shot; but no attempts have been made to tame them,
for though indispensable to the Laplander, they are quite
superfluous in Iceland, which is too rugged and too much
intersected by streams to admit of sledging. They are, in
fact, generally considered as a nuisance, as they eat away the
Icelandic moss, which the islanders would willingly keep for
their own use.

The Polar bear is but a casual visitor in Iceland. About
a dozen come drifting every year with the ice from Jan
Mayen, or Spitzbergen, to the northern shores. Ravenous
with hunger, they immediately attack the first herds they
meet with; but their ravages do not last long, for the
neighbourhood, arising in arms, soon puts an end to their
existence.

In Iceland the ornithologist finds a rich field for his
favourite study, as there are no less than eighty-two different
species of indigenous birds, besides twenty-one that are only
casual visitors, and six that have been introduced by man.

The swampy grounds in the interior of the country are
peopled with legions of golden and king plovers, of snipes
and red-shanks; the lakes abound with swans, ducks, and
geese of various kinds; the snow-bunting enlivens the
solitude of the rocky wilderness with his lively note, and,
wherever grass grows, the common pipit (*Anthus pratensis*)
builds its neat little nest, well lined with horse-hair. Like
the lark, he rises singing from the ground, and frequently
surprises the traveller with his melodious warbling, which
sounds doubly sweet in the lifeless waste.

The eider-duck holds the first rank among the useful birds
of Iceland. Its chief breeding-places are small flat islands
on various parts of the coast, where it is safe from the attacks
of the Arctic fox, such as Akurey, Flatey, and Videy, which,
from its vicinity to Reykjavik, is frequently visited by
travellers. All these breeding-places are private property,
and several have been for centuries in the possession of the

same families, which, thanks to the birds, are among the wealthiest of the land. It may easily be imagined that the eider-ducks are guarded with the most sedulous care. Whoever kills one is obliged to pay a fine of thirty dollars; and the secreting of an egg, or the pocketing of a few downs, is punished with all the rigour of the law. The chief occupation of **Mr.** Stephenson, the aged proprietor of Videy, who dwells alone on the islet, is to examine through his telescope all the boats that approach, so as to be sure that there are no guns on board. During the breeding season no one is allowed to land without his special permission, and all noise, shouting, or loud speaking is strictly prohibited. But, in spite of these precautions, we are informed by recent travellers that latterly the greater part of the ducks of Videy have been tempted to leave their old quarters for the neighbouring Engey, whose proprietor hit upon the plan of laying hay upon the strand so as to afford them greater facilities for nest-building. The eider-down is easily collected, as the birds are quite tame. The female having laid five or six pale greenish-olive eggs, in a nest thickly lined with her beautiful down, the collectors, after carefully removing the bird, rob the nest of its contents, after which they replace her. She then begins to lay afresh, though this time only three or four eggs, and again has recourse to the down on her body. But her greedy persecutors once more rifle her nest, and oblige her to line it for the third time. Now, however, her own stock of down is exhausted, and with a plaintive voice she calls her mate to her assistance, who willingly plucks the soft feathers from his breast to supply the deficiency. If the cruel robbery be again repeated, which in former times was frequently the case, the poor eider-duck abandons the spot, never to return, and seeks for a new home where she may indulge her maternal instinct undisturbed.

Mr. Shepherd thus describes his visit to Vigr in the Isafjardardjup, one of the head-quarters of the eider-duck in the north of Iceland:—" As the island was approached, we could see flocks upon flocks of the sacred birds, and could hear their cooings at a great distance. We landed on a rocky wave-worn shore, against which the waters scarcely rippled, and set off to investigate the island. The shore was the most

F

wonderful ornithological sight conceivable.  The ducks and
their nests were everywhere in a manner that was quite
alarming.  Great brown ducks sat upon their nests in
masses, and at every step started up from under our feet.  It
was with difficulty that we avoided treading on some of the
nests.  The island being but three-quarters of a mile in
width, the opposite shore was soon reached.  On the coast
was a wall built of large stones, just above the high-water
level, about three feet in height and of considerable thickness.  At the bottom, on both sides of it, alternate stones
had been left out, so as to form a series of square compartments for the ducks to make their nests in.  Almost every
compartment was occupied ; and, as we walked along the
shore, a long line of ducks flew out one after another.  The
surface of the water also was perfectly white with drakes, who
welcomed their brown wives with loud and clamorous cooing.
When we arrived at the farmhouse we were cordially welcomed by its mistress.  The house itself was a great marvel.
The earthen wall that surrounded it and the window em-
brasures were occupied by ducks.  On the ground, the house
was fringed with ducks.  On the turf-slopes of the roof we
could see ducks ; and a duck sat in the scraper.

' A grassy bank close by had been cut into square patches
like a chess-board (a square of turf of about eighteen inches
being removed, and a hollow made), and all were filled with
ducks.  A windmill was infested, and so were all the out-
houses, mounds, rocks, and crevices.  The ducks were everywhere.  Many of them were so tame that we could stroke
them on their nests ; and the good lady told us that there
was scarcely a duck on the island which would not allow her
to take its eggs without flight or fear.  When she first
became possessor of the island, the produce of down from the
ducks was not more than fifteen pounds weight in the year,
but under her careful nurture of twenty years it had risen to
nearly one hundred pounds annually.  It requires about one
pound and a half to make a coverlet for a single bed, and the
down is worth from twelve to fifteen shillings per pound.  Most
of the eggs are taken and pickled for winter consumption,
one or two only being left to hatch.'

Though not so important as the eider, the other members

of the duck family which during the summer season enliven the lakes and swamps of Iceland are very serviceable. On the Myvatn, or Gnat Lake, one of their chief places of resort, the eggs of the long-tailed duck, the wild duck, the scoter, the common goosander, the red-breasted merganser, the scaup-duck, &c., and other anserines are carefully gathered and preserved in enormous quantities for the winter, closely packed in a fine grey volcanic sand.

The wild swan is frequently shot or caught for his feathers, which bring in many a dollar to the fortunate huntsman. This noble bird frequents both the salt and brackish waters along the coast, and the inland lakes and rivers, where it is seen either in single pairs or congregated in large flocks. To build its nest, which is said to resemble closely that of the flamingo, being a large mound, composed of mud, rushes, grass, and stones, with a cavity at top lined with soft down, it retires to some solitary uninhabited spot. Much has been said in ancient times of the singing of the swan, and the beauty of its dying notes; but, in truth, the voice of the swan is very loud, shrill, and harsh, though when high in the air, and modulated by the winds, the note or whoop of an assemblage of them is not unpleasant to the ear. It has a peculiar charm in the unfrequented wastes of Iceland, where it agreeably interrupts the profound silence that reigns around.

The raven, one of the commonest land-birds in Iceland, is an object of aversion to the islanders, as it not only seizes on their young lambs and eider-ducks, but also commits great depredations among the fishes laid out to dry upon the shore. Poles to which dead ravens are attached, to serve as a warning to the living, are frequently seen in the meadows; and the Icelander is never so happy as when he has succeeded in shooting a raven. This, however, is no easy task, as no bird is more cautious, and its eyes are as sharp as those of the eagle. Of all Icelandic birds, the raven breeds the earliest, laying about the middle of March its five or six pale-green eggs spotted with brown in the inaccessible crevices of rocks. Towards the end of June, Preyer saw many young ravens grown to a good size, and but little inferior to the old ones in cunning.

In the gloomy Scandinavian mythology the raven occupies

a rank equal to that of the eagle in the more cheerful fables of ancient Greece. It was dedicated to Odin, who, as the traditional history of Iceland informs us, had two ravens which were let loose every morning to gather tidings of what was going on in the world, and which on returning in the evening perched upon Odin's shoulders to whisper the news in his ear: the name of one was *Hugin*, or spirit; of the other, *Mumin*, or memory. Even now many superstitious notions remain attached to the raven; for the Icelanders believe this bird to be not only acquainted with what is going on at a distance, but also with what is to happen in future, and are convinced that it foretells when any of a family is about to die, by perching on the roof of the house, or wheeling round in the air with a continual cry, varying its voice in a singular and melodious manner.

The white-tailed sea-eagle is not uncommon in Iceland, where he stands in evil repute as a kidnapper of lambs and eider-ducks. He is sometimes found dead in the nets of the fishermen; for, pouncing upon a haddock or salmon, he gets entangled in the meshes, and is unable to extricate himself. The skins of the bird, which seems to attain a larger size than in Great Britain, most likely from being less disturbed by man, are sold at Reykjavik and Akureyre for from three to six rixdollars.

The jerfalcon (*Falco gyrfalco*), generally considered as the boldest and most beautiful of the falcon tribe, has its head-quarters in Iceland. As long as the noble sport of falconry was in fashion, for which it was highly esteemed, the trade in falcons was worth from 2000 to 3000 rixdollars annually to the islanders, and even now high prices are paid for it by English amateurs.

The rarest bird of Iceland, if not entirely extinct, is the giant-auk, or Geirfugl. The last pair was caught about seventeen years ago near the Geirfuglaskers, a group of solitary rocks to the south of the Westman Isles, its only known habitat besides some similar cliffs on the north-eastern coast. Since that time it is said to have been seen by some fishermen; but this testimony is extremely doubtful, and the question of its existence can only be solved by a visit to the Geirfuglaskers themselves—an undertaking which, if practicable at all, is attended with extreme difficulty and danger, as these rocks are completely isolated in the sea, which even in calm weather breaks with such violence against their abrupt declivities that for years it must be absolutely impossible to approach them.

In 1858 two English naturalists determined at least to make the attempt, and settled for the season in a small hamlet on the neighbouring coast, eager to seize the first opportunity for storming the Geirfugl's stronghold. They waited for several months, but in vain, the stormy summer being more than usually unfavourable for their undertaking; and they were equally unsuccessful in the north, whither they had sent an Icelandic student specially instructed for the purpose. The giant-auk is three feet high, and has a black bill four inches and a quarter long, both mandibles being crossed obliquely with several ridges and furrows. Its wings are mere stumps, like those of the Antarctic penguins. Thirty pounds have been paid for its egg, which is larger than that of any other European bird; and there is no knowing the price the Zoological Society would pay for a live bird, if this truly ' rara avis ' could still be found.

The waters of Iceland abound with excellent fish which not only supply the islanders with a great part of their food and furnish them with one of their chief articles of exportation, but also attract a number of foreign seamen. Thus about 300 French, Dutch, and Belgian fishing sloops, manned with crews amounting in all to 7000 men, annually make their appearance on the southern and western coasts of Iceland, particularly those of the Guldbringe Syssel, or gold-bringing country: thus named, not from any evidence of the precious metal, but from the golden cod-harvests reaped on its shores. Between thirty and forty English fishing-smacks yearly visit the northern coast. When they have obtained a good cargo they run to Shetland to discharge it, and return again for more.

The Icelandic fishing-season, which begins in February and ends in June, occupies one-half of the male inhabitants of the island, who come flocking to the west, even from the remotest districts of the north and east, to partake of the rich harvest of the seas. Many thus travel for more than 200 miles, in

the midst of winter, while the storm howls over the naked
waste, and the pale sun scarcely dispels for a few hours the
darkness of the night.   In every hut where they tarry on
the road they are welcome, and have but rarely to pay for their
entertainment, for hospitality is still reckoned a duty in Iceland.   On reaching the fishing-station an agreement is soon
made with the proprietor of a boat.   They usually engage to
assist in fishing from February 12 to May 12, and receive in
return a share of the fish which they help to catch, besides
forty pounds of flour and a daily allowance of sour curds
or 'skier.'

All the men belonging to a boat generally live in the same
damp and narrow hut.   At daybreak they launch forth to
brave for many hours the inclemencies of the weather and the
sea, and while engaged in their hard day's work their sole
refreshment is the chewing of tobacco or a mouthful of skier.
On returning to their comfortless hut, their supper consists
of the fishes of inferior quality they may have caught, or of
the heads of the cod or ling, which are too valuable for
their own consumption.   These are split open and hung upon
lines or exposed on the shore to the cold winds and the hot
sun ; this renders them perfectly hard, and they keep good
for years.   In this dried state the cod is called stockfish.
About the middle of May the migratory fishermen return to
their homes, leaving their fish which are not yet quite dry to
the care of the fishermen dwelling on the spot.   Towards the
middle of June, when the horses have so far recovered from
their long winter's fast as to be able to bear a load, they come
back to fetch their stockfish, which they convey either to their
own homes for the consumption of their own families, or to
the nearest port for the purpose of bartering it against other
articles.   Haddocks, flatfish, and herrings are also very
abundant in the Icelandic seas ; and along the northern and
north-western coasts the basking shark is largely fished for
all the summer.   Strong hooks baited with mussels or pieces
of fish, and attached to chains anchored at a short distance
from the shore, serve for the capture of this monster, which is
scarcely, if at all, inferior in size to the white shark, though
not nearly so formidable, as it rarely attacks man.   The
skin serves for making sandals; the coarse flesh is eaten by

the islanders, whom necessity has taught not to be overnice in their food; and the liver, the most valuable part, is stewed for the sake of its oil.

'We had observed,' says Mr. Shepherd, 'that the horrible smell which infested Jsa-fjordr varied in intensity as we approached or receded from a certain black-looking building at the northern end of the town. On investigating this building, we discovered that the seat of the smell was to be found in a mass of putrid sharks' livers, part of which were undergoing a process of stewing in a huge copper. It was a noisome green mass, fearful to contemplate. The place was endurable only for a few seconds; yet dirty-looking men stirred up the mass with long poles, and seemed to enjoy the reeking vapours.'

The salmon of Iceland, which formerly remained undisturbed by the phlegmatic inhabitants, are now caught in large numbers for the British market. A small river bearing the significant name of Laxaa, or Salmon-river, has been rented for the trifling sum of 100l. a year by an English company, which sends every spring its agents to the spot well provided with the best fishing apparatus. The captured fish are immediately boiled, and hermetically packed in tin boxes, so that they can be eaten in London almost as fresh as if they had just been caught.

The mineral kingdom contributes but little to the prosperity of Iceland. It affords neither metals, nor precious stones, nor rock-salt, nor coal; for the seams of 'surturbrand,' or 'lignite,' found here and there, are too unimportant to be worked. The solfataras of Krisuvik and Husavik, though extremely interesting to the geologist, likewise furnish sulphur in too impure a condition or too thinly scattered to afford any prospect of being worked with success, not to mention the vast expense of transport over the almost impassable lava tracts that separate them from the nearest ports. In 1839–40, when, in consequence of the monopoly granted by the Neapolitan government to a French company, sulphur had risen to more than three times its usual price, Mr. Knudsen, an enterprising Danish merchant, undertook to work the mines of Krisuvik, but even then it would not answer.

In 1859 a London company, founded by Mr. Bushby,—who having explored the sulphur districts, had raised great expectations on what he considered their dormant wealth,—renewed the attempt, but after a year's trial it was abandoned as perfectly hopeless. The 'solfataras of Iceland,' says Professor Sartorius of Waltershausen, 'cannot compete with those of Sicily, where more sulphur is wantonly wasted and trodden under foot than all Iceland possesses. While the "Namars" of the north, which are far richer than those of Krisuvik, annually furnish scarcely more than ten tons, the sulphur mines of Sicily produce at least 50,000, and, if necessary, could easily export double the quantity.'

As coal is too expensive a fuel for any but the rich in the small seaport towns, and peat, though no doubt abundantly scattered over the island, is dug only in a few places, the majority of the people make use of singular substitutes. The commonest is dried cow's and sheep's dung; but many a poor fisherman lacks even this 'spicy' material, and is fain to use the bones of animals, the skeletons of fishes or dried sea-birds, which, with a stoical contempt for his olfactory organs, he burns, feathers and all. There is, however, no want of fuel in those privileged spots where driftwood is found, and here the lava hearth of the islander cheerfully blazes either with the pine conveyed to him by the kindly Polar currents from the Siberian forests, or with some tropical trunk, wafted by the Gulf Stream over the Atlantic to his northern home.

The Eider-duck.

Herdu-Breid, from Krabla.

# CHAPTER VI.

## HISTORY OF ICELAND.

Discovery of the Island by Naddodr in 861—Gardar—Floki of the Ravens—Ingolfr
and Leif—Ulfliot the Lawgiver—The Althing—Thingvalla—Introduction of
Christianity into the Island—Frederick the Saxon and Thorwald the Traveller
—Thangbrand—Golden Age of Icelandic Literature—Snorri Sturleson—The
Island submits to Hakon, King of Norway, in 1254—Long Series of Calamities
—Great Eruption of the Skapta Jökull in 1783—Commercial Monopoly—
Better Times in Prospect.

THE Norse vikings were, as is well known, the boldest of
navigators. They possessed neither the sextant nor the
compass; they had neither charts nor chronometers to guide
them; but trusting solely to fortune, and to their own indomitable courage, they fearlessly launched forth into the
vast ocean. Many of these intrepid corsairs were no doubt
lost on their adventurous expeditions, but frequently a favourable chance rewarded their temerity, either with some rich
booty or some more glorious discovery.

Thus in the year 861, Naddodr, a Norwegian pirate,
while sailing from his native coast to the Faeroe Islands, was
drifted by contrary winds far to the north. For several days
no land was visible—nothing but an interminable waste of
waters; when suddenly the snow-clad mountains of Iceland

were seen to rise above the mists of the ocean. Soon after
·Naddodr landed with part of his crew, but discovered no
traces of man in the desert country. The viking tarried but
a short time on this unpromising coast, on which he bestowed
the appropriate name of Snowland.

Three years later, Gardar, another northern freebooter,
while sailing to the Hebrides, was likewise driven by stormy
weather to Iceland. He was the first circumnavigator of
the island, which he called, after himself, Gardar's holm, or
the island of Gardar. On his return to his native port, he
gave his countrymen so flattering an account of the newly
discovered land, that Floki, a famous viking, resolved to
settle there. Trusting to the augury of birds, Floki took
with him three ravens to direct him on his way. Having
sailed a certain distance beyond the Faeroe Islands, he gave
liberty to one of them, which immediately returned to the
land. Proceeding onwards, he loosed the second, which, after
circling for a few minutes round the ship, again settled on
its cage, as if terrified by the boundless expanse of the sea.
The third bird, on obtaining his liberty a few days later,
proved at length a faithful pilot, and flying direct to the
North, conducted Floki to Iceland. As the sea-king entered
the broad bay, which is bounded on the left by the huge
Snäfells Jökull, and on the right by the bold promontory of
the Guldbringe Syssel, Faxa, one of his companions, remarked
that a land with such noble features must needs be of considerable extent. To reward him for this remark, which
flattered the vanity or the ambition of his leader, the bay
was immediately named Faxa Fiord, as it is still called to
the present day. The new colonists, attracted by the abundance of fish they found in the bay, built their huts on the
borders of a small outlet, still bearing the name of Rafna
Fiord, or the Raven's Frith; but as they neglected to make
hay for the winter, the horses and cattle they had brought
with them died of want. Disappointed in his expectations,
Floki returned home in the second year, and, as might
naturally have been expected from an unsuccessful settler,
gave his countrymen but a dismal account of Iceland, as he
definitively named it.

Yet, in spite of his forbidding description, the political

disturbances which took place about this time in Norway led to the final colonisation of the island. Harold Haarfager, or the Fair-haired, a Scandinavian yarl, having by violence and a successful policy reduced all his brother-yarls to subjection, first consolidated their independent domains into one realm, and made himself absolute master of the whole country. Many of his former equals submitted to his yoke; but others, animated by that unconquerable love of liberty innate in men who for many generations have known no superior, preferred seeking a new home across the ocean to an ignominious vassalage under the detested Harold. Ingolfr and his cousin Leif were the first of these high-minded nobles that emigrated (869–870) to Iceland.

On approaching the southern coast, Ingolfr cast the sacred pillars belonging to his former dwelling into the water, and vowed to establish himself on the spot to which they should be wafted by the waves. His pious intentions were for the time frustrated, as a sudden squall separated him from his penates, and forced him to locate himself on a neighbouring promontory, which to this day bears the name of Ingolfrshofde. Here he sojourned three years, until the followers he had sent out in quest of the missing pillars at length brought him the joyful news that they had been found on the beach of the present site of Reykjavik, whither, in obedience to what he supposed to be the divine summons, he instantly removed. Ingolfr's friend and relative Leif was shortly after assassinated by some Irish slaves whom he had captured in a predatory descent on the Hibernian coast. The surviving chieftain deplored the loss of his kinsman, lamenting 'that so valiant a man should fall by such villains,' but found consolation by killing the murderers and annexing the lands of their victim. When, in course of time, he himself felt his end approaching, he requested to be buried on a hill overlooking the fiord, that from that elevated site his spirit might have a better view of the land of which he was the first inhabitant.

Such are the chronicles related in the 'Landnama Bok,' or 'Book of Occupation,' one of the earliest records of Icelandic history.

Ingolfr and his companions were soon followed by other

emigrants desirous of escaping from the tyranny of Harold Haarfager, who at first favoured a movement that removed far beyond the sea so many of his turbulent opponents, but subsequently alarmed at the drain of population, or desirous of profiting by the exodus, levied a fine of four ounces of silver on all who left his dominions to settle in Iceland. Yet such were the attractions which the island at that time presented, that, in spite of all obstacles, not half a century elapsed before all its inhabitable parts were occupied, not only by Norwegians, but also by settlers from Denmark and Sweden, Scotland and Ireland.

The Norwegians brought with them their language and idolatry, their customs and historical records, which the other colonists, but few in numbers, were compelled to adopt. At first the udal or free land-hold system of their own country was in vigour, but every leader of a band of emigrants being chosen by force of circumstances as the acknowledged chief of the district occupied by himself and companions, speedily paved the way for a demi-feudal system of vassalage and subservience. As the arrival of new settlers rendered the possession of the land more valuable, endless contests between these petty chiefs arose for the better pastures and fisheries. To put an end to this state of anarchy, so injurious to the common weal, Ulfliot the Wise was commissioned to frame a code of laws, which the Icelanders, by a single simultaneous and peaceful effort, accepted as their future constitution.

The island was now divided into four provinces and twelve districts. Each district had its own judge, and its own popular 'Thing,' or assembly; but the national will was embodied and represented by the 'Althing,' or supreme parliament of Iceland, which annually met at Thingvalla, under an elective president, or 'Logmathurman,' the chief magistrate of this northern republic.

On the banks of the river Oxerá, where the rapid stream, after forming a magnificent cascade, rushes into the lake of Thingvalla, lies the spot where, for many a century, freemen met to debate, while despotic barbarians still reigned over the milder regions of Europe. Isolated on all sides by deep volcanic chasms, which some great revolution of nature has

rent in the vast lava-field around, and embosomed in a wide
circle of black precipitous hills, the situation of Thingvalla is
extremely romantic, but the naked dark-coloured rocks, and
the traces of subterranean fire visible on every side, impart a
stern melancholy to the scene. The lake, the largest sheet of
water in the island, is about thirty miles in circumference;
its boundaries have undergone many changes, especially
during the earthquakes of the past century, when its northern
margin collapsed, while the opposite one was raised. The
depth of its crystal waters is very great, and in its centre
rise two small crater-islands, the result of some unknown
eruption. The mountains on its south bank have a picturesque appearance, and large volumes of steam issuing from
several hot sources on their sides prove that, though all
be tranquil now, the volcanic fires are not extinct. Only a
few traces of the ancient Althing are left—three small
mounds, where sat in state the chiefs and judges of the
land—for as the assembly used to pitch their tents on the
borders of the stream, and the deliberations were held in
the open air, there are no imposing ruins to bear witness to a
glorious past. But though all architectural pomp be absent,
the scene hallowed by the recollections of a thousand years
is one of deep interest to the traveller. The great features
of nature are the same as when the freemen of Iceland
assembled to settle the affairs of their little world; but the
raven now croaks where the orator appealed to the reason
or the passions of his audience, and the sheep of the neighbouring pastor crop undisturbed the grass of desecrated
Thingvalla.

Christianity was first preached in Iceland about the year
981, by Friedrich, a Saxon bishop, to whom Thorwald the
traveller, an Icelander, acted as interpreter. Thorwald
having been treated with great severity by his father, Kodran, had fled to Denmark, where he had been converted by
Friedrich. He returned with the pious bishop to his paternal
home, where the solemn service of the Christians made
some impression on Kodran, but still the obstinate pagan
could not be prevailed upon to renounce his ancient gods.
' He must believe,' said he, ' the word of his own priest, who
was wont to give him excellent advice.' ' Well then,' replied

Thorwald, 'this venerable man whom I have brought to thy dwelling is weak and infirm, while thy well-fed priest is full of vigour. Wilt thou believe in the power of our God if the bishop drives him hence?' Friedrich now cast a few drops of holy-water on the priest, which immediately burnt deep holes into his skin, so that he fled, uttering dreadful curses. After this convincing proof, Kodran adopted the Christian faith. But persuasion and miracles acted too slowly for the fiery Thorwald, who would willingly have converted all Iceland at once with fire and sword. His sermons were imprecations, and the least contradiction roused him to fury. Unable to bear so irascible an associate, the good bishop Friedrich, giving up his missionary labours, returned to Saxony. As to Thorwald, his restless disposition led him to far distant lands. He visited Greece and Syria, Jerusalem and Constantinople, and ultimately founded a convent in Russia, where he died in the odour of sanctity.

Soon after Thangbrand was sent by the Norwegian king Olaf Truggeson as missionary to Iceland. His method of conversion appears to have been very like that of his erratic predecessor; for while he held the cross in one hand, he grasped the sword with the other. 'Thangbrand,' says an ancient chronicler, 'was a passionate ungovernable person, and a great manslayer, but a good scholar and clever. He was two years in Iceland, and was the death of three men before he left it.'

Other missionaries of a more evangelical character took his place, and proved by their success that mild reasoning is frequently a far more effectual means of persuasion than brutal violence. They made a great number of proselytes, and the whole island was now divided into two factions ready to appeal to the sword for the triumph of Christ or of Odin. But before coming to this dreadful extremity, the voice of reason was heard, and the contending parties agreed to submit the question to the decision of the Althing.

The assembly met, and the momentous debate was proceeding, when suddenly a loud crash of subterranean thunder was heard, and the earth shook under their feet. 'Listen!' exclaimed a follower of Odin, 'and beware of the anger of our gods: they will consume us with their fires, if we venture to question their authority.' The Christian party hesitated; but their confidence was soon restored by the presence of mind of their chief orator, Thorgeir, who, pointing to the lava-fields around, asked with whom the gods were angry when these rocks were melted: a burst of eloquence which at once decided the question in favour of the Cross.

The new faith brought with it a new spirit of intellectual development, which attained its highest splendour in the twelfth century. Classical studies were pursued with the utmost zeal, and learned Icelanders travelled to Germany and France to extend their knowledge in the schools of Paris, or Cologne. The Icelandic bards, or scalds, were renowned throughout all Scandinavia; they frequented the courts of Sweden, Denmark, and Norway, and were everywhere received with the highest honours.

The historians, or sagamen, of Iceland were no less renowned than its scalds. They became the annalists of the whole Scandinavian world, and the simplicity and truth by which their works are distinguished fully justify their high reputation. Among the many remarkable men who at that time graced the literature of the Arctic isle, Sämund Frode, the learned author of the 'Voluspa' (a work on the ancient Icelandic mythology) and the 'Havamal' (a general chronicle of events from the beginning of the world); Are Thorgilson, whose 'Landnama Bok' relates with the utmost accuracy the annals of his native land; and Gissur, who about the year 1180 described his voyages to the distant Orient, deserve to be particularly mentioned; but great above all in genius and fame was Snorri Sturleson, the Herodotus of the North, whose eventful life and tragic end would well deserve to be recounted at greater length.

Gifted with the rarest talents, and chief of the most powerful family of the island, Snorri was elected in 1215 to the high office of Logmathurman; but disgusting his sturdy countrymen by his excessive haughtiness, he was obliged to retire to the court of Hakon, king of Norway. During this exile he collected the materials for his justly celebrated 'Heimskringla,' or Chronicle of the Kings of Norway. Returning home in 1221, he was again named Logmathurman; but as he endeavoured to pave the way for the annexation of his

native country to the Norwegian realm, his foreign intrigues
caused a rising against his authority, and he was once
more compelled to take refuge in Norway. Here he remained several years, until the triumph of his own faction
allowed him to return to his family estate at Reikholt, where
he was murdered on a dark September night in the year
1241. Thus perished the most remarkable man Iceland has
ever produced. The republic itself did not long survive his
fall; for, weary of the interminable feuds of their chiefs,
the people voluntarily submitted to Hakon in 1254, and
the middle of the thirteenth century was signalised by
the transfer of the island to the Norwegian crown, after
three hundred and forty years of a turbulent but glorious
independence.

From that time the political history of the Icelanders offers
but little interest. With their annexation to an European
monarchy perished the vigour, restlessness and activity which
had characterised their forefathers; and though the Althing
still met at Thingvalla, the national spirit had fled. It was
still further subdued by a long chain of calamities—plagues,
famines, volcanic eruptions, and piratical invasions—which
following each other in rapid succession, devastated the land
and decimated its unfortunate inhabitants.

In 1402 that terrible plague, the memory of which is still
preserved under the name of the ' Black Death,' carried off
nearly two-thirds of the whole population, and was followed
by such an inclement winter that nine-tenths of the cattle in
the island died. The miseries of a people suffering from
pestilence and famine were aggravated by the English fishermen, who, in spite of the remonstrances of the Danish government, frequented the defenceless coast in considerable
numbers, and were in fact little better than the old sea-robbers
who first colonised the island, plundering and burning on the
main, and holding the wealthy inhabitants to ransom. Their
predatory incursions were frequently repeated during the
seventeenth century, and even the distant Mediterranean sent
its Algerine pirates to add to the calamities of Iceland.

The eighteenth century was ushered in by the small-pox,
which carried off sixteen thousand of the inhabitants. In
the middle of the century—severe winters following in rapid

succession—vast numbers of cattle died, inducing a famine that again swept away ten thousand inhabitants.

Since the first colonisation of Iceland, its numerous volcanoes had frequently brought ruin upon whole districts—twenty-five times had Hecla, eleven times Kötlugiá, six times Trölladyngja, five times Oraefa, vomited forth their torrents of molten stone, without counting a number of submarine volcanic explosions, or where the plain was suddenly rent and flames and ashes burst out of the earth; but the eruption of Skaptar Jökull in 1783 was the most frightful visitation ever known to have desolated the island. The preceding winter and spring had been unusually mild, and the islanders looked forward to a prosperous summer; but in the beginning of June repeated tremblings of the earth, increasing in violence from day to day, announced that the subterranean powers that had long been slumbering under the icy mantle of the Skaptar were ready to awake. All the neighbouring peasants abandoned their huts and erected tents in the open field, anxiously awaiting the result of these terrific warnings. On the 9th, immense pillars of smoke collected over the hill country towards the north, and rolling down in a southerly direction, covered the whole district of Sitha with darkness. Loud subterranean thunders followed in rapid succession, and innumerable fire-spouts were seen leaping and flaring through the dense canopy of smoke and ashes that enveloped the land. The heat raging in the interior of the volcano melted enormous masses of ice and snow, which caused the river Skapta to rise to a prodigious height; but on the 11th torrents of fire usurped the place of water, for a vast lava-stream breaking forth from the mountain, flowed down in a southerly direction, until reaching the river, a tremendous conflict arose between the two hostile elements. Though the channel was six hundred feet deep and two hundred feet wide, the lava-flood, pouring down one fiery wave after another into the yawning abyss, ultimately gained the victory, and blocking up the stream, overflowed its banks. Crossing the low country of Medalland, it poured into a great lake, which after a few days was likewise completely filled up, and having divided into two streams, the unexhausted torrent again poured on, overflowing in one direction

G

some ancient lava fields, and in another re-entering the channel of the Skapta and leaping down the lofty cataract of Stapafoss. But this was not all, for while one lava flood had chosen the Skapta for its bed, another, descending in a different direction, was working similar ruin along the banks of the Hverfisfliot. Whether the same crater gave birth to both, it is impossible to say, as even the extent of the lava-flow can only be measured from the spot where it entered the inhabited districts. The stream which followed the direction of Skapta is calculated to have been about fifty miles in length by twelve or fifteen at its greatest breadth; that which rolled down the Hverfisfliot at forty miles in length by seven in breadth.

Where it was inclosed, between the precipitous banks of the Skapta, the lava is five or six hundred feet thick, but as soon as it spread out into the plain its depth never exceeded one hundred feet. The eruption of sand, ashes, pumice, and lava continued till the end of August when at length the vast subterranean tumult subsided.

But its direful effects were felt for a long time after, not only in its immediate vicinity, but over the whole of Iceland, and added many a mournful page to her long annals of sorrow. For a whole year a dun canopy of cinder-laden clouds hung over the unhappy island. Sand and ashes, carried to an enormous height into the atmosphere, spread far and wide and overwhelmed thousands of acres of fertile pasturage. The Faeroes, the Shetlands, and the Orkneys were deluged with volcanic dust which perceptibly contaminated even the skies of England and Holland. Mephitic vapours obscured the rays of the sun, and the sulphurous exhalations tainted both the grass of the field and the waters of the lake, the river and the sea, so that not only the cattle died by thousands, but the fish also perished in their poisoned element. The unhealthy air, and the want of food—for hunger at last drove them to have recourse to untanned hides and old leather—gave rise to a disease resembling scurvy among the unfortunate Icelanders. The head and limbs began to swell, the bones seemed to be distending. Dreadful cramps forced the patient to strange contortions. The gums loosened, the decomposed blood oozed from the mouth and the ulcerous skin, and a few days of torment and prostration were followed by death.

In many a secluded vale whole families were swept away, and those that escaped the scourge had hardly strength sufficient to bury the dead.

> Sorrow and anguish
> And evil and dread,
>   Envelope a nation—
> The blest are the dead,
> Who see not the sight
>   Of their own desolation.

So great was the ruin caused by this one eruption that in the short space of two years no less than 9336 men, 28,000 horses, 11,461 cattle, and 190,000 sheep—a large proportion of the wealth and population of the island—were swept away.

After this dreadful catastrophe followed a long period of volcanic rest, for the next eruption of the Eyjafialla did not take place before 1821. A twelfth eruption of Kötlugja occurred in 1823, the twenty-sixth of Hecla in 1845–46; and ultimately the thirteenth of Kötlugja in 1860. Since then there has been repose; but who knows what future disasters may be preparing beneath those icy ridges and fields of snow of Skapta and his frowning compeers, where no human foot has ever wandered, or how soon they may awaken their dormant thunders?

Besides the sufferings caused by the elements, the curse of monopoly weighed for many a long year upon the miserable Icelanders. The Danish kings, to whom on the amalgamation of the three Scandinavian monarchies the allegiance of the people of Iceland was passively transferred, considered their poor dependency as a private domain, to be farmed out to the highest bidder. In the 16th century the Hanseatic Towns purchased the exclusive privilege of trading with Iceland; and in 1594 a Danish company was favoured with the monopoly, for which it had to pay the paltry sum of 16 rixdollars for each of the ports of the island.

In the year 1862 a new company paid 4000 dollars for the Icelandic monopoly; but at the expiration of the contract, each of the ports was farmed out to the highest bidder—a financial improvement which raised the revenue to 16,000 dollars a year, and ultimately to 22,000. The incalculable misery produced by the eruption of the Skapta had at least the beneficial consequence that it somewhat loosened the bonds of monopoly, as it now became free to every Danish merchant to trade with the island; but it is only since April 1855 that the last restrictions have fallen and the ports of Iceland been opened to the merchants of all nations. It is to be hoped that the beneficial effects of free trade will gradually heal the wounds caused by centuries of neglect and misfortune; but great progress must be made before Iceland can attain the degree of prosperity which she enjoyed in the times of her independence.

Then she had above a hundred thousand inhabitants, now she has scarcely half that number; then she had many rich and powerful families, now mediocrity or poverty is the universal lot; then she was renowned all over the North as the seat of learning and the cradle of literature, now were it not for her remarkable physical features, no traveller would ever think of landing on her rugged shores.

The Long-tailed Duck.

The Lava Field of Surts-Hellir.

# CHAPTER VII.

## THE ICELANDERS.

Skalholt—Reykjavik—The Fair—The Peasant and the Merchant—A Clergyman in his Cups—Hay-making—The Icelander's Hut—Churches—Poverty of the Clergy—Jon Thorlaksen—The Seminary of Reykjavik—Beneficial Influence of the Clergy—Home Education—The Icelander's Winter's Evening—Taste for Literature—The Language—The Public Library at Reykjavik—The Icelandic Literary Society—Icelandic Newspapers—Longevity—Leprosy—Travelling in Iceland—Fording the Rivers—Crossing of the Skeidara by Mr. Holland—A Night's Bivouac.

NEXT to Thingvalla, there is no place in Iceland so replete with historical interest as Skalholt, its ancient capital. Here in the eleventh century was founded the first school in the island; here was the seat of its first bishops; here flourished a succession of great orators, historians, and poets; Isleif, the oldest chronicler of the North; Gissur, who in the beginning of the twelfth century had visited all the countries of Europe and spoke all their languages; the philologian Thorlak, and Finnur Johnson, the learned author of the 'Ecclesiastical History of Iceland.' The cathedral of Skalholt was renowned far and wide for its size, and in the year 1100, Latin, poetry, music, and rhetoric, the four liberal arts, were taught in its school, more than they were at that time in many of the large European cities. As a proof how early the study of the ancients flourished in Skalholt, we find it recorded that in the twelfth century, a bishop once caught a scholar reading Ovid's 'Art of Love,' and as the story relates that the venerable pastor flew into a violent passion at the sight of the unholy book, we may without injustice conclude that he must have read it himself in some of his leisure hours, to know its character so well.

Of all its past glories, Skalholt has retained nothing but its name. The school and the bishopric have been removed, the old church has disappeared, and been replaced by a small wooden building, in which divine service is held once a month; three cottages contain all the inhabitants of the once celebrated city, and the extensive churchyard is the only memorial of its former importance. Close by are the ruins of the old schoolhouse, and on the spot where the bishop resided, a peasant has erected his miserable hovel.

But the ever-changing tide of human affairs has not bereft the now lonely place of its natural charms, for the meadow-lands of Skalholt are beautifully imbedded in an undulating range of hills, overlooking the junction of the Bruara and Huita, and backed by a magnificent theatre of mountains, amongst which Hecla and the Eyafyalla are the most prominent.

Reykjavik, the present capital of the island, has risen into importance at the expense both of Skalholt and Thingvalla. At the beginning of the present century the courts of justice were transferred from the ancient seat of legislature to the new metropolis, and in 1797 the bishoprics of Hoolum and Skalholt, united into one, had their seats likewise transferred to Reykjavik. The ancient school of Skalholt, after having first migrated to Bessestadt, has also been obliged to follow the centralising tendency, so powerful in our times, and now contributes to the rising fortunes of the small seaport town.

But in spite of all these accessions, the first aspect of Reykjavik by no means corresponds to our ideas of a capital. 'The town,' says Lord Dufferin*, 'consists of a collection of wooden sheds, one story high—rising here and there into a gable end of greater pretensions—built along the lava track, and flanked at either end by a suburb of turf huts. On every side of it extends a desolate plain of lava, that once must have boiled up red-hot from some distant gateway of hell, and fallen hissing into the sea. No tree or bush relieves the dreariness of the landscape, and the mountains are too distant to serve as a background to the buildings; but before the door of each merchant's house facing the sea, there flies a gay little pennon; and as you walk along the silent streets, whose dust no carriage-wheel has ever desecrated, the rows of flower-pots that peep out of the windows, between curtains of white muslin, at once convince you, that notwithstanding their unpretending appearance, within each dwelling reign the elegance and comfort of a woman-tended home.'

Twenty years since, Reykjavik was no better than a wretched fishing village, now it already numbers 1,400 inhabitants, and free-trade promises it a still greater increase for the future. It owes its prosperity chiefly to its excellent port, and to the abundance of fish-banks in its neighbourhood, which have induced the Danish merchants to make it their principal settlement. Most of them, however, merely visit it in summer like birds of passage, arriving in May with small cargoes of foreign goods, and leaving it again in August, after having disposed of their wares. Thus Reykjavik must be lonely and dreary enough in winter, when no trade animates its port, and no traveller stays at its solitary inn; but the joy of the inhabitants is all the greater, when the return of spring reopens their intercourse with the rest of the world, and the delight may be imagined, with which they hail the first ship that brings them the long-expected news from Europe, and perhaps some wealthy tourist, eager to admire the wonders of the Geysirs.

The most busy time of the town, is however the beginning of July, when the annual fair attracts a great number of fishermen and peasants within its walls. From a distance

---

* 'Letters from High Latitudes,' p. 35.

of forty and fifty leagues around, they come with long trains
of pack-horses; their stock-fish slung freely across the
animals' backs, their more damageable articles close pressed
and packed in boxes or skin bags.

The greater part of the trade in this and other small
seaports, such as Akreyri, Hafnafjord, Eyrarbacki, Beru-
fjord, Vapnafjord, Isafjord, Grafaros, Budenstadt; which,
taken all together, do not equal Reykjavik in traffic and
population—is carried on by barter.*

Sometimes the Icelander desires to be paid in specie for
part of his produce, but then he is obliged to bargain for a
long time with the merchant, who of course derives a double
profit by an exchange of goods, and is loth to part with his
hard cash. The dollars thus acquired are either melted
down, and worked into silver massive girdles, which in point
of execution as well as design are said, on good authority,†
to be equal to anything of the kind fashioned by English
jewellers, or else deposited in a strong box, as taxes and
wages are all paid in produce, and no Icelander ever thinks
of investing his money in stocks, shares, or debentures.

He is, however, by no means so ignorant of mercantile
affairs as to strike at once a bargain with the Danish traders.
Pitching his tent before the town, he first pays a visit to all
the merchants of the place. After carefully noting their
several offers (for as each of them invariably treats him to a
dram, he with some justice mistrusts his memory), he returns
to his caravan and makes his calculations as well as his
somewhat confused brain allows him. If he is accompanied
by his wife, her opinion of course is decisive, and the following
morning he repairs with all his goods to the merchant who
has succeeded in gaining his confidence.

After the business has been concluded, the peasant empties
one glass to the merchant's health, another to a happy

---

* In 1855, Iceland imported among others: 65,712 pieces of timber, 148,038 lbs.
of iron, 37,700 lbs. hemp, 15,179 fishing lines, 20,312 lbs. salt, 6,539 tons of coal.
The chief exportations of the same year were tallow 932,906 lbs., wool 1,569,323
lbs., 69,305 pairs of stockings, 27,109 pairs of gloves, 12,712 salted sheepskins, 4116
lbs. eiderdowns, 25,000 lbs. other feathers, 244 horses, and 24,079 ship's pounds
(the ship's pound = 320 lbs.) salt fish.
† Barrow, ' Visit to Iceland,' 1834.

meeting next year, a third to the king, a fourth because three have been drunk already. At length, after many embraces, and protestations of eternal friendship, he takes his leave of the merchant. Fortunately there is no thief to be found in all Iceland; but in consequence of these repeated libations, one parcel has not been well packed, another negligently attached to the horse, and thus it happens that the poor peasant's track is not unfrequently marked with sugar, coffee-beans, salt or flour, and that when he reaches home, he finds some valuable article or other missing.

It would, however, be doing the Icelanders an injustice to regard them as generally intemperate; for though within the last twelve years the population has increased only ten per cent., and the importation of brandy thirty, yet the whole quantity of spirits consumed in the island amounts to less than three bottles per annum for each individual, and, of this allowance, the people of Reykjavik and of the other small seaports have more than their share, while many of the clergy and peasantry in the remoter districts hardly ever taste spirituous liquors. Dr. Hooker mentions the extraordinary effect which a small portion of rum produced on the good old incumbent of Middalr, whose stomach had been accustomed only to a milk-diet and a little coffee. 'He begged me,' says the Doctor,* 'to give him some rum to bathe his wife's breast; but having applied a portion of it to that purpose, he drank the rest without being at all aware of its strength, which, however, had no other effect than in causing this clerical blacksmith† with his lame hip to dance in the most ridiculous manner in front of the house. The scene afforded a great source of merriment to all his family, except his old wife, who was very desirous of getting him to bed, while he was no less anxious that she should join him in the dance.'

Dr. Hooker justly remarks that this very circumstance is a convincing proof how unaccustomed this priest was to spirituous liquors, as the quantity taken could not have exceeded a wine-glass full.

After his visit to the fair, the peasant sets about hay-

* 'Journal of a Tour in Iceland,' p. 110.

† All the clergymen are blacksmiths, for a reason that will be stated hereafter.

making, which is to him the great business of the year, for he is most anxious to secure winter-fodder for his cattle, on which his whole prosperity depends. The few potatoes and turnips about the size of marbles, or the cabbage and parsley, which he may chance to cultivate, are not worth mentioning; grass is the chief, nay the only produce of his farm, and that Heaven may grant clear sunshiny days for hay-making is now his daily prayer.

Every person capable of wielding a scythe or rake is pressed into the work. The best hay is cut from the ' tún,' a sort of paddock comprising the lands adjoining the farm-house, and the only part of his grounds on which the peasant bestows any attention, for in spite of the paramount importance of his pasture-land he does but little for its improvement, and a meadow is rarely seen, where the useless or less nutritious herbs are not at least as abundant as those of a better quality. The ' tún ' is encircled by a turf or stone wall, and is seldom more than ten acres in extent, and generally not more than two or three. Its surface is usually a series of closely packed mounds, like graves, most unpleasant to walk over, the gutter, in some places, being two feet in depth between the mounds. After having finished with the ' tun,' the farmer subjects to a process of cutting all the broken hill-sides and boggy undrained swamps that lie near his dwelling. The blades of the scythes are very short. It would be impossible to use a long-bladed scythe, owing to the unevenness of the ground.

The cutting and making of hay is carried on, when the weather will permit, through all the twenty-four hours of the day. When the hay is made it is tied in bundles by cords and thongs, and carried away by ponies to the earthen houses prepared for it, which are similar to, and adjoin those in which the cattle are stalled. ' It is a very curious sight,' says Mr. Shepherd, ' to see a string of hay-laden ponies returning home. Each pony's halter is made fast to the tail of the preceding one, and the little animals are so enveloped in their burdens, that nothing but their hoofs and the connecting ropes are visible, and they look as though a dozen huge haycocks, feeling themselves sufficiently made, were crawling off to their resting-places.'

When the harvest is finished, the farmer treats his family and labourers to a substantial supper, consisting of mutton, and a soup of milk and flour; and although the serious and taciturn Icelander has perhaps of all men the least taste for music and dancing, yet these simple feasts are distinguished by a placid serenity, no less pleasing than the more boisterous mirth displayed at a southern vintage.

Almost all labour out of doors now ceases for the rest of the year. A thick mantle of snow soon covers mountain and vale, meadow and moor; with every returning day, the sun pays the cold earth a decreasing visit, until finally he hardly appears above the horizon at noon, the wintry storm howls over the waste, and for months the life of the Icelander is confined to his hut, which frequently is but a few degrees better than that of the filthy Lap.

Its lower part is built of rude stones to about the height of four feet, and between each row layers of turf are placed with great regularity to serve instead of mortar, and keep out the wind. A roof of such wood as can be procured rests upon these walls, and is covered with turf and sods. On one side (generally facing the south) are several gable-ends and doors, each surmounted with a weathercock. These are the entrances to the dwelling-house proper, to the smithy, store-room, cow-shed, &c. A long narrow passage, dark as pitch, and redolent of unsavoury odours, leads to the several apartments, which are separated from each other by thick walls of turf, each having also its own roof, so that the peasant's dwelling is in fact a conglomeration of low huts, which sometimes receive their light through small windows in the front, but more frequently through holes in the roof, covered with a piece of glass or skin. The floors are of stamped earth; the hearth is made of a few stones clumsily piled together, a cask or barrel, with the two ends knocked out, answers the purpose of a chimney, or else the smoke is allowed to escape through a mere hole in the roof.

The thick turf walls, the dirty floor, the personal unclean-liness of the inhabitants, all contribute to the pollution of the atmosphere. No piece of furniture seems ever to have been cleaned, since it was first put into use; all is disorder and confusion. Ventilation is utterly impossible and the whole family, frequently consisting of twenty persons or more, sleep in the same dormitory, as well as any strangers who may happen to drop in. On either side of this apartment are bunks three or four feet in width, on which the sleepers range themselves.

Such are in general the dwellings of the farmers and clergy, for but very few of the more wealthy inhabitants live in any way according to our notions of comfort, while the cots of the poor fisherman are so wretched that one can hardly believe them to be tenanted by human beings.

The farmhouses are frequently isolated, and, on account of their grass-covered roofs and their low construction, are not easily distinguished from the neighbouring pasture-grounds; where four or five of them are congregated in a grassy plain, they are dignified with the name of a village, and become the residence of a Hrepstior, or parish-constable.

Then also a church is seldom wanting, which however is distinguished from the low huts around merely by the cross planted on its roof. An Icelandic house of prayer is generally from eight to ten feet wide, and from eighteen to twenty-four long, but of this about eight feet are devoted to the altar, which is divided off by a partition stretching across the church, and against which stands the pulpit. A small wooden chest or cupboard, placed at the end of the building, between two very small square windows not larger than a common sized pane of glass, constitutes the communion-table, over which is generally a miserable representation of the Lord's Supper painted on wood. The height of the walls, which are wainscoted, is about six feet, and from them large wooden beams stretch across from side to side. On these beams are placed in great disorder a quantity of old bibles, psalters, and fragments of dirty manuscripts. The interior of the roof, the rafters of which rest on the walls, is also lined with wood. On the right of the door, under which one is obliged to stoop considerably on entering, is suspended a bell, large enough to make an intolerable noise in so small a space. A few benches on each side the aisle, so crowded together as almost to touch one another, and affording accommodation to thirty or forty persons when squeezed very tight, leave room for a narrow passage.

These churches, besides their proper use, are also made to answer the purpose of the caravanserais of the East, by affording a night's lodging to foreign tourists. They are indeed neither free from dirt, nor from bad smells; but the stranger is still far better off than in the intolerable atmosphere of a peasant's hut.

The poverty of the clergy corresponds with the meanness of their churches. The best living in the island is that of Breide'-Bolstadr, where the nominal stipend amounts to 180 specie dollars, or about 40l. a year; and Mr. Holland states that the average livings do not amount to more than 10l. for each parish in the island. The clergymen must therefore depend almost entirely for subsistence on their glebe land, and a small pittance to which they are entitled for the few baptisms, marriages, and funerals that occur among their parishioners. The bishop himself has only 2000 rix-dollars, or 200l. a year, a miserable pittance to make a decent appearance, and to exercise hospitality to the clergy who visit Reykjavik from distant parts.

It cannot be wondered at that pastors, thus miserably paid, are generally obliged to perform the hardest work of day labourers to preserve their families from starving, and that their external appearance corresponds less with the dignity of their office than with their penury. Besides hay-making and tending the cattle, they may be frequently seen leading a train of pack-horses from a fishing station to their distant hut. They are all blacksmiths also from necessity, and the best shoers of horses on the island. The feet of an Iceland horse would be cut to pieces over the sharp rock and lava if not well shod. The great resort of the peasantry is the church, and should any of the numerous horses have lost a shoe, or be likely to do so, the priest puts on his apron, lights his little charcoal fire in his smithy (one of which is always attached to every parsonage), and sets the animal on his legs again. The task of getting the necessary charcoal is not the least of his labours, for whatever the distance may be to the nearest thicket of dwarf-birch, he must go thither to burn the wood, and to bring it home when charred across his horse's back. His hut is scarcely better than that of the meanest fisherman; a bed, a rickety table, a few chairs, and a chest or two, are all his furniture. This is, as long as he lives, the condition of the Icelandic clergyman, and learning, virtue, and even genius are but too frequently buried under this squalid poverty.

But few of my readers have probably ever heard of the poet Jon Thorlakson, but who can withhold the tribute of his admiration from the poor priest of Backa, who with a fixed income of less than 6*l.* a year, and condemned to all the drudgery which I have described, finished at seventy years of age a translation of Milton's ' Paradise Lost,' having previously translated Pope's ' Essay on Man.'

Three of the first books only of the ' Paradise Lost ' were printed by the Icelandic Literary Society, when it was dissolved in 1796, and to print the rest at his own expense was of course impossible. In a few Icelandic verses, Thorlakson touchingly alludes to his penury:—' Ever since I came into this world, I have been wedded to Poverty, who has now hugged me to her bosom these seventy winters, all but two; and whether we shall ever be separated here below, is only known to Him who joined us together.'

As if Providence had intended to teach the old man that we must hope to the last, he soon after received the unexpected visit of Mr. Henderson, an agent of the British and Foreign Bible Society, who thus relates his interview.

' Like most of his brethren, at this season of the year, we found him in the meadow assisting his people in hay-making. On hearing of our arrival, he made all the haste home, which his age and infirmity would allow, and bidding us welcome to his lowly abode, ushered us into the humble apartment where he translated my countrymen into Icelandic. The door is not quite four feet in height, and the room may be about eight feet in length by six in breadth At the inner end is the poet's bed, and close to the door, over against a small window, not exceeding two feet square, is a table where he commits to paper the effusions of his Muse. On my telling him that my countrymen would not have forgiven me, nor could I have forgiven myself, had I passed through this part of the island without paying him a visit, he replied that the translation of Milton had yielded him many a pleasant hour, and often given him occasion to think of England.'*

This visit was followed by agreeable consequences for the venerable bard. The Literary Fund soon afterwards sent him a present of 30*l.*, a modest sum according to our ideas, but a mine of wealth in the eyes of the poor Icelandic priest. His life, however, was now near its close, as it is stated in a short view 'Of the Origin, Progress, and Operations of the Society,' dated March 3rd, 1821, that 'the poet of Iceland is now in his grave; but it is satisfactory to know that the attention, in this instance, of a foreign and remote society to his gains and his fortunes was highly gratifying to his feelings, and contributed not immaterially to the comfort of his concluding days.'

He wrote a letter in very elegant Latin, expressing his heartfelt gratitude for the kindness and generosity of the Society, so accordant with the character of the British nation, and accompanied it with a MS. copy of his translation. The latter was first printed in Iceland in 1828, but his own original poems did not appear before 1842.

The school where most of the Icelandic clergymen, so poor and yet generally so respectable in their poverty, are educated, is that of Reykjavik, as few only enjoy stipends which enable them to study at Copenhagen. There they live several years under a milder sky, they become acquainted with the splendour of a large capital, and thus it might be supposed that the idea of returning to the dreary wastes of their own land must be intolerable. Yet this is their ardent desire, and, like banished exiles, they long for their beloved Iceland, where privations and penury await them.

In no Christian country, perhaps with the sole exception of Lapland, are the clergy so poor as in Iceland, but in none do they exert a more beneficial influence.

Though the island has but the one public school at Reykjavik, yet perhaps in no country is elementary education more generally diffused. Every mother teaches her children to read and write, and the peasant, after providing for the wants of his family by the labour of his hands, loses no opportunity, in his leisure hours, of inculcating a sound morality. In

* Henderson's 'Travels in Iceland,' 1818.

these praiseworthy efforts the parents are supported by the pastor.

He who, judging from the sordid condition of an Icelandic hut, might imagine its inhabitants to be no better than savages, would soon change his opinion were he introduced on a winter evening into the low ill-ventilated room where the family of a peasant or a small landholder is assembled. Vainly would he seek a single idler in the whole company. The women and girls spin or knit; the men and boys are all busy mending their agricultural implements and household utensils, or else chiselling or cutting with admirable skill ornaments or snuff boxes in silver, ivory, or wood. By the dubious light of a tallow lamp, just making obscurity visible, sits one of the family who reads with a loud voice an old ' saga ' or chronicle, or maybe the newest number of the ' Northurfari,' an Iceland literary almanack, published during the last few years by Mr. Gisle Brinjulfsson. Sometimes poems or whole sagas are repeated from memory, and there are even itinerant story-tellers who, like the troubadours and trouvères of the middle ages, wander from one farm to another, and thus gain a scanty livelihood. In this manner the deeds of the ancient Icelanders remain fixed in the memory of their descendants, and Snorre Sturleson, Sämund, Frodi, and Eric Rauda are unforgotten. Nine centuries have elapsed; but every Icelander still knows the names of the proud yarls who first peopled the fiords of the island; and the exploits of the brave vikings who spread terror and desolation along all the coasts of Europe still fill the hearts of the peaceful islanders of our days with a glow of patriotic pride.

Where education is so general, one may naturally expect to find a high degree of intellectual cultivation among the clergy, the public functionaries, and the wealthier part of the population. Their classical knowledge is one of the first things that strike the stranger with astonishment. He sees men whose appearance too frequently denotes an abject poverty conversant with the great authors of antiquity, and keenly alive to their beauties. Travelling to the Geysirs he is not seldom accosted in Latin by his guide, and stopping at a farm, his host greets him in the same language.

I have specially named Jon Thorlakson, but Iceland has produced and still produces many other men who, without the hope of any other reward but that which proceeds from the pure love of literature, devote their days and nights to laborious studies, and live with Virgil and Homer under the sunny skies of Italy and Greece. In the study of the modern languages, the Icelanders are as far advanced as can be expected from their limited intercourse with the rest of the world.

The English language, in which they find so many words of their own and so many borrowed from the Latin, is cultivated by many of the clergy. The German they find still more easy, and as all the Scandinavian languages proceed from the same root, they have no difficulty in understanding the Danish and the Norwegian tongues. Of all the modern languages or dialects which have sprung from the ancient Norse, spoken a thousand years ago, all over Denmark, Sweden, and Norway, none has undergone fewer changes than the Icelandic. In the sea-ports it is mixed up with many Danish words and phrases, but in the interior of the island it is still spoken as it was in the times of Ingolfr and Eric the Red, and in the whole island there is no fisherman or day labourer who does not perfectly understand the oldest writings.

It may easily be imagined that among a people so fond of literature, books must be in great request. Too poor to be constantly increasing their small collections of modern publications or of old 'sagas' or chronicles by new acquisitions, one assists the other. When the peasant goes on Sundays to church, he takes a few volumes with him, ready to lend his treasures to his neighbours, and, on his part, selects from among those which they have brought for the same purpose. When he is particularly pleased with a work, he has it copied at home, and it may be here remarked that the Icelanders are frequently most excellent caligraphists.

The foundation of a public library at Reykjavik in 1821, at the instigation of the learned Professor Rafn of Copenhagen, was a great boon to the people. It is said to contain about 12,000 volumes, which are kept under the roof of the cathedral. Books are freely lent for months, or even for a whole year, to the inhabitants of remote districts. This liberality is, of course, attended with some inconvenience, but it has the inestimable advantage of rendering a number of good works accessible to numerous families too poor to purchase them.

Another excellent institution is the New Icelandic Literary Society founded in 1816. It has two seats, one in Copenhagen the other in Reykjavik, and its chief object is the publication of useful works in the language of the country. Besides an annual grant of 100 specie dollars (24*l.*) awarded to it by the Danish government, its income is confined to the yearly contributions of its members,* and with this scanty means it has already published many excellent works.

Though remote from the busy scenes of the world, Iceland has three newspapers, the Thyodtholfr and the Islendingur, which appear at Reykjavik, and the Northri, which is published at Akreyri, on the borders of the Polar Ocean. The Islendingur is said to contain many excellent articles, but it would sorely task the patience of those who are accustomed to the regular enjoyment of the 'Times' at breakfast; as it sometimes appears but once in three weeks, and then again, as if to make up for lost time, twice in eight days.

In spite of their ill-ventilated dwellings and the hardships entailed upon them by the severity of the climate, the Icelanders frequently attain a good old age. Of the 2,019 persons who died in 1858, 25 had passed the age of ninety, and of these 20 belonged to the fair sex. The mortality among the children is, however, very considerable; 993, or nearly one-half of the entire number having died before the age of five in the year above mentioned. Cutaneous affections are very common among Icelanders, as may easily be supposed from their sordid woollen apparel, and the uncleanliness of their huts; and the northern leprosy, or 'likthra,' is constantly seeking out its victims among them. This dreadful disease, which is also found among the fishermen in Norway, in Greenland, in the Faeroes, in Lapland, and in short wherever the same mode of life exists, begins with a swelling of the hands and feet. The hair falls off; the senses

* Their number in 1860 was 991. During his voyage to Iceland in 1850 Prince Napoleon was named honorary president, a distinction he shares with the bishop of Reykjavik. Among the 46 honorary members I find the name of Lord Dufferin.

become obtuse. Tumours appear on the arms and legs, and on the face, which soon loses the semblance of humanity. Severe pains shoot through the joints, an eruption covers the whole body, and finally changes into open sores, ending with death. He whom the leprosy has once attacked is doomed, for it mocks all the efforts of medical art. Fortunately the victims of this shocking complaint are rather objects of pity than of disgust, and as it is not supposed to be contagious, they are not so cruelly forsaken by their relations as their fellow-sufferers in the East. In the hut of the priest of Thingvalla, Marmier saw a leper busy grinding corn. Some of the poorest and most helpless of these unfortunate creatures find a refuge in four small hospitals, where they are provided for at the public expense.

Since a regular steam-boat communication has been opened between Iceland, Denmark, and Scotland, the number of tourists desirous of viewing the matchless natural wonders of the island has considerably increased. But travelling in the island itself is still attended with considerable difficulties and no trifling expense, to say nothing of the want of all comforts, so that most of its visitors are content with a trip to Thingvalla and the Geysir, which are but a couple of days' journey from Reykjavik, and very few, like Mr. Holland, make the entire circuit of the island, or, like Mr. Shepherd, plunge into the *terra incognita* of its north-western peninsula. The only mode of travelling is on horseback, as there are no roads and therefore no carriages in Iceland. The distances between the places are too great, the rivers are too furious, and the bogs too extensive to allow of a walking tour being made. Even the tourist with the most modest pretensions requires at least two riding horses for himself, two for his guide, and two packhorses, and when a larger company travels, it always forms a cavalcade of from twenty to thirty horses, tied head to tail, the chief guide mounted on the first and leading the string, the other accelerating its motions by gesticulation, sundry oaths, and the timely application of the whip. The way, or the path, lies either over beds of lava, so rugged that the horses are allowed to pick their way, or over boggy ground where it is equally necessary to avoid those places into which the animals might sink up to their belly, but which, when left to themselves, they are remarkably skilful in detecting. With the solitary exception of a few planks thrown across the Bruera, and a kind of swing bridge, or *kláfr*, contrived for passing the rapid Jökulsa, there are no bridges over the rivers, so that the only way to get across is to ride through them—a feat which, considering the usual velocity of their current, is not seldom attended with considerable danger, as will be seen by the following account of the crossing of the Skeidara by Mr. Holland.*

'Our guide,' says this intrepid traveller, 'urged on his horse through the stream, and led the way towards the mid

Klafr.

channel. We followed in his wake, and soon were all stemming the impetuous and swollen torrent. In the course of our journey we had before this crossed a good many rivers more or less deep, but all of them had been mere child's play compared to that which we were now fording. The angry water rose high against our horses' sides, at times almost coming over the tops of their shoulders. The spray from their broken crests was dashed up into our faces. The stream was so swift that it was impossible to follow the individual waves as they rushed past us, and it almost made us dizzy to look down at it. Now, if ever, is the time for firm hand or rein, sure seat, and steady eye; not only is the stream so strong, but the bottom is full of large stones, that the horse cannot see through the murky waters; if he should fall, the torrent will sweep you down to the sea—its white breakers are plainly visible as they run along the shore at scarcely a mile's distance, and they lap the beach as if they

* 'Peaks, Passes, and Glaciers.'

waited for their prey. Happily, they will be disappointed. Swimming would be of no use, but an Icelandic water-horse seldom makes a blunder or a false step. Not the least of the risks we ran in crossing the Skeidara, was from the masses of ice carried down by the stream from the Jökull, many of them being large enough to knock a horse over.

'Fortunately we found much less ice in the centre and swiftest part of the river, where we were able to see and avoid it, than in the side channels. How the horses were able to stand against such a stream was marvellous; they could not do so unless they were constantly in the habit of crossing swift rivers. The Icelanders who live in this part of the island keep horses known for their qualities in fording difficult rivers, and they never venture to cross a dangerous stream unless mounted on a tried water-horse. The action of the Icelandic horses when crossing a swift river is very peculiar. They lean all their weight against the stream, so as to resist it as much as possible, and move onwards with a peculiar side-step. This motion is not agreeable. It feels as if your horse were marking time without gaining ground, and the progress made being really very slow, the shore from which you started seems to recede from you, whilst that for which you are making appears as far as ever.

'When we reached the middle of the stream, the roar of the waters was so great that we could scarcely make our voices audible to one another; they were overpowered by the crunching sound of the ice, and the bumping of large stones against the bottom. Up to this point a diagonal line, rather down stream, had been cautiously followed; but when we came to the middle, we turned our horses' heads a little against the stream. As we thus altered our course, the long line of baggage-horses appeared to be swung round altogether, as if swept off their legs. None of them, however, broke away, and they continued their advance without accident; and at length we all reached the shore in safety.'

After a day's journey in Iceland, rest, as may well be supposed, is highly acceptable. Instead of passing the night in the peasant's hut, the traveller, when no church is at hand, generally prefers pitching his tent near a running stream on a grassy plain; but sometimes, in consequence of the great distance from one habitable place to another, he is obliged to encamp in the midst of a bog where the poor horses find either bad herbs, scarcely fit to satisfy their hunger, or no food at all. After they have been unloaded, their fore-legs are bound together above their hoofs, so as to prevent them straying too far, while their masters arrange themselves in the tent as comfortably as they can.

The Great Auk.

Hver-Fjall.

# CHAPTER VIII.

### THE WESTMAN ISLANDS.

The Westmans—Their extreme Difficulty of Access—How they became peopled—
Heimaey—Kaufstathir and Ofanleyte—Sheep Hoisting—Egg Gathering—Dread-
ful Mortality among the Children — The Ginklofi — Gentleman John — The
Algerian Pirates—Dreadful Sufferings of the Islanders.

RISING abruptly from the sea to a height of 916 feet, the
small Westman Islands are no less picturesque than
difficult of access. Many a traveller while sailing along the
south coast of Iceland has admired their towering rock-
walls, but no modern tourist has ever landed there. For so
stormy a sea rolls between them and the mainland, and so
violent are the currents, which the slightest wind brings
forth in the narrow channels of the archipelago, that a
landing can be effected only when the weather is perfectly
calm. The Drifanda foss, a cascade on the opposite mainland, rushing from the brow of the Eyafyalla range in a
column of some 800 or 900 feet in height, is a sort of
barometer, which decides whether a boat can put off with a
prospect of gaining the Westmans. In stormy weather the

wind eddying among the cliffs converts the fall, though considerable, into a cloud of spray, which is dissipated in the atmosphere, so that no cascade is visible from the beach. In calm weather, the column is intact, and if it remains so two days in succession, then the sea is usually calm enough to allow boats to land, and they venture out. As the Icelanders, through stormy weather, are frequently cut off from Europe, so the inhabitants of the Westmans are still more frequently cut off from Iceland, and it is seldom more than once a year that the mails are landed direct. The *few* letters from Denmark (for the correspondence is in all probability not very active) are landed in Iceland at Reykjavik, and thence forwarded to the islands by boat, as chance may offer, for, during the whole winter and the greater part of the summer, communication is impossible. It will now be understood why tourists are so little inclined to visit the Westmans, despite the magnificence of their coast scenery, for who has the patience to tarry in a miserable hut on the opposite mainland, till the cascade informs him that they are accessible, or is inclined to run the risk of being detained by a sudden change of the weather, for weeks or even months on these solitary rocks?

The puffin, or the screeching sea-mew, seem the only inhabitants for which nature has fitted the Westmans, and yet they have a history which leads us back to the times when Iceland itself first became known to man.

About 875, a few years after Ingolfr followed his household gods to Reykjavik, a Norwegian pirate, perchance one of the associates of that historical personage, landed on the coast of Ireland, attacked with fire and sword the defenceless population, captured forty or fifty persons, men, women, and children, and carried them off as slaves. The passage must have been anything but pleasant, for it gave the Hibernians such a foretaste of the wretchedness that awaited them in Iceland, their future abode, that taking courage from despair, they rose on their captors, threw them overboard, and went ashore on the first land they met with.

A day of rare serenity must have witnessed their arrival on the Westmans, a spot which of all others seemed most unlikely to become their home. Why they remained there, is a secret of the past; most likely they had no other alternative, and freedom on a rock was, at all events, better than slavery under a cruel viking.

Thus these weather-beaten islets were first peopled by men from the west, whence they derive their name, and it is supposed that the present inhabitants are the descendants of those children of Erin. No one will be inclined to envy them the heritage bequeathed to them by their fathers.

The Westmans are fourteen in number; but of these only one, called Heimaey, or Home Island, is inhabited. It is fifteen miles from the coast of Iceland, and forty-five from Hekla. Though larger than all the others put together, its entire surface is not more than ten square miles. It is almost surrounded with high basaltic cliffs, and an otherwise iron-bound shore; its interior is covered with black ashy-looking cones, bearing undoubted evidence of volcanic action; in fact, the harbour, which lies on its north-east side, and is only accessible to small craft, is formed out of an old crater, into which the sea has worn an entrance. The inhabitants are located in two villages; Kaupstathir on a little grassy knoll, near the landing-place, and Ofanleyti on the grassy platform of the island. Only three of the other islets produce any vegetation or pasturage, and it is said that, on one of these, the sheep are hoisted with a rope out of the boats by an islander, who, at the risk of his neck, has climbed to the top of the precipitous rock. The others are mere naked cliffs or basaltic pillars, the abode of innumerable sea-birds, which, when accessible, are a precious resource to the islanders. For, as may well be supposed, the scanty grass lands afford nourishment but to a few cows and sheep; and as the unruly waters too often prevent their fishing-boats from putting to sea, they depend in a great measure for their subsistence upon the sea-birds, in whose capture they exhibit wonderful courage and skill. In the egg-season they go to the top of the cliff, and putting a rope round a man's waist, let him down the side of the perpendicular rock, one, two, or three hundred feet; on arriving at the long, narrow, horizontal shelves, he proceeds to fill a large bag with the brittle treasures deposited by the birds. When his bag is full, he and his eggs are drawn to the top by his companions. If the rope breaks, or is cut off by the sharp corners of the rock, which, however, happens but seldom, nothing can save the luckless fowler, who is either precipitated into the sea, or dashed to pieces on the rocks below.

At a later period in the season they go and get the young birds, and then they have often desperate battles with the old ones, who will not give up fighting for their offspring till their necks are broken, or their brains knocked out with a club. Where the cliffs are not accessible from the top, they go round the bottom in boats, and show a wonderful agility and daring in scaling the most terrible precipices.

In summer they eat the eggs and the fresh meat of the young birds, which they also salt for the winter. The feathers form their chief article of export, besides dried and salted codfish, and with these they procure their few necessaries and luxuries, consisting principally of clothing, tobacco and snuff, spirits, fish-hooks and lines, and salt. As there is no peat on these islands, nor dried fish-bones in sufficient quantity, they also make use of the tough old seabirds as fuel. For this purpose they split them open, and dry them on the rocks.

The Westmans form a separate Syssel or county, and they have a church, and usually two clergymen. Their church was rebuilt of stone, at the expense of the Danish government, in 1774, and is said to be one of the best in Iceland. Unfortunately the two clergymen to whom the spiritual care of the islanders is confided seem to have but a very indifferent flock, for their neighbours on the mainland give rather a bad character to the inhabitants of Heimaey, describing them as great sluggards and drunkards.

The population, which was formerly more considerable, amounts to about 200 souls, but even this is more than might be expected from the dreadful mortality which reigns among the children. The eggs and the oily flesh of seabirds furnish a miserable food for infants, particularly when weaned, as is here customary, at a very early age; but the poor islanders have nothing else to give them, except some fish, and a very insufficient quantity of cow's or sheep's milk. This unhealthy diet, along with the boisterous air, gives rise to an incurable infantile disease called Ginklofi (*tetanus*). Its first symptoms are squinting and rolling of the eyes, the muscles of the back are seized with incipient cramps and become stiff. After a day or two lock-jaw takes place, the back is bent like a bow, either backwards or forwards. The lock-jaw prevents swallowing, and the cramps become more frequent and prolonged until death closes the scene. The same disease is said to decimate the children on St. Kilda in consequence of a similar mode of life.

The only means of preserving the infants of Heimaey from the Ginklofi, is to send them as soon as possible to the mainland to be reared, and thus a long continuance of bad weather is a death-warrant to many.

Who would suppose that the Westman islanders, doubly guarded by their poverty and their almost inaccessible cliffs, could ever have become the prey of freebooters? and yet they have been twice attacked and pillaged, and well-nigh exterminated by sea-rovers.

I have already mentioned, in a previous chapter, that before the discovery of the banks of Newfoundland, the English cod-fishers used to resort in great numbers to the coasts of Iceland, where some of them—now and then—appeared also in the more questionable character of corsairs. One of these worthies, who like Paul Clifford, or Captain Macheath, so effectually united the *suaviter in modo* with the *fortiter in re*, as to have merited the name of 'Gentleman John,' came to the Westmans in 1614, and set the church on fire, after having previously removed the little that was worth taking. After this exploit he returned to Great Britain, but King James I. had him hung, and ordered the church ornaments which he had robbed to be restored to the poor islanders. It was, however, written in the book of fate that they were not to enjoy them long, for in 1627, a vessel of Algerine pirates, after plundering several places on the eastern and southern coasts of Iceland, fell like a thunderbolt on Heimaey. These miscreants, compared with whom John was a 'gentleman' indeed, cut down every man who ventured to oppose them, plundered and burnt the new-built church, and every hovel of the place, and carried away about 400 prisoners—men, women, and children. One of the two

clergymen of the island, Jon Torsteinson, was murdered
at the time.   This learned and pious man had translated the
Psalms of David and the Book of Genesis into Icelandic
verse, and is spoken of as the ' martyr ' in the history of
the land.   The other clergyman, Olaf Egilson, with his
wife and children, and the rest of the prisoners, was sold into
slavery in Algiers.   The account of his sufferings and privations, which he wrote in the Icelandic language, was
afterwards translated and published in Danish.

It was not until 1636, nine years after their capture, that
the unfortunate Heimaeyers were released, and then only by
being ransomed by the king of Denmark.   Such was the
misery they had endured from their barbarous taskmasters,
that only thirty-seven of the whole number survived, and of
these but thirteen lived to return to their native island.

The Wild Goose.

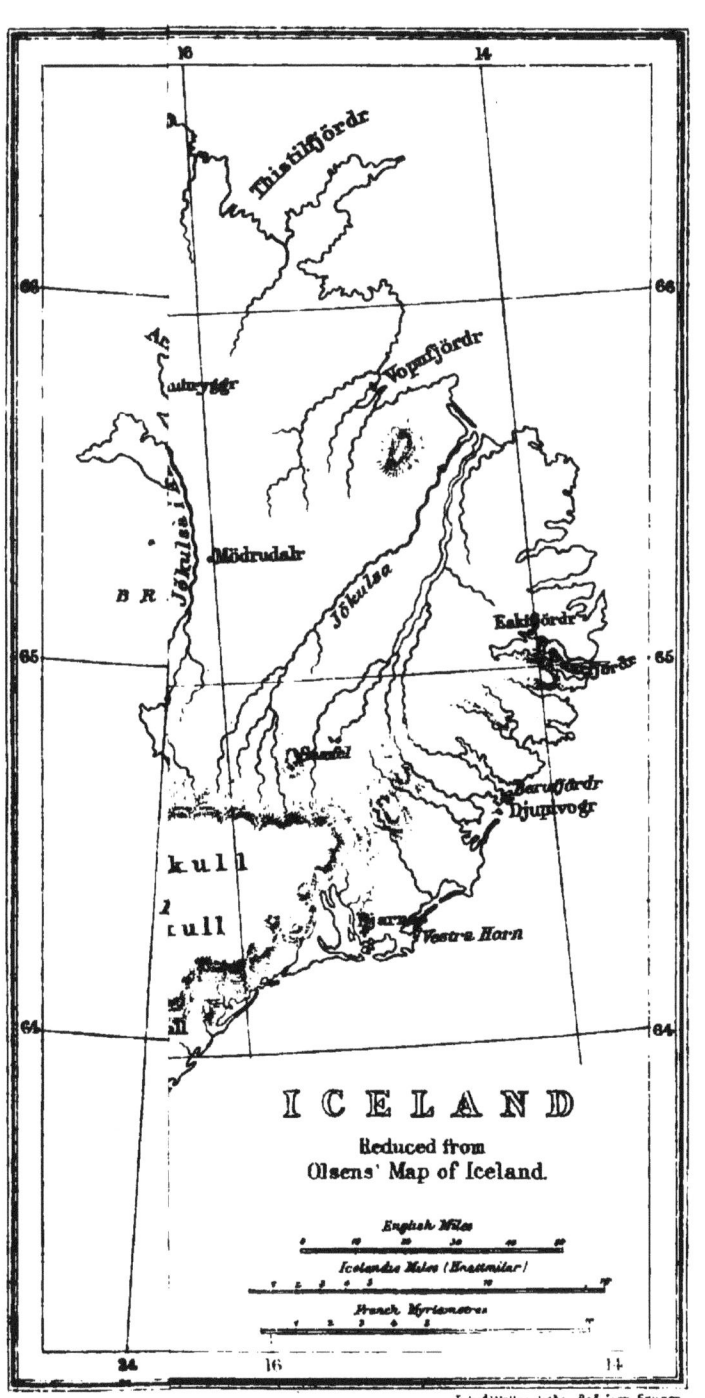

ICELAND

Reduced from
Olsens' Map of Iceland.

English Miles

Icelandic Miles (Bræmmilar)

French Myriametres

Vaager Kallen, Lofoten Islands.

# CHAPTER IX.

## FROM DRONTHEIM TO THE NORTH CAPE.

Mild Climate of the Norwegian Coast—Its Causes—The Norwegian Peasant—
Norwegian Constitution—Romantic Coast Scenery—Drontheim—Greiffenfeld
Holme and Väre—The Sea-Eagle—The Herring Fisheries—The Lofoten
Islands—The Cod Fisheries—Wretched Condition of the Fishermen—Tromso—
Altenfiord—The Copper Mines—Hammerfest the most Northern Town in the
World—The North Cape.

OF ALL the lands situated either within or near the Arctic
Circle none enjoys a more temperate climate than the
Norwegian coast. Here, and nowhere else throughout the
northern world, the birch and the fir tree climb the mountain-
slopes to a height of 700 or 800 feet above the level of the
sea, as far as the 70th degree of latitude; here we still find a

flourishing agriculture in the interior of the Malanger Fjord in 69°.

On the opposite side of the Polar Ocean extends the in-accessible ice belt of East Greenland; Spitzbergen and Novaya Zemlya are not 400 miles distant from Talvig and Hammerfest, and yet these ports are never blocked with ice, and even in the depth of winter remain constantly open to navigation.

What are the causes which in this favoured region banish the usual rigors of the Arctic Zone? How comes it that the winter even at the North Cape (mean temperature +22°) is much less severe than at Quebec (mean temperature +14°), which is situated 25° of latitude nearer to the equator?

The high mountain chains which separate Norway from Sweden and Finland, and keep off the eastern gales issuing from the Siberian wastes, while its coasts lie open to the mild south-westerly winds of the Atlantic, no doubt account in some measure for the comparative mildness of its climate; but the main cause of this phenomenon must no doubt be sought for in the sea.

Flowing into the Atlantic Ocean between Florida and Cuba, the warm gulf-stream traverses the sea from west to east, and although about the middle of its course it partly turns to the south, yet a considerable portion of its waters flows on-wards to the north-east, and streaming through the wide portal between Iceland and Great Britain, eventually reaches the coasts of Norway. Of course its warmth diminishes as it advances to the north, but this is imparted to the winds that sweep over it, and thus it not merely brings the seeds of tropical plants, from equatorial America, to the coasts of Norway, but also the far more important advantages of a milder temperature.

The soil of Norway is generally rocky and sterile, but the sea amply makes up for the deficiencies of the land, and with the produce of their fisheries, of their forests, and their mines, the inhabitants are able to purchase the few foreign articles which they require. Though poor, and not seldom obliged to reap the gifts of nature amidst a thousand hardships and dangers, they envy no other nation upon earth.

The Norwegian peasant is a free man on the scanty bit of

ground which he has inherited from his fathers, and he has all the virtues of a freeman—an open character, a mind clear of every falsehood, an hospitable heart for the stranger. His religious feelings are deep and sincere, and the Bible is to be found in every hut.

He is said to be indolent and phlegmatic, but when necessity urges he sets vigorously to work, and never ceases till his task is done. His courage and his patriotism are abundantly proved by a history of a thousand years.

Norway owes her present prosperity chiefly to her liberal constitution. The press is completely free, and the power of the king extremely limited. All privileges and hereditary titles are abolished. The parliament or the 'storthing,' which assembles every three years, consists of the 'odelthing' or upper house, and of the 'logthing' or legislative assembly. Every new law requires the royal sanction, but if the storthing has voted it in three successive sittings, it is definitively adopted in spite of the royal veto. Public education is admirably cared for. There is an elementary school in every village, and where the population is too thinly scattered, the schoolmaster may truly be said to be abroad, as he wanders from farm to farm, so that the most distant families have the benefit of his instruction. Every town has its public library, and in many districts the peasants annually contribute a dollar towards a collection of books, which, under the care of the priest, is lent out to all subscribers. No Norwegian is confirmed who does not know how to read, and no Norwegian is allowed to marry who has not been confirmed. He who attains his twentieth year without having been confirmed has to fear the House of Correction. Thus ignorance is punished as a crime in Norway, an excellent example for far richer and more powerful nations.

The population of Norway amounts to about 1,350,000, but these are very unequally distributed, for while the southern province of Aggerhuus has 513,000 inhabitants on a surface of 35,200 square miles, Nordland has only 59,000 on 16,325, and Finmark, the most northern province of the land, but 38,000 on 29,925, or hardly more than one inhabitant to every square mile. But even this scanty population is immense when compared with that of Eastern Siberia or of the

Hudson's Bay territories, and entirely owes its existence to the mildness of the climate and the open sea, which at all seasons affords its produce to the fisherman.

It is difficult to imagine a more secluded, solitary life than that of the 'bonders,' or peasant proprietors, along the northern coasts of Norway. The farms, confined to the small patches of more fruitful ground scattered along the fjords, at the foot or on the sides of the naked mountains, are frequently many miles distant from their neighbours, and the stormy winter cuts off all communication between them. Thus every family, reduced to its own resources, forms as it were a small commonwealth, which has but little to do with the external world, and is obliged to rely for its happiness on internal harmony, and a moderate competency. Strangers seldom invade their solitude, for they are far from the ordinary tracks of the tourist, and yet a journey from Drontheim to Hammerfest and the North Cape affords many objects of interest well worthy of a visit. The only mode of communication is by sea, for the land is everywhere intersected by deep fjords, bounded by one continuous chain of precipitous cliffs and rocks, varying from one thousand to four thousand feet in height. Formerly, even the sea-voyage was attended with considerable difficulties, for the miserable " yoegt," or Scandinavian sloop, the only means of conveyance at the disposal of the traveller, required at the best of times at least a month to perform the voyage from Drontheim to Hammerfest, and in case of stormy weather, or contrary wind, had often to wait for weeks in some intermediate port. Now, however, a steamer leaves the port of Drontheim every week, and conveys the traveller in five or six days to the remote northern terminus of his journey. Innumerable isles, of every size, from a few yards in diameter to as many miles, stud the line of coast, and between these and the mainland the steamer ploughs its way. Sometimes the channel is as narrow as the bed of a river, at others it expands into a mighty lake, and the ever-varying forms of the isles, of the fjords, and of the mountains, constantly open new and magnificent prospects to the view. One grand colossal picture follows upon another, but unfortunately few or none show the presence of man. From time to time only some fishing-boat makes its appearance on the sea, or some wooden farmhouse rises on the solitary beach. On advancing further to the north, the aspect of nature becomes more and more stern, vegetation diminishes, man is more rarely seen, and the traveller feels as if he were on the point of entering the gloomy regions of perpetual death.

With the sole exception of Archangel, Drontheim is the most populous and important town situated in so high a latitude as 63° 24'. Although the cradle of ancient Scandinavian history, and the residence of a long line of kings, it looks as if it had been built but yesterday, as its wooden houses have frequently been destroyed by fire. The choir of its magnificent cathedral, built in the eleventh century, and once the resort of innumerable pilgrims who came flocking to the shrine of St. Olave from all Scandinavia, is the only remaining memorial of the old Tronyem of the Norse annalists and scalds. The modern town has a most pleasing and agreeable appearance, and the lively colours with which the houses are painted harmonize with the prosperity of its inhabitants, which is due in a great measure to its thriving fisheries and to the rich iron and copper mines in its neighbourhood. The tall chimneys of many smelting-huts, iron foundries, and other manufactories, bear evidence that modern industry has found its way to the ancient capital of Norway. In point of picturesque beauty, the bay, on a peninsula of which the town is situated, does not yield to that of Naples. Up and down, in every direction, appear the villas of the merchants, and ships of all burden riding at anchor in the bay, and boats passing and repassing. In a small island of the bay, fronting the town, is the celebrated castle of Munkholm, where in former times many a prisoner of state has bewailed the loss of his liberty. Here, among others, Greiffenfeld, who had risen from obscurity to the rank of an all-powerful minister, was incarcerated for eighteen years (1680- 98).

At Hildringen, where the potato is still cultivated with success, and barley ripens every four or five years, begins the province of Nordland, which extends from 65° to 69° 30' N. lat. The mostly uninhabited isles along the coast are called 'Holme,' when rising like steep rocks out of the water, and ' Väre ' when flat and but little elevated above the level of the sea. The latter are the breeding-places of numberless sea-fowls, whose eggs yield a welcome harvest to the inhabitants of the neighbouring mainland, or of the larger islands. A well-stocked egg-vär is a valuable addition to a farm, and descends from father to son, along with the pasture-grounds and the herds of the paternal land. When the proprietor comes to plunder the nests, the birds remain quiet, for they know by experience that only the superfluous eggs are to be removed. But not unfrequently strangers land, and leave not a single egg behind. Then all the birds, several thousands at once, rise from their nests, and fill the air with their doleful cries. If such disasters occur repeatedly they lose courage, and abandoning the scene of their misfortunes, retire to another vär. Most of these birds are sea-gulls (*Maasfugl*, or *Maage*), their eggs are large, and of a not disagreeable taste. The island of Lovunnen is the favourite breeding-place of the puffin, which is highly esteemed on account of its feathers. This silly bird is very easily caught. The fowler lets down an iron hook, or sends a dog trained on purpose into the narrow clefts or holes of the rock, where the puffins sit crowded together. The first bird being pulled out, the next one bites and lays hold of his tail, and thus in succession, till the whole family, clinging together like a chain, is dragged to light.

This rocky coast is also much frequented by the sea-eagle, who is very much feared over the whole province, as he not only carries away lambs and other small animals, but even assails and not seldom overpowers the Norwegian oxen. His mode of attack is so singular that if Von Buch had not heard it so positively and so circumstantially related in various places, situated at great distances from each other, he would willingly have doubted its truth. The eagle darts down into the waves, and then rolls about with his wet plumage on the beach until his wings are quite covered with sand. Then he once more rises into the air and hovers over his intended victim. Swooping down quite close to him, he claps his wings, flings the sand into the eyes of the unfortunate brute, and thoroughly scares it by repeated blows of his pinions. The blinded ox rushes away to avoid the eagle's attacks, until he is completely exhausted, or tumbles down some precipitous cliff.

The sea coast from Alsten to Rodoë, which is crossed by the Arctic Circle, is particularly rich in herrings, as it furnishes more than one-half of the fish exported to Bergen.

In respect of the capital invested, the cod-fishery must be regarded as the most important of the Norwegian deep-sea fisheries, but in the number of hands employed, the herring-fishery takes precedence. The number of men actually engaged in the latter is not less than 60,000, and considerably more than double that number are directly or indirectly interested in the result of their operations. The herrings taken in 1866 filled 750,000 barrels, each weighing 224 lbs., the largest catch ever taken on the Norwegian coast, at least in recent years. As the movements of the fish are extremely erratic, large shoals being found one year in a part of the coast where none will be seen the year following, the fishermen are forced to move from place to place, and formerly the herrings frequently escaped altogether for want of hands to capture them. Now this difficulty is in a great measure removed. Telegraph stations are erected at different places on the coast, from which the movements of the shoals are carefully watched; and field-telegraphs are kept in readiness to be joined on to the main line, so as to summon the fishermen from every part of the country on the first appearance of the fish at any new point. The best time for the herring-fishery is from January to March, and in 1866, 200,000 barrels, or more than one-fourth of the total catch, were caught between February 11 and 14.

At the northern extremity of the province of Nordland, between 68° and 69° N. lat., are situated the Lofoten Islands, or Vesteraalen Oerne, which are separated from the mainland by the Vestfjord. This broad arm of the sea is remarkable both for its violent currents and whirlpools, among which the Malstrom has attained a world-wide celebrity, and also from its being the most northerly limit where the oyster has been found. But it is chiefly as the resort of the cod that the Vestfjord is of the highest importance, not only to Nordland, but to the whole of Norway. No less than 6,000 boats from all parts of the coast, manned probably by more than half of the whole adult male population of Nordland, annually assemble at Vaage, on the island of Ost Vaagoe, and besides these, more

than 300 yœegts, or larger fishing sloops, from Bergen, Chris-
tiansand, and Molde, appear upon the scene.   The banks of
Newfoundland hardly occupy more hands than the fishing
grounds of the Vestfjord, which, after the lapse of a thousand
years, continue as prolific as ever;* nor is there an instance
known of its having ever disappointed the fisherman's hopes.
In Harold Haarfagr's times, Vaage was already renowned
for its fisheries, and several yarls had settled in this northern
district, to reap the rich harvest of the seas.   At a later
period, under the reign of Saint Olave (1020), the annual
parliament of Nordland was held at Vaage, and, in 1120, the
benevolent King Eystein, brother of Sigurd the Crusader,
caused a church to be erected here in honour of his saintly
predecessor, along with a number of huts, to serve as a
shelter to the poor fishermen, a deed which he himself prized
more highly than all his chivalrous brother's warlike exploits
in the East, for 'these men,' said he, ' will still remember in
distant times that a King Eystein once lived in Norway.'

The reason why the fish never cease visiting this part of
the coast is, that the Lofoten Isles enclose, as it were, an
inland or mediterranean sea, which only communicates with
the ocean by several narrow channels between the islands,
and where the fish find the necessary protection against
stormy weather.   They assemble on three or four banks well
known to the fishermen, seldom arriving before the middle
of January, and rarely later than towards the end of February.
They remain in the sheltered fjord no longer than is necessary for spawning, and in April have all retired to the deeper
waters, so that the whole of the fishing season does not last
longer than a couple of months.   The fish are either caught
by hooks and lines, or more frequently in large nets about
twenty fathoms long and seven or eight feet broad, buoyed
with pieces of light wood, and lested with stones, so as to
maintain a vertical position when let down in the water.
The fish, swimming with impetuous speed, darts into the
meshes, which effectually bar his retreat.   The nets are
always spread in the evening and hauled up in the morning,

* In 1866 the total catch of cod was 21,000,000, about 12,000,000 of which
were salted (clip-fish) and the remainder dried (stock-fish); each fish making on
un average 2 lbs. of clip-fish and one-fourth less of stock-fish.

for as long as it is daylight, the fish sees and avoids them, even at a depth of sixty or eighty fathoms. A single haul of the net frequently fills half the boat, and the heavy fish would undoubtedly tear the meshes if they were not immediately struck with iron hooks, and flung into the boat as soon as they are dragged to the surface.

Claus Niels Sliningen, a merchant of Borgund, first introduced the use of these nets in the year 1685, an innovation which more than doubled the total produce of the fisheries. But (as with all useful inventions) loud complaints were raised against him in Norway, and as late as 1762, no nets were allowed at Drontheim 'to prevent the ruin of the poor people who had not the capital to provide themselves with them.'

The life of a fisherman is everywhere full of privations and dangers, but nowhere more so than at the Lofoten Islands. Here, after toiling on the stormy sea for many hours, he has nothing but the miserable shelter of a damp, filthy, over-crowded hut, which affords him neither the rest nor the warmth needed after his fatiguing day's work. Even the iron-framed sons of the North are frequently unable to resist such continuous hardships, and bring home with them the seeds of contagion and death. Malignant fevers have frequently decimated the population of Norway, and their origin may generally be traced to the fishing-grounds. 'The Arab and the Persian,' says Leopold von Buch, 'build cara-vansaries for the wayfarers through the desert; the in-habitants of the Alps have founded "hospices" on the summits of the mountain passes; and the Norwegian has erected houses of refuge on Dovrefeld, but none for the fishermen of Lofoten. Near Rodoë there is a large hospital for the sick of Nordland; would it not be as well to build houses in Lofoten, so as not to crowd the hospitals and churchyards?' This was written at the beginning of the present century, but the poor fishermen are still as neglected as ever, for a more recent traveller, Marmier, beheld with pity the wretched huts in which they spend three winter months, far from their families.

In the channel between Hvalö and the mainland lies, in 69° 45′ N. lat., the small island of Tromsö, where about fifty years since only a few fishermen resided, whose huts have gradually expanded into a thriving little town of about 3,000 inhabitants, along the shore opposite the mainland. Its staple exports are dried and salted cod, and train-oil. The livers of the cod are put in open barrels and placed in the sun, and the melted portion which rises to the surface is skimmed off, being the purest oil. The coarse refuse is boiled in great iron pots by the side of the sea, and yields the common 'train-oil.' The muscular matter which remains is collected into barrels and exported as a powerful manure; some of it is sent to England.

The town consists mainly of one long straggling street, following the windings of the shore, and has a picturesque appearance from the harbour. The houses are all of wood painted with lively colours, and the roofs mostly covered with grass, diversified with bright clusters of yellow and white flowers, look pretty in summer.

Tromsö has a Latin school, and even boasts of a newspaper, the 'Tromsö Tidende et Blad for Nordland og Finmarken' ('The Tromsö Gazette, a paper for Nordland and Finmark'). This paper is published twice a week, and as only one mail arrives at Tromsö every three weeks, the foreign news is given by instalments, spreading over six successive numbers, until a fresh despatch arrives.

The island of Tromsö is beautifully situated, being on all sides environed by mountains, so that it seems to lie in the midst of a huge salt-lake. Its surface rises in gentle slopes to a tolerable elevation, and no other Arctic isle contains richer pasturage, and dwarf plantations of greater luxuriance. Many meadows are yellow with buttercups and picturesque underwood, and the heathy hills are covered with shrubs, bearing bright berries of many hues.

The pride of the Tromsöites in their island and town, and their profound attachment to it, are remarkable. No Swiss can be more enthusiastically bound to his mountains and vales, than they are to their circumscribed domain.

To the north of Tromsö lies the broad and deep Altenfjord, whose borders are studded with numerous dwellings, and where the botanist meets with a vegetation that may well raise his astonishment in so high a latitude. Here the common birch-tree grows 1,450 feet, and the *Vaccinium myr-*

*tillus* 2,030 feet above the level of the sea; the dwarf birch (*Betula nana*) still vegetates at a height of 2,740 feet, and the Arctic willow is even found as high as 3,500 feet, up to the limits of perennial snow.

Alten is moreover celebrated through its copper mines. A piece of ore having been found by a Lap-woman in the year 1825, accidentally fell into the hands of Mr. Crowe, an English merchant in Hammerfest. This gentleman immediately took measures for obtaining a privilege from government for the working of the mines, and all preliminaries being arranged, set off for London, where he founded a company, with a capital of 75,000*l.* When Marmier visited the Altenfjord in 1842, more than 1,100 workmen were employed in these *most northerly mining works* of the world, and not seldom more than ten English vessels at a time were busy unloading coals at Kaafjord for the smelting of the ores. New copper works had recently been opened on the opposite side of the bay at Raipass—and since then the establishment has considerably increased.

Hammerfest, the capital of Finmark, situated on the west side of the island of Hvalö, in 70° 39′ 15″, is the most *northern* town in the world. Half a century since, it had but 44 inhabitants; at present its population amounts to 1,200. As at Tromsö, very many of the houses, forming one long street winding round the shore, have grass sown on their roofs, which gives the latter the appearance of little plots of meadows. With us the expression, 'he sleeps with grass above his head' is equivalent to saying 'he is in his grave;' but here it may only mean that he sleeps beneath the verdant roof of his daily home. Many large warehouses are built on piles projecting into the water, with landing quays before them; and numerous ranges of open sheds are filled with reindeer skins, wolf and bear skins, walrus tusks, reindeer horns, train-oil and dried fish, ready for exportation. The chief home traffic of Hammerfest consists in barter with the Laps, who exchange their reindeer skins for brandy, tobacco, hardware, and cloth. Some enterprising merchants annually fit out vessels for walrus and seal-hunting at Spitzbergen and Bear Island, but the principal trade is with Archangel, and is carried on entirely in 'lodjes' or White Sea ships, with three single upright masts, each hoisting a huge try-sail. These vessels supply Hammerfest with Russian rye, meal, candles, &c., and receive stock-fish and train-oil in exchange. Sometimes, also, an English ship arrives with a supply of coals.

The fishing grounds off the coast of Finmark, whose produce forms the staple article of the merchants of Hammerfest, are scarcely inferior in importance to those of Lofoten, the number of cod taken here in 1866 amounting to 15,000,000. A great part of the fish is purchased by the Russians as it comes out of the water. Of the prepared cod, Spain takes the largest quantity, as in 1865 upwards of 44,000,000 lbs. of clip-fish (nearly the whole yield for the year) was consigned to that country. Of the dried variety, 10,000,000 lbs. were exported to the Mediterranean, and upwards of 4,000,000 lbs. more to Italy. Sweden and Holland come next in order, the supply in each case being over 5,000,000 lbs. Great Britain takes scarcely any stock-fish, but 1,500,000 lbs. of clip-fish, and the large export to the West Indies is almost entirely composed of the latter article.

The winter, though long and dark, has no terrors for the jolly Hammerfesters, for all the traders and shopkeepers form a united aristocracy, and rarely a night passes without a feast, a dance, and a drinking bout. The day when the sun reappears is one of general rejoicing, the first who sees the great luminary proclaims it with a loud voice, and everybody rushes into the street to exchange congratulations with his neighbours. The island of Hvalö has a most dreary sterile aspect, and considerable masses of snow fill the ravines, even in summer. The birch, however, is still found growing 620 feet above the sea, but the fir has disappeared.

It may well be supposed that no stranger has ever sojourned in this interesting place, the furthest outpost of civilisation towards the Pole, without visiting, or at least attempting to visit, the far-famed North Cape, situated about sixty miles from Hammerfest, on the island of Magerö, where a few Norwegians live in earthen huts, and still manage to rear a few heads of cattle. The voyage to this magnificent headland, which fronts the sea with a steep rock wall nearly a thousand feet high, is frequently difficult and precarious, nor can it be scaled without considerable fatigue; but the view from the summit amply rewards the trouble, and it is no small satisfaction to stand on the brink of the most northern promontory of Europe.

'It is impossible,' says Mr. W. Hurton,* 'adequately to describe the emotion experienced by me as I stepped up to the dizzy verge. I only know that I devoutly returned thanks to the Almighty for thus permitting me to realise one darling dream of my boyhood. Despite the wind, which here blew violently and bitterly cold, I sat down, and wrapping my cloak around me, long contemplated the spectacle of Nature in one of her sublimest aspects. I was truly alone.

'Not a living object was in sight; beneath my feet was the boundless expanse of ocean, with a sail or two on its bosom, at an immense distance; above me was the canopy of heaven flecked with fleecy cloudlets; the sun was luridly gleaming over a broad belt of blood-red mist; the only sounds were the whistling of the wandering winds and the occasional plaintive scream of the hovering sea-fowl. The only living creature which came near me was a bee, which hummed merrily by. What did the busy insect seek there? Not a blade of grass grew, and the only vegetable matter on this point was a cluster of withered moss at the very edge of the awful precipice, and this I gathered, at considerable risk, as a memorial of my visit.'

* *Voyage from Leith to Lapland.*

The Osprey.

Magdalena Bay, Spitzbergen.

# CHAPTER X.

## SPITZBERGEN—BEAR ISLAND—JAN MEYEN.

The west coast of Spitzbergen—Ascension of a Mountain by Dr. Scoresby—His
Excursion along the Coast—A stranded Whale—Magdalena Bay—Multitudes of
Sea-birds—Animal Life—Midnight Silence—Glaciers—A dangerous Neighbour-
hood—Interior Plateau—Flora of Spitzbergen—Its Similarity with that of the
Alps above the Snow-line—Reindeer—The hyperborean Ptarmigan—Fishes—
Coal—Driftwood—Discovery of Spitzbergen by Barentz, Heemskerk, and Ryp
—Brilliant Period of the Whale-fishery—Coffins—Eight English Sailors winter
in Spitzbergen, 1630—Melancholy Death of some Dutch Volunteers—Russian
Hunters—Their Mode of Wintering in Spitzbergen—Scharostin—Walrus Ships
from Hammerfest and Tromsö—Bear or Cherie Island—Bennet—Enormous
Slaughter of Walruses—Mildness of its Climate—Mount Misery—Adventurous
Boat Voyage of some Norwegian Sailors—Jan Meyen—Beerenberg.

THE archipelago of Spitzbergen consists of five large
islands: West Spitzbergen, North-East Land, Stans
Foreland, Barentz Land, Prince Charles Foreland; and of a
vast number of smaller ones, scattered around their coasts.
Its surface is about equal to that of two-thirds of Scotland;
its most southern point (76° 30′ N. lat.) lies nearer to the

Pole than Melville Island; and Ross Islet, at its northern
extremity (80° 49′ N. lat.), looks out upon the unknown ocean,
which perhaps extends without interruption as far as the
Straits of Behring.

Of all the Arctic countries that have hitherto been discovered, Grinnell Land and Washington alone lie nearer to
the Pole; but while these ice-blocked regions can only be
reached with the utmost difficulty, the western and north-
western coasts of Spitzbergen, exposed to the mild south-
westerly winds, and to the influence of the Gulf Stream, are
frequently visited, not only by walrus-hunters and Arctic
explorers, but by amateur travellers and sportsmen.

The eastern coasts are far less accessible, and in parts have
never yet been accurately explored. As far as they are
known, they are not so bold and indented as the western
and north-western coasts, which, projecting in mighty capes
or opening a passage to deep fjords, have been gnawed into
every variety of fantastic form by the corroding power of
an eternal winter, and justify, by their endless succession of
jagged spikes and break-neck acclivities, the name of Spitzbergen, which its first Dutch discoverers gave to this land of
' serrated peaks.'

The mountains on the west coast are very steep, many of
them inaccessible, and most of them dangerous to climb,
either from the smooth hard snow with which they are encrusted even in summer, or from the looseness of the disintegrated stones which cover the parts denuded by the sun,
and give way under the slightest pressure of the foot.

More than one daring seaman has paid dearly for his
temerity in venturing to scale these treacherous heights.
The supercargo, or owner of the very first Dutch whaler
that visited Spitzbergen (1612), broke his neck in attempting
to climb a steep mountain in Prince Charles Foreland, and
Barentz very nearly lost several of his men under similar
circumstances. Dr. Scoresby, who in the course of his
whaling expeditions touched at Spitzbergen no less than
seventeen times, was more successful in scaling a mountain
3,000 feet high, near Mitre Cape, though the approach to the
summit was by a ridge so narrow, that he could only advance
by sitting astride upon its edge. But the panorama which

he beheld, after having attained his object, amply repaid him for the danger and fatigue of clambering for several hours over loose stones, which at every step rolled with fearful rapidity into the abyss beneath.

'The prospect,' says the distinguished naturalist, 'was most extensive and grand. A fine sheltered bay was seen to the east of us; an arm of the same on the north-east; and the sea, whose glassy surface was unruffled by a breeze, formed an immense expanse on the west; the icebergs, rearing their proud crests almost to the tops of the mountains between which they were lodged, and defying the power of the solar beams, were scattered in various directions about the sea-coast and in the adjoining bays. Beds of snow and ice, filling extensive hollows and giving an enamelled coat to adjoining valleys, one of which, commencing at the foot of the mountain where we stood, extended in a continued line towards the north, as far as the eye could reach; mountain rising above mountain, until by distance they dwindled into insignificance; the whole contrasted by a cloudless canopy of deepest azure, and enlightened by the rays of a blazing sun, and the effect aided by a feeling of danger—seated, as we were, on the pinnacle of a rock, almost surrounded by tremendous precipices; all united to constitute a picture singularly sublime.

'Our descent we found really a very hazardous, and in some instances a painful undertaking. Every movement was a work of deliberation. Having by much care and with some anxiety made good our descent to the top of the secondary hills, we took our way down one of the steepest banks, and slid forward with great facility in a sitting posture. Towards the foot of the hill, an expanse of snow stretched across the line of descent. This being loose and soft, we entered upon it without fear, but on reaching the middle of it, we came to a surface of solid ice, perhaps a hundred yards across, over which we launched with astonishing velocity, but happily escaped without injury. The men, whom we left below, viewed this latter movement with astonishment and fear.'

After this perilous descent, Scoresby continued his excursion on the flat land next the sea, where he found scattered here and there many skulls and other bones of sea-horses,

whales, narwals, foxes and seals. Two Russian lodges, formed
of logs of pine, with a third in ruins, were also seen; the
former, from a quantity of fresh chips about them and other
appearances, gave evidence of having been recently inhabited.
These huts were built upon a ridge of shingle, adjoining the
sea. Among the boulders heaped upon the shore, numerous
sea-birds had built their nests or laid their eggs, which they
defended with loud cries and determined courage against
the attacks of gulls.

The only insect he perceived was a small green fly, but the
water along the coast was filled with medusæ and shrimps.
The strong north-west winds had covered the strand with
large heaps of *Fucus vesiculosus* and *Laminaria saccharina*,
the same which the storms also cast out upon our shores.

The view of this high northern life was extremely interesting, but Dr. Scoresby was still further rewarded by the
discovery of a dead whale, found stranded on the beach,
which, though much swollen and not a little putrid, proved
a prize worth at least 400*l*.

By a harpoon found in its body, it appeared to have been
struck by some of the fishers on the Elbe, and having
escaped from them, it had probably stranded itself on the
spot where it was found. When the first incision was made,
the oil gushed forth like a fountain. It was a slow and
laborious work to transport the blubber to the ship, which
on account of the dangerous nature of the coast was obliged
to remain two miles off at sea. After five boat-loads had
safely been brought on board, the wind suddenly changed,
so that the ship was driven far out to sea, and the boat
reached it with great difficulty.

Of the numerous fjords of Spitzbergen, once the busy
resort of whole fleets of whalers, and now but rarely visited
by man, none has been more accurately described by modern
Arctic voyagers than the magnificent harbour of Magdalena
Bay. Here the 'Dorothea' and the 'Trent' anchored in
1818, on their way to the North Pole; here also the French
naturalists, who had been sent out in the corvette 'La Re-
cherche' (1835–36) to explore the high northern latitudes,
sojourned for several weeks.

The number of the sea-birds is truly astonishing. On the

ledges of a high rock, at the head of the bay, Beechey saw the little auks (*Arctica alle*) extend in an uninterrupted line full three miles in length, and so closely congregated that about thirty fell at a single shot. He estimated their numbers at about 4,000,000. When they took flight they darkened the air; and at the distance of four miles their chorus could distinctly be heard.

On a fine summer's day, the bellowing of the walruses and the hoarse bark of the seals are mingled with the shrill notes of the auks, divers, and gulls. Although all these tones produce a by no means harmonious concert, yet they have a pleasing effect, as denoting the happy feelings of so many creatures. When the sun verges to the pole, every animal becomes mute, and a silence broken only by the bursting of a glacier reigns over the whole bay—a remarkable contrast to the tropical regions, where Nature enjoys her repose during the noon-day heat, and it is only after sunset that life awakens in the forest and the field.

Four glaciers reach down this noble inlet: one, called the Waggon Way, is 7,000 feet across at its terminal cliff, which is 300 feet high, presenting a magnificent wall of ice. But the whole scene is constructed on so colossal a scale, that it is only on a near approach, that the glaciers of Magdalena Bay appear in all their imposing grandeur. In clear weather the joint effect of the ice under the water, and the reflection of the glacier wall above, causes a remarkable optical delusion. The water assumes a milk-white colour, the seals appear to gambol in a thick cream-like liquid, and the error only becomes apparent when, on leaning over the side of the boat, the spectator looks down into the transparent depth below.

It is extremely dangerous to approach these cliffs of ice, as every now and then large blocks detach themselves from the mass, and frequently even a concussion of the air is enough to make them fall.

During the busy period of Spitzbergen history, when its bay used to be frequented by whalers who anchored under the glacier-walls, these ice-avalanches often had disastrous consequences. Thus, in the year 1619, an English ship was driven by a storm into Bell Sound. While it was passing under a precipice of ice, a prodigious mass came thundering down upon it, broke the masts, and threw the ship so violently upon one side, that the captain and part of the crew were swept into the sea. The captain escaped unhurt, but two sailors were killed and several others wounded.

One day a gun was fired from a boat of the 'Trent,' when about half a mile from one of the glaciers of Magdalena Bay. Immediately after the report of the musket, a noise resembling thunder was heard in the direction of the ice-stream, and in a few seconds more, an enormous mass detached itself from its front, and fell into the sea. The men in the boat, supposing themselves to be beyond the reach of its influence, were tranquilly contemplating the magnificent sight, when suddenly a large wave came sweeping over the bay, and cast their little shallop to a distance of ninety-six feet upon the beach.

Another time, when Franklin and Beechey had approached one of these ice-walls, a huge fragment suddenly slid from its side, and fell with a crash into the sea. At first the detached mass entirely disappeared under the waters, casting up clouds of spray, but soon after it shot up again at least 100 feet above the surface, and then kept rocking several minutes to and fro. When at length the tumult subsided, the block was found to measure no less than 1,500 feet in circumference; it projected 60 feet above the water, and its weight was calculated at more than 400,000 tons.

Besides the glaciers of Magdalena Bay, Spitzbergen has many others that protrude their crystal walls down to the water's edge; and yet but few icebergs, and the largest not to be compared with the productions of Baffin's Bay, are drifted from the shores of Spitzbergen into the open sea. The reason is that the glaciers usually terminate where the sea is shallow, so that no very large mass if dislodged can float away, and they are at the same time so frequently dismembered by heavy swells, that they cannot attain any great size.

The interior of Spitzbergen has never been explored. According to the Swedish naturalists,* who climbed many

---

* Within the last few years, no less than three scientific expeditions have been sent out to Spitzbergen at the expense of the Swedish government. During the summer of 1858, Messrs. Otto Torell, Guennerstedt, and Nordenskjold visited the western parts of the archipelago. In 1861 the whole coast, from Ice Sound to Dove Bay in North-East Land was accurately investigated by Messrs. Torell, Malmgren, Chydenius, &c., and in 1864 Messrs. Nordenskjold, Duner, and Malmgren visited the southern shores and Wjde Jan's Water. A fourth expedition has just left the port of Gothenburg (June 1868).

of the highest mountains in various parts of the coast, all the central regions of the archipelago form a level ice-plateau, interrupted only here and there by denuded rocks, projecting like islands from the crystal sea in which they are imbedded. The height of this plateau above the level of the ocean is in general from 1,500 to 2,000 feet, and from its frozen solitudes descend the various glaciers above described. During the summer months, the radiation of the sun at Spitzbergen is always very intense, the thermometer in some sheltered situations not seldom rising at noon to 62°, 67°, or even 73°. Even at midnight, at the very peak of the high mountain ascended by Scoresby, the power of the sun produced a temperature several degrees above the freezing point, and occasioned the discharge of streams of water from the snow-capped summit. Hence, though even in the three warmest months the temperature of Spitzbergen does not average more than 34½°, yet in the more southern aspects, and particularly where the warmth of the sun is absorbed and radiated by black rock-walls, the mountains are not seldom bared at an elevation nearly equal to that of the snow-line of Norway, and various Alpine plants and grasses frequently flourish, not only in sheltered situations at the foot of the hills, but even to a considerable height, wherever the disintegrated rocks lodge and form a tolerably good soil.

The Flora of Spitzbergen consists of about ninety-three species of flowering or phenogamous plants, which generally grow in isolated tufts or patches; but the mosses which carpet the moist lowlands, and the still more hardy lichens, which invest the rocks with their thin crusts or scurfs as far as the last limits of vegetation, are much more numerous. Some of the plants of Spitzbergen are also found on the Alps, beyond the snow-line, at elevations of from 9,000 to 10,000 feet above the level of the sea. According to Mr. Martins, nothing can give a better idea of Spitzbergen than the vast circus of *névé*, in the centre of which rises the triangular rock known to the visitors of Chamouny as the Jardin or the Courtil. Let the tourist, placed on this spot at a time when the sun rises but little above the horizon, or better still, when wreaths of mist hang over the neighbouring mountains, fancy the sea bathing the foot of the amphitheatre of which he occupies the centre, and he has a complete Spitzbergen prospect before him. Supposing him to be a botanist, the sight of the *Ranunculus glacialis, Cerastium alpinum, Arenaria biflora,* and *Erigeron uniflorus,* will still further increase the illusion.

The only esculent plant of Spitzbergen is the *Cochlearia fenestrata,* which here loses its acrid principles, and can be eaten as a salad. The grasses which Keilhau found growing near some Russian huts in Stans Foreland, are during the summer a precious resource for the reindeer, which, though extremely shy, make their appearance from time to time in every part of the land from the Seven Islands to South Cape, and are more abundant than could have been expected. The Polar bears are probably their only native enemies on these islands, and their fleetness furnishes them with ample means of escape from a pursuer so clumsy on land. Lord Mulgrave's crew killed fifty deer on Vogelsang, a noted hunting place, and on Sir Edward Parry's polar expedition about seventy deer were shot in Treurenberg Bay by inexperienced deer-stalkers, and without the aid of dogs. During the winter these large herbivora live on the Icelandic moss which they scent under the snow, but it may well be asked where they find shelter in a naked wilderness without a single tree. In May and June they are so thin as scarcely to be eatable, but in July they begin to get fat, and then their flesh would everywhere be reckoned a delicacy.

Besides the reindeer, the only land-quadrupeds of Spitzbergen are the Polar bear, the Arctic fox, and a small field-mouse, which in summer has a mottled, and in winter a white fur.

Of the birds, the hyperborean Ptarmigan (*Lagopus hyperborea*), which easily procures its food under the snow, undoubtedly winters in Spitzbergen, and probably also the lesser red-pole, which perhaps finds grass seeds enough for its subsistence during the long polar nights, while the snow bunting (*Plectrophanes nivalis*), and the twenty species of water-fowl and waders that frequent the shores of the high northern archipelago during the summer, all migrate southwards when the long summer's day verges to its end.

Until very lately, the Spitzbergen waters were supposed to be poor in fishes, though the numerous finbacks, which towards the end of summer frequent the southern and south-western coasts, and, unlike the large smooth-back whales, chiefly live on herrings, as well as the troops of salmon-loving white dolphin seen about the estuaries of the rivers, sufficiently proved the contrary, not to mention the herds of seals, and the hosts of ichthyophagous sea-birds that breed on every rocky ledge of the archipelago.   Phipps and Scoresby mention only three or four species of fishes occurring in the seas of Spitzbergen, while the Swedish naturalist Malmgren, the first who seems to have paid real attention to this interesting branch of zoology, collected no less than twenty-three species in 1861 and 1864.   The northern shark (*Scymnus microcephulus*) is so abundant that of late its fishery has proved highly remunerative.   The first ship, which was fitted out for this purpose in 1863 by Hilbert Pettersen, of Tromsö, returned from Bell and Ice Sounds with a full cargo of sharks' livers, and in 1865 the same enterprising merchant sent out no less than five shark-ships to Spitzbergen.   The cod, the common herring, the shell-fish, the halibut have likewise been caught in the waters of the archipelago, and there is every reason to believe that their fishery, which has hitherto been entirely neglected, might be pursued with great success.

The mineral riches of Spitzbergen are, of course, but little known.   Coal of an excellent quality, which might easily be worked, as it nearly crops out on the surface at a short distance from the sea, has, however, been discovered lately by Mr. Blomstrand in King's Bay, and similar strata exist in various parts of Bell Sound and Ice Sound.   Large quantities of drift wood, probably from the large Siberian rivers, are deposited by the currents, particularly on the north coasts of North East Land, and on the southern coasts of Stans Fore Land.   In English Bay, Lord Dufferin saw innumerable logs of unhewn timber, mingled with which lay pieces of broken spars, an oar, a boat's flagstaff, and a few shattered fragments of some long lost vessel's planking.

Most probably the Norwegians had their attention directed at a very early period to the existence of a land lying to

the north of Finmarken by the troops of migratory birds
which they saw flying northwards in spring, and by the
casual visits of sea-bears, which the drift-ice carried to the
south. There can be no doubt that they were the first
discoverers of Spitzbergen, but their history contains no
positive records of the fact, and it was not before the six-
teenth century that Europe first became acquainted with
that desolate archipelago. Sir Hugh Willoughby may
possibly have seen it in 1559, but it is certain that on
June 19, 1596, Barentz, Heemskerke, and Ryp, who had
sailed in two ships from Amsterdam to discover the north-
eastern passage to India, landed on its western coast, and
gave it the name it bears to the present day. In the year
1607 it was visited by the unfortunate Henry Hudson, and
four years later the first English whalers were fitted out by
the Russia Company in London to fish in the bays of
Spitzbergen or East Greenland, as it was at that time called,
being supposed to be the eastern prolongation of that
vast island. Here our countrymen met with Dutchmen,
Norwegians, and Biscayans from Bayonne and the ports of
northern Spain, and commercial rivalry soon led to the
usual quarrels. In the year 1613, James I. granted the
Russia Company a patent, giving them the exclusive right
to fish in the Spitzbergen waters, and seven ships of war
were sent out to enforce their pretensions. The Dutch,
the Norwegians, and the Biscayans were driven away; a
cross with the name of the King of England was erected on
the shore, and Spitzbergen received the name of 'King
James his Newland.' This triumph, however, was but of
short duration, and after a struggle, in which none of the
combatants gained any decisive advantage, all parties came
at last to an amicable agreement. The English received for
their share the best stations on the southwestern coast,
along with English Bay and Magdalena Bay. The Dutch
were obliged to retreat to the north, and chose Amsterdam
Island, with Smeerenberg Bay, as the seat of their operations.
The Danes or Norwegians established their headquarters on
Dane's Island; the Hamburgers, who also came in for their
share, in Hamburg Bay; and the French or Biscayans on
the north coast, in Red Bay. At present a right or smooth-

backed whale rarely shows itself in the Spitzbergen waters, but at that time it was so abundant that frequently no less than forty whalers used to anchor in a single bay, and send out their boats to kill these cetaceans, who came there for the purpose of casting their young in the sheltered friths and channels. The fat of the captured whales was immediately boiled in large kettles on the shore, and the bays of Spitzbergen presented a most animated spectacle during the summer season.

Numerous coffins—an underground burial being impossible in this frost-hardened earth—still bear witness to those busy times, and also to the great mortality among the fishermen, caused doubtless by their intemperate habits. They are particularly abundant at Smeerenberg, where Admiral Beechey saw upwards of one thousand of them; boards with English inscriptions were erected over a few, but the greater number were Dutch, and had been deposited in the eighteenth century. Some coffins having been opened, the corpses were found in a state of perfect preservation, and even the woollen caps and stockings of the mariners, who might perhaps have rested for more than a century on this cold earth, were still apparently as new as if they had been but recently put on.

In the seventeenth century, the English and the Dutch made several attempts to establish permanent settlements in Spitzbergen. The Russia Company tried to engage volunteers by the promise of a liberal pay, and as none came forward, a free pardon was offered to criminals who would undertake to winter in Bell Sound. A few wretches, tired of confinement, accepted the proposal, but when the fleet was about to depart, and they saw the gloomy hills, and felt the howling north-eastern gales, their hearts failed them, and they entreated the captain who had charge of them to take them back to London and let them be hanged. Their request to be taken back was complied with, but the company generously interceded for them, and obtained their pardon.

Some time after, in the year 1630, an English whaler landed eight men in Bell Sound to hunt reindeer. They remained on shore during the night, but meanwhile a storm had arisen, and on the following morning their ship had vanished out of sight.  It was towards the end of August, and they had no hope of rescue at this advanced period of the year.

Their despair may be imagined, but they soon recovered their courage, and wisely determined to make preparations for the impending winter, instead of losing time in useless lamentations.  Their first care was to lay in a stock of food, and in a short time they had killed nineteen reindeer and four bears.  Fortunately they found in Bell Sound the necessary materials for the erection of a hut.  A large shed fifty feet long and thirty-eight broad, had been built as a workshop for the men of the Russia Company, and they very judiciously constructed their small hut of stones and thick planks within this enclosed space.  They thus gained a better protection against the icy wind and room for exercise during stormy weather, one of the best preservatives against the scurvy. They made their beds and winter dresses of the skins of the animals they had killed, sewing them together with needles made of bone splinters and using disentangled rope ends as thread.

Their hut was ready by September 12, and to preserve their supply of meat as long as possible, they lived four days of the week on the offal of whales' fat which lay scattered about in great plenty.  From October 26 to February 15, they saw no sun, and from the 13th to the 31st of December no twilight. The new year began with excessive cold ; every piece of metal they touched stuck to their fingers like glue, and their skin became blistered when exposed to the air.  The reappearance of the sun was as a resurrection from death.  To increase their joy, they saw two bears on the ice, one of which they killed, but they found, what has since been frequently experienced by others, that the liver of the animal has poisonous qualities, or is at least very unwholesome, for, after eating it, they were all attacked with a kind of eruptive fever, and their skin peeled off.  Towards the middle of March, their provisions were well nigh exhausted, but the polar bears appearing more frequently replenished their stock.  Soon also the migratory birds arrived from the south, the foxes crept out of their burrows, and many were caught in traps.  On June 5, the ice began to break up, and on the following morning one-half of the bay was open. A gale forced them to seek the shelter of their hut. There seated round the fire, they spoke of their approaching delivery, when suddenly a loud halloo was heard. They immediately rushed out into the open air, and hardly believed their eyesight, for they were greeted by their comrades of the previous summer, and saw their own well-known ship at anchor in the bay. Thus were these brave-hearted men rescued after a ten months' exile in the latitude of 77°.

The possibility of wintering in Spitzbergen having thus been proved, some volunteers belonging to the Dutch fleet were induced by certain emoluments to attempt the same enterprise on Amsterdam Island; but, less fortunate than their predecessors, they all fell victims to the scurvy. A diary which they left behind recorded the touching history of their sufferings. 'Four of us,' these were its last words, 'are still alive, stretched out flat upon the floor, and might still be able to eat if one of us had but the strength to rise and fetch some food and fuel, but we are all so weak, and every movement is so painful, that we are incapable of stirring. We constantly pray to God soon to release us from our sufferings, and truly we cannot live much longer without food and warmth. None of us is able to help the others, and each must bear his burthen as well as he can.'

Since that time both the English and the Dutch have given up the idea of forming permanent settlements in Spitzbergen, but scarcely a year passes that some Russians and Norwegians do not winter in that high northern land. As far back as the seventeenth century, the former used to send out their clumsy but strongly built 'lodjes' of from 60 to 160 tons from the ports of Archangel, Mesen, Onega, Kola, and other places bordering the White Sea, to chase the various animals of Spitzbergen, the reindeer, the seal, the beluga, but chiefly the walrus, the most valuable of all. These vessels leave home in July, or as soon as the navigation of the White Sea opens, and as the shortness of the season hardly allows them to return in the same year, they pass the winter in some sheltered bay. Their first care on landing is to erect a large cross on the shore, a ceremony they repeat on leaving, and such is their religious faith that under the protection of that holy symbol they mock all the terrors of the

Arctic winter. Near the place where their vessels are laid up, they build a large hut from twenty to twenty-five feet square, which is used as a station and magazine; but the huts used by the men who go in quest of skins, and which are erected at distances of from ten to fifty versts along the shore, are only seven or eight feet square. The smaller huts are usually occupied by two or three men, who take care to provide themselves from the storehouse with the necessary provisions for the winter. Scoresby visited several of these huts, some constructed of logs, others of deal two inches in thickness. They are of the same kind as those used by the peasants in Russia, and, being taken out in pieces, are erected with but little trouble in the most convenient situation. The stoves are built with bricks, or with clay found in the country. During the stay of the hunters, they employ themselves in killing seals or walruses in the water, and bears, foxes, deer, or whatever else they meet with on land. Each ship is furnished with provisions for eighteen months, consisting of rye flour for bread, oatmeal, barley-meal, peas, salt beef, salt cod, and salt halibut, together with curdled milk, honey, and linseed oil; besides which they enjoy the flesh of the animals which they kill. Their drink consists chiefly of *quas*, a national beverage made from rye flour and water; malt or spirituous liquors being entirely forbidden to prevent drunkenness, as, when they were allowed it, they drank so immoderately that their work was often altogether neglected. Their fuel for the most part is brought with them from Russia, and drift wood is used for the same purpose.

The hunters, seldom travelling far in winter, make their short excursions on foot on snow-skates, and draw their food after them on hand sledges. Not seldom they are overtaken by terrific snowstorms, which force them to throw themselves flat upon the ground, and sometimes even cost them their lives. Their best preservation against the scurvy is bodily exercise; they also use the *Cochlearia fenestrata*, which grows wild in the country, either eating it without any preparation, or drinking the liquor prepared from it by infusion in water. Yet, in spite of all their precautions, they often fall a prey to this terrible scourge. In the year 1771, Mr. Steward, of Whitby, landed in King's Bay to gather drift wood, and found a Russian hut. After having vainly called for admittance, they opened it, and found a corpse stretched out on the ground, its face covered with green mould. Most likely the unfortunate man, having buried all his comrades, had as the last survivor found no one to perform the same kind office for himself. Generally the Russian hunters, after spending the winter in Spitzbergen, return home in the following August on September; but their stay is often prolonged during several years; and Scharostin, a venerable Russian, who died in 1826 in Ice Sound, is deservedly remarkable for having spent no less than thirty-two winters of his long life in that high northern land, where he once remained during fifteen consecutive years. Surely this man ought to have been crowned king of Spitzbergen—

> On a throne of rocks, in a robe of clouds,
> With a diadem of snow !

Every year, at the beginning of summer, about a dozen vessels leave the ports of Hammerfest and Tromsö for Spitzbergen. Formerly it was a very common thing for them to procure three cargoes of walrus and seals in a season, and less than two full cargoes was considered very bad luck indeed; now, however, it is a rare thing to get more than one cargo in a season, and many vessels return home after four months' absence only half full. Yet, in spite of this diminution, the numbers of walruses still existing in that country are very considerable, particularly on the northern banks and skerries, which are only accessible in open seasons, or perhaps once in every three or four summers, and where consequently the persecuted animals get a little breathing time to breed and replenish their numbers.

About midway between Hammerfest and Spitzbergen lies Bear Island, originally discovered by Barentz on June 9, 1596. Seven years later, Stephen Bennet, a shipmaster in the service of the Muscovy Company, while on a voyage of discovery in a north-easterly direction, likewise saw Bear Island on August 16. Ignorant of its previous discovery by Barentz, he called it Cherie Island, after Sir Francis Cherie, a member of the company, and to this day both names are used.

Bennet found some walruses on its desert shores, and returned in the following year with a vessel fitted out by a merchant of the name of Welden, to wage war with these sea-monsters. His first operations were not very successful. Of a herd of at least a thousand walruses, he killed no more than fifteen, and a later attack upon an equally enormous troop raised the entire number of his victims to no more than fifty. Their tusks alone were brought away, and along with some loose ones collected on the beach formed the chief produce of the expedition. At first the unwieldy creatures were fired at, but as the bullets made no great impression on their thick hides, grape shot was now discharged into their eyes, and the blinded animals were finally killed with axes.

In the following year, Welden himself proceeded to Bear Island, and the art of walrus-killing gradually improving by practice, this second expedition proved far more profitable than the first. Care had also been taken to provide large kettles and the necessary fuel to boil their fat on the spot, so that besides the tusks a quantity of oil was gained. In 1606, Bennet again appeared on the field of action, and the dexterity of the walrus-hunters had now become so great that in less than six hours they killed more than 700, which yielded twenty-two tons of oil. During the following voyage, Welden, who seems to have acted in partnership with Bennet, each taking his turn, killed no less than 1,000 walruses in seven hours. Thus Bear Island proved a mine of wealth to these enterprising men, and though the walruses are not now so abundant as in the good old times, yet they are still sufficiently numerous to attract the attention of speculators. Every year several expeditions proceed to its shores from the Russian and Norwegian ports, and generally some men pass the winter in huts erected on its northern and south eastern coasts.

Considering its high northern latitude of 75°, the climate of Bear Island is uncommonly mild. According to the reports of some Norwegian walrus-hunters, who remained there from 1824 to 1826, the cold was so moderate during the first winter that, until the middle of November, the snow which fell in the night melted during the daytime. It rained at Christmas, and seventy walruses were killed during Christmas week by the light of the moon and that of the Aurora. Even in February the weather was so mild that the men were able to work in the open air under the same latitude as Melville Island, where mercury is a solid body during five

months of the year.   The cold did not become intense before
March, and attained its maximum in April, when the sea
froze fast round the island, and the white bears appeared
which had been absent during the whole winter.   The second
winter was more severe than the first, but even then the sea
remained open till the middle of November—evidently in
consequence of the prevailing south-westerly winds.   The
greater part of Bear Island is a desolate plateau raised about
100 or 200 feet above the sea.   Along its western shores
rises a group of three mountains, supposed to be about 200
feet high, and towards the south it terminates in a solitary
hill to which the first discoverers gave the appropriate name
of Mount Misery.   At the northern foot of this terrace-
shaped elevation, the plateau is considerably depressed, and
forms a kind of oasis, where grass (*Poa pratensis*), enlivened
with violet cardamines and white polygonums and saxifragas,
grows to half a yard in height.   The general character of the
small island is, however, a monotony of stone and morass,
with here and there a patch of snow, while the coasts have
been worn by the action of the waves into a variety of fantastic shapes, bordered in some parts by a flat narrow strand,
the favorite resort of the walrus, and in others affording
convenient breeding-places to hosts of sea-birds.   In Coal
Bay, four parallel seams of coal, about equidistant from each
other, are visible on the vertical rock walls, but they are too
thin to be of any practical use.

Bear Island has no harbours, and is consequently a rather
dangerous place to visit.   During the first expedition sent
out from Hammerfest, it happened that some of the men
who had been landed were abandoned by their ship, which
was to have cruised along the coast, while they were hunting
on shore.   But the current, the wind, and a dense fog so
confused the ignorant captain that, leaving them to their
fate, he at once returned to Hammerfest.   When the men
became aware of their dreadful situation, they determined to
leave the island in their boat, and taking with them a quantity
of young walrus flesh, they luckily reached Northkyn after
a voyage of eight days.   It seems almost incredible that
these same people immediately after revisited Bear Island in
the same ship, and were again obliged to return to Norway
in the same boat.   The ship had anchored in the open bay of

North Haven, and having taken in its cargo, consisting of 180 walruses, which had all been killed in a few days, was about to leave when a storm arose which cast it ashore, and broke it to pieces. The Russians had built some huts in the neighbourhood, and the provisions might probably have been saved, but rather than winter in the island the crew resolved to venture home again in the boat. This was so small that one-half of them were obliged to lie down on the bottom while the others rowed; the autumn was already far advanced, and they encountered so savage a storm, that an English ship they fell in with at the North Cape vainly endeavoured to take them on board. After a ten days' voyage, however, they safely arrived at Magerö, thus proving the truth of the old saying that " Fortune favours the bold." The distance from Bear Island to North Cape is about sixty nautical miles.

In a straight line between Spitzbergen and Iceland lies Jan Meyen, which, exposed to the cold Greenland current, almost perpetually veiled with mists, and surrounded by drift ice, would scarcely ever be disturbed in its dreary solitude but for the numerous walrus and seal herds that frequent its shores. The ice-bears and the wild sea birds are its only inhabitants; once some Dutchmen attempted to winter there, but the scurvy swept them all away. Its most remarkable features are the volcano Esk and the huge mountain Beerenberg, towering to the height of 6,870 feet, with seven enormous glaciers sweeping down its sides into the sea.

Abandoned Vessel on an Arctic Shore.

# CHAPTER XI.

### NOVAYA ZEMLYA.

The Sea of Kara—Loschkin—Rosmysslow—Lütke—Krotow—Pachtussow—Sails along the Eastern Coast of the Southern Island to Matoschkin Schar—His Second Voyage and Death—Meteorological Observations of Ziwolka—The Cold Summer of Novaya Zemlya—Von Baer's scientific Voyage to Novaya Zemlya —His Adventures in Matoschkin Schar—Storm in Kostin Schar—Sea Bath and Votive Cross—Botanical Observations—A natural Garden—Solitude and Silence —A Bird-Bazaar—Hunting Expeditions of the Russians to Novaya Zemlya.

THE sea of Kara, bounded on the west by Novaya Zemlya, and on the east by the vast peninsula of Tajmurland, is one of the most inhospitable parts of the inhospitable Polar Ocean. For all the ice which the east-westerly marine currents drift during the summer along the Siberian coasts accumulates in that immense land-locked bay, and almost constantly blocks the gate of Kara, as the straits have been named that separate Novaya Zemlya from the island of Waigatz.

The rivers Jenissei and Obi, which remain frozen over until late in June, likewise discharge their vast masses of ice

ARCTIC BIRD MOUNTAIN.

into the gulf of Kara, so that we cannot wonder that the eastern coast of Novaya Zemlya, fronting a sea which opposes almost insuperable obstacles to the Arctic navigator, has remained almost totally unknown until 1833, while the western coast, exposed to the Gulf Stream, and bathed, in summer at least, by a vast open ocean, has long been traced in all its chief outlines on the map.

The walrus-hunter Loschkin is indeed said to have sailed along the whole eastern coast of Novaya Zemlya in the last century, but we have no authentic records of his voyage, and at a later period Rosmysslow, who, penetrating through Mathew's Straits, or Matoschkin Schar, found Novaya Zemlya to consist of two large islands, investigated but a small part of those unknown shores. From 1819 to 1824, the Russian government sent out no less than five expeditions to the sea of Kara; the famous circumnavigator Admiral Lütke endeavoured no less than four times to advance along the eastern coast of Novaya Zemlya, but all these efforts proved fruitless against the superior power of a stormy and ice-blocked sea. Yet in spite of these repeated failures, two enterprising men—Klokow, a chief inspector of forests, and Brandt, a rich merchant of Archangel—fitted out three ships in 1832 for the purpose of solving the mysteries of the sea of Kara.

One of these vessels, commanded by Lieutenant Krotow, was to penetrate through Mathew's Straits, and, having reached their eastern outlet, to sail thence across the sea, to the mouth of the Obi and the Jenissei; but nothing more was heard of the ill-fated ship after its first separation from its companions at Kanin Nos.

The second ship, which was to sail along the western coast of Novaya Zemlya, and, if possible, to round its northern extremity, was more fortunate, for though it never reached that point, it returned home with a rich cargo of walrus-teeth.

The third ship, finally, under Pachtussow's command, was to penetrate through the gate of Kara, and from thence to proceed along the eastern coast. When Pachtussow, according to his instructions, had reached the straits, all his efforts to effect a passage proved ineffectual. It was in vain he more than once steered to the east, the stormy weather and large

masses of drift ice constantly threw him back, the short
summer approached its end, and thus he was obliged to put
off all further attempts to the next year, and to settle for the
winter in Rocky Bay within the gate of Kara. A small hut
was built out of the drift-wood found on the spot, and joined
by means of a gallery of sail-cloth to a bathing-room, that
indispensable comfort of a Russian. The laying of traps in
which many Arctic foxes were caught, and the carrying of
the wood, which had sometimes to be fetched from a distance
of ten versts, occupied the crew during fair weather. In
April, a party under Pachtussow's command set out for the
purpose of exploring the western coast. On this expedition
they were overtaken on the twenty-fourth day of the month
by a terrible snow storm, which obliged them to throw themselves flat upon the ground, to avoid being swept away by the
wind. They remained three days without food under the
snow, as it was impossible for them to reach the depot of provisions buried a few versts off.

On June 24, the gate of Kara was at length open, and
Pachtussow would gladly have sailed through the passage,
but his ship was fast in the ice. He therefore resolved, in
order to make the best use of his time, to examine the eastern
coast in a boat, and reached in this manner the small
Sawina River, where he found a wooden cross with the date
of 1742. Most likely it had been placed there by Loschkin,
his predecessor on the path of discovery. He now returned
with his boat to the ship, which, after an imprisonment of
297 days, was at length, July 11, able to leave the bay.

On Stadolski Island, near Cape Menschikoff, they found a
wretched hut, which proved that they were not the first to
penetrate into these deserts. But the hut was tenantless,
and a number of human bones were strewn over the ground.
One of Pachtussow's companions now related that in 1822 a
Samojede, named Mawei, had gone with his wife and children
to Novaya Zemlya, and had never returned. On gathering
the bones, they were found to compose the skeletons of two
children and of a woman, but no remains could be discovered
of the man. Most likely the unfortunate savage had been
surprised by a snow storm, or had fallen a prey to a hungry
ice-bear, on one of his excursions, and his family, deprived
of their support, had died of hunger in the hut.

On July 19, they reached the river Stawinen, and on the 21st Lütke's Bay, where a number of white dolphins and seals of an unknown species were found. Here contrary winds arrested the progress of the navigators during eighteen days. On August 13, Pachtussow entered Matoschkin Schar, and reached its western mouth on the 19th. Thus he succeeded at least in circumnavigating the southern island, which no one had achieved before him, and as his exhausted provisions did not allow him to spend a second winter in Novaya Zemlya, he resolved to return at once to Archangel. But contrary winds drove him to the island of Kolgujew, and thence to the mouth of the Petschora, where, on September 3, a dreadful storm at length shattered his crazy vessel. The crew found refuge in a hut, but this also was filled by the water; so that they had to wade several versts before they could reach the dry land.

Pachtussow now travelled by way of Archangel and Onega to St. Petersburgh, where he communicated the results of his journey to the minister of marine, who gave him a most flattering reception, well merited by his ability and courage. The success he had already obtained encouraged the hope that a second expedition would be able to complete the undertaking, and consequently, by an imperial order, the schooner Krotow and a transport were fitted out, with which Pachtussow once more sailed from the port of Archangel on August 5. His instructions were to winter in Mathew's Straits, and thence to attempt in the following summer the exploration of the eastern coast of the northern island. The winter hut he built at the western entrance of the straits was ready for his reception by October 20. It was of stately dimensions for a Novaya Zemlya residence, 25 feet long, 21 broad, 8 feet high in the centre, 5 at the sides; and consisted of two compartments, one for the officers and the other for the crew. They found the cold very endurable, but were rather incommoded by the smoke, which did not always find a ready passage through the opening in the roof. Sometimes the snow accumulated in such masses, or the storm raged so furiously round the hut, that they could not leave it for eight days running, and frequently the hole in the roof had to serve them for a door.

Eleven white bears were killed about the hut during the

winter; one on the roof, another in the passage. Pachtussow, well aware that occupation is the best remedy against
melancholy, kept his crew in constant activity. They were
obliged to fetch wood from distances of ten or eleven versts,
not seldom during a cold of −36°, which, thanks to their
thick fur-dresses, they bore remarkably well, particularly as
a temperature lower than −25° never occurred, unless during
perfectly calm weather. He also made them lay fox traps at
considerable distances from the hut, and amused them with
shooting at a mark and gymnastic exercises.

By this means he succeeded in preserving their health,
and warding off the attacks of the scurvy.

As early as April, the indefatigable Pachtussow fitted out
two sledge-parties, for the exploration of the eastern coast.
The one, consisting of seven men, he commanded in person;
the other was led by the steersman Ziwolka. Both parties
travelled in company as far as the eastern entrance of the
straits, where one of the huts in which Rosmysslow had wintered seventy years since was still found in a good condition.

Pachtussow now returned for the purpose of accurately
surveying the straits, while Ziwolka proceeded along the
east coast, with a small tent and provisions for a month.
All his men had Samojede dresses, but they were already so
hardened that they did not wear the upper coat with the
hood even during the night, although snow storms not seldom
occurred. Once their boots were frozen so hard that they
could not pull them off before they had been previously
thawed, and as drift-wood was nowhere to be found, they
were obliged to burn the poles of their tent, and to keep
their feet over the fire, until the leather became soft. On
May 18, the thirty-fourth day of his journey, Ziwolka returned to his commander after having explored the east
coast northwards to a distance of 150 versts.

Meanwhile Pachtussow had been busy building a boat
eighteen feet long, with which he intended to proceed along
the western coast, to the northern extremity of the island,
and, the elements permitting, to return to the straits along
its eastern shores. About the beginning of June, the migratory birds made their appearance, and introduced a very
agreeable change in the monotonous fare of the navigators,

who, a few weeks later, enjoyed the sight of blooming flowers, and gathered antiscorbutic herbs in large quantities.

Thus the high northern land had assumed its most friendly aspect, and looked as cheerfully as it possibly could, when on July 11, Pachtussow and Ziwolka set out for the north, with the boat and the transport; the schooner being left behind in the straits with the surgeon and a few invalids. At first the wind and weather favoured their course, but on July 21, the boat was smashed between two pieces of ice, so that they had hardly time to escape upon the land with the nautical instruments, a sack of flour and some butter.

In this unpleasant situation, they were obliged to remain for thirteen days, until at last a walrus hunter appeared, who took the shipwrecked explorers on board, and brought them safely back to their winter-quarters on August 22.

Thus this first attempt ended in complete disappointment, and the season was already too far advanced to permit of its renewal. Yet Pachtussow, resolving with praiseworthy zeal to make the most of the last days of the short summer, set out again on August 26, for the eastern entrance of the straits, and proceeded along the coast, until he was stopped by the ice, at some distance beyond the small islands which bear his name.

Convinced of the fruitlessness of all further efforts, Pachtussow bade adieu with a sorrowful heart to the coast, which still stretched out before him in undiscovered mystery, and sailed back again to Archangel on September 20. Soon after his return, he fell ill, and four weeks later his mourning friends carried him to his grave.

The Arctic Ocean is so capricious that in the following year the walrus-hunter Issakow, of Kem, who had no discoveries in view, was able to round without difficulty the north-eastern extremity of Novaya Zemlya, but fearful of encountering the dangers of that dreadful coast, he almost immediately returned.

During the two winters he spent in Novaya Zemlya, the steersman Ziwolka had daily consulted the thermometer, and the result of his observations gave to the western entrance of Mathew's Straits a mean annual temperature of $+17°$.

Thus Novaya Zemlya is colder than the west coast of

Spitzbergen, which, although still further to the north, is more favourably situated with regard to the winds and currents, and from five to ten degrees warmer than the high northern parts of Siberia and continental America, which sustain a comparatively numerous population, while Novaya Zemlya is uninhabited. Hence this want and the circumstance that the vegetation of these islands scarcely rises a span above the ground, while the forest region still penetrates far within the confines of the colder continental regions above mentioned, are to be ascribed not to the low mean annual temperature of Novaya Zemlya, but to the unfavourable distribution of warmth over the various seasons of the year. For although high northern Siberia and America have a *far colder* winter, they enjoy a *considerably warmer* summer, and this it is which in the higher latitudes determines the existence or the development of life on the dry land. During the winter, the organic world is partly sheltered under the snow, or else it migrates, or it produces within itself sufficient warmth to defy the cold—and thus a few degrees more or less at that time of the year are of no material consequence, while the warmth of summer is absolutely indispensable to awaken life and determine its development.

The comparatively *mild winter* of Novaya Zemlya (no less than thirty-three degrees warmer than that of Jakutsk) is therefore of but little benefit to vegetable life, which on the other hand suffers considerably from a summer inferior even to that of Melville Island and Boothia Felix. A coast where the sun, in spite of a day of several months' continuance, generates so small a quantity of heat, and where yet some vegetation is able to flourish, must necessarily be well worthy the attention of botanists, or rather of all those who take an interest in the geographical distribution of plants. For if in the primitive forests of Brazil the naturalist admires the effects of a tropical sun and an excessive humidity in producing the utmost exuberance of vegetation, it is no less interesting for him to observe how Flora under the most adverse circumstances still wages a successful war against death and destruction.

Thus a few years after Pachtussow's expedition, the desire to explore a land so remarkable in a botanical point of view,

and to gather new fruits for science in the wilderness, induced
Herr von Baer, though already advanced in years, to undertake the journey to Novaya Zemlya.

Accompanied by two younger naturalists, Mr. Lehmann and
Mr. Röder, the celebrated Petersburg academician arrived
on July 29, 1837, at the western entrance of Mathew's Straits,
sailed through them the next day in a boat and reached
the sea of Kara, where he admired a prodigious number of
jelly-fishes (*Pleurobrachia pileus*) swimming about in the
ice-cold waters, and displaying a marvellous beauty of colouring in their ciliated ribs. This excursion might, however, have
had very disagreeable consequences, for a dreadful storm,
blowing from the west, prevented their boat from returning,
and forced them to pass the night with some walrus-hunters,
whom they had the good fortune to meet with.

On the following day, the storm abated, so that the return
could be attempted; they were, however, obliged to land on
a small island in the Beluga Bay, where, wet to the skin,
and their limbs shaking with cold, they fortunately found
a refuge in the ruins of a hut in which Rosmysslow had
wintered in 1767.

Meanwhile the wind had veered to the east, accompanied
by a very disagreeable cold rain, which on the mountains
took the form of snow; they were now, however, able to make
use of their sail, and arrived late at night at the spot where
their ship lay at anchor, completely wet, but in good health
and spirits.

'We could esteem ourselves happy,' says Von Baer,* 'in
having paid so slight a penalty for neglecting the precaution,
so necessary to all travellers in Novaya Zemlya, of providing
for a week when you set out for a day's excursion.'

On August 4, after a thorough botanical examination of
the straits, the party proceeded along the west coast. The
wind, blowing from the north, brought them to the Kostin
Schar, a maze of passages between numerous islets, where
the walrus-hunters in Novaya Zemlya chiefly assemble.

On August 9, an excursion was made up the river Nech-

* In his instructive and entertaining account of his journey in the *Bulletins de
l'Académie de St. Pétersbourg.*

watowa, where they rested in a hut which had been
erected by some fisherman employed in catching 'golzi,' or
Arctic salmon.   On returning to the ship, a dreadful storm
arose from the north-east, which lasted nine days, and, very
fortunately for the botanists, caught them in the Kostin
Schar, and not on the high sea.

Although they were anchored in a sheltered bay, the waves
frequently swept over the deck of their vessel, and compelled
them to remain all the time in their small low cabin.   Only
once they made an attempt to land, but the wind was so
strong that they could hardly stand.   Their situation was
rendered still more terrible and anxious, as part of the crew
which had been sent out hunting before the storm began,
had not yet returned.

When at last the storm ceased, winter seemed about to
begin in good earnest.   Every night ice formed in the river,
and the land was covered with snow, which had surprised the
scanty vegetation in its full bloom.   At length the hunters
returned, after having endured terrible hardships, and now
preparations were made for a definitive departure.

A general bath was taken, without which no anchorage in
Novaya Zemlya is ever left, and according to ancient custom
a votive cross was likewise erected on the strand, as a memorial of the expedition.

On August 28, the anchors were weighed, but they were
soon dropped again in the Schar, to examine on a small
island the vegetable and animal products of the land
and of the shore.   The former offered but few objects of
interest, but they were astonished at the exuberance of
marine life.   After having been detained by a thick fog in
this place for several days, they at length sailed towards
the White Sea, where they were obliged by contrary winds
to run into Tri Ostrowa.   Dreary and desolate as the
tundras at this extreme point of Lapland had appeared to
them on their journey outwards, they were now charmed with
their green slopes, a sight of which they had been deprived
in Novaya Zemlya.

On September 11, they at length reached the port of
Archangel, with the agreeable prospect of passing the
winter in a comfortable study at St. Petersburg instead of

spending it, like Barentz and his associates, as might easily have happened, in a wretched hut, beyond the 70th degree of northern latitude.

Having thus briefly sketched Von Baer's adventures, I will now notice some of the most interesting scientific results of his journey.

The rocky west-coast of Novaya Zemlya has about the same appearance as the analogous part of Spitzbergen, for here also the mountains, particularly in the northern island, rise abruptly to a height of three or four thousand feet from the sea, while the eastern coast is generally flat. In both countries, angular blocks of stone, precipitated from the summits, cover the sides of the hills, and frequently make it impossible to ascend them. In fact, no rock, however hard or finely grained, is able to withstand the effects of a climate where the summer is so wet and the winter so severe. Nowhere in Novaya Zemlya is a grass-covered spot to be found deserving the name of a meadow. Even the foliaceous lichens, which grow so luxuriantly in Lapland, have here a stunted appearance, but, as Von Baer remarks, this is owing less to the climate than to the nature of the soil, as plants of this description thrive best on chalky ground. The crustaceous lichens, however, cover the blocks of augite and porphyry with a motley vesture, and the dingy carpet with which *Dryas octopetala* invests here and there the dry slopes, formed of rocky detritus, reminds one of the tundras of Lapland.

The scanty vegetable covering which this only truly social plant of Novaya Zemlya affords is, however, but an inch thick, and can easily be detached like a cap from the rock beneath.

On a clayey ground in moist and low situations, the mosses afford a protection to the polar willow (*Salix polaris*), which raises but two leaves and a catkin over the surface of its covering.

Even the most sparing sheet of humus has great difficulty to form in Novaya Zemlya, as in a great number of the plants which grow there the discoloured leaf dries on the stalk, and is then swept away by the winds, so that the land would appear still more naked if many plants, such as the snow ranunculus (*Ranunculus nivalis*), were not so extremely

abstemious as to require no humus at all, but merely a rocky
crevice or some loose gravel capable of retaining moisture in
its interstices.

But even in Novaya Zemlya there are some more favoured
spots. Thus when Von Baer landed at the foot of a high
slate mountain fronting the south-west, and reflecting the
rays of the sun, he was astonished and delighted to see a
gay mixture of purple silenes, golden ranunculuses, peach-
coloured parryas, white cerastias, and blue palemones, and was
particularly pleased at finding the well-known forget-me-
not among the ornaments of this Arctic pasture. Between
these various flowers the soil was everywhere visible, for the
dicotyledonous plants of the high latitudes produce no more
foliage than is necessary to set off the colours of the blossoms,
and have generally more flowers than leaves.

The entire vegetation of the island is confined to the
superficial layer of the soil and to the lower stratum of the
air. Even those plants which in warm climates have a descending or vertical root have here a horizontal one, and
none, whether grasses or shrubs, grow higher than a span
above the ground.

In the polar willow, a single pair of leaves sits on a stem
about as thick as a straw, although the whole plant forms
an extensive shrub with numerous ramifications. Another
species of willow (*Salix lanata*) attains the considerable
height of a span, and is a perfect giant among the Novaya
Zemlyan plants, for the thick subterranean trunk sometimes
measures two inches in diameter, and can be laid bare for a
length of ten or twelve feet without finding the end. Thus
in this country the forests are more *in* than *above* the earth.

This horizontal development of vegetation is caused by
the sun principally heating the superficial sheet of earth,
which imparts its warmth to the stratum of air immediately
above it, and thus confines the plants within the narrow
limits which best suit their growth. Hence also the influence of position on vegetation is so great that, while a
plain open to the winds is a complete desert, a gentle mountain slope not seldom resembles a garden.

The absence of all trees or shrubs, or even of all vigorous
herbage, imparts a character of the deepest solitude to the

Novaya Zemlyan landscape, and inspires even the rough sailor with a kind of religious awe. 'It is,' says Von Baer, 'as if the dawn of creation had but just begun, and life were still to be called into existence.' The universal silence is but rarely broken by the noise of an animal. But neither the cry of the sea-mew, wheeling in the air, nor the rustling of the lemming in the stunted herbage are able to animate the scene. No voice is heard in calm weather. The rare land-birds are silent as well as the insects, which are comparatively still fewer in number. This tranquillity of nature, particularly during serene days, reminds the spectator of the quiet of the grave; and the lemmings seem like phantoms as they glide noiselessly from burrow to burrow. In our fields even a slight motion of the air becomes visible in the foliage of the trees, or in the waving of the corn; here the low plants are so stiff and immovable that one might suppose them to be painted. The rare sand-bee (*Andrena*), which on sunny days and in warm places flies about with languid wings, has scarcely the spirit to hum, and the flies and gnats, though more frequent, are equally feeble and inoffensive.

As a proof of the rarity of insects in Novaya Zemlya, Von Baer mentions that not a single larva was to be found in a dead walrus which had been laying at least fourteen days on the shore. The hackneyed phrase of our funeral sermons cannot therefore be applied to these high latitudes, where even above the earth the decay of bodies is extremely slow.

However poor the vegetation of Novaya Zemlya may be, it still suffices to nourish a number of lemmings, which live on leaves, stems, and buds, but not on roots. The slopes of the mountains are often undermined in all directions by their burrows. Next to these lemmings, the Arctic foxes are the most numerous quadrupeds, as they find plenty of food in the above-mentioned little rodents, as well as in the young birds, and in the bodies of the marine animals which are cast ashore by the tides. White bears are scarcely ever seen during the summer, and the reindeer seems to have decreased in numbers, at least on the west coast, where they are frequently shot by the Russian morse-hunters.

The hosts of sea-birds in some parts of the coast prove

that the waters are far more prolific than the land. The foolish guillemots (*Uria troile*), closely congregated in rows, one above the other, on the narrow ledges of vertical rock-walls, make the black stone appear striped with white. Such a breeding place is called by the Russians a bazaar. On the summit of isolated cliffs, and suffering no other bird in his vicinity, nestles the large grey sea-mew (*Larus glaucus*), to whom the Dutch whale-catchers have given the name of burghermaster. While the ice-bear is monarch of the land animals, this gull appears as the sovereign lord of all the seabirds around, and no guillemot would venture to dispute the possession of a dainty morsel claimed by the imperious burghermaster.

This abundance of the sea has also attracted man to the desert shores of Novaya Zemlya. Long before Barentz made western Europe acquainted with the existence of Novaya Zemlya (1594–96), the land was known to the Russians as a valuable hunting or fishing ground; for the Dutch discoverer met with a large number of their vessels on its coast. Burrough, who visited the port of Kola in 1556, in search of the unfortunate Willoughby, and thence sailed as far as the mouth of the Petschora, likewise saw in the gulf of Kola no less than thirty lodjes, all destined for walrus-hunting in Novaya Zemlya.

Whether, before the Russians, the adventurous Norsemen ever visited these desolate islands is unknown, but so much is certain, that ever since the times of Barentz the expeditions of the Muscovites to its western coast have been uninterruptedly continued. As is the case with all fishing speculations, their success very much depends upon chance. The year 1834 was very lucrative, so that in the following season about eighty ships, with at least 1,000 men on board, sailed for Novaya Zemlya from the ports of the White Sea, but this time the results were so unsatisfactory that in 1836 scarce half the number were fitted out. In 1837 no more than twenty vessels were employed, and Von Baer relates that but one of them which penetrated into the sea of Kara made a considerable profit, while all the rest, with but few exceptions, did not pay one-half of their expenses.

The most valuable animals are the walrus and the white

dolphin, or beluga. Among the seals, the *Phoca albigena* of Pallas distinguishes itself by its size, the thickness of its skin, and its quantity of fat; *Phoca grœnlandica* and *Phoca hispida* rank next in estimation. The Greenland whale never extends his excusions to the waters of Novaya Zemlya, but the fin-back and the grampus are frequently seen.

The Alpine salmon (*Salmo alpinus*), which towards autumn ascends into the mountain-lakes, is caught in incredible numbers; and, finally, the bean-goose (*Anser segetum*) breeds so frequently, at least upon the southern island, that the gathering of its quill feathers is an object of some importance.

The Arctic Fox.

Lapps moving.

# CHAPTER XII.

## THE LAPPS.

THE nation of the Lapps spreads over the north of Scandinavia and Finland, from about degree of latitude to the confines of the Polar their number, hardly amounting to more than sand, bears no proportion to the extent of the in which they are found. Although now sub crowns of Russia, Sweden, and Norway, the possessed the whole Scandinavian peninsula

REINDEER HERD.

Lapps moving.

# CHAPTER XII.

## THE LAPPS.

Their ancient History and Conversion to Christianity—Self-denial and Poverty of the Lapland Clergy—Their singular Mode of Preaching—Gross Superstition of the Lapps—The Evil Spirit of the Woods—The Lapland Witches—Physical Constitution of the Lapps—Their Dress—The Fjälllappars—Their Dwellings—Store Houses—Reindeer Pens—Milking the Reindeer—Migrations—The Lapland Dog—Skiders, or Skates—The Sledge, or Pulka—Natural Beauties of Lapland—Attachment of the Lapps to their Country—Bear Hunting—Wolf Hunting—Mode of Living of the wealthy Lapps—How they kill the Reindeer—Visiting the Fair—Mammon Worship—Treasure Hiding—"Tabak, or Brænde"—Affectionate Disposition of the Lapps—The Skogslapp—The Fisherlapp.

THE nation of the Lapps spreads over the northern parts of Scandinavia and Finland, from about the 63rd degree of latitude to the confines of the Polar Ocean; but their number, hardly amounting to more than twenty thousand, bears no proportion to the extent of the vast regions in which they are found. Although now subject to the crowns of Russia, Sweden, and Norway, they anciently possessed the whole Scandinavian peninsula, until the

REINDEER HERD.

sons of Odin drove them further and further to the north, and, taking possession of the coasts and valleys, left them nothing but the bleak mountain and the desolate tundra. In the thirteenth century, under the reign of Magnus Ladislas, King of Sweden, their subjugation was completed by the Birkarls, a race dwelling on the borders of the Bothnian Gulf. These Birkarls had to pay the crown a slight tribute, which they wrang more than a hundredfold from the Lapps, until at length Gustavus I. granted the persecuted savages the protection of more equitable laws, and sent missionaries among them to relieve them at the same time from the yoke of their ancient superstitions. In 1600, Charles IX. ordered churches to be built in their country, and, some years after, his son and successor, the celebrated Gustavus Adolphus, founded a school for the Lapps at Pitea, and ordered several elementary works to be translated into their language. In the year 1602, Christian IV., King of Denmark and Norway, while on a visit to the province of Finmark, was so incensed at the gross idolatry of the Lapps that he ordered their priests or sorcerers to be persecuted with bloody severity. A worthy clergyman, Eric Bredal, of Drontheim, used means more consonant with the spirit of the Gospel, and, having instructed several young Lapps, sent them back again as missionaries to their families. These interpreters of a purer faith were, however, received as apostates and traitors by their suspicious countrymen, and cruelly murdered, most likely at the instigation of the sorcerers. In 1707, Frederic IV. founded the Finmark mission, and in 1716 Thomas Westen, a man of rare zeal and perseverance, preached the Gospel in the wildest districts of the province. Other missionaries and teachers followed his example, and at length succeeded in converting the Lapps, and in some measure conquering their ancient barbarism. Nothing can be more admirable than the self-denial and heroic fortitude of these ministers of Christ, for to renounce all that is precious in the eyes of the world to follow nomads little better than savages through the wilds of an Arctic country surely requires a courage not inferior to that of the soldier

Who seeks preferment at the cannon's mouth.

The Lapland schoolmaster enjoys an annual salary of twenty-five dollars, and receives besides half a dollar for every child instructed. But the priest is not much better off, as his stipend amounts to no more than thirty dollars in money, and to about 150 dollars in produce. Among this miserably paid clergy there are, as in Iceland, men worthy of a better lot. The famous Löstadius was priest at Karesuando, seventy-five leagues from Tromsö, the nearest town, and a hundred leagues from Tornea. His family lived upon rye bread and fishes, and but rarely tasted reindeer flesh. Chamisso mentions another Lapland priest who had spent seven years in his parish, which lay beyond the limits of the forest region. In the summer he was completely isolated, as then the Lapps wandered with their herds to the cool shores of the icy sea; and in the winter, when the moon afforded light, he travelled about in his sledge, frequently bivouacking at the temperature of freezing mercury to visit his Lapps. During all that time his solitude had been but twice broken by civilised man : a brother had come to see him, and a botanist had strayed to his dwelling. He well knew how to appreciate the pleasure of such meetings, but neither this pleasure nor any other, he said, was equal to that of seeing the sun rise again above the horizon after the long winter's night.

It is a singular custom that the pastors preaching to the Lapps deliver their harangues in a tone of voice as elevated as if their audience, instead of being assembled in a small chapel, were stationed upon the top of a distant mountain, and labour as if they were going to burst a bloodvessel. Dr. Clarke, who listened to one of these sermons, which lasted one hour and twenty minutes, ventured to ask the reason of the very loud tone of voice used in preaching. The minister said he was aware that it must appear extraordinary to a stranger, but that, if he were to address the Laplanders in a lower key, they would consider him as a feeble and impotent missionary, wholly unfit for his office, and would never come to church; that the merit and abilities of the preacher, like that of many a popular politician, are always estimated by the strength and power of his lungs.

Though the Lapps (thanks to the efforts of their spiritual

guides) hardly even remember by name the gods of their fathers—Aija, Akka, Tuona—they still pay a secret homage to the Saidas, or idols of wood or stone, to whom they were accustomed to sacrifice the bones and horns of the reindeer. They are in fact an extremely superstitious race, faithfully believing in ghosts, witchcraft, and above all in Stallo, or Troller, the Evil Spirit of the woods.

Many of them, when about to go hunting, throw a stick into the air, and then take their way in the direction to which it points. The appearance of the Aurora borealis fills them with terror, as they believe it to be a sign of divine wrath, and generally shout and howl during the whole duration of the grand phenomenon, which their ignorance connects with their own petty existence.

The pretended gift of being able to predict future events is common among the Laplanders. The sorcerers fall into a magic sleep, during which their soul wanders. In this state, like the somnambules of more polished nations, they reveal things to come, or see what passes at a distance. Men and women affect the power of fortune-telling by the common trick of palmistry, or by the inspection of a cup of liquor; and this, to ensure the greatest possible certainty, must be a cup of brandy, which at once explains the whole business of the prophecy. The Lapland witches pretended, or perhaps still pretend, to the power of stilling the wind or causing the rain to cease, and such was their reputation that English seamen trading to Archangel made it a point to land and buy a wind from these poor creatures.

The Lapps are a dwarfish race. On an average, the men do not exceed five feet in height, many not even reaching four, and the women are considerably less. Most of them are, however, very robust, the circumference of their chest nearly equalling their height. Their complexion is more or less tawny and copper-coloured, their hair dark, straight, and lank, its dangling masses adding much to the wildness of their aspect. They have very little beard, and as its want is considered a beauty, the young men carefully eradicate the scanty supply given them by nature.

Their dark piercing eyes are generally deep sunk in their heads, widely separated from each other, and, like those of

the Tartars or Chinese, obliquely slit towards the temples.
The cheek-bones are high, the mouth pinched close, but
wide, the nose flat.  The eyes are generally sore, either in
consequence of the biting smoke of their huts, or of the refraction from the snow, so that a Lapp seldom attains a high
age without becoming blind.  Their countenances generally
present a repulsive combination of stolidity, low cunning, and
obstinacy.  Hogguer, who dwelt several months among them
and saw during this time at least 800 Lapps, found not
twenty who were not decidedly ugly; and Dr. Clarke says
that many of them, when more advanced in years, might, if
exhibited in a menagerie of wild beasts, be considered as the
long-lost link between man and ape.

Their legs are extremely thick and clumsy, but their hands
are as small and finely shaped as those of any aristocrat.
The reason for this is that from generation to generation
they never perform any manual labour, and the very trifling
work which they do is necessarily of the lightest kind.  Their
limbs are singularly flexible, easily falling into any posture,
like all the Oriental nations, and their hands are constantly
occupied in the beginning of conversation with filling a short
tobacco-pipe, the head being turned over one shoulder to
the person addressed.  Such are the traits by which the whole
tribe is distinguished from the other inhabitants of Europe,
and in which they differ from the other natives of the land
in which they live.

The summer garb of the men consists of the 'poesk,'
a sort of tunic, generally made of a very coarse light-coloured
woollen cloth, reaching to the knees, and fastened round
the waist with a belt or girdle.  Their woollen caps are
shaped precisely like a night-cap, or a Turkish fez, with a
red tassel and red worsted band round the rim, for they are
fond of lively hues strongly contrasted.  Their boots or
shoes are made of the raw skin of the reindeer, with the
hair outwards, and have a peaked shape.  Though these
shoes are very thin, and the Lapp wears no stockings, yet
he is never annoyed by the cold or by striking against
stones, as he stuffs them with the broad leaves of the *Carex
vesicaria*, or cyperus grass, which he cuts in summer and
dries.  This he first combs and rubs in his hands, and then

places it in such a manner that it covers not only his feet but his legs also, and being thus guarded, he is quite secured against the intense cold. With this grass, which is an admirable non-conductor of heat, he likewise stuffs his gloves in order to preserve his hands. But as it wards off the cold in winter, so in summer it keeps the feet cool, and is consequently used at all seasons. The women's apparel differs very little from that of the other sex, but their girdles are more ornamented with rings and chains. In winter both sexes are so packed up in skins as to look more like bears than human beings, and, when squatting according to the fashion of their country, exhibit a mound of furs, with the head resting upon the top of it.

According to their different mode of life, the Lapps may be aptly subdivided into Fjälllappars, or Mountain Lapps; Skogslappars, or Wood Lapps; and Fisherlapps.

The Fjälllappars, who form the greater and most characteristic part of the nation, lead an exclusively pastoral life, and are constantly wandering with their herds of reindeer from place to place, for the lichen which forms the chief food of these animals during the greater part of the year is soon cropped from the niggard soil, and requires years for its reproduction. For this reason, also, this people do not herd together, and never more than three or four families pitch their huts, or tuguria, upon the same spot. Of course the dwelling of the nomad Lapp harmonises with his vagrant habits; a rude tent, which can easily be taken to pieces, and as easily erected, is all he requires to shelter his family and chattels. It consists of flexible stems of trees, placed together in a conical form, like a stack of poles for hops, and covered in the summer with a coarse cloth, in winter with additional skins, to be better fenced against the inclemencies of the climate. To form the entrance, a part of the hanging, about eighteen inches wide at the bottom, and terminating upwards in a point, is made to turn back, as upon hinges. The hearth, consisting of several large stones, is in the centre, and in the roof immediately above it is a square opening for the escape of smoke and the admission of rain, snow, and air. All the light which the den receives when the door is closed comes from this hole. The diameter of one of these conical huts generally measures at its base no more than six feet; its whole circumference, of course, does not exceed eighteen feet, and its extreme height may be about ten feet. The floor is very nearly covered with reindeer skins, on which the inmates squat during the day, and sleep at nights, contracting their limbs together and huddling round their hearth, so that each individual of this pigmy race occupies scarcely more space than a dog. On the sides of the tent are suspended a number of pots, wooden bowls, and other household utensils; and a small chest contains the holiday apparel of the family. Such are the dwellings of those among the Laplanders who are called wealthy, and who sometimes possess very considerable property.

Near the tent is the dairy or storehouse of the establishment. It consists of nothing more than a shelf or platform, raised between two trees, so as to be out of the reach of the dogs or wolves. The means of ascent to this treasury of curds, cheese, and dried reindeer flesh, is simply a tree stripped of its branches, but presenting, at every foot or so, knobs, which serve the same purpose as staves on a ladder, the tree being obliquely reared against the platform.

Another characteristic feature of a Lapp encampment is found in the enclosures in which the reindeer are penned during the night, or for the purpose of milking. These are circus-like open places, each of a diameter of about one hundred and fifty feet, and are formed by stumps of trees and poles set upright on the ground, and linked together by horizontal poles. Against the latter are reared birch poles and branches of trees, varying from six to ten feet in height, without the slightest attempt at neatness, the whole being as rude as well can be, a sufficient security against the wolves being all that its builders desire. The milking of a herd of reindeer presents a most animated scene. When they have been driven within the enclosure, and all outlets are secured, a Lapp, selecting a long thong or cord, takes a turn of both ends round his left hand, and then gathers what sailors call the bight in loose folds, held in his right. He now singles out a reindeer, and throws the bight with unerring aim over the antlers of the victim. Sometimes the latter makes no resistance, but in general the moment it feels the touch of the thong, it breaks away from the spot, and is only secured by the most strenuous exertions. Every minute may be seen an unusually powerful deer furiously dragging a Lapp round and round the enclosure, and sometimes it fairly overcomes the restraint of the thong, and leaves its antagonist prostrate on the sod. This part of the scene is highly exciting, and it is impossible not to admire the trained skill evinced by all the Lapps, women as well as men. The resistance of the deer being overcome, the Lapp takes a dexterous hitch of the thong round his muzzle and head, and then fastens him to the trunk of a prostrate tree, many of which have been brought within the level enclosure for that especial purpose. Men and women are indiscriminately engaged both in singling out milch reins, and in milking them. Every one is fully occupied, for even the little children are practising the throwing of the lasso, in which they evince great dexterity, although their strength is insufficient to hold the smallest doe.

When the pasture in the neighbourhood is fully exhausted, which generally takes place in about a fortnight, the encampment is broken up, to be erected again on some other spot. In less than half an hour the tent is taken to pieces, and packed with all the household furniture upon the backs of reindeer, who by long training acquire the capacity of serving as beasts of burden. On the journey they are bound together, five and five, with thongs of leather, and led by the women over the mountains, while the father of the family precedes the march to select a proper place for the new encampment, and his sons or servants follow with the remainder of the herd.

Towards the end of spring the Lapps descend from the mountains to the sea. When they approach its borders, the reindeer, sniffing the sea air from a distance, rush tumultuously to the fjord, where they take long draughts of the salted water. This, as the Lapps believe, is essential to their health. As the summer advances, and the snow melts, they ascend higher and higher into the mountains. At the approach of winter, they retreat into the woods, where, with the assistance of their dogs and servants, they have enough to do to keep off the attacks of the wolves. The reindeer dog is about the size of a Scotch terrier, but his head bears a wonderful resemblance to that of the lynx. His colour varies considerably, but the hair is always long and shaggy. Invaluable as are his services, he is nevertheless treated with great cruelty.

For their winter journeys the Lapps use sledges or skates. One of their skates, or 'skiders,' is usually as long as the person who wears it; the other is about a foot shorter. The feet stand in the middle, and to them the skates are fastened ·by thongs or withes. The skiders are made of fir-wood, and covered with the skins of young reindeer, which obstruct a retrograde movement by acting like bristles against the snow—the roots pointing towards the forepart of the skate, and thus preventing their slipping back. With these skiders, the Lapp flies like a bird over the snow, now scaling the mountains by a tortuous ascent, and now darting down into the valley:

Ocior cervis et agente nimbos
Ocior Euro.

Such is the rapidity of his course, that he will overtake the swiftest wild beasts; and so violent the exercise, that during the most rigorous season of the year, when earnestly engaged in the chase; he will divest himself of his furs. A long pole with a round ball of wood near the end, to prevent its piercing too deep in the snow, serves to stop the skater's course when he wishes to rest. The Laplander is no less expert in the use of the sledge, or 'pulka,' which is made in the form of a small boat with a convex bottom, that it may slide all the more easily over the snow; the prow is sharp and pointed, but the sledge is flat behind. The traveller is swathed in this carriage like an infant in a cradle, with a stick in his hand to steer the vessel, and disengage it from the stones or stumps of trees which it may chance to encounter in the route. He must also balance the sledge with his body, to avoid the danger of being overturned. The traces by which this carriage is fastened to the reindeer, are fixed to a collar about the animal's neck, and run down over the breast between the fore and hind-legs, to be connected with the prow of the sledge; the reins managed by the traveller are tied to the horns, and the trappings are furnished with little bells, the sound of which the animal likes. With this draught at his tail, the reindeer will travel sixty or seventy English

miles in a day; often persevering fifty miles without inter-
mission, and without taking any refreshment, except occasionally moistening his mouth with the snow.  His Lapland
driver knows how to find his way through the wilderness
with a surprising certainty; here a rock, there a fir-tree, is
impressed as a landmark on his faithful memory, and thus,
like the best pilot, he steers his sledge to the distant end
of his journey.  Frequently the Aurora lights him on his
way, illumining the snow-covered landscape with a magic
brilliancy, and investing every object with a dream-like,
supernatural beauty.

But even without the aid of this mysterious coruscation,
Lapland is rich in grand and picturesque features, and has all
the romance of the mountain and the forest.  In summer
countless rivulets meander through valleys of alpine verdure, and broad pellucid rivers rush down the slopes in
thundering cataracts, embracing islands clothed with pine-
trees of incomparable dignity and grace.  Whoever has
grown up in scenes like these, and been accustomed from
infancy to the uncontrolled freedom of the nomad state, receives impressions never to be erased; and thus we cannot
wonder that the wild Laplander believes his country to be a
terrestrial paradise, and feels nowhere happy but at home.

In the year 1819, a Scotch gentleman attempted to ac-
climatise the reindeer in Scotland, and induced two young
Laplanders to accompany the herd which he had bought for
that purpose.  The reindeer soon perished, and the Laplanders would have died of nostalgia if they had not been
sent home by the first opportunity.  Prince Jablonowsky, a
Polish nobleman, who travelled about thirty years since
through a part of Russian Lapland, took a Lapp girl with
him to St. Petersburg.  He gave her a superior education,
and she was well treated in every respect.  She made rapid
progress, and seemed to be perfectly reconciled to her new
home.  About two years after her arrival, it happened that
a Russian gentleman, who possessed extensive estates
near the capital, bought a small herd of reindeer, which
arrived under the guidance of a Lapp family.  As it was
winter-time, and these people had brought with them their
tents, their sledges, and their snow-shoes, they soon became

objects of curiosity, and crowds of fashionable visitors flocked to their encampment; among others the good-natured prince, who imprudently conducted his pupil, the young Lapland girl, to see her countrymen, an interview which he supposed would give her great pleasure. But from that moment she became an altered being; she lost her spirits and her appetite, and, in spite of every care and attention, her health declined from day to day. One morning she disappeared, and it was found on inquiry that she had returned to her family, where she remained ever after.

Another very remarkable instance of the Laplanders' love of their country is related by Hogström. During the war of Gustavus III. with Russia, a young Laplander enlisted in a regiment which was passing through Tornea. He served in several campaigns as a common soldier, was made a sergeant in consequence of his good conduct and courage; and having given himself the greatest trouble to improve his education and acquire military knowledge, at length, after twenty years of service, attained the rank of captain in the Swedish army. After this long time spent in the civilised world, and having become accustomed to all its enjoyments and comforts, he felt a strong desire to revisit his family and his country. Scarcely had he seen his native mountains, and spent a few days among his countrymen and the reindeer, than he at once quitted the service, and resumed the nomad life of his youth.

The Laplander's chief desire is for peace and tranquillity. Exposed to all the privations of a vagrant life, and to every inclemency of weather, he endures the greatest hardships with equanimity, desiring only not to be disturbed in the enjoyment of the little that is his—not to be interfered with in his old customs and habits.

Yet this same peaceful Laplander, who has so easily submitted to a foreign yoke, is one of the boldest hunters, and not only pursues the elk or the wild reindeer, but engages in single combat with the bear. Like all the other Arctic nations of Russia and Siberia, he has strange notions about this animal, which in his opinion is the most cunning and gifted of all created beings. Thus he supposes that the bear knows and hears all that is said about him, and for this reason he takes good care never to speak of him disrespectfully. It may seem strange that he should venture to slay an animal which ranks so high in his esteem; but the temptation is too strong, as its flesh has an excellent flavour, and its fur, though not near so valuable as that of the American black-bear, is still worth from fifteen to twenty dollars.

At the beginning of winter, the bear, as is well known, retires either into a rocky cave, or under a cover of branches, leaves, and moss, and remains there without food, and plunged in sleep, until the next spring recalls him to a more active existence. After the first fall of snow, the Lapp hunters go into the forest, and look out for traces of the bear. Having found them they carefully mark the spot, and returning after a few weeks disturb the slumbering brute, and excite him to an attack. It is not considered honourable to shoot him while sleeping; and in many parts of Lapland, the hunter who would kill a bear with any other weapon but a lance, would be universally despised. Hogguer accompanied two Lapps, well-armed with axes and stout lances with barbed points, on one of these bear-hunts. When about a hundred paces from the lair, the company halted, while one of the Lapps advanced shouting, telling his comrades to make as much noise as they could. When about twenty paces from the cavern, he stood still and flung several stones into it. For some time all was quiet, so that Hogguer began to fear that the lair was deserted, when suddenly an angry growl was heard. The hunters now redoubled their clamour, until slowly, like an honest citizen disturbed in his noonday slumbers, the bear came out of his cavern. But this tranquillity did not last long, for the brute, as soon as he perceived his nearest enemy, uttered a short roar, and rushed upon him. The Lapp coolly awaited the onset with his lance in rest, until the bear, coming quite near, raised himself on his haunches, and began to strike at him with his forepaws. The hunter bent down to avoid the strokes, and then, suddenly rising, with a sure eye and with all his might, plunged his lance into the heart of the bear. During this short conflict the Lapp had received a slight wound on the hand, but the marks of the bear's teeth were found deeply impressed upon the iron of the lance. According to an ancient custom, the wives of the hunters assemble in the hut of one of them; and as soon as they hear the returning sportsmen, begin chanting or howling a song in praise of the bear. When the men, laden with the skin and flesh of the

animal, approach, they are received by the women with op-
probrious epithets, and forbidden ingress through the door;
so that they are obliged to make a hole in the wall, through
which they enter with their spoils. This comedy, which
is meant to pacify the manes of the victim, is still acted,
though not so frequently as formerly; but the custom
of begging the bear's pardon with many tears, is completely out of date. The animal's interment, however, still
takes place with all the ancient honours and ceremonies.
After having been skinned, and its flesh cut off, the body is
buried in anatomical order—the head first, then the neck,
the forepaw, &c. This is done from a belief in the resurrection of the bear, who having been decently buried, will, it is
hoped, allow himself to be killed a second time by the same
Lapp; while a neglect of the honours due to him would ex-
asperate the whole race of bears, and cause them to wreak a
bloody vengeance on the disrespectful hunter.

The wolf is treated with much less ceremony. Many a
wealthy Lapp, the owner of a thousand reindeer, has been reduced to poverty by the ravages of this savage beast, which
is constantly prowling about the herds. Hence one of
the first questions they put to each other when they meet
is, 'Lekor rauhe?' 'Is it peace?'—which means nothing
more than, 'Have the wolves molested you?' Such is their
detestation of these animals, that they believe them to be
creatures of the devil, contaminating all that touches them
while alive. Thus they will never shoot a wolf, as the gun
that killed him would ever after be accursed.

At the first alarm that wolves have appeared, the neighbours assemble, and the chase begins. For miles they pursue
him over hills and valleys on their 'skiders,' and kill him
with clubs, which they afterwards burn. They will not
even defile themselves with skinning him, but leave his hide
to the Finnish or Russian colonists, who, being less scru-
pulous or superstitious, make a warm cloak of it, or sell it for
a few dollars at the fair.

Among the Fjall Lapps there are many rich owners of
1,000 or 1,500 reindeer, 300 of which fully suffice for the
maintenance of a family. In this case the owner is able
to kill as many as are necessary for providing his household with food and raiment, while the sale of the super-

fluous skins and horns enables him to purchase cloth, flour, hardware, and other necessary articles—not to forget the tobacco or the brandy in which he delights. The price of the entire carcase of a reindeer, skin and all, varies from one to three dollars Norsk (four shillings and sixpence to thirteen shillings and sixpence). A fine skin will always sell for one dollar in any part of the North. It will thus be seen that a Lapp possessing a herd of 500 or 1,000 deer is virtually a capitalist in every sense of the word, far richer than the vast majority of his Norwegian, Swedish, or Russian fellow-subjects, although they all affect to look upon him with supreme contempt.

The daily food of the mountain Laplanders consists of the fattest reindeer venison, which they boil, and eat with the broth in which it has been cooked. Their summer diet consists of cheese and reindeer-milk. The rich also eat bread baked upon hot iron plates.

Their mode of killing the reindeer is the method used by the butchers in the South of Italy—the most ancient and best method of slaying cattle, because it is attended with the least pain to the animal and the greatest profit to its possessor. They thrust a sharp-pointed knife into the back part of the head, between the horns, so as to divide the spinal marrow from the brain. The beast instantly drops, and dies without a groan or struggle. As soon as it falls, and appears to be dead, the Laplander plunges the knife dexterously behind the off-shoulder into the heart; then opening the animal, its blood is found in the stomach, and ladled out into a pot. Boiled with fat and flour it forms a favourite dish.

An important epoch in the life of the Fjall Lapp is his annual visit to one of the winter fairs held in the chief towns or villages which the more industrious Swedes, Norwegians, or Fins have founded on the coasts here and there, or in the well-watered valleys of his fatherland, and which he attends frequently from an immense distance. After a slight duty to Government has been paid, business begins; but as every bargain is ratified with a full glass of brandy, his thoughts get confused before the day is half over—a circumstance which the cunning merchant does not fail to turn to account. On awaking the next morning, the vexation of the nomad at his bad bargains is so much the greater, as no people are

more avowed mammon-worshippers than the Lapps, or more
inclined to sing, with our Burns :—

O wae on the siller, it is sae prevailin' !

Their sole object seems to be the amassing of treasure, for
the sole purpose of hoarding it.   The avarice of a Lapp is
gratified in collecting a number of silver vessels, or pieces of
silver coin ; and being unable to carry this treasure with him
on his journeys, he buries the whole, not even making his
wife acquainted with the secret of its deposit, so that when
he dies the members of his family are often unable to discover
where he has hidden it.    Some of the Lapps possess a
hundredweight of silver, and those who own 1,500 or 1,000
reindeer have much more ; in short, an astonishing quantity
of specie is dispersed among them.    Silver plate, when
offered to them for sale, must be in a polished state, or they
will not buy it; for such is their ignorance, that when the
metal, by being kept buried, becomes tarnished, they conceive
that its value is impaired, and exchange it for other silver,
which, being repolished, they believe to be new.    The merchants derive great benefit from this traffic.

Brandy and tobacco are the chief luxuries of the Lapps.
The tobacco-pipe is never laid aside, except during meals ; it
is even used by the women, who also swallow spirits as
greedily as the men ; in fact, both sexes will almost part with
life itself for the gratification of dram-drinking.   If you
walk up to a Lapp, uncouthly squatted before his tent,
his very first salutation is made by stretching forth a tawny
hand, and demanding, in a whining tone, 'Tabak,' or
'Braendi.'    Dr. Clarke relates an amusing instance of their
propensity for spirituous liquors.    On his very first visit to
one of their tents, he gave the father of the family about a
pint of brandy, thinking he would husband it with great
care, as he had seen him place it behind him, upon his bed,
near the skirting of the tent.    The daughter now entered, and
begged for a taste of the brandy, as she had lost her share by
being absent.    The old man made no answer, but when the
request was repeated, he slily crept round the outside of the
tent, until he came to the spot where the brandy was, when,
thrusting his arm beneath the skirting, he drew it out, and
swallowed the whole contents of the bottle at a draught.

The practice of dram-drinking is so general that mothers pour the horrid dose down the throats of their infants. Their christenings and funerals become mere pretexts for indulging in brandy. But their mild and pacific disposition shows itself in their drunkenness, which is manifested only in howling, jumping, and laughing, and in a craving for more drams with hysteric screams, until they fall senseless on the ground —while at the same time they will suffer kicks, cuffs, blows, and provocations of any kind, without the smallest irascibility. When sober they are as gentle as lambs, and the softness of their language, added to their effeminate shrill tone of voice, remarkably corresponds with their placable disposition. An amiable trait in the character of the Lapp is the warmth of his affection towards his wife, his children, and his dependents. Nothing can exceed the cordiality of their mutual greetings after separation, and it is to be feared that but few married men in England could match the Lapp husband, who assured Castrén that during thirty years of wedlock no worse word had passed between himself and his wife than 'Loddadsham,' or 'My little bird.'

In spite of his fatiguing life, and the insufficient shelter afforded him by his hut, the Fjall Lapp is generally vigorous and healthy, and not seldom lives to a hundred years age. Continual exercise in the open air braces his constitution, his warm clothing protects him against the cold of winter, and his generous meat diet maintains his strength. To prevent the scurvy, he eats the berries of the *Empetrum nigrum*, or *Rubus Chamæmorus*, and mixes the stems of the Angelica among his food. But his chief remedy against this and every other bodily evil is warm reindeer-blood, which he drinks with delight as a universal panacea.

The Skogs Lapp, or Forest Lapp, occupies an intermediate grade between the Fjall Lapp and the Fisher Lapp, as fishing is his summer occupation, and hunting and the tending of his reindeer that of the winter months. His herds not being so numerous as those of the Fjall Lapp, he is not driven to constant migration to procure them food; but they require more care than his divided pursuits allow him to bestow upon them, and hence he inevitably descends to the condition of the Fisher Lapp. Lästadius describes his life as one of the happiest on earth— as a constant change between the agreeable pastime of fishing and the noble amusement of the chase. He is not, like the Mountain Lapp, exposed to all the severity of the Arctic winter, nor so poor as the Fisher Lapp. He is often heard to sing under the green canopy of the firs.

The villages of the Fisher Lapps—as they are found, for instance, on the banks of Lake Enara—afford a by no means pleasing spectacle.

About the miserable huts, which are shapeless masses of mingled earth, stones, and branches of trees, and scarcely equal to the dwellings of the wretched Fuegians, heaps of stinking fish and other offal taint the air with their pestilential odours. When a stranger approaches, the inmates come pouring out of their narrow doorway, so covered with dirt and vermin as to make him recoil with disgust. Not in the least ashamed, however, of their appearance, they approach the stranger and shake his hand, according to the code of Lapp politeness. After this preliminary, he may expect the following questions: ' Is peace in the land? How is the emperor, the bishop, and the captain of the district? ' The more inquisitive of the filthy troop then ask after the home of the stranger, and being told that it is beyond the mountains, they further inquire if he comes from the land where tobacco grows. For as our imagination loves to wander to the sunny regions,

> Where the citron and olive are fairest of fruit,
> And the voice of the nightingale never is mute;

so the fancy of the Lapp conceives no greater paradise than that which produces the weed that, along with the brandy-bottle, affords him his highest luxury.

The Glutton.

Tornea River.

# CHAPTER XIII.

### MATTHIAS ALEXANDER CASTRÉN.

His Birthplace and first Studies—Journey in Lapland, 1838—The Iwalojoki—
The Lake of Enara—The Pastor of Utzjoki—From Rowanièmi to Kemi— Se-
cond Voyage, 1841-44—Storm on the White Sea—Return to Archangel—The
Tundras of the European Samojedes—Mesen—Universal Drunkenness—Sledge
Journey to Pustosersk—A Samojede Teacher—Tundra Storms—Abandoned
and alone in the Wilderness—Pustosersk—Our Traveller's Persecutions at
Ustsylmsk and Ishemsk—The Uusa—Crossing the Ural—Obdorsk—Second
Siberian Journey, 1845-48—Overflowing of the Obi—Surgut—Krasnojarsk
—Agreeable Surprise—Turuchansk—Voyage down the Jenissei—Castrén's
Study at Plachina—From Dudinka to Tolstoi Noss—Frozen Feet—Return
Voyage to the South—Frozen fast on the Jenissei—Wonderful Preservation—
Journey across the Chinese Frontiers, and to Transbaikalia—Return to Finland
—Professorship at Helsingfors—Death of Castrén, 1855.

MATTHIAS ALEXANDER CASTRÉN, whose interesting journeys form the subject of the present chapter,
was born in the year 1813, at Rowanièmi, a Finland village
situated about forty miles from the head of the Gulf of
Bothnia, immediately under the Arctic Circle; so that, of
all men who have attained celebrity, probably none can

boast of a more northern birthplace. While still a scholar
at the Alexander's College of Helsingfors, he resolved to
devote his life to the study of the nations of Finnish origin
(Fins, Laplanders, Samojedes, Ostjaks, &c.); and as books
gave but an insufficient account of them, each passing year
strengthened his desire to visit these tribes in their own
haunts, and to learn from themselves their languages, their
habits, and their history.

We may imagine, therefore, the joy of the enthusiastic
student, whom poverty alone had hitherto prevented from
carrying out the schemes of his youth, when Dr. Ehrström,
a friend and medical fellow-student, proposed to take him as
a companion, free of expense, on a tour in Lapland. No
artist that ever crossed the Alps on his way to sunny Italy
could feel happier than Castrén at the prospect of plunging
into the wildernesses of the Arctic zone.

On June 25, 1838, the friends set out, and arrived on the
30th at the small town of Muonioniska, where they remained six weeks—a delay which Castrén put to good
account in learning the Lapp language from a native catechist. At length the decreasing sun warned the travellers
that it was high time to continue their journey, if they
wished to see more of Lapland before the winter set in; and
after having, with great difficulty, crossed the mountain-
ridge which forms the watershed between the Gulf of
Bothnia and the Polar Sea, they embarked on the romantic
Iwalojoki, where for three days and nights the rushing
waters roared around them. In spite of these dangerous
rapids, they were obliged to trust themselves to the stream,
which every now and then threatened to dash their frail
boat to pieces against the rocks. Armed with long oars,
they were continually at work during the daytime to guard
against this peril; the nights were spent near a large fire
kindled in the open air, without any shelter against the rain
and wind.

The Iwalo river is, during the greater part of its course,
encased between high rocks; but a few miles before it discharges itself into the large Lake of Enara, its valley
improves into a fine grassy plain. Small islands covered
with trees divide the waters, which now flow more tranquilly; soon also traces of culture appear, and the astonished

traveller finds in the village of Kyrö, not wretched Lapland huts, but well-built houses of Finnish settlers, with green meadows and cornfields.

The beautiful Lake of Enara, sixty miles long and forty miles broad, is so thickly studded with islands that they have never yet been counted. After the travellers had spent a few days among the Fisher Lapps who sojourn on its borders, they proceeded northwards to Utzjoki, the limit of their expedition, and one of the centres of Lapland civilisation, as it boasts of a church, which is served by a man of high character and of no little ability. On accepting his charge, this self-denying priest had performed the journey from Tornea in the depth of winter, accompanied by a young wife and a female relation of the latter, fifteen years of age. He had found the parsonage, vacated by his predecessor, a wretched building, distant some fifteen miles from the nearest Lapp habitation. After establishing himself and his family in this dreary tenement, he had returned from a pastoral excursion to find his home destroyed by a fire, from which its inmates had escaped with the loss of all that they possessed. A miserable hut, built for the temporary shelter of the Lapps who resorted thither for divine service, afforded the family a refuge for the winter. He had since contrived to build himself another dwelling, in which our party found him, after five years' residence, the father of a family, and the chief of a happy household. Gladly would the travellers have remained some time longer under his hospitable roof, but the birds of passage were moving to the south, warning them to follow their example.

Thus they set out, on August 15, for their homeward voyage, which proved no less difficult and laborious than the former. At length, after wandering through deserts and swamps—frequently wet to the skin, and often without food for many hours—they arrived at Rowaniemi, where they embarked on the Kemi river. 'With conflicting feelings,' says Castrén, 'I descended its stream; for every cataract was not only well-known to me from the days of my earliest childhood, but the cataracts were even the only acquaintances which death had left me in the place of my birth. Along with the mournful impressions which the loss of beloved relations made upon my mind, it was delightful to renew my intercourse with the rapid stream and its waterfalls — those boisterous playfellows, which had often brought me into peril when a boy. Now, as before, it was a pleasant sport to me to be hurried along by their tumultuous waters, and to be wetted by their spray. The boatmen often tried to persuade me to land before passing the most dangerous waterfalls, and declared that they could not be answerable for my safety. But, in spite of all their remonstrances, I remained in the boat, nor had I reason to repent of my boldness, for He who is the steersman of all boats granted us a safe arrival at Kemi, where our Lapland journey terminated.' *

In 1841 Castrén published a metrical translation, into the Swedish language, of the ' Kalewala,' a cycle of the oldest poems of the Fins; and at the end of the same year proceeded on his first great journey to the land of the European Samojedes, and from thence across the northern Ural Mountains to Siberia. In the famous convent of Solovetskoi, situated on a small island in the White Sea, he hoped to find a friendly teacher of the Samojede language in the Archimandrite Wenjamin, who had laboured as a missionary among that savage people; but the churlish dignitary jealously refused him all assistance, and as the tundras of the Samojedes are only accessible during the winter, he resolved to turn the interval to account by a journey among the Terski Lapps, who inhabit the western shores of the White Sea. With this view, in an evil hour of the 27th June, 1842, though suffering at this time from illness severe enough to have detained any less persevering traveller, he embarked at Archangel, in a large corn-laden vessel, with a reasonable prospect of being landed at Tri Ostrowa in some twenty-four hours; but a dead calm detained him eight days, during which he had no choice but to endure the horrible stench of Russian sea-stores in the cabin, or the scorching sun on deck. At length a favourable wind arose, and after a few hours' sailing nothing was to be seen but water and sky. Soon the Terski coast came in view, with its white ice-capped shore, and Castrén hoped soon to be released from his floating prison, when suddenly the wind changed, and,

* *Reisen in Lappland, &c.*

increasing to a storm, threatened to dash them on the cliffs of the Solovetzkoi Islands.

'Both the captain and the ship's company began to despair of their lives; and prayers having been resorted to in vain, to conjure the danger, general drunkenness was the next resource. The captain, finding his own brandy too weak to procure the stupefaction he desired, left me no peace till I had given him a bottle of rum. After having by degrees emptied its contents, he at length obtained his end, and fell asleep in the cabin. The crew, following his example, dropped down one by one into their cribs, and the ship was left, without guidance, to the mercy of the winds and waves. I alone remained on deck, and gloomily awaited the decisive moment. But I soon discovered that the wind was veering to the east, and awakening the captain from his drunken lethargy, sent him on deck, and took possession of his bed. Exhausted by the dreadful scenes of the day, I soon fell into a deep slumber; and when I awoke the following morning, I found myself again on the eastern coast of the White Sea, at the foot of a high sheltering rock-wall.'

Continued bad weather and increasing illness now forced Castrén to give up his projected visit to the Lapps, and when he returned to Archangel, both his health and his purse were in a sad condition. He had but fifteen roubles in his pocket, but fortunately he found some Samojede beggars still poorer than himself, one of whom, for the reward of an occasional glass of brandy, consented to become at once his host, his servant, and his private tutor in the Samojede language. In the hut and society of this savage, he passed the remainder of the summer; his health improved, and soon also his finances changed wonderfully for the better—the Government of Finland having granted him a thousand silver roubles for the prosecution of his travels. With a light heart he continued his linguistic studies until the end of November, when he started with renewed enthusiasm for the land of the European Samojedes. These immense tundras extend from the White Sea to the Ural mountains, and are bounded on the north by the Polar Sea, and on the south by the region of forests, which here reaches as high as the latitudes of 66° and 67°.

The large river Petschora divides these dreary wastes into two unequal halves, whose scanty population, as may easily be imagined, is sunk in the deepest barbarism. It consists of nomadic Samojedes, and of a few Russians, who inhabit some miserable settlements along the great stream and its tributary rivers.

To bury himself for a whole year in these melancholy deserts, Castrén left Archangel in November, 1842. As far as Mesen, 345 versts north of Archangel, the scanty population is Russ and Christian. At Mesen civilisation ceases, and further north the Samojede retains, for the most part, with his primitive habits and language, his heathen faith— having, in fact, borrowed nothing from occasional intercourse with civilised man but the means and practice of drunkenness. Castrén's first care, on his arrival at Mesen, was to look for a Samojede interpreter and teacher; but he was as unsuccessful here as at Somsha, a village some forty versts further on, where drunkenness was the order of the day. He took the most temperate person he could find in all Somsha into his service, but even this moderate man would, according to our ideas, have been accounted a perfect drunkard. He now resolved to try the fair sex, and engaged a female teacher, but she also could not remain sober. At length a man was introduced to him as the most learned person of the tundra, and at first it seemed as if he had at length found what he wanted; but after a few hours the Samojede began to get tired of his numerous questions, and declared himself ill. He threw himself upon the floor, wailed and lamented, and begged Castrén to have pity on him, until at length the incensed philologist turned him out-of-doors. Soon after, he found him lying dead drunk in the snow, before the 'Elephant and Castle' of the place.

Thus obliged to look for instruction elsewhere, Castrén resolved to travel, in the middle of winter, to the Russian village of Pustosersk, at the mouth of the Petschora, where the fair annually attracts a number of Samojedes. During this sledge-journey of 700 versts, he had to rest sometimes in the open air on the storm-beaten tundra, and sometimes in the rickety tent of the Samojede, or in the scarcely less wretched hut of the Russian colonist—where the snow

penetrated through the crevices of the wall, where the flame
of the light flickered in the wind, and a thick cloak of wolf-
skin afforded the only protection against the piercing cold of
the Arctic winter.

For this arduous tour, two sledges, with four reindeer
attached to each, were employed—the traveller's sledge, which
was covered, being attached to an uncovered one occupied by
the guide. The Kanin Tundra stretched out before them, as
they flew along—almost as naked as the sea, of which they
saw the margin in the east; and had not the wind here and
there driven away the snow which Heaven in its mercy strews
over this gloomy land, they might have been in doubt on
which element they were travelling. Daily, from time to
time, some dwarf firs made their appearance, or clumps of
low willows, which generally denote the presence of some
little brook slowly winding through the flat tundra.

The village of Ness, on the north coast, was the first
halting-place, and here Castrén flattered himself he had at
length found what his heart desired, in the person of a
Samojede teacher who knew Russian, and was gifted with a
clearer head than is usually possessed by his race.

' The man was conscious of his superiority, and while acting
as a professor looked down with contempt upon his weaker
brethren. Once, some other Samojedes venturing to correct
one of his translations, he commanded them to be silent,
telling them they were not learned. I tried by all possible
means to secure the services of this Samojede phenomenon.
I spoke kindly with him, I paid him well, gave him every
day his allowance of brandy, and never once forbad him to
get drunk when he felt inclined to do so. Yet, in spite of
all my endeavours to please, he felt unhappy, and sighed for
the liberty of the tundra. "Thou art kind, and I love thee,"
said he one day to me, "but I cannot endure confinement.
Be therefore merciful, and give me my freedom."

' I now increased his daily pay and his rations of brandy,
sent for his wife and child, treated his wife also with
brandy, and did all I could to dispel the melancholy of the
Samojede. By these means I induced him to remain a few
days longer with me.

' While I was constantly occupying him, the wife was busy

N

sewing Samojede dresses, and sometimes assisted her husband in his translations. I often heard her sighing deeply,
and having asked for the reason, she burst into tears, and
answered that she grieved for her husband, who was thus
imprisoned in a room. "Thy husband," was my reply, "is
not worse off than thyself. Tell me, what do you think of
your own position?" "I do not think of myself—I am sorrowful for my husband," was her ingenuous reply. At
length both the husband and the wife begged me so earnestly
to set them at liberty, that I allowed them to depart.'

On the way from Pjoscha to Pustosersk, after Castrén had
once more vainly endeavoured to discover that *rara avis*, a
Samojede teacher, he became thoroughly acquainted with
the January snowstorms of the tundra: 'The wind arose
about noon, and blew so violently, that we could not see the
reindeer before our sledges. The roof of my vehicle, which at
first had afforded me some protection, was soon carried away
by the gale. Anxious about my fate, I questioned my guides,
whenever they stopped to brush off the snow which had accumulated upon me, and received the invariable answer, "We
do not know where we are, and see nothing." We proceeded
step by step, now following one direction, now another, until
at length we reached a river well known to the guides. The
leader of the first sledge hurried his reindeer down the precipitous bank, and drove away upon the ice to seek a more
convenient descent; but as he did not return, the other guide
likewise left me to look after his companion, and thus I was
kept waiting for several hours on the tundra, without knowing where my guides had gone to.

'At first I did not even know that they had left me, and
when I became aware of the fact, I thought that they had
abandoned me to my fate. I will not attempt to describe
my sensations; but my bodily condition was such, that when
the cold increased with the approach of night, I was seized
with a violent fever. I thought my last hour was come, and
prepared for my journey to another world.'

The reappearance of the guides relieved Castrén of his
anxiety, and when the little party reached some Samojede
huts, the eldest of the guides knelt down at the side of our
traveller's sledge, and expressed his joy in a prayer to God;

begging Castrén to join him in his thanksgivings, ' for He, and not I, has this night saved thee.'

The next morning, as the weather seemed to improve, and the road (along the Indiga river) to the next Russian settlement was easy to find, Castrén resolved to pursue his journey. ' But the storm once more arose, and became so dreadfully violent that I could neither breathe, nor keep my eyes open against the wind. The roaring of the gale stupefied my senses. The moist snow wetted me during the day, and the night converted it into ice. Half frozen, I arrived after midnight at the settlement. The fatigues of the journey had been such that I could scarcely stand; I had almost lost my consciousness, and my sight had suffered so much from the wind, that I repeatedly ran with my forehead against the wall. The roaring of the storm continually resounded in my ears for many hours after.'

A few days later, Castrén arrived at Pustosersk, undoubtedly one of the dreariest places in the world. With scarcely a trace of arboreal vegetation, the eye, during the greater part of the year, rests on an interminable waste of snow, where the cold winds are almost perpetually raging. The storms are so violent as not seldom to carry away the roofs of the huts, and to prevent the wretched inhabitants from fetching water and fuel. In this Northern Eden our indefatigable ethnologist tarried several months, as it afforded him an excellent opportunity for continuing his studies of the language, manners, and religion of the Samojedes, who come to the fair of Pustosersk during the winter, to barter their reindeer-skins for flour and other commodities, and at the same time to indulge in their favourite beverage—brandy. At length the Samojedes retired, the busy season of the place was evidently at an end, and Castrén, having no further inducement to remain at Pustosersk, left it for the village of Ustsylmsk, situated 150 versts higher up the Petschora, where he hoped still to find some straggling Samojedes. The road to Ustsylmsk leads through so desolate a region, that, according to the priests of the neighbourhood, it cannot have been originally created by God with the rest of the world, but must have been formed after the deluge. Near Ustsylmsk (65° 30′ N. lat.) the country improves, as most of the northern trees grow about the place ; but, unfortunately, a similar praise cannot be awarded to its inhabitants, whom Castrén found to be the most brutal and obstinate Raskolniks (or sectarians) he had ever seen. Without in the least caring for the Ten Commandments, and indulging in every vice, these absurd fanatics fancied themselves better than the rest of mankind, because they made the sign of the cross with the thumb and the two last fingers, and stood for hours together before an image in stupid contemplation. Our homeless traveller soon became the object of their persecutions ; they called him 'wizard,' 'a poisoner of rivers and wells,' and insulted him during his walks. At length they even attempted to take his life, so that he thought best to retreat to Ishemsk, on the Ishma, a hundred versts farther to the south. But, unfortunately, his bad reputation had preceded him, and although the Isprawnik (or parish official) and his wife warmly took his part, the people continued to regard him with suspicion.

Towards the end of June, Castrén ascended the Petschora and its chief tributary, the Uusa, as far as the village of Kolwa, where he spent the remainder of the summer, deeply buried as usual, in Samojede studies. Beyond Kolwa, which he left on September 16 for Obdorsk, there is not a single settlement along the Uusa and its tributaries.

As he ascended the river, the meadows on its low banks appeared coloured with the grey tints of autumn. Sometimes a wild animal started from its lair, but no vestige of man was to be seen. Countless flocks of wild ducks and geese passed over the traveller's head, on their way southwards.

After many a tedious delay, caused by storms and contrary winds, Castrén reached (on September 27) a wretched hut, about forty versts from the Ural, where he was obliged to wait a whole month, with fourteen other persons, until the snow-track over the mountains became practicable for sledges.

The total want of every comfort, the bad company, the perpetual rain, and the dreary aspect of the country, made his prolonged stay in this miserable tenement almost unbearable. At length, on October 25, he was able to depart, and on November 3, he saw the Ural Mountains raising their snow-capped summits to the skies. 'The weather is mild,' said his Samojede driver, 'and thou art fortunate, but the Ural can be very different.' He then described the dreadful storms that rage over the boundary-chain which separates Europe from Asia, and how they precipitate stones and rocks from the mountain-tops.

This time the dreaded pass was crossed in safety, and on November 9, 1843, Castrén arrived at Obdorsk, on the Obi, exhausted in strength and shattered in health, but yet delighted to find himself in Asia, the land of his early dreams. Obdorsk—the most northerly colony in Western Siberia, and, as may easily be imagined, utterly deficient in all that can be interesting to an ordinary traveller—was as much as a university to the zealous student, for several thousands of Samojedes and Ostjaks congregate to its fair from hundreds of versts around.

No better place could possibly be found for the prosecution of his researches; but the deplorable condition of his health did not allow him to remain as long as he would have desired at this fountain-head of knowledge. He was thus obliged to leave for Tobolsk, and to return, in March 1844, by the shortest road to Finland.

In the following summer (1845), we again find him on the banks of the Irtysch and the Obi, plunged in Ostjak studies with renewed energy and enthusiasm. After having sojourned for several weeks at Toropkowa, a small island at the confluence of these two mighty streams, he ascended the Obi in July as far as Surgut, where he arrived in the beginning of August.

In consequence of the overflowing of its waters, the river had spread into a boundless lake, whose monotony was only relieved, from time to time, by some small wooded island or some inundated village. The rising of the stream had spread misery far and wide, for many Ostjak families had been obliged to abandon their huts, and to seek a refuge in the forests. Those who had horses and cows had the greatest difficulty to keep them alive; and as all the meadows were under water, and the autumn, with its night-frosts, was already approaching, there was scarcely any hope of making hay for the winter.

As Castrén proceeded on his journey, the low banks of the river rose above the waters, and appeared in all their wild and gloomy desolation. The number of inhabitants along the Obi is utterly insignificant when compared with the wide extent of the country; and as hunting and fishing are their chief occupations, nothing is done to subdue the wilderness. The weary eye sees but a dull succession of moors, willow-bushes, dry heaths, and firs on the higher grounds. Near every flourishing tree stands another, bearing the marks of decay. The young grass is hemmed in its growth by that of the previous year, which even in July gives the meadow a dull ash-grey colour. Cranes, wild ducks, and geese are almost the only living creatures to be seen. From Siljarski to Surgut, a distance of 200 versts, there are but three Russian villages; and the Ostjaks, who form the main part of the population, generally live along the tributary rivers, or erect their summer huts on the smaller arms of the Obi, where they can make a better use of their very imperfect fishing implements than on the principal stream.

Surgut, once a fortress, and the chief town of the Cossack conquerors of Siberia, is now reduced to a few miserable huts, scattered among the ruins of repeated conflagrations.

Here Castrén remained till September 24, occupied with the study of the various dialects of the neighbouring Ostjak tribes, and then ascended the Obi as far as Narym, a distance of 800 versts. Most of the fishermen had already retired from the banks of the river, and a deathlike stillness, rarely interrupted by an Ostjak boat rapidly shooting through the stream, reigned over its waters.

Fortunately the weather was fine, at least during the first days of the journey; and the green river-banks, the birds singing in the trees, and the sunbeams glancing over the wide mirror of the Obi, somewhat enlivened the monotony of the scene.

After having enjoyed at Narym a *remarkably mild* Siberian winter, as *no crows had been frozen to death*, and having increased his knowledge of the Ostjak dialects, Castrén proceeded in the following spring, by way of Tomsk, to Krasnojarsk, on the Jenisei, where he arrived in April 1846, and was welcomed in a most agreeable and unexpected manner. It will be remembered that during his stay at Ishemsk, in the tundra of the Samojedes, he found warm-hearted friends and protectors against the insane bigotry of the Raskolniks in the Isprawnik and his young and amiable wife. Of the latter, it might truly be said that she was like a flower born to blush unseen in the desert. Remarkably eloquent, she was no less talented in expressing her thoughts by writing; and yet she was only the daughter of a serf who had been exiled to Krasnojarsk, and had spent a great part of a small property, acquired by industry and economy, in the education of his gifted daughter. The Isprawnik, a young Pole of insinuating manners, having gained her affections, she had accompanied him to Ishemsk as his wife.

From what Castrén had told her three years since about his future plans, she knew that he would probably arrive about this time at Krasnojarsk, and had written a letter, which reached its destination only a few hours before him. It was to her father, earnestly begging him to pay every attention to the homeless stranger. The feelings of Castrén may easily be imagined when the old man knocked at his door, and brought him these friendly greetings from a distance of 6,000 versts.*

But his stay at Krasnojarsk was not of long duration, for he was impatient to proceed northwards, for the purpose of becoming acquainted with the tribes dwelling along the Jenisei, after having studied their brethren of the Obi. From June till the end of July, his literary pursuits detained him at Turuchansk, where, in the vicinity of the Arctic Circle, he had much to suffer from the heat and the mosquitoes. In the beginning of August, the signs of approaching winter made their appearance, the cold north-wind swept away the leaves from the trees, the fishermen retired to the woods, and the ducks and geese prepared to migrate to the south. And now Castrén also took leave of Turuchansk—not however, like the birds, for a more sunny region, but to bury himself still deeper in the northern wilds of the Jenisei. Below Turuchansk, the river begins to flow so languidly, that

---

* The verst is about three-fifths of a mile.

when the wind is contrary, the boat must be dragged along by dogs, and advances no more than from five to ten versts during a whole day. Thus the traveller has full time to notice the willows on the left bank, and the firs on the right; the ice-blocks, surviving memorials of the last winter, which the spring inundations have left here and there on the banks of the vast stream; and the countless troops of wild birds that fly with loud clamour over his head.

About 365 versts below Turuchansk is situated Plachina, the fishing-station of a small tribe of Samojedes, among whom Castrén tarried three weeks. He had taken possession of the *best* of the three huts of which the place consisted, but even this would have been perfectly intolerable to any one but our zealous ethnologist. Into his study the daylight penetrated so sparingly through a small hole in the wall, that he was often obliged to write by the light of a resinous torch in the middle of the day.

The flame flickering in the wind, which blew through a thousand crevices, affected his eyes no less severely than the smoke, which at the same time rendered respiration difficult. Although the roof had been repaired, yet during every strong rain—and it rained almost perpetually—he was obliged to pack up his papers, and to protect himself from the wet as if he had been in the open air. From this delightful residence Castren, still pursuing his study of the Samojede dialects, proceeded down the river to Dudinka, and finally, in November, to Tolstoi Noss, whose pleasant climate may be judged of by the fact that it is situated in the latitude of 71°. This last voyage was performed in a 'balok' or close sledge, covered with reindeer-skins. The tediousness of being conveyed like a corpse in a dark and narrow box, induced him to exchange the 'balok' for an open sledge; but the freezing of his feet, of his fingers, and of part of his face, soon caused him to repent of his temerity. As soon as this accident was discovered at the next station, Castrén crept back again into his prison, and was heartily glad when, after a nine-days' confinement, he at length arrived at Tolstoi Noss, which he found to consist of four wretched huts. Here again he spent several weeks studying by torchlight, for the sun had made his last appearance in November,

and the day was reduced to a faint glimmering at noon.   In
January we find him on his return-voyage to Turuchansk, a
place which, though not very charming in itself, appeared
delightful to Castrén after a six-months' residence in the
tundras beyond the Arctic Circle.

Turuchansk can boast at least of seeing some daylight at
all seasons of the year, and this may be enjoyed even within-
doors, for Turuchansk possesses no less than four houses
with glass windows.   Longing to reach this comparatively
sunny place, Castrén, against his usual custom, resolved to
travel day and night without stopping, but his impatience
wellnigh proved fatal to him.   His Samojede guide had not
perceived in the dark that the waters of the Jenisei, over
which they were travelling, had oozed through fissures in the
ice, and inundated the surface of the river far and wide.
Thus he drove into the water, which of course was rapidly
congealing; the reindeer were unable to drag the sledge back
again upon the land, and Castrén stuck fast on the river,
with the agreeable prospect of being frozen to death.   From
this imminent danger he was rescued by a wonderful circumstance.   Letters having arrived from the Imperial Academy of St. Petersburg, a courier had been despatched from
Turuchansk to convey them to Castrén.   This courier fortunately reached him while he was in this perilous situation,
helped him on land, and conducted him to a Samojede hut,
where he was able to warm his stiffened limbs.

After such a journey, we cannot wonder that, on arriving
at Turuchansk, he was so tormented with rheumatism and
toothache as to be obliged to rest there several days.   With
sore joints and an aching body, he slowly proceeded to
Jeniseisk, where he arrived on April 3, 1847, in a wretched
state of health, which however had not interrupted his Ostjak
studies on the way.   I rapidly glance over his subsequent
travels, as they are but a repetition of the same privations
and the same hardships, all cheerfully sustained for the love
of knowledge.   Having somewhat recruited his strength at
Jeniseisk, he crossed the Sajan mountains to visit some
Samojedes beyond the Russian frontier—a journey which,
besides the usual fatigues, involved the additional risk of
being arrested as a spy by the Chinese authorities—and the

year after he visited Transbaikalia, to make inquiries among the Buriat priests about the ancient history of Siberia.

Having thus accomplished his task, and thoroughly investigated the wild nations of the Finnish race, from the confines of the Arctic Sea to the Altaï—a task which cost him his health, and the best part of his energies—he longed to breathe the air of his native country. But neither the pleasures of home, nor a professorship at the University of Helsingfors, richly earned by almost superhuman exertions, were able to arrest the germs of disease, which journeys such as these could scarcely fail to plant even in his originally robust constitution. After lingering some years, he died in 1855, universally lamented by his countrymen, who justly mourned his early death as a national loss.

The Souslik.

Samojedes and their Dwellings.

# CHAPTER XIV.

## THE SAMOJEDES.

Their Barbarism—Num, or Jilibeambaertje—Shamanism—Samojede Idols—Sja-
dæi—Hahe—The Tadebtsios, or Spirits—The Tadibes, or Sorcerers—Their
Dress—Their Invocations—Their conjuring Tricks—Reverence paid to the Dead
—A Samojede Oath—Appearance of the Samojedes—Their Dress—A Samojede
Belle—Character of the Samojedes—Their decreasing Numbers—Traditions of
ancient Heroes.

THE Samojedes, the neighbours of the Laplanders, are still
further removed from civilised society, and plunged in
even deeper barbarism. The wildest tundras and woods of
Northern Russia and Western Siberia are the home of the
Samojede. With his reindeer herds he wanders over the
naked wastes, from the eastern coast of the White Sea to
the banks of the Chatanga, or hunts in the boundless forests
between the Obi and the Jenisei. His intercourse with the
Russians is confined to his annual visits at the fairs of such
miserable settlements as Obdorsk and Pustosersk, where, far
from improving by their company, he but too often becomes
the prey of their avarice, and learns to know them merely as
cheats and oppressors. Protestant missionaries have long

since brought instruction to the Laplander's hut, but the
majority of the less fortunate Samojedes still adhere to the
gross superstitions of their fathers.  They believe in a Supreme Being—Num, or Jilibeambaertje—who resides in the
air, and, like the Jupiter of old, sends down thunder and
lightning, rain and snow; and as a proof that something of
a poetic fancy is to be found even among the most savage
nations, they call the rainbow 'the hem of his garment.'  As
this deity, however, is too far removed from them to leave
them any hope of gaining his favour, they never think of
offering him either prayer or sacrifice.  But, besides Num,
there are a great many inferior spirits, or idols, who directly
interfere in human concerns—capricious beings, who allow
themselves to be influenced by offerings, or yield to magical
incantations; and to these, therefore, the Samojede has recourse when he feels the necessity of invoking the aid or
averting the wrath of a higher Power.

The chief of all Samojede idols is in the island of Way-
gatz—a cold and melancholy Delos—where it was already
found by old Barentz.  This idol is a mere block of stone,
with its head tapering to a point.  It has thus been
fashioned, not by a mortal artist, but by a play of nature.
After this original the Samojedes have formed many idols of
stone or wood of various sizes, which they call 'Sjadæi,' from
their possessing a human physiognomy (sja).  These idols
they dress in reindeer-skins, and ornament them with all
sorts of coloured rags.  But a resemblance to the human
form is not the necessary attribute of a Samojede idol; any
irregularly-shaped stone or tree may be thus distinguished.
If the object is small, the savage carries it everywhere about
with him, carefully wrapped up; if too cumbersome to be
transported, it is reserved as a kind of national deity.  As
with the Ostjaks, each Samojede tribe has in its train a
peculiar sledge—the Hahengan—in which the household
idols (or Hahe) are placed.  One of these Penates protects
the reindeer, another watches over the health of his wor-
shippers, a third is the guardian of their connubial happiness, a fourth takes care to fill their nets with fish.  Whenever his services are required, the Hahe is taken from his
repository, and erected in the tent or on the pasture-ground,

in the wood or on the river's bank. His mouth is then smeared with oil or blood, and a dish with fish or flesh is set before him, in the full expectation that his good offices will amply repay the savoury repast. When his aid is no longer necessary, he is put aside without any further ceremony, and as little noticed as the Madonna of the Neapolitan fisherman after the storm has ceased.

The Hahe, or idols, are very convenient objects of reverence to the Samojede, as he can consult them, or ask their assistance, without being initiated in the secrets of magic; while the Tadebtsios, or invisible spirits, which everywhere hover about in the air, and are more inclined to injure than to benefit man, can only be invoked by a Tadibe, or sorcerer, who, like the Cumæan Sibyl, works himself into a state of ecstatic frenzy. When his services are required, the first care of the Tadibe is to invest himself with his magical mantle—a kind of shirt made of reindeer leather, and hemmed with red cloth. The seams are covered in a similar manner, and the shoulders are decorated with epaulettes of the same gaudy material. A piece of red cloth veils the eyes and face—for the Tadibe requires no external organs of sight to penetrate into the world of spirits—and a plate of polished metal shines upon his breast.

Thus accoutred, the Tadibe seizes his magical drum, whose sounds summon the spirits to his will. Its form is round, it has but one bottom, made of reindeer-skin, and is more or less decorated with brass rings and other ornaments, according to the wealth or poverty of its possessor. During the ceremony of invocation, the Tadibe is generally assisted by a disciple, more or less initiated in the magic art. They either sit down, or walk about in a circle. The chief sorcerer beats the drum, at first slowly, then with increasing violence, singing at the same time a few words to a mystic melody. The disciple immediately falls in, and both repeat the same monotonous chant.

At length the spirits appear, and the consultation is supposed to begin; the Tadibe from time to time remaining silent, as if listening to their answers, and but gently beating his drum, while the assistant continues to sing. Finally, this mute conversation ceases, the song changes into a wild howling, the drum is violently struck, the eye of the Tadibe glows with a strange fire, foam issues from his lips—when suddenly the uproar ceases, and the oracular sentence is pronounced. The Tadibes are consulted not only for the purpose of recovering a strange reindeer, or to preserve the herd from a contagious disorder, or to obtain success in fishing; the Samojede, when a prey to illness, seeks no other medical advice; and the sorcerer's drum either scares away the malevolent spirits that cause the malady, or summons others to the assistance of his patient.

The office of Tadibe is generally hereditary, but individuals gifted by nature with excitable nerves and an ardent imagination not seldom desire to be initiated in these supernatural communications. No one can teach the candidate. His morbid fancy is worked upon by solitude, the contemplation of the gloomy aspect of nature, long vigils, fasts, the use of narcotics and stimulants, until he becomes persuaded that he too has seen the apparitions which he has heard of from his boyhood. He is then received as a Tadibe with many ceremonies, which are held in the silence of the night, and invested with the magic drum. Thus the Tadibe partly believes in the visions and fancies of his own overheated brain. Besides dealing with the invisible world, he does not neglect the usual arts of an expert conjuror, and knows by this means to increase his influence over his simple-minded countrymen. One of his commonest tricks is similar to that which has been practised with so much success by the Brothers Davenport. He sits down, with his hands and feet bound, on a reindeer-skin stretched out upon the floor, and, the light being removed, begins to summon the ministering spirits to his aid. Strange unearthly noises now begin to be heard— bears growl, snakes hiss, squirrels rustle about the hut. At length the tumult ceases, the audience anxiously awaits the end of the spectacle, when suddenly the Tadibe, freed from his bonds, steps into the hut—no one doubting that the spirits have set him free.

As barbarous as the poor wretches who submit to his guidance, the Tadibe is incapable of improving their moral condition, and has no wish to do so. Under various names

—Schamans among the Tungusi, Angekoks among the Esqui-
muax, medicine-men among the Crees and Chepewyans, &c.
—we find similar magicians or impostors assuming a spiritual
dictatorship over all the Arctic nations of the Old and the
New World, wherever their authority has not been broken by
Christianity or Buddhism; and this dreary faith still extends
its influence over at least half a million of souls, from the
White Sea to the extremity of Asia, and from the Pacific to
Hudson's Bay.

Like the Ostjaks and other Siberian tribes, the Samojedes
honour the memory of the dead by sacrifices and other ceremonies. They believe that their deceased friends have still
the same wants, and pursue the same occupations, as when in
the land of the living; and thus they place in or about their
graves a sledge, a spear, a cooking-pot, a knife, an axe, &c.,
to assist them in procuring and preparing their food. At
the funeral, and for several years afterwards, the relations
sacrifice reindeer over the grave. When a person of note,
a prince, a Starschina, the proprietor of numerous herds of
reindeer, dies (for even among the miserable Samojedes we
find the social distinctions of rich and poor), the nearest
relations make an image, which is placed in the tent of the
deceased, and enjoys the respect paid to him during his life-
time. At every meal the image is placed in his former seat,
and every evening it is undressed and laid down in his bed.
During three years the image is thus honoured, and then
buried; for by this time the body is supposed to be decayed,
and to have lost all sensation of the past. The souls of the
Tadibes, and of those who have died a violent death, alone
enjoy the privilege of immortality, and after their terrestrial
life hover about in the air as unsubstantial spirits.

Yet in spite of this privilege, and of the savoury morsels
that fall to their share at every sacrificial feast, or of the
presents received for their services, the Tadibes are very
unhappy beings. The ecstatic condition into which they
so frequently work themselves, shatters their nerves and
darkens their mind. Wild looks, bloodshot eyes, an uncer-
tain gait, and a shy manner, are among the effects of this
periodical excitement.

Like the Ostjaks, the Samojedes consider the taking of an

oath as an action of the highest religious importance. When
a crime has been secretly committed against a Samojede, he
has the right to demand an oath from the suspected person.

If no wooden or stone Hahe is at hand, he manufactures
one of earth or snow, leads his opponent to the image, sacrifices a dog, breaks the image, and then addresses him with
the following words :—' If thou hast committed this crime,
then must thou perish like this dog ! '  The ill-consequences
of perjury are so much dreaded by the Samojedes—who,
though they have but very faint ideas of a future state,
firmly believe that crime will be punished in this life, murder
with violent death, or robbery by losses of reindeer—that the
true criminal, when called upon to swear, hardly ever submits
to the ceremony, but rather at once confesses his guilt and
pays the penalty.

The most effectual security for an oath is that it should be
solemnised over the snout of a bear—an animal which is
highly revered by all the Siberian tribes, from the Kamtschatkans to the Samojedes, as well as by the Laplanders.
Like the Laplanders, they believe that the bear conceals under
his shaggy coat a human shape with more than human
wisdom, and speak of him in terms of the highest reverence.
Like the Lapps also, when occasion offers, they will drive an
arrow or a bullet through his skin; but they preface the
attack with so many compliments, that they feel sure of dis-
arming his anger.

The appearance of the Samojedes is as wild as the country
which they inhabit.  The dwarfish stature of the Ostjak, or
the Lapp, thick lips, small eyes, a low forehead, a broad
nose so much flattened that the end is nearly upon a level
with the bone of the upper jaw (which is strong and greatly
elevated), raven-black shaggy hair, a thin beard, and a
yellow-brown complexion, are their characteristic features,
and in general they do nothing to improve a form which has
but little natural beauty to boast of.  The Samojede is satisfied if his heavy reindeer-dress affords him protection against
the cold and rain, and cares little if it be dirty or ill-cut ;
some dandies, however, wear furs trimmed with cloth of a
gaudy colour.  The women, as long as they are unmarried,
take some pains with their persons ; and when a Samojede girl,

with her small and lively black eyes, appears in her reindeer jacket tightly fitting round the waist, and trimmed with dog-skin, in her scarlet mocassins, and her long black tresses ornamented with pieces of brass or tin, she may well tempt some rich admirer to offer a whole herd of reindeer for her hand. For amongst the Samojedes no father ever thinks of bestowing a portion on his daughter: on the contrary, he expects from the bridegroom an equivalent for the services which he is about to lose by her marriage. The consequence of this degrading custom is that the husband treats his consort like a slave, or as an inferior being. A Samojede, who had murdered his wife, was quite surprised at being summoned before a court of justice for what he considered a trifling offence; 'he had honestly paid for her,' he said, 'and could surely do what he liked with his own.'

The senses and faculties of the Samojedes correspond to their mode of life as nomads and hunters. They have a piercing eye, delicate hearing, and a steady hand: they shoot an arrow with great accuracy, and are swift runners. On the other hand, they have a gross taste, generally consuming their fish or their reindeer-flesh raw; and their smell is so weak that they appear quite insensible to the putrefying odours arising from the scrapings of skins, stinking fish, and other offal which is allowed to accumulate in and about their huts.

The Samojede is good-natured, melancholy, and phleg-matic. He has, indeed, but indistinct notions of right and wrong, of good and evil; but he possesses a grateful heart, and is ready to divide his last morsel with his friend. Cruelty, revenge, the darker crimes that pollute so many of the savage tribes of the tropical zone, are foreign to his character. Constantly at war with a dreadful climate, a prey to igno-rance and poverty, he regards most of the things of this life with supreme indifference. A good meal is of course a mat-ter of importance in his eyes; but even the want of a meal he will bear with stoical apathy, when it can only be gained by exertion, for he sets a still higher value on repose and sleep.

A common trait in the character of all Samojedes, is the gloomy view which they take of life and its concerns; their internal world is as cheerless as that which surrounds them. True men of ice and snow, they relinquish, without a murmur, a life which they can hardly love, as it imposes upon them many privations, and affords them but few pleasures in return.

They are suspicious, like all oppressed nations that have much to suffer from their more crafty or energetic neighbours. Obstinately attached to their old customs, they are opposed to all innovations; and they have been so often deceived by the Russians, that they may well be pardoned if they look with a mistrustful eye upon all benefits coming from that source.

The wealth of the Samojedes consists in the possession of herds of reindeer, and P. von Krusenstern, in 1845, calculated the number owned by the Samojedes of the Lower Petschora, near Pustosersk, at 40,000 head—a much smaller number than what they formerly had, owing to a succession of misfortunes. The Russian settlers along that immense stream and its tributaries gradually obtain possession of their best pasture-grounds, and force them to recede within narrower and narrower limits. Thus many have been reduced to the wretched condition of the Arctic fisherman, or have been compelled to exchange their ancient independence for a life of submission to the will of an imperious master.

The entire number of the European and Asiatic Samojedes is estimated at no more than about 10,000, and this number, small as it is when compared to the vast territory over which they roam, is still decreasing from year to year. Before their subjugation by the Russians, the Samojedes were frequently at war with their neighbours, the Ostjaks, the Woguls, and the Tartars, and the rude poems which celebrate the deeds of the heroes of old are still sung in the tents of their peaceful descendants. The *minstrel*, or *troubadour*—if I may be allowed to use these names while speaking of the rudest of mankind—is seated in the centre of the hut, while the audience squat around. His gesticulations endeavour to express his sympathy with his hero. His body trembles, his voice quivers, and during the more pathetic parts of his story, tears start to his eyes, and he covers his face with his left hand, while the right, holding an arrow, directs its point to the ground. The audience generally keep silence, but their groans accompany the hero's death; or when he soars upon an eagle to the clouds, and thus escapes the malice of his enemies, they express their delight by a triumphant shout.

The Snow Bunting.

Group of Ostjaks.

# CHAPTER XV.

## THE OSTJAKS.

What is the Obi?—Inundations—An Ostjak Summer Jurt—Poverty of the Ostjak Fishermen—A Winter Jurt—Attachment of the Ostjaks to their ancient Customs—An Ostjak Prince—Archery—Appearance and Character of the Ostjaks —The Fair of Obdorsk.

WHAT is the Obi?—'One of the most melancholy rivers on earth,' say the few European travellers who have ever seen it roll its turbid waters through the wilderness, 'its monotonous banks a dreary succession of swamps and dismal pine-forests, and hardly a living creature to be seen, but cranes, wild ducks, and geese.' If you address the same question to one of the few Russians who have settled on its banks, he answers, with a devout mien, 'Obi is our mother;' but if you ask the Ostjak, he bursts forth, in a laconic but energetic phrase—'Obi is the god whom we honour above all our other gods.'

To him the Obi is a source of life. With its salmon and sturgeon he pays his taxes and debts, and buys his few

luxuries; while the fishes of inferior quality which get entangled in his net he keeps for his own consumption, and
that of his faithful dog, eating them mostly raw, so that the
perch not seldom feels his teeth as soon as it is pulled
out of the water. In spring, when the Obi and its tributaries burst their bonds of ice, and the floods sweep
over the plains, the Ostjak is frequently driven into the
woods, where he finds but little to appease his hunger;
at length, however, the waters subside, the flat banks of
the river appear above their surface, and the savage erects
his summer hut close to its stream. This hovel has
generally a quadrangular form, low walls, and a high
pointed roof, made of willow-branches covered with large
pieces of bark. These, having first been softened by
boiling, are sewn together, so as to form large mats or
carpets, easily rolled up and transported. The hearth, a mere
hole enclosed by a few stones, is in the centre, and the smoke
escapes through an aperture at the top. Close to the hut there
is also, generally, a small storehouse erected on high poles,
as in Lapland; for the provisions must be secured against
the attacks of the glutton, the wolf, or the owner's dogs.

Although the Obi and its tributaries—the Irtysch, the
Wach, the Wasjugan—abundantly provide for the wants
of the Ostjaks, yet those who are exclusively fishermen
vegetate in a state of the greatest poverty, in indolence,
drunkenness, and vice. The wily Russian settlers have got
them completely in their power, by advancing them goods
on credit, and thus securing the produce of their fisheries
from year to year. During the whole summer Russian
speculators from Obdorsk, Beresow, and Tobolsk, sail about
on the Obi, to receive from their Ostjak debtors the salmon
and sturgeon which they have caught, or to fish on their own
account, which, as having better nets and more assistance,
they do with much greater success than the poor savages.

The Russian Government has, indeed, confirmed the Ostjaks
in the possession of almost all the land and water in the
territories of the Lower Obi and Irtysch, but the Russian
traders find means to monopolise the best part of the
fisheries; for ignorance and stupidity, in spite of all laws in
their favour, are nowhere a match for mercantile cunning.

At the beginning of winter, the Ostjaks retire into the woods, where they find at least some protection against the Arctic blasts, and are busy hunting the sable or the squirrel; but as fishing affords them at all times their chief food, they take care to establish their winter huts on some eminence above the reach of the spring inundations, near some small river, which, through holes made in the ice, affords their nets and anglers a precarious supply. Their winter jurt is some-what more solidly constructed than their summer residence, as it is not removed every year. It is low and small, and its walls are plastered with clay. Light is admitted through a piece of ice inserted in the wall, or on the roof. In the better sort of huts, the space along one or several of the walls is hung with mats made of sedges, and here the family sits or sleeps. Sometimes a small antechamber serves to hang up the clothes, or is used as a repository for household utensils. Besides those who live solely upon fishes and birds of passage, there are other Ostjaks who possess reindeer herds, and wander in summer to the border of the Polar sea, where they also catch seals and fish. When winter approaches, they slowly return to the woods. Finally, in the more southernly districts, there are some Ostjaks who, having entirely adopted the Russian mode of life, cultivate the soil, keep cattle, or earn their livelihood as carriers.

In general, however, the Ostjak, like the Samojede, obsti-nately withstands all innovations, and remains true to the customs of his forefathers. He has been so often deceived by the Russians that he is loth to receive the gifts of civili-sation from their hands. He fears that if his children learn to read and write, they will no longer be satisfied to live like their parents, and that the school will deprive him of the support of his age. He is no less obstinately attached to the religion of his fathers, which in all essential points is identical with that of the Samojedes. In some of the southern districts, along the Irtysch, at Surgut, he has in-deed been baptized, and hangs up the image of a saint in his hut, as his Russian pope or priest has instructed him to do; but his Christianity extends no further Along the tribu-taries of the Obi, and below Obdorsk, he is still plunged in Schamanism.

Like the Samojedes, the Ostjaks, whose entire number

amounts to about 25,000, are subdivided into tribes, reminding one of the Highland clans. Each tribe consists of a number of families, of a common descent, and sometimes comprising many hundred individuals, who, however distantly related, consider it a duty to assist each other in distress. The fortunate fisherman divides the spoils of the day with his less fortunate clansman, who hardly thanks him for a gift which he considers as his due. In cases of dispute the Starschina, or elder, acts as a judge; if, however, the parties are not satisfied with his verdict, they appeal to the higher authority of the hereditary chieftain or prince—a title which has been conferred, by the Empress Catherine II., on the Ostjak magnates who, from time immemorial, have been considered as the heads of their tribes. These princes are, of course, subordinate to the Russian officials, and bound to appear, with the Starschinas, at the fairs of Beresow or Obdorsk, as they are answerable for the quantity and quality of the various sorts of furs which the Ostjaks are obliged to pay as a tribute to Government. Their dignity is hereditary, and, in default of male descendants, passes to the nearest male relation. It must, however, not be supposed that these princes are distinguished from the other Ostjaks by their riches, or a more splendid appearance; for their mode of life differs in no way from that of their inferiors in rank, and like them they are obliged to fish or to hunt for their daily subsistence.

On entering the hut of one of these dignitaries, Castrén found him in a ragged jacket, while the princess had no other robe of state but a shirt. The prince, having liberally helped himself from the brandy-bottle which the traveller offered him, became very communicative, and complained of the sufferings and cares of the past winter. He had exerted himself to the utmost, but without success. Far from giving way to indolence in his turf-hut, he had been out hunting in the forest, after the first snow-fall, but rarely pitching his bark-tent, and frequently sleeping in the open air. Yet, in spite of all his exertions, he had often not been able to shoot a single ptarmigan. His stores of meal and frozen fishes were soon exhausted, and sometimes the princely family had been reduced to eat the flesh of wolves.

The Ostjaks are excellent archers, and, like all the other hunting tribes of Siberia, use variously constructed arrows for the different objects of their chase. Smaller shafts, with a knob of wood at the end, are destined for the squirrels and other small animals whose fur it is desirable not to injure; while large arrows with strong triangular iron points bring down the wolf, the bear, and sometimes the fugitive exile. For, to prevent the escape of criminals sentenced to banishment in Siberia, the Russian Government allows the Ostjaks to shoot any unknown person, not belonging to their race, whom they may meet with on their territory. Although well aware of this danger, several exiles have attempted to escape to Archangel along the border of the Arctic sea; but they either died of hunger, or were devoured by wild beasts, or shot by the Ostjaks. There is but one instance known of an exile, who, after spending a whole year on the journey, at length reached the abodes of civilised man, and he was pardoned in consideration of the dreadful sufferings he had undergone.

The Ostjaks are generally of a small stature, and most of them are dark-complexioned, with raven-black hair like the Samojedes; some of them, however, have a fairer skin and light-coloured hair. They have neither the oblique eyes nor the broad projecting cheek-bones of the Mongols and Tungus, but bear a greater resemblance to the Finnish, Samojede, and Turkish cast of countenance. They are a good-natured, indolent, honest race; and though they are extremely dirty, yet their smoky huts are not more filthy than those of the Norwegian or Icelandic fisherman. As among the Samojedes, the women are in a very degraded condition, the father always giving his daughter in marriage to the highest bidder. The price is very different, and rises or falls according to the circumstances of the parent; for while the rich man asks fifty reindeer for his child, the poor fisherman is glad to part with his daughter for a few squirrel-skins and dried sturgeon.

Before taking leave of the Ostjaks, we will still tarry a moment at the small town of Obdorsk, which may be considered as the capital of their country, and entirely owes its existence to the trade carried on between them and the Russians. Formerly the merchants from Beresow and Tobolsk used merely to visit the spot, but the difficulties of the journey soon compelled them to establish permanent dwell-

ings in that dreary region. A certain number of exiles
serves to increase the scanty population, which consists of a
strange medley of various nations, among whom Castrén
found a Calmuck, a Kirghis, and a Polish cook, who bitterly
complained that he had but few opportunities of showing his
skill in a town where people lived à la Ostjak. In fact, most
of the Russian inhabitants of the place have in so far adopted
the Ostjak mode of life, as to deem the cooking of their
victuals superfluous. When Castrén, on his arrival at Obdorsk,
paid a visit to a Tobolsk merchant, who had been for some
time settled in the place, he found the whole family lying on
the floor, regaling on raw fish, and the most civilised person
he met with told him that he had tasted neither boiled nor roast
flesh or fish for half a year. Yet fine shawls and dresses, and
now no doubt the crinoline and the chignon, are found amidst
all this barbarism. Edifices with the least pretensions to architectural beauty it would of course be vain to look for in
Obdorsk. The houses of the better sort of Russian settlers are
two-storied, or consisting of a ground-floor and garrets; but
as they are built of wood, and are by no means wind-tight,
the half-famished Ostjaks, who have settled in the town, are
probably more comfortably housed in their low turf-huts,
than the prosperous Russian inhabitants of the place. The
latter make it their chief occupation to cheat the Ostjaks
in every possible way; some of them, however, add to this
profitable, if not praiseworthy occupation, the keeping of
reindeer herds, or even of cows and sheep.

The fair lasts from the beginning of winter to February,
and during this time the Ostjaks who assemble at Obdorsk
pitch their bark-tents about the town. With their arrival a
new life begins to stir in the wretched place. Groups of the
wild sons and daughters of the tundra, clothed in heavy
skins, make their appearance, and stroll slowly through the
streets, admiring the high wooden houses, which to them
seem palaces. But nothing is to be seen of the animation
and activity which usually characterise a fair. Concealing
some costly fur under his wide skin mantle, the savage pays
his cautious visit to the trader, and makes his bargain amid
copious libations of brandy. He is well aware that this
underhand way of dealing is detrimental to his interests;
but his timorous disposition shrinks from public sales, and

frequently he is not even in the situation to profit by competition; for among the thousands that flock to the fair,
there are but very few who do not owe to the traders of
Obdorsk much more than they possess, or can ever hope to
repay. Woe to the poor Ostjak whose creditor should find
him dealing with some other trader!—for the seizure of all his
moveable property, of his tent and household utensils, would
be the least punishment which the wretch turned adrift into
the naked desert would have to expect. The fair is not
opened before Government has received the furs which are
due to it, or at least a guarantee for the amount from the
merchants of the place. Then the magazines of the traders
gradually fill with furs—with clothes of reindeer-skin ready-
made, with feathers, reindeer-flesh, frozen sturgeon, mammoth tusks, &c. For these goods the Ostjaks receive flour,
baked bread, tobacco, pots, kettles, knives, needles, brass
buttons and rings, glass pearls, and other trifling articles.
An open trade in spirits is not allowed; but brandy may be
sold as a medicine, and thus many an Ostjak takes advantage
of the fair for undergoing a cure the reverse of that which
is recommended by hydropathic doctors.

Towards the end of February, when the Ostjaks have retired into the woods—where they hunt or tend their reindeer
herds until the opening of the fishing season recalls them to
the Obi—the trader prepares for his journey to Irbit, where
he hopes to dispose of his furs at an enormous profit, and
Obdorsk is once more left until the following winter to its
deathlike solitude.

The Sable.

Tobolsk.

# CHAPTER XVI.

## CONQUEST OF SIBERIA BY THE RUSSIANS—THEIR VOYAGES OF DISCOVERY ALONG THE SHORES OF THE POLAR SEA.

Ivan the Terrible—Strogonoff—Yermak the Robber and Conqueror—His Expeditions to Siberia—Battle of Tobolsk—Yermak's Death—Progress of the Russians to Ochotsk—Semen Deshnew—Condition of the Siberian Natives under the Russian Yoke—Voyages of Discovery in the Reign of the Empress Anna—Prontschischtschew—Chariton and Demetrius Laptew—An arctic Heroine—Schalaurow—Discoveries in the Sea of Behring and in the Pacific Ocean—The Lächow Islands—Fossil Ivory—New Siberia—The Wooden Mountains—The past Ages of Siberia.

IN the beginning of the thirteenth century, the now huge Empire of Russia was confined to part of her present European possessions, and divided into several independent principalities, the scene of disunion and almost perpetual warfare. Thus when the country was invaded, in 1236, by the Tartars, under Baaty Khan, a grandson of the famous Gengis Khan, it fell an easy prey to its conquerors. The miseries of a foreign yoke, aggravated by intestine discord, lasted about 250 years, until Ivan Wasiljewitsch I. (1462-

1505) became the deliverer of his country, and laid the
foundations of her future greatness. This able prince subdued, in 1470, the *Great Novgorod*, a city until then so powerful as to have maintained its independence, both against the
Russian grand princes and the Tartar khans; and, ten years
later, he not only threw off the yoke of the Khans of Khip-
sack, but destroyed their empire. The conquest of Constantinople by the Turks placed the spiritual diadem of the
ancient Cæsars on his head, and caused him, as chief of the
Greek orthodox Church, to exchange his old title of Grand
Prince for the more significant and imposing one of Czar.

His grandson, Ivan Wasiljewitsch II., a cruel but energetic
monarch, conquered Kasan in 1552, and thus completely and
permanently overthrew the dominion of the Tartars. Two
years later he subdued Astrakhan, and planted the Greek
cross on the borders of the Caspian Sea, where until then
only the Crescent had been seen.

In spite of the inhuman cruelty that disgraced his character, and earned for him the name of *Terrible*, Ivan sought,
like his illustrious successor Peter the Great, to introduce
the arts and sciences of Western Europe into his barbarous
realm, and to improve the Russian manufactures by encouraging German artists and mechanics to settle in the
country. It was in his reign that Chancellor discovered the
passage from England to the White Sea, and Ivan gladly
seized the opportunity thus afforded. Soon after this the
port of Archangel was built, and thus a new seat was opened
to civilisation at the northern extremity of Europe.

After the conquest of Kasan, several Russians settled in
that province; among others, a merchant of the name of
Strogonoff, who established some salt-works on the banks
of the Kama, and opened a trade with the natives. Among
these he noticed some strangers, and having heard that they
came from a country ruled by a Tartar khan, who resided in
a capital called Sibir, he sent some of his people into their
land. These agents returned with the finest sable-skins,
which they had purchased for a trifling sum; and Strogonoff,
not so covetous as to wish to keep all the advantage of his
discovery to himself, immediately informed the Government
of the new trade he had opened. He was rewarded with

the gift of considerable estates at the confluence of the
Kama and Tschinsova, and his descendants, the Counts
Strogonoff, are, as is well known, reckoned among the richest
of the Russian nobility.

Soon after Ivan sent some troops to Siberia, whose prince
Jediger acknowledged his supremacy, and promised to pay
him an annual tribute of a thousand sable-skins. But this con-
nection was not of long duration, for a few years after Jediger
was defeated by another Tartar prince, named Kutchum Khan;
and thus, after Russian influence had taken the first step to
establish itself beyond the Ural, it once more became doubtful
whether Northern Asia was to be Christian or Mahometan.
The question was soon after decided by a fugitive robber.

The conquests of Ivan on the Caspian Sea had called into
life a considerable trade with Bokhara and Persia, which,
however, was greatly disturbed by the depredations of the
Don Cossacks, who made it their practice to plunder the
caravans. But Ivan, not the man to be trifled with by a
horde of freebooters, immediately sent out a body of troops
against the Don Cossacks, who, not venturing to meet them,
sought their safety in flight. At the head of the fugitives,
whose number amounted to no less than 6,000 men, was
Yermak Timodajeff, a man who, like Cortez or Pizarro, was
destined to lay a new empire at the feet of his master.
But while the troops of the Czar were following his track,
Yermak was not yet dreaming of future conquests; his only
aim was to escape the executioner; and he considered himself
extremely fortunate when, leaving his pursuers far behind, he
at length arrived on the estates of Strogonoff. Here he was
well received—better, no doubt, than if he had come single-
handed and defenceless; and Strogonoff having made him
acquainted with Siberian affairs, he at once resolved to try
his fortunes on this new scene of action. As the tyranny of
Kutchum Khan had rendered him odious to his subjects, he
hoped it would be an easy task to overthrow his power; the
prospect of a rich booty of sable-skins was also extremely
attractive; and, finally, there could be no doubt that the
greatest dangers were in his rear, and that any choice was
better than to fall into the hands of Ivan the Terrible. Strogonoff, on his part, had excellent reasons for encouraging the

adventure. If it succeeded, a considerable part of the profits was likely to fall to his share; if not, he at least was rid of his unbidden guest.

Thus Yermak, in the summer of 1578, advanced with his Cossacks along the banks of the Tschinsova into Siberia. But, either from a want of knowledge of the country, or from not having taken the necessary precautions, he was overtaken by winter before he could make any progress; and when spring appeared, famine compelled him to return to his old quarters, where, as may easily be imagined, his reception was none of the most cordial. But, far from losing courage from this first disappointment, Yermak was firmly resolved to persevere. He had gained experience—his self-confidence was steeled by adversity; and when Strogonoff attempted to refuse him further assistance, he pointed to his Cossacks, with the air of a man who has the means of enforcing obedience to his orders. This time Yermak took better measures for ensuring success; he compelled Strogonoff to furnish him with an ample supply of provisions and ammunition, and in the June of the following year, we again find him, with his faithful Cossacks, on the march to Siberia. But such were the impediments which the pathless swamps and forests, the severity of the climate, and the hostility of the natives opposed to his progress, that towards the end of 1580, his force (now reduced to 1,500 men) had reached no farther than the banks of the Tara. The subsequent advance of this little band was a constant succession of hardships and skirmishes, which caused it to melt away like snow in the sunshine; so that scarcely 500 remained when, at the confluence of the Tobol and the Irtysch, they at length reached the camp of Kutchum Khan, whose overwhelming numbers seemed to mock their audacity.

But Yermak felt as little fear at sight of the innumerable tents of the Tartar host, as the wolf when meeting a herd of sheep; he knew that his Cossacks, armed with their matchlocks, had long since disdained to count their enemies, and, fully determined to conquer or to die, he gave the order to attack. A dreadful battle ensued, for though the Tartars only fought with their bows and arrows, yet they were no less brave than their adversaries, and their vast superiority of numbers made up for the inferior quality of their weapons. The struggle was long doubtful—the Tartars repeating attack upon attack like the waves of a storm-tide, and the Cossacks receiving their assaults as firmly and immoveably as rocks; until, finally, the hordes of Kutchum Khan gave way to their stubborn obstinacy, and his camp and all its treasures fell into the hands of the conquerors.

The subsequent conduct of Yermak proved that he had all the qualities of a general and a statesman, and that his talents were not unequal to his fortunes. Without losing a single moment, he, immediately after this decisive battle, sent part of his small band to occupy the capital of the vanquished Kutchum, for he well knew that a victory is but half-gained if one delays to reap its fruits. The Cossacks found the place evacuated, and soon after Yermak made his triumphal entry into Sibir. His weakness now became a source of strength, for, daunted by the wonderful success of this handful of strangers, the people far and wide came to render him homage. The Ostjaks of the Soswa freely consented to yield an annual tribute of 280 sable-skins, and other tribes of the same nation, who were more backward in their submission, were compelled by his menaces to pay him a tax or *jassak* of eleven skins for every archer.

It was not without reason that Yermak thus sought to collect as many of these valuable furs as he possibly could, for his aim was to obtain from Ivan a pardon of his former delinquencies, by presenting him with the richest spoils of his victories, and he well knew that it would be impossible for him to maintain his conquests without further assistance from the Czar. Great was Ivan's astonishment when an envoy of the fugitive robber brought him the welcome gift of 2,400 sable-skins, and informed him that Yermak had added a new province to his realm. He at once comprehended that the hero who with small means had achieved such great successes, was the fittest man to consolidate or enlarge his acquisitions; he consequently not only pardoned all his former offences, but confirmed him in the dignity of governor and commander-in-chief in the countries which he had subdued. Thus Yermak's envoy, having been received with the greatest distinction at Moscow, returned to his fortunate master with a robe of honour which had been worn by the Czar him-self, and the still more welcome intelligence that reinforce-ments were on the march to join him.

Meanwhile Yermak had continued to advance into the valley of the Obi beyond its confluence with the Irtysch; and when at length his force was augmented by the arrival of 500 Russians, he pursued his expeditions with increasing audacity. On his return from one of these forays, he en-camped on a small island in the Irtysch. The night was dark and rainy, and the Russians, fatigued by their march, relied too much upon the badness of the weather or the terror of their name. But Kutchum Khan, having been informed by his spies of their want of vigilance, crossed a ford in the river, and falling upon the unsuspecting Russians, killed them all except one single soldier, who brought the fatal intelligence to Sibir. Yermak, when he saw his warriors fall around him like grass before the scythe, without losing his presence of mind for a moment, cut his way through the Tartars, and endeavoured to save himself in a boat. But in the medley he fell into the water and was drowned.

By the orders of Kutchum, the body of the hero was exposed to every indignity which the rage of a barbarian can think of; but after this first explosion of impotent fury, his followers, feeling ashamed of the ignoble conduct of their chief, buried his remains with princely pomp, and ascribed miraculous powers to the grave in which they were deposited. The Russians have also erected a monument to Yermak in the town of Tobolsk, which was built on the very spot where he gained his first decisive victory over Kutchum. It is inscribed with the dates of that memorable event, and of the unfortunate day when he found his death in the floods of the Irtysch. His real monument, however, is all Siberia from the Ural to the Pacific; for as long as the Russian nation continues to exist, it will remember the name of Yermak Timodajeff. The value of the man became at once apparent after his death, for scarcely had the news of the disaster arrived, when the Russians immediately evacu-ated Sibir, and left the country. But they well knew that this retreat was to be but temporary, and that the present ebb of their fortunes would soon be followed by a fresh tide

of success. After a few years they once more returned, as
the definitive masters of the country. Their first settlement
was Tjumen, on the Tara, and before the end of 1587 Tobolsk
was founded. They had, indeed, still many a conflict with
the Woguls and Tartars, but every effort of the natives to
shake off the yoke proved fruitless.

As gold had been the all-powerful magnet which led the
Spaniards from Hispaniola to Mexico and Peru, so a small
fur-bearing animal (the sable) attracted the Cossacks farther
and farther to the east; and although the possession of fire-
arms gave them an immense advantage over the wild inhabitants of Siberia, yet it is astonishing with what trifling
means they subdued whole nations, and perhaps history
affords no other example of such a vast extent of territory
having been conquered by so small a number of adventurers.

As they advanced, small wooden forts (or *ostrogs*) were
built in suitable places, and became in their turn the starting-
posts for new expeditions. The following dates give the
best proof of the uncommon rapidity with which the tide of
conquest rolled onwards to the east. Tomsk was founded
in 1604; and the ostrog Jeniseisk, where the neighbouring nomads brought their sable-skins to market, in 1621.
The snow-shoes of the Tunguse, which they sometimes
saw ornamented with this costly fur, induced the Cossacks
to follow their hordes, of which many had come from the
middle and inferior Tunguska, and thus, in 1630, Wassiljew
reached the banks of the Lena. In 1636, Jelissei Busa was
commissioned to ascend that mighty river, and to impose
*jassak* on all the natives of those quarters. He reached the
western mouth of the Lena, and after navigating the sea for
twenty-four hours came to the Olekma, which he ascended.
In 1638 he discovered the Tana, on whose banks he spent another winter; and in 1639, resuming his voyage eastward by
sea, he reached the Tchendoma, and wintering for two years
among the Jukahirs, made them also tributary to Russia.

In that same year another party of Cossacks crossed the
Altai Mountains, and, traversing forests and swamps, arrived
at the coasts of the inhospitable Sea of Ochotsk; while a
third expedition discovered the Amur, and built a strong
ostrog, called Albasin, on its left bank. The report soon

spread that the river rolled over gold-sand, and colonists came flocking to the spot, both to collect these treasures, and to enjoy the fruits of a milder climate and of a more fruitful soil. But the Chinese destroyed the fort in 1680, and carried the garrison prisoners to Peking.

Albasin was soon after rebuilt; but as Russia at that time had no inclination to engage in constant quarrels with the Celestial Empire about the possession of a remote desert, all its pretensions to the Amur were given up by the treaty of Nertschinsk (1689). This agreement, however, like so many others, was doomed to last no longer than it pleased the more powerful of the contracting parties to keep it, and came to nothing as soon as the possession of the Amur territory became an object of importance, and the increasing weakness of China was no longer able to dispute its possession. Thus, when Count Nicholas Mourawieff was appointed Governor-General of Eastern Siberia in 1847, one of his first cares was to appropriate or annex the Amur. He immediately sent a surveying expedition to the mouth of the river, where, in 1851, regardless of the remonstrances of the Chinese Government, he ordered the stations of Nikolajewsk and Mariinsk to be built; and in 1854 he himself sailed down the Amur, with a numerous flotilla of boats and rafts, for the purpose of personally opening this new channel of intercourse with the Pacific. Other expeditions soon followed, and the Chinese, finding resistance hopeless, ceded to Russia in the year 1858, by the treaty of Aigun, the left bank of the Amur as far as the influx of the Ussuri, and both its banks below the latter river. Thus the Czar found some consolation for the losses of the Crimean campaign in the acquisition of a vast territory in the distant East, which, though at present a mere wilderness, may in time become a flourishing colony.

In 1644, a few years after the discovery of the Amur, the Cossack Michael Staduchin formed a winter establishment on the delta of the Kolyma, which has since expanded into the town of Nishnei-Kolymsk, and afterwards navigated the sea eastward to Cape Schelagskoi, which may be considered as the north-eastern cape of Siberia.

In 1648 Semen Deschnew sailed from the Kolyma with the intention of reaching the Anadyr by sea, and by this remarkable voyage—which no one else, either before or after him, has ever performed—*discovered* and passed through the strait, which properly should bear his name, instead of Behring's, who, sailing from Kamtschatka northwards in 1728, did not go beyond East Cape, being satisfied with the westerly trending of the cape beyond the promontory. Some of Deschnew's companions subsequently reached Kamtschatka, and were put to death by the people of that peninsula, which was conquered, in 1699, by Atlassoff, a Cossack officer who came from Jakutsk.

After having thus rapidly glanced at the progress of the Russian dominion from the Ural to the Sea of Ochotsk, it may not be uninteresting to inquire whether the natives had reason to bless the arrival of their new masters, or to curse the day when they were first made to understand the meaning of the word *yassak* or tribute. Unfortunately, history tells us that, while the conquerors of Siberia were fully as bold and persevering as the companions of Cortez and Pizarro, they also equalled them in avarice and cruelty. Under their iron yoke whole nations, such as the Schelagi, Aniujili, and Omoki, melted away; others, as the Woguls, Jukahires, Koriaks, and Itälmenes, were reduced to a scanty remnant.

The history of the subjugation of the Itälmenes, or natives of Kamtschatka, as described by Steller, may suffice to show how the Cossacks made and how they abused their conquests.

When Atlassoff, with only sixteen men, came to the river of Kamtschatka, the Itälmene chieftain inquired, through a Koriak interpreter, what they wanted, and whence they came; and received for answer, that the powerful sovereign, to whom the whole land belonged, had sent them to levy the tribute which they owed him as his subjects. The chieftain was naturally astonished at this information, and offering the strangers a present of costly furs, he requested them to leave the country, and not to repeat their visit. But the Cossacks thought proper to remain, and built a small wooden fort, Verchnei Ostrog, whence they fell on the neighbouring villages, robbing or destroying all they could lay hands upon. Exasperated by these acts the Itälmenes resolved to attack the fort; but as the wary Cossacks had kept up a friendly intercourse with some of them, and had moreover ingratiated themselves with the women, the plans of their enemies were always revealed to them in proper time, and led to a still greater tyranny. At length the savages appeared before the ostrog in such overwhelming numbers, that the Cossacks began to lose courage; yet by their superior tactics they finally managed to gain a complete victory, and those who escaped their bullets were either drowned or taken prisoners, and then put to death in the most cruel manner.

Convinced that a lasting security was impossible as long as the natives retained their numbers, the Cossacks lost no opportunity of goading them to revolt, and then butchering as many of them as they could. Thus, in less than forty years, the Kamtschatkans were reduced to a twelfth part of their original numbers; and the Cossacks, having made a solitude, called it peace.

In former times, the nomads of the North used freely to wander with their reindeer herds over the tundra, but after the conquest they were loaded with taxes, and confined to certain districts. The consequence was that their reindeer gradually perished, and that a great number of wandering herdsmen were now compelled to adopt a fisherman's life— a change fatal to many.

It would, however, be unjust to accuse the Russian Government of having wilfully sought the ruin of the aboriginal tribes; on the contrary, it has constantly endeavoured to protect them against the exactions of the Cossacks, and, in order to secure their existence, has even granted them the exclusive possession of the districts assigned to them. Thus the Ostjaks and Samojedes, the Koriaks and the Jakuts, have their own land, their own rivers, forests, and tundri. But if it is a common saying in European Russia, 'that heaven is high, and the Czar distant,' it may easily be imagined that beyond the Ural the weak indigenous tribes found the law but a very inefficient barrier against the rapacity of their conquerors.

Thus, in spite of the Government, the *yassak* was not unfrequently raised, under various pretences, to six or ten times its original amount; and the natives were, besides, obliged to bring the best of their produce, from considerable distances, to the ostrog.

Nor could the Government prevent the accumulation of usurious debts, nor the leasing of the best pasturages or fishing-stations for a trifling sum quite out of proportion to their value; so that the natives no longer had the means of feeding their herds, and sank deeper and deeper into poverty.

And if we consider, finally, of what elements Yermak's band was originally composed, we can easily conceive that, under such masters, the lot of the Siberian natives was by no means to be envied.

The year 1734 opens a new epoch in the history of Siberian discoveries. Until then they had been merely undertaken for purposes of traffic; bold Cossacks and Promyschlenniki (or fur-hunters) had gradually extended their excursions to the Sea of Behring; but now, for the first time, scientific expeditions were sent out, for the more accurate investigation of the northern coasts of Siberia.

Prontschischtschew, who sailed westwards from the Lena to circumnavigate the icy capes of Taimurland, was accompanied by his youthful wife, who wintered with him at the Olenek, in 72° 54' of latitude, and in the following summer took part in his fruitless endeavours to double those most northernly points of Asia. He died in consequence of the fatigues he had to undergo, and a few days after she followed him to the grave. A similar example of female devotion is not to be met with in the annals of Arctic discovery.

After Prontschischtschew's death, Lieutenant Chariton Laptew was appointed to carry out the project in which the former had failed. Having been repulsed by the drift-ice, he was obliged to winter on the Chatanga (1739–40); but renewed the attempt in the following summer, which however exposed him to still severer trials. The vessel was wrecked in the ice; the crew reached the shore with difficulty, and many of them perished, from fatigue and famine, before the rivers were sufficiently frozen to enable the feeble survivors to return to their former winter-station at Chatanga. Notwithstanding the hardships which he and his party had endured, Laptew prosecuted the survey of the promontory in the following spring.

Setting out with a sledge-party across the tundra on April 24, 1741, he reached Taimur Lake on the 30th; and following the Taimur river, as it flows from the lake, ascertained its mouth to be situated in lat. 75° 36' N. On

August 29, he safely returned to Jeniseisk, after one of the most difficult voyages ever performed by man. The resolution with which he overcame difficulties, and his perseverance amid the severest distresses, entitle him to a high rank among Arctic discoverers.

While Chariton Laptew was thus gaining distinction in the wilds of Taimurland, his brother, Dimitri Laptew, was busy extending geographical knowledge to the east of the Lena. He doubled the *Sviatoi-noss*, wintered on the banks of the Indigirka, surveyed the Bear Islands, passed a second winter on the borders of the Kolyma; and in a fourth season extended his survey of the coast to the Baranow Rock, which he vainly endeavoured to double during two successive summers. After having passed seven years on the coasts of the Polar Ocean, he returned to Jakutsk in 1743.

Fourteen years later, Schalaurow, a merchant of Jakutsk, who sailed from the Jana in a vessel built at his own expense, at length succeeded in doubling the Baranow Rock, and proceeded eastwards as far as Cape Schelagskoi, which prevented his farther progress. After twice wintering on the dreary Kolyma, he resolved, with admirable perseverance, to make a third attempt, but his crew would no longer follow him. From a second sea-journey, which he undertook in 1764 to that cape, he did not return. 'His unfortunate death is the more to be lamented,' says Wrangell, 'as he sacrificed his property and life to a disinterested aim, and united intelligence and energy in a remarkable degree.' On his map, the whole coast from the Jana to Cape Schelagskoi is marked, with an accuracy which does him the greatest honour. In 1785, Billings and Sarytchew were equally unsuccessful in the endeavour to sail round the cape which had defeated all Schalaurow's endeavours; nor has the voyage been accomplished to the present day.

As the sable had gradually led the Russian fur-hunters to Kamtschatka, so the still more valuable sea-otter gave the chief impulse to the discovery of the Aleutic chain and the opposite continent of America. When Atlassow and his band arrived at Kamtschatka by the end of the seventeenth century, they found the sea-otter abounding on its coasts; but the fur-hunters chased it so eagerly that, before the middle of the eighteenth century, they had entirely extir-

pated it in that country. On Behring's second voyage of
discovery (1741–42), it was again found in considerable
numbers. Tschirigow is said to have brought back 900
skins, and on Behring's Island 700 sea-otters—whose skins,
according to present prices, would be worth about 20,000*l.*
—were killed almost without trouble. These facts, of course,
encouraged the merchants of Jakutsk and Irkutsk to undertake new expeditions.

Generally, several of them formed an association, which
fitted out some hardly seaworthy vessel at Ochotsk, where
also the captain and the crew, consisting of fur-hunters and
other adventurers, were hired. The expenses of such an expedition amounted to the considerable sum of about 30,000
roubles, as pack-horses had to transport a great part of the
necessary outfit all the distance from Jakutsk, and the
vessel generally remained four or five years on the voyage.
Passing through one of the Kurile Straits, these expeditions
sailed at first along the east coast of Kamtschatka, bartering
sables and sea-otters for reindeer-skins and other articles;
and as the precious furs became more rare, ventured out
farther into the Eastern Ocean. Thus Michael Nowodsikoff
discovered the Western Aleuts in 1745; Paikoff the Fox
Islands in 1759; Adrian Tolstych almost all the islands of
the central group, which still bear his name, in 1760;
Stephen Glottoff the island of Kadiak in 1763, and Krenitzin
the peninsula of Aljaska in 1768. When we consider the
scanty resources of these Russian navigators, the bad condition of their miserable barks, their own imperfect nautical
knowledge, and the inhospitable nature of the seas which
they traversed, we cannot but admire their intrepidity.

In the Polar Sea there are neither sables nor otters, and thus
the islands lying to the north of Siberia might have remained
unknown till the present day, if the search after mammoth-
teeth had not, in a similar manner, led to their discovery.

In March 1770, while a merchant of the name of Lächow
was busy collecting fossil ivory about Cape Svatoinoss, he saw
a large herd of deer coming over the ice from the north.

Resolute and courageous, he at once resolved to follow
their tracks, and after a sledge-journey of seventy versts, he
came to an island, and twenty versts further reached a
second island, at which, owing to the roughness of the ice,

his excursion terminated.    He saw enough, however, of the
richness of the two islands in mammoth-teeth, to show him
that another visit would be a valuable speculation ; and on
making his report to the Russian Government, he obtained an
exclusive privilege to dig for mammoth-bones on the islands
which he had discovered, and to which his name has been
given.    In the summer of 1773 he consequently returned,
and ascertained the existence of a third island, much larger
than the others, mountainous, and having its coasts covered
with driftwood.    He then went back to the first island,
wintered there, and returned to Ustjansk in spring, with a
valuable cargo of mammoth-tusks.

There hardly exists a more remarkable article of commerce than these remains of an extinct animal.    In North
Siberia, along the Obi, the Jenisei, the Lena, and their
tributaries, from lat. 58° to 70°, or along the shores of the
Polar Ocean as far as the American side of Behring Strait, the
remains of a species of elephant are found imbedded in the
frozen soil, or become exposed, by the annual thawing and
crumbling of the river-banks.    Dozens of tusks are frequently found together, but the most astonishing deposit
of mammoth-bones occurs in the Lächow Islands, where, in
some localities, they are accumulated in such quantities as
to form the chief substance of the soil.    Year after year the
tusk-hunters work every summer at the cliffs, without producing any sensible diminution of the stock.    The solidly-
frozen matrix, in which the bones lie, thaws to a certain
extent annually, allowing the tusks to drop out, or to be
quarried.    In 1821, 20,000 lbs. of fossil ivory were procured
from the island of New Siberia.

The ice in which the mammoth remains are imbedded
sometimes preserves their entire bodies, in spite of the
countless ages which must have elapsed since they walked on
earth.    In 1799 the carcase of a mammoth was discovered,
so fresh that the dogs ate the flesh for two summers.    The
skeleton is preserved at St. Petersburg, and specimens of
the woolly hair—proving that the climate of Siberia, though
then no doubt much milder than at present, still required
the protection of a warm and shaggy coat—were presented to
the chief museums of Europe.

The remains of a rhinoceros, very similar to the Indian species, are likewise found in great numbers along the shores, or on the steep and sandy river-banks of Northern Siberia, along with those of fossil species of the horse, the musk-ox, and the bison, which have now totally forsaken the Arctic wilds.

The Archipelago of New Siberia, situated to the north of the Lächow Islands, was discovered by Sirowatsky in 1806, and since then scientifically explored by Hedenström in 1808, and Anjou in 1823. These islands are remarkable no less for the numerous bones of horses, buffaloes, oxen, and sheep scattered over their desolate shores, than for the vast quantities of fossil-wood imbedded in their soil. The hills, which rise to a considerable altitude, consist of horizontal beds of sandstone, alternating with bituminous beams or trunks of trees. On ascending them, fossilised charcoal is everywhere met with, encrusted with an ash-coloured matter, which is so hard that it can scarcely be scraped off with a knife. On the summit there is a long row of beams resembling the former, but fixed perpendicularly in the sandstone. The ends, which project from seven to ten inches, are for the most part broken, and the whole has the appearance of a ruinous dyke. Thus a robust forest vegetation once flourished where now only hardy lichens can be seen; and many herbivorous animals feasted on grasses where now the reindeer finds but a scanty supply of moss, and the polar bear is the sole lord of the dreary waste.

The Argali Sheep.

Siberian Exiles en route.

## CHAPTER XVII.

### SIBERIA—FUR-TRADE AND GOLD-DIGGINGS.

SIBERIA is at least thirty times more extensive than Great Britain and Ireland, but its scanty population forms a miserable contrast to its enormous size. Containing scarcely three millions of inhabitants, it is comparatively three hundred times less peopled than the British Islands. This small population is, moreover, very unequally distributed, consisting chiefly of Russians and Tartars, who have settled in the south or in the milder west, along the rivers and the principal thoroughfares which lead from the territory of

SABLE AND ARCTIC FOX.

one large stream to the other. In the northern and eastern districts, as far as they are occupied, the settlements are likewise almost entirely confined to the river-banks; and thus the greater part of the enormous forest-lands, and of the interminable tundras, are either entirely uninhabited by man, or visited only by the huntsman, the gold-digger, or the migratory savage.

And yet Siberia has not been so niggardly treated by Nature as not to be able to sustain a far more considerable population. In the south there are thousands of square miles fit for cultivation; the numbers of the herds and flocks might be increased a hundredfold, and even the climate would become milder after the labour of man had subdued the chilling influences of the forest and the swamp. But it is easier to express than to realise the wish to see Siberia more populous, for its reputation is hardly such as to tempt the free colonist to settle within its limits; and thus the Russian Government, which would willingly see its more temperate regions covered with flourishing towns and villages, can only expect an increase of population from the slow growth of time, aided by the annual influx of the involuntary emigrants which it sends across the Ural to the East.

Many a celebrated personage has already been doomed to trace this melancholy path, particularly during the last century, when the all powerful-favourite of one period was not seldom doomed to exile by the next palace revolution. This fate befel, among others, the famous Prince Mentschikoff. In a covered cart, and in the dress of a peasant, the confidential minister of Peter the Great, the man who for years had ruled the vast Russian Empire, was conveyed into perpetual banishment. His dwelling was now a simple hut, and the spade of the labourer replaced the pen of the statesman. Domestic misfortunes aggravated his cruel lot. His wife died from the fatigues of the journey; one of his daughters soon after fell a victim to the smallpox; his two other children, who were attacked by the same malady, recovered. He himself died in the year 1729, and was buried near his daughter at Beresow, the seat of his exile. Like Cardinal Wolsey, after his fall he remembered God, whom he had forgotten during the swelling tide of his prosperity. He considered his punishment as a blessing, which showed him the way to everlasting happiness. He built a chapel, assisting in its erection with his own hands, and after the services gave instruction to the congregation. The inhabitants of Beresow still honour his memory, and revere him as a saint. They were confirmed in this belief by the circumstance that his body, having been disinterred in 1821, was found in a state of perfect preservation, after a lapse of ninety-two years.

One day, as his daughter walked through the village, she was accosted by a peasant from the window of a hut. This peasant was Prince Dolgorouky, her father's enemy—the man who had caused his banishment, and was now, in his turn, doomed to taste the bitterness of exile. Soon after, the princess and her brother were pardoned by the Empress Anna, and Dolgorouky took possession of their hut. Young Mentschikoff was finally reinstated in all the honours and riches of his father, and from him descends, in a direct line, the famous defender of Sebastopol.

Marshal Münich, the favourite of the Empress Anna, was doomed, in his sixtieth year, to a Siberian exile, when Elizabeth ascended the throne. His prison consisted of three rooms—one for his guards or gaolers, the second for their kitchen, the third for his own use. A wall twenty feet high prevented him from enjoying the view even of the sky. The man who had once governed Russia had but half a rouble daily to spend; but the love of his wife—who, although fifty-five years old, had the courage and the self-denial to accompany him in his banishment—alleviated the sorrows of his exile. The venerable couple spent twenty-one years in Siberia, and on their return from exile, fifty-two children, grandchildren, and great-grandchildren were assembled to meet them at Moscow. The revolution which placed Catherine the Second on the throne, had nearly once more doomed the octogenarian statesman to banishment, but he fortunately weathered the storm, and died as governor of St. Petersburg.

In this century, also, many an unfortunate exile, guiltless at least of ignoble crimes, has been doomed to wander to Siberia. There many a soldier of the *grande armée* has ended his life; there still lives many a patriotic Pole, banished for having loved his country 'not wisely but too well;' there also the conspirators who marked with so bloody an episode the accession of Nicholas, have had time to reflect on the dangers of plotting against the Czar.

Most of the Siberian exiles are, however, common criminals—such as in our country would be hung or transported, or sentenced to the treadmill: the assassin, the robber—to Siberia; the smuggler on the frontier, whose free-trade principles injure the imperial exchequer—to Siberia; even the vagabond who is caught roaming, and can give no satisfactory account of his doings and intentions, receives a fresh passport—to Siberia.

Thus the annual number of the exiles amounts to about 12,000, who, according to the gravity of their offences, are sent further and further eastwards. On an average, every week sees a transport of about 300 of these 'unfortunates,' as they are termed by popular compassion, pass through Tobolsk. About one-sixth are immediately pardoned, and the others sorted. Murderers and burglars are sent to the mines of Nertschinsk, after having been treated in Russia, before they set out on their travels, with fifty lashes of the knout. In former times their nostrils used to be torn off, a barbarity which is now no longer practised.

According to Sir George Simpson's 'Narrative of a Journey Round the World' (1847), Siberia is the best penitentiary in the world. Every exile who is not considered bad enough for the mines—those black abysses, at whose entrance, as at that of Dante's hell, all hope must be left behind—receives a piece of land, a hut, a horse, two cows, the necessary agricultural implements, and provisions for a year. The first three years he has no taxes to pay, and, during the following ten, only the half of the usual assessment. Thus, if he choose to exert himself, he has every reason to hope for an improvement in his condition, and at the same time fear contributes to keep him in the right path; for he well knows that his first trespass would infallibly conduct him to the mines, a by no means agreeable prospect. Under the influence of these stimulants, many an exile attains a degree of prosperity which would have been quite beyond his reach had he remained in European Russia.

Hofmann gives a less favourable account of the Siberian exiles. In his opinion, the prosperity and civilisation of the country has no greater obstacle than the mass of criminals sent to swell its population. In the province of Tomsk, which seems to be richly stocked with culprits of the worst description, all the waggoners belong to this class. They endeavoured to excite his compassion by hypocrisy. 'It was the will of God!' is their standing phrase, to which they tried to give a greater emphasis by turning up the whites of their eyes. But, in spite of this pious resignation to the Divine will, Hofmann never met with a worse set of drunkards, liars, and thieves.

As to the free Siberian peasant, who is generally of exile extraction, all travellers are agreed in his praise. 'As soon as one crosses the Ural,' says Wrangell, 'one is surprised by the extreme friendliness and good-nature of the inhabitants, as much as by the rich vegetation, the well-cultivated fields, and the excellent state of the roads in the southern part of the government of Tobolsk. Our luggage could be left without a guard in the open air. "Neboss!" "Fear not!" was the answer when we expressed some apprehension; "there are no thieves among us." This may appear strange, but it must be remembered that the Tomsk waggoners, described above, are located far more to the east, and that every exiled criminal has his prescribed circuit, the bounds of which he may not pass without incurring the penalty of being sent to the mines.

According to Professor Hansteen,* the Siberian peasants are the finest men of all Russia, with constitutions of iron. With a sheepskin over their shirt, and their thin linen trousers, they bid defiance to a cold of 30° and more. They have nothing of the dirty avarice of the European Russian boor; they have as much land as they choose for cultivation, and the soil furnishes all they require for their nourishment and clothing. Their cleanliness is exemplary. Within the last thirty years the gold-diggings have somewhat spoilt this

---

* Travels in Siberia, 1828–1830.

state of primitive simplicity, yet even Hofmann allows that the West-Siberian peasant has retained much of the honesty and hospitality for which he was justly celebrated.

Besides agriculture, mining, fishing, and hunting, the carriage of merchandise is one of the chief occupations of the Siberians, and probably, in proportion to the population, no other country employs so large a number of waggoners and carriers. The enormous masses of copper, lead, iron, and silver, produced by the Altai and the Nertschinsk mountains, have to be conveyed from an immense distance to the Russian markets. The gold from the East-Siberian diggings is indeed easier to transport, but the provisions required by the thousands of workmen employed during the summer in working the auriferous sands, have to be brought to them, frequently from a distance of many hundred versts.

The millions of furs, from the squirrel to the bear, likewise require considerable means of transport; and, finally, the highly important caravan-trade with China conveys thousands of bales of tea from Kiachta to Irbit. Siberia has indeed many navigable rivers, but a glance at the map shows us at once, that they are so situated as to afford far less facilities to commerce than would be the case in a more temperate climate. They all flow northwards into an inhospitable sea, which is for ever closed to navigation, and are themselves ice-bound during the greater part of the year. Enormous distances separate them from each other, and there are no navigable canals to unite them.

On some of the larger rivers, steamboats have indeed been introduced, and railroads are *talked of*; but there can be no doubt that, for many a year to come, the cart and the sledge will continue to be the chief means of transport in a country which, in consequence of its peculiar geographical position, is, even in its more southern parts, exposed to all the rigours of an Arctic winter.

Thus at Jakutsk (62° N. lat.), which is situated but six degrees further to the north than Edinburgh (55° 58′), the mean temperature of the coldest month is −40°, and mercury a solid body during one-sixth part of the year; while at Irkutsk (52° 16′ N. lat.) situated but little further to the north than Oxford (51° 46′), the thermometer frequently falls to −30°, or even −40°; temperatures which are, of course, quite unheard of on the banks of the Isis. For these dreadful winters in the heart of Siberia, and under comparatively low degrees of latitude, there are various causes. The land is, in the first place, an immense plain slanting to the north; moreover, it is situated at such a distance from the Atlantic, that beyond the Ural the western sea-winds, which bring warmth to our winters, assume the character of cold land-winds; and, finally, it merges in the south into the high Mongolian plateau, which, situated 4,000 feet above the level of the sea, has of course but little warmth to impart to it in winter; so that, from whatever side the wind may blow at that season, it constantly conveys cold. But in summer the scene undergoes a total change. Under the influence of the sun circling for months round the North Pole, floods of warmth are poured into Central Siberia, and rapidly cause the thermometer to rise; no neighbouring sea refreshes the air with a cooling breeze; whether the wind come from the heated Mongolian deserts, or sweep over the Siberian plains, it imbibes warmth on every side. Thus the terrible winter of Jakutsk is followed by an equally *immoderate* summer (58° 3′), so that rye and barley are able to ripen on a soil which a few feet below the surface is perpetually frozen.

The boundless woods of Siberia harbour a number of fur-bearing animals, whose skins form one of the chief products of the country. Among these persecuted denizens of the forest, the sable (*Martes zibellina*), which closely resembles the pine-marten (*Martes abietum*) in shape and size, deserves to be particularly noticed, both for the beauty of its pelt, and its importance in the fur-trade. Sleeping by day, the sable hunts his prey by night; but though he chiefly relishes animal food, such as hares, young birds, mice, and eggs, he also feeds on berries, and the tasteful seeds of the *Pinus cembra*. His favourite abode is near the banks of some river, in holes of the earth, or beneath the roots of trees. Incessant persecution has gradually driven him into the most inaccessible forests; the days are no more when the Tunguse hunter willingly gave for a copper kettle as many sable-skins as it would hold, or when the Kamtschatkan trapper could easily catch seventy or eighty sables in one winter; but Von Baer still estimates the annual produce of all Siberia at 45,000 skins. The finest are caught in the forests between the Lena and the Eastern Sea, but Kamtschatka furnishes the greater number. A skin of the finest quality is worth about forty roubles on the spot, and at least twice as much in St. Petersburg or Moscow, particularly when the hair is long, close, and of a deep blackish-brown, with a thick brown underwool. Skins with long dark hair tipped with white are highly esteemed, but still more so those which are entirely black—a colour to which the Russians give the preference, while the Chinese have no objection to reddish tints. In consequence of this difference of taste, the sables from the Obi, which are generally larger but of a lighter colour, are sent to Kiachta, while the darker skins, from Eastern Siberia, are directed to St. Petersburg and Leipsic.

The chase of the sable is attended with many hardships and dangers. The skins are in the highest perfection at the commencement of the winter; accordingly, towards the end of October, the hunters assemble in small companies, and proceed along the rivers in boats, or travel in sledges to the place of rendezvous—taking with them provisions for three or four months. In the deep and solitary forest they erect their huts, made of branches of trees, and bank up the snow round them, as a further protection against the piercing wind. They now roam and seek everywhere for the traces of the sable, and lay traps or snares for his destruction. These are generally pitfalls, with loose boards placed over them, baited with fish or flesh; firearms or crossbows are more rarely used, as they damage the skins. The traps must be frequently visited, and even then the hunter often finds that a fox has preceded him, and left but a few worthless remnants of the sable in the snare. Or sometimes a snowstorm overtakes him, and then his care must be to save his own life. Thus sable-hunting is a continual chain of disappointments and perils, and at the end of the season it is frequently found that the expenses are hardly paid. Until now the sable has been but rarely tamed. One kept in the palace of the Archbishop of Tobolsk was so perfectly domesticated, that it was allowed to stroll about the town as it

Q

liked. It was an arch-enemy of cats, raising itself furiously on its hind-legs as soon as it saw one, and showing the greatest desire to fight it.

In former times the ermine (*Mustela erminea*) ranked next to the sable as the most valuable fur-bearing animal of the Siberian woods; at present the skin is worth no more than from five to eight silver kopeks at Tobolsk, so that the whole produce of its chase hardly amounts to 200,000 roubles. This little animal resembles in its general appearance the weasel, but is considerably larger, as it attains a length of from twelve to fourteen inches. Its colour, which is reddish-brown in summer, becomes milk-white during the winter in the northern regions, with the exception of the tip of the tail, which always remains black. Its habits likewise greatly resemble those of the weasel; it is equally alert in all its movements, and equally courageous in defending itself when attacked. It lives on birds, poultry, rats, rabbits, leverets, and all kinds of smaller animals, and will not hesitate to attack a prey of much greater size than itself. Although various species of ermine are distributed over the whole forest region of the north, yet Siberia produces the finest skins. The largest come from the Kolyma, or are brought to the fair of Ostrownoje by the Tchutchi, who obtain them from the coldest regions of America.

The Siberian weasel (*Viverra siberica*), which is much smaller than the ermine, is likewise hunted for its soft and perfectly snow-white winter dress—the tip of the tail not being black, as in the latter.

The sea-otter, or kalan (*Enhydris lutris*), the most valuable of all the Russian fur-bearing animals, as 110 silver roubles is the average price of a single skin, is nearly related to the weasel tribe. The enormous value set upon the glossy, jet-black, soft, and thick fur of the kalan sufficiently explains how the Russian hunters have followed his traces from Kamtschatka to America, and almost entirely extirpated him on many of the coasts and islands of Behring's Sea and the Northern Pacific, where he formerly abounded. His habits very much resemble those of the seal; he haunts sea-washed rocks, lives mostly in the water, and loves to bask in the sun. His hind-feet have a membrane skirting the outside of the exterior toe, like that of a goose, and the elongated form of his flexible body enables him to swim with the greatest celerity. The love of the sea-otters for their young is so great that they reckon their own lives as nothing to protect them from danger; and Steller, who had more opportunities than any other naturalist for observing their habits, affirms that, when deprived of their offspring, their grief is so strong that in less than a fortnight they waste away to skeletons. On their flight they carry their young in their mouths, or drive them along before them. If they succeed in reaching the sea, they begin to mock their baffled pursuer, and express their joy by a variety of antics. Sometimes they raise themselves upright in the water, rising and falling with the waves, or holding a forepaw over their eyes, as if to look sharply at him; or they throw themselves on their back, rubbing their breast with their forepaws; or cast their young into the water, and catch them again, like a mother playing with her infant. The sea-otter not only surpasses the fish-otter by the beauty of his fur, but also in size, as he attains a length of from three to four feet exclusive of the tail. His food consists of small fishes, molluscs, and crustaceous animals, whose hard calcareous covering his broad grinders are well adapted to crush.

Next to the sea-otter, the black fox, whose skin is of a rich and shining-black or deep brown colour, with the longer or exterior hairs of a silvery-white, furnishes the most costly of all the Siberian furs. The average price of a single skin amounts to 60 or 70 silver roubles, and rich amateurs will willingly pay 300 roubles, or even more, for those of first-rate quality. The skin of the Siberian red fox, which ranks next in value, is worth no more than 20 roubles; the steel-grey winter dress of the Siberian crossed fox (thus named from the black cross on his shoulders), from 10 to 12 roubles; and that of the Arctic fox, though very warm and close, no more than 6 or 8.

The bear family likewise furnishes many skins to the Siberian furrier. That of the young brown bear (*Ursus arctos*) is highly esteemed for the trimming of pelisses; but that of the older animal has little value, and is used, like that of the Polar bear, as a rug or a foot-cloth in sledges.

The lynx is highly prized for its very thick, soft, rust-
coloured winter dress striped with darker brown. It attains
the size of the wolf, and is distinguished from all other
members of the cat tribe, by the pencils of long black hair
which tip its erect and pointed ears. It loves to lie in
ambush for the passing reindeer or elk, on some thick branch
at a considerable distance from the ground. With one prodigious bound it leaps upon the back of its victim, strikes
its talons into its flesh, and opens with its sharp teeth the
arteries of its neck.

Though singly of but little value, as a thousand of its
skins are worth no more than one sea-otter, the squirrel
plays in reality a far more important part in the Siberian
fur-trade than any of the before-mentioned animals, as the
total value of the grey peltry which it furnishes to trade is
at least seven times greater than that of the sable. Four
millions of grey squirrel-skins are, on an average, annually
exported to China, from two to three millions to Europe,
and the home-consumption of the Russian Empire is beyond
all doubt still more considerable, as it is the fur most commonly used by the middle-classes. The European squirrels
are of inferior value, as the hair of their winter dress is still
a mixture of red and grey; in the territory of the Petschora,
the grey first becomes predominant, and increases in beauty
on advancing towards the east. The squirrels are caught in
snares or traps, or shot with blunted arrows. Among the
fur-bearing animals of Siberia, we have further to notice the
varying hare, whose winter dress is entirely white, except
the tips of the ears, which are black; the Baikal hare; the
ground-squirrel, whose fur has fine longitudinal dark-brown
stripes, alternating with four light-yellow ones; and the
suslik, a species of marmot, whose brown fur, with white
spots and stripes, fetches a high price in China. It occurs
over all Siberia as far as Kamtschatka. Its burrows are
frequently nine feet deep; this, however, does not prevent its
being dug out by the hunters, who likewise entrap it in
spring when it awakes from its winter sleep.

Summing together the total amount of the Russian fur-
trade, Von Baer estimates the value of the skins annually
brought to the market by the Russian American Fur Com-

pany at half a million of silver roubles, the produce of European Russia at a million and a half, and that of Siberia at three millions. As agriculture decreases on advancing to the north, the chase of the fur-bearing animals increases in importance. Thus, in the most northern governments of European Russia—Wjatka, Wologda, Olonez, and Archangel —it is one of the chief occupations of the inhabitants. In Olonez about four hundred bears are killed every year, and the immense forests of Wologda furnish from one hundred to two hundred black foxes, three hundred bears, and three millions of squirrels.

Although the sable and the sea-otter are not so numerous as in former times, yet, upon the whole, the Russian fur-trade is in a very flourishing condition; nor is there any fear of its decreasing, as the less valuable skins—such as those of the squirrels and hares, which from their numbers weigh most heavily in the balance of trade—are furnished by rodents, which multiply very rapidly, and find an inexhaustible supply of food in the forests and pasture-grounds of Siberia.

The chase of the fur-bearing animals affords the North Siberian nomads—such as the Ostjaks, Jakuts, Tungusi, and Samojedes—the only means of procuring the foreign articles they require; hence it taxes all their ingenuity, and takes up a great deal of their time. On the river-banks and in the forests, they lay innumerable snares and traps, all so nicely adapted to the size, strength, and peculiar habits of the various creatures they are intended to capture, that it would be almost impossible to improve them. An industrious Jakut will lay about five hundred various traps as soon as the first snow has fallen; these he visits about five or six times in the course of the winter, and generally finds some animal or other in every eighth or tenth snare.

The produce of his chase he brings to the nearest fair, where the tax-gatherer is waiting for the yassak, which is now generally paid in money (five paper roubles=four shillings). With the remainder of his gains he purchases iron kettles, red cloth for hemming his garments, powder and shot, rye-meal, glass pearls, tobacco, and brandy—which, though forbidden to be sold publicly, is richly supplied to him in private—and then retires to his native wilds. From the smaller fairs, the furs are sent by the Russian merchants to the larger staple places, such as Jakutsk, Nertchinsk, Tobolsk, Kiachta, Irbit, Nishne-Nowgorod, and finally St. Petersburg and Moscow; for by repeatedly sorting, and matching the size and colour of the skins, their value is increased.

About thirty years ago, furs were still the chief export article of Siberia—to China, European Russia, and Western Europe—but since then the discovery of its rich auriferous deposits has made gold its most important produce. The precious metal is found on the western slopes of the Ural chain and in West Siberia; but the most productive diggings are situated in East Siberia, where they give occupation to many thousands of workmen, and riches to a few successful speculators.

The vast territory drained by the Upper Jenisei and its tributaries, the Superior and the Middle Tunguska, consists for the greater part of a dismal and swampy primeval forest, which scarcely thirty years since was almost totally unknown. A few wretched nomads and fur-hunters were the only inhabitants of the Taiga—as those sylvan deserts are called—and squirrel-skins seemed all they were ever likely to produce. A journey through the Taiga is said to be one of the most fatiguing and tedious tours which it is possible to make. Uphill and downhill, a narrow path leads over a swampy ground, into which the horses sink up to their knees. The rider is scarcely less harassed than the patient animal which carries him over this unstable soil. No bird enlivens the solitary forest with its song; the moaning of the wind in the crowns of the trees alone interrupts the gloomy silence. The eternal sameness of the scene—day after day one constant succession of everlasting larches and fir-trees—is as wearying to the mind as the almost impassable road to the body.

But suddenly the sound of the axe or the creaking of the waterwheel is heard; the forest opens, a long row of huts extends along the banks of a rivulet, and hundreds of workmen are seen moving about as industrious as a hive of bees. What is the cause of all this activity — of this sudden change from a deathlike quiet to a feverish life? These are the goldfields; the sands of these swampy grounds are

mixed, like those of the Pactolus, with gold, and their fortunate possessors would not exchange them for the finest
meadows, cornfields, or vineyards.

Fedor Popow, a hunter of the province of Tomsk, is said
to have been the first discoverer of gold in Siberia; and
Government having granted permission to private persons
to search for the precious metal, a few enterprising men
directed their attention to the wild spurs of the Sajan Mountains. A brilliant success rewarded their endeavours. In
the year 1836 an exploring party, sent out by a merchant
named Jakin Resanow, discovered a rich deposit of auriferous sand near the banks of the Great Birussa; and in
1839–40, similar deposits were found along several of the
tributaries of the Upper Tunguska, and still farther to the
north, on the Oktolyk, a rivulet that flows into the Pit.

The expenses of a searching party amount, on an average,
to 3,000 silver roubles (600l.), and as very often no gold
whatever is found, these hazardous explorations not seldom
put both the purse and the perseverance of their undertakers
to a severe trial. Thus Nikita Maesnikow had spent no less
than 260,000 silver roubles (52,000l.) in fruitless researches,
when he at length discovered the rich goldfield on the Peskin, which, as we shall presently see, amply remunerated him
for his previous losses.

Of the difficulties which await the gold-searchers, a faint
idea may be formed, on considering that the whole of the
auriferous region, which far surpasses in size most of the
European kingdoms, consists of one vast forest like that
above described. Patches of grass-land on which horses can
feed are of very rare occurrence, and damp moss is the only
bed the Taiga affords. As the gold-searchers are very often
at work some hundreds of versts from the nearest village,
they are obliged to carry all their provisions along with
them. Their clothes are almost constantly wet, from their
sleeping in the damp forest, from the frequent rains to which
they are exposed, and from their toiling in the swampy
ground. Scarcely have they dug a few feet deep when the
pit fills with water, which they are obliged to pump out as
fast as it gathers, and thus standing up to their knees in the
mud, they work on until they reach the solid rock, for then

only can they be certain that no auriferous layer has been neglected in their search. When we consider, moreover, that all this labour is very often totally useless, their perseverance cannot but be admired; nor is it to be wondered at that exploring parties have sometimes encamped on the site of rich gold-deposits without examining the spot, their patience having been exhausted by repeated failures in the vicinity. When the winter, with its deep snowfalls, suddenly breaks in upon the searchers, their hardships become dreadful. The frost and want of food kill their horses, their utensils have to be left behind; and dragging their most indispensable provisions along with them, on small sledges, they are not seldom obliged to wade for weeks through the deep snow before they reach some inhabited place.

But even the severity of a Siberian winter does not prevent the sending out of exploring parties. Such winter expeditions are only fitted out for the more accurate examination of *very* swampy auriferous grounds that have been discovered in the previous year, and where it is less difficult to work in the frozen soil than to contend with the water in summer. A winter-party travels without horses, the workmen themselves transporting all that they require on light sledges. They are obliged to break up the obdurate soil with pickaxes, and the sand thus loosened has to be thawed and washed in warm water. After their day's work, they spend the night in huts made of the branches of trees, where they sleep on the hard ground. It requires the iron constitution of a Siberian to bear such hardships, to which many fall a prey, in spite of their vigorous health.

A gold-deposit having been found, the fortunate discoverer obtains the grant of a lot of ground, 100 sashens (600 feet) broad, and 2,500 sashens (or 5 versts) long. Two adjoining lots are never granted to the same person, but a subsequent purchase or amalgamation is permitted. At first Government was satisfied with a moderate tax of 15 per cent. of the produce; subsequently, however, this was doubled until within the last few years, when, the gold production having been found to decrease, the primitive impost was returned to, or even reduced to 5 per cent. for the less productive mines. Besides this tax, from four to eight gold roubles per pound of gold, according to the richness of the diggings, have to be paid for police expenses. Only a twelve years' lease is granted, after which the digging reverts to the crown, and a new lease has to be purchased. As the severe climate of the Taiga limits the working-time to four months (from May to September), the period of the concession is thus in reality not more than four years.

The first care of the lessee is, of course, to collect the necessary provisions and working apparatus. The distant steppe of the Kirghese furnishes him with dried or salted meat; his iron utensils he purchases in the factories of the Ural; the fairs of Irbit and Nishne-Nowgorod supply him with every other article; and rye-meal and fishes he easily obtains from the Siberian peasants or traders. By water and by land, all these various stores have to be transported in summer to the *residence* or establishment of the gold-digger on the border of the Taiga. The transport through the Taiga itself takes place during the winter, on sledges, at a very great cost; and the expense is still more increased if time has been lost through inattention, as then all that may still be wanting has to be conveyed to the spot on the backs of horses.

Most of the men that are hired for working in the diggings are exiles—the remainder generally free peasants, who have been reduced in their circumstances by misfortunes or misconduct. The procuring of the necessary workmen is an affair of no small trouble and expense. Before every summer campaign the agents of the gold-diggers travel about the country like recruiting-sergeants, and after giving many fair words and some hand-money, they take the passport of the man engaged as a security for his appearance. But although a passport is an indispensable document in Siberia, yet it not seldom happens that the workman finds means to obtain a new one under some other name, and, engaging himself to a new master, defrauds the first of his hand-money.

It may easily be imagined that, as the workmen only consist of the refuse of society, the greatest discipline is necessary to keep them in order. The system of a secret police, so cherished by all arbitrary governments, is here extended

to its utmost limits; scarcely has a suspicious word fallen
among the workmen, when the director is immediately informed of it, and takes his measures accordingly. Every
man knows that he is watched, and is himself a spy upon his
companions.

Hofman relates an instance of a plot singularly nipped
in the bud. In one of the gold-diggings on the Noiba,
the workmen, at the instigation of an under-overseer, had
refused to perform a task assigned to them. It was to
be feared that the spirit of insubordination would gain
ground, and extend over all the neighbouring diggings. The
director, consequently, sent at once for military assistance;
this, however, proved to be unnecessary, for when the Cossacks arrived at the Noiba, a thunderstorm arose, and at
the very moment they came riding up to the digging, a flash
of lightning killed the ringleader in the midst of the mutineers. As soon as the men recovered from the first shock of
their surprise and terror, they all exclaimed, ' This is the
judgment of God!' and, without any further hesitation, at
once returned to their duty.

Besides free rations, the ordinary wages of a common
workman are 15 roubles banco, or 12 shillings a month, but
more experienced hands receive 50 or even 60 roubles. The
pay dates from the day when the workman makes his appearance at the residence, and thenceforward, also, his rations
are served out to him. They consist of a pound of fresh or
salt-meat, or an equivalent portion of fish on fasting-days,
cabbage and groats for soup, besides fresh rye-bread and
*quas* (the favourite national beverage) *ad libitum*. The
whole number of workmen employed in a gold-digging sub-
divide themselves into separate societies, or artells. Each of
these elects a chief, or headman, to whom the provisions for
his artell are weighed out, and to whom all the other common
interests are entrusted. The sale of spirituous liquor is
strictly forbidden, for its use would render it impossible to
maintain order; and, according to law, no gin-shop is allowed
to be opened within 60 versts of a digging.

The pay and the liberal rations received would alone be
insufficient to allure workmen to the diggings, for, as we
have seen, the voyage there and back is extremely irksome,
and the labour very fatiguing. An excellent plan has con-

sequently been devised for their encouragement. The contract of each workman distinctly specifies the quantity of his daily work, consisting of a certain number of wheelbarrows of sand—from 100 to 120, according to the distance of the spot where it is dug to the place where it is washed out—each reckoned at three pouds,* which one party has to fill, another to convey to the wash-stands, and a third to wash.

The task is generally completed by noon, or early in the afternoon. For the labour they perform during the rest of the day, or on Sundays and holidays, they receive an extra pay of two or three roubles for every solotnik of gold they wash. Every evening the workmen come with the produce of their free labour to the office, the gold is weighed in their presence, and the artell credited for the amount of its share. This free-work is as advantageous for the masters as the labourers. The former enjoy a net profit of eight or ten roubles per solotnik, and all the working expenses are of course put to the charge of the contract labour; and the latter earn a great deal of money, according to their industry or good-luck, for when fortune favours an artell, its share may amount to a considerable sum. During Hofman's stay at the Birussa, each workman of a certain artell earned in one afternoon 72 roubles, and the Sunday's work of another of these associations gave to each of its members 105 roubles, or 4l. The artisans—who, though employed in a gold-mine, are not engaged in digging or washing the auriferous sand—are also rewarded from time to time by a day's free-labour in places which are known to be rich. On one of these occasions a Cossack on the Oktolyk received 300 roubles for his share of the gold that was washed out of 49 wheelbarrows of sand. These of course are extraordinary cases, but they show how much a workman *may* gain; and being of course exaggerated by report, are the chief inducements which attract the workmen, and keep them to their duty.

If the free-labour is unproductive, many of the workmen desert or give up free-labour altogether, and in both cases the master is a loser. To prevent this, it is customary, in many of the diggings, to pay the workmen a fixed sum for their extra work.

---

* The poud is equal to 40 pounds. The poud is divided into 96 solotniks.

At the end of the season the workmen are paid off, and receive provisions for their home-journey. Generally, the produce of their summer's labour is spent, in the first villages they reach, in drinking and gambling; so that, to be able to return to their families, they are obliged to bind themselves anew for the next season, and to receive hand-money from the agent, who, knowing their weakness, is generally on the spot to take advantage of it. After spending a long winter full of want and privations, they return to the Taiga in spring, and thus, through their own folly, their life is spent in constant misery and hard labour.

During the winter the digging is deserted, except by an under-overseer and a few workmen, who make the necessary preparations for the next campaign, receive and warehouse the provisions as they arrive, and guard the property against thieves or wanton destruction. The upper-overseer or director, meanwhile, is fully occupied at the residence, in forwarding the provisions and stores that have arrived there during the summer to the mine, in making the necessary purchases for the next year, in sending his agents about the country to engage new workmen; and thus the winter is, in fact, his busiest time. With the last sledge transport he returns to the digging, to receive the workmen as they arrive, and to see that all is ready for the summer. As his situation is one of great trust and responsibility, he enjoys a considerable salary. Maesnikow, for instance, paid his chief director 40,000 roubles a year; and 6,000 or 8,000 roubles, besides free station, and a percentage of the gold produced, is the ordinary emolument.

It is thus evident that the expenses of a Siberian gold-mine are enormous, but when fortune favours the undertaker he is amply rewarded for his outlay; an annual produce of 10, 15, or 20 pouds of gold is by no means uncommon. In the year 1845, 458 workmen employed in the gold-mine of Mariinsk, belonging to Messrs. Golubdow and Kusnezow, produced 81 pouds 19½ lbs. of the much-coveted metal; in the year 1843 the mine of Olginsk, belonging to Lieutenant Malewinsky, yielded 82 pouds 37¼ lbs.; and in 1844, the labour of 1,014 workmen, employed in the mine of Kresdowosdwishensk, belonging to Messrs. Kusnezow and Schtschegolow, produced no less than 87 pouds 14 lbs. of gold.

But even Kresdowosdwishensk has been distanced by the mine of Spasky, situated near the sources of the Peskin, which, in the year 1842, yielded its fortunate possessor, the above-mentioned Counsellor Nikita Maesnikow (one of the few men who were already extremely rich before the Siberian auriferous deposits were discovered), the enormous quantity of 100 pouds of gold! From 1840 to 1845, Maesnikow extracted from this mine no less than 348 pouds 6 lbs. of gold, worth 4,135,174 silver roubles, or about 640,000l. Still more recently, in 1860, the Gawrilow mine, belonging to the house of Rjasanow, produced 102½ pouds of pure gold.

But in Siberia, as elsewhere, mining operations are frequently doomed to end in disappointment, particularly if the space destined to be worked in the following summer has not been carefully examined beforehand, as the ore is often very unequally distributed. A speculator, having discovered a gold-mine, examined four or five samples of the sand, which gave a highly satisfactory result. Delighted with his good fortune, he made his arrangements on a grand scale, and collected provisions for 500 workmen; but when operations began, it was found that he had, unfortunately, hit upon a small patch of auriferous sand, the vicinity of which was totally void of gold, so that his 500 workmen produced no more than a few pounds of ore, and he lost at least 10,000l. by his adventure.

The entire gold produce of East Siberia amounted, in 1845, to 848 pouds 36 lbs., and in 1856 to about 1,100 pouds; but latterly, in consequence of the increasing wages and dearness of provisions, which has caused many of the less productive mines to be abandoned, it has somewhat diminished. In 1860, 31,796 men, 919 women, and 8,751 horses and oxen, were employed in the Siberian gold-mines.

As may easily be imagined, the discovery of these sources of wealth in the desert has caused a great revolution in the social state of Siberia. The riches so suddenly acquired by a few favourites of fortune, have raised luxury to an unexampled height, and encouraged a senseless prodigality. Some *sterlets* * having been offered for 300 roubles to a miner

---

* A species of sturgeon highly esteemed by epicures.

suddenly raised from penury to wealth, 'Fool!' said the
upstart, with the superb mien of a conquering hero, to the
fish-dealer, 'wilt thou sell me these excellent sterlets so
cheap? Here are a thousand roubles; go, and say that thou
hast dealt with *me!*'

The small town of Krasnojarsk, romantically situated on
the Jenisei, is the chief seat of the rich miners.  Here may
be seen the choicest toilettes, the most showy equipages,
and champagne (which in Siberia costs at least 1*l.* a bottle)
is the daily beverage of the gold aristocracy.  Unfortunately, Krasnojarsk had, until very recently, not a single
bookseller's shop to boast of; and while thousands were
lavished on vanity and sensual enjoyments, not a rouble was
devoted to the improvement of the mind.

Less rich in gold than the province of Jeniseisk, but
richer in copper and iron, and above all in platina, is the
Ural, where mining industry was first introduced, by Peter
the Great, in the last years of the seventeenth century, and
has since acquired a colossal development.  Though gold
was discovered in the Uralian province of Permia as early as
1745, yet its production on a large scale is of more modern
date.  In the year 1816, the whole quantity of gold furnished
by the Ural amounted only to 5 pouds 35 lbs., while in 1834 it
had increased to 405 pouds.

The discovery of the precious metals on the estates of the
large mine-proprietors of the Ural, who already before that
time were among the wealthiest men of the empire, has increased their riches to an enormous extent, and given an
European celebrity to the names of Jakowlew and Demidoff.
Werch Issetsk and Werchne Tagilsk, in the province of
Permia, belonging to the Jakowlew family, have an extent of
more than three millions of acres, with a population of
11,000 souls.  Besides iron and copper, their chief produce,
these estates yielded, in 1834, 58 pouds of gold.

Nishne-Tagilsk, belonging, since 1725, to the Demidoffs,
is a still more magnificent possession; for it may truly be
said, that perhaps nowhere in the world are greater mineral riches congregated in one spot than here, where,
besides vast quantities of iron and copper, the washing of
the sands produced, in 1834, no less than 29 pouds of gold,

and 113 pouds 3 lbs. of platina. The estate extends over four millions of acres, and its population, in 1834, amounted to 20,000 souls.

The town of Nishne-Tagilsk has about 15,000 inhabitants, and Helmersen ('Travels in the Ural') praises the Demidoffs for their zeal in carrying the civilisation of Europe to the wilds of the Ural. In an excellent elementary school, 150 boys are clothed, fed, and educated at their expense. Those pupils who distinguish themselves by their abilities are then sent to a higher school, such as the Demidoff Lyceum in Jaroslaw, or the University of Moscow, and after the termination of their studies obtain a situation on the estates of the family. The palace of the Demidoffs has a fine collection of paintings by the first Italian masters; but it is seldom if ever inhabited by the proprietors, who prefer Florence. Paris to the Ural. The founder of the family was an eminent gunsmith of the town of Tula, whose abilities gained him the favour of Peter the Great, and the gift of the mines on which the colossal fortune of his descendants has been raised.

The Sea-Otter.

Group of Russian Sledges.

# CHAPTER XVIII.

### MIDDENDORFF'S ADVENTURES IN TAIMURLAND.

For what Purpose was Middendorff's Voyage to Taimurland undertaken?—Difficulties and Obstacles—Expedition down the Taimur River to the Polar Sea—Storm on Taimur Lake—Loss of the Boat—Middendorff ill and alone in 75° N. Lat.—Saved by a grateful Samojede—Climate and Vegetation of Taimurland.

ON following the contours of the Siberian coast, we find, to the east of Novaya Zemlya, a vast tract of territory projecting towards the Pole, and extending its promontories far into the Icy sea. This country—which, from its principal river, may be called Taimurland—is the most northern, and, I need hardly add, the most inhospitable part of the Old World. The last huts of the Russian fishermen are situated about the mouth of the Jenisei, but the whole territory of the Taimur river, and the regions traversed by the lower course of the Chatanga and the Päsina, are completely uninbited.

Even along the upper course of these two last-named rivers,

the population is exceedingly scanty and scattered; and the few Samojedes who migrate during the summer to the banks of the Taimur, gladly leave them at the approach of winter, the cold of which no thermometer has ever measured. As may easily be imagined, Taimurland has but few attractions for the trader or the fur-hunter, but for the naturalist it is by no means without interest.

We have seen in a former chapter how Von Baer, prompted by the disinterested love of science, travelled to Novaya Zemlya, to examine the productions of a *cold insular* summer, beyond the 70th degree of latitude. The instructive results of his journey rendered it doubly desirable to obtain information about the effects of summer in a *continental* climate, situated if possible still farther to the north; and as no region could be better suited to this purpose than the interior of the broad mass of Taimurland, the Academy of Sciences of St. Petersburg resolved to send thither a scientific expedition. Fortunately for the success of the undertaking, Von Middendorff, the eminent naturalist, whose offer of service was gladly accepted, was in every respect the right man in the right place; for to the most untiring scientific zeal, and an unwavering determination, he joined a physical strength and a manual dexterity rarely found united with learning. In the Lapland moors he had learned to bivouac for nights together, while chasing the waterfowl, and on foot he was able to tire the best-trained walrus-hunter. He understood how to construct a boat, and to steer it with his own hand, and every beast or bird was doomed that came within reach of his unerring ball. In one word, no traveller ever plunged into the Arctic wilds more independent of baggage, followers, or the means of transport.

On April 4 we find Middendorff, accompanied by Mr. Brandt, a Danish forester, and a single servant, on the ice of the Jenisei between Turuchansk and Dudino. Here his companions were attacked by measles; but as it was high time to reach the Chatanga before the melting of the snow, the patients were carefully packed up in boxes lined with skins, and the whole party—whose numbers, meanwhile, had been increased by the addition of a topographer and of three Cossacks—emerged from the region of forests on April 13, having to face a cold of −36°, and a storm that almost overturned their sledges. With Tunguse guides they traversed the tundra in a north-easterly direction as far as the Päsina, and thence passing on from one Samojede horde to another, at length reached Koronnoje Filippowskoj (71° 5′ lat.) on the Boganida, an affluent of the Cheta, which is itself a tributary of the Chatanga. Here a halt was made, partly because all the party except Middendorff were by this time attacked with the reigning epidemic, and partly to wait for the Samojedes, whom they intended to join on their summer migration to the north. During this interval Middendorff made an excursion to the Chatanga, for the purpose of gathering information about the voyage down that river, and to make the necessary preparations. In the village of Chatangsk, however, he found nearly all the inhabitants suffering from the measles, and as no assistance was to be expected from them, he resolved to alter his route, and to proceed as soon as possible to the river Taimur, which would in all probability afford him the best means for penetrating to the extreme confines of continental Asia. As this most *northerly* river of the old world lies far beyond the boundaries of arboreal growth, a boat frame of twelve feet on the keel had to be made at Koronnoje before setting out. Brandt was left behind, with part of the company, to make a prolonged series of meteorological observations, and to gather as complete a collection as possible of the animals and plants of the country, while Middendorff started on his adventurous tour (May 19), with sixty-eight reindeer, under the guidance of a few Samojedes on their progress to the north, and accompanied only by the topographer, an interpreter, and two Cossacks. The difficulties of this journey, since a boat-frame, fuel, provisions, physical instruments, apparatuses for the preservation of objects of natural history, forming altogether a load for many sledges, had to be transported along with the travellers, would have been great at all times, but were now considerably increased by the epidemic having also seized the tribe of Samojedes which Middendorff expected to find near the small river Nowaja, and which was to guide him farther on to the Taimur. At length, after a search of three days, he found the remnant of the horde, which had been decimated and reduced to a deplorable condition by the epidemic. In vain he sought for the well-known faces of the chief personages of the horde, with whom he had negotiated on the Boganida—'they were all dead.' Of thirty-five persons, one only was completely healthy; a second could hardly crawl about; but the others lay prostrate in their tents, coughing and groaning under their skin coverings. Leaving seven corpses on the road, they had advanced by slow journeys to join Middendorff, until they broke down, so that, instead of receiving aid at their hands, he was now obliged to help them in their distress--- an assistance which they amply repaid, as we shall see in the sequel.

Unfortunately the illness had prevented the Samojede women from sewing together, as they had promised, the skins that were necessary to complete the covering of the travellers' tent, so that they had much to suffer during a violent snow-storm, which raged from May 27 to 30. Thus after another long delay and an irreparable loss of time, considering the extreme shortness of the summer, Middendorff was not able to start from the Nowaja before May 31. The softening of the snow rendered the advance of the sledges extremely difficult, so that it was not before June 14 that he reached the Taimur at a considerable distance above the point where the river discharges its waters into the lake. Encamping on a steep declivity of its bank, Middendorff now set about building his boat. On June 30, the ice on the river began to break up, and on July 5, the navigation of the stream was free. By the light of the midnight sun the boat was launched, and christened 'The Tundra,' to commemorate the difficulties of its construction in the deserts of 74° N. lat. Constant north winds retarded the voyage down the river and over the lake, beyond which the Taimur, traversing a hilly country, is enclosed within steep and picturesque rocks. The increasing rapidity of the stream now favoured the travellers, and the storms were less troublesome between the mighty rock-walls; but unfortunately Middendorff, instead of being able, as he had expected, to fill his nets with fish as he advanced, and to establish depôts for his return journey, found himself obliged to consume the provisions he

had taken with him in the boat. On August 6, the first
night frost took place, and from that time was regularly
repeated. Yet in spite of these warnings, Middendorff
continued his journey down the river, and reached the sea
on August 24, in 76° N. lat. But now it was high time to
return.

'The fear of leaving my undertaking half unfinished,'
says Middendorff, 'had hitherto encouraged me to persevere. The great distance from any human habitation, the
rapid stream, against which we had now to contend, and the
advanced season, with its approaching dark nights and
frosts, made our return an imperative necessity, and I could
have but little reliance on our remaining strength. The
insufficient food and the fatigues of our journey, often
prolonged to extreme exhaustion, had reduced our vigour,
and we all began to feel the effects of our frequent wading
through cold water, when, as often happened, our boat had
grounded upon a shallow, or when the flat mud banks of the
river gave us no other alternative for reaching the dry land.
It was now also the second month since we had not slept under
a tent, having all the time passed the nights behind a screen
erected on the oars of the boat, as a shelter against the wind.
Provided with a good load of drift-wood, collected on the
shore of the Polar Ocean, we began our return voyage on
August 26. The borders of the river were already encrusted
with ice. Wading became extremely irksome, the river
having meanwhile fallen above six feet, and the shallows
frequently forcing us to step into the water, and pull the
boat along.

'Fortunately the wind remained favourable, and thus by
rowing to the utmost of our strength, and with the assistance
of the broad sails of our "Tundra," we surmounted two rapids
which, encased between abrupt rocks, seemed to defy our utmost efforts.

'On the 31st, a malicious gust of wind, bursting out of a
narrow gorge, threw our boat against the rocks and broke the
rudder. The frost and wet, together with the shortness of
our provisions, tried us sorely. Not a day passed without
sleet and snow.

'On September 5, while endeavouring to double during a

violent storm a rocky island at the northern extremity of
Lake Taimur, one wave after another dashed into the boat,
which I could only save by letting her run upon a sand-bank.
The violent wind, with a temperature of only $+27°$ at noon,
covered our clothes with solid ice-crusts. We were obliged
to halt four days till the storm ceased; our nets and my double-
barrelled gun proved daily more and more unsuccessful, so that
hunger combined with cold to render our situation almost intolerable. On the 8th, while on the look-out for ptarmigan,
I saw through my telescope a long stripe of silver stretching
over the lake, and returning to my comrades informed them
that we must absolutely set off again the next morning, regardless of wind and weather.

'On the following day the ominous indications of the telescope rendered it necessary to approach the more open
west side of the lake; which I followed until stopped by the
ice, along whose borders I then sailed in order to reach the
river, which must still be open. Meanwhile the wind had
completely fallen, and to our astonishment we saw the water
in our wake cover itself with a thin crust of ice as soon as
we passed. The danger of freezing fast in the middle of the
lake was evident.'

Unfortunately, while endeavouring to reach the river, the
boat was crushed between two ice floes, and was with great
difficulty dragged on shore. The only chance of rescue now
was to meet with some Samojedes on the upper course of
the river, for these nomads never wander northwards beyond the southern extremity of the lake, and from this our
travellers were still at a great distance.

'We made a large hand-sledge,' continues Middendorff, 'and
set off without loss of time on the 10th, in spite of the rainy
weather, which had completely dissolved the sparing snow
upon the hills. The sharp stones cut into our sledge-runners
like knives, and after having scarcely made three versts, the
vehicle fell to pieces. The bad weather forced us to stop for
the night. The fatigues of our boat journey, the want of
proper food, and mental anxiety, had for several weeks been
undermining my health: a total want of sleep destroyed
the remainder of my strength, so that, early on the 11th, I
felt myself quite unable to proceed.'

In this extremity Middendorff adopted with heroic self-
denial the best and only means for his own preservation and
that of his comrades.  If, by departing without loss of time,
they were fortunate enough to reach the Samojedes before
these nomads had left the Taimur country for the south, he
also might be rescued; if they found them very late, they
at least might expect to save their lives; if the Samojedes
could not be found, then, of course, the whole party was
doomed.  Thus Middendorff resolved to separate at once
from his comrades.  A remnant of flesh extract, reserved for
extreme cases, was divided into five equal portions; the
naturalist's dog, the faithful companion of all his previous
journeys, was killed, though reduced to a mere skeleton, and
his scanty flesh similarly distributed among the party.  The
blood and a soup made of the bones served for the parting
repast.  Thus of his own free will, the winter having already
set in, Middendorff, ill and exhausted, remained quite alone
in the icy desert, behind a sheltering rock, in 75° N. lat.,
several hundred versts from all human dwellings, almost
without fuel, and with a miserable supply of food.  The
three first days he was still able to move.  He saw the lake
cover itself completely with ice, and the last birds depart for
the south.  Then his strength utterly failed him, and for the
next three days he was unable to stir.  When he was again
able to move, he felt an excessive thirst.  He crawled to the
lake, broke the ice, and the water refreshed him.  But he was
not yet free from disease, and this was fortunate, as want of
appetite did not make him feel the necessity of food.  Now
followed a succession of terrible snow-storms, which completely imprisoned the solitary traveller, but at the same time
afforded him a better shelter against the wind.

'My companions,' he writes in a letter to a relation, 'had
now left me twelve days; human assistance could no longer
be expected; I was convinced that I had only myself to rely
upon, that I was doomed, and as good as numbered with the
dead.  And yet my courage did not forsake me.  Like our
squirrels, I turned myself according to the changes of the
wind.  During the long sleepless nights fancy opened her
domains, and I forgot even hunger and thirst.  Then Boreas
broke roaring out of the gullies as if he intended to sweep

me away into the skies, and in a short time I was covered
with a comfortable snow-mantle. Thus I lay three days,
thinking of wretches who had been immured alive, and
grown mad in their dreadful prison. An overwhelming
fear of insanity befell me—it oppressed my heart—it became
insupportable. In vain I attempted to cast it off—my
weakened brain could grasp no other idea. And now suddenly—like a ray of light from heaven—the saving thought
flashed upon me.

' My last pieces of wood were quickly lighted—some water
was thawed and warmed—I poured into it the spirits from a
flask containing a specimen of natural history, and drank.
A new life seemed to awaken in me; my thoughts returned
again to my family, to the happy days I had spent with the
friends of my youth. Soon I fell into a profound sleep—
how long it lasted I know not—but on awakening I felt like
another man, and my breast was filled with gratitude. Appetite returned with recovery, and I was reduced to eat
leather and birch-bark—when a ptarmigan fortunately came
within reach of my gun. Having thus obtained some food
for the journey, I resolved, although still very feeble, to set
out and seek the provisions we had buried. Packing some
articles of dress, my gun and ammunition, my journal, &c.,
on my small hand sledge, I proceeded slowly, and frequently
resting. At noon I saw, on a well-known declivity of the hills,
three black spots which I had not previously noticed, and as
they changed their position, I at once altered my route to
join them. We approached each other—and, judge of my
delight, it was Trischun, the Samojede chieftain, whom I
had previously assisted in the prevailing epidemic, and who
now, guided by one of my companions, had set out with
three sledges to seek me. Eager to serve his benefactor, the
grateful savage had made his reindeer wander without food
over a space of 150 versts where no moss grew.

' I now heard that my companions had fortunately reached
the Samojedes, four days after our separation; but the
dreadful snow storms had prevented the nomads from
coming sooner to my assistance, and had even forced them
twice to retrace their steps.

' On September 30, the Samojedes brought me to my tent

and, on October 9, we bade the Taimur an eternal farewell. After five months we hailed with delight, on October 20, the verge of the forest, and on the following day we reached the smoky hut on the Boganida where we had left our friends.'

Having thus accompanied Middendorff on his adventurous wanderings through Taimuria, I will now give a brief account of his observations on the climate and natural productions of this northern land.

The remark of Saussure that the difference of temperature between light and shade is greatest in summer, and in the high latitudes, was fully confirmed by Middendorff. While the thermometer marked $-37°$ in the shade, the hill sides exposed to the sun were dripping with wet, and towards the end of June, though the mean temperature of the air was still below the freezing point of water, the snow had already entirely disappeared on the sunny side of the Taimur river. Torrents came brawling down the hills; the swollen rivers rose forty or sixty feet above their winter level, and carried their icy covering along with them to the sea.

On August 3, in the very middle of the short Taimurian summer in $74° 15'$ of latitude, Middendorff hunted butterflies under the shelter of a hill, bare-footed and in light under-clothes. The thermometer rose in the sun to $+68°$, and close to the ground to $+86°$, while at a short distance on a spot exposed to the north-eastern air-current, it fell at once to $+27°$.

The moisture of the air was very remarkable. In May thick snow fogs almost perpetually obscured the atmosphere, so that it was impossible to ascertain the position of the sun. It appeared only in the evening, or about midnight, and then regularly a perpendicular column of luminous whiteness descended from its orb to the earth, and, widening as it approached the horizon, took the form and the appearance of a colossal lamp flame, such as the latter appears when seen through the mists of a vapour bath. From the same cause parhelia and halos were very frequent.

During the daytime the snow fogs, in perpetual motion, either entirely veiled the nearest objects, or magnified their size, or exhibited them in a dancing motion. In June, the snow-fog became a vapour-fog, which daily from time to time precipitated its surplus of moisture in form of a light rain, but even then the nights, particularly after eleven o'clock, were mostly serene.

Experience proved contrary to Arago's opinion that thunderstorms take place within the Arctic zone. The perpetual motion of the air was very remarkable. The sun had merely to disappear behind a cloud, to produce at once a gust of wind. Towards the end of August, the southern and the northern air-currents, like two contending giants, began to strive for the mastery, until finally the storms raged with extreme violence. But in these treeless deserts their fury finds nothing to destroy.

It is impossible to form anything like a correct estimate of the quantity of snow which annually falls in the highest latitudes. So much is certain that it cannot be small, to judge by the violence and swelling of the rivers in spring. The summits of the hills, and the declivities exposed to the reigning winds, are constantly deprived of snow, which, however, fills up the bottom of the valleys to a considerable height. Great was Middendorff's astonishment, while travelling over the tundra at the end of winter, to find it covered with no more than two inches, or at the very utmost half a foot, of snow; the dried stems of the Arctic plants everywhere peeping forth above its surface. This was the natural consequence of the north-easterly storms, which, sweeping over the naked plain, carry the snow along with them, and form the snow-waves, the compass of the northern nomads.

It is extremely probable that, on advancing towards the pole, the fall of snow gradually diminishes, as in the Alps, where its quantity likewise decreases on ascending above a certain height.

On measuring the thickness of the ice, Middendorff was very much surprised to find it nowhere, both in the lakes and on the river, thicker than eight feet, and sometimes only four and a half; its thickness being constantly proportionate to the quantity of snow with which it was covered. At first he could hardly believe that this simple covering could afford so efficacious a protection against the extreme

cold of winter in the 74th degree of latitude, but the fact is
well known to the Samojedes, who, whenever they require
water, always make the hole where the snow lies deepest.

The tundras of Taimuria were found to consist principally
of arid plateaux and undulating heights, where the vegetation
cannot conceal the boulders and the sand of which the crust
of the earth is formed.

The withered tips of the grasses scarcely differ in colour
from the dirty yellow-brown moss, and the green of the
lower part of the stalks appears as through a veil. Nothing
can be of a more dreary monotony than this vegetation when
spread over a wide surface, but in the hardly perceptible
depressions of the plains where the spring water is able to
collect, a fresher green gains the upper hand, the stalks are
not only longer but stand closer together, and the grass,
growing to a height of three or even four inches, usurps the
place of the moss. Here and there small patches of *Dryas
octopetala*, or *Cassiope tetragona*, and much more rarely a
dwarf ranunculus, diversify the dingy carpet, yet without
being able to relieve its wearisome character. But very
different, and indeed truly surprising, is the aspect of the
slopes which, facing the Taimur lake or river, are protected
against the late and early frosts. Here considerable patches
of ground are covered with a lively green, intermingled with
gaily coloured flowers, such as the brilliant yellow Sieversia,
the elegant Oxytropis, the blue and white Saxifragas, the red
*Armeria alpina*, and a beautiful new species of Delphinium.
All these various flowers are not dwarfs of stunted growth,
for Polemones, Sisymbrias, Polygonums, and Papavers, above
a foot high, decorate the slopes, and Middendorff found an
islet in the Taimur covered like a field with a Senecio, of
which some of the most conspicuous specimens were more
than a foot and a half high, and bore no less than forty
flowers above an inch in diameter.

The progress of vegetation is uncommonly rapid, so that,
as Middendorff remarks, if any one wishes to see the grass
grow, he must travel to the Taimur. Scarcely do the first
leaves peep forth when the blossoms also appear, as if,
conscious of the early approach of autumn, they felt the

necessity of bringing their seeds to a rapid maturity under this wintry sky.

With regard to the animal creation, the general law of polar uniformity was fully confirmed in Taimur Land. The same lemmings were found which people the whole north of Asia and America, and as high as 75° N. lat. they found the traces of the snow-hare, which inhabits the complete circle of the Arctic regions of the globe. The Arctic fox, everywhere at home in the treeless wastes, is here also pursued by the northern glutton; and following the herds of the reindeer, the wolves, and the Samojedes, roams up and down the tundra. The ptarmigan, which in Scandinavia and on Melville Island feeds on berries and buds, appears also as a summer visitor at the mouth of the Taimur in 75° 4′ N. lat., and the ivory gull of the northern European seas likewise builds its nest on the rocks of that distant shore.

The more vigorous vegetation on the sheltered declivities of the Taimur provides food for a comparatively greater number of insects than is found on the coasts of Novaya Zemlya. Bees, hornets, and three different species of butterflies, buzzed or hovered round the flowers, and caterpillars could be gathered by dozens on the tundra, but their mortal enemies had pursued them even here; and ichneumon flies crept out of most of them. Two spiders, several flies, gnats, and tipulæ, a curculio, and half-a-dozen carabi completed Middendorff's entomological list, to which, no doubt, further researches would have considerably added.

Thus, at the northern extremity of Asia, as in every other part of the world, the naturalist finds the confirmation of the general law that, where the means of life are given, life is sure to come forth.

The Ivory Gull.

Jakuts.

# CHAPTER XIX.

### THE JAKUTS.

Their energetic Nationality—Their Descent—Their gloomy Character—Summer and Winter Dwellings—The Jakut Horse—Incredible Powers of Endurance of the Jakuts—Their Sharpness of Vision—Surprising local Memory—Their manual Dexterity—Leather, Poniards, Carpets—Jakut Gluttons—Superstitious Fear of the Mountain Spirit Ljeschei—Offerings of Horse-hair—Improvised Songs—The River Jakut.

THE Jakuts are a remarkably energetic race, for though subject to the Muscovite yoke, they not only successfully maintain their language and manners, but even impose their own tongue and customs upon the Russians who have settled in their country. Thus in Jakutsk, or the 'capital of the Jakuts,' as with not a little of national pride and self-complacency they style that dreary city, their language is much more frequently spoken than the Russian, for almost all the artisans are Jakuts, and even the rich fur-merchant has not seldom a Jakut wife, as no Russian now disdains an alliance with one of that nation.

At Amginskoje, an originally Russian settlement, Midden-dorff found the greatest difficulty in procuring a guide able to speak the Russian language, and all the Tunguse whom he met with between Jakutsk and Ochotsk understood and spoke Jakut, which is thus the dominant language from the basin of the Lena to the extreme eastern confines of Siberia. In truth, no Russian workmen can compete with the Jakuts, whose cunning, and effrontery would make it difficult even for a Jew to prosper among them.

Though of a Mongolian physiognomy, their language, which is said to be intelligible at Constantinople, distinctly points to a Turk extraction, and their traditions speak of their original seats as situated on the Baikal and Angora, whence, retreating before more powerful hordes, they advanced to the Lena, where in their turn they dispossessed the weaker tribes which they found in possession of the country. At present, their chief abode is along the banks of that immense river, which they occupy at least as far southward as the Aldan. Eastward they are found on the Kolyma, and westward as far as the Jenisei. Their total number amounts to about 200,000, and they form the chief part of the population of the vast but almost desert province of Jakutsk.

They are essentially a pastoral people, and their chief wealth consists in horses and cattle, though the northern portion of their nation is reduced to the reindeer and the dog. Besides the breeding of horses, the Russian fur-trade has developed an industrial form of the hunter's state, so that amongst the Jakuts property accumulates, and we have a higher civilisation than will be found elsewhere in the same latitude, Iceland, Finland, and Norway alone excepted. Of an unsocial and reserved disposition, they prefer a solitary settlement, but at the same time they are very hospitable, and give the stranger who claims their assistance a friendly welcome. Villages consisting of several huts, or *jurts*, are rare, and found only between Jakutsk and the Aldan, where the population is somewhat denser. Beyond the Werchojansk ridge, the solitary huts are frequently several hundred versts apart, so that the nearest neighbours sometimes do not see each other for years.

In summer the Jakut herdsmen live in 'Urossy,' light conical tents fixed on poles and covered with birch rind, and during this whole season they are perpetually employed in making hay for the long winter.

In 62° N. lat. and in a climate of an almost unparalleled severity, the rearing of their cattle causes them far more trouble than is the case with any other pastoral people. Their supply of hay is frequently exhausted before the end of the winter, and from March to May their oxen must generally be content with willow and birch twigs or saplings.

At the beginning of the cold season, the Jakut exchanges his summer tent for his warm winter residence, or *jurt*, a hut built of beams or logs, in the form of a truncated pyramid, and thickly covered with turf and clay. Plates of ice serve as windows, and are replaced by fishbladders or paper steeped in oil, as soon as the thaw begins. The earthen floor, for it is but rarely boarded, is generally sunk two or three feet below the surface of the ground. The seats and sleeping berths are ranged along the sides, and the centre is occupied by the *tschuwal*, or hearth, the smoke of which finds its exit through an aperture in the roof. Clothes and arms are suspended from the walls, and the whole premises exhibit a sad picture of disorder and filth. Near the jurt are stables for the cows, but when the cold is very severe, these useful animals are received into the family room. As for the horses, they remain night and day without a shelter, at a temperature when mercury freezes, and are obliged to feed on the withered autumnal grass, which they find under the snow. These creatures, whose powers of endurance are almost incredible, change their hair in summer like the other quadrupeds of the Arctic regions. They keep their strength, though travelling perhaps for months through the wilderness without any other food than the parched, half-rotten grass met with on the way. They retain their teeth to old age, and remain young much longer than our horses. 'He who thinks of improving the Jakut horse,' says Von Middendorff, 'aims at something like perfection. Fancy the worst conceivable roads, and for nourishment the bark of the larch and willow, with hard grass-stalks instead of oats; or merely travel on the post-road to Jakutsk, and see the horses that have just run forty versts without stopping, and are covered with perspiration and foam, eating their hay in the open air without the slightest covering, at a temperature of −40°.'

But the Jakut himself is no less hardened against the cold than his faithful horse. 'On December 9,' says Wrangell, 'we bivouacked round a fire, at a temperature of −28°, on an open pasture ground, which afforded no shelter against the northern blast. Here I had an excellent opportunity for admiring the unparalleled powers of endurance of our Jakut attendants. On the longest winter journey they take neither tents nor extra coverings along with them, not even one of the larger fur-dresses. While travelling, the Jakut contents himself with his usual dress; in this he generally sleeps in the open air; a horse rug stretched out upon the snow is his bed, a wooden saddle his pillow. With the same fur jacket which serves him by daytime as a dress, and which he pulls off when he lies down for the night, he decks his back and shoulders, while the front part of his body is turned towards the fire, almost without any covering. He then stops his nose and ears with small pieces of skin, and covers his face so as to leave but a small opening for breathing—these are all the precautions he takes against the severest cold. Even in Siberia the Jakuts are called "men of iron." Often have I seen them sleeping at a temperature of −4° in the open air, near an extinguished bivouac fire, and with a thick ice-rind covering their almost unprotected body.'

Most of the Jakuts have an incredible sharpness of vision. One of them told Lieutenant Anjou, pointing to the planet Jupiter, that he had often seen yonder blue star devour a smaller one, and then after a time cast it out again.* Their local memory is no less astonishing; a pool of water, a large stone, a solitary bush imprints itself deeply into their remembrance, and guides them after a lapse of years through the boundless wilderness. In manual dexterity they surpass all other Siberian nations, and some of their articles, such as their poniards and their leather, might figure with credit in any European exhibition. Long before the Russian con-

* Humboldt likewise mentions an artisan of Breslau whose sight was so sharp as to enable him to point out the position of Jupiter's satellites.

quest they made use of the iron ore on the Wilui to manufacture their own knives and axes, which, either from the
excellence of the material or of the workmanship, rarely
break, even in the severest cold—a perfection which the
best Sheffield ware does not attain.  Since time immemorial
they have been acquainted with the art of striking fire with
flint and steel, an invention unknown even to the ancient
Greeks and Romans.  Their leather is perfectly water-tight,
and the women make carpets of white and coloured skins
which are even exported to Europe.  It is almost superfluous to mention that a people so capable of bearing hardships, so sharp-witted and so eager for gain, as the Jakuts,
must needs pursue the fur-bearing animals with which their
forests abound with untiring zeal and a wonderful dexterity.

The horse renders the Jakut services not less important
than those of the reindeer to the Samojede or the Lapp.
Besides using it for carrying or riding, the Jakut makes
articles of dress out of its skin, and fishing-nets of its hair;
boiled horse meat is his favourite food, and sour mare's milk,
or *kumyss*, his chief beverage.  Of the latter he also makes a
thick porridge, or *salamat*, by mixing it with rye flour, or the
inner rind of the larch or fir-tree, to which he frequently
adds dried fish and berries, and, to render it perfect, a quantity of rancid fat, of which he is immoderately fond.  He is
in fact a gross feeder, and some professional gluttons are
capable of consuming such astonishing masses as to shame
the appetite even of an Esquimaux.  During his stay at
Jakutsk, Sir George Simpson put the abilities of two distinguished artists to the test, by setting two pouds of boiled
beef and a poud of melted butter before them.  Each of them
got a poud of meat for his share; the butter they were allowed
to ladle out and drink ad libitum.  The one was old and
experienced, the other young and full of zeal.  At first the
latter had the advantage.  'His teeth are good,' said the
elder champion, 'but with the assistance of my saint (crossing
himself), I will soon come up to him.'

When about half of their task was finished, Sir George
left his noble guests to the care and inspection of his secretary, but when he returned a few hours after, he was informed
that all was consumed, while the champions, stretched out on

the floor, confirmed the secretary's report, and expressed their thanks for the exorbitant meal they had enjoyed by respectfully kissing the ground. After one of these disgusting feats, the gorged gluttons generally remain for three or four days plunged in a torpid state like boa snakes, without eating or drinking, and are frequently rolled about on the ground to promote digestion. It may also be noticed, as a proof of the low state of intellectual culture among the Jakuts, that at every wedding among the richer class two professed virtuosi in the art of gormandizing are regularly invited for the entertainment of the guests. One of them is treated at the bridegroom's expense, the other at that of the bride, and the party whose champion gains the victory considers it as a good omen for the future.

The Jakuts, besides being a pre-eminently pastoral people, are also the universal carriers to the east of the Lena. For beyond Jakutsk, the only roads are narrow paths leading through swamps, dense forests, or tangled bushes, so that the horse affords the only means of reaching the more even and lower countries where reindeer or dogs can be attached to sledges. Without the Jakut and his horse, the Russian would never have been able to penetrate to the sea of Ochotsk, and from thence to the Aleutian chain; but for him, they never would have settled on the Kolyma, nor have opened a commercial intercourse with the Tchuktchi and the western Esquimaux.

Before the possession of the Amur had opened a new road to commerce, thousands of pack-horses used annually to cross the Stanowoi hills on the way to Ochotsk; and when we consider the dreadful hardships of the journey, we cannot wonder that the road was more thickly strewn with the skeletons of fallen horses than the caravan routes through the desert with the bones of famished camels. But the Jakut fears neither the icy cold of the bivouac nor the pangs of hunger, which, in spite of his wolfish voracity, he is able to support with stoical fortitude. He fears neither the storm on the naked hill, nor the gloom of the forest, nor the depth of the morass; and, bidding defiance to everything else, fears only the invisible power of 'Ljeschei,' the spirit of the mountain and the wood. The traveller wonders when he sees on an eminence crowned with firs, an old tree from whose branches hang bunches of horse-hair. The Jakut who leads the caravan soon explains the mystery. He dismounts, and plucking a few hairs from the mane of his horse, attaches them with a great show of respect to a branch, as an offering to propitiate the favour of Ljeschei on the journey. Even those Jakuts who pass for Christians, still pay this mark of respect to the dethroned divinity of their fathers; and there can be no doubt that they still retain the old belief in Schamanism, and an abject fear of all sorts of evil spirits.

While travelling they sing almost perpetually melancholy tunes, corresponding with the habitual gloom of their national character. The text has more variety and poetry, and generally celebrates the beauties of nature, the stately growth of the pine, the murmuring of the brook, or the grandeur of the mountain. The singers are mostly improvisators, and to conciliate the favour of Ljeschei, they praise the desert through which they pass, as if it were a paradise.

Like the impoverished Samojede or Lapp, the indigent Jakut, who possesses neither cattle nor horses, settles near some stream. His only domestic animal is his dog, who carries the fish on a light sledge from the river bank to his hut, or follows him into the woods on his hunting expeditions. With the skins of fur-bearing animals he pays his Jassak, and is glad if the surplus allows him to indulge from time to time in the luxury of a pipe of Circassian tobacco.

The Whistling Swan.

Russian Dog-sledge.

## CHAPTER XX.

### WRANGELL.

His distinguished Services as an Arctic Explorer—From Petersburgh to Jakutsk
in 1820—Trade of Jakutsk—From Jakutsk to Nishne Kolymsk—The Badarany—Dreadful Climate of Nishne Kolymsk—Summer Plagues—Vegetation—
Animal Life—Reindeer Hunting—Famine—Inundations—The Siberian Dog—
First Journeys over the Ice of the Polar Sea, and Exploration of the Coast
beyond Cape Shelagskoi in 1821—Dreadful Dangers and Hardships—Matiuschkin's Sledge Journey over the Polar Sea in 1822—Last Adventures on the Polar
Sea—A Run for Life—Return to St. Petersburgh.

THE expeditions which had been sent out during the
reign of the Empress Anna for the exploration of the
Arctic shores of eastern Siberia, had performed their task
so badly, as to leave them still almost totally unknown.
To fill up this blank in geography, the Emperor Alexander
ordered two new expeditions to be fitted out in 1820, for the
purpose of accurately ascertaining the limits of these extreme frontiers of his immense empire. Of the one which,
under Lieutenant Anjou, commenced its operations from the
mouth of the Jana, and comprised within its range New
Siberia and the other islands of the Lächow group, but

little has been communicated to the public, all his papers
having been accidentally burnt; but the travels of Lieutenant
von Wrangell, the commander of the second expedition,
have obtained a world-wide celebrity.  Starting from the
mouths of the Kolyma, he not only rectified the errors of
the coast-line of Siberia, from the Indigirka in the west to
Koliutschin Island in the east, but more than once ventured
in a sledge upon the Polar Ocean, in the hopes of discovering
a large country supposed to be situated to the northward of
Kotelnoi and New Siberia.

Wrangell left St. Petersburg on March 23, 1820, and
experiencing in his journey of 3,500 miles repeated alter-
nations of spring and winter, arrived at Irkutsk, where the
gardens were in full flower, on May 20.

After a month's rest, a short journey brought him to the
banks of the Lena, on which he embarked on June 27, to
descend to Jakutsk, which he reached on July 27.  This
small town of 4,000 inhabitants bears the gloomy stamp of
the frigid north, for though it has a few good houses, its
dwellings chiefly consist of the winter jurts of the Jakuts,
with turf-covered roofs, doors of skins, and windows of talc
or ice.  The only 'sight' of this dreary place is the old
ruinous ostrog or wooden fort built by the Cossacks, the conquerors of the country, in 1647.  Jakutsk is the centre of
the interior trade of Siberia.  To this place are brought, in
enormous quantities, furs of all kinds, walrus teeth and
mammoth tusks, from distances of many thousand versts, to
an amount of half a million of pounds.

The commercial sphere of the Jakutsk merchants is of
an immense extent.  During a cold of ten and twenty
degrees they set out for the Lächow Isles, for the fair of
Ostrownoje, for Ochotsk, or Kjachta.  Jakutsk merchants
were the first who ventured in crazy ships across the sea of
Kamtschatka, and discovered the island of Kadjiak, eighty
degrees of longitude from their home.

On September 12, Wrangell left Jakutsk, where regular
travelling ends, as from thence to Kolymsk, and generally
throughout Northern Siberia, there are no beaten roads.
The utmost that can be looked for are foot or horse-tracks
leading through morasses or tangled forests, and over rocks

and mountains. Travellers proceed on horseback through the hilly country, and on reaching the plains, use sledges drawn either by reindeer or dogs.

In this manner Wrangell crossed from the basin of the Lena to that of the Yana, never experiencing a higher temperature than $+2°$, and frequently enduring a cold of more than $-12°$, during the journey over the intervening hills, and then turning eastward, traversed the Badarany, a completely uninhabited desert, chiefly consisting of swamps. These Badarany never entirely dry up, even after the longest summer-drought. At that time a solid crust is formed, through which the horses frequently break, but they are preserved from totally sinking in the mire, by the perpetually frozen underground. Nothing can be more dismal and dreary than the Badarany. As far as the eye reaches, nothing is to be seen but a covering of dingy moss, relieved here and there on some more elevated spots by wretched specimens of dwarf-larches. The winter is the only season for traversing this treacherous waste, but woe to the traveller should he be overtaken by a snow-storm, as for miles and miles there is no shelter to be found but that of some ruinous powarni, or post-station.

At length, fifty-two days after leaving Jakutsk, Wrangell arrived on November 2 at Nishne Kolymsk, the appointed head-quarters of the expedition, where he was welcomed with a cold of $-40°$, or $72°$ below the freezing point of water.

Even in Siberia the climate of this place is ill-reputed for its severity, which is as much due to its unfavourable position as to its high latitude ($68°$ N.). The town stands on a low swampy island of the Kolyma, having on the west the barren tundra, and on the north the Arctic Ocean, so that the almost constant north-west winds have full scope for their violence, and cause frequent snow-storms even in summer.

The mean temperature of the whole year is only $+14°$. The river at Nishne Kolymsk freezes early in September, but lower down, where the current is less rapid, loaded horses can sometimes cross on the ice as early as August 20, nor does the ice ever melt before June.

Although the sun remains fifty-two days above the horizon, the light, obscured by almost perpetual mists, is accompanied with little heat, and the solar disk, compressed by refraction into an elliptical form, may be looked at with the naked eye without inconvenience. In spite of the constant light, the common order of the parts of the day is plainly discernible. When the sun sinks down to the horizon, all nature is mute, but when, after a few hours, it rises in the skies, everything awakens, the few little birds break out in feeble twitter, and the shrivelled flowers venture to open their petals.

Although winter and summer are in reality the only seasons, yet the inhabitants fancy they have spring when about noon the rays of the sun begin to make themselves felt, which generally takes place about the middle of March, but this so-called spring has frequent night frosts of twenty degrees. Their autumn is reckoned from the time when the rivers begin to freeze over, that is, from the first days of September, when a cold of thirty degrees is already by no means uncommon. As may easily be supposed in a climate like this, the vegetation of summer is scarcely more than a struggle for existence.

In the latter end of May the stunted willow-bushes put out little wrinkled leaves, and those banks which slope towards the south become clothed with a semi-verdant hue; in June the temperature at noon attains 72°; the flowers show themselves, and the berry-bearing plants blossom, when sometimes an icy blast from the sea destroys the bloom. The air is clearest in July, and the temperature is usually mild, but then a new plague arises for the torment of man. Millions and millions of mosquitoes issue from the swamps of the tundra, and compel the inhabitants to seek refuge in the dense and pungent smoke of the ' dymokury,' or large heaps of fallen leaves and damp wood, which are kindled near the dwellings and on the pasture grounds, as the only means of keeping off those abominable insects.

These tormentors, however, are not without use, for they compel the reindeer to migrate from the forests to the sea-shore and the ice, thus exposing them to the attack of the hunters, and they also prevent the horses from straying in the plains, and wandering beyond the protection of the smoke.

Scarcely is the mosquito plague at an end, when the dense autumn fogs rising from the sea spoil the enjoyment of the last mild hours which precede the nine months' winter. In January, the cold increases to −45°; breathing then becomes difficult; the wild reindeer, the indigenous inhabitant of the Polar region, withdraws to the thickest part of the forest, and stands there motionless, as if deprived of life.

With the 22nd November begins a night of thirty-eight days, relieved in some degree by the strong refraction and the white of the snow, as well as by the moon and the aurora. On the 28th December the first pale glimmering of dawn appears, which even at noon does not obscure the stars. With the reappearance of the sun the cold increases, and is most intense in February and March at the rising of the sun. Even in winter, completely clear days are very rare, as the cold sea wind covers the land with mists and fogs.

The character of the vegetation corresponds with that of the climate. Moss, stunted grass, dwarfish willow shrubs, are all that the place produces. The neighbouring valleys of the Aniuj, protected by mountains against the sea wind, have a somewhat richer flora, for here grow berry-bearing plants, the birch, the poplar, absinth, thyme, and the low creeping cedar. This poverty, however, of the vegetable world is strongly contrasted with the profusion of animal life over these shores and on the Polar Sea. Reindeer, elks, bears, foxes, sables, and grey squirrels fill the upland forests, while stone foxes burrow in the low grounds. Enormous flights of swans, geese, and ducks arrive in spring, and seek deserts where they may moult and build their nests in safety. Eagles, owls, and gulls pursue their prey along the sea-coast; ptarmigan run in troops among the bushes; little snipes are busy among the brooks. In the morasses the crows gather round the huts of the natives; and when the sun shines in spring, the traveller may even sometimes hear the note of the finch, and in autumn that of the thrush. But the landscape remains dreary and dead; all denotes that here the limits of the habitable earth are passed, and one asks with astonishment what could induce human beings to take up their abode in so comfortless a region?

In the district of Kolymsk, which surpasses in size many an European kingdom, the population, at the time of Wrangell's visit, consisted of 325 Russians, 1,034 Jakuts, and 1,139 Jukahires of the male sex, of whom 2,173 had to pay the Jassak, consisting of 803 fox and 28 sable skins, worth 6,704 roubles, besides which they were taxed to the amount of 10,847 roubles in money. Thus the Russian double-eagle made, and no doubt still makes, the poor people of Kolymsk pay rather dear for the honour of living under the protection of its talons.

The Cossacks, in virtue of their descent from the original conquerors of the country, enjoy the enviable privilege of being tax free; they are, however, obliged to render military service when required. They form the small garrison of Nishne Kolymsk, and every year twenty-five of them repair to the fair of Ostrownoje, to keep the wild Tchuktchi in check. The Russians are chiefly the descendants of fur-hunters or of exiles; and though they have adopted the native clothing and mode of life, they are still distinguishable by their more muscular frame. The women, who are somewhat better looking than the female Jakuts and Jukahires, are fond of music, and their traditional songs dwell on the beauties of nature—the rustling brook, the flowery mead, the nightingale's note—all things belonging to a world of which they have no idea.

The dwellings of the Russians are hardly to be distinguished from the jurts of the native tribes. They are made of drift-wood, and, as may easily be imagined, are very small and low. The interstices are carefully stopped up with moss, and the outside is covered with a thick layer of clay. An external mud wall rises to the height of the roof to keep off the wind. In a hut like this Wrangell spent many a winter month, but when the cold was very intense, he was not able to lay aside any part of his fur clothing, though sitting close to a large fire. When he wanted to write he had to keep the inkstand in hot water; and at night, when the fire was allowed to go out for a short time, his bedclothes were always covered with a thick snow-like rime.

The existence of the people of Kolymsk depends upon fishing and hunting, in which they are assisted by their dogs. These faithful, but cruelly-treated animals, are said to resemble the wolf, having long, pointed, projecting noses, sharp and upright ears, and long bushy tails. Their colour is black, brown, reddish-brown, white, and spotted, their howling that of a wolf. In summer they dig holes in the ground for coolness, or lie in the water to escape the mosquitoes; in winter they burrow in the snow, and lie curled up, with their noses covered with their bushy tails. The preparation of these animals for a journey must be carefully attended to; for a fortnight at least they should be put on a small allowance of hard food, to convert their superfluous fat into firm flesh; they must also be driven from ten to twenty miles daily, after which they have been known to travel a hundred miles a day without being injured by it. A team consists commonly of twelve dogs, and it is of importance that they should be accustomed to draw together. The quick and steady-going of the team, as well as the safety of the traveller, mainly depends on the docility and sagacity of the foremost dog or leader. No pains are therefore spared in his education, so that he may understand and obey his master's orders, and prevent the rest from starting off in pursuit of the stone foxes or other animals that may chance to cross their path. Their usual food is frozen fish, and ten good herrings are said to be a proper daily allowance for each dog while on duty. When not actively employed, they are obliged to content themselves with offal, and towards spring, when the winter's provisions are generally exhausted, they suffer the keenest hunger.

This season is also a hard time for the wandering tribes of the neighbourhood. Then they flock to Nishne Kolymsk, and to the other Russian settlements on the Kolyma, but here also famine stares them in the face. There is, indeed, a public corn magazine, but the price of flour is raised by the cost of transport to such an exorbitant height, as to be completely beyond the reach of the majority of the people. Three such dreadful springs did Wrangell pass at Kolymsk, witnessing scenes of misery never to be forgotten.

But when the distress of the people has reached its highest

point, relief is generally at hand. Troops of migratory birds
come from the south, and furnish some food for the despairing
population. The supply is increased in June, when the
ice breaks on the Kolyma, for in spite of the faultiness of
the nets and the want of skill of the fishermen, the river
is the principal source of plenty during the summer, and
supplies, moreover, the chief provisions for the following
winter. But with these gifts the Kolyma brings the plague
of inundations, so that during the summer of 1822 Wrangell was obliged to spend a whole week on the flat roof of
his hut.

The chief resource of the Jukahires of the river Aniuj is
the reindeer chase, the success of which mainly decides
whether famine or some degree of comfort is to be their lot
during the coming winter. The passage of the reindeer
takes place twice a year; in spring, when the mosquitoes
compel them to seek the sea-shore, where they feed on the
moss of the tundra, and in autumn, when the increasing
cold forces them to retire from the coast. The spring
migration, which begins about the middle of May, is not very
profitable, partly because the animals are meagre, and their
furs in bad condition, and partly because it is more difficult to
kill them as they pass the frozen rivers. The chief hunting
is in August and September, when the herds, consisting each
of several thousand deer, return to the forests. They invariably cross the river at a particular spot, where a flat
sandy bank makes their landing easier; and here they press
more closely together, under the guidance of the strongest
animals of the herd.

The passage takes place after some hesitation, and in a
few minutes the river is covered with swimming reindeer.
The hunters, hidden in creeks or behind stones and bushes,
now shoot forth in their small boats and wound as many as
they can. While they are thus busy, they run some risk of
being overturned in the turmoil, for the bucks defend themselves with their horns, their teeth, and their hind legs,
while the roes generally attempt to spring with their fore-
feet upon the edge of the boat. When the hunter is thus
overset, his only chance of safety is to cling to a strong
animal, which safely brings him to the shore. But the

dexterity of the hunters renders such accidents rare. A good hunter will kill a hundred reindeer and more in half an hour. In the meantime the other boats seize the killed animals, which become their property, while those that are merely wounded and swim ashore belong to the hunters, who, in the midst of the tumult, where all their energies are taxed to the utmost, direct their strokes in such a manner as only severely to wound the larger animals. The noise of the horns striking against each other, the waters tinged with blood, the cries of the hunters, the snorting of the affrighted animals, form a scene not to be described.

The people of the Aniuj were already suffering great distress when, on September 12, 1821, the eagerly expected reindeer herds made their appearance on the right bank of the river. Never had such a multitude been seen, they covered the hills, and their horns might have been mistaken at a distance for a moving forest. In a short time numbers of the Siberian tribes had assembled, ready to destroy them. But the wary animals, alarmed by some circumstance or other, took another road, and leaving the banks of the river, vanished on the mountains. The despair of the people may be imagined; some lamented aloud and wrung their hands, others threw themselves upon the ground and scratched up the snow, others stood motionless like statues—a dreadful image of the universal misery. The later fishing season likewise failed in this deplorable year, and many hundreds died in the following winter.

While the men of Kolymsk are busily employed during the short summer in hunting, fishing, and hay-making, the women wander over the country, particularly in the mountains, to gather edible roots, aromatic herbs, and berries of various kinds, which latter, however, do not every year arrive at maturity. The berry-gathering here, like the vintage elsewhere, is a time of merriment. The younger women and girls go together in large parties, passing whole days and nights in the open air. When the berries are collected, cold water is poured over them, and they are preserved in a frozen state for a winter treat. Social parties are not unknown at Kolymsk, and are perhaps not less entertaining than in more refined communities. Floods of weak tea (for the aromatic leaves 'which cheer, but not inebriate' are very dear at Kolymsk) form the staple of the entertainment; and as sugar is also an expensive article, every guest takes a lump of candy in his mouth, lets the tea which he sips flow by, and then replaces it upon the saucer. It would be considered very unmannerly were he to consume the whole piece, which thus is able to do duty at more than one *soirée*. Next to tea, brandy is a chief requisite of a Kolymsk party.

The busiest time at Kolymsk is in February, when the caravan from Jakutsk arrives on its way to the fair of Ostrownoje. It consists of about twenty merchants, each of whom leads from ten to forty sumpter horses. This is the time not only for sale and purchase, but also for hearing the last news from the provincial capital Jakutsk, and receiving intelligence six months old from Moscow and St. Petersburgh.

From this short account of Kolymsk life it may well be imagined what a sensation it must have made in so secluded a place when Wrangell arrived there in November, and informed the people that he was come to spend the better part of the next three years among them.

The winter was passed in preparation for the next spring expeditions, for during the long Arctic night the darkness prevents travelling, and the snow acquires a peculiar hardness or sharpness from the extreme cold, so that then four times the number of dogs would be needed. But as in summer the thawing is likewise a hindrance, Wrangell had in reality only about ten weeks every year, from March till the end of May, for the accomplishment of his task.

As may easily be supposed, it was no easy matter to make the necessary arrangements for an expedition requiring some hundreds of dogs, and provisions for several weeks; but such was the energy displayed by Wrangell and his colleagues, that on February 19, 1821, they were able to start on their first journey over the ice of the Polar Sea, which they reached on the 25th. Nine sledges, with the usual team of twelve dogs to each, were provided for the present excursion, six of which were to carry provisions and stores, to be distributed in different depôts, and then to return. The provisions for the dogs consisted of 2,400 fresh herrings, and as much 'jukola' as was equivalent to 8,150 dried herrings. The increasing cold and the violence of the wind made travelling very difficult. To guard the dogs from being frozen, the drivers were obliged to put clothing on their bodies, and a kind of boots on their feet, which greatly impeded their running. At times the frost was so intense, that the mercury congealed while Wrangell was making his observations. He thus describes the manner in which he passed the nights on the Polar Sea in his tent :—

'Between tea and supper the sledge-drivers went out to attend and feed their dogs, which were always tied up for the night, lest they should be tempted away by the scent of some wild animal. Meanwhile, we were engaged in comparing our observations, and in laying down on the map the ground which we had gone over in the course of the day; the severe cold, and the smoke which usually filled the tent, sometimes made this no easy task. Supper always consisted of a single dish of fish or meat soup, which was boiled for us all in the same kettle, out of which it was eaten. Soon after we had finished our meal, the whole party lay down to sleep. On account of the cold we could not lay aside any part of our travelling dress, but we regularly changed our boots and stockings every evening, and hung those we had taken off, with our fur caps and gloves, on the tent poles to dry. This is an essential precaution, particularly in respect to stockings, for with damp clothing there is the greatest risk of the part being frozen. We always spread the bearskins between the frozen ground and ourselves, and the fur coverings over us, and being well tired we usually slept very soundly. As long as all the sledge-drivers continued with us we were so crowded that we had to place ourselves like the spokes of a wheel, with our feet towards the fire and our heads against the tent wall. In the morning we generally rose at six, lit the fire, and washed ourselves before it with fresh snow; we then took tea, and immediately afterwards dinner (which was similar to the supper of the night before). The tent was then struck, and everything packed and stowed on the sledges, and at nine we usually took our departure.'

The chief impediments to journeying on the ice were

found to be the hummocks, often eighty feet high, which lie in ridges at certain distances, parallel perhaps to the shore. Along the line or lines where the ice is periodically broken, it is forced by pressure and the tossing of a tempestuous sea into those irregular ridges through which Wrangell had sometimes to make a way with crowbars for half a mile. The 'polinyas,' or spaces of open water in the midst of the ice, offered less hindrance, as they might be avoided; but in this neighbourhood, and sometimes even where no hole in the ice was visible, layers of salt were met with, which cut the dogs' feet, and at the same time increased the labour of the draft, the sledges moving over the salt with as much difficulty as they would over gravel.

In spite of all these hindrances, Wrangell extended his exploration of the coast fifty versts beyond Cape Shelagskoi, where the want of fuel and provisions compelled him to return. The depôts which he had made as he advanced, were found partly devoured by the stone foxes and gluttons, so that the party was compelled to fast during the two last days of the journey. After an absence of three weeks Nishne Kolymsk appeared like a second Capua to Wrangell, but time being precious he allowed himself but a few days' rest, and started afresh, on March 26, for Cape Shelagskoi, with the intention of penetrating as far as possible to the North, on the ice of the Polar Sea. The caravan consisted of twenty-two sledges, laden with fuel and provisions for thirty days, including food for 240 dogs. So imposing a train had certainly never been seen before in these desolate regions, for the part of the coast between the Kolyma and Cape Shelagskoi is wholly uninhabited; on one side the occasional excursions of the Russians terminate at the Baranow rocks, and on the other the Tchuktchi do not cross the larger Baranow river. The intervening eighty versts of coast are never visited by either party, but considered as neutral ground. On April 1, Wrangell reached the borders of the Polar Sea, and proceeding northward to 71° 31', found the thickness of the ice, which he measured by means of a hole, to be about a foot, very rotten, and full of salt; the soundings twelve fathoms, with a bottom of soft green mud. The wind increasing in violence, he heard the sound of the water beneath, and felt the undulatory motion of the thin crust of ice.

'Our position,' says the bold explorer, 'was at least an anxious one; the more so as we could take no step to avoid the impending danger. I believe few of our party slept, except the dogs, who alone were unconscious of the great probability of the ice being broken up by the force of the waves. Next day, the wind having fallen, I had two of the best sledges emptied, and placed in them provisions for twenty-four hours, with the boat and oars, some poles and boards, and proceeded northwards to examine the state of the ice; directing M. von Matiuschkin, in case of danger, to retire with the whole party as far as might be needful, without awaiting my return. After driving through the thick brine with much difficulty for seven versts, we came to a number of large fissures, which we passed with some trouble by the aid of the boards which we had brought with us. At last the fissures became so numerous and so wide, that it was hard to say whether the sea beneath us was really still covered by a connected coat of ice, or only by a number of detached floating fragments, having everywhere two or more feet of water between them. A single gust of wind would have been sufficient to drive these fragments against each other, and being already thoroughly saturated with water, they would have sunk in a few minutes, leaving nothing but sea on the spot where we were standing. It was manifestly useless to attempt going farther; we hastened to rejoin our companions, and to seek with them a place of greater security. Our most northern latitude was 71° 43′ at a distance of 215 versts in a straight line from the lesser Baranow rock.' After rejoining his companions, and while still on the frozen sea, so thick a snow-storm came on, that those in the hindmost sledge could not see the leading ones. Unable either to pitch their tent or to light a fire, they were exposed during the night to the whole fury of the storm, with a temperature of + 7°, without tea or soup, and with nothing to quench their thirst or satisfy their hunger but a few mouthfuls of snow, a little rye biscuit, and half spoilt fish. On April 28, they arrived at Nishne Kolymsk, after an absence of thirty-six days, during which they had travelled above 800 miles with the same dogs, men and animals having equally suffered from cold, hunger, and fatigue.

Neither discomfort, however, nor danger prevented Wrangell from undertaking a third excursion in the following spring. He had great difficulty in procuring the necessary dogs, a disease which raged among them during the winter having carried off more than four-fifths of these useful animals. At length his wants were supplied by the people of the Indigirka, where the sickness had not extended, and on March 14, 1822, he again set out for the borders of the Polar Sea. During this expedition a large extent of coast was accurately surveyed by Wrangell, who sent out his worthy assistant Matiuschkin, with two companions, in an unloaded sledge, to see if any further advance could be made to the north. Having accomplished ten versts, Matiuschkin was stopped by the breaking up of the ice. Enormous masses, raised by the waves into an almost vertical position, were driven against each other with a dreadful crash, and pressed downwards by the force of the billows to reappear again on the surface covered with the torn-up green mud which here forms the bottom of the sea. It would tire the reader were I to relate all the miseries of their return voyage; suffice it to say, that worn out with hunger and fatigue, they reached Nishne Kolymsk on May 5, after an absence of fifty-seven days. Such sufferings and perils might have excused all further attempts to discover the supposed land in the Polar Sea, but nothing daunted by his repeated failures, Wrangell determined on a fourth expedition in 1823, on which he resolved to start from a more easterly point. On reaching the coast, the obstacles were found still greater than on his previous visits to that fearful sea. The weather was tempestuous, the ice thin and broken. It was necessary at times to cross wide lanes of water on pieces of ice; at times the thin ice bent beneath the weight of the sledges, which were then saved only by the sagacity of the dogs, who, aware of the danger, ran at their greatest speed till they found a solid footing. At length, about sixty miles from shore, they arrived at the edge of an immense break in the ice, extending east and west further than the eye could reach.

'We climbed one of the loftiest hummocks,' says Wrangell,

'whence we obtained an extensive view towards the north, and whence we beheld the wide ocean spread before our gaze. It was a fearful and magnificent, but to us a melancholy spectacle! Fragments of ice of enormous size floated on the surface of the water, and were thrown by the waves with awful violence against the edge of the ice-field on the further side of the channel before us. The collisions were so tremendous, that large masses were every instant broken away, and it was evident that the portion of ice which still divided the channel from the open ocean, would soon be completely destroyed. Had we attempted to ferry ourselves across upon one of the floating pieces of ice, we should not have found firm footing upon our arrival. Even on our own side fresh lines of water were continually forming, and extending in every direction in the field of ice behind us. We could go no further. With a painful feeling of the impossibility of overcoming the obstacles which nature opposed to us, our last hope vanished of discovering the land, which we yet believed to exist. We saw ourselves compelled to renounce the object for which we had striven through three years of hardships, toil, and danger. We had done what honour and duty demanded; further attempts would have been absolutely hopeless, and I decided to return.'

They turned, but already the track of their advance was scarcely discernible, as new lanes of water had been formed, and fresh hummocks raised by the sea. To add to their distress, a storm arose, which threatened every moment to swallow up the ice island, on which they hoped to cross a wide space of water which separated them from a firmer ground.

'We had been three long hours in this position, and still the mass of ice beneath us held together, when suddenly it was caught by the storm, and hurled against a large field of ice: the crash was terrific, and the mass beneath us was shattered into fragments. At that dreadful moment, when escape seemed impossible, the impulse of self-preservation, implanted in every living being, saved us. Instinctively we all sprang at once on the sledges, and urged the dogs to their full speed. They flew across the yielding fragments to the field on which we had been stranded, and safely reached a

T

part of it of firmer character, on which were several hummocks, where the dogs immediately ceased running, conscious, apparently, that the danger was past. We were saved! We joyfully embraced each other, and united in thanks to God for our preservation from such imminent peril.'

But their misfortunes did not end here; they were cut off from the deposit of their provisions; they were 360 versts from their nearest magazines, and the food for the dogs was now barely sufficient for three days. Their joy may be imagined when, after a few versts' travelling, they fell in with Matiuschkin and his party, bringing with them an abundant supply of provisions of all kinds.

To leave nothing undone which could possibly be effected, Wrangell advanced to the eastward along the coast, past Cape North, seen in Cook's last voyage, and proceeded as far as Koliutschin Island, where he found some Tchuktchi, who had come over from Behring's Straits to trade.

With this journey terminated Wrangell's labours on the coasts, or on the surface of the Polar Sea, and, at the beginning of the following winter, we find him taking a final leave of Nishne Kolymsk. On January 10, 1824, he arrived at Jakutsk, and a few months later at Petersburg. If we consider the difficulties he had to encounter, and his untiring zeal and courage, in the midst of privations and dangers, it is only fair to admit that his name deserves to be ranked among the most distinguished explorers of the Arctic world.

The Black Guillemot.

Ochotsk.

# CHAPTER XXI.

## THE TUNGUSI.

Their Relationship to the Mandschu—Dreadful Condition of the Outcast Nomads
—Character of the Tungusi—Their Outfit for the Chase—Bear-hunting—
Dwellings—Diet—A Night's Halt with Tungusi in the Forest—Ochotsk.

THOUGH both belonging to the same stock, the fate of the
Tungusi and Mandschu has been very different; for at
the same time when the latter conquered the vast Chinese
empire, the former, after having spread over the greatest
part of East Siberia, and driven before them the Jakuts, the
Jukahiri, the Tchuktchi, and many other aboriginal tribes,
were in their turn subjugated by the mightier Russians. In
the year 1640 the Cossacks first encountered the Tungusi,
and in 1644 the first Mandschu emperor mounted the
Chinese throne. The same race which here imposes its yoke
upon millions of subjects, there falls a prey to a small number
of adventurers. However strange the fact, it is, however,
easily explained, for the Chinese were worse armed and less
disciplined than the Mandschu, while the Tungusi had nothing

but bows and arrows to oppose to the Cossack fire-arms; and
history (from Alexander the Great to Sadowa) teaches us that
victory constantly sides with the best weapons.

In their intellectual development we find the same difference as in their fortunes between the Mandschu and the
Siberian Tungusi. Two hundred and fifty years ago the
former were still nomads, like their northern kinsfolk, and
could neither read nor write, and already they have a rich
literature, and their language is spoken at the court of
Peking; while the Tungusi, oppressed and sunk in poverty,
are still as ignorant as when they first encountered the
Cossacks.

According to their occupations, and the various domestic
animals employed by them, they are distinguished by the
names of Reindeer, Horse, Dog, Forest, and River Tungusi;
but although they are found from the basins of the Upper,
Middle, and Lower Tunguska, to the western shores of the
Sea of Ochotsk, and from the Chinese frontiers and the
Baikal to the Polar Ocean, their whole number does not
amount to more than 30,000, and diminishes from year to
year, in consequence of the ravages of the small-pox and
other epidemic disorders transmitted to them by the Russians. Only a few rear horses and cattle, the reindeer being
generally their domestic animal; and the impoverished
Tunguse, who has been deprived of his herd by some contagious disorder, or the ravages of the wolves, lives as a
fisherman on the borders of a river, assisted by his dog, or
retires into the forests as a promyschlenik or hunter. Of the
miseries which here await him, Wrangell relates a melancholy
instance. In a solitary hut in one of the dreariest wildernesses imaginable, he found a Tunguse and his daughter.
While the father, with his long snow-shoes, was pursuing a
reindeer for several days together, this unfortunate girl remained alone and helpless in the hut, which even in summer
afforded but an imperfect shelter against the rain and wind,
exposed to the cold, and frequently to hunger, and without
the least occupation. No wonder that the impoverished
Tungusi not seldom sink into cannibalism. Neither the
reindeer nor the dogs, nor the wives and children of their more

fortunate countrymen, are secure from the attacks and voracity of these outcasts, who, in their turn, are treated like wild beasts, and destroyed without mercy. A bartering trade is, however, carried on with them, but only at a distance, and by signs; each party depositing its goods, and following every motion of the other with a suspicious eye.

The Russian Government, anxious to relieve the misery of the impoverished nomads, has given orders to settle them along the river-banks, and to provide them with the necessary fishing implements; but only extreme wretchedness can induce the Tunguse to relinquish the free life of the forest. His careless temper, his ready wit, and sprightly manner, distinguish him from the other Siberian tribes—the gloomy Samojede, the uncouth Ostjak, the reserved Jakut— but he is said to be full of deceit and malice. His vanity shows itself in the quantity of glass beads with which he decorates his dress of reindeer leather, from his small Tartar cap to the tips of his shoes. When chasing or travelling on his reindeer through the woods, he of course lays aside most of his finery, and puts on large water-tight boots or sari, well greased with fat, to keep off the wet of the morass. His hunting apparatus is extremely simple. A small axe, a kettle, a leathern bag containing some dried fish, a dog, a short gun, or merely a bow and a sling, is all he requires for his expeditions into the forest. With the assistance of his long and narrow snow-shoes, he flies over the dazzling plain, and protects his eyes, like the Jakut, with a net made of black horse-hair. He never hesitates to attack the bear single handed, and generally masters him. The nomad Tunguse naturally requires a movable dwelling. His tent is covered with leather, or large pieces of pliable bark, which are easily rolled up and transported from place to place. The jurt of the sedentary Tunguse resembles that of the Jakut, and is so small, that it can be very quickly and thoroughly warmed by a fire kindled on the stone hearth in the centre. In his food the Tunguse is by no means dainty. One of his favourite dishes consists of the contents of a reindeer's stomach mixed with wild berries, and spread out in thin cakes on the rind of trees, to be dried in the air or in the sun.

Those who have settled on the Wiluj and in the neighbour-hood of Nertschinsk, likewise consume large quantities of brick tea, which they boil with fat and berries into a thick porridge, and this unwholesome food adds no doubt to the yellowness of their complexion.

But few of the Tungusi have been converted to Christi-anity, the majority being still addicted to Shamanism. They do not like to bury their dead, but place them, in their holiday dresses, in large chests, which they hang up between two trees. The hunting apparatus of the deceased is buried beneath the chest. No ceremonies are used on the occasion, except when a Schaman happens to be in the neighbourhood, when a reindeer is sacrificed, on whose flesh the sorcerer and the relations regale themselves, while the spirits to whom the animal is supposed to be offered are obliged to content themselves with the smell of the burnt fat. As among the Samojedes or the Ostjaks, woman is a marketable ware among the Tungusi. The father gives his daughter in marriage for twenty or a hundred reindeer, or the bridegroom is obliged to earn her hand by a long period of service.

In East Siberia, the Tungusi divide with the Jakuts the task of conveying goods or travellers through the forests, and afford the stranger frequent opportunities for admiring their agility and good humour. On halting after a day's journey, the reindeer are unpacked in an instant, the saddles and the goods ranged orderly on the ground, and the bridles collected and hung on branches of trees. The hungry animals soon disappear in the thicket, where they are left to provide for themselves. The men, who meanwhile have been busy with their axes, drag a larch tree or two to the place of encamp-ment. The smaller branches are lopped off and collected to serve as beds or seats upon the snow, while the resinous wood of the larger trunks is soon kindled into a lively fire. The kettle, filled with snow, is suspended from a strong forked branch placed obliquely in the ground over the fire, and in a few minutes the tea is ready—for the Tungusi pro-ceed every evening according to the same method, and are consequently as expert as long and invariable practice can make them. . Comfortably seated on his reindeer saddle, the

traveller may now amuse himself with the dances, which the
Tungusi accompany with an agreeable song, or if he choose
to witness their agility in athletic exercises, it only costs him
a word of encouragement, and a small donation of brandy.
Two of the Tungusi hold a rope, and swing it with all their
might, so that it does not touch the ground. Meanwhile a
third Tunguse skips over the rope, picks up a bow and arrow,
spans the bow and shoots the arrow, without once touching
the rope. Some particularly bold and expert Tungusi will
dance over a sword which a person, lying on his back on the
ground, is swinging about with the greatest rapidity. Should
our traveller be a friend of chess, the Tungusi are equally at
his service, as they are passionately fond of this noblest of
games, especially in the Kolymsk district. Like all other
Siberian nomads, they visit at least once a year the various
fairs which are held in the small towns scattered here and
there over their immense territory—such as Kirensk, Olek-
minsk, Bargusin, Tschita, and Ochotsk, which, before the
opening of the Amur to trade, was the chief port of East
Siberia. Ochotsk is one of the dreariest places imaginable;
at least no traveller who ever visited it has a word to say in
its favour. Not a single tree grows for miles and miles around,
and the wretched huts of which the town is composed, lie
in the midst of a swamp, which in summer is a fruitful
source of malaria and pestilence. The river Ochota, at whose
mouth Ochotsk is situated, does not break up before the end
of May, and the ice masses continue to pass the town till the
15th or 20th of June. Soon after begins the most unpleasant
time of all the year, or ' buss ' of the Siberians, characterised
by thick fog and a perpetually drizzling rain. The weather
clears up in July, but as early as August the night frosts
cover the earth with rime. Salmon, of which no less than
fourteen different species live in the sea of Ochotsk, are the
only food which the neighbourhood affords; all other necessaries of life come from Jakutsk, and are of course enormously
dear. Meat appears only from time to time on the tables of
the wealthier merchants, and bread is an article of luxury.
No wonder that the scurvy ravages every winter a place so
ill-provisioned, and that at the time when the first caravan of

packhorses is expected to cross the Aldan Mountains, the people of Ochotsk, unable to restrain their impatience, go out a long way to meet it. As the former trade of the place has now no doubt been transferred to the settlements on the Amur, it may well be supposed that Ochotsk has lost most of its former inhabitants, who can only be congratulated on their change of residence.

The Scoter, or Black Diver.

The Aleutian Islands.
(From an original sketch by Frederick Whymper.)

## CHAPTER XXII.

### GEORGE WILLIAM STELLER.

His Birth—Enters the Russian Service—Scientific Journey to Kamtschatka—Accompanies Behring on his second Voyage of Discovery—Lands on the Island of Kaiak—Shameful Conduct of Behring—Shipwreck on Behring Island—Behring's Death—Return to Kamtschatka—Loss of Property—Persecutions of the Siberian Authorities—Frozen to death at Tjumen.

GEORGE WILLIAM STELLER, one of the most distinguished naturalists of the past century, was born at Winsheim, a small town in Franconia in the year 1709. After completing his studies at the universities of Wittenberg and Halle, he turned his thoughts to Russia, which, since the reforms of Czar Peter the Great, and the protection which that monarch and his successors afforded to German learning, had become the land of promise for all adventurous spirits.

Having been appointed surgeon in the Russian army, which at that time was besieging Danzig, he went with a transport of wounded soldiers, after the surrender of that town, to

St. Petersburg, where he arrived in 1734. Here his talents were soon appreciated; after a few years he was named a member of the Imperial Academy of Sciences, and sent by Government, in 1738, to examine the natural productions of Kamtschatka.

The ability and zeal with which he fulfilled this mission is proved by the valuable collections which he sent to the Academy, and by his numerous memoirs, which are still read with interest in the present day.

In 1741 he accompanied Behring on his second voyage of discovery, the object of which was to determine the distance of America from Kamtschatka, and to ascertain the separation or the junction of both continents in a higher latitude—a question which his first voyage had left undecided. Nothing could be more agreeable to a man like Steller, than the prospects held out to him by an expedition to unknown regions; and we can easily imagine the delight with which the naturalist embarked on board of the 'Saint Peter,' commanded by Behring in person. Accompanied by the 'Saint Paul,' under Tschirigow, they sailed on June 4 from the bay of Awatscha.

The expedition had cost ten years of preparation, and brought misery and ruin upon many of the wild Siberian tribes, for all that was necessary for the outfit had to be conveyed by compulsory labour from the interior of the continent over mountains and rivers, through dense forests and pathless wilds, and it seemed from the very beginning of the voyage as if the curses of the unfortunate natives clung to it. Much valuable time had been lost, for the ships ought to have sailed at least a month earlier, and Behring, who from illness constantly kept to his cabin, was by no means a fit commander for a scientific expedition.

After a few days a dense fog separated the vessels, which were never to meet again; and as the 'St. Peter' held her course too much to the south, the Aleutic chain remained undiscovered, and the first land was only sighted after four weeks in the neighbourhood of Behring's Bay. During the whole of this passage Steller had to endure all the vexations which arrogant stupidity could inflict upon a man anxious to do his duty. It was in vain that he repeatedly pointed out the signs which indicated the presence of land not far to the north, in vain that he entreated the commander to steer but one day in that direction. At last, on July 15, the high mountains of America were seen to rise above the horizon, and the vessel anchored on the 19th near to the small island of Kaiak.

On the following day a boat was sent out to fetch some fresh water, but it was with the utmost difficulty that Steller could obtain permission to join the party. All assistance was obstinately denied him, and accompanied by his only servant, a Cossack, he landed on the unknown shore, eager to make the most of the short time allotted him for his researches. He immediately directed his steps towards the interior, and had scarcely walked a mile when he discovered the hollowed trunk of a tree, in which, a few hours before, the savages had boiled their meat with red hot stones. He also found several pots filled with esculent herbs, and a wooden instrument for making fire, like those which are used by the inhabitants of Kamtschatka. Hence he conjectured that the aborigines of this part of the American coast must be of the same origin as the Kamtschatkans, and that both countries must necessarily approach each other towards the north, as their inhabitants could not possibly traverse such vast extents of ocean in their rudely-constructed boats.

Pursuing his way, Steller now came to a path which led into a dense and shady forest. Before entering, he strictly forbade his Cossack to act without commands, in case of a hostile encounter. The Cossack had a gun with a knife and hatchet; Steller himself only a Jakut poniard, which he had taken with him to dig out plants or stones.

After half an hour's walking they came to a place strewn with grass. This was immediately removed, and a roof or platform discovered, consisting of strips of bark laid upon poles and covered with stones. This platform opened into a cellar containing a large quantity of smoked fishes, and a few bundles of the inner bark of the larch or fir tree, which, in case of necessity, serves as food throughout all Siberia. There were also some arrows, dyed black and smoothed, of a size far superior to those used in Kamtschatka.

After Steller, in spite of the danger of being surprised by

the savages, had accurately examined the contents of the
cellar, he sent his Cossack back again to the place where the
boatmen were watering.  He gave him specimens of the
various articles which he had found, ordering him to take
them to Captain Behring, and to request that two or three
men might be sent to him for further assistance.  In the
meantime, though quite alone, he continued his investiga-
tions of the strange land, and having reached the summit of
a hill, he saw smoke rising from a forest at some distance.
Overjoyed at the sight, for he now could hope to meet with
the natives and to complete his knowledge of the island, he
instantly returned to the landing-place, with all the eagerness of a man who has something important to communicate ;
and as the boat was just about to leave, told the sailors to
inform the captain of his discovery, and to beg that the small
pinnace, with a detachment of armed men, might be sent out
to him.

Meanwhile, exhausted with fatigue, he sat down on the
beach, where he described in his pocket-book some of the
more delicate plants he had collected, which he feared might
speedily wither, and regaled himself with the excellent
water.

After waiting for about an hour, he at length received an
answer from Behring, telling him to return immediately on
board, unless he chose to be left behind; and we can easily
imagine the indignation of the disappointed naturalist at
this shameful command.

On the morning of July 21, Behring, contrary to his
custom, appeared on deck, ordered the anchors to be weighed,
and gave directions to sail back again on the same course.
The continent he had discovered was not even honoured with
a single visit, so that Steller could not help telling the
Russians they had merely come thus far for the purpose of
carrying American water to Asia.

Any conscientious commander would have continued to sail
along the unknown shore, or, considering that the season was
already far advanced, would have determined to winter there,
and to pursue his discoveries next spring ; but, unfortunately
for Behring and his companions, the course he adopted proved
as disastrous as it was dishonourable.

Three months long the ship was tossed about by contrary winds and storms; the islands of the Aleutic chain, though frequently seen through the mists, were but seldom visited; the scurvy broke out amongst the dispirited, ill-fed crew, their misery increased from day to day, and their joy may be imagined when at length, on November 5, a land was seen which they firmly believed to be Kamtschatka—though in reality it was merely the desert Behring's Island, situated a hundred miles from that peninsula. Even those who were nearly half-dead crept upon deck to enjoy the welcome sight; every one thanked God, and the ignorant officer, convinced that they were at the entrance of the bay of Awatscha, even named the several mountains, but their mistake soon became apparent when, on rounding a small promontory, some well-known islets were missed. As they had no doubt, however, that the land was really Kamtschatka, and the bad weather and the small number of hands fit to do duty rendering it difficult to reach the gulf of Awatscha, it was resolved to run into the bay that lay before them, and to send notice from thence to Nishne Kamtschatsk of their safe arrival.

Steller was among the first to land, and probably the very first of the party who discovered the mistake of the *excellent* navigators to whom the expedition had been entrusted. Sea-otters came swimming to him from the land, and he well knew that these much persecuted animals had long since disappeared from the coast of Kamtschatka. The number of Arctic foxes, too, who showed no fear at his approach, and the sea-cows gambolling in the water, were sure signs that the foot of man had not often trodden this shore.

Steller was also the first to set the good example of making the best of a bad situation, instead of uselessly bewailing his misfortunes. He began to erect a hut for the following winter, and formed an association with several of the crew, who, whatever might await them, promised to stand by each other.

During the following days the sick were gradually conveyed on shore. Some of them died on board as soon as they were brought into the open air, others in the boat, others as soon as they were landed. 'On all sides,' says Steller, in his interesting account of this ill-fated voyage,* 'nothing was to be seen but misery. Before the dead could be buried, they were mangled by the foxes, who even ventured to approach the helpless invalids who were lying without cover on the beach. Some of these wretched sufferers bitterly complained of the cold, others of hunger and thirst—for many had their gums so swollen and ulcerated with the scurvy as to be unable to eat.'

'On November 13,' continues the naturalist, 'I went out hunting for the first time with Messieurs Plenisner and Betge; we killed four sea-otters, and did not return before night. We ate their flesh thankfully, and prayed to God that He might continue to provide us with this excellent food. The costly skins, on the other hand, were of no value in our eyes; the only objects which we now esteemed were knives, needles, thread, ropes, &c., on which before we had not bestowed a thought. We all saw that rank, science, and other social distinctions were now of no avail, and could not in any way contribute to our preservation: we therefore resolved, before we were forced to do so by necessity, to set to work at once. We introduced among us five a community of goods, and regulated our housekeeping in such a manner, as not to be in want before the winter was over. Our three Cossacks were obliged to obey our orders, when we had decided upon something in common; but we began to treat them with greater politeness, calling them by their names and surnames, and we soon found that Peter Maximowitsch served us with more alacrity than formerly Petrucha (a diminutive of Peter).

'Nov. 14. The whole ship's company was formed into three parties. The one had to convey the sick and provisions from the ship; the second brought wood; the third, consisting of a lame sailor and myself, remained at home—the former busy making a sledge, while I acted as cook. As our party was the first to organise a household, I also performed the duty of bringing warm soup to some of our sick, until they had so far recovered as to be able to help themselves.

'The barracks being this day ready to receive the sick,

---

* Beschreibung der Seereise von Kamtschatka nach Amerika.  Frankfurt, 1774.

many of them were transported under roof; but for want of room, they lay everywhere on the ground, covered with rags and clothes. No one could assist the other, and nothing was heard but lamentations and curses—the whole affording so wretched a sight, as to make even the stoutest heart lose courage.

'On November 15 all the sick were at length landed. We took one of them, named Boris Sänd, into our hut, and by God's help he recovered within three months.

'The following days added to our misery, as the messengers we had sent out brought us the intelligence that we were on a desert island, without any communication with Kamtschatka. We were also in constant fear that the stormy weather might drive our ship out to sea, and along with it all our provisions, and every hope of ever returning to our homes. Sometimes it was impossible to get to the vessel for several days together, so boisterous was the surge; and about ten or twelve men, who had hitherto been able to work, now also fell ill. Want, nakedness, frost, rain, illness, impatience, and despair, were our daily companions.'

Fortunately the stormy sea drove the ship upon the strand, better than it could probably have been done by human efforts.

Successively many of the scorbutic patients died, and on December 8, the unfortunate commander of the expedition paid his debt to nature.

Titus Behring, by birth a Dane, had served thirty-six years with distinction in the Russian navy, but age and infirmities had completely damped his energies, and his death is a warning to all who enter upon undertakings above their strength.

In the meantime the whole ship's company had established itself for the winter in five subterranean dwellings; the general health was visibly improving, merely by means of the excellent water, and by the fresh meat furnished by sea-otters, seals, and manatees; and the only care now was to gain sufficient strength to be able to undertake the work of deliverance in spring.

In April the shipwrecked mariners began to build a smaller ship out of the timbers of the 'St. Peter,' and such was the alacrity with which all hands set to work, that on August 13 they were able to set out.

'When we were all embarked,' says Steller, 'we first perceived how much we should be inconvenienced for want of room; the water-casks, provisions, and baggage taking up so much space, that our forty-two men (the three ship's officers and myself were somewhat better off in the cabin) could hardly creep between them and the deck. A great quantity of the bedding and clothing had to be thrown overboard. Meanwhile we saw the foxes sporting about our deserted huts, and greedily devouring remnants of fat and meat.

'On the 14th, in the morning, we weighed anchor, and steered out of the bay. The weather being beautiful, and the wind favourable, we were all in good spirits, and as we sailed along the island, pointed out to each other the well-known mountains and valleys which we had frequently visited in quest of game, or for the purpose of reconnoitring. Towards evening we were opposite the furthest point of the island, and on the 15th, the wind continuing favourable, we steered direct towards the bay of Awatscha. About midnight, however, we perceived, to our great dismay, that the vessel began to fill with water from an unknown leak, which, in consequence of the crowded and overloaded state of the vessel, it was extremely difficult to find out. The pumps were soon choked by the shavings left in the hold, and the danger rapidly increased, as the wind was strong and the vessel badly built. The sails were immediately taken in; some of the men removed the baggage to look for the leak, others kept continually pouring out the water with kettles, while others again cast all superfluous articles overboard. At length, after the lightening of the ship, the carpenter succeeded in stopping the leak, and thus we were once more saved from imminent danger. . . . On the 17th we sighted Kamtschatka, but as the wind was contrary, we did not enter the harbour before the evening of the 27th.

'In spite of the joy we all felt at our deliverance, yet the news we heard on our arrival awakened in us a host of conflicting emotions. We had been given up for lost, and all our property had passed into other hands, and been mostly carried away beyond hope of recovery. Hence joy and sorrow alternated within a few moments in our minds, though we were all so accustomed to privation and misery, as hardly to feel the extent of our losses.'

In the year 1744 Steller was ordered to return to St. Petersburg; but his candour had made him powerful enemies. Having reached Novgorod, and rejoicing in the idea of once more mixing with the civilised world, he was suddenly ordered to appear before the imperial court of justice at Irkutsk, on the charge of having treacherously sold powder to the enemies of Russia. Thus obliged to return once more into the depths of Siberia, he was at length dismissed by his judges, after waiting a whole year for their verdict.

Once more on his way to St. Petersburg, he had already reached Moscow, when he was again summoned to appear without delay before the court of Irkutsk. A journey to Siberia is, under all circumstances, an arduous undertaking; what, then, must have been Steller's feelings when, instead of enjoying the repose he had so well merited, he saw himself obliged to retrace his steps for the fourth time, for the purpose of vindicating his conduct before a rascally tribunal? On a very cold day, his Cossack guards stopped to refresh themselves with some brandy at an inn by the road-side, and Steller, who remained in the sledge waiting for their return, fell asleep, and was frozen to death.

He lies buried near the town of Tjumen, and no monument apprises the naturalist, whom the love of knowledge may lead into the Siberian wilds, that his unfortunate predecessor was thus basely requited after years of exertion in the interests of science.

The Silvery Fox.

Petropaulowsk.
(From an original sketch by Frederick Whymper.)

## CHAPTER XXIII.

### KAMTSCHATKA.

Climate — Fertility — Luxuriant Vegetation — Fish — Sea Birds — Kamtschatkan Birdcatchers—The Bay of Awatscha—Petropaulowsk—The Kamtschatkans—Their physical and moral Qualities—The Fritillaria Sarrana—The Muchamor—Bears—Dogs.

THE peninsula of Kamtschatka though numbering no more than 6,000 or 7,000 inhabitants, on a surface equalling Great Britain in extent, has so many natural resources that it could easily maintain a far greater number. The climate is much more temperate and uniform than that of the interior of Siberia, being neither so excessively cold in winter, nor so intensely hot in summer; and though the late and early night frosts, with the frequent fogs and rains, prevent the cultivation of corn, the humid air produces a very luxuriant herbaceous vegetation. Not only along the banks of the rivers and lakes, but in the forest glades, the grass grows to a height of more than twelve feet, and many of the Compositæ and Umbelliferæ attain a size so colossal, that the *Heraclium dulce* and the *Senecio cannabifolius* not seldom overtop the rider on horseback. The pasture grounds are so excellent, that the grass can generally be cut thrice during the short summer, and thus a comparatively small extent of land affords the winter supply for all the cattle of a hamlet.

Though the cold winds prevent the growth of trees along the coast, the more inland mountain slopes and valleys are clothed with woods richly stocked with sables and squirrels.

No country in the world has a greater abundance of excellent fisheries. In spring the salmon ascend the rivers in such amazing numbers, that on plunging a dart into the stream one is almost sure to strike a fish; and Steller affirms that the bears and dogs of Kamtschatka catch on the banks more fish with their paws and mouths, than man in other countries with all his cunning devices of net or angle. As the various birds of passage do not all wander at the same time to the north, so also the various kinds of fishes migrate, some sooner, others later, and consequently profusion reigns during the whole of the summer. Ermann was astonished at this incalculable abundance of the Kamtschatkan rivers, for in one of them, when the water was only six inches deep, he saw multitudes of Chaekos (*Slagocephalus*) as long as his arm partly stranded on the banks, partly still endeavouring to ascend the shallow stream. As the waters contain such an incredible multitude of fishes, we cannot wonder that the rocky coasts of the peninsula swarm with sea-fowl, whose breeding and roosting places are as densely peopled as any others in the world. At the entrance of the Awatscha Bay lies a remarkable labyrinth of rocks, separated from each other by narrow channels of water, like the intricate streets of an old-fashioned city. The flood has everywhere scooped out picturesque cavities and passages in these stupendous masses of stone, and the slightest wind causes the waves to beat with terrific violence against their feet. Every ledge, platform, and projection, every niche, hollow, and crevice, is peopled with sea birds of strange and various forms. In the capture of these birds the Kamtschatkans display an intrepidity equal to that of the islanders of St. Kilda or Feroe, and trust solely to their astonishing agility in climbing. Barefooted, without ropes or any other assistance, they venture down the steepest declivities, which are frequently only accessible from the top, as the foaming breakers cut off all access from below. The left arm clasps a basket which they fill with eggs as they advance, while the right hand grasps a short stick with an iron hook to drag the birds from the crevices of the rock. When a bird is caught, a dexterous grip wrings its neck, and it is then attached to the girdle of the fowler. In this manner an expert climber will kill in one day from seventy to eighty birds, and gather above a hundred eggs.

Thus the population of Kamtschatka is quite out of proportion to the riches of its pastures and waters. Its scanty inhabitants are moreover concentrated on a few spots along the chief rivers and bays, so that almost the whole peninsula is nothing but an uninhabited wilderness.

Before the conquest of the country by the Russians it had at least twenty times its present population, but the cruelty of the Cossacks and the ravages of the small-pox caused it to melt away almost as rapidly as that of Cuba or Haiti after the arrival of the Spaniards. At that time the sable and the sea-otter were considered of far greater importance than man; and unfortunately Russia has too many deserts to people, before she can think of repairing past errors and sparing inhabitants for this remotest corner of her vast Asiatic empire.

As the peninsula is too distant from the highways of the world to attract the tide of emigration, it is also seldom visited by travellers. The few strangers, however, who have sailed along the coasts, or made excursions into the interior of the country, speak with enthusiasm of the boldness of its rocky promontories, the magnificence of its bays and mountains, and only regret that during the greater part of the year an Arctic winter veils the beauties of the landscape under mists and snow.

Throughout its whole length Kamtschatka is traversed by an Alpine chain rising in some of its peaks to a height of 14,000 or 16,500 feet, and numbering no less than 28 active volcanoes along with many others whose fires are extinct. A land thus undermined with subterranean fires must be possessed of many mineral riches, but as yet no one has ever thought of seeking for them or putting them to use.

Owing to the great humidity of the climate and the quantities of rain attracted by the mountains, Kamtschatka abounds in springs. In the lowlands they gush forth in such numbers as to render it very difficult to travel any distance on foot or horseback, even in winter, as they prevent the rivers from freezing. No doubt many a mineral spring—cold, tepid, or warm—that would make the fortune of a German spa, here flows unnoticed into the sea.

Kamtschatka has many excellent harbours, and the magnificent Bay of Awatscha would alone be able to afford room to all the navies of the world. Its steep rocky shores are almost everywhere clothed with a species of beech (*Betula Ermanni*), intermingled with luxuriant grasses and herbs, and the higher slopes are generally covered with a dense underwood of evergreens and shrubs of deciduous foliage, whose changes of colour in autumn tinge the landscape with yellow, red, and brown tints. But the chief beauty of the Bay of Awatscha is the prospect of the distant mountains, forming a splendid panorama of fantastic peaks and volcanic cones, among which the Streloshnaja Sopka towers pre-eminent to the height of 14,000 feet. Close to this giant, but somewhat nearer to the coast, rises the active volcano of Awatscha, which frequently covers the whole country with ashes.

The vast Bay of Awatscha forms several minor creeks: among others the haven of Saint Peter and Paul, one of the finest natural harbours in the world, where the Russians have established the seat of their government in the small town of Petropaulowsk, which hardly numbers 500 inhabitants, but has acquired some celebrity from the unsuccessful attack of the English and French forces in 1854.

Besides some Jakut immigrants, the chief stock of the scanty population of the country consists of the descendants of the primitive Kamtschatkans, who, in spite of frequent intermarriages with their conquerors the Cossacks, have still retained many of their ancient manners. They are of a small stature, but broad shouldered, their cheek bones are prominent, their jaws uncommonly broad and projecting, their noses small, their lips very full, their hair black. The colour

of the men is dark brown, or sometimes yellow; the women
have fairer complexions, which they endeavour to preserve
by means of bears' guts, stuck upon their faces in spring with
fish lime, so as not to be burnt by the sun. They also paint
their cheeks with a sea-weed, which, when rubbed upon
them with fat, gives them a beautiful red colour.

The Kamtschatkans are a remarkably healthy race. Many
of them attain an age of seventy or eighty years, and are
able to walk and to work until their death. Their hair
seldom turns grey before their sixtieth year, and even the
oldest men have a firm and elastic step. The weight of their
body is greater than that of the Jakuts, though the latter
live on milk and flesh, while fish is the almost exclusive
food of the Kamtschatkans. The round tubercles of the
*Fritillaria Sarrana*, a species of lily with a dark purple flower,
likewise play an important part in their diet, and serve them
instead of bread and meal. ' If the fruits of the bread-fruit
tree,' says Kittlitz—who has seen both plants in the places
of their growth—' are pre-eminent among all others, as affording man a perfect substitute for bread, the roots of the Sarrana,
which are very similar in taste, rank perhaps immediately
after them. The collecting of these tubers in the meadows
is an important summer occupation of the women, and one
which is rather troublesome, as the plant never grows gre-
gariously, so that each root has to be sought and dug out
separately with a knife. Fortunately the wonderful activity
of the Siberian field-vole facilitates the labour of gathering
the tubers. These remarkable animals burrow extensive
winter nests, with five or six storehouses, which they fill
with various roots, but chiefly with those of the Sarrana.
To find these subterranean treasures, the Kamtschatkans use
sticks with iron points, which they strike into the earth.
The contents of three of these nests are as much as a man
can carry on his back.

A species of fungus, called Muchamor, affords a favourite
stimulant. It is dried and eaten raw. Besides its exhila-
rating effects, it is said to produce, like the Peruvian Coca, a
remarkable increase of strength, which lasts for a considerable time.

Fishing and hunting supply all the wants of the Kamtschatkans, for they have not yet learnt to profit in any degree worth mentioning by the luxuriance of their meadow-lands. They pay their taxes and purchase their foreign luxuries—meal and tea, tobacco and brandy—with furs. The chase of the costly sea-otter (which from excessive persecution had at one time almost become extinct) has latterly improved. Besides the fur animals, they also hunt the reindeer, the argali, the wolf, and the bear, whose skins supply them with clothing.

Bears abound in Kamtschatka, as they find a never-failing supply of fishes and berries, and Ermann assures us that they would long since have extirpated the inhabitants, if (most probably on account of the plenty in which they live) they were not of a more gentle disposition than any others in the world. In spring they descend from the mountains to the mouths of the rivers, to levy their tribute on the migratory troops of the fishes, frequently eating only the heads. Towards autumn they follow the fishes into the interior of the country as they ascend the streams.

The most valuable domestic animal in Kamtschatka is the dog, who has the usual characters of the Esquimaux race. He lives exclusively on fish, which he catches very dexterously. From spring to autumn he is allowed to roam at liberty, no one troubling himself about him ; but in October, every proprietor collects his dogs, binds them to a post, and lets them fast for a time, so as to deprive them of their superfluous fat, and to render them more fit for running. During the winter they are fed with dried fish every morning and evening, but while travelling they get nothing to eat, even though they run for hours. Their strength is wonderful. Generally no more than five of them are harnessed to a sledge, and will drag with ease three full-grown persons, and sixty pounds weight of luggage. When lightly laden, such a sledge will travel from 30 to 40 versts in a day over bad roads and through the deep snow ; on even roads from 80 to 140. The horse can never be used for sledging, on account of the deep snow, into which it would sink, and of the numerous rivers and sources, which are either never frozen, or merely covered with a thin sheet of ice, unable to bear the weight of so large an animal.

Travelling with dogs is, however, both dangerous and difficult. Instead of the whip, the Kamtschatkans use a crooked stick with iron rings, which, by their jingling, give the leader of the team the necessary signals. When the dogs do not sufficiently exert themselves, the stick is cast among them to rouse them to greater speed; but then the traveller must be dexterous enough to pick it up again while the sledge shoots along. During a snow-storm, the dogs keep their master warm, and will lie quietly near him for hours, so that he has merely to prevent the snow from covering him too deeply and suffocating him. The dogs are also excellent weather prophets, for when, while resting, they dig holes in the snow, a storm may with certainty be expected.

The sledge-dogs are trained to their future service at a very early period. Soon after birth they are placed with their mother in a deep pit, so as to see neither man nor beast, and after having been weaned, they are again condemned to soli-tary confinement in a pit. After six months they are attached to a sledge with other older dogs, and being extremely shy, they run as fast as they can. On returning home, they are again confined in their pit, where they remain until they are perfectly trained, and able to perform a long journey. Then, but not before, they are allowed their summer liberty. This severe education completely sours their temper, and they constantly remain gloomy, shy, quarrelsome, and suspicious.

To return to the Kamtschatkans—travellers praise their goodnature, their hospitality, and their natural wit. Of a sanguine disposition, they are happy and content in their poverty, and have no cares for the morrow. Being extremely indolent, they never work unless when compelled. They readily adopt strange manners, and no doubt education might produce valuable results in so pliable and sharp-witted a race. Unfortunately the Russians and Cossacks who have settled among them do not afford them the best examples. They have long since been converted to the Greek Church, but it is supposed that baptism has not fully effaced all traces of Schamanism. Formerly they had many gods, the chief of whom was Kutka, the creator of heaven and earth. But far from honouring Kutka, they continually ridiculed him, and made him the constant butt of their satire. Kutka, however, had a wife Chachy, who was endowed with all the intelligence in which her spouse was supposed to be deficient, and who, as is the case in many mortal housekeepings, was constantly exerting her ingenuity in repairing the blunders of her lord and master.

The Esquimaux Dog.

The Sedentary Tchuktchi and their Tents.
(From an original sketch by Frederick Whymper.)

# CHAPTER XXIV.

## THE TCHUKTCHI.

The Land of the Tchuktchi—Their independent Spirit and commercial Enterprise—Perpetual Migrations—The Fair of Ostrownoje—Visit in a Tchuktch Polog—Races—Tchuktch Bajaderes—The Tennygk or Reindeer Tchuktchi—The Onkilon or Sedentary Tchuktchi—Their Mode of Life.

AT the extreme north-eastern point of Asia, bounded by the Polar Ocean on one side and the sea of Behring on the other, lies the land of the Tchuktchi. The few travellers who have ever visited that bleak promontory describe it as one of the dreariest regions of the earth. The climate is dreadfully cold, as may be expected in a country confined between icy seas. Before July 20th there is no appearance of summer, and winter already sets in about August 20th. The lower grounds shelving to the north are intersected with numerous streams, which, however, enjoy their liberty but a short time of the year; the valleys are mostly swampy and filled with small lakes or ponds; while on the bleak hill slopes the Vaccinium and the dwarf birch or willow sparingly vegetate under a carpet of mosses and lichens.

The eastern, north-eastern, and partly also the southern coasts abound with walruses, sea-lions and seals, while the reindeer, the argali, the wolf, and the Arctic fox occupy the land. During the short summer, geese, swans, ducks, and wading birds frequent the marshy grounds; but in winter the snow-owl and the raven alone remain, and constantly follow the path of the nomadic inhabitants.

In this desolate nook of the Old World lives the only aboriginal people of North Asia which has known how to maintain its liberty to the present day, and which, proud of its independence, looks down with sovereign contempt upon its relations, the Korjaks, who, without offering any resistance, have yielded to the authority of Russia.

The rulers of Siberia have indeed confined the Tchuktchi within narrower limits—but here at least they obey no foreign ruler, and wander unmolested by the stranger, with their numerous reindeer herds, over the naked tundras. A natural distrust of their powerful neighbours has rendered them long unwilling to enter into any commercial intercourse with the Russians and to meet them at the fair of Ostrownoje, a small town, situated not far from their frontiers, on a small island of the Aniuj, in 68° N. lat.

This remotest trading-place of the Old World is not so unimportant as might be supposed from the sterile nature of the country, for the Tchuktchi are not satisfied, like the indolent Lapps or Samojedes, with the produce of their reindeer herds, but strive to increase their enjoyments or their property by an active trade. From the East Cape of Asia, where, crossing Behring's Straits in boats covered with skins, they barter furs and walrus teeth from the natives of America, the Tchuktchi come with their goods and tents drawn on sledges to the fair of Ostrownoje. Other sledges laden with lichens, the food of the reindeer, follow in their train, as in their wanderings, however circuitous, they not seldom pass through regions so stony and desert as not even to afford these frugal animals the slightest repast. Thus regulating their movements by the wants of their herds, they require five or six months for a journey which, in a direct line, would not be much longer than a thousand versts, and are almost constantly wandering from place to place, though, as they always carry their dwellings along with them, they at the same time never leave home. One of these snail-like caravans generally consists of fifty or sixty families, and one fair is scarcely at an end when they set off to make their arrangements for the next.

Tobacco is the primum mobile of the trade which centres in Ostrownoje. The desire to procure a few of its narcotic leaves induces the American Esquimaux, from the Icy Cape to Bristol Bay, to send their produce from hand to hand as far as the Gwosdew Islands in Behring's Straits, where it is bartered for the tobacco of the Tchuktchi, and these again principally resort to the fair of Ostrownoje to purchase tobacco from the Russians. Generally the Tchuktchi receive from the Americans as many skins for half a pood or eighteen pounds of tobacco-leaves as they afterwards sell to the Russians for two poods of tobacco of the same quality. These cost the Russian merchant about 160 roubles at the very utmost, while the skins which he obtains in barter are worth at least 260 at Jakutsk, and more than double that sum at St. Petersburg.

The furs of the Tchuktchi principally consist of black and silver grey foxes, stone foxes, gluttons, lynxes, otters, beavers, and a fine species of marten which does not occur in Siberia, and approaches the sable in value. They also bring to the fair bear-skins, walrus-thongs and teeth, sledge-runners of whale-ribs, and ready-made clothes of reindeer-skin. The American furs are generally packed in sacks of seal-skin, which are made in an ingenious manner by extracting the bones and flesh through a small opening made in the abdomen.

The Russian traders on their part bring to the fair, besides tobacco, iron-ware—particularly kettles and knives—for the Tchuktchi, and tea, sugar, and various stuffs for their countrymen who have settled along the Kolyma.

But Ostrownoje attracts not only Tchuktchi and Russians; a great number of the Siberian tribes from a vast circuit of 1,000 or 1,500 versts—Jukahires, Lamutes, Tungusi, Tschuwanzi, Koriaks—also come flocking in their sledges, drawn partly by dogs, partly by horses, for the purpose of bartering their commodities against the goods of the Tchuktchi. Fancy this barbarous assembly meeting every year during the intense cold and short days of the beginning of March. Picture to yourself the fantastic illumination of their red watch-fires blazing under the starry firmament, or mingling their ruddy glare with the Aurora flickering through the skies, and add to the strange sight the hollow sound of the Schaman's drum, and the howling of several hundreds of hungry dogs, and you will surely confess that no fair has a more original character than that of Ostrownoje. A government commissary, assisted by some Cossacks, superintends the fair, and receives the inconsiderable market-tax which the Tchuktchi pay to the Emperor.

All preliminaries having been arranged, the orthodox Russians repair to the chapel for the purpose of hearing a solemn mass, after which, the hoisting of a flag on the tower of the Ostrog announces the opening of the market. At this welcome sign the Tchuktchi, completely armed with spears, bows and arrows, advance with their sledges, and form a wide semicircle round the fort, while the Russians, and the other visitors of the fair, ranged opposite to them, await in breathless silence the tolling of the bell, which is to begin the active business of the day. At the very first sound, each trader, grotesquely laden with packages of tobacco, kettles, knives, or whatever else he supposes best able to supply some want, or to strike some fancy of the Tchuktchi, rushes as fast as he can towards the sledges, and in the jumble not seldom knocks down a competitor, or is himself stretched at full length on the snow. But, unmindful of the loss of cap and gloves, which he does not give himself time to pick up, he starts afresh, to make up for the delay by redoubled activity. Before he reaches the first Tchuktch, his eloquence breaks forth in an interminable flow, and in a strange jargon of Russian, Tchuktch, and Jakute, he praises the excellence of his tobacco, or the solidity of his kettles. The imperturbable gravity of the Tchuktch forms a remarkable contrast with the greedy eagerness of the Russian trader; without replying to his harangue, he merely shakes his head if the other offers him too little for his goods, and never for an instant loses his self-possession; while the Russian, in his hurry, not seldom hands over two poods of tobacco for one, or pockets a red fox instead of a black one. Although the

Tchuktch have no scales with them, it is not easy to deceive them in the weight, for they know exactly by the feeling of the hand whether a quarter of a pound is wanting to the pud. The whole fair seldom lasts longer than three days, and Ostrownoje, which must have but very few stationary inhabitants indeed (as it is not even mentioned in statistical accounts, which cite towns of seventeen souls), is soon after abandoned for many months to its ultra-Siberian solitude.

But before we allow the Tchuktchi to retire to their deserts, we may learn something more of their habits by accompanying Mr. Matiuschkin—Wrangell's companion—on a visit to the ladies of one of their first chiefs. ' We enter the outer tent or " namet," consisting of tanned reindeer skins supported on a slender framework. An opening at the top to let out the smoke, and a kettle in the centre, announce that antechamber and kitchen are here harmoniously blended into one. But where are the inmates? Most probably in that large sack made of the finest skins of reindeer calves, which occupies, near the kettle, the centre of the " namet." To penetrate into this "sanctum sanctorum" of the Tchuktch household, we raise the loose flap which serves as a door. creep on all fours through the opening, cautiously re-fasten the flap by tucking it under the floor-skin, and find ourselves in the reception or withdrawing-room—the " polog." A snug box no doubt for a cold climate, but rather low, as we cannot stand upright in it, and not quite so well ventilated as a sanitary commissioner would approve of, as it has positively no opening for light or air. A suffocating smoke meets us on entering, we rub our eyes, and when they have at length got accustomed to the biting atmosphere, we perceive, by the gloomy light of a train-oil lamp, the worthy family squatting on the floor in a state of almost complete nudity. Without being in the least embarrassed, Madame Leütt and her daughter receive us in their primitive costume : but to show us that the Tchuktchi know how to receive company, and to do honour to their guests, they immediately insert strings of glass beads in their greasy hair. Their hospitality equals their politeness ; for, instead of a cold reception, a hot dish of boiled reindeer-flesh, copiously irrigated with rancid train-oil by the experienced hand of the mistress of the household, is soon after smoking before us. Unfortunately our effeminate taste is not up to the *haut goût* of her culinary art, and while Mr. Leütt does ample justice to the artistic talent of his spouse, by rapidly bolting down pieces as large as a fist, we are hardly able to swallow a morsel.'

During his visit at Ostrownoje, Matiuschkin had a favourable opportunity of becoming acquainted with the sports of the Tchuktchi, the chieftain Makomol having set out prizes for a race. These consisted of a valuable silver fox, a first-rate beaver skin, and two fine walrus teeth. Nothing can be more admirable than the fleetness of the reindeer, or the dexterity of their drivers; and the agility displayed in the foot-race by the Tchuktchi, running at full speed in their heavy winter dresses over a distance of fifteen versts, gives a high idea of their muscular powers. After the races, the spectators are treated to a grand choregraphic display. The arctic bajaderes, muffled from head to foot in their stiff skin garments, form a narrow circle, slowly moving their feet backwards and forwards, and fiercely gesticulating with their hands, whilst their faces are distorted into a thousand horrible grimaces. The singing that accompanies the ballet has no doubt its charm for native ears, but to strangers it seems no better than a kind of grunt. The representation is closed by three first-rate *artistes* executing a particularly favourite dance. The faces of their countrymen express the same intense admiration with which a European dilettante follows the graceful pirouettes of a Taglioni, while the Russian guests see only three greasy monsters alternately rushing towards each other and starting back, until at length they stop from sheer exhaustion. As a token of their satisfaction, the Russians regale the fair performers with a cup of brandy and a roll of tobacco, and both parties take leave of each other with mutual protestations of satisfaction and friendship.

Though most of the reindeer or nomadic Tchuktchi have been baptized, yet Wrangell supposes the ceremony to have been a mere financial speculation on their part, and is convinced that the power of the Schamans is still as great as ever. An epidemic had carried off a great number of persons, and also whole herds of reindeer. In vain the Schamans had recourse to their usual conjurations, the plague continued. They consulted together, and directed that one of their most respected chiefs, named Kotschen, must be sacrificed, to appease the irritated spirits. Kotschen was willing to submit to the sentence, but none could be found to execute it, until his own son, prevailed on by his father's exhortations, and terrified by his threatened curse, plunged a knife into his heart, and gave his body to the Schamans.

Polygamy is general among the Tchuktchi, and they change their wives as often as they please. Still, though the women are certainly slaves, they are allowed more influence, and are subjected to less labour than among many savages. Amongst other heathenish and detestable customs, is that of killing all deformed children, and all old people as soon as they become unfit for the hardships and fatigues of a nomade life. Two years before Wrangell's arrival at Kolyma, there was an instance of this in the case of one of their richest chiefs. Waletka's father became infirm and tired of life, and was put to death at his own express desire, by some of his nearest relations.

Besides the wandering, or reindeer Tchuktchi, who call themselves Tennygk, there are others dwelling in fixed habitations along the borders of the sea at Behring's Straits and the Gulf of Anadyr, who differ considerably from the former in appearance and language. These Onkilon, or stationary Tchuktchi, belong to the wide-spread Esquimaux family, and, like most of their race, subsist by hunting the whale, the walrus, and the seal. They live in a state of abject dependence on the nomad Tchuktchi, and are poor, like all fishermen, while some of the Tennygk chieftains possess several thousands of reindeer, and are continually adding to their wealth by trade. Of course there is an active exchange of commodities between the two; the Onkilon furnishing thongs of walrus hide, walrus teeth, train oil, &c., and receiving reindeer skins, or ready-made clothes of the same material, in return.

They live in small settlements or villages spread along the

coast; their huts, raised on frameworks of whale rib and covered with skins, resemble a large irregular cone reposing on its side, with the apex directed to the north and the base shelving abruptly to the south. Here is the small opening, closed by a flap of loose skin, which serves as a door, while the smoke escapes and the light enters through a round hole in the roof. At the further or northern end of this structure is a second low square tent covered with double reindeer skins, the polog, which in winter serves both as the dining and bed-room of the family.

The Onkilon catch seals in a kind of net made of leather straps, which they spread out under the ice, and in which the animal entangles itself with the head or flippers. When the walrus, which is particularly abundant about Koliutschin Island, creeps on shore, they steal upon it unawares, cut off its retreat and kill it with their spears. Like the Esquimaux, they use dogs to drag their sledges.

The number of the Tchuktchi is greater than one might expect to find in so sterile a country. According to the Russian missionaries, there were, some years back, 52 ulusses or villages of the Onkilon, with 1,568 tents and 10,000 inhabitants; and Wrangell tells us that the Tennygk are at least twice as numerous, so that the entire population of the land of the Tchuktchi may possibly amount to 30,000.

The Polar Hare.

Natives of Unalaschka.

# CHAPTER XXV.

## BEHRING SEA—THE RUSSIAN FUR COMPANY—THE ALEÜTS.

Behring Sea—Unalaschka—The Pribilow Islands—St. Matthew—St. Laurence
—Behring's Straits—The Russian Fur Company—The Aleüts—Their Character
—Their Skill and Intrepidity in Hunting the Sea-otter—The Sea-bear—Whale
Chasing—Walrus Slaughter—The Sea-lion.

BEHRING SEA is extremely interesting in a geographical point of view, as the temperature of its coasts and
islands exhibit so striking a contrast with that part of the
Arctic Ocean which extends between Greenland, Iceland,
Norway, and Spitzbergen, and affords us the most convincing
proof of the benefits we owe to the Gulf Stream and to the
mild south-westerly winds which sweep across the Atlantic.
While through the sea, between Iceland and Scotland, a part of
the warmth generated in the tropical zone penetrates by means
of marine and aërial currents as far as Spitzbergen and
the western coast of Novaya Zemlya, the Sea of Behring is
completely deprived of this advantage. The long chain of
mountainous islands which bounds it on the south serves
as a barrier against the mild influence of the Pacific, and in-

stead of warm streams mixing with its waters many considerable rivers and deep bays yearly discharge into it enormous masses of ice.

Thus as soon as the navigator enters Behring Sea he perceives at once a considerable fall in the temperature, and finds himself suddenly transferred from a temperate oceanic region to one of a decidedly Arctic character.

In spite, therefore, of their comparatively southerly position (for the Straits of Behring do not even reach the Arctic circle, and the Andrianow Islands are ten degrees farther to the south than the Feroës), those frigid waters are, with regard to climate, far less favourably situated than the seas of Spitzbergen.

The same gradual differences of temperature and vegetation which we find in Unalaschka, the Pribilow Islands, St. Laurence, and the Straits of Behring, within 10° of latitude, occur in the Shetland Islands, Iceland, Bear Island, and Spitzbergen at distances of almost 20°; so that in the Sea of Behring the increase of cold on advancing to the north is about twice as rapid as in the waters between North Europe and North America.

The long and narrow peninsula of Aljaska, which forms the south-eastern boundary of this inhospitable sea, shows us its influence in a very marked degree, for while the climate of the northern side of that far projecting land-tongue has a decidedly Arctic character, its southern coasts fronting the Pacific enjoy a temperate climate. The mountain-chain which, rising to a height of five or six thousand feet, forms the back-bone of the peninsula, serves as the boundary of two distinct worlds, for while the northern slopes are bleak and treeless like Iceland, the southern shores are covered from the water's edge with magnificent forests. While on the northern side the walrus extends his excursions down to 56° 30′ N. L., on the southern exposure the humming-bird is seen to flit from flower to flower as high as 61°, the most northerly point it is known to attain.

The Feroe islands (64° N. lat.) have undoubtedly a no very agreeable climate to boast of, but they may almost be said to enjoy Italian skies when compared with Unalaschka (54° N. lat.), the best known of the Aleütian chain.

The Scandinavian archipelago is frequently obscured with fogs, but here they are perpetual from April to the middle of July. From this time till the end of September, the weather improves, as then the southerly winds drive the foggy region more to the north, and enable the sun to shine during a few serene days upon the bleak shores of Unalaschka. But soon the Polar air-streams regain the supremacy, and a dismal veil once more shrouds the melancholy island. Snow generally begins to fall early in October, and snow-storms occur to the very end of May. There are years in which it rains continually during the whole winter. In the Feroës some service trees are to be seen twelve feet high or more, while nothing like a tree ever grew in Unalaschka. The difference between the temperatures of the summer and winter, which in the Feroës is confined to very narrow limits, is much more considerable in Unalaschka, though here also the moderating influence of the sea makes itself felt. Thus in summer the thermometer rarely rises above 66°, but on the other hand in winter it still more rarely falls below -2°.

Of course no corn of any kind can possibly ripen in a climate like this, but the damp and cool temperature favours the growth of herbs. In the moist lowlands the stunted willow bushes are stifled by the luxuriant grasses; and even on the hills, the vegetation, which is of a decidedly Alpine character, covers the earth up to the line of perpetual snow; while several social plants, such as the Lupinus nootkeanus and the Rhododendron kamtschadalicum, decorate these dismal regions with their brilliant colour. The lively green of the meadows reminds one of the valley of Urseren, so well known to all Alpine tourists. The mosses and lichens begin already at Unalaschka to assume that predominance in the Flora, which characterises the frigid zone.

A few degrees to the north of the Aleütian chain, which extends in a long line from the promontory of Aljaska to Kamtschatka, are situated the Pribilow Islands, St. George and St. Paul, which are celebrated in the history of the fur trade, the former as the chief breeding-place of the sea-bear, the latter as that of the sea-lion. Chamisso was struck with their wintry aspect, for here no sheltered valleys and lowlands promote, as at Unalaschka, a more vigorous vegetation. The rounded backs of the hills and the scattered rocks are covered with black and grey lichens; and where the melting snows afford a sufficient moisture, sphagnum, mosses, and a few weeds occupy the marshy ground. The frozen earth has no springs, and yet these desolate islands have a more southerly situation than the Orkneys, where barley grows to ripeness. Before these islands were discovered by the Russians they had been for ages the undisturbed home of the sea birds and the large cetacean seals. Under Russian superintendence some Aleüts have now been settled on both of them. The innumerable herds of sea-lions, which cover the naked shores of St. George as far as the eye can reach, present a strange sight. The guillemots have taken possession of the places unoccupied by their families and fly fearlessly among them, or nestle in the crevices of the wave-worn rock-walls, or between the large boulders which form a bank along the strand.

Still farther to the north lies the uninhabited island of St. Matthew (62° N. lat.). A settlement was once attempted; but as the animals which had been reckoned upon for the winter supply of food departed, the unfortunate colonists all died of hunger.

Fogs are so frequent about the island of St. Laurence, that navigators have often passed close by it (65° N. lat.) without seeing it. Chamisso was surprised at the beauty and the numbers of its dwarfish flowering herbs, which reminded him of the highlands of Switzerland, while the neighbouring St. Laurence Bay, in the land of the Tchuktchi, was the image of wintry desolation. In July the lowlands were covered with snow-fields, and the few plants bore the Alpine character in the most marked degree. Under this inclement sky the mountains, unprotected by vegetation, rapidly fall into decay. Every winter splits the rocks, and the summer torrents carry the fragments down to their feet. The ground is everywhere covered with blocks of stone, unless where the sphagnum, by the accumulation of its decomposed remains, has formed masses of peat in the swampy lowlands.

On sailing through Behring's Straits the traveller may see, in clear weather, both the Old and the New World. On both sides rise high mountains precipitously from the water's edge in Asia, but separated from the sea by a broad alluvial belt on the American side. The sea is deepest on the Asiatic border, where the current, flowing from the south with considerable rapidity, has also the greatest force. Here also whales may be often seen, and large herds of walruses.

In former times the baidar of the Esquimaux was the only boat ever seen in the straits, and since Semen Deshnew, who first sailed round the eastern point of Asia, European navigators had but rarely passed them to explore the seas beyond; but recently this remotest part of the world has become the scene of an active whale fishery.

The shores of Behring Sea are naked and bleak; and the numerous volcanoes of the Aleütian chain pour out their lava streams over unknown wildernesses. But the waters of the sea are teeming with life. Gigantic algæ, such as are never seen in the torrid zone, form, round the rocky coasts, vast submarine forests. A host of fishes, whales, walruses, and seals, fill the sea and its shores, and innumerable sea birds occupy the cliffs. But these treasures of the ocean, which for ages furnished the Aleüts and other wild tribes with the means of existence, have also been the cause of their servitude. Had the sea-otter not existed, the wild children of the soil might possibly still be in possession of their ancient freedom; and but for the sea-bear and the walrus, the whale and the seal, the banners of the Czar would scarcely have met the flag of England on the continent of America.

As the whole fur trade of the Hudson's Bay Territory is concentrated in the hands of one mighty company, thus also one powerful association enjoys the exclusive commerce of the eastern possessions of Russia. The regions under the authority of the Russian fur company* occupy an immense space, as they comprise not only all the islands of Behring Sea but also the American coasts down to 55° N. lat. The extreme points of this vast territory are situated at a greater distance from each other than London from Tobolsk, but

---

* Since last year, the Russian Government has sold her American possessions to the United States, but as it is not yet known how far the interests of the Russian fur company have been affected by the change, I may be allowed to speak of her in the present tense.

the importance of its trade bears no proportion to its extent.

The company, which was founded, in the year 1799, under the Emperor Paul, had, in 1839, thirty-six hunting settlements on its own territory (the Kurile islands, the Aleütic chain, Aljaska, Bristol Bay, Cook's Inlet, Norton Sound, &c.), besides a chain of agencies from Ochotsk to St. Petersburg. Its chief seat is New Archangel on Sitcha, one of the many islands of King George III.'s Archipelago, first accurately explored by Vancouver. The magnificent bay of Norfolk, at the head of which the small town is situated, greatly resembles a Norwegian fjord, as we here find the same steep rockwalls bathing their precipitous sides in the emerald waters, and clothed with dense pine forests wherever a tree can grow.

A number of islets scattered over the surface of the bay add to the beauty of the scene. The furs collected by the company are chiefly those of sea-bears, sea-otters, foxes, beavers, bears, lynxes, American martens, &c., and are partly furnished by the subjects of its own territory (Aleüts, Kadjacks, Kenaïzes, Tchugatchi, Aljaskans), who are compelled to hunt on its account, and partly obtained by barter from the independent tribes of the mainland, or from the Hudson's Bay Company. The greater part is sent to Ochotsk, or the Amur, and from thence through Siberia to St. Petersburg; the rest to the Chinese ports, where the skins of the young sea-bear always find a ready market.

Of all the aboriginal tribes which inhabit the vast territory of Russian America, the most worthy of notice is that of the Aleüts. Less fortunate than their independent relatives, the Esquimaux of the north—who in the midst of privations maintain an imperturbable gaiety of temper—these islanders have been effectually spirit-broken under a foreign yoke. In 1817, the cruel treatment of their masters had reduced them to about a thousand; since that time their number has somewhat increased, the company having at length discovered that man is, after all, the most valuable production of a land, and that if depopulation increased still further, they would soon have no more hunters to supply them with furs.

Every Aleüt is bound, after his eighteenth year, to serve the company *three years*; and this forced labour-tax does not seem at first sight immoderate, but if we consider that the islanders, to whom every foreign article is supplied from the warehouses of the company, are invariably its debtors, we cannot doubt that as long as the Aleüt is able to hunt he is obliged to do so for the wages of a slave. The Bishop Ivan Weniaminow, who resided ten years at Unalaschka, draws a picture of this people which exhibits evident marks of a long servitude. They never quarrel among each other, and their patience is exemplary. Nothing can surpass the fortitude with which they endure pain. On the other hand they never show excessive joy; it seems impossible to raise their feelings to the pitch of delight. Even after a long fast, a child never grasps with eagerness the proffered morsel, nor does it on any occasion exhibit the mirth so natural to its age.

In hunting the marine animals the Aleüts exhibit a wonderful skill and intrepidity. To catch the sea-otter they assemble in April or May, at an appointed spot, in their light skin boats or baidars, and choose one of their most respected chiefs for the leader of the expedition, which generally numbers from fifty to a hundred boats. Such hunting parties are annually organised from the Kurile Islands to Kadjack, and consequently extend their operations over a line of 3,000 miles. On the first fine day the expedition sets out and proceeds to a distance of about forty versts from the coast, when the baidars form into a long line, leaving an interval of about 250 fathoms from boat to boat, as far as a sea-otter diving out of the water can be seen, so that a row of thirty baidars occupies a space of from ten to twelve versts. When the number of the boats is greater the intervals are reduced. Every man now looks upon the sea with great attention. Nothing escapes the eye of the Aleüt; in the smallest black spot appearing but one moment over the surface of the waters, he at once recognises a sea-otter. The baidar which first sees the animal rows rapidly towards the spot where the creature dived, and now the Aleüt, holding his oar straight up in the air, remains motionless on the spot. Immediately, the whole squadron is on the move, and the long straight line changes into a wide circle, the centre of which is occupied by the baidar with the raised oar. The otter not being able to remain long under water reappears, and the nearest Aleüt immediately greets him with an arrow. This first attack is seldom mortal; very often the missile does not even reach its mark, and the sea-otter instantly disappears. Again the oar rises from the next baidar; again the circle forms, but this time narrower than at first; the fatigued otter is obliged to come oftener to the surface, arrows fly from all sides, and finally the animal, killed by a mortal shot, or exhausted by repeated wounds, falls to the share of the archer who has hit it nearest to the head. If several otters appear at the same time, the boats form as many rings, provided their number be sufficiently great.

The boldest of all hunters, the Aleüts of the Fox Islands, pursue the sea-otter also in winter. If, during the summer chase, the rapidity and regularity with which all the movements are performed, and the sure eye and aim of the archers command the spectator's admiration, this winter chase gives him occasion to wonder at their courage. During the severest winter-storms the otter shelters himself on the shore of some small uninhabited island, or on a solitary rock, and after having carefully ascertained that no enemy is near coils himself up and falls asleep. While the storm still rages, two Aleüts approach the rock in two single baidars, from the leeward. The hunter in the foremost baidar stands upright, a gun or a club in his hand, and waits in this position till a wave brings him near to the summit of the rock. He now springs on land, and while his companion takes care of the baidar, approaches the sleeping otter and shoots it or kills it with his club. With the assistance of his companion who has remained on the water, he springs back into his baidar as soon as the crest of a wave brings it within his reach.

The sea-bear is nearly as valuable as the sea-otter to the fur company, as the woolly skin of the young animal is the only one of the whole seal tribe which is reckoned among the finer peltry. The sea-bears are chiefly killed on the Commodore and Pribilow Islands, particularly on St. Paul, where they are hunted by a certain number of Aleüts located there under Russian superintendence. The chase begins in the latter part of September, on a cold foggy day, when the wind blows from the side where the animals are assembled on the rocky shore. The boldest huntsmen open the way, then follow the older people and the children, and the chief personage of the band comes last, to be the better able to direct and survey the movements of his men, who are all armed with clubs. The main object is to cut off the herd as quickly as possible from the sea. All the grown up males and females are spared and allowed to escape, but most of the younger animals are sentenced to death. Those which are only four months old (their furs being most highly prized) are doomed without exception; while of the others that have attained an age of one, two, or three years, only the males are killed. For several days after the massacre, the mothers swim about the island, seeking and loudly wailing for their young.

From October 5, St. Paul is gradually deserted by the sea-bears, who then migrate to the south and reappear towards the end of April, the males arriving first. Each seeks the same spot on the shore which he occupied during the preceding year, and lies down among the large stone blocks with which the flat beach is covered. About the middle of May the far more numerous females begin to make their appearance, and the sea-bear families take full possession of the strand. Each male is the sultan of a herd of females, varying in number according to his size and strength; the weaker brethren contenting themselves with half-a-dozen, while some of the sturdier and fiercer fellows preside over harems 200 strong. Jealousy and intrusion frequently give rise to terrible battles. The full-grown male sea-bear, who is about four or five times larger than the female, grows to the length of eight feet, and owes his name to his shaggy blackish fur, and not to his disposition, which is far from being cruel or savage.

Armed with a short spear a single Aleüt does not hesitate to attack the colossal whale. Approaching cautiously from behind in his baidar until he reaches the head he plunges his weapon into the animal's flank, under the fore-fin, and then retreats as fast as his oar can carry him. If the spear has penetrated into the flesh, the whale is doomed, it dies within the next two or three days and the currents and the waves drift the carcase to the next shore. Each spear has its peculiar mark by which the owner is recognised. Sometimes

the baidar does not escape in time, and the whale, maddened
by pain, furiously lashes the waters with its tail, and throws
the baidar high up into the air, or sinks it deep into the
sea. The whale fishers are highly esteemed among the Aleüts,
and their intrepidity and skill well deserve the general admiration. Of course many of the whales are lost. In the
summer of 1831, 118 whales were wounded near Kadjack, of
which only forty-three were found. The others may have been
wafted far out into the sea to regale the sharks and sea-birds,
or driven to more distant shores, whose inhabitants no doubt
gladly welcomed their landing. Wrangell informs us, that
since 1833 the Russians have introduced the use of the
harpoon, and engaged some English harpooners to teach the
Aleüts a more profitable method of whale-catching, but we
are not told how the experiment has succeeded.

The company, besides purchasing a great quantity of walrus
teeth from the Tchuktchi of the Behring's Straits and
Bristol Bay, send every year a detachment of Aleüts to the
north coast of Aljaska, where generally a large number of
young walruses, probably driven away by the older ones, who
prefer the vicinity of the polar ice, spend the summer
months.

The walruses herd on the lowest edge of the coast which is
within reach of the spring tides. When the Aleüts prepare
to attack the animals, they take leave of each other as if
they were going to face death, being no less afraid of the
tusks of the walruses than of the awkwardness of their
own companions. Armed with lances and heavy axes,
they stealthily approach the walruses, and having disposed
their ranks, suddenly fall upon them with loud shouts, and
endeavour to drive them from the sea, taking care that none
of them escape into the water, as in that case the rest would
irresistibly follow and precipitate the huntsmen along with
them. As soon as the walruses have been driven far enough
up the strand, the Aleüts attack them with their lances,
striking at them in places where the hide is not so thick, and
then pressing with all their might against the spear, to render the wound deep and deadly. The slaughtered animals
tumble one over the other and form large heaps, whilst the
huntsmen, uttering furious shouts and intoxicated with

carnage, wade through the bloody mire. They then cleave
the jaws and extract the tusks, which are the chief objects
of the slaughter of several thousand walruses, since neither
their flesh nor their fat is made use of in the colony. The
carcases are left on the shore to be washed away by the
spring-tides, which soon efface the mark of the massacre,
and in the following year the inexhaustible north sends new
victims to the coast.

Sir George Simpson, in his 'Overland Journey round the
World,' relates that the bales of fur sent to Kjachta are
covered with walrus hide; it is then made to protect the tea-
chests which find their way to Moscow, and after all these
wanderings, the far-travelled skin returns again to New
Archangel, where, cut into small pieces and stamped with the
company's mark, it serves as a medium of exchange.

The skin of the sea-lion (*Otaria Stelleri*) has but little
value in the fur trade, as its hair is short and coarse, but in
many other respects the unwieldy animal is of considerable
use to the Aleüt. Its hide serves to cover his baidar; with
the entrails he makes his water-tight kamleika, a wide, long
shirt which he puts on over his dress to protect himself
against the rain or the spray; the thick webs of its flippers
furnish excellent soles for his boots, and the bristles of its
lip figure as ornaments in his head-dress.

The Sea Bear.

WALRUS HUNTING.

Esquimaux watching a Seal Hole.

# CHAPTER XXVI.

## THE ESQUIMAUX.

Their wide Extension—Climate of the Regions they inhabit—Their physical Appearance—Their Dress—Snow Huts—The Kayak or the Baidar—Hunting Apparatus and Weapons—Enmity between the Esquimaux and the Red Indian —The 'Bloody Falls'—Chase of the Reindeer—Bird Catching—Whale Hunting —Various Stratagems employed to catch the Seal—The Keep Kuttuk—Bear Hunting—Walrus Hunting—Awaklok and Myouk—The Esquimaux Dog— Games and Sports—Angekoks—Moral Character—Self-reliance—Intelligence— Iligliuk—Commercial Eagerness of the Esquimaux—Their Voracity—Seasons of Distress.

OF all the uncivilised nations of the globe none range over a wider space than the Esquimaux, whose various tribes extend from Greenland and Labrador, over all the coasts of Arctic America, to the Aleütic chain and the extreme north-eastern point of Asia. Many are independent, others subject to the Russian, Danish, or British rule. In Baffin's Bay and Lancaster Sound, they accost the whale-fisher; they meet him in the Icy Sea beyond Behring's Straits; and while their most southerly tribes dwell as low as the latitude of

Vienna, others sojourn as high as the 80th degree of northern latitude—and probably roam even still higher on the still undiscovered coasts beyond—a nearness to the pole no other race is known to reach.

The old Scandinavian settlers in Greenland expressed their dislike for them in the contemptuous name of Skraelingers (screamers or wretches); the seamen of the Hudson's Bay ships, who trade annually with the natives of northern Labrador and the Savage Islands, have long called them ' Seymos ' or ' Suckemos,' names evidently derived from the cries of ' Seymo,' or ' Teymo,' with which they greet the arrival of the ships; they speak of themselves simply as ' Inuit,' or men.

With few exceptions the whole of the vast region they inhabit lies beyond the extremest limits of forest growth, in the most desolate and inhospitable countries of the globe. The rough winds of the Polar Sea almost perpetually blow over their bleak domains, and thus only a few plants of the hardiest nature—lichens and mosses, grasses, saxifragas, and willows— are able to subsist there, and to afford a scanty supply of food to a few land animals and birds.

Ill indeed would it fare with the Esquimaux, if they were reduced to live upon the niggardly produce of the soil; but the sea, with its cetaceans and fishes, amply provides for their wants. Thus they are never found at any considerable distance from the ocean, and they line a considerable part of the coasts of the Arctic seas without ever visiting the interior.

It may easily be supposed that a race whose eastern branches have for several centuries been under the influence of the Danes and English, while in the extreme west it has long been forced to submit to Russian tyranny, and whose central and northern tribes rarely come into contact with Europeans—must show some variety in its manners and mode of life, and that the same description is not applicable in all points to the disciples of the Moravian brothers in Labrador or Greenland, to the Greek-Catholic Aleüts, and to the far more numerous heathen Esquimaux of continental America, or of the vast archipelago beyond its northern shores. Upon the whole, however, it is curious to observe how exactly, amidst all diversity of time and place, these people have preserved unaltered their habits and manners. The broad, flat face, widest just below the eyes, the forehead generally narrow and tapering upwards; the eyes narrow and more or less oblique; all indicate a mongol or tartar type, differing greatly from the features of the conterminous Red Indian tribes. Their complexion, when relieved from smoke and dirt, also approaches more nearly to white than that of their copper-coloured neighbours. Most of the men are rather under the medium English size, but they cannot be said to be a dwarfish race. Thus Simpson saw in Camden Bay three Esquimaux who measured from five feet ten inches to six feet; and among the natives of Smith Strait, Kane met with one a foot taller than himself. The females, however, are all comparatively short. The Esquimaux are all remarkably broad shouldered, and though their muscles are not so firm as those of the European seamen, yet they surpass in bodily strength all the other natives of America. In both sexes the hands and feet are remarkably small and well formed. From exercise in hunting the seal and walrus, the muscles of the arms and back are much developed in the men, who are moreover powerful wrestlers. When young the Esquimaux looks cheerful and good humoured, and the females exhibit, when laughing, a set of very white teeth. Could they be induced to wash their faces, many of these savage beauties would be found to possess a complexion scarcely a shade darker than that of a deep brunette; but though disinclined to ablutions, for which the severity of their climate may serve as an excuse, they are far from neglecting the arts of the toilette.

Unlike the Hare Indian and Dog Rib females, in whom the hard rule of their lords and masters has obliterated every trace of female vanity, the Esquimaux women tastefully plait their straight, black, and glossy hair; and hence we may infer that greater deference is paid to them by the men. They also generally tattoo their chin, forehead, and cheeks, not, however, as in the South Sea Islands, with elaborate patterns, but with a few simple lines, which have a not unpleasing effect.

From Behring's Straits eastward, as far as the Mackenzie,

the males pierce the lower lip near each angle of the mouth, and fill the apertures with labrets of blue or green quartz, or of ivory resembling buttons. Many also pierce the septum of the nose, and insert a dentalium shell or ivory needle. Like the Red Indians, they are fond of beads, but their most common ornament consists in strings of teeth of the fox, wolf, or musk-ox—sometimes many hundreds in number— which are either attached to the lower part of the jacket, or fastened as a belt round the waist.

Their dress is admirably adapted to the severity of their climate. With their two pair of breeches made of reindeer or seal-skin, the outer one having the hair outside and the inner one next the body, and their two jackets—of which the upper one is provided with a great hood; with their water-tight seal-skin boots, lined with the downy skins of birds, and their enormous gloves, they bid defiance to the severest cold, and, even in the hardest weather, pursue their occupations in the open air whenever the moon is in the sky, or during the doubtful meridian twilight. The women are perfect in the art of making water-tight shirts, or ' kamleikas,' of the entrails of the seal or walrus, which in summer serve to replace their heavy skin jackets. They also sew their boots so tight, that not the slightest wet can penetrate, and with a neatness of which the best shoemaker in Europe might be proud. The dress of the two sexes is much alike, the outer jacket having a pointed skirt before and behind, but that of the females is a little longer. The women also wear larger hoods, in which they carry their children; and sometimes (as in Labrador) the inner boot has in front a long, pointed flap, to answer the same purpose.

The Esquimaux are equally expert in the construction of their huts. As soon as the lengthening days induce the tribes about Cape Bathurst and the mouth of the Mackenzie to move seaward on the ice to the seal hunt, a marvellous system of architecture comes into use, unknown among any other American nations. The fine pure snow has by that time acquired, under the action of the winds and frosts, sufficient coherence to form an admirable light building material, which the Esquimaux skilfully employ for the erection of most comfortable dome-shaped houses. A circle

is first traced on the smooth surface of the snow, and slabs
for raising the walls cut from within, so as to clear a space
down to the ice, which is to form the floor of the dwelling,
and whose evenness was previously ascertained by probing.
The slabs for the dome are cut from some neighbouring spot.
The crevices between the slabs are plugged up, and the
seams closed, by throwing a few shovelfuls of loose snow
over the fabric. Two men generally work together, and
when the dome is completed, the one within cuts a low door,
and creeps out. The walls being only three or four inches
thick, admit a very agreeable light, which serves for ordinary
purposes; if more is required, a window of transparent ice is
introduced. The proper thickness of the walls is of some
importance; one of a few inches excludes the wind, yet keeps
down the damp so as to prevent dripping from the interior.
The furniture of this crystal hut is also formed of snow (the
seats, the table, the sleeping-places), and when covered with
skins is very comfortable. By means of ante-chambers and
porches, with the opening turned to leeward, warmth is
insured, and social intercourse facilitated by contiguous
building, doors of communication, and covered passages.
By constant practice, the Esquimaux can raise such huts
almost as quickly as we could pitch a tent. When M'Clintock
for a few nails hired four Esquimaux to build a hut for his
party, they completed it in an hour, though it was 8 ft. in
diameter, and 5½ ft. high.

In spite of its fragile materials, this snow-house is durable,
for the wind has little effect on its dome-like form, and it
resists the thaw until the sun acquires a very considerable
power. Of course a strong fire could not possibly be made
within, but such is not needed by the Esquimaux. The
train-oil lamp suffices to dry his wet clothes and boots when
he returns from hunting; and the crowding of the inmates
engenders a sufficiently high temperature to keep him warm.
Having also a decided predilection for raw flesh and fat, he
requires no great expenditure of fuel to cook his dinner.
The lower part of his dwelling being under the surface of
the snow, likewise promotes its warmth.

But of whatever materials the hut of the Esquimaux may
be constructed—of snow, as I have just described, or, as is

Y

frequently the case, of stones, or earth, or drift-wood—everywhere, from Behring's Straits to Smith Sound, it is equally well adapted to the climate and to circumstances. Thus when Dr. Scoresby landed in 1822 on the eastern coast of Greenland, he discovered some deserted Esquimaux huts, which gave proof both of the severity of the climate, and of the ingenuity evinced in counteracting its rigours. A horizontal tunnel about fifteen feet long, and so low as to render it necessary to creep through on hands and feet, opens with one end to the south, and leads through the other into the interior of the hut. This rises but little above the surface of the earth, and, as it is generally overgrown with moss or grass, is scarcely to be distinguished from the neighbouring soil. The floor of the tunnel is frequently on a level with that of the hut, but often also it is made to slant downwards and upwards, so that the colder, and consequently heavier, air without is still more effectually kept off from the warmer air within; and thus the Esquimaux, without ever having studied physics, make a practical use of one of its fundamental laws. But their most ingenious invention is unquestionably that of the one-seated boat, the 'kayak,' or the 'baidar.' A light, long, and narrow frame of wood, or seal or walrus bone, is covered water-tight with seal-skin, leaving but one circular hole in the middle. In this the Esquimaux sits with outstretched legs, and binds a sack (which is formed of the intestines of the whale, or of the skins of young seals, and fits in the opening) so tightly round his middle, that even in a heavy sea not a drop of water can penetrate into the boat. Striking with his light oar (which is paddled at each extremity) alternately to the right and to the left, his spear or harpoon before him, and maintaining his equilibrium with all the dexterity of a rope-dancer, he flies like an arrow over the water; and should a wave upset him, he knows how to right himself by the action of the paddle. The 'oomiak,' or women's boat, likewise consists of a framework covered with seal-skins, and is roomy enough to hold ten or twelve people, with benches for the women who row or paddle. The mast supports a triangular sail made of the entrails of seals, and easily distended by the wind. The men would consider it beneath their dignity to row in one of these omnibus boats; they leave this labour entirely to the women, who, to the tact of a monotonous song, slowly propel the oomiak through the water. Judging of foreign customs by their own, the Esquimaux between the Mackenzie and Coppermine rivers made the strange mistake, as Sir John Richardson relates, of supposing that the English sailors whom they saw rowing in company were women. One of them even asked whether all white females had beards.

The weapons of the Esquimaux, and their various fishing and hunting implements, likewise show great ingenuity and skill. Their oars are tastefully inlaid with walrus teeth; they have several kinds of spears or darts, adapted to the size of the various animals which they hunt; and their elastic bows, strongly bound with strings of seal-gut, drive a six-foot arrow with unerring certainty to a distant mark. To bring down a larger animal, the shaft is armed with a sharp flint, or a pointed bone; if intended to strike a bird, it is smaller, and blunted.

The harpoons and lances used in killing whales or seals have long shafts of wood or of the narwhal's tooth, and the barbed point is so constructed that, when the blow takes effect, it is left sticking in the body of the animal, while the shaft attached to it by a string is disengaged from the socket, and becomes a buoy of wood. Seal-skins, blown up like bladders, are likewise used as buoys for the whale-spears, being adroitly stripped from the animal so that all the natural apertures are easily made air-tight.

With equal industry and skill the Esquimaux put to use almost every part of the land and marine animals which they chase. Knives, spear-points, and fish-hooks are made of the horns and bones of the deer. The ribs of the whale are used in roofing huts, or in the construction of sledges, where drift-timber is scarce. Strong cord is made from strips of seal-skin hide, and the sinews of musk-oxen and deer furnish bow-strings or cord to make nets or snares. In default of drift-wood, the bones of the whale are employed for the construction of their sledges, in pieces fitted to each other with neatness, and firmly sewed together.

During the long confinement to their huts or 'igloos,' in the dark winter months, the men execute some very fair figures in bone and in walrus or fossil ivory; besides making fish-hooks, knife-handles, and other instruments neatly of these materials, or of metal or wood.

Thus in all these respects the Esquimaux are as superior to the Red Indians as they are in strength and personal courage; and yet no Norwegian can more utterly despise the filthy Lapp, and no orthodox Mussulman look down with greater contempt upon a 'giaour,' than the Loucheux or Chepewayan upon the Esquimaux, who in his eyes is no better than a brute, and whom he approaches only to kill.

In his 'Voyage to the Coppermine River' Hearne relates a dreadful instance of this bloodthirsty hatred. The Indians who accompanied him having heard that some Esquimaux had erected their summer huts near the mouth of that river, were at once seized with a tiger-like fury. Hearne, the only European of the party, had not the power to restrain them, and he might as well have attempted to touch the heart of an ice-bear as to move the murderous band to pity. As craftily and noiselessly as serpents they drew nigh, and when the midnight sun verged on the horizon, with a dreadful yell they burst on the huts of their unsuspecting victims. Not one of them escaped, and the monsters delighted to prolong the misery of their death-struggle by repeated wounds. An old woman had both her eyes torn out before she received the mortal blow. A young girl fled to Hearne for protection, who used every effort to save her, but in vain.

In 1821 some human skulls lying on the spot still bore testimony to this cruel slaughter, and the name of the 'Bloody Falls,' given by Hearne to the scene of the massacre, will convey its memory to distant ages.

No wonder that the hate of the Esquimaux is no less intense, and that they also pursue the Indians, wherever they can, with their spears and arrows, like wild beasts.

'Year after year,' says Sir John Richardson, 'sees the Esquimaux on the polar coast of America occupied in a uniform circle of pursuits. When the rivers open in spring, they proceed to the rapids and falls to spear the salmon, which at that season come swimming stream upwards. At the same time, or earlier in more southern localities, they hunt the reindeer, which drop their young on the coasts and islands while the snow is only partially melted. Where the open country affords the huntsman no opportunity of approaching his game unperceived, deep pits are dug in the snowy ravines and superficially covered with snow-tablets. The wind soon effaces the traces of the human hand, and thus many reindeer are snared.'

In summer the reindeer are killed partly by driving them from islands or narrow necks of land into the sea, and then spearing them from their kayaks; and partly by shooting them from behind heaps of stones raised for the purpose of watching them, and imitating their peculiar bellow or grunt. Among the various artifices which they employ for this purpose, one of the most ingenious consists in two men walking directly *from* the deer they wish to kill, when the animal almost always follows them. As soon as they arrive at a large stone, one of the men hides behind it with his bow, while the other, continuing to walk on, soon leads the deer within range of his companion's arrows.

The multitudes of swans, ducks, and geese resorting to the morasses of the northern coasts to breed, likewise aid in supplying the Esquimaux with food during their short but busy summer of two months. For their destruction a very ingenious instrument has been invented. Six or eight small balls made of walrus-tooth and pierced in the middle are separately attached to as many thongs of animal sinew, which are tied together at the opposite end. When cast into the air the diverging balls describe circles—like the spokes of a wheel—and woe to the unfortunate bird that comes within their reach.

On the coasts frequented by whales, the month of August is devoted to the pursuit of these animals; a successful chase ensuring a comfortable winter to a whole community. Their capture requires an association of labour: hence along the coasts of the Polar Sea, the Esquimaux unite their huts into villages, for whose site a bold point of coast is generally chosen, where the water is deep enough to float a whale.

When one of these huge creatures is seen lying on the water, a dozen kayaks or more cautiously paddle up astern of him, till a single canoe, preceding the rest, comes close to him on one quarter, so as to enable the men to drive the spear into the animal with all the force of both arms. This spear has a

long line of thong and an inflated seal-skin attached to it.
The stricken whale immediately dives; but when he reappears
after some time, all the canoes again paddle towards him,
some warning being given by the seal-skin buoy floating on
the surface. Each man being furnished like the first, they
repeat the blow as often as they find an opportunity, till
perhaps every line has been thus employed. After chasing
him in this manner sometimes for half a day, he is at length
so wearied by the resistance of the buoys and exhausted by
loss of blood as to be obliged to rise more and more often to
the surface, and is finally killed and towed ashore.

Though in many parts seals are caught at every season of
the year, yet the great hunt takes place in spring, when they
play in the open lanes near the coasts, or come out on the
ice to bask in the sun. In spite of their wariness, they are
no match for the Esquimaux, who have carefully studied
all their habits from infancy. Sometimes the hunter approaches them by imitating their forms and motions so
perfectly that the poor animals are not undeceived until one
of them is struck with his lance; or else, by means of a
white screen pushed forward on a sledge, the hunter comes
within range and picks out the best conditioned of the band.
As the season draws near midsummer, the seals are more
approachable; their eyes being so congested by the glare of
the sun, that they are sometimes nearly blind. In winter
they are assaulted while working at their breathing-holes, or
when coming up for respiration.

If an Esquimaux has any reason to suppose that a seal is
busy gnawing beneath the ice, he immediately attaches himself to the place, and seldom leaves it, even in the severest
frost, till he has succeeded in killing the animal. For this
purpose he first builds a snow-wall about four feet in height,
to shelter him from the wind, and seating himself under the
lee of it, deposits his spears, lines, and other implements
upon several little forked sticks inserted into the snow, in
order to prevent the smallest noise being made in moving
them when wanted. But the most curious precaution consists
in tying his own knees together with a thong so securely as to
prevent any rustling of his clothes, which might otherwise
alarm the animal. In this situation a man will sit quietly

sometimes for hours together, attentively listening to any noise
made by the seal, and sometimes using the 'keep-kuttuk'
in order to ascertain whether the animal is still at work
below.  This simple little instrument—which affords another
striking proof of Esquimaux ingenuity—is merely a slender
rod of bone (as delicate as a fine wire, that the seal may not
see it) nicely rounded, and having a point at one end, and a
knob at the other.  It is inserted into the ice, and the knob
remaining above the surface informs the fisherman by its
motion whether the seal is employed in making his hole; if
not, it remains undisturbed, and the attempt is given up in
that place.  When the hunter supposes the hole to be nearly
completed, he cautiously lifts his spear (to which the line
has been previously attached), and as soon as the blowing of
the seal is distinctly heard—and the ice consequently very
thin—he drives it into him with the force of both arms, and
then cuts away with his 'panna,' or well-sharpened knife,
the remaining crust of ice, to enable him to repeat the
wounds, and get him out.  The 'neituk' (*phoca hispida*),
being the smallest seal, is held while struggling, either simply
by hand, or by putting the line round a spear with the point
stuck into the ice.  For the 'oguke' (*phoca barbata*), the
line is passed round the man's leg or arm; and for a walrus,
round his body, his feet being at the same time firmly set
against a hummock of ice, in which position these people
can, from habit, hold against a very heavy strain.  A boy of
fifteen is equal to the killing of a 'neituk,' but it requires a
full-grown person to master either of the larger animals.
This sport is not without the danger which adds to the excitement of success, particularly if the creature struck by the
hunter be a large seal or walrus; for woe betide him if he
does not instantly plant his feet firmly in the ice, and throw
himself in such a position, that the strain on the line is as
nearly as possible brought into the direction of the length of
the spine of his back, and axis of his lower limbs.  A trans-
verse pull from one of these powerful animals would double
him up across the air-hole, and perhaps break his back; or
if the opening be large, as it often is when the spring is advanced, he would be dragged under water and drowned.

As the Polar bear is as great a seal-hunter as the

Esquimaux, one of the usual methods employed by the latter to catch these bears is to imitate the motions of the seal by lying flat on the ice until the bear approaches sufficiently near to ensure a good aim; but a gun is necessary to practise this stratagem with success. Seeman ('Voyage of the Herald') mentions another ingenious mode of capturing the bear by taking advantage of the well-known voracity of the animal, which generally swallows its food without much mastication. A thick and strong piece of whalebone, about four inches broad and two feet long, is rolled up into a small compass, and carefully enveloped in blubber, forming a round ball. It is then placed in the open air at a low temperature, where it soon becomes hard and frozen. The natives, armed with their knives, bows and arrows, together with this frozen bait, proceed in quest of the bear. As soon as the animal is seen, one of the natives discharges an arrow at it; the monster, smarting from this assault, chases the party, then in full retreat, until, meeting with the frozen blubber dropped in his path, he greedily swallows it, and continues the pursuit—doubtless fancying that there must be more where that came from. The natural heat of the body soon causes the blubber to thaw, when the whalebone, thus freed, springs back, and frightfully lacerates the stomach. The writhing brute falls down in helpless agony, and the Esquimaux, hurrying to the spot, soon put an end to his sufferings.

The Esquimaux of Smith Sound hunt the bear with the assistance of their dogs, which are carefully trained not to engage in contest with the bear, but to retard his flight. While one engrosses his attention ahead, a second attacks him in the rear, always alert, and each protecting the other; and thus it rarely happens that they are seriously injured, or that they fail to delay the animal until their masters come up. If there be two hunters, the bear is killed easily; for one makes a feint of thrusting a spear at the right side, and, as the animal turns, with his arms towards the threatened attack, the left is unprotected, and receives the death-wound. But if the hunter is alone, he grasps the lance firmly in his hands, and provokes the animal to pursue him by moving rapidly across its path, and then running as if to escape. But hardly is its long, unwieldy body extended for the chase, than, with a rapid jump, the hunter doubles on his track, and runs back towards his first position. The bear is in the act of turning after him again, when the lance is plunged into the left side below the shoulder. So dexterously has this thrust to be made, that an unpractised hunter has often to leave his spear in the side of his prey, and run for his life; but even then, if well aided by the dogs, a cool, skilful man seldom fails to kill his adversary.

While the seal, narwhal, and white whale furnish the staple food of the more southern Greenlander, the walrus is the chief resource of the Smith Sound Esquimaux. The manner of hunting this animal depends much on the season of the year. In spring, or the breeding season, when the walrus is in his glory, he is taken in two ways. Sometimes he has risen by the side of an iceberg, where the currents have worn away the floe, or through a tide crack, and, enjoying the sunshine too long, finds his retreat cut off by the freezing up of the opening; for, like the seal, the walrus can only work from below at his breathing-hole. When thus caught, the Esquimaux, who with keen hunter-craft are scouring the floes, scent him out by their dogs, and spear him. Frequently the female and her calf, accompanied by the grim-visaged father, are seen surging, in loving trios, from crack to crack, and sporting in the openings. While thus on their tour, they invite their vigilant enemies to the second method of capture. This also is by the lance and harpoon; but it often becomes a regular battle, the male gallantly fronting the assault, and charging the hunters with furious bravery. In the fall, when the pack is but partially closed, the walrus are found in numbers, hanging around the neutral region of mixed ice and water, and, as this becomes solid with the advance of winter, following it more and more to the south.

The Esquimaux at this season approach them over the young ice, and assail them in cracks and holes with harpoon and line. This fishery, as the season grows colder, darker, and more tempestuous, is fearfully hazardous. Kane relates how, during a time of famine, two of his Esquimaux friends, Awaklok and Myouk, determined to seek the walrus on the open ice. They succeeded in killing a large male, and were returning to their village, when a north wind broke up the

ice, and they found themselves afloat. The impulse of a
European would have been to seek the land; but they knew
that the drift was always most dangerous on the coast, and
urged their dogs towards the nearest iceberg. They reached
it after a struggle, and, by great efforts, made good their
landing, with their dogs and the half-butchered carcase of
the walrus. It was at the close of the last moonlight of
December, and a complete darkness settled around them.
They tied the dogs down to knobs of ice, to prevent their
losing their foot-hold, and prostrated themselves, to escape
being blown off by the violence of the wind. At first the sea
broke over them, but they gained a higher level, and built a
sort of screen of ice. On the fifth night afterwards, so far
as they could judge, one of Myouk's feet was frozen, and
Awaklok lost his great toe by frost-bite. But they did not
lose courage, and ate their walrus-meat as they floated slowly
to the south. It was towards the close of the second moonlight, after a month's imprisonment, such as only these iron
men could endure, that they found the berg had grounded.
They liberated their dogs as soon as the young ice could
bear their weight, and attaching long lines to them, which
they cut from the hide of the dead walrus, they succeeded in
hauling themselves through the water space which always
surrounds an iceberg, and reaching safe ice. They returned
to their village like men raised from the dead, to meet a
welcome, but to meet famine along with it.

In the form of their bodies, their short pricked ears, thick
furry coat, and bushy tail, the dogs of the Esquimaux so
nearly resemble the wolf of these regions, that when of a
light or brindled colour, they may easily at a little distance
be mistaken for that animal; but an eye accustomed to
both, perceives that the wolf always keeps his head down
and his tail between his legs in running, whereas the
dogs almost always carry their tails handsomely curled
over the back. Their hair in the winter is from three to
four inches long; but, besides this, nature furnishes them
during this rigorous season with a thick under-coating of
close, soft wool, which enables them to brave the most
inclement weather. They do not bark, but have a long,
melancholy howl, like that of the wolf. When drawing a

sledge, they have a simple harness of deer or seal-skin going round the neck by one bight, and another for each of the fore-legs, with a single thong leading over the back, and attached to the sledge as a trace. Though they appear at first sight to be huddled together without regard to regularity, considerable attention is really paid to their arrangement, particularly in the selection of a dog of peculiar spirit and sagacity, who is allowed by a longer trace to precede the rest as leader, and to whom, in turning to the right or left, the driver usually addresses himself, using certain words as the carters do with us. To these a good leader attends with admirable precision (especially if his own name be repeated at the same time), looking behind over his shoulder with great earnestness, as if listening to the directions of the driver, who sits quite low on the fore-part of the sledge, his whip in hand, and his feet overhanging the snow on one side.

On rough ground, as among hummocks of ice, the sledge would be frequently overturned if the driver did not repeatedly get off, and by lifting or drawing it to one side, steer it clear of those obstacles. At all times, indeed, except on a smooth and well-made road, he is pretty constantly employed thus with his feet, and this, together with his never-ceasing vociferations and frequent use of the whip, renders the driving of one of these vehicles by no means a pleasant or easy task.

'The whip,' says Kane, who from assiduous practice at length attained a considerable proficiency in its use, 'is six yards long, and the handle but sixteen inches—a short lever to throw out such a length of seal hide. Learn to do it, however, with a masterly sweep, or else make up your mind to forego driving sledges; for the dogs are guided solely by the lash, and you must be able to hit not only any particular dog out of a team of twelve, but to accompany the feat also with a resounding crack. After this you find that to get your lash back involves another difficulty; for it is apt to entangle itself among the dogs and lines, or to fasten itself cunningly round bits of ice, so as to drag you head over heels into the snow. The secret by which this complicated set of requirements is fulfilled consists in properly describing an arc from the shoulder with a stiff elbow, giving the jerk to the whip-handle

from the hand and wrist alone. The lash trails behind as you
travel, and when thrown forward is allowed to extend itself
without an effort to bring it back. You wait patiently after
giving the projectile impulse until it unwinds its slow length,
reaches the end of its tether, and cracks to tell you that it is
at its journey's end. Such a crack on the ear or fore-foot of
an unfortunate dog is signalised by a howl quite unmistake-
able in its import.'

The mere labour of using this whip is such that the Esquimaux travel in couples, one sledge after the other. The
hinder dogs follow mechanically, and thus require no whip;
and the drivers change about so as to rest each other.

In the summer, when the absence of snow prevents the use
of sledges, the dogs are still made useful, on journeys and
hunting excursions, by being employed to carry burdens in
a kind of saddle-bags laid across their shoulders. A stout
dog thus accoutred will accompany his master laden with a
weight of about twenty or twenty-five pounds.

The scent of the Esquimaux dog is excellent, and this property is turned to account in finding the seal-holes, which
they will discover entirely by the smell at a very great distance. The track of a single deer upon the snow will in like
manner set them off at a full gallop, at least a quarter of a
mile before they arrive at it, and with the same alacrity they
pursue the bear or the musk-ox. Indeed, the only animal
which they are not eager to chase is the wolf, of which they
seem to have an instinctive dread, giving notice at night of
their approach to the huts by a loud and continued howl.

In spite of their invaluable services they are treated with
great severity by their masters, who never caress them, and,
indeed, scarcely ever take any notice of them except to punish
them. But, notwithstanding this rough treatment, the attachment of the dogs to their masters is very great, and this
they display, after a short absence, by jumping up and licking
their faces all over with extreme delight.

It may be supposed that among so cheerful a people as the
Esquimaux there are many games or sports practised. One of
their exhibitions consists in making hideous faces by drawing
both lips into the mouth, poking forward the chin, squinting
frightfully, occasionally shutting one eye, and moving the
head from side to side, as if the neck had been dislocated.

Another performance consists in repeating certain words with a guttural tone resembling ventriloquism, staring at the same time in such a manner as to make their eyes appear ready to burst out of their sockets with the exertion. Two or more will sometimes stand up face to face, and, with great quickness and regularity, respond to each other, keeping such exact time that the sound appears to come from one throat instead of several. They are fond of music, both vocal and instrumental, but their singing is not much better than a howl.

The Esquimaux have neither magistrates nor laws, yet they are orderly in their conduct towards each other. The constitution of their society is patriarchal, but there is no recognition of mastership except such as may be claimed by superior prowess. The rule of the head of a family lasts only as long as he has vigour enough to secure success in hunting. When his powers of mind and body are impaired by age, he at once sinks in the social scale, associates with the women, and takes his seat in the oomiak. They rarely quarrel among themselves, and settle their disputes either by boxing, the parties sitting down and striking blows alternately, until one of them gives in; or before a court of honour, where, after the accuser and the accused have richly abused and ridiculed each other, the case is decided by the priests or 'angekoks.' These wonder-workers, who enjoy a great reputation as sorcerers, soothsayers, or medicine-men, employ ventriloquism, swallow knives, extract stones from various parts of their bodies, and use other deceptions to impress their dupes with a high opinion of their supernatural powers. Like the members of the learned professions elsewhere, they have a certain language or jargon of their own, in which they communicate with each other. The heathen Esquimaux do not appear to have any idea of the existence of one Supreme Being, but believe in a number of spirits, with whom on certain occasions the angekoks pretend to hold mysterious intercourse. Even in Old Greenland the influence and teachings of the missionaries have not entirely obliterated the old superstitions, and the mysteries of the angekok, though not openly recognised near the Danish settlements, still hold their secret power over many a native who is professedly a Christian.

Captain Hall highly praises the goodnature of the Esquimaux; but in their behaviour to the old and infirm they
betray the insensibility, or rather inhumanity, commonly
found among savage nations, frequently abandoning them to
their fate on their journeys, and allowing them to perish in
the wilderness.

Among themselves 'Tiglikpok' (he is a thief) is a term of reproach, but they steal without scruple from strangers, and are
not ashamed when detected, nor do they blush when reproved.
Parry taxes them with want of gratitude; and though they
have no doubt rendered good services to many of our Arctic
navigators, yet sometimes, when they fancied themselves
the stronger party, they have not hesitated to attack or to
murder the strangers, and their good behaviour can only be
relied upon as long as there is the power of enforcing it.

One of the most amiable traits of their character is the
kindness with which they treat their children, whose gentleness and docility are such as to occasion their parents little
trouble, and to render severity towards them quite unnecessary.  Even from their earliest infancy they possess that
quiet disposition, gentleness of demeanour, and uncommon
evenness of temper, for which, in mature age, they are for the
most part distinguished.  'They are just as fond of play,'
says Parry, 'as any other young people, and of the same
kind, only that while an English child draws a cart of wood,
an Esquimaux of the same age has a sledge of whalebone,
and for the superb baby-house of the former, the latter builds
a miniature hut of snow, and begs a lighted wick from her
mother's lamp to illuminate the little dwelling.'

When not more than eight years old, the boys are taken
by their fathers on their sealing excursions, where they
begin to learn their future business; and even at that early
age they are occasionally entrusted to bring home a sledge
and dogs from a distance of several miles over the ice. At the
age of eleven we see a boy with his water-tight boots, a spear
in his hand, and a small coil of line at his back, accompanying
the men to the fishery under every circumstance; and from
this time his services daily increase in value to the whole tribe.

In intelligence and susceptibility of civilisation the Esquimaux are far superior to the neighbouring Indians.  They

have such a good idea of the hydrography and bearings of the sea coasts which they frequent as to draw accurate charts of them. Thus Parry, in his second voyage, was guided in his operations by the sketches of the talented Iligliuk; and while Beechey was at Kotzebue Sound, the natives constructed a chart of the coast upon the sand, first marking out the coast-line with a stick, and regulating the distance by the day's journey. The hills and ranges of mountains were next shown by elevations of sand or stone, and the islands represented by heaps of pebbles, their proportions being duly attended to. When the mountains and islands were erected, the villages and fishing-stations were marked by a number of sticks placed upright, in imitation of those which are put up on the coast wherever these people fix their abode. In this manner a complete hydrographical plan was drawn from Cape Derby to Cape Krusenstern.

The Esquimaux have a decided predilection for commercial pursuits, and undertake long voyages for the purposes of trade. Thus on the continental line of coast, west of the Mackenzie, the Point Barrow Esquimaux proceed every summer with sledges laden with whale or seal oil, whalebone, walrus tusks, thongs of walrus hide, and seal skins, to the Colville River, where they meet the Esquimaux from Kotzebue Sound, who offer them in exchange articles procured from the Tchuktchi in the previous summer, such as iron and copper kettles, knives, tobacco, beads, and tin for making pipes. About ten days are spent in bartering, dancing, and revelry, on the flat ground between the tents of each party, pitched a bow-shot apart. The time is one of pleasant excitement, and is passed nearly without sleep. About July 20 this friendly meeting is at an end: the Kotzebue Sound Esquimaux ascend the Colville on their way homewards, while those from Point Barrow descend to the sea, to pursue their voyage eastward to Barter Reef, where they obtain in traffic from the eastern Esquimaux various skins, stone lamps, English knives, small white beads, and lately guns and ammunition, which, in the year following, they exchange for the Kotzebue Sound articles at the Colville, along with the produce of their own sea hunts.

In this manner, articles of Russian manufacture, originally

purchased at the fair of Ostrownoje by the Tchuktchi, or from the factors of the Russian Fur Company on Sledge Island in Behring's Strait, find their way from tribe to tribe along the American coast as far as Repulse Bay, and compete among the tribes of the Mackenzie with articles from Sheffield or Birmingham.

A hunter's life is always precarious—a constant alternation between abundance and want; and though the Esquimaux strikes many a seal, white-fish, or walrus in the course of the year, yet these animals do not abound at all seasons, and there are other causes, besides improvidence, which soon exhaust the stores laid by in times of abundance. Active exercise and constant exposure to cold are remarkable promoters of atomic change in the human body, and a very large supply of food is absolutely necessary to counterbalance the effects of a rapid organic combustion. As a matter of curiosity, Parry once tried how much an Esquimaux lad would, if freely supplied, consume in the course of a day. The undermentioned articles were weighed before being given to him : he was twenty hours in getting through them, and certainly did not consider the quantity extraordinary.

|  | | | | | lb. | oz. |
|---|---|---|---|---|---|---|
| Sea-horse flesh, hard frozen | . | . | . | . | 4 | 4 |
| „ „ boiled | . | . | . | . | 4 | 4 |
| Bread and bread-dust | . | . | . | . | 1 | 12 |
| | | | Total of solids | | 10 | 4 |

The fluids were in fair proportion, viz. rich gravy soup, 1¼ pint ; raw spirits, 3 wine glasses ; strong grog, 1 tumbler ; water, 1 gallon, 1 pint.*

Kane averages the Esquimaux ration in a season of plenty at eight or ten pounds a-day, with soup and water to the extent of half a gallon, and finds in this excessive consumption—which is rather a necessity of their peculiar life and organisation than the result of gluttony—the true explanation of the scarcity from which they frequently suffer. In times of abundance they hunt indomitably without the loss of a day, and stow away large quantities of meat. An ex-

* Captain Hall, who in his search after the remains of the Franklin expedition has now spent several years among the Esquimaux, has so far acquired their appetite that he is able to consume 9 lbs. of meat a day without any inconvenience.

cavation is made either on the main-land—or, what is preferred, on an island inaccessible to foxes—and the flesh is
stacked inside and covered with heavy stones. One such
cache, which Kane met on a small island, contained the flesh
of ten walrus, and he knew of others equally large. But by
their ancient custom, all share with all ; and as they migrate
in numbers as their necessities prompt, the tax on each particular settlement is not seldom so excessive, that even considerable stores are unable to withstand the drain, and soon
make way for pinching hunger, and even famine.

The Narwhal.

Hudson's Bay Post.

# CHAPTER XXVII.

## THE FUR TRADE OF THE HUDSON'S BAY TERRITORIES.

The Coureur des Bois—The Voyageur—The Birch-bark Canoe—The Canadian
Fur Trade in the last Century—The Hudson's Bay Company—Bloody Feuds
between the North-West Company of Canada and the Hudson's Bay Company
—Their Amalgamation into a New Company in 1821—Reconstruction of the
Hudson's Bay Company in 1863—Forts or Houses—The Attihawmeg—Influence
of the Company on its savage Dependents—The Black Bear or Baribal—The
Brown Bear—The Grisly Bear—The Racoon—The American Glutton—The
Pine Marten—The Pekan or Woodshock—The Chinga—The Mink—The Cana-
dian Fish-otter—The Crossed Fox—The Black or Silvery Fox—The Canadian
Lynx or Pishu—The Ice Hare—The Beaver—The Musquash.

AS the desire to reach India by the shortest road first made
the civilised world acquainted with the eastern coast
of North America, so the extension of the fur trade has been
the chief, or rather the only, motive which originally led the
footsteps of the white man from the Canadian Lakes and
the borders of Hudson's Bay into the remote interior of that
vast continent.

The first European fur traders in North America were
French Canadians—coureurs des bois—a fitting surname for
men habituated to an Indian forest life. Three or four of
these 'irregular spirits' agreeing to make an expedition into
the backwoods would set out in their birch-bark canoe, laden

A PORTAGE IN THE HUDSON'S BAY TERRITORIES.

with goods received on trust from a merchant, for a voyage of great danger and hardship, it might be of several years, into the wilderness.

On their return the merchant who had given them credit of course received the lion's share of the skins gathered among the Hurons or the Iroquois; the small portion left as a recompense for their own labour was soon spent, as sailors spend their hard-earned wages on their arrival in port; and then they started on some new adventure until finally old age, infirmities, or death prevented their revisiting the forest.

The modern '*voyageur*,' who has usurped the place of the old '*coureurs*,' is so like them in manners and mode of life, that to know the one is to become acquainted with the other. In short, the voyageur is merely a coureur subject to strict law and serving for a fixed pay; while the coureur was a voyageur trading at his own risk and peril, and acknowledging no control when once beyond the pale of European colonisation.

The camel is frequently called the 'ship of the desert,' and with equal justice the birch-bark canoe might be named the 'camel of the North American wilds.' For if we consider the rivers which, covering the land like a net-work, are the only arteries of communication; the frequent rapids and cataracts; the shallow waters flowing over a stony ground whose sharp angles would infallibly cut to pieces any boat made of wood; and finally the surrounding deserts, where, in case of an accident, the traveller is left to his own resources, we must come to the conclusion that in such a country no intercourse could possibly be carried on without a boat made of materials at once flexible and tough, and capable moreover of being easily repaired without the aid of hammer and nails, of saw and plane. This invaluable material is supplied by the rind of the paper-birch, a tree whose uses in the Hudson's Bay territories are almost as manifold as those of the palm trees of the tropical zone. Where the skins of animals are rare, the pliant bark, peeled off in large pieces, serves to cover the Indian's tent. Carefully sewn together and ornamented with the quills of the porcupine,

it is made into baskets, sacks, dishes, plates, and drinking
cups, and in fact in one word the chief material of which
the household articles of the Crees are formed. The wood
serves for the manufacture of oars, snow-shoes, and sledges;
and in spring the sap of the tree furnishes an agreeable beverage, which, by boiling, may be inspissated into a sweet syrup.
Beyond the Arctic Circle the paper-birch is a rare and
crooked tree, but it is met with as a shrub as far as 69° N. lat.
It grows to perfection on the northern shores of Lake Superior, near Fort William, where the canoes of the Hudson's
Bay Company are chiefly manufactured.

A birch-bark canoe is between thirty and forty feet long,
and the rinds of which it is built are sewn together with
filaments of the root of the Canadian fir. In case of a hole
being knocked into it during the journey, it can be patched
like an old coat, and is then again as good as new. As it has
a flat bottom, it does not sink deep into the water; and the
river must be almost dried up which could not carry such
a boat. The cargo is divided into bales or parcels of from
90 to 100 pounds; and although it frequently amounts to
more than four tons, yet the canoe itself is so light that the
crew can easily transport it upon their shoulders. This
crew generally consists of eight or ten men, two of whom
must be experienced boatmen, who receive double pay, and
are placed one at the helm, the other at the poop. When
the wind is fair, a sail is unfurled and serves to lighten
the toil.

The Canadian voyageur combines the light-heartedness
of the Frenchman with the apathy of the Indian, and his
dress is also a mixture of that of the Red-skins and of
the European colonists. Frequently he is himself a mixture of Gallic and Indian blood—a so-called ' bois-brûlé,'
and in this case doubly light-hearted and unruly. With
his woollen blanket as a surcoat, his shirt of striped
cotton, his pantaloons of cloth, or his Indian stockings of
leather, his mocassins of deer-skin, and his sash of gaudily
dyed wool, in which his knife, his tobacco-bag, and various
other utensils are stuck, he stands high in his own esteem.
His language is a French jargon, richly interlarded with
Indian and English words—a jumble fit to drive a gram-

marian mad, but which he thinks so euphonious that his tongue is scarcely ever at rest. His supply of songs and anecdotes is inexhaustible, and he is always ready for a dance. His politeness is exemplary : he never calls his comrades otherwise than 'mon frère,' and 'mon cousin.' It is hardly necessary to remark that he is able to handle his boat with the same ease as an expert rider manages his horse.

When after a hard day's work they rest for the night, the axe is immediately at work in the nearest forest, and in less than ten minutes the tent is erected and the kettle simmering on the fire. While the passengers—perhaps some chief-trader on a voyage to some distant fort, or a Back or a Richardson on his way to the Polar Ocean—are warming or drying themselves, the indefatigable 'voyageurs' drag the unloaded canoe ashore, turn it over, and examine it carefully, either to fasten again some loose stitches, or to paint over some damaged part with fresh resin. Under the cover of their boat, which they turn against the wind, and with a flaming fire in the foreground, they then bid defiance to the weather. At one o'clock in the morning ' Lève ! lève ! lève !' is called ; in half-an-hour the encampment is broken up, and the boat reladen and launched. At eight in the morning a halt is made for breakfast, for which three quarters of an hour are allowed. About two in the afternoon half an hour's rest suffices for a cold dinner. Eighteen hours' work and six hours' rest make out the day. The labour is incredible ; yet the ' voyageur ' not only supports it without a murmur, but with the utmost cheerfulness. Such a life requires, of course, an iron constitution. In rowing, the arms and breast of the ' voyageur' are exerted to the utmost; and in shallow places he drags the boat after him, wading up to the knees and thighs in the water. Where he is obliged to force his way against a rapid, the drag rope must be pulled over rocks and stumps of trees, through swamps and thickets ; and at the portages the cargo and the boat have to be carried over execrable roads to the next navigable water. Then the ' voyageur ' takes upon his back two packages, each weighing 90 pounds, and attached by a leathern belt running over the forehead, that his hands may be free to clear the way ; and such portages sometimes occur ten or eleven times in one day.

For these toils of his wandering life he has many compensations, in the keen appetite, the genial sensation of muscular strength, and the flow of spirits engendered by labour in the pure and bracing air.  Surely many would rather breathe with the 'voyageur' the fragrance of the pine forest, or share his rest upon the borders of the stream, than lead the monotonous life of an artisan, pent up in the impure atmosphere of a city.

During the first period of the American fur trade the 'coureurs des bois' used to set out on their adventurous expeditions from the village 'La Chine,' one of the oldest and most famous settlements in Canada, whose name points to a time when the St. Lawrence was still supposed to be the nearest way to China.  How far some of them may have penetrated into the interior of the continent is unknown; but so much is certain, that their regular expeditions extended as far as the Saskatchewan, 2,500 miles beyond the remotest European settlements.  Several factories or forts protected their interests on the banks of that noble river; and the French would no doubt have extended their dominion to the Rocky Mountains or to the Pacific if the conquest of Canada by England, in 1761, had not completely revolutionized the fur trade.  The change of dominion laid it prostrate for several years, but our enterprising countrymen soon opened a profitable intercourse with the Indian tribes of the west, as their predecessors had done before them.  Now, however, the adventurous 'coureur des bois,' who had entered the wilds as a semi-independent trader, was obliged to serve in the pay of the British merchant, and to follow him, as his 'voyageur,' deeper and deeper into the wilderness, until finally they reached on the Athabasca and the Churchill River the Indian hunters who used to sell their skins in the settlements of the Hudson's Bay Company.

This Company was founded in the year 1670 by a body of adventurers and merchants under the patronage of Prince Rupert, second cousin of Charles II.  The charter obtained from the Crown was wonderfully liberal, comprising not only the grant of the exclusive trade, but also of full territorial possession to all perpetuity of the vast lands within the watershed of Hudson's Bay. The Company at once established some forts along the shores of the great inland sea from which it derived its name, and opened a very lucrative trade with the Indians, so that it never ceased paying rich dividends to the fortunate shareholders until towards the close of the last century, when, as I have already mentioned, its prosperity began to be seriously affected by the energetic competition of the Canadian fur traders.

In spite of the flourishing state of its affairs, or rather because the monopoly which it enjoyed allowed it to prosper without exertion, the Company, as long as Canada remained in French hands, had conducted its affairs in a very indolent manner, waiting for the Indians to bring the produce of their chase to the Hudson's Bay settlements, instead of following them into the interior and stimulating them by offering greater facilities for exchange.

For eighty years after its foundation the Company possessed no more than four small forts on the shores of Hudson's Bay; and only when the encroachments of the Canadians at length roused it from its torpor, did it resolve likewise to advance into the interior, and to establish a fort on the eastern shore of Sturgeon Lake, in the year 1774. Up to this time, with the exception of the voyage of discovery which Hearne (1770-71) made under its auspices to the mouth of the Coppermine River, it had done but little for the promotion of geographical discovery in its vast territory.

Meanwhile the Canadian fur traders had become so hateful to the Indians, that these savages formed a conspiracy for their total extirpation.

Fortunately for the white men, the small-pox broke out about this time among the Red-skins, and swept them away as the fire consumes the parched grass of the prairies. Their unburied corpses were torn by the wolves and wild dogs, and the survivors were too weak and dispirited to be able to undertake anything against the foreign intruders. The Canadian fur traders now also saw the necessity of combining their efforts for their mutual benefit, instead of

ruining each other by an insane competition; and consequently formed, in 1783, a society which, under the name of
the North-West Company of Canada, at first consisted of
sixteen, later of twenty partners or shareholders, some of
whom lived in Canada, while the others were scattered
among the various stations in the interior. The whole
Canadian fur trade was now greatly developed; for while
previously each of the associates had blindly striven to do as
much harm as possible to his present partners and thus indirectly damaged his own interests, they now all vigorously
united to beat the rival Hudson's Bay Company out of the
field. The agents of this North-West Company, in defiance of their charter, were indefatigable in exploring the
lakes and woods, the plains and the mountains, for the purpose of establishing new trading-stations at all convenient
points.

The most celebrated of these pioneers of commerce,
Alexander Mackenzie, reached, in the year 1789, the mouth
of the great river which bears his name, and saw the white
dolphins gambol about in the Arctic Sea. In a second voyage
he crossed the Rocky Mountains, and followed the course
of the Fraser River until it discharges its waters into the
Georgian Gulf, opposite to Vancouver's Island. Here he
wrote with perishable vermilion the following inscription on
a rock-wall fronting the gulf:—

> A. Mackenzie
> arrived from Canada by land,
> 22 July, 1792.

The words were soon effaced by wind and weather, but the
fame of the explorer will last as long as the English language is spoken in America.

The energetic North-West Company thus ruled over
the whole continent from the Canadian Lakes to the Rocky
Mountains, and in 1806 it even crossed that barrier and
established its forts on the northern tributaries of the
Columbia River. To the north it likewise extended its
operations, encroaching more and more upon the privileges
of the Hudson's Bay Company, which, roused to energy, now
also pushed on its posts further and further into the interior,

and established in 1812 a colony on the Red River to the south of Winipeg Lake, thus driving, as it were, a sharp thorn into the side of its rival. But a power like the North-West Company, which had no less than 50 agents, 70 interpreters, and 1,120 voyageurs in its pay, and whose chief managers used to appear at their annual meetings at Fort William, on the banks of Lake Superior, with all the pomp and pride of feudal barons, was not inclined to tolerate this encroachment; and thus, after many quarrels, a regular war broke out between the two parties, which, after two years' duration, led to the expulsion of the Red River colonists and the murder of their Governor, Semple. This event took place in the year 1816, and is but one episode of the bloody feuds which continued to reign between the two rival Companies until 1821. At first sight it may seem strange that such acts of violence should take place between British subjects and on British soil, but then we must consider that, at that time, European law had little power in the American wilderness.

The dissensions of the fur traders had most deplorable consequences for the Redskins; for both Companies, to swell the number of their adherents, lavishly distributed spirituous liquors—a temptation which no Indian can resist.

The whole of the hunting-grounds of the Saskatchewan and Athabasca were but one scene of revelry and bloodshed. Already decimated by the small-pox, the Indians now became the victims of drunkenness and discord, and it was to be feared that if the war and its consequent demoralisation continued, the most important tribes would soon be utterly swept away.

The finances of the belligerent Companies were in an equally deplorable state; the produce of the chase diminished from year to year with the increase of their expenditure; and thus the Hudson's Bay Company, which used to gratify its shareholders with dividends of 50 and 25 per cent., was unable, from 1808 to 1814, to distribute a single shilling among them. At length wisdom prevailed over passion, and the enemies came to a resolution which, if taken from the very beginning, would have saved them both a great deal of treasure and many crimes. Instead of continuing to swing the tomahawk,

they now smoked the calumet, and amalgamated in 1821
under the name of the 'Hudson's Bay Company,' and under
the wing of the charter. The British Government, as a
dowry to the impoverished couple, presented them with a
licence of exclusive trade throughout the whole of that
territory which, under the name of the Hudson's Bay and
North-West territories, extends from Labrador to the
Pacific, and from the Red River to the Polar Ocean. This
licence was terminable in 21 years, but in 1838 it was renewed
again for the same period. The good effects of peace and
union soon became apparent, for after a few years the Company was enabled to pay half-yearly dividends of five per
cent., and the Indians, to whom brandy was now no longer
supplied unless as a medicine, enjoyed the advantages of a
more sober life.

About 1848 the Imperial Government, fearing that Vancouver's Island might be annexed by the United States,
resolved to place it under the management of the Hudson's Bay Company. This was accordingly done in 1849. A
licence of exclusive trade and management was granted for
ten years, terminable therefore in 1859 (the time of expiration of the similar licence over the Indian territory).

These were the palmy days of the Hudson's Bay Company.
They held Rupert's Land by the Royal charter, which was
perpetual ; they held Vancouver's Island and the whole
Indian territory to the Pacific by exclusive licences terminable in 1859 ; and thus maintained under their sole sway
about 4,000,000 square miles—a realm larger than the whole
of Europe.

For the ten years ending May 31, 1862, the average net
annual profits of the Company amounted to 81,000l. on a
paid up capital of 400,000l., but a portion only of this income
was distributed as dividend.

In 1863 the Company was reconstructed with a capital of
2,000,000l., for the purpose of enlarging its operations—such
as opening the southern and more fruitful districts of the
Saskatchewan or the Winipeg to European colonisation ; but
the northern, and by far the larger portion of the vast
domains over which, after the dismemberment of British
Columbia and the Stikine territory, it still holds sway, have

too severe a climate ever to be cultivated, and, unless their mineral wealth be made available, must ever be what they are now—a fur-bearing region of gloomy pine-forests, naked barren-grounds, lakes, and morasses.

Over this vast extent of desert the Company has established about 150 trading posts, called 'houses,' or 'forts,' which, however, consist merely of a few magazines and dwelling-houses protected by a simple wall, stockade, or palisade, sufficiently strong to resist any sudden attack of the Indians. Among the tribes with whom a friendly intercourse has long subsisted, and whose fidelity may implicitly be trusted, no guard is ever kept, and it is only in forts more recently built in remote parts that precautions are taken.

These forts are always situated on the borders of a lake or river, both for facility of transport and for the purpose of catching fish, particularly the species of Coregonus or white-fish, which, from its importance to all the natives of Rupert's Land between the great Canada Lakes and the Arctic Sea, the Crees call Attihawmeg, or the 'reindeer of the waters.' In many of the trading posts it forms the chief food of the white residents; and it is asserted that though deprived of bread and vegetables, a man may live upon it for months or even years without tiring. According to Sir John Richardson, no fish in any country or sea excels the white fish in flavour and wholesomeness, and it is the most beneficial article of diet to the Red Indians near the Arctic Circle, being obtained with more certainty than the reindeer, and with less change of abode in summer and winter.

Each of the principal forts is the seat of a chief factor, or general administrator of a district, and of a chief trader, who transacts the business with the Indians.

Besides these principal functionaries—out of whom the governor is chosen—the Company employed, in 1860, 5 surgeons, 87 clerks, 67 postmasters, 1,200 permanent servants, and 500 voyageurs, besides temporary employés of different ranks, so that the total number of persons in its pay was at least 3,000. Besides this little army of immediate dependents, the whole male Indian population of its vast territory, amounting to about 100,000 hunters and trappers, may be considered as actively employed in the service of the

Company. Armed vessels, both sailing and steam, are employed on the north-west coast, to carry on the fur trade with the warlike natives of that distant region. More than twenty years ago this trade alone gave employment to about 1,000 men, occupying 21 permanent establishments, or engaged in navigating 5 armed sailing vessels, and 1 armed steamer, varying from 100 to 300 tons in burden.

The influence of the Company over its savage dependents may justly be called beneficial. Both from motives of humanity and self-interest, every effort is made to civilise them. No expense is spared to preserve them from the want into which their improvidence too often plunges them ; and the example of an inflexible straightforwardness serves to gain their confidence. This moral preponderance, and the admiration of the Indian for the superior knowledge and arts of the Europeans, explain how a mere handful of white men, scattered over an enormous territory, not only lead a life of perfect security, but exercise an almost absolute power over a native population outnumbering them at least several hundred times. The Indians have in course of time acquired many new wants, and have thus become more and more dependent on the white traders. The savage hunter is no longer the free, self-dependent man, who, without any foreign assistance, was able to make and manufacture, with his own hands, all the weapons and articles needed for his maintenance. Without English fire-arms and fishing gear, without iron-ware and woollen blankets, he could no longer exist, and the unfortunate tribe on which the Company should close its stores would soon perish for want. ' History,' says Professor Hind,* 'does not furnish another example of an association of private individuals exerting a powerful influence over so large an extent of the earth's surface, and administering their affairs with such consummate skill and unwavering devotion to the original objects of their incorporation.'

The standard of exchange in all mercantile transactions with the natives is a beaver-skin, the relative value of which as originally established by the traders, differs considerably from the present worth of the articles represented by it; but

* Narrative of the Canadian Red River Exploring Expedition, vol. ii. p. 211.

the Indians are averse to change. They receive their principal outfit of clothing and ammunition on credit in the autumn, to be repaid by their winter hunts; the amount entrusted to each of the hunters varying with their reputations for industry and skill.

The furs which, in the course of the year, are accumulated in the various forts or trading stations, are transported in the short time during which the rivers and lakes are navigable, and in the manner described at the beginning of the chapter, to York Factory, or Moose Factory, on Hudson's Bay, to Montreal or Vancouver, and shipped from thence mostly to London. From the more distant posts in the interior, the transport often requires several seasons; for travelling is necessarily very slow when rapids and portages continually interrupt navigation, and the long winter puts a stop to all intercourse whatever.

The goods from Europe, consisting (besides those mentioned above) of printed cotton, or silk handkerchiefs, or neck-cloths, of beads, and the universal favourite tobacco, require at least as much time to find their way into the distant interior; and thus the Company is not seldom obliged to wait for four, five, or six years before it receives its returns for the articles sent from London. It must, however, be confessed, that it amply repays itself for the tediousness of delay, for Dr. Armstrong was told by the Esquimaux of Cape Bathurst—a tribe in the habit of trading with the Indians from the Mackenzie, who are in direct communication with the Hudson's Bay Company's agents—that for three silver fox skins—which sometimes fetch as high a price as twenty-five or thirty guineas a-piece at the annual sale of the Company—they had got from the traders cooking utensils which might be worth eight shillings and sixpence!

The value of the skins annually imported into England by the Company amounts to about 150,000*l.* or 200,000*l.* Besides, many of its furs are bartered for Russian-American peltry, and a large quantity is exported direct to China.

After this brief account of one of the most remarkable mercantile associations of any age, some remark on the chief fur-bearing animals of the Hudson's Bay territory may not be without interest. Among these, the black bear, muskwa, or baribal (*Ursus americanus*), is one of the most valuable, as his long hair—unlike that of the brown or the white bear—is beautifully smooth and glossy. He inhabits the forest regions of North America, but migrates according to the seasons. In spring he seeks his food in the thickets along the banks of the rivers or lakes; in summer he retreats into the forests; in winter he either wanders further to the south, or hollows out a kind of lair beneath the root of an overthrown tree, where, as the cold is more or less severe, he either finds a retreat after his excursions, or hybernates buried in the snow. He feeds chiefly on berries, grain, acorns, roots, eggs, and honey; though, when pressed by hunger, he will attack other quadrupeds. He climbs upon trees or rocks with great agility, and, being very watchful, is not easily got at in summer. Sometimes, however, his caution brings about his destruction; for, from fear of some possible danger, or at the slightest noise, he rises on his hind legs to look over the bushes under which he lies concealed, and thus offers a mark to the bullet of the hunter. In the winter, when the snow betrays his traces, he is more easily shot, and his skin and flesh are then also in the best condition. In spite of his apparent clumsiness and stolidity, the muskwa is more alert than the brown bear, whom he nearly approaches in size; he runs so fast that no man can overtake him, and is an excellent swimmer and climber. When attacked, he generally retreats as fast as possible into the forest; but, if escape is impossible, he turns furiously upon his pursuers, and becomes exceedingly dangerous. Dogs alone are incapable of mastering him, as he is always ready to receive them with a stroke of his forepaw; but they are very useful in driving him up a tree, and thus giving the hunter an opportunity of hitting him in the right spot. When in a state of captivity, the baribal, in his mild and good-humoured disposition, is distinguished from the brown and white bear. His fur is also much more valuable than that of the brown bear.

It is not yet fully ascertained whether the American brown bear is identical with that of Europe; the resemblance, however, is close. In summer he wanders to the shores of the Polar Sea, and indulges more frequently in animal food than the baribal. He is even said to attack man when pressed by hunger; but all those whom Sir John Richardson met with, ran away as soon as they saw him.

As the grisly bear (*Ursus ferox*) is found on the Rocky Mountains up to the latitude of 61°, he undoubtedly deserves a place among the sub-arctic animals. The skin of this most formidable of the ursine race, who is about nine feet long and is said to attain the weight of eight hundred pounds, is but little prized in the fur trade. He is the undoubted monarch of his native wilds, for even the savage bison flies at his approach.

Although the racoon (*Procyon lotor*) is more commonly found in Canada and the United States, yet he is also an inhabitant of the Hudson's Bay territories, where he is met with up to 56° N. lat. This interesting little animal, which, like the bears, applies the sole of its foot to the ground in walking, has an average length of two feet from the nose to the tail, which is about ten inches long. Its colour is greyish-brown, with a dusky line running from the top of the head down the middle of the face, and ending below the eyes. The tail is very thickly covered with hair, and is annulated with several black bars on a yellowish-white ground. Its face is very like that of the fox, whom it equals in cunning, while its active and playful habits resemble those of the monkey. Its favourite haunts are the woods, near streams or lakes, for one of its most marked peculiarities, from which it has received its specific name of *lotor*, or the washer, is its habit of plunging its dry food into water before eating it. The racoon devours almost anything that comes in his way—fruits and grain of all sorts, birds' nests, mice, grasshoppers, beetles: while the waters yield him fishes, crabs, and oysters, which he is very expert in opening. His fur forms no inconsiderable article of commerce, and is very fashionable in Russia. In 1841, 111,316 racoon skins were imported into St. Petersburg, and more than half a million were stapled in Leipzig, intended, no doubt, for smuggling across the frontier.

The fur of the American glutton, or wolverine, is much used for muffs and linings; yet, from its being a notorious robber of their traps, the animal is as much hated by the Indian hunters as the dog-fish by the northern fishermen.

The Hudson's Bay territories cannot boast of the sable, but the American pine marten (*Martes abietum*) is not much inferior in value, as its dark brown fur is remarkably fine, thick, and glossy. It frequents the woody districts, where it preys on birds, and all the smaller quadrupeds from the hare to the mouse. Even the squirrel is incapable of escaping the pine marten, and after having vaulted and climbed from tree to tree, sinks at last exhausted into its gripe.

The pekan, or woodshock (*Martes canadensis*), the largest of the marten family, is also the one which most richly supplies the fur market. It is found over the whole of North America, and generally lives in burrows near the banks of rivers, as it principally feeds on the small quadrupeds that frequent the water.

Several species of ermine inhabit the Hudson's Bay territories, but their skins are of no great importance in the fur trade. Like many other species of the marten family, they eject, when irritated or alarmed, a fluid of a fetid odour; but in this respect they are far surpassed by the chinga (*Mephitis chinga*), whose secretion has so intolerable a smell that the least quantity suffices to produce nausea and a sense of suffocation. This animal is frequently found near Hudson's Bay, whence it extends further to the north. In spite of the formidable means of defence with which it has been armed by nature, it is of use to man, for its black and white striped fur (which, as may easily be supposed, never appears in the European market) provides the Indians with coverings or tobacco pouches. Before seizing the chinga, they irritate it with a long switch, until it has repeatedly emptied the glands from which the noxious vapour issues; then suddenly springing upon it, they hold it up by the tail and despatch it.

The mink (*Vison americanus*), another member of the weasel family, is one of the most important fur-bearing animals of the Hudson's Bay territories. It resembles the small European fish-otter (*Vison lutreola*), but its skin is far more valuable—the brown hair with which it is covered being much softer and thicker. As its toes are connected by a small web, it is an excellent swimmer, and as formidable to the salmon or trout in the water as to the hare on land.

The Canadian fish-otter (*Lutra canadensis*) far surpasses

the European species, both in size and in the beauty of its glossy brown skin. It occurs as far northwards as 66° or 67° lat., and is generally taken by sinking a steel trap near the mouth of its burrow. It has the habit of sliding or climbing to the top of a ridge of snow in winter, or of a sloping moist bank in summer, where, lying on the belly, with the fore-feet bent backwards, it gives itself with the hind legs an impulse, which sends it swiftly down the eminence. This school-boy sport it continues for a long time.

The red fox (*Vulpes fulvus*), which is found throughout the Hudson's Bay territories, has likewise a much finer fur than our common fox. It is of a bright ferruginous red on the head, back, and sides; beneath the chin it is white, while the throat and neck are of a dark grey, and the under parts of the body, towards the tail, are of a very pale red. The crossed fox (*Canis decussatus*), thus named from the black cross on its shoulders, is still more valuable; its skin—the colour of which is a sort of grey, resulting from the mixture of black and white hair—being worth four or five guineas. Peltry, still more costly, is furnished by the black or silvery fox (*Canis argentatus*), whose copious and beautiful fur is of a rich and shining black, or deep brown colour, with the longer or exterior hairs of a silvery white. Unfortunately it is of such rare occurrence, that not more than four or five are annually brought to a trading post.

The Canada lynx, or pishu (*Lynx canadensis*), is smaller than the European species, but has a finer fur, those skins being most valued which approach to a pale or whitish colour, and on which the spots are most distinct. It chiefly feeds on the hare (*Lepus americanus*), which is not much larger than a rabbit, and is found on the banks of the Mackenzie as far north as 68° or 69°.

Still nearer to the Pole, the ice-hare (*Lepus glacialis*) ranges as far as the Parry Islands (75° N. lat.), where it feeds on the arctic willow, and other high northern plants. Its favourite resorts are the stony districts, where it easily finds a refuge; in winter it burrows in the snow. In summer its back is greyish white, but as the cold increases, it becomes white, with the exception of the tips of the ears, which remain constantly black.

A A

Formerly the beaver (*Castor fiber*) was the most important of the fur-bearing animals of the Hudson's Bay territories. In the year 1743, 127,000 beaver skins were exported from Montreal to La Rochelle, and 26,700 by the Hudson's Bay Company to London. At present, the exportation hardly amounts to one-third of this quantity. As the beaver chiefly lives on the barks of the willow, the beech, and the poplar, it is not found beyond the forest region; but along the banks of the Mackenzie it reaches a very high latitude.

The musk rat, ondatra or musquash (*Fiber sibethicus*)—which is about the size of a small rabbit, and of a reddish-brown colour—is called by the Indians the younger brother of the beaver, as it has similar instincts. Essentially a bank haunting animal, it is never to be seen at any great distance from the water, where it swims and dives with consummate ease, aided greatly by the webs which connect the hinder toes. It drives a large series of tunnels into the bank, branching out in various directions, and having several entrances, all of which open under the surface of the water. If the animal happens to live upon a marshy and uniformly wet soil, it becomes a builder, and lives in curiously constructed huts, from three to four feet in height, plastered with great neatness in the inside, and strengthened externally with a kind of basket-work of rushes, carefully interlaced together. The judgment of the animal shows itself in the selection of the site, invariably choosing some ground above the reach of inundation, or else raising its hut on an artificial foundation; for, though obliged to reside near flat, submerged banks, where the soft soil is full of nourishing roots, it requires a dry home to rest in.

In winter the musquash villages—for the huts are sometimes built in such numbers together as to deserve that name —are generally covered with thick snow, under which this rodent is able to procure water, or to reach the provisions laid up in its storehouse. Thus it lives in ease and plenty, for the marten is too averse to the water, and the otter too bulky, to penetrate into its tunnels. But when the snow melts, and the huts of the musquash appear above the ground, the Indian, taking in his hand a large four-barbed spear, steals up to the house, and driving his weapon through the walls, is sure to pierce the animals inside. Holding the spear firmly with one hand, he takes his tomahawk from his belt, dashes the house to pieces and secures the inmates. Another method employed by the Indians to capture the musquash, is to block up the different entrances to their tunnels, and then to intercept the animals as they try to escape. Sometimes the gun is used, but not very frequently, as the musquash is so wary, that it dives at the least alarm, and darts into one of its holes. The trap, however, is the ordinary means of destruction. The soft and glossy fur of the musquash, though worth no more than from 6d. to 9d., is still a not inconsiderable article of trade, as no less than half a million skins are annually imported into England for hat making; nor is there any fear of the musquash being extirpated, in spite of its many enemies, as it multiplies very fast, and is found near every swamp or lake with grassy banks, as far as the confines of the Polar Sea.

The Black Bear.

Cree Wigwams in Summer.

# CHAPTER XXVIII.

### THE CREE INDIANS, OR EYTHINYUWUK.

The various Tribes of the Crees—Their Conquests and subsequent Defeat—Their
Wars with the Blackfeet—Their Character—Tattooing—Their Dress—Fondness
for their Children—The Cree Cradle—Vapour Baths—Games—Their religious
Ideas—The Cree Tartarus and Elysium.

THE various tribes of the Crees, or Eythinyuwuk, range
from the Rocky Mountains and the plains of the Saskatchewan to the swampy shores of Hudson's Bay. Towards
the west and north they border on the Tinné, towards the
east and south on the Ojibbeway or Sauteurs, who belong
like them to the great family of the Lenni-lenape Indians,
and inhabit the lands between Lake Winipeg and Lake
Superior.

About sixty years since, at the time when Napoleon
was deluging Europe with blood, the Crees likewise played
the part of conquerors, and subdued even more extensive,
though less valuable domains.

Provided with fire-arms, which at that time were unknown

to their northern and western neighbours, they advanced as far as the Arctic Circle, imposing tribute on the various tribes of the Tinné. But their triumphs were not more durable than those of the great European conqueror.

The small-pox broke out among them and swept them away by thousands. Meanwhile the Tinné tribes had remained untouched by this terrible scourge; and as the agents of the Hudson's Bay Company, advancing further and further to the west and north, had likewise made them acquainted with the use of fire-arms, they in their turn became the aggressors, and drove the Crees before them. Their former conquerors now partly migrated to the south, and leaving the forest region, where they had hunted the reindeer and the elk, spread over the prairies of the Saskatchewan, where, mounted on horseback, they now pursued the herds of bison. But in their new abodes they became engaged in constant feuds with their new neighbours the Assiniboins and Blackfeet, who of course resented their intrusion.

The romance in which the manners and character of the Indians are portrayed might lead us to attribute to these people a loftiness of soul for which it would be vain to look in the present day, and which without much scepticism we may assert they never really possessed. Actions, prompted only by the caprice of a barbarous people, have been considered as the results of refined sentiment; and savage cunning, seen through the false medium of prejudice, assumed the nobler proportions of a far-sighted policy. But though the history of the wars of the Indians among themselves and with the Europeans affords but few instances of heroism, it abounds in traits of revolting cruelty, and in pictures of indescribable wretchedness.

A large party of Blackfeet once made a successful foray in the territory of the Crees. But meanwhile the latter surprised the camp where the aggressors had left their wives and children; and thus, when the Blackfeet returned to their tents, they found desolation and death where they looked for a joyful welcome. In their despair they cast away their arms and their booty, and retired to the mountains, where for three days and nights they wailed and mourned.

In the year 1840 a bloody war broke out between the

Crees and the Blackfeet, arising as in general from a very trifling cause. Peace was at length concluded, but while the two nations were celebrating this fortunate event with games and races, a Cree stole a ragged blanket, and a new fight immediately began. Returning home the Blackfeet met a Cree chieftain with two of his warriors and killed them after a short altercation. Soon after the Crees surprised and murdered some of the Blackfeet, and thus the war raged more furiously than ever. Sir George Simpson, who was travelling through the country at the time, visited the hut of a Cree who had been wounded in the conflict at the peace-meeting. As in his flight he bent over his horse's neck, a ball had struck him on the right side, and remained sticking near the articulation of the left shoulder. In this condition he had already lain for three and thirty days, his left arm frightfully swollen, and the rest of his body emaciated to a skeleton. Near the dying savage, whose glassy eye and contracted features spoke of the dreadful pain of which he disdained to speak, lay his child, reduced to skin and bones, and expressing by a perpetual moaning the pangs of illness and hunger, while most to be pitied perhaps of this wretched family was the wife and mother, who seemed to be sinking under the double load of care and fatigue. During the night the 'medicine-man' was busy beating his magic drum and driving away the evil spirits from the hut.

Although the Crees show great fortitude in enduring hunger and the other evils incident to a hunter's life, yet any unusual accident dispirits them at once, and they seldom venture to meet their enemies in open warfare, or even to surprise them, unless they have a great advantage in point of numbers. Instances of personal bravery like that of the Esquimaux are rare indeed among them. Superior in personal appearance to the Tinné, they are less honest, and though perhaps not so much given to falsehood as the Tinné, are more turbulent and more prompt to invade the rights of their countrymen, as well as of neighbouring nations.

Tattooing is almost universal among them. The women are in general content with having one or two lines drawn from the corners of the mouth towards the angles of the lower jaw, but some of the men have their bodies covered with lines and figures. It seems to be considered by most rather as a proof of courage than an ornament, as the operation is both painful and tedious. The lines on the face are formed by dexterously running an awl under the cuticle, and then drawing a cord, dipped in charcoal and water, through the canal thus formed. The punctures on the body are made by needles of various sizes, set in a frame. A number of hawk-bells attached to this frame, serve, by their noise, to cover the groans of the sufferer, and probably for the same reason the process is accompanied with singing. An indelible stain is produced by rubbing a little finely-powdered willow-charcoal into the puncture. A half-breed, whose arm was amputated by Sir John Richardson, declared that tattooing was not only the more painful operation of the two, but rendered infinitely more difficult to bear by its tediousness, having lasted, in his case, three days.

The Crees are also fond of painting their faces with vermilion and charcoal. In general the dress of the male consists of a blanket thrown over the shoulders, a leathern shirt or jacket, and a piece of cloth tied round the middle. The women have in addition a long petticoat, and both sexes wear a kind of wide hose, which, reaching from the ankle to the middle of the thigh, are suspended by strings to the girdle. These hose, or 'Indian stockings,' are commonly ornamented with beads or ribands, and from their convenience have been universally adopted by the white residents, as an essential part of their winter-clothing. Their shoes, or rather soft boots (for they tie round the ankle), are made of dressed moose-skins; and during the winter they wrap several pieces of blanket round their feet. They are fond of European articles of dress, such as great-coats, shawls, and calicoes, which, however showy they may be at first, are soon reduced to a very filthy condition by their custom of greasing the face and hair with soft fat or marrow. This practice they say preserves the skin soft, and protects it from cold in the winter and the mosquitoes in summer; but it renders their presence disagreeable to Europeans who may chance to be seated near them in a close tent and near a hot fire.

The Cree women are not in general treated harshly by their husbands: a great part of the labour, however, falls to the lot of the wife. She makes the hut, cooks, dresses the skins, and for the most part carries the heaviest load; but when she is unable to perform her task, the husband does not consider it beneath his dignity to assist her.

The Crees are extremely indulgent to their children. The father never chastises them; and the mother, though more hasty in her temper, seldom bestows a blow on a troublesome child.

The cradle in use among them is well adapted to their mode of life, and is one of their neatest articles of furniture, being generally ornamented with beads and bits of scarlet cloth, but it bears a very strong resemblance in its form to a mummy-case. The infant is placed in this bag, having its lower extremities wrapped up in soft sphagnum or bog-moss, and may be hung up in the tent, or to the branch of a tree, without the least danger of tumbling out; or in a journey may be suspended on the mother's back, by a band which crosses the forehead so as to leave her hands free. The sphagnum forms a soft elastic bed, which absorbs moisture very readily, and affords such a protection from the winter cold, that its place would be ill supplied by any other material.

The ordinary wigwams, skin tents, or 'lodges' of the Tinné and Crees are exactly alike in form, being extended on poles set up in a conical manner; but as a general rule the tents of the latter are more commodious and more frequently supplied with a fresh lining of the spray of the balsam fir. They also occasionally erect a larger dwelling of lattice work, covered with birch-bark, in which forty men or more can assemble for feasting, debating, or performing some of their religious ceremonies. The entire nation of the Eythinyuwuk cultivate oratory more than their northern neighbours, who express themselves more simply and far less fluently.

Vapour baths are in common use with the Crees, and form one of the chief remedies of their medicine-men. The operator shuts himself up with his patient in the small

sweating-house, in which red-hot stones besprinkled with
water, and having a few leaves of a species of prunus strewed
around them, produce a damp atmosphere of a stifling heat,
and shampoos him, singing all the time a kind of hymn.  As
long as the medicine-man can hold out, so long must the
patient endure the intense heat of the bath, and then, if the
invalid be able to move, they both plunge into the river.   If
the patient does not recover, he is at least more speedily released from his sufferings by this powerful remedy.

The Crees are a vain, fickle, improvident, indolent, and
ludicrously boastful race.  They are also great gamblers, but,
instead of cards or dice, they play with the stones of a species
of *prunus*.  The difficulty lies in guessing the number of
stones which are tossed out of a small wooden dish, and the
hunters will spend whole nights at this destructive sport,
staking their most valuable articles.  They have, however, a
much more manly amusement termed the 'cross,' although
they do not engage even in it without depositing considerable
stakes.  An extensive meadow is chosen for this sport, and the
articles staked are tied to a post, or deposited in the custody
of two old men.  The combatants being stripped and painted,
and each provided with a kind of racket, in shape resembling
the letter P, with a handle about two feet long, and a head
loosely wrought with network, so as to form a shallow bag,
range themselves on different sides.  A ball being now tossed
up in the middle, each party endeavours to drive it to their
respective goals, and much dexterity and agility is displayed
in the contest.  When a nimble runner gets the ball in his
*cross*, he sets off towards the goal with the utmost speed, and
is followed by the rest, who endeavour to jostle him and
shake it out, but, if hard pressed, he discharges it with a jerk,
to be forwarded by his own party, or bandied back by their
opponents until the victory is decided by its passing the
goal.

Neither the Esquimaux nor the Tinné have any visible
objects of worship, but the Crees carry with them small
wooden figures rudely carved, or merely the tops of a few
willow-bushes tied together, as the representatives of a malicious, or at least capricious being, called Kepoochikann.

Their most common petition to this being is for plenty of food, but as they do not trust entirely to his favour, they endeavour at the same time to propitiate the *animal,* an imaginary representative of the whole race of larger quadrupeds that are objects of the chase.

Though often referring to the Kitche-manito, the 'Great Spirit' or 'Master of Life,' they do not believe that he cares for his creatures, and consequently never think of praying to him. They have no legend about the creation, but they speak of a deluge caused by an attempt of the fish to drown Woesack-ootchacht, a kind of demi-god, with whom they had quarrelled. Having constructed a raft, this being embarked with his family and all kinds of birds and beasts. After the flood had continued for some time, he ordered several waterfowl to dive to the bottom. They were all drowned; but a musk-rat, dispatched on the same errand, returned with a mouthful of mud, out of which Woesack-ootchacht, imitating the mode in which the rats construct their houses, formed a new earth. First a small conical hill of mud appeared above the water; by and by, its base gradually spreading out, it became an extensive bank, which the rays of the sun at length hardened into firm land. Notwithstanding the power that Woesack-ootchacht here displayed, his person is held in very little reverence by the Indians, who do not think it worth while to make any effort to avert his wrath.

Like the Tinné, the Crees also have a Tartarus and an Elysium. The souls of the departed are obliged to scramble with great labour up the sides of a steep mountain, upon attaining the summit of which, they are rewarded with the prospect of an extensive plain abounding in all sorts of game, and interspersed here and there with new tents, pitched in pleasant situations. Whilst they are absorbed in the contemplation of this delightful scene, they are descried by the inhabitants of the happy land, who, clothed in new skin-dresses, approach and welcome, with every demonstration of kindness, those Indians who have led good lives, but the bad Indians are told to return from whence they came, and without more ceremony are hurled down the precipice.

As yet Christianity has made but little progress among the

Indians of British North America, its benefits being hitherto confined to the Ojibbeways of Lake Huron, and to a small number of the Crees of the Hudson's Bay territory. The well-fed Sauteurs of the Winipeg are as disinclined to be converted as the buffalo hunters of the prairies.

The Mink.

The Rocky Mountains, at the bend of the Mackenzie.

## CHAPTER XXIX.

### THE TINNÉ INDIANS.

The various Tribes of the Tinné Indians—The Dog Ribs—Clothing—The Hare
Indians—Degraded State of the Women—Practical Socialists—Character—
Cruelty to the Aged and Infirm.

THE Tinné Indians, whose various tribes range from the
Lower Mackenzie to the Upper Saskatchewan, and
from New Caledonia to the head of Chesterfield Inlet, occupy
a considerable part of the territories of the Hudson's Bay
Company. To their race belong the Strongbows of the
Rocky Mountains; the Beaver Indians between Peace
River and the west branch of the Mackenzie; the Red
Knives, thus named from the copper knives of which their
native ores furnish the materials, and who roam between the
Great Fish River and the Coppermine; the Hare Indians
who inhabit the thickly-wooded district of the Mackenzie
from Slave Lake downwards; the Dog Ribs who occupy the
inland country on the east, from Martin Lake to the Cop-
permine; the Athabascans who frequent the Elk and Slave
Rivers, and many other tribes of inferior note.

The Tinné, in general, have more regular features than

the Esquimaux, and, taken on the whole, exhibit all the characteristics of the Red races dwelling farther south; but their utter disregard of cleanliness and their abject behaviour (for when in the company of white people they exhibit the whine and air of inveterate mendicants) give them a wretched appearance. Mackenzie, the first European who became acquainted with the Dog Ribs, describes them as an ugly emaciated tribe, covered with dirt and besmeared with grease from head to foot. More than sixty years have passed since Mackenzie's journey, but his account of them is true to the present day. The women are even uglier and more filthy than the men, for the latter at least paint their unwashed faces and wear trinkets on festive occasions, while the females leave even their hair without any other dressing than wiping their greasy hands on the matted locks, when they have been rubbing their bodies with marrow. The clothing of the men in summer consists of reindeer leather dressed like shammy, which, when newly made, is beautifully white and soft. 'A shirt of this material,' says Sir John Richardson, to whom we are indebted for the best account of the various nations inhabiting the Hudson's Bay territory, 'cut evenly below, reaches to the middle; the ends of a piece of cloth secured to a waist-band hang down before and behind; the hose, or Indian stockings, descend from the top of the thigh to the ankle, and a pair of mocassins or shoes of the same soft leather with tops which fold round the ankle, complete the costume. When the hunter is equipped for the chase he wears, in addition, a stripe of white hare-skin, or of the belly part of a deer-skin, in a bandana round the head, with his lank, black elf-locks streaming from beneath; a shot pouch suspended by an embroidered belt, a fire-bag or tobacco-pouch tucked into the girdle, and a long fowling-piece thrown carelessly across the arm, or balanced on the back of the neck. The several articles here enumerated are ornamented at the seams and hems with leather thongs wound round with porcupine quills, or more or less embroidered with bead-work, according to the industry of the wife or wives. One of the young men, even of the slovenly Dog Ribs, when newly equipped, and tripping jauntily over the mossy ground with an elastic step, displays his slim and not ungraceful figure to advantage. But this fine dress once donned is neither laid aside nor cleaned while it lasts, and soon acquires a dingy look and an odour which betrays its owner at some distance. In the camp a greasy blanket of English manufacture is worn over the shoulders by day, and forms with the clothes the bedding by night.'

In winter they clothe themselves with moose or reindeer skins, retaining the hair, while a large robe of the same material is thrown over the shoulders, and hangs down to the feet in place of the blanket. The women's dress resembles the men's, but the skirt is somewhat longer, and generally accompanied by a petticoat which reaches nearly to the knee. The form of dress here described is common to the whole Tinné nation, and also to the Crees, but the material varies with the district. Thus moose-deer, red-deer, and bison leather are in use among the more southern and western tribes, and the Hare Indians make their skirts of the skins of the animal from which they derive their surname. As this, however, is too tender to be used in the ordinary way, it is torn into narrow strips twisted slightly, and plaited or worked into the required shape. Such is the closeness and fineness of the fur, that these hare-skin dresses are exceedingly warm, notwithstanding the looseness of their texture.

The Hare Indian and Dog Rib women are certainly at the bottom of the scale of humanity in North America. Not that they are treated with cruelty, but that they are looked upon as inferior beings, and in this belief they themselves acquiesce. In early infancy, the boy discovers that he may show any amount of arrogance towards his sisters, who, as soon as they can walk, are harnessed to a sledge, while the tiny hunter struts in his snow shoes after the men and apes their contempt of the women. All the work, except hunting and fishing, falls to their share; yet they are in general not discontented with their lot.

It would be vain to look among the Dog Ribs for the stoicism popularly attributed to the Indians, for they shrink from pain, shed tears readily, and are very timorous; but all, young and old, enjoy a joke heartily, and when young are lively and cheerful. When bands of their nation meet each other after a long absence, they perform a kind of dance. A piece of ground is cleared for the purpose, and the dance frequently lasts for two or three days, the parties relieving each other as they get tired. The two bands commence the dance with their backs turned to each other, the individuals following one another in Indian file, and holding the bow in the left hand, and an arrow in the right. They approach obliquely after many turns, and when the two bands are closely back to back, they feign to see each other for the first time, and the bow is instantly transferred to the right hand and the arrow to the left, signifying that it is not their intention to use them against their friends. Their dancing, which they accompany by a chorus of groans, compared by Sir John Richardson to the deep sigh of a paviour as he brings his rammer down upon the pavement, has not the least pretensions to grace; their knees and body are half bent, and from their heavy stamping, they appear as if desirous of sinking into the ground.

The Dog Ribs are practical socialists, and their wretched condition results in a great measure from this cause. All may avail themselves of the produce of a hunter's energy or skill, and do not even leave him the distribution of his own game. When it becomes known in a camp that deer have been killed, the old men and women of each family sally forth with their sledges and divide the quarry, leaving the owner nothing but the ribs and tongue—all he can claim of right. Unable to restrain their appetite, all the community feast in times of abundance, however little many of the men (and there are not a few idle ones) may have contributed to the common good. Taught by frequent sufferings, the more active hunters frequently withdraw from the worthless drones, leaving them at some fishing-station, where, with proper industry, they may subsist comfortably. Fish-diet is, however, not agreeable to their taste, and as soon as reports of a successful chase arrive, a general movement to the hunting-ground ensues. If on their march the craving multitude discover a hoard of meat, it is devoured on the spot; but they are not always so fortunate. The deer and the hunters may have gone off, and then they are obliged to retrace their steps, many perishing by the way.

The Dog Ribs are not conspicuous for hospitality. When a stranger enters a tent he receives no welcome and proffer of food, though he may help himself from a piece of meat hanging on the wall, or join the repast. Though great liars, they do not steal the white man's property like the Esquimaux and Crees, and when visiting a fort, they may be trusted in any of the rooms. As to their religious belief, the majority of the nation recognise a Great Spirit, while others doubt his existence, assigning as a reason their miserable condition. They are in great fear of evil spirits, which, as they imagine, assume the forms of the bear, wolf, and wolverine, and in the woods, waters, and desert-places, they fancy they hear them howling in the winds, or moaning by the graves of the dead. They never make offerings to the Great Spirit, but deprecate the wrath of an evil being by the promise of a sacrifice, or by scattering a handful of deer-hair or a few feathers. They believe in a state of future happiness or torment. The soul, after death, crosses a broad river in a boat, and thus endeavours to reach the opposite shore, which is adorned with all the beauties of paradise. If laden with crime, the boat sinks under the weight, and the unfortunate soul, immersed in water, strives in vain to reach the blissful abode from which it is for ever banished.

Formerly when a Tinné warrior died, it was customary for the family to abandon every article they possessed, and betake themselves, in a perfectly destitute condition, to the nearest body of their own people or trading post. The advice of traders is gradually breaking down this absurd practice, which would alone suffice to keep this people in a state of perpetual poverty. In other respects also European influence begins to make itself felt. Since 1846, Roman Catholic missionaries are at work among the Chepewyans, and have taught many of their converts to read and write. The Athabascans had formerly but a small breed of dogs, now a stouter race has, in some respects, ameliorated the condition of the females, and the introduction of the horse, which has more recently taken place, holds out prospects of a still greater improvement. The Tinné are as giddy and thought- less as children. When accompanied by a white man they will perform a long journey carefully, but cannot be depended upon to carry letters, however high the reward may be that has been promised them on reaching their destination, as the least whim suffices to make them forget their commission.

They are generally content with one wife at a time, and none but the chiefs have more than two. The successful wrestler takes the wife of his weaker countryman, who con- soles himself for his loss by endeavouring to find one weaker than himself.

Tender and affectionate parents, the Tinné are totally in- different to the sorrows of helpless age. During the stay of Sir George Back at Fort Reliance, an old woman arrived there on Easter Sunday, clothed in ragged reindeer skins, worn down to a skeleton, and grasping with both her hands a stick to support her body, bent double by age and want. The story of the poor creature was soon told. She had be- come a burden to her family; her former services had all been forgotten, and she had been told, 'that though she still seemed to live, she was in reality dead, and must be abandoned to her fate. In the new fort she might find assistance, for the white strangers were powerful medicine-men.' This had happened a month before, and all this time she had slowly crept along, appeasing her hunger with the berries she found here and there on the way. When she reached the fort it was too late, she died a few days after her arrival.

The Lynx.

Kutchin Natives.
(From an original sketch by Frederick Whymper.)

## CHAPTER XXX.

### THE LOUCHEUX, OR KUTCHIN INDIANS.

The Countries they inhabit—Their Appearance and Dress—Their Love of Finery
—Condition of the Women—Strange Customs—Character--Feuds with the
Esquimaux—Their suspicious and timorous Lives—Pounds for catching Rein-
deer—Their Lodges.

ON the banks of the Lower Mackenzie, to the west of
Great Bear Lake, in the territories drained by the Peel
River and by the Upper Yukon, dwell the Loucheux, or
Kutchin Indians, whose language is totally different from
that of the other North American tribes, and whose customs
and manners also vary considerably from those of all their
neighbours, both Red-skins and Esquimaux.

They are an athletic and fine looking people, with regular
features and a complexion of a lighter copper colour than
that of the other Red Indians, so that many of their women
would be reckoned handsome in any country. The females
tattoo their chins and use a black pigment when they paint
their faces, while the men employ both red and black on all

occasions of ceremony, and always to be ready each carries a small bag with red clay and black lead suspended to his neck. Most commonly the eyes are encircled with black, a stripe of the same runs down the middle of the nose, and a blotch is daubed on the upper part of each cheek. The forehead is crossed by many narrow red stripes, and the skin is streaked alternately with red and black.

The outer shirt of the Kutchin is made of the skins of fawn reindeer, dressed with the hair on after the manner of the Hare, Dog Rib, and other Chepewyan tribes, but resembles in form the analogous garment of the Esquimaux, being furnished with peaked skirts though of smaller size. The men wear these skirts before and behind; the women have larger back skirts but none in front. In winter, shirts of hare-skin are worn, and the pantaloons of deer-skin have the fur next the skin.

None of the neighbouring nations pay so much attention to personal cleanliness, or are so studious in adorning their persons. A broad band of beads is worn across the shoulders and breast of the shirt, and the hinder part of the dress is fringed with tassels wound round with dyed porcupine quills and strung with the silvery fruit of the oleaster (*Elæagnus argentea*); a stripe of beads, strung in alternate red and white squares, ornament the seams of the trousers, and bands of beads encircle the ankles. The poorer sort, or the less fortunate hunters, who are unable to procure these costly trinkets in the same enviable abundance as the rich, strive to wear at least a string of beads, and look down with contemptuous pity upon the still more needy class, which is reduced to adorn itself with porcupine quills only.

In consequence of this passionate fondness for beads, these ornaments serve as a medium of exchange among the Kutchin, and Sir John Richardson remarks that no such near approach to money has been invented by the nations to the eastward of the Rocky Mountains. The standard bead, and one of the most value, is a large one of white enamel, manufactured in Italy only, and is with difficulty procured in sufficient quantity to satisfy the demand, as beads are more prized than English cloth and blankets.

Another article very much in request among the Kutchin, is the large ribbed dentalium shell which is collected in the archipelago between Oregon and Cape Fairweather, and passes by trade from tribe to tribe until it finds its way at length to the Yukon. With this shell they adorn their mittens, and even attach it to their guns, which have been lately introduced, and are in great demand. All men carry powder and ball, whether they own a gun or not, and obtain for it a share of the game.

The tribes on the Yukon tie their hair behind in a cue, or 'chignon,' and daub it with grease and the down of geese and ducks, until, by the repetition of the process continued from infancy, it swells to an enormous thickness, so that the weight of the accumulated load of hair, dirt, and ornaments, causes the wearer to stoop forwards habitually. The tail-feathers of the eagle and fishing-hawk are stuck into the hair on the back of the head, and are removed only when the owner retires to sleep, or when he wishes to wave them to and fro in a dance.

The principal men have two or three wives each, while the bad hunters are obliged to remain bachelors. A good wrestler, however, even though poor, can always obtain a wife.

The women do all the drudgery in winter, except cooking, and do not eat till the husband is satisfied. In summer they labour little, except in drying meat or fish for its preservation. The men alone paddle while the women sit as passengers, and husbands even carry their wives to the shore on their arms, that they may not wet their feet—an instance of gallantry almost unparalleled in savage life. The Esquimaux women row their own 'oomiaks,' and the Chepewyan women assist the men in paddling their canoes. On the whole, the social condition of the Kutchin women is far superior to that of the Tinné women, but scarcely equal to that of the Esquimaux dames.

They do not carry their children in their hoods or boots like the Esquimaux, nor do they stuff them into a bag with moss like the Tinné and Crees, but they place them in a seat of birch-bark, with a back and sides like those of an arm-chair, and a pommel in front resembling the peak of a Spanish saddle, by which they hang it from their back. The child's feet are bandaged to prevent them growing, small feet being thought handsome, and consequently short unshapely feet are characteristic of the people of both sexes. A more ridiculous or insane custom can hardly be imagined among a nation of hunters.

The Kutchin are a lively cheerful people, fond of dancing and singing, in which they excel all other Indians; leaping, wrestling, and other athletic exercises are likewise favourite amusements. They are inveterate talkers. Every new-comer arriving at a trading-post makes a long speech which must not be interrupted. The belief in Shamanism is still in full vigour among them.

Though a treacherous people, they have never yet imbrued their hands in European blood, but there are frequent feuds among their various tribes, by which one-half of the population of the banks of the Yukon has been cut off within the last twenty years. From a constant dread of ambuscade, they do not travel except in large parties; and thus a perpetual feeling of insecurity embitters their lives, which are already rendered sufficiently hard by the severity of an Arctic climate. The agents of the Hudson's Bay Company have endeavoured by good advice, and the distribution of large presents, to establish peace, but have only met with partial success.

Like the Tinné, the Kutchin are in a state of perpetual warfare with the Esquimaux; and though they always charge the latter with treachery, yet there can be no doubt that the accusation might, with full justice, be retorted upon themselves. One of the hostile encounters, mentioned by Sir J. Richardson, deserves notice, on account of its resemblance in some particulars to the meeting of Joab and Abner, recorded in the Second Book of Samuel. A party of each of the two nations having met on the banks of a river, the young men of both parties rose up as if for a friendly dance. The stream glides peacefully along, the setting sun gilds the pine forest and sparkles in the waters, all nature breathes peace. But the Esquimaux having, according to their custom, concealed their long knives in the sleeves of their deer-skin shirts, suddenly draw them in one of the evolutions of the dance, and plunge them into their opponents. A general conflict ensues, in which the Kutchin, thanks to their guns, ultimately prove victorious. 'Another incident,' says Sir John Richardson, 'which occurred on the banks of the Yukon in 1845, gives us a further insight into the suspicious and timorous lives of these people. One night four strangers from the lower part of the river arrived at the tent of an old man who was sick, and who had with him only two sons, one of them a mere boy. The new comers entered in a friendly manner, and when the hour of repose came, lay down; but as they did not sleep, the sons, suspecting from their conduct that they meditated evil, feigned a desire of visiting their moose-deer snares. They intimated their purpose aloud to their father and went out, taking with them their bows and arrows. Instead, however, of continuing their way into the wood, they stole back quietly to the tent, and listening on the outside, discovered, as they fancied, from the conversation of the strangers, that their father's life was in danger. Knowing the exact position of the inmates, they thereupon shot their arrows through the skin covering of the tent and killed two of the strange Indians; and the other two, in endeavouring to make their escape by the door, shared the fate of their companions. This is spoken of in the tribe as an exceedingly brave action.'

During the summer the Yukon Kutchin dry, for their winter use, the white fish (*Coregonus albus*), which they catch by planting stakes across the smaller rivers and narrow parts of the lakes and closing the openings with wicker-baskets. They take the moose-deer in snares, and towards spring mostly resort to the mountains to hunt reindeer, and lay in a stock of dried venison. On the open pasture grounds frequented by this animal they construct large pounds. Two rows of posts firmly planted in the ground, and united by the addition of strong horizontal bars into a regular fence, extend their arms for nearly the length of a mile in the form of a Roman V. The extremity of the avenue is closed by stakes with sharp points sloping towards the entrance, on which the reindeer, driven together and hotly pursued by the Indians, may impale themselves in their desperate flight. The structure is erected with great labour, as the timber has to be transported into the open country from a considerable distance. Some of these may be a century old, and they are the hereditary possession of the families or tribes by whom they were originally constructed.

But in spite of all their contrivances and the use of fire-arms, the Kutchin, whose numbers on the banks of the Yukon are estimated at about a thousand men and boys able to hunt, are frequently reduced to great distress. Hence the old and infirm are mercilessly left to their fate when game is scarce, and famine makes itself felt. Attempts have been vainly made to better the condition of the northern Indians by inducing them to tame the reindeer. Their superstition is one of the obstacles against this useful innovation, for they fear that were they to make some of the reindeer their captives, the remainder would immediately leave the country. 'And why,' they add, 'should we follow like slaves a herd of tame animals, when the forest and the barren ground provide us with the elk, the wild reindeer, and the musk-ox, and our rivers and lakes are filled with fishes that cost us nothing but the trouble of catching them?'

Each family possesses a deer-skin tent or lodge, which in summer, when in quest of game, is rarely erected. The winter encampment is usually in a grove of spruce-firs; the ground being cleared of snow, the skins, which are prepared with the hair, are extended over flexible willow-poles which take a semi-circular form. This hemispherical shape of lodges is not altogether unknown among the Chepewyans and Crees, being that generally adapted for their vapour baths, framed of willow-poles, but their dwelling places are conical, as stiff poles are used for their construction.

When the tent is erected the snow is packed on outside to half its height, and it is lined equally high within with the young spray of the spruce-fir, that the bodies of the inmates may not rest against the cold wall. The doorway is filled up by a double fold of skin, and the apartment has the closeness and warmth but not the elegance of the Esquimaux snow-hut, which it resembles in shape. Though only a very small fire is kept in the centre of the lodge, yet the warmth is as great as in a log-house. The provisions are stored on the outside under fir-branches and snow, and further protected from the dogs by sledges being placed on top.

The Pine Marten.

Hill at Rapids on Bear Lake River.

## CHAPTER XXXI.

### ARCTIC VOYAGES OF DISCOVERY FROM THE CABOTS TO BAFFIN.

First Scandinavian Discoverer of America—The Cabots—Willoughby and Chancellor (1553–1554)—Stephen Burrough (1556)—Frobisher (1576–1578)—Davis (1585–1587)—Barentz, Cornelis, and Brant (1594)—Wintering of the Dutch Navigators in Novaya Zemlya (1596–1597)—John Knight (1606)—Murdered by the Esquimaux—Henry Hudson (1607–1609)—Baffin (1616).

LONG before Columbus sailed from the port of Palos (1492) on that ever memorable voyage which changed the geography of the world, the Scandinavians had already found the way to North America. From Greenland, which was known to them as early as the ninth century, and which they began to colonise in the year 985, they sailed farther to the west, and gradually extended their discoveries from the coasts of Labrador, Nova Scotia, and Newfoundland, to those of the present state of Rhode Island, which, from the wild vines they there found growing in abundance, they called the ' good Vinland.'

But a long series of disasters destroyed their Greenland colonies about the end of the fourteenth century, and as Scandinavia itself had at that time but very little intercourse with the more civilised nations of Southern Europe, it is not to be wondered at that, despite the discoveries of Günnbjorn and Eric the Red, the great western continent remained unknown to the world in general.

One of the first consequences of the achievements of Columbus was the *re-discovery* of the northern part of America, for the English merchants longed to have a share of the commerce of India; and as the Pope had assigned the eastern route to the Portuguese and the western one to the Spaniards, they resolved to ascertain whether a third and shorter way to the Spice Islands, or to the fabulous golden regions of the east, might not be found by steering to the north-west. In pursuance of these views John and Sebastian Cabot sailed in 1497 from Bristol, at that time our first commercial port, and discovered the whole American coast from Labrador to Virginia. They failed indeed in the object of their mission, but they laid the first foundations of the future colonial greatness of England.

A second voyage in 1498 by Sebastian Cabot alone, without the companionship of his father, had no important results, but in a third voyage which he undertook in search of a north-west passage, at Henry VIII.'s expense, in 1516 or 1517, it is tolerably certain that that great navigator discovered the two straits which now bear the names of Davis and Hudson.

The French expeditions of Verazzani (1523) and Jacques Cartier (1524), however memorable in other respects, having been as unsuccessful as those of Cortereal (1500) or Gomez (1524) in discovering the desired north-western passage, Sebastian Cabot, who in 1549 was created Grand Pilot of England, started in his old age another idea, which has become almost equally momentous in the history of Arctic discovery—the search for a north-eastern route to China. Accordingly, in the year 1553, a squadron of three small vessels, under the command of Sir Hugh Willoughby, Chancellor, and Durfoorth, set sail from Ratcliffe, with the vain hope of reaching India by sailing round North Asia, the formation and vast extent of which were at that time totally unknown.

Off Senjan, an island on the Norwegian coast in lat. 69¼°, the ships parted company in a stormy night never to meet again.     Willoughby and Durfoorth reached the coast of Novaya Zemlya, and ultimately sought a harbour in Lapland on the west side of the entrance into the White Sea, where the captain-general, officers, and crews of both ships were miserably frozen to death, as some Russian fishermen ascertained in the following spring.   How long they sustained the severity of the weather is not known, but the journals and a will found on board the 'Admiral' proved that Sir Hugh Willoughby and most of that ship's company were alive in January, 1554.   They died the victims of inexperience, for had they, as Sir John Richardson remarks, been skilled in hunting and clothing themselves, and taken the precaution moreover of laying in, at the beginning of the winter, a stock of mossy turf, such as the country produces for fuel, and above all had they secured a few of the very many seals and belugæ which abounded in the sea around them, they might have preserved their lives and passed an endurable winter.

Chancellor was either more fortunate or more skilful, for after having long been buffeted about by stormy weather, he eventually reached St. Nicholas in the White Sea.   From thence he proceeded overland to Moscow, and delivered his credentials to the Czar, Ivan Vasilovitch, from whom he obtained many privileges for the company of merchants who had fitted out the expedition.   In 1554 he returned to England, and shortly afterwards was sent back to Russia by Queen Mary for the purpose of negotiating a treaty of commerce between the two nations.   Having satisfactorily accomplished his mission, he once more set sail from the White Sea, accompanied by a Muscovite ambassador.   But this time the return voyage was extremely unfortunate, for Chancellor, after losing two of his vessels off the coast of Norway, was carried by a violent tempest into the bay of Pitsligo in Scotland, where his ship was wrecked.   He endeavoured to save the ambassador and himself in a boat, but the small pinnace was upset; and although the Russian safely reached the strand, the Englishman, after having escaped so many dangers in the Arctic Ocean, was drowned within sight of his native shores.

· In 1556 the Muscovy Company fitted out the Serchthrift pinnace, under the command of Stephen Burrough, for discovery towards the River Obi and further search for a north-east passage. This small vessel reached the strait between Novaya Zemlya and Vaigats, called by the Russians the Kara Gate, but the enormous masses of ice that came floating through the channel compelled it to return.

In spite of these repeated disappointments, the desire to discover a northern route to India was too great to allow an enterprising nation like the English to abandon the scheme as hopeless.

Thus in the days of Elizabeth the question of the N.W. passage was again revived, and Martin Frobisher, who had solicited merchants and nobles during fifteen years for means to undertake ' *the only great thing left undone in the world*,' sailed in the year 1576 with three small vessels of 35, 30, and 10 tons, on no less an errand than the circumnavigation of northern America. The reader may smile at the ignorance which encouraged such efforts, but he cannot fail to admire the iron-hearted man who ventured in such wretched nut- shells to face the Arctic seas. The expedition safely reached the coasts of Greenland and Labrador, and brought home some glittering stones, the lustre of which was erroneously attributed to gold. This belief so inflamed the zeal for new expeditions to 'Meta Incognita,' as Frobisher had named the coasts he had discovered, that he found no difficulty in equipping three ships of a much larger size, that they might be able to hold more of the anticipated treasure. At the entrance of the straits which still bear his name, he was prevented by the gales and drift-ice from forcing a passage to the sea beyond, but having secured about 200 tons of the supposed golden ore the expedition was considered eminently successful. A large squadron of fifteen vessels was conse- quently fitted out in 1578 for a third voyage, and commissioned not only to bring back an untold amount of treasure but also to take out materials and men to establish a colony on those desolate shores. But this grand expedition, which sailed with such extravagant hopes, was to end in disappointment. One of the largest vessels was crushed by an iceberg at the entrance of the strait, and the others were so beaten about by

storms and obstructed by fogs that they were at length glad
to return to England without having done anything for the
advancement of geographical knowledge. The utter worth-
lessness of the glittering stones having meanwhile been
discovered, Frobisher relinquished all further attempts to
push his fortunes in the northern regions, and sought new
laurels in a sunnier clime. He accompanied Drake to the
West Indies, commanded subsequently one of the largest
vessels opposed to the Spanish Armada, and ended his heroic
life while attacking a small French fort in behalf of Henry IV.
during the war with the League.

The discovery of the north-western passage was, however,
still the great enterprise of the day, and thus sundry London
merchants again 'cast in their adventure,' and sent out
John Davis in 1585, with his two ships, 'Sunshine' and
'Moonshine,' carrying, besides their more necessary equip-
ments, a band of music 'to cheer and recreate the spirits of
the natives.' Davis arrived in sight of the south-western
coast of Greenland, where he saw a high mountain (Sukkertoppen) towering like a cone of silver over the fog which
veiled the dismal shore. The voyagers were glad to turn
from the gloomy scene, and to steer through the open water
to the north-west, where, on August 6, they discovered land
in latitude 66° 40′ altogether free from 'the pesters of ice,
and ankered in a very fair rode.' A friendly understanding was established with the Esquimau·, and a lively
traffic opened, the natives eagerly giving their skins and
furs for beads and knives, until a brisk wind separated the
strange visitants from their simple-minded friends. The
remainder of the season was spent in exploring Cumberland Sound and the entrance to Frobisher's and Hudson's
Straits.

In the following year Davis undertook a second voyage to
the north-west, for which the 'Sunshine' and 'Moonshine'
were again engaged, with two other vessels. On June 29,
1586, he landed on the coast of Greenland, in latitude 64°,
and soon after steered to the west. The enormous ice-floes
which, as is well known, come drifting from Baffin's Bay
until the season is far advanced, opposed his progress. For
some days he coasted these floating islands, when a fog came

on, during which ropes, sails, and cordage, were alike fast
frozen, and the seamen, hopeless of accomplishing the passage, warned their commander that ' by his over-boldness he
might cause their widows and fatherless children to give him
bitter curses.'

Touched by this appeal, Davis ordered two of his ships to
return home, and pushing on in the 'Moonshine' with the
boldest of his followers, he reached the American shore,
which he coasted from 67° to 57° of latitude. Off the
coast of Labrador, two of his sailors were killed by the
natives, and September being ushered in by violent gales,
he gave up farther attempts for the year, and returned to
England.

On June 16, 1587, we once more find him on the coast of
Greenland, in his old tried bark the 'Sunshine,' in company
with the 'Elizabeth' and a pinnace. The supplies for this
third voyage being furnished under the express condition
that the expenses should be lightened as much as possible
by fishing at all suitable times, the two larger ships were
stationed for the purpose near the part of the coast which
they had formerly visited, while Davis steered forward in the
small and ill-conditioned vessel which alone remained at his
disposal. He first sailed along the Greenland coast as far as
72° lat., where, having fairly entered Baffin's Bay, he named
the point at which he touched Sanderson's Hope, in honour
of his chief patron, and then steered to the west, until he
once more fell in with the ice-barrier, which had prevented
his progress the year before. Time and perseverance, however, overcame all obstacles, and by July 19 he had crossed
to the opposite side of the strait which bears his name. He
then sailed for two days up Cumberland Strait—which, it will
be remembered, he discovered on his first expedition—but
believing this passage to be an enclosed gulf, he returned, and
again passing the entrance to Hudson's Bay, without an effort
to investigate it, repaired to the rendezvous appointed for
the two whaling vessels, to meet him on their way to England.
But who can paint his astonishment and consternation, when
he found that his companions had sailed away, leaving him
to find his way home in his miserable pinnace, which, however, landed him safely on his native shores. This was the

last of the Arctic voyages of that great navigator, for the spirit of the nation was chilled by his three successive disappointments; and all the zeal with which he pleaded for a fourth expedition proved fruitless.

He subsequently made five voyages to the East Indies, and was killed on December 27, 1605, on the coast of Malacca, in a fight with the Malays.

Seven years after Davis's last Arctic voyage, the Dutch made their first appearance on the scene of northern discovery. This persevering people had just then succeeded in casting off the Spanish yoke, and was now striving to gain, by the development of its maritime trade, a position among the neighbouring states, which the smallness of its territory seemed to deny to it. All the known avenues to the treasures of the south were at that time too well guarded by the fleets of Portugal and Spain to admit of any rivalry; but if fortune favoured them in finding the yet unexplored northern passage to India, they might still hope to secure a lion's share in that most lucrative of trades.

Animated by this laudable spirit of enterprise, the merchants of Amsterdam, Enkhuizen, and Middelburg fitted out in 1594 an expedition in quest of the north-eastern passage, which they entrusted to the command of Cornelius Corneliszoon, Brant Ysbrantzoon, and William Barentz, one of the most experienced seamen of the day. The three vessels sailed from the Texel on June 6, and having reached the coast of Lapland, separated into two divisions; Barentz choosing the bolder course of coasting the west side of Novaya Zemlya, as far as the islands of Orange, the most northerly points of the archipelago; while his less adventurous comrades were contented to sail along the Russian coast, until they reached a strait to which they gave the very appropriate name of Vaigats, or 'Wind Hole.' Forcing their way through the ice, which almost constantly blocks up the entrance to the Kara Sea, they saw, on rounding a promontory at the other end of the strait, a clear expanse of blue open sea, stretching onward as far as the eye could reach, while the continent trended away rapidly towards the south-east. They now no longer doubted that they had sailed round the famous Cape Tabin—a fabulous headland, which, according to Pliny (an indisputable authority in those times of geographical ignorance), formed the northern extremity of Asia, from whence the voyage was supposed to be easy to its eastern and southern shores. Little did Brant and Cornelius dream, that within the Arctic Circle the Asiatic coast still stretched 120° to the east; and fully trusting their erroneous impressions, they started in full sail for Holland, eager to bring to their countrymen the news of their imaginary success. Off Russian Lapland they fell in with Barentz, who, having arrived at the northern extremity of Novaya Zemlya—a higher latitude than any navigator is recorded to have reached before—had turned back before strong opposing winds and floating ice, and the three vessels returned together to Texel.

Such were the hopes raised by the discovery of the imaginary Cape Tabin, that, losing sight of their habitual caution, the merchants of Middelburg, Enkhuizen, Rotterdam, and Amsterdam immediately fitted out a fleet of six ships, laden with all sorts of merchandise fit for the Indian market. A little yacht was added, which was to accompany the fleet as far as that promontory, and thence to return with the good news, that the squadron had been left steering with a favourable wind right off to India. But, as may well be supposed, these sanguine hopes, built on the unsubstantial fabric of a vision, were doomed to a woful disappointment, for the 'Wind Hole Strait,' doing full justice to its name, did not allow the vessels to pass; and after fruitless efforts to force their way through the ice-blocks which obstructed that inhospitable channel, they returned crestfallen to the port whence they had sailed a few months before with such brilliant expectations.

Although great disappointment was felt at this failure, the scheme of sailing round Cape Tabin to India was, however, not abandoned by the persevering Amsterdamers; and, on May 16, 1596, Heemskerk, Barentz, and Cornelis Ryp once more started for the north-east. Bear Island and Spitzbergen were discovered, whereupon the ships separated, Cornelis and Heemskerk returning to Holland, while Barentz, slowly making his way through the fog and ice, advanced to the most northern point of Novaya Zemlya, the

crew being encouraged by the tidings, that from the high
cliffs of Orange Island clear open water had been seen to
the south-east. The effort to reach this inviting channel
was frustrated by the ice, which gathered about the ship
as it lay near shore, and gradually collecting under and
around it, raised it far above the level of the sea. All hope
of return before the next summer now vanished, but these
brave sailors submitted with resignation to their fate, ' though
much grieved,' says Gerrit de Veer, who was himself an eye-
witness of all the incidents he relates, ' to live there all that
cold winter, which we knew would fall out to be extremely
bitter.' Fortunately a quantity of drift-wood was found on
the strand, which served the Dutchmen both for the construction of a small hut and for fuel.

As early as September, the ground was frozen so hard that
they tried in vain to dig a grave for a dead comrade, and
their cramped fingers could hardly build the hut, which was
the more necessary, as the vessel, cracking under the pressure
of the ice, gave signs of speedily breaking up altogether.
By the middle of October the rude dwelling was completed,
and though its accommodation was scanty, they were glad
to take up their abode in it at once. The best place by the
central fire was assigned to a sick comrade, while all the rest
arranged their beds as best they could on shelves which had
been built round the walls. An examination into the state
of their provisions showed the necessity of reducing their
daily rations of bread, cheese, and wine, but by setting traps
they caught a good many Arctic foxes, which gave them an
occasional supply of fresh food. The sun had now entirely
taken his departure, and the long winter night of the 75°
43' of latitude set in, during which snowdrifts and impetuous
winds confined them to their miserable hut.

' We looked pitifully one upon the other,' says De Veer,
' being in great fear that if the extremity of the cold grew to
be more and more, we should all die there of cold, for that
what fire soever we made would not warm us.'

The ice was now two inches thick upon the walls, and even
on the sides of their sleeping cots, and the very clothes they
wore were whitened with frost. Yet in the midst of all their
sufferings these brave men maintained cheerful hearts; and

so great was their elasticity of spirit, that remembering January 5 was Twelfth Eve, they resolved to celebrate it as best they might. 'And then,' says the old chronicler, 'we prayed our Maister that we might be merry that night, and said that we were content to spend some of the wine that night which we had spared, and which was our share (one glass) every second day, and whereof for certaine days we had not dranke, and so that night we made merry and drew for king. And therewith we had two pounds of meal, whereof we made pancakes with oyle, and every man had a white biscuit which we sopt in the wine. And so supposing that we were in our owne country and amongst our friends, it comforted us well as if we had made a great banquet in our owne house. And we also made trinkets, and our gunner was king of Novaya Zemlya, which is at least 800 miles long and lyeth between two seas.'

On January 24, the edge of the sun appeared above the horizon, and the sight was a joyful one indeed. Now also the furious snow-storms ceased, and though the severity of the cold continued unabated, they were better able to brave the outer air and to recruit their strength by exercise. With the return of daylight the bears came again about the house, and some being shot, afforded a very seasonable supply of grease, so that they were able to burn lamps and pass the time in reading.

When summer returned, it was found impossible to disengage the ice-bound vessel, and the only hopes of escaping from this dreary prison now rested on two small boats, in which they finally quitted the scene of so much suffering on June 14, 1596. On the fourth day of their voyage, their barks became surrounded by enormous masses of floating ice, which so crushed and injured them, that the crews, giving up all hope, took a solemn leave of each other. But in this desperate crisis they owed their preservation to the presence of mind and agility of De Veer, who, with a well secured rope, leaped from one ice block to another, till he reached a larger floe, on which first the sick, then the stores, the crews, and finally the boats themselves were fairly landed. Here they were obliged to remain while the boats underwent the necessary repairs, and during this detention upon a floating ice raft, the gallant Barentz closed the eventful voyage of his life. He died as he had lived, calmly and bravely, thinking less of himself than of the welfare of his fellow-sufferers, for his last words were directions as to the course in which they were to steer. His death was bitterly mourned by the rough men under his command, and even the prospect of a return to their homes could not console them for the loss of their beloved leader. After a most tedious passage (for by July 28 they had only reached the southern extremity of Novaya Zemlya) they at length, at the end of August, arrived at Kola in Russian Lapland, where, to their glad surprise, they found their old comrade John Cornelison Ryp, with whom they returned to Amsterdam.

Meanwhile the spirit of discovery had once more recovered in England from the chill thrown upon it by so many previous disappointments. In 1602, Weymouth, while attempting to sail up the promising inlet, now so well-known as the entrance to Hudson's Bay, was repulsed by a violent storm, and in 1606 a melancholy issue awaited the next expedition to the north-west, which sailed under the command of John Knight, a brave and experienced sailor. Driven by stormy weather among the drift-ice on the coast of Labrador, Knight was fain to take shelter in the first cove that presented itself, and lost no time in ordering his damaged ship of forty tons to be drawn high up on the dry sand beyond the tide mark, where she might undergo the necessary repairs.

This position, however, not proving satisfactory, he manned his boat next day, and while the rest of the crew were busy at work, sailed across to the other side of the inlet to seek for some more convenient anchorage. Leaving two men in charge of the boat, he landed with his mate and three of his men to explore the strange coast. They climbed the steep acclivity of the shore, lingered for a moment on the summit of the cliffs, and before disappearing on the other side exchanged greetings of farewell with their messmates in the boat, who little imagined that it was a parting for ever. Evening came on and then darkened into night, muskets were fired and trumpets sounded, but no answer was made, and eleven o'clock arriving without any sign or signal of the missing party, the men who had tarried on shore mournfully returned to the ship with the dismal tidings of the loss of their brave commander and his comrades.

During this melancholy night, passed in alternate lamentations and plans for search and rescue, the ice had so accumulated in the channel which the unfortunate Knight crossed the day before, that though the boat was speedily rigged for the expedition, and the party who occupied it were one and all uncontrollably eager to start, the morning light convinced the most sanguine of the utter impossibility of forcing their way across the gulf. Thus passed two wretched days of uncertainty, rendered doubly miserable by the inactivity to which they were condemned, when on the night of the second day the little encampment was attacked by a large party of natives, whose hostility left no doubt about the fate which had befallen their missing friends. A volley of musketry soon dispersed the savages, but fearing future attacks, the crew, now only eight in number, at once resolved to put to sea in their crazy bark, which, though deprived of its rudder, and so leaky that the pumps were obliged to be constantly at work, safely carried them to Newfoundland.

In the year 1607, Henry Hudson made the first attempt to sail across the North Pole, a plan started in 1527 by Robert Thorne, but not yet acted upon by any one during the eighty years that had since passed. He reached the east coast of Greenland in 73° of latitude, and then proceeded to the northern extremity of Spitzbergen, but all his efforts to launch forth into the unknown ocean beyond, were baffled by the ice fields that opposed his progress.

In his next voyage (1608) he vainly tried for the north-east passage, but his third voyage (1609), which he performed in the service of the Dutch, led to the discovery of the magnificent river which still bears his name, and at whose mouth the ' Empire City ' of the great American republic has arisen.

In April, 1610, we find him setting sail on the last and most celebrated of his voyages. In all but its commander, this expedition was miserably inadequate to the object of its mission, for it consisted only of one vessel of fifty-five tons provisioned for six months, and manned by a crew who speedily proved themselves to be utterly unworthy of their leader.

On entering Hudson's Straits, the large masses of ice which encumbered the surface of the water and the thickness of the constant fogs, made them lose all courage, and they earnestly begged their commander to return at once to England. But Hudson pressed on until at last his little bark emerged into a vast open water rippling and sparkling in the morning sunshine. Hudson's Bay expanded before him, and the enraptured discoverer was fully convinced that the north-western route to India now lay open to the mariners of England.

It was the beginning of August, and the dastardly crew considering the passage effected, urged an immediate return; but Hudson was determined on completing the adventure, and wintering, if possible, on the sunny shores of India. For three months he continued tracking the south coasts of that vast northern mediterranean, but all his hopes of finding a new channel opening to the south proved vain, until at length the ship was frozen in on November 10 in the south-east corner of James's Bay. A dreary winter awaited the ice-bound seamen, with almost exhausted provisions, and unfortunately without that heroic patience and concord which had sustained the courage of Barentz and his companions under trials far more severe. But spring came at last and revived the spirits of their leader. His ship was once more afloat, once more his fancy indulged in visions of the sunny east, when as he stepped on deck on the morning of June 21, his arms were suddenly pinioned, and he found himself in the power of three of his men.

Inquiry, remonstrance, entreaty, command, all failed to draw a word from the stubborn mutineers, and Hudson resigned himself bravely to his fate, and with the quiet dignity of a noble nature, looked on calmly at the ominous preparations going forward. A small open boat was in waiting, and into this Hudson—his hands being previously tied behind his back—was lowered; some powder and shot, and the carpenter's box came next, followed by the carpenter himself, John King, whose name ought to be held in honourable remembrance, as he alone among the crew remained true to his master. Six invalids were also forced into the boat, which was then cut adrift, and the vessel sailed onwards on its homeward course. Nothing more was ever heard of

Hudson; but the ringleaders of that dark conspiracy soon paid a terrible penalty. Some fell in a fight with the Esquimaux, and others died on the homeward voyage, during which they suffered from the extremest famine.

The account of the great expanse of sea which had been reached gave new vigour to the spirit of discovery, and new expeditions sallied forth (Sir Thomas Button 1612, Gibbons 1614, Bylot 1615), to seek along the western shores of Hudson's Bay the passage which was to open the way to India. All efforts in this direction were of course doomed to disappointment, but Baffin, who sailed in 1616, with directions to try his fortune beyond Davis' Straits, enriched geography with a new and important conquest, by sailing round the enormous bay which still bears his name. During this voyage, he discovered the entrances of Smith's, Jones', and Lancaster Sounds, without attempting to investigate these broad highways to fields of later exploration. He believed them to be mere enclosed gulfs, and this belief became so firmly grounded in the public mind, that two full centuries elapsed before any new attempt was made to seek for a western passage in this direction, while Jens Munk, a Dane, sent out in 1619 with two good vessels, under the patronage of his king, Christian IV.; Fox and James (1631–1632), Knight and Barlow (1719), Middleton (1741), Moor and Smith (1746), confined their efforts to Hudson's Bay, and, by their repeated disappointments, made all expeditions in quest of a north-western passage appear well-nigh as chimerical as those of the knight-errants of romance.

The Musquash.

The Torso Rock, near Point Deas Thompson, North Coast of America.

# CHAPTER XXXII.

## ARCTIC VOYAGES OF DISCOVERY, FROM BAFFIN TO M'CLINTOCK.

Buchan and Franklin—Ross and Parry (1818)—Discovery of Melville Island—Winter Harbour (1819–1820)—Franklin's First Land Journey—Dreadful Sufferings—Parry's Second Voyage (1821–1823)—Iligliuk—Lyon (1824)—Parry's Third Voyage (1824)—Franklin's Second Land Journey to the Shores of the Polar Sea—Beechey—Parry's Sledge Journey towards the Pole—Sir John Ross's Second Journey—Five Years in the Arctic Ocean—Back's Discovery of Great Fish River—Dease and Simpson (1837–1839)—Franklin and Crozier's Last Voyage (1845)—Searching Expeditions—Richardson and Rae—Sir James Ross—Austin—Penny—De Haven—Franklin's First Winter Quarters discovered by Ommaney—Kennedy and Bellot—Inglefield—Sir E. Belcher—Kellett—M'Clure's Discovery of the North-West Passage—Collinson—Bellot's Death—Dr. Rae learns the Death of the Crews of the 'Erebus' and 'Terror'—Sir Leopold M'Clintock.

THE failure of Captain Phipps (afterwards Lord Mulgrave) in the Spitzbergen seas (1773), and that of the illustrious Cook (1776), in his attempt to circumnavigate the northern shores of America or Asia by way of the Straits of Behring, entirely damped, for the next forty years, the spirit of Arctic discovery; but hope revived when it became known that Captain Scoresby, on a whaling expedition in the Greenland seas (1806), had attained 81° 30′ N. lat., and thus approached

the Pole to within 540 miles. No previous navigator had
ever reached so far to the north; an open sea lay temptingly
before him, and the absence of the ice-blink proved, that for
miles beyond the visible horizon no ice-field or no snow-
covered land opposed his onward course; but as the object
of Scoresby's voyage was strictly commercial, and he himself
answerable to the owners of his vessel, he felt obliged to
sacrifice his inclinations to his duty, and to steer again to
the south.

During the Continental war, indeed, England had but
little leisure to prosecute discoveries in the Arctic Ocean:
but not long after the conclusion of peace, four stout vessels
(1818) were sent out on that mission by Government. Two
of these, the 'Dorothea,' Captain Buchan, and the 'Trent,'
Commander Lieutenant John Franklin, were destined to
proceed northwards by way of Spitzbergen, and to endeavour
to cross the Polar Sea. After unnumbered difficulties, the
expedition was battling with the ice to the north-west of
that wintry archipelago, when, on July 30, a sudden gale
compelled the commander, as the only chance of safety, to
'take the ice'—that is, to thrust the ships into any opening among the moving masses that could be perceived.
In this very hazardous operation, the 'Dorothea'—having
received so much injury that she was in danger of sinking
—was therefore turned homewards as soon as the storm subsided, and the 'Trent' of necessity accompanied her.

The other two ships which sailed in the same year, the 'Isabella,' commanded by Captain John Ross, and the 'Alexander,'
by Lieutenant William Edward Parry, had been ordered
to proceed up the middle of Davis' Strait to a high northern
latitude, and then to stretch across to the westward, in the
hope of being able to pass the northern extremity of America,
and reach Behring's Strait by that route. As respects the
purposes for which it was sent out, this expedition likewise
ended in disappointment; for though Ross defined more
clearly the Greenland coast to the north of the Danish
possessions between Cape Melville and Smith's Sound, he
was satisfied with making a very cursory examination of all
the great channels leading from Baffin's Bay into the Polar

Sea. After sailing for some little distance up Lancaster Sound, he was arrested by the atmospheric deception of a range of mountains, extending right across the passage, and concluding it useless to persevere, he at once—to the great astonishment and mortification of his officers—abandoned a course which was to render his successor illustrious. As may easily be imagined, the manner in which Ross had conducted this expedition failed to satisfy the authorities at home; and thus, in the following year, the 'Hecla' and 'Griper' were commissioned for the purpose of exploring the sound, whose entrance only had been seen by Baffin and Ross. The former ship was placed under the command of Parry, and the latter under that of Lieutenant Matthew Liddon.

With this brilliant voyage, the epoch of modern discoveries in the Arctic Ocean may properly be said to begin. Sailing right through Lancaster Sound, over the site of Ross's imaginary Croker mountains, Parry passed Barrow's Strait, and after exploring Prince Regent Inlet, whence the ice compelled him to return to the main channel, he discovered Wellington Channel (August 22), and soon after had the satisfaction of announcing to his men, that, having reached 110° W. long., they were entitled to the king's bounty of 5,000l., secured by order of council to 'such of His Majesty's subjects as might succeed in penetrating thus far to the west within the Arctic Circle.' After passing and naming Melville Island, a little progress was still made westward; but the ice was now rapidly gathering, the vessels were soon beset, and, after getting free with great difficulty, Parry was only too glad to turn back and settle down in Winter Harbour. It was no easy task to attain this dreary port, as a canal, two miles and a third in length, had first to be cut through solid ice of seven inches average thickness; yet such was the energy of the men, that the herculean labour was executed in three days. The two vessels were immediately unrigged, the decks housed over, a heating apparatus arranged, and everything made as comfortable as possible. To relieve the monotony of the long winter's night, plays were acted every fortnight, a school established, and a newspaper set on foot—certainly the first periodical ever issued in so high a latitude. During the day, the men were employed for exercise in banking up the ships with snow, or making excursions within a certain distance; and when the weather forbade their leaving shelter, they were obliged to run round the decks to the tune of a barrel-organ.

In January the cold became more and more intense. On the 12th it was 51° below zero in the open air, and on the 14th, the thermometer fell to 54°. On February 24, a fire broke out in a small house which had been built near the ships, to serve as an observatory for Captain Sabine, who accompanied the expedition as astronomer. All hands rushed to the spot to endeavour to subdue the flames, but having only snow to throw on it, it was found impossible to extinguish it. The snow, however, covered the astronomical instruments, and secured them from the fire. The thermometer was at the time 44° below zero, and the faces of nearly the whole party grew white and frost-bitten after five minutes' exposure, so that the surgeon and two or three assistants were busily employed in rubbing the faces of their comrades with snow, while the latter were working might and main to extinguish the flames. One poor fellow, in his anxiety to save the dipping needle, carried it out without putting on his gloves; his hands were so benumbed in consequence, that when plunged into a basin of cold water, it instantly froze, from the intense coldness imparted to it, and it was found necessary to resort, some time after, to the amputation of a part of four fingers on one hand and three on the other.

February 3 was a memorable day—the sun being visible from the maintop of the 'Hecla,' from whence it was last seen on November 11. The weather got considerably milder in March; on the 6th the thermometer rose to zero, for the first time since December 17; and on April 30 it stood at the freezing point, which it had not done since September 12.

At length May appeared, bringing the long summer's day of the high northern latitudes; but as many a week must still pass before the vessels could move out of their ice-bound harbour, Parry started on June 1 to explore the interior of the island, which at this early period of the season still wore a very dreary aspect. But such was the rapidity of vegetation, that by the end of the month the land, now completely clear of snow, was covered with the purple-coloured saxifrage in blossom, with mosses, and with sorrel, and the grass was from two to three inches long. The pasturage appeared to be excellent in the valleys, and, to judge by the numerous tracks of musk-oxen and reindeer, there was no lack of animals to enjoy its abundance.

It was not before August 1 that the ships were released from their ten months' blockade in Winter Harbour, when Parry once more stood boldly for the west; but no amount of skill or patience could penetrate the obstinate masses of ice that blocked the passage, or insure the safety of the vessels under the repeated shocks sustained from them. Finding the barriers insuperable, he gave way, and steering homeward, reached London on November 3, 1820, where, as may well be imagined, his reception was most enthusiastic.

While Parry was engaged on this wonderful voyage, Lieutenant Franklin and Dr. Richardson, accompanied by two midshipmen, George Back and Robert Hood, and a sailor John Hepburn, to whom were added during the course of the journey a troop of Canadians and Indians, were penetrating by land to the mouth of the Coppermine River, for the purpose of examining the unexplored shores of the Polar Sea to the east. An idea of the difficulties of this undertaking may be formed, when I mention that the travellers started from Fort York, Hudson's Bay, on August 30, 1819, and after a boat voyage of 700 miles up the Saskatchewan arrived before winter at Fort Cumberland. The next winter found them 700 miles further on their journey, established during the extreme cold at Fort Enterprise, as they called a log-house built by them on Winter Lake, where they spent ten months, depending upon fishing and the success of their Indian hunters. During the summer of 1821 they accomplished the remaining 334 miles to the mouth of the Coppermine, and on July 21, Franklin and his party embarked in two birch-bark canoes on their voyage of exploration. In these frail shallops they skirted the desolate coast of the American

continent 555 miles to the east of the Coppermine as far as
Point Turnagain, when the rapid decrease of their provisions
and the shattered state of the canoes imperatively compelled
their return (August 22).   And now began a dreadful land-
journey of two months, accompanied by all the horrors of
cold, famine, and fatigue.   An esculent lichen (tripe de
roche), with an occasional ptarmigan, formed their scanty
food, but on very many days even this poor supply could not
be obtained, and their appetites became ravenous.   Sometimes they had the good fortune to pick up pieces of skin,
and a few bones of deer which had been devoured by the
wolves in the previous spring.   The bones were rendered
friable by burning, and now and then their old shoes were
added to the repast.   On reaching the Coppermine, a raft had
to be framed, a task accomplished with the utmost difficulty
by the exhausted party.   One or two of the Canadians had
already fallen behind and never rejoined their comrades, and
now Hood and three or four more of the party broke down
and could proceed no farther, Dr. Richardson kindly volun-
teering to remain with them, while Back, with the most
vigorous of the men, pushed on to send succour from Fort
Enterprise, and Franklin followed more slowly with the others.
On reaching the log-house this last party found that wretched
tenement desolate, with no deposit of provisions and no trace
of the Indians whom they had expected to meet there.   ‘ It
would be impossible,’ says Franklin, ‘ to describe our sensations after entering this miserable abode and discovering how
we had been neglected ; the whole party shed tears, not so
much for our own fate as for that of our friends in the rear,
whose lives depended entirely on our sending immediate relief
from this place.’   Their only consolation was a gleam of
hope afforded them by a note from Back, stating that he had
reached the deserted hut two days before, and was going in
search of the Indians.   The fortunate discovery of some
cast-off deer-skins, and of a heap of acrid bones, a provision
worthy of the place, sustained their flickering life-flame,
and after eighteen miserable days they were joined by Dr.
Richardson and Hepburn, the sole survivors of their party,
Lieutenant Hood, a young officer of great promise, having
been murdered by a treacherous Canadian, whom Richardson

was afterwards obliged to shoot through the head in self-defence.

'Upon entering the desolate dwelling,' says Richardson, 'we had the satisfaction of embracing Captain Franklin, but no words can convey an idea of the filth and wretchedness that met our eyes on looking around. Our own misery had stolen upon us by degrees, and we were accustomed to the contemplation of each other's emaciated figures; but the ghastly countenances, dilated eyeballs, and sepulchral voices of Captain Franklin and those with him, were more than we could at first bear.' At length, on November 7, when the few survivors of the ill-fated expedition (for most of the voyagers died from sheer exhaustion) were on the point of sinking under their sufferings, three Indians sent by Back, whose exertions to procure them relief had been beyond all praise, brought them the succour they had so long been waiting for. The eagerness with which they feasted on dried meat and excellent tongues may well be imagined; but severe pains in the stomach soon warned them that after so long an abstinence they must be exceedingly careful in the quantity of food taken. In a fortnight's time they had sufficiently recruited their strength to be able to join Back at Moose Deer Island, and in the following year they returned to England.

Parry's second voyage of discovery (1821–1823) was undertaken for the purpose of ascertaining whether a communication might be found between Regent's Inlet and Rowe's Welcome, or through Repulse Bay and thence to the north-western shores of America. The first summer (1821) was spent in the vain attempt of forcing a way through Frozen Strait, Repulse Bay, the large masses of ice in these waters holding the ships helplessly in their grasp, and often carrying them back in a few days to the very spot which they had left a month before. Owing to these rebuffs, the season came to an end while their enterprise was yet scarcely begun, and the ships took up their quarters in an open roadstead at Winter Island to the south of Melville Peninsula. Besides the winter amusements and occupations of the first voyage, the monotony of the winter was pleasantly broken during February by friendly visits from a party of Esquimaux.

Among these a young woman Iligliuk distinguished herself by her talents. Her love for music amounted to a passion, and her quickness of comprehension was such that she soon became an established interpreter between her own people and the English. The nature of a map having been explained to her, she readily sketched with chalk upon the deck the outlines of the adjoining coast, and continuing it farther, delineated the whole eastern shore of Melville Peninsula, rounding its northern extremity by a large island and a strait of sufficient magnitude to afford a safe passage for the ships. This information greatly encouraged the whole · party, whose sanguine anticipations already fancied the worst part of their voyage overcome, and its truth was eagerly tested as soon as the ships could once more be set afloat, which was not till July 2.

After running the greatest dangers from the ice, they at length reached the small island of Igloolik near the entrance of the channel, the situation of which had been accurately laid down by the Esquimaux woman. But all their efforts to force a passage through the narrow strait proved vain, for after struggling sixty-five days to get forward, they had only in that time reached forty miles to the westward of Igloolik. The vessels were therefore again placed in winter-quarters in a channel between Igloolik and the land; but having ascertained by boat excursions the termination of the strait, Parry thought it so promising for the ensuing summer, that he at once named it the 'Hecla and Fury Strait.' But his hopes were once more doomed to disappointment by the ice-obstructed channel, and he found it utterly impossible to pass through it with his ships. His return to England with his crews in health, after two winters in the high latitudes, was another triumph of judgment and discipline.

In the following year two new expeditions set sail for Polar America. Captain Lyon was sent out in the 'Griper,' with orders to land at Wager River off Repulse Bay, and thence to cross Melville Peninsula, and proceed overland to Point Turnagain, where Franklin's journey ended. But a succession of dreadful storms so crippled the 'Griper,' while endeavouring to proceed onward up Rowe's

Welcome, that it became necessary to return at once to England.

Such was the esteem and affection Parry had acquired among the companions of his two former voyages, that when he took the command of a third expedition, with the intention of seeking a passage through Prince Regent's Inlet, they all volunteered to accompany him. From the middle of July till nearly the middle of September (1824), the 'Hecla' and the 'Fury' had to contend with the enormous ice masses of Baffin's Bay, which would infallibly have crushed vessels less stoutly ribbed; and thus it was not before September 10 that they entered Lancaster Sound, which they found clear of ice, except here and there a solitary berg. But new ice now began to form, which, increasing daily in thickness, beset the ship, and carried them once more back again into Baffin's Bay. By perseverance, however, and the aid of a strong easterly breeze, Parry regained the lost ground, and on September 27 reached the entrance of Port Bowen, on the eastern shore of Prince Regent Inlet, where he passed the winter. By July 19, the vessels were again free, and Parry now sailed across the inlet, to examine the coast of North Somerset; but the floating ice so injured the 'Fury,' that it was found necessary to abandon her. Her crew and valuables were therefore received on board the 'Hecla;' the provisions, stores, and boats were landed, and safely housed on Fury Point, off North Somerset, for the relief of any wandering Esquimaux, or future Arctic explorers who might chance to visit the spot, and the crippled ship was given up to the mercy of the relentless ice, while her companion made the best of her way to England.

In spite of the dreadful sufferings of Franklin, Richardson, and Back during their first land journey, we find these heroes once more setting forth in 1825, determined to resume the survey of the Arctic coasts of the American continent. A far more adequate preparation was made for the necessities of their journey than before, and before they settled down for the winter at 'Fort Franklin,' on the Shores of Great Bear Lake, a journey of investigation down the Mackenzie River to the sea had been brought to a successful end. As soon as the ice broke in the following summer, they set out in

four boats, and separated at the point where the river divides
into two main branches, Franklin and Back proposing to
survey the coast-line to the westward, while Richardson set
out in an easterly direction to the mouth of the Coppermine
River. Franklin arrived at the mouth of the Mackenzie
on July 7, where a large tribe of Esquimaux pillaged his
boats, and it was only by great prudence and forbearance
that the whole party were not massacred. A full month was
now spent in the tedious survey of 374 miles of coast, as far
as Return Reef, more than 1,000 miles distant from their
winter-quarters on Great Bear Lake. The return journey to
Fort Franklin was safely accomplished, and they arrived at
their house on September 21, where they had the pleasure of
finding Dr. Richardson and Lieutenant Kendall, who, on their
part, had reached the Coppermine, thus connecting Sir John
Franklin's former discoveries to the eastward in Coronation
Gulf with those made by him on this occasion to the westward of the Mackenzie. The cold during the second winter
at Fort Franklin was intense, the thermometer standing at
one time at 58° below zero; but the comfort they now enjoyed
formed a most pleasing contrast to the squalid misery of
Fort Enterprise.

When Franklin left England to proceed on this expedition, his first wife was then lying at the point of death, and
indeed expired the day after his departure. But with heroic
fortitude she urged him to set out on the very day appointed,
entreating him, as he valued her peace and his own glory,
not to delay a moment on her account. His feelings may
be imagined, when he raised on Garry Island a silk flag
—which she had made and given him as a parting gift, with
the instruction that he was only to hoist it on reaching the
Polar Sea.

While Parry and Franklin were thus severally employed
in searching for a western passage, a sea expedition, under
the command of Captain Beechey, had been sent to Behring's
Straits, to co-operate with them, so as to furnish provisions
to the former and a conveyance home to the latter—a task
more easily planned than executed; and thus we cannot
wonder, that when the 'Blossom' reached the appointed
place of rendezvous at Chamisso Island, in Kotzebue Sound

(July 25, 1826), she found neither Parry (who had long since returned to England) nor Franklin. Yet the barge of the ' Blossom '—which was despatched to the eastward under charge of Mr. Elson—narrowly missed meeting the latter; for when she was stopped by the ice at Point Barrow, she was only about 150 miles from Return Reef, the limit of his discoveries to the westward of the Mackenzie.

In the year 1827, the indefatigable Parry undertook one of the most extraordinary voyages ever performed by man; being no less than an attempt to reach the North Pole by boat and sledge travelling over the ice. His hopes of success were founded on Scoresby's authority, who reports having seen ice-fields so free from either fissure or hummock, that, had they not been covered with snow, a coach might have been driven many leagues over them in a direct line; but when Parry reached the ice-fields to the north of Spitzbergen, he found them of a very different nature, composed of loose, rugged masses, intermixed with pools of water, which rendered travelling over them extremely arduous and slow. The strong flat-bottomed boats, specially prepared for an amphibious journey, with a runner attached to each side of the keel, so as to adapt them for sledging, had thus frequently to be laden and unladen, in order to be raised over the hummocks, and repeated journeys backward and forward over the same ground were the necessary consequence. Frequently the crew had to go on hands and knees to secure a footing. Heavy showers of rain often rendered the surface of the ice a mass of slush, and in some places the ice took the form of sharp-pointed crystals, which cut the boots like penknives. But in spite of all these obstacles, they toiled cheerfully on, until at length, after thirty-five days of incessant drudgery, the discovery was made, that while they were apparently advancing towards the pole, the ice-field on which they were travelling was drifting to the south, and thus rendering all their exertions fruitless. Yet, though disappointed in his hope of planting his country's standard on the northern axis of the globe, Parry had the glory of reaching the highest authenticated latitude ever yet attained (82° 40′ 30″). On their return to the ' Hecla,' which awaited them, under Captain Forster, in Treurenberg Bay, on the

northern coast of Spitzbergen, the boats encountered a
dreadful storm on the open sea, which obliged them to bear
up for Walden Island—one of the most northerly rocks
of the archipelago—where, fortunately, a reserve supply of
provisions had been deposited. 'Everything belonging to
us,' says Sir Edward Parry, 'was now completely drenched
by the spray and snow; we had been fifty-six hours without
rest, and forty-eight at work in the boats, so that by the
time they were unloaded, we had barely strength to haul
them up on the rocks. However, by dint of great exertion,
we managed to get the boats above the surf, after which, a
hot supper, a blazing fire of drift-wood, and a few hours'
quiet rest, restored us.' He who laments over the degene-
racy of the human race, and supposes it to have been more
vigorous or endowed with greater powers of endurance in
ancient times, may perhaps come to a different opinion when
reading of Parry and his companions.

Thus ended the last of this great navigator's Arctic voyages.
Born in the year 1790, of a family of seamen, Parry, at an
early age, devoted himself, heart and soul, to the profession
in which his father had grown old. In his twenty-eighth
year he discovered Melville Island, and his subsequent expedition confirmed the excellent reputation he had acquired by
his first brilliant success. From the years 1829 to 1834 we
find him in New South Wales, as Resident Commissioner of
the Australian Agricultural Company. In the year 1837, he
was appointed to organise the mail packet service, then
transferred to the Admiralty; and after filling the post of
Captain Superintendent of the Royal Naval Hospital at
Haslar, was finally appointed Governor of Greenwich Hospital.
He died in the summer of 1855, at Ems.

Ten years had elapsed since Captain John Ross's first
unsuccessful voyage, when the veteran seaman, anxious to
obliterate the reproach of former failure by some worthy
achievement, was enabled, through the munificence of Sir
Felix Booth, to accomplish his wishes. A small Liverpool
steamer, bearing the rather presumptuous name of the ' Victory,' was purchased for the voyage, a rather unfortunate
selection, for surely nothing can be more unpractical than
paddle-boxes among ice-blocks; but to make amends for this

error, the commander of the expedition was fortunate in being accompanied by his nephew, Commander James Ross, who, with every quality of the seaman, united the zeal of an able naturalist. He it was who, by his well-executed sledge journeys, made the chief discoveries of the expedition, but the voyage of the 'Victory' is far less remarkable for successes achieved than for its unexampled protraction during a period of five years.

The first season ended well. On August 10, 1829, the 'Victory' entered Prince Regent's Inlet and reached on the 13th the spot where Parry, on his third voyage, had been obliged to abandon the 'Fury.' The ship itself had been swept away; but all her sails, stores, and provisions on land were found untouched. The hermetically sealed tin canisters in which the flour, meat, bread, wine, spirits, sugar, &c., were packed, had preserved them from the attacks of the white bears, and they were found as good after four years as they had been on the day when the 'Fury' started on her voyage. It was to this discovery that the crew of the 'Victory' owed their subsequent preservation, for how else could they have passed four winters in the Arctic wastes?

On August 15, Cape Garry was attained, the most southern point of the inlet which Parry had reached on his third voyage. Fogs and drift-ice greatly retarded the progress of the expedition, but Ross moved on, though slowly, so that, about the middle of September, the map of the northern regions was enriched by some 500 miles of newly-discovered coast. But now, at the beginning of winter, the 'Victory' was obliged to take refuge in Felix Harbour, where the useless steam engine was thrown overboard as a nuisance, and the usual preparations made for spending the cold season as pleasantly as possible.

The following spring (from May 17 to June 13) was employed by James Ross on a sledge journey, which led to the discovery of King William's Sound and King William's Land, and during which that courageous mariner penetrated so far to the west, that he had only ten days' provisions—scantily measured out—for a return voyage of 200 miles through an empty wilderness.

After twelve months' imprisonment, the 'Victory' was

released from the ice on September 17, and proceeded once more on her discoveries. But the period of her liberty was short, for after advancing three miles in one continual battle against the currents and the drift-ice, she again froze fast on the 27th of the same month.

In the following spring we again see the indefatigable James Ross extending the circle of his sledge excursions, and planting the British flag on the site of the Northern Magnetic Pole—which, however, is not invariably fixed to one spot, as was then believed, but moves from place to place within the glacial zone.

On August 28, 1831, the 'Victory'— after a second imprisonment of eleven months—was warped into open water; but after spending a whole month to advance four miles, she was encompassed by the ice on September 27 and once more fettered in the dreary wilderness.

As there seemed no prospect of extricating her, next summer, they resolved to abandon her and travel over the ice to Fury Beach, there to avail themselves of the boats, provisions, and stores, which would assist them in reaching Davis' Straits. Accordingly, on May 29, 1832, the colours of the 'Victory' were hoisted and nailed to the mast, and after drinking a parting glass to the ship with the crew, and having seen every man out in the evening, the captain took his own leave of her. 'It was the first vessel,' says Ross, 'that I had ever been obliged to abandon, after having served in thirty-six, during a period of forty-two years. It was like the last parting with an old friend, and I did not pass the point where she ceased to be visible, without stopping to take a sketch of this melancholy desert, rendered more melancholy by the solitary, abandoned, helpless home of our past years, fixed in immovable ice, till time should perform on her his usual work.'

After having, with incredible difficulty, reached Fury Beach, where, thanks to the forethought of Sir Edward Parry, they fortunately found a sufficient number of boats left for their purpose, and all the provisions in good condition, they set out on August 1—a considerable extent of open sea being visible—and, after much buffeting among the ice, reached the north of the inlet by the end of the month. But here they were doomed to disappointment, for, after several fruitless attempts to run along Barrow's Strait, the ice obliged them to haul their boats on shore, and pitch their tents. Day after day they lingered, till the third week in September, but the strait continuing one impenetrable mass of ice, it was unanimously agreed that their only resource was to fall back again on the stores at Fury Beach, and there spend a fourth long winter within the Arctic Circle. They were only able to get half the distance in the boats, which were hauled on shore in Batty Bay on September 24, and performed the rest of their journey on foot, the provisions being dragged in sledges. On October 7 they once more reached the canvas hut, dignified with the name of 'Somerset House,' which they had erected in July, on the scene of the 'Fury's' wreck, and which they had vainly hoped never to see again.

They now set about building a snow-wall four feet thick round their dwelling, and strengthening the roof with spars, for the purpose of covering it with snow, and by means of this shelter, and an additional stove, made themselves tolerably comfortable, until the increasing severity of the cold, and the furious gales, confined them within doors and sorely tried their patience. Scurvy now began to appear, and several of the men fell victims to the scourge. At the same time, cares for the future darkened the gloom of their situation; for, should they be disappointed in their hopes of escaping in the ensuing summer, their failing strength and diminishing stores gave them but little hope of surviving another year.

It may easily be imagined how anxiously the movements of the ice were watched when the next season opened, and with what beating hearts they embarked at Batty Bay on August 15. Making their way slowly among the masses of ice, with which the inlet was encumbered, they, to their great joy, found, on the 17th, the wide expanse of Barrow's Strait open to navigation.

Pushing on with renewed spirits, Cape York soon lay behind them, and alternately rowing and sailing, on the night of the 25th they rested in a good harbour, on the eastern shore of Navy Board Inlet. At 4 o'clock on the following morning, they were roused from their slumber by the joyful intelligence of a ship being in sight, and never did men more hurriedly and energetically set out; but the elements were against them, and the ship disappeared in the distant haze.

After a few hours' suspense, the sight of another vessel, lying to in a calm, relieved their despair. This time their exertions were successful, and, strange to say, the ship which took them on board was the same 'Isabella'—now reduced to the rank of a private whaler—in which Ross had made his first voyage to the Arctic Seas.

The seamen of the 'Isabella' told him of his own death—of which all England was persuaded—and could hardly believe that it was really he and his party who now stood before them. But when all doubts were cleared away, the rigging was instantly manned to do them honour, and thundering cheers welcomed Ross and his gallant band on board! The scene that now followed cannot be better told than in Ross's own words.

'Though we had not been supported by our names and characters, we should not the less have claimed from charity the attentions that we received; for never was seen a more miserable set of wretches. Unshaven since I know not when, dirty, dressed in the rags of wild beasts, and starved to the very bones, our gaunt and grim looks, when contrasted with those of the well-dressed and well-fed men around us, made us all feel (I believe for the first time) what we really were, as well as what we seemed to others. But the ludicrous soon took the place of all other feelings; in such a crowd and such confusion, all serious thought was impossible, while the new buoyancy of our spirits made us abundantly willing to be amused by the scene which now opened. Every man was hungry, and was to be fed; all were ragged, and were to be clothed; there was not one to whom washing was not indispensable, nor one whom his beard did not deprive of all human semblance. All, everything too, was to be done at once: it was washing, dressing, shaving, eating, all intermingled: it was all the materials of each jumbled together, while in the midst of all there were interminable questions to be asked and answered on both sides; the adventures of the "Victory," our own escapes, the politics of England, and the news which was now four years old. But all subsided into peace at last. The sick were accommodated, the seamen disposed of, and all was done for us which care and kindness could perform. Night at length brought quiet and serious thoughts, and I trust there was not a man among us who did not then express where it was due, his gratitude for that interposition which had raised us all from a despair which none could now forget, and had brought us from the borders of a most distant grave, to life, and friends, and civilisation. Long accustomed, however, to a cold bed on the hard snow, or the bare rocks, few could sleep amid the comfort of our new accommodations. I was myself compelled to leave the bed which had been kindly assigned me, and take my abode in a chair for the night; nor did it fare much better with the rest. It was for time to reconcile us to this sudden and violent change, to break through what had become habit, and to inure us once more to the usages of our former days.'

The 'Isabella' remained some time longer in Baffin's Bay, to prosecute the fishery, and thus our Arctic voyagers did not return to England before October 15, 1833, when they were received as men risen from the grave. Wherever Ross appeared, he was met and escorted by a crowd of sympathisers; orders, medals, and diplomas from foreign states and learned societies rained down upon him. London, Liverpool, Bristol, and Hull presented him with the freedom of their respective cities; he received the honour of knighthood; and, though last, not least, Parliament granted him 5,000*l.* as a remuneration for his pecuniary outlay and privations.

It may easily be imagined, that his long, protracted absence had not been allowed to pass without awakening a strong desire to bring him aid and assistance. Thus, when Captain (afterwards Rear-Admiral Sir George) Back, that noble Paladin of Arctic research, volunteered to lead a land expedition in quest of Ross, to the northern shore of America, 4,000*l.* were immediately raised by public subscription to defray expenses. While deep in the American wilds, Back was gratified with the intelligence that the object of his search had safely arrived in England; but, instead of returning home, the indefatigable explorer resolved to trace the unknown course of the Thlu-it-scho, or Great Fish River, down to the distant outlet where it pours its waters into the Polar Seas.

It would take a volume to relate his adventures in this expedition, the numberless falls, cascades, and rapids that obstructed his progress; the storms and snow-drifts, the horrors of the deserts through which he forced his way, until he finally (July 28) reached the mouth of the Thlu-it-scho, or, rather, the broad estuary through which it disembogues itself into the Polar Sea. His intention was to proceed to Point Turnagain, but the obstacles were insurmountable, even by him. For ten days, the exploring party had a continuation of wet, chilly, foggy weather, and the only vegetation (fern and moss) was so damp, that it would not burn; being thus without fuel, they had only during this time one hot meal. Almost without water, without any means of warmth, and sinking knee-deep as they proceeded on land, in the soft slush and snow, no wonder that some of the best men, benumbed in their limbs, and dispirited by the prospect before them, broke out for a moment in murmuring at the hardness of their duty.

On August 15, seeing the impossibility of proceeding even a single mile further, Back assembled the men around him, and unfurling the British flag, which was saluted with three cheers, he announced to them his determination to return. The difficulties of the river were of course doubled in the ascent, from having to go against the stream. All the obstacles of rocks, rapids, sand-banks, and long portages had to be faced. They found, as they went on, that many of the deposits of provisions, on which they relied, had been destroyed by wolves. After thus toiling on for six weeks, they were ultimately stopped by one most formidable perpendicular fall, which obliged them to abandon their boat; and proceeding on foot—each laden with a pack of about 75 lbs. weight—they ultimately arrived at their old habitation, Fort Reliance, after an absence of nearly four months, exhausted and worn out, but justly proud of having accomplished so difficult and dangerous a voyage.

The Fish River has since been named Back's River, in

honour of its discoverer; and surely no geographical distinction has ever been more justly merited.

This indefatigable explorer had scarcely returned to England (Sept. 8, 1835), when he once more set out on his way to the Arctic regions; but his ship, the 'Terror,' was so disabled by the ice, that she was scarcely able to accomplish the return voyage across the Atlantic, without allowing her to make any new discoveries.

The land expedition sent out by the Hudson's Bay Company (1837-39), under the direction of Peter Warren Dease, one of their chief factors, and Mr. Thomas Simpson, proved far more successful.  Descending the Mackenzie to the sea, they surveyed, in July, 1837, that part of the northern coast of America which had been left unexamined by Franklin and Elson in 1825, from Return Reef to Cape Barrow.

Although it was the height of summer, the ground was found frozen several inches below the surface, and the spray froze on the oars and rigging of their boats, which the drift ice along the shore ultimately obliged them to leave behind.

As they went onwards on foot, heavily laden, the frequent necessity of wading up to the middle in the ice-cold water of the inlets, together with the constant fogs and the sharp north wind, tried their powers of endurance to the utmost; but Simpson, the hero of the expedition, was not to be deterred by anything short of absolute impossibility; nor did he stop till he had reached Point Barrow.  Indeed, no man could be more fit than he to lead an expedition like this, for he had once before travelled 2,000 miles on foot in the middle of winter from York Factory to Athabasca, walking sometimes not less than 50 miles in one day, and without any protection against the cold but an ordinary cloth mantle.

After wintering at Fort Confidence, on Great Bear Lake, the next season was profitably employed in descending the Coppermine River, and tracing nearly 140 miles of new coast beyond Cape Turnagain, the limit of Franklin's survey in 1821.  The third season (1839) was still more favoured by fortune, for Simpson succeeded in discovering the whole coast beyond Cape Turnagain, as far as Castor and Pollux River (August 20, 1839), on the eastern side of the vast arm of the sea which receives the waters of the Great Fish River.   On his return voyage, he traced sixty miles of the south coast of King William's Island, and a considerable part of the high, bold shores of Victoria Land, and reached Fort Confidence on September 24, after one of the longest and most successful boat voyages ever performed in the Polar waters, having traversed more than 1,600 miles of sea.

Unfortunately he was not destined to reap the rewards of his labour, for in the following year, while travelling from the Red River to the Mississippi, where he intended to embark for England, he was assassinated by his Indian guides; and thus died, in the thirty-sixth year of his age, one of the best men that have ever served the cause of science in the frozen north.

On May 26, 1845, Sir John Franklin, now in the sixtieth year of his age, and Captain Crozier, sailed from England, to make a new attempt at the north-west passage. Never did stouter vessels than the ' Erebus ' and ' Terror,' well-tried in the Antarctic Seas, carry a finer or more ably commanded crew; never before had human foresight so strained all her resources to ensure success; and thus, when the commander's last despatches from the Whalefish Islands, Baffin's Bay (July 12), previous to his sailing to Lancaster Sound, arrived in England, no one doubted but that he was about to add a new and brilliant chapter to the history of Arctic discovery.

His return was confidently expected towards the end of 1847; but when the winter passed and still no tidings came, the anxiety at his prolonged absence became general, and the early part of 1848 witnessed the beginning of a series of searching expeditions fitted out at the public cost or by private munificence, on a scale exceeding all former examples. The ' Plover ' and the ' Herald ' (1848) were sent to Behring's Straits to meet Franklin with supplies should he succeed in getting thither. In spring Sir John Richardson hurried to the shores of the Polar Sea, anxious to find the traces of his lost friend. He was accompanied by Dr. Rae, who had just returned from the memorable land expedition (1846–47), during which, after crossing the isthmus which joins Melville Peninsula to the mainland, he traced the shores of Committee Bay and the east coast of Boothia as far as the Lord Mayor's

Bay of Sir John Ross, thus proving that desolate land to be likewise a vast peninsula.

But in vain did Rae and Richardson explore all the coasts between the Mackenzie and the Coppermine. The desert remained mute; and Sir James Ross ('Enterprize') and Captain Bird ('Investigator'), who set sail in June 1848, three months after Dr. Richardson's departure, and minutely examined all the shores near Barrow Strait, proved equally unsuccessful.

Three years had now passed since Franklin had been expected home, and even the most sanguine began to despair; but to remove all doubts, it was resolved to explore once more all the gulfs and channels of the Polar Sea. Thus in the year 1850, no less than twelve ships sailed forth, some to Behring's Straits, some to the sounds leading from Baffin's Bay.* Other expeditions followed in 1852 and 1853, and though none of them succeeded in the object of their search, yet they enriched the geography of the Arctic World with many interesting discoveries, the most important of which I will now briefly mention.

Overcoming the ice of Baffin's Bay by the aid of their powerful steam-tugs, Austin, Ommaney, and Penny reached the entrance of Lancaster Sound. Here they separated, and while the 'Resolute' remained behind to examine the neighbourhood of Pond's Bay, Ommaney found at Cape Riley (North Devon) the first traces of the lost expedition. He was soon joined by Ross, Austin, Penny, and the Americans, and a minute investigation soon proved that Cape

* 1850–1854. 'Investigator,' Captain M'Clure, ⎫
  1850–1855. 'Enterprise,' Captain Collinson, ⎬ Behring's Straits.
  1850, 1851. 'Resolute,' Captain Austin, ⎫ Lancaster Strait and
  1850, 1851. 'Assistance,' Captain Ommaney, ⎬ Cornwallis Island.
      Accompanied by two steam tenders, officered by Lieutenant Sherard Osborne and Lieutenant F. L. M'Clintock.
  1850, 1851. 'Lady Franklin,' Master Penny, accompanied by the 'Sophia, Master A. Stewart, under Admiralty Orders to Lancaster Strait and Wellington Channel.
  1850. . 'Prince Albert,' Captain Forsyth, belonging to Lady Franklin, to Regent's Inlet and Beechey Island.
  1850, 1851. 'Advance,' Lieutenant De Haven, U.S.N. ⎫
  1850, 1851. 'Rescue,' S. P. Griffin, Esq., U.S.N. ⎬
      Fitted at the expense of H. Grinnell, Esq., of New York, to Lancaster Strait and Wellington Channel.

Spencer and Beechey Island, at the entrance of Wellington Channel, had been the site of Franklin's first winter-quarters, distinctly marked by the remains of a large storehouse, staves of casks, empty pemmican-tins, and most touching relic of all—a little garden shaped into a neat oval, by some flower-loving sailor, and filled with the few hardy plants which that bleak clime can nourish. Meanwhile winter approached, and little more could be done that season; so all the vessels which had entered Barrow's Strait now took up their winter-quarters at the southern extremity of Cornwallis Land; with the exception of the 'Prince Albert,' which set sail for England before winter set in, and of the Americans, who, perceiving the impolicy of so many ships pressing to the westward on one parallel, turned back, but were soon shut up in the pack-ice, which for eight long months kept them prisoners. The 'Rescue' and 'Advance' were drifted backwards and forwards in Wellington Channel, until in December a terrific storm drove them into Barrow's Strait, and still farther on into Lancaster Sound. Several times during this dreadful passage they were in danger from the ice opening round them and closing suddenly again, and only escaped being 'nipped' by their small size and strong build, which enabled them to rise above the opposing edges instead of being crushed between them. Even on their arrival in Baffin's Bay, the ice did not release them from its hold, and it was not till June 9, 1851, that they reached the Danish settlement at Disco. After recruiting his exhausted crew, the gallant De Haven determined to return and prosecute the search during the remainder of the season; but the discouraging reports of the whalers induced him to change his purpose, and the ships and crews reached New York at the beginning of October, having passed through perils such as few have endured and still fewer have lived to recount.

Meanwhile the English searching expeditions had not remained inactive. As soon as spring came, well organised sledge expeditions were despatched in all directions, but they all returned with the same invariable tale of disappointment.

As soon as Wellington Channel opened, Penny boldly entered the ice-lanes with a boat, and after a series of adventures and difficulties, penetrated up Queen's Channel, as far as Baring Island and Cape Beecher, where most reluctantly he was compelled to turn back.

A fine open sea stretched invitingly away to the north, but his fragile boat was ill-equipped for a voyage of discovery. Fully persuaded that Franklin must have followed this route, he failed, however, in convincing Captain Austin of the truth of his theory, and as, without that officer's co-operation, nothing could be effected, he was compelled to follow the course pointed out by the Admiralty squadron, which, after two ineffectual attempts to enter Smith's and Jones's Sounds, returned to England.

The 'Prince Albert' having brought home in 1850 the intelligence of the discoveries at Beechey Island, it was resolved to prosecute the search during the next season, and no time was lost to refit the little vessel and send her once more on her noble errand, under the command of William Kennedy (1851–52), to examine Prince Regent's Inlet on the coast of North Somerset. Finding the passage obstructed by a barrier of ice, Kennedy was obliged to take a temporary refuge in Port Bowen, on the eastern shore of the inlet. As it was very undesirable, however, to winter on the opposite coast to that along which lay their line of search, Kennedy with four of his men crossed to Port Leopold, amid masses of ice, to ascertain whether any documents had been left at this point by previous searching parties. None having been found, they prepared to return; but to their dismay they now found the inlet so blocked with ice as to render it absolutely impossible to reach the vessel either by boat or on foot. Darkness was fast closing round them, the ice-floe on which they stood threatened every instant to be shivered in fragments by the contending ice-blocks which crashed furiously against it: unless they instantly returned to shore, any moment might prove their last. A bitter cold night (September 10, 1851), with no shelter but their boat, under which each man in turn took an hour's rest—the others, fatigued as they were, seeking safety in brisk exercise—was spent on this inhospitable shore, and on the following morning they discovered that the ship had disappeared. The drift-ice had carried her away, leaving Kennedy and his companions to brave the winter as well as they could, and to endeavour in the spring to rejoin their vessel, which must have drifted down the inlet, and was most likely by this time imprisoned by the ice. Fortunately a depôt of provisions, left by Sir James Ross at Whaler Point, was tolerably near, and finding all in good preservation, they began to fit up a launch, which had been left at the same place as the stores, for a temporary abode. Here they sat on October 17, round a cheerful fire, manufacturing winter garments and completely resigned to their lot, when suddenly to their inexpressible joy they heard the sound of well known voices, and Lieutenant Bellot, the second in command of the ' Prince Albert,' appeared with a party of seven men. Twice before had this gallant French volunteer made unavailing attempts to reach the deserted party, who soon forgot their past misery as they accompanied their friends back to the ship. In the following spring Kennedy and Bellot explored North Somerset and Prince of Wales' Land, traversing with their sledge 1,100 miles of desert, but without discovering the least traces of Franklin or his comrades. Yet in spite of these frequent disappointments, the searching expeditions were not given over, and as Wellington Channel and the sounds to the north of Baffin's Bay appeared to offer the best chances, the spring of 1852 witnessed the departure of Sir Edward Belcher and Captain Inglefield* for those still unknown regions.

The voyage of the latter proved one of the most successful in the annals of Arctic navigation. Boldly pushing up Smith's Sound, which had hitherto baffled every research, Inglefield examined this noble channel as far as 78° 30' N. lat., when stormy weather drove him back. He next attempted Jones's Sound, and entered it sufficiently to see it expand into a wide channel to the northward.

* 1852.     . ' Isabel,' Captain E. Inglefield. Lady Franklin's vessel.
  1852–1854. 'Assistance,' Sir Edward Belcher, to Lancaster Sound, Wellington Channel.
  1852–1854. ' Resolute,' Captain Kellett, Lancaster Strait, Melville, and Banks' Island.
  1852–1854. ' Pioneer,' Lieutenant Sherard Osborne.
  1852–1854. ' Intrepid,' Captain M'Clintock.
  1852–1854. ' North Star,' Captain Pullen.

The squadron which sailed under the command of Sir Edward Belcher was charged with the double mission of prosecuting the discoveries in Wellington Channel, and of affording assistance to Collinson and M'Clure, who, it will be remembered, had sailed in 1850 to Behring's Straits.

At Beechey Island, where the 'North Star' was stationed as depôt-ship, the squadron separated, Belcher proceeding with the 'Assistance' and the 'Pioneer' up Wellington Channel, while Kellett, with the 'Resolute' and 'Intrepid,' steered to the west. Scarcely had the latter reached his winter-quarters (September 7, 1852) at Dealy Island, on the south coast of Melville Island, when parties were sent out to deposit provisions at various points of the coast, for the sledge parties in the ensuing spring.

The difficulties of transport over the broken surface of the desert when denuded of snow, may be estimated from the fact, that though the distance from the north to the south coast of Melville Island is no more than 36 miles in a direct line, Lieutenant M'Clintock required no less than 19 days to reach the Hecla and Griper Gulf. Similar difficulties awaited Lieutenant Mechan on his way to Liddon Gulf, but he was amply rewarded by finding at Winter Harbour despatches from M'Clure, showing that, in April, 1851, the 'Investigator' was lying in Mercy Bay, on the opposite side of Banks' Strait, and that consequently the north-west passage, the object of so many heroic efforts, was at last discovered.

On March 9, 1853, the 'Resolute' opened her spring campaign with Lieutenant Pym's sledge journey to Mercy Bay, to bring assistance to M'Clure, or to follow his traces in case he should no longer be there.

A month later three other sledge expeditions left the ship. The one under M'Clintock proceeded from the Hecla and Griper Gulf to the west, and returned after 106 days, having explored 1,200 miles of coast,—a sledge journey without a parallel in the history of Arctic research, though nearly equalled by the second party under Lieutenant Mecham, which likewise started to the west from Liddon Gulf, and travelled over a thousand miles in ninety-three days. The third party, under Lieutenant Hamilton, which proceeded to the north-east, towards the rendezvous appointed by Sir

Edward Belcher the preceding summer, was the first that returned to the ship, but before its arrival another party had found its way to the 'Resolute,'—pale, worn, emaciated figures, slowly creeping along over the uneven ice. A stranger might have been surprised at the thundering hurrahs which hailed the ragged troop from a distance, or at the warm and cordial greetings which welcomed them on deck, but no wonder that M'Clure and his heroic crew were thus received by their fellow-seamen, after a three years' imprisonment in the ice of the Polar Sea.

On August 1, 1850, the 'Investigator,' long since separated from her consort, the 'Enterprise,' had met the 'Herald' and 'Plover'* at Cape Lisburne, beyond Behring's Straits, and now plunged alone into the unknown wildernesses of the Arctic Ocean. She reached the coast of Banks' Land on September 6, discovered Prince Albert Land on the 9th, and then sailed up Prince of Wales' Strait, where, on October 9, she froze in for the winter. In the same month, however, a sledge expedition was sent to the northern extremity of the strait, which established the fact of its communication with Parry Sound and Barrow's Strait. In the following July the 'Investigator,' though set free, was prevented from penetrating into the sound, by impassable barriers of ice. Nothing now remained but to return to the southern extremity of the strait, and then to advance along the west coast of Banks' Land to the north. This course was followed with tolerable ease till August 20, when the ship was driven between the ice and the beach, a little north of Prince Albert Cape. Here she lay in comparative safety till the 29th, when the immense floe to which she was attached was raised edgeways out of the water, from the pressure of surrounding ice, and lifted perpendicularly some twenty-five feet. The slightest additional pressure would have thrown the delicately poised vessel entirely over, but, fortunately, a large piece from underneath was rent away, and after one or two frightful oscillations the floe righted itself, and drifted onwards, bearing the ship unharmed upon its course.

During the succeeding month, every day brought its perils.

* These two vessels had been sent in the year 1847 to the Polar Sea beyond Behring's Straits, when they discovered the 'Herald' and 'Plover' Islands.

Now forced ashore by the pressure of the ice, now hurried along amidst its enclosing masses, the adventurers, slowly working their way along the north coast of Banks' Land, at length found refuge in a harbour to which the appropriate name of Mercy Bay was thankfully given. Here they spent two winters—the intervening summer having failed to release the ship. In the spring of 1853, Lieutenant Pym brought them the joyful news that the 'Resolute' was not far off. Such had been the adventures of M'Clure up to the moment when Kellett welcomed him on board.

Meanwhile neither the sledge parties of the 'Resolute,' nor those which Sir Edward Belcher had sent out in all directions from his first winter-quarters in Northumberland Sound (76° 52′ N. lat.), on the west side of Grinnell Peninsula, had been able to discover the least traces of Franklin. The winter (1853-54) passed, and in the following April, Lieutenant Mecham found in Prince of Wales' Strait, and later on Ramsay Island at its southern outlet, documents from Collinson, bearing date August 27, 1852, and giving full intelligence of his proceedings since his separation from the 'Investigator.' While M'Clure was achieving in 1850 the discovery of the north-west passage, Collinson, having arrived in Behring's Straits later in the season, was unable to double Point Barrow. In 1851, however, he succeeded in getting round that projection and pursuing the continental channel as easily as his precursor had done, followed him through Prince of Wales' Strait; but, though he penetrated a few miles further into Melville Sound, he found no passage, and returning to the south end of the strait passed the winter of 1851-52 in Walker Bay. Next summer he carried his ship through Dolphin and Union Straits and Dease Strait to Cambridge Bay, where he spent his second winter (1852-53). His sledge parties explored the west side of Victoria Strait, but a deficiency of coals compelled him to return the way he came, instead of attempting to force a passage through the channel. He did not, however, get round Barrow Point on his return, without passing a third winter on the northern coast of America.

On returning to the 'Resolute' Lieutenant Mecham found all hands busy preparing to leave the ship, Sir E. Belcher having given orders to abandon her as well as the 'Assistance,' 'Pioneer,' and 'Intrepid,' which had now been blocked up above a year in the ice, and had no chance of escaping.

Thus the summer of 1854 witnessed the return to England of the 'North Star,' with all those brave crews which had spent so many unavailing efforts, and in numerous boat and sledge excursions had explored so many known and unknown coasts in search of Franklin; and thus also M'Clure and his comrades, abandoning the 'Investigator' in Mercy Bay, returned home through Davis' Straits, after having entered the Polar Ocean at the Strait of Behring. He had, however, been preceded by Lieutenant Cresswell and Mr. Wynniat, who, on an excursion to Beechey Island in the summer of 1858, had there met with and joined the 'Phœnix,' Captain Inglefield, who, accompanied by his friend Lieutenant Bellot, had conveyed provisions to Sir E. Belcher's squadron and was about to return to England. During this expedition Bellot, whose many excellent qualities had made him a universal favourite, was unfortunately drowned by a fall into an ice-crevice during a sledge excursion. A stone monument erected before Greenwich Hospital reminds England of the gallant volunteer whose name is gloriously linked with that of Franklin in Arctic history.

Years had thus passed without bringing any tidings of the 'Erebus' and 'Terror' since the discovery of their first winter-quarters, until at last, in the spring of 1854, Dr. Rae, of the Hudson's Bay Company, while engaged in the survey of the Boothian isthmus, fell in with a party of Esquimaux, who informed him that in the spring of 1850 some of their countrymen on King William's Island had seen a party of white men making their way to the mainland. None of them could speak the Esquimaux language intelligibly, but by signs they gave them to understand that their ships had been crushed by ice, and that they were now going to where they expected to find deer to shoot. At a later date of the same season, but before the breaking up of the ice, the bodies of some thirty men were discovered on the continent a day's journey from Back's Great Fish River, and five on an island near it. Some of the bodies had been buried (probably those of the first victims of famine), some were in a tent, others under the boat which had been turned over to form a shelter, and several lay scattered about in different directions. Of those found on the island, one was supposed to have been an officer, as he had a telescope strapped over his shoulder and his double-barrelled gun lay underneath him. The mutilated condition of several of the corpses, and the contents of the kettles, left no doubt that our wretched countrymen had been driven to the last resource of cannibalism, as a means of prolonging existence. Some silver spoons and forks, a round silver plate, engraved 'Sir John Franklin, K.C.B.,' a star or order, with the motto, 'Nec aspera terrent,' which Dr. Rae purchased of the Esquimaux, corroborated the truth of their narrative.

Thus it was now known how part of the unfortunate mariners had perished, but the fate of the expedition was still enveloped in mystery. What had become of the ships and of the greater part of their crews? And was Franklin one of the party seen by the Esquimaux, or had an earlier death shortened his sufferings?

To solve at least this mournful secret—for every hope that he might still be alive had long since vanished—his noble widow resolved to spend all her available means—since Government would no longer prosecute the search—and with the assistance of her friends, but mostly at her own expense, fitted out a small screw steamer, the 'Fox,' which the gallant M'Clintock, already distinguished in perilous Polar voyages, volunteered to command. Another Arctic officer, Lieutenant Hobson, likewise came forward to serve without pay.

At first it seemed as if all the elements had conspired against the success of this work of piety, for in the summer of 1857 the floating ice off Melville Bay, on the coast of Greenland, seized the 'Fox,' and after a dreary winter, various narrow escapes, and eight months of imprisonment, carried her back nearly 1,200 geographical miles, even to 63¼° N. lat. in the Atlantic.

At length, on April 25, 1858, the 'Fox' got free, and having availed herself of the scanty stores and provisions which the small Danish settlement of Holstenburg afforded, sailed into Barrow Strait. Finding Franklin Channel ob-

structed with ice, she then turned back, and steaming up
Prince Regent Inlet, arrived at the eastern opening of Bellot's
Strait. Here the passage to the west was again found
blocked with ice, and after five ineffectual attempts to pass,
the 'Fox' at length took up her winter-quarters in Port
Kennedy, on the northern side of the strait.

On his first sledge excursion in the following spring,
M'Clintock met, at Cape Victoria, on the south-west coast of
Boothia, with a party of Esquimaux, who informed him that
some years back a large ship had been crushed by the ice
out in the sea to the west of King William's Island, but that
all the people landed safely.

Meeting with the same Esquimaux on April 20, he learned,
after much anxious inquiry, that besides the ship which had
been seen to sink in deep water, a second one had been forced
on shore by the ice, where they supposed it still remained,
but much broken. They added that it was in the fall of
the year—that is, August or September—when the ships
were destroyed; that all the white people went away to
the Great Fish River, taking a boat or boats with them,
and that in the following winter their bones were found
there.

These first indications of the fate of Franklin's expedition
were soon followed by others. On May 7, M'Clintock heard
from an old Esquimaux woman on King William's Island,
that many of the white men dropped by the way as they
went to the Great River; that some were buried, and some
were not. They did not themselves witness this, but discovered their bodies during the winter following.

Visiting the shore along which the retreating crews must
have marched, he came, shortly after midnight of May 25,
when slowly walking along a gravel ridge near the beach,
which the winds kept partially bare of snow, upon a human
skeleton, partly exposed, with here and there a few fragments
of clothing appearing through the snow.

'A most careful examination of the spot,' says M'Clintock,
'was of course made, the snow removed, and every scrap of
clothing gathered up. A pocket-book, which being frozen hard
could not be examined on the spot, afforded strong grounds
for hope that some information might be subsequently ob-

tained respecting the owner, and the march of the lost crews. The victim was a young man, slightly built, and perhaps above the common height; the dress appeared to be that of a steward. The poor man seems to have selected the bare ridge top, as affording the least tiresome walking, and to have fallen upon his face in the position in which we found him. It was a melancholy truth that the old woman spake, when she said, "they fell down and died as they walked along." '

Meanwhile Lieutenant Hobson, who was exploring with another sledge party the north-western coast of King William's Land, had made the still more important discovery of a record, giving a laconic account of the Franklin expedition up to the time when the ships were lost and abandoned. It was found on May 6 in a large cairn at Point Victory. It stated briefly, that in 1845 the 'Erebus' and 'Terror' had ascended Wellington Channel to lat. 77°, and returned by the west side of Cornwallis Island to Beechey Island, where they spent the first winter. In 1846 they proceeded to the southwest, through Peel Sound and Franklin Sound, and eventually reached within twelve miles of the north extremity of King William's Land, when their progress was arrested by the ice. Sir John Franklin died on June 11, 1847, having completed—two months before his death—the sixty-first year of an active, eventful, and honourable life. On April 22, 1848, the ships were deserted, having been beset since Sept. 12, 1846. The officers and crew, consisting of 105 souls, under the command of Captain Crozier, landed with the intention of starting for Back's Fish River, which, as we have seen, they were never destined to reach.

Quantities of clothing, and articles of all kinds, were found lying about the cairn, as if these men, aware that they were retreating for their lives, had then abandoned everything which they considered superfluous.

Thus all doubts about Sir John Franklin's fate were at length removed. He at least had died on board his ship, and been spared the miserable end of his comrades, as they fell one by one in the dreary wilderness.

The two wrecks have disappeared, without leaving a trace behind. A single document, some coins and pieces of plate—

this is all that remains of the gallant ships which so hope-
fully sailed forth, under one of the noblest seamen that ever
served in the navy of Great Britain.

It is a curious circumstance, that Franklin's ships perished
within sight of the headlands named Cape Franklin and Cape
Jane Franklin, by their discoverer, Sir James Ross, eighteen
years before.

The Great Northern Diver.

The Great Humboldt Glacier.
(From an original Sketch by Frederick Whymper.)

# CHAPTER XXXIII.

### KANE AND HAYES.

Kane sails up Smith's Sound in the 'Advance' (1853)—Winters in Rensselaer
Bay — Sledge Journey along the Coast of Greenland — The Three Brother
Turrets—Tennyson's Monument—The Great Humboldt Glacier—Dr. Hayes
crosses Kennedy Channel—Morton's Discovery of Washington Land—Mount
Parry—Kane resolves upon a Second Wintering in Rensselaer Bay—Departure
and Return of Part of the Crew—Sufferings of the Winter—The Ship abandoned
—Boat Journey to Upernavik—Kane's Death in the Havannah (1857)—Dr.
Hayes' Voyage in 1860—He winters at Port Foulke—Crosses Kennedy Channel
—Reaches Cape Union, the most Northern known Land upon the Globe—
Koldewey—Plans for future Voyages to the North Pole.

IN point of dramatic interest, few of the Arctic expeditions
can rival the second and last voyage of Dr. Kane, which,
to avoid interrupting the narrative of the discovery of Franklin's fate by Dr. Rae and Sir James M'Clintock, I have re-
frained from mentioning in chronological order.

Weak in body, but great in mind, this remarkable man,
who had accompanied the first Grinnell expedition in the
capacity of surgeon, sailed from Boston, in 1853, as commander

of the 'Advance,' with a crew of 17 officers and men, to which two Greenlanders were subsequently added. His plan was to pass up Baffin's Bay, to its most northern attainable point, and thence pressing on towards the Pole, as far as boats or sledges could reach, to examine the coast-lines for vestiges of Franklin.

Battling with storms and icebergs, he passed, on August 7, 1853, the rocky portals of Smith's Sound, Cape Isabella, and Cape Alexander, which had been discovered the year before by Inglefield; left Cape Hatherton—the extreme point attained by that navigator—behind, and after many narrow escapes from shipwreck, secured the 'Advance' in Rensselaer Bay, from which she was destined never to emerge. His diary gives us a vivid account of the first winter he spent in this haven, in lat. 78° 38', almost as far to the north as the most northern extremity of Spitzbergen, and in a far more rigorous climate.

'*Sept.* 10, +14° F.—The birds have left. The sea-swallows, which abounded when we first reached here, and even the young burgomasters that lingered after them, have all taken their departure for the south. The long "night in which no man can work" is close at hand; in another month we shall lose the sun. Astronomically, he should disappear on Oct. 24, if our horizon were free; but it is obstructed by a mountain ridge; and, making all allowance for refraction, we cannot count on seeing him after the 10th.

'*Sept.* 11.—The long staring day, which has clung to us for more than two months, to the exclusion of the stars, has begun to intermit its brightness. Even Aldebaran, the red eye of the bull, flared out into familiar recollection as early as 10 o'clock; and the heavens, though still somewhat reddened by the gaudy tints of midnight, gave us Capella and Arcturus, and even that lesser light of home memories, the Polar star. Stretching my neck to look uncomfortably at the indication of our extreme northernness, it was hard to realise that he was not directly overhead; and it made me sigh, as I measured the few degrees of distance that separated our zenith from the Pole over which he hung.

'*Oct.* 28.—The moon has reached her greatest northern declination of about 25° 35'. She is a glorious object; sweeping around the heavens, at the lowest part of her curve, she is still 14° above the horizon. For eight days she has been making her circuit with nearly unvarying brightness. It is one of those sparkling nights that bring back the memory of sleigh-bells and songs, and glad communings of hearts in lands that are far away.

'*Nov.* 7.—The darkness is coming on with insidious steadiness, and its advances can only be perceived by comparing one day with its fellow of some time back. We still read the thermometer at noonday without a light, and the black masses of the hills are plain for about five hours, with their glaring patches of snow; but all the rest is darkness. The stars of the sixth magnitude shine out at noonday. Except upon the island of Spitzbergen, which has the advantages of an insular climate, and tempered by ocean currents, no Christians have wintered in so high a latitude as this.* They are Russian sailors who made the encounter there—men inured to hardships and cold. Our darkness has ninety days to run before we shall get back again even to the contested twilight of to-day. Altogether our winter will have been sunless for one hundred and forty days.

'*Nov.* 9.—Wishing to get the altitude of the cliffs on the south-west cape of our bay before the darkness set in thoroughly, I started in time to reach them with my Newfoundlanders at noonday, the thermometer indicating 23° below zero. Fireside astronomers can hardly realise the difficulties in the way of observations at such low temperatures. The breath, and even the warmth of the face and body, cloud the sextant-arc and glasses with a fine hoar frost. It is, moreover, an unusual feat to measure a base line in the snow at 55° below freezing.

'*Nov.* 21.—We have schemes innumerable to cheat the monotonous solitude of our winter—a fancy ball; a newspaper, "The Ice Blink;" a fox chase round the decks.

'*Dec.* 15.—We have lost the last vestige of our midday twilight. We cannot see print, and hardly paper; the fingers cannot be counted a foot from the eyes. Noonday and mid-

---

* Rensselaer Harbour is situated 1° 46' higher than Sir E. Belcher's winter-quarters in Northumberland Sound, 76° 52'.

night are alike; and except a vague glimmer in the sky that seems to define the hill outlines to the south, we have nothing to tell us that this Arctic world of ours has a sun. In the darkness, and consequent inaction, it is almost in vain that we seek to create topics of thought, and, by a forced excitement, to ward off the encroachments of disease.

'*Jan.* 21.—First traces of returning light, the southern horizon having for a short time a distinct orange tinge.

'*Feb.* 21.—We have had the sun for some days, silvering the ice between the headlands of the bay; and to-day, towards noon, I started out to be the first of my party to welcome him back. It was the longest walk and toughest climb that I have had since our imprisonment; and scurvy and general debility have made me "short o' wind." But I managed to attain my object. I saw him once more, and upon a projecting crag nestled in the sunshine. It was like bathing in perfumed water.'

Thus this terrible winter night drew to its end, and the time came for undertaking the sledge journeys, on which the success of the expedition mainly depended. Unfortunately, of the nine magnificent Newfoundlanders, and the thirty-five Esquimaux dogs originally possessed by Kane, only six had survived an epizootic malady which raged among them during the winter; their number was, however, increased by some new purchases from the Esquimaux who visited the ship at the beginning of April.

Thus scantily provided with the means of transport, Kane, though in a very weak condition, set out on April 25, 1854, to force his way to the north. He found the Greenland coast beyond Rensselaer Bay extremely picturesque, the cliffs rising boldly from the shore line to a height of sometimes more than a thousand feet, and exhibiting every freak and caprice of architectural ruin. In one spot the sloping rubbish at the foot of the coast-wall led up, like an artificial causeway, to a gorge that was streaming at noon-day with the southern sun, while everywhere else the rock stood out in the blackest shadow. Just at the edge of this bright opening, rose the dreamy semblance of a castle, flanked with triple towers, completely isolated and defined. These were called the 'Three Brother Turrets.'

'Farther on, to the north of latitude 79°, a single cliff of greenstone rears itself from a crumbled base of sandstone, like the boldly chiselled rampart of an ancient city. At its northern extremity, at the brink of a deep ravine which has worn its way among the ruins, there stands a solitary column or minaret tower, as sharply finished as if it had been cast for the Place Vendôme. Yet the length of the shaft alone is 480 ft., and it rises on a pedestal, itself 280 ft. high. 'I remember well the emotions of my party, as it first broke upon our view. Cold and sick as I was, I brought back a sketch of it, which may have interest for the reader, though it scarcely suggests the imposing dignity of this magnificent landmark. Those who are happily familiar with the writings of Tennyson, and have communed with his spirit in the solitudes of a wilderness, will apprehend the impulse that inscribed the scene with his name.'

But no rock formation, however striking or impressive, equalled in grandeur the magnificent glacier to which Kane has given the name of Humboldt. Its solid glassy wall, diminishing to a well-pointed wedge in the perspective, rises 300 ft. above the water level, with an unknown, unfathomable depth below it and its curved face, 60 miles in length— from Cape Agassiz to Cape Forbes—vanishes into unknown space at not more than a single day's railroad travel from the Pole.

In spite of the snow which had so accumulated in drifts that the travellers were forced to unload their sledges and carry forward the cargo on their backs, beating a path for the dogs to follow in, Kane came within sight of the Great Glacier on May 4; but this progress was dearly earned, as it cost him the last remnant of his strength.

'I was seized with a sudden pain,' says the intrepid explorer, 'and fainted. My limbs became rigid, and certain obscure tetanoid symptoms of our winter enemy, the scurvy, disclosed themselves. I was strapped upon the sledge, and the march continued as usual, but my powers diminished so rapidly that I could not resist the otherwise comfortable temperature of 5° below zero. My left foot becoming frozen caused a vexatious delay, and the same night it became evident that the immovability of my limbs was due to drop-

sical effusion. On the 5th, becoming delirious and fainting
every time that I was taken from the tent to the sledge, I
succumbed entirely. My comrades would kindly persuade
me that, even had I continued sound, we could not have proceeded on our journey. The snows were very heavy and
increasing as we went; some of the drifts perfectly impassable, and the level floes often four feet deep in yielding
snow.

'The scurvy had already broken out among the men, with
symptoms like my own, and Morton, our strongest man, was
beginning to give way. It is the reverse of comfort to me
that they shared my weakness. All that I should remember
with pleasurable feeling is that to my brave companions,
themselves scarcely able to travel, I owe my preservation.

'They carried me back by forced marches. I was taken
into the brig on the 14th, where for a week I lay fluctuating
between life and death. Dr. Hayes regards my attack as
one of scurvy complicated by typhoid fever.'

Fortunately summer was now fast approaching with his
cheering sunbeams and his genial warmth. The seals
began to appear on the coast in large numbers, and there
was now no want of fresh meat, the chief panacea against
the scurvy. The snow-buntings returned to the ice-crusted
rocks; and the gulls and eider ducks came winging their way
to their northern breeding-places.

Vegetation likewise sprang into life with marvellous
rapidity, and the green sloping banks not only refreshed
the eye, but yielded juicy, anti-scorbutic herbs.

Kane's health slowly but steadily improved. He was,
however, obliged to give up all further sledge excursions for
the season, and to leave the execution of his plans to his
more able-bodied companions.

Thus Dr. Hayes, crossing the sound in a north-easterly
direction, reached the opposite coast of Grinnell Land, which
he surveyed as far as Cape Frazer in lat. 79° 45'.

This journey was rendered uncommonly slow and tedious
by the excessively broken and rugged character of the ice.
Deep cavities filled with snow intervened between lines of
hummocks frequently exceeding twenty or thirty feet in
height. Over these the sledge had to be lifted by main

strength, and it required the most painful efforts of the
whole party to liberate it from the snow between them. Dr.
Hayes returned on June 1, and a few days later Morton left
the brig to survey the Greenland coast beyond the Great
Glacier. The difficulties were great, for, besides the usual
impediments of hummocks, the lateness of the season had
in many places rendered the ice extremely unsafe, or even
entirely destroyed the ice-ledge along the shore. Thus for
the last days of his onward journey, he was obliged to toil
over the rocks and along the beach of a sea which, like the
familiar waters of the south, dashed in waves at his feet.
Morton and his companion Hans, the Esquimaux, reached
on June 26, 1854, Cape Constitution, a bold headland, where
the surf rolled furiously against high overhanging cliffs,
which it was found impossible to pass. Climbing from rock
to rock, in hopes of doubling the promontory, Morton stood
at this termination of his journey, and from a height of 300
feet looked out upon a great waste of waters, stretching to
the unknown north. Numerous birds—sea-swallows, kittiwakes, brent-geese—mixed their discordant notes with the
novel music of dashing waves ; and among the flowering plants
growing on the rocks, was found a crucifer (Hesperis pygmæa),
the dried pods of which, still containing seed, had survived
the wear and tear of winter. From Cape Constitution the
coast of Washington Land trended to the east, but far to the
north-west, beyond the open waters of the channel, a peak,
terminating a range of mountains similar in their features to
those of Spitzbergen, was seen towering to a height of from
2,500 to 3,000 feet. This peak, the most remote northern
land at that time known upon our globe, received the name
of Mount Parry.

Meanwhile the short summer was wearing on, and, as far
as the eye could reach, the ice remained inflexibly solid.
It was evident that many days must still elapse before
the vessel could possibly be liberated—but then most likely
winter would almost have returned—a dismal prospect for
men who knew by experience the long fearful night of the 79°
of latitude, and who, broken in health and with very insufficient supplies of provisions and fuel, were but ill armed for a
second encounter. No wonder that many of Kane's com-

panions thought it better to abandon the vessel than to tarry
any longer in those frozen solitudes.

But though it was horrible to look another winter in the
face, the resolution of Kane could not be shaken.   On
August 24, when the last hope of seeing the vessel once more
afloat had vanished, he called the officers and crew together,
and explained to them frankly the considerations which
determined him to remain.   To abandon the vessel earlier
would have been unseemly, and to reach Upernavik so late
in the season was next to impossible.   To such of them,
however, as were desirous of making the attempt, he freely
gave his permission so to do, assuring them of a brother's
welcome should they be driven back.   He then directed the
roll to be called, and each man to answer for himself.   In result eight out of the seventeen survivors of the party resolved
to stand by the brig.   The others left on the 28th, with
every appliance which the narrow circumstances of the brig
could furnish to speed and guard them.   When they disappeared among the hummocks, the stern realities of their
condition pressed themselves with double force on those
whom they left behind.

The reduced numbers of the party, the helplessness of
many, the waning efficiency of all, the impending winter,
with its cold, dark nights, the penury of their resources, the
dreary sense of increased isolation—all combined to depress
them.   But their energetic leader, leaving them no time for
these gloomy thoughts, set them actively to work to make
the best possible preparations they could for the long cold
night to come.

He had carefully studied the Esquimaux, and determined
that their form of habitations and their mode of diet, without
their unthrift and filth, were the safest and best that could
be adopted.   The deck was well padded with moss and turf,
so as to form a nearly cold-proof covering, and, down below,
a space some eighteen feet square—the apartment of all uses
—was enclosed and packed from floor to ceiling with inner
walls of the same non-conducting material.   The floor itself,
after having been carefully calked, was covered with Manilla
oakum a couple of inches deep, and a canvas carpet.   The
entrance was from the hold, by a low moss-lined tunnel, with

as many doors and curtains to close it up as ingenuity could devise. Large banks of snow were also thrown up along the brig's sides to keep off the cold wind.

All these labours in the open air wonderfully improved the health of the exiles, and their strength increased from day to day. A friendly intercourse was opened with the Esquimaux of the winter settlements of Etah and Anoatok, distant some thirty and seventy miles from the ship, who, for presents of needles, pins, and knives, engaged to furnish walrus and fresh seal meat, and to show the white men where to find the game. Common hunting parties were organised, visits of courtesy and necessity paid, and even some personal attachments established deserving of the name. As long as the Americans remained prisoners of the ice, they were indebted to their savage friends for invaluable counsel in relation to their hunting expeditions, and in the joint hunt they shared alike.

The Esquimaux gave them supplies of meat at critical periods, and they were able to do as much for them. In one word, without the natives, Kane and his companions would most likely have succumbed to the winter, and the Esquimaux on their part learned to look on the strangers as benefactors, and mourned their departure bitterly.

On December 12, the party which had abandoned the ship returned, having been unable to penetrate to the south, and was received, as had been promised, with a brotherly welcome. They had suffered bitterly from the cold, want of food, and the fatigues of their march among the hummocks.

'The thermometer,' says Kane, 'was at minus 50°; they were covered with rime and snow, and were fainting with hunger. It was necessary to use caution in taking them below; for, after an exposure of such fearful intensity and duration as they had gone through, the warmth of the cabin would have prostrated them completely. They had journeyed three hundred and fifty miles; and their last run from the bay near Etah, some seventy miles in a right line, was through the hummocks at this appalling temperature. One by one they all came in and were housed. Poor fellows! as they threw open their Esquimaux garments by the stove, how they relished the scanty luxuries which we had to offer

them. The coffee, and the meat-biscuit soup, and the
molasses, and the wheat-bread, even the salt pork, which our
scurvy forbade the rest of us to touch—how they relished it
all! For more than two months they had lived on frozen
seal and walrus-meat.'

Thus Kane, by his determination not to abandon the ship,
proved the saviour of all his comrades, for what would have
become of them, had he been less firm in his resolution, or if
his courage had failed him during the trials of that dreadful
winter?

'February closes,' says the heroic explorer, 'thank God
for the lapse of its twenty-eight days! Should the thirty-
one of the coming March not drag us farther downward, we
may hope for a successful close to this dreary drama. By
April 10 we should have seals; and when they come, if we
remain to welcome them, we can call ourselves saved. But
a fair review of our prospects tells me that I must look the
lion in the face. The scurvy is steadily gaining on us. I do
my best to sustain the more desperate cases, but as fast as I
partially build up one, another is stricken down. Of the six
workers of our party, as I counted them a month ago, two
are unable to do out-door work, and the remaining four
divide the duty of the ship among them. Hans musters
his remaining energies to conduct the hunt. Petersen is his
disheartened, moping assistant. The other two, Bonsall and
myself, have all the daily offices of household and hospital.
We chop five large sacks of ice, cut six fathoms of eight
inch hawser into junks of a foot each, serve out the meat
when we have it, hack at the molasses, and hew out with
crowbar and axe the pork and dried apples; pass up the foul
slop and cleansings of our dormitory, and in a word, cook,
scullionize, and attend the sick. Added to this, for five nights
running I have kept watch from 8 P.M. to 4 A.M., catching
such naps as I could in the day without changing my clothes,
but carefully waking every hour to note thermometers.'

With March came an increase of sufferings. Every man
on board was tainted with scurvy, and there were seldom more
than three who could assist in caring for the rest. The
greater number were in their bunks, absolutely unable to stir.
Had Kane's health given way, the whole party, deprived of
its leading spirit, must inevitably have perished.

To abandon the ship was now an absolute necessity, for a third winter in Rensselaer Bay would have been certain death to all; but before the boats could be transported to the open water, many preparations had to be made, and most of the party were still too weak to move. The interval was employed by Kane in an excursion with his faithful Esquimaux to the Great Glacier.

At length on May 20, 1855, the entire ship's company bade farewell to the 'Advance,' and set out slowly on their homeward journey. It was in the soft, subdued light of a Sunday evening, June 17, that after hauling their boats with much hard labour through the hummocks, they stood beside the open sea-way. But fifty-six days had still to pass before they could reach the port of Upernavik. Neither storms nor drift-ice rendered this long boat-journey dangerous, but they had to contend with famine, when they at length reached the open bay, and found themselves in the full line of the great ice-drift to the Atlantic, in boats so unseaworthy as to require constant baling to keep them afloat. Their strength had decreased to an alarming degree; they breathed heavily; their feet were so swollen that they were obliged to cut open their canvas boots; they were utterly unable to sleep, and the rowing and baling became hourly more difficult.

It was at this crisis of their fortunes that they saw a large seal floating—as is the custom of these animals—on a small patch of ice, and seemingly asleep. 'Trembling with anxiety,' says Kane, 'we prepared to crawl down upon him. Petersen, with a large English rifle, was stationed in the bow, and stockings were drawn over the oars as mufflers. As we neared the animal, our excitement became so intense that the men could hardly keep stroke. He was not asleep, for he reared his head when we were almost within rifle-shot; and to this day I can remember the hard, careworn, almost despairing expression of the men's thin faces as they saw him move; their lives depended on his capture. I depressed my hand nervously, as a signal for Petersen to fire. M'Gary hung upon his oar, and the boat, slowly but noiselessly surging ahead, seemed to me within certain range. Looking at Petersen, I saw that the poor fellow was paralysed by his anxiety, trying vainly to obtain a rest for his gun against the cut-water of the boat. The seal rose on his fore flippers, gazed at us for a moment with frightened curiosity, and coiled himself for a plunge. At that instant, simultaneously with the crack of our rifle, he relaxed his long length on the ice, and, at the very brink of the water, his head fell helpless to one side. I would have ordered another shot, but no discipline could have controlled the men. With a wild yell, each vociferating according to his own impulse, they urged their boats upon the floes. A crowd of hands seized the seal, and bore him up to safer ice. The men seemed half crazy. I had not realised how much we were reduced by absolute famine. They ran over the floe, crying and laughing, and brandishing their knives. It was not five minutes before every man was sucking his bloody fingers, or mouthing long strips of raw blubber. Not an ounce of this seal was lost.'

Within a day or two another seal was shot, and from that time forward they had a full supply of food.

When Kane, after an absence of thirty months, returned on October 11, 1855, to New York, he was enthusiastically received. Well deserved honours of all sorts awaited him on both sides of the Atlantic; but his health, originally weak, was completely broken by the trials of his journey, and on February 16, 1857, he died at the Havannah, in the thirty-seventh year of his age. In him the United States lost one of their noblest sons, a true hero, whose name will ever shine among the most famous navigators of all times and of all nations.

In 1860, Dr. Hayes, who had accompanied Kane on his journey, once more sailed from America for the purpose of completing the survey of Kennedy's Channel, and, if possible, of pushing on to the Pole itself. After several narrow escapes from ice-fields and icebergs, his schooner, the 'United States,' was at length compelled to take up her winter-quarters at Port Foulke, on the Greenland coast, about twenty miles in latitude to the south of Rensselaer Harbour. Thanks to an abundant supply of fresh meat (for the neighbourhood abounded with reindeer), and also no doubt to the inexhaustible fund of good humour which prevailed in the ship's company, they passed the winter without suffering from the scurvy; but most of the dogs on which Dr. Hayes relied for his sledge expeditions in the ensuing spring were destroyed by the same epidemic which had been so fatal to the teams of Dr. Kane. Fortunately some fresh dogs could be purchased and borrowed of the friendly Esquimaux, and thus, early in April, 1861, Dr. Hayes left the schooner to plunge into the icy wilderness. Having previously ascertained that an advance along the Greenland shore was utterly impossible, he resolved to cross the sound, and to try his fortunes along the coast of Grinnell Land. Of the difficulties which he had to encounter his own words will give the best idea.

'By winding to the right and left, and by occasionally retracing our steps when we had selected an impracticable route, we managed to get over the first few miles without much embarrassment, but further on the tract was rough, past description. I can compare it to nothing but a promiscuous accumulation of rocks closely packed together and piled up over a vast plain in great heaps and endless ridges, leaving scarcely a foot of level surface. The interstices between these closely accumulated ice-masses are filled up, to some extent, with drifted snow. The reader will readily imagine the rest. He will see the sledges winding through the tangled wilderness of broken ice-tables, the men and dogs pulling and pushing up their respective loads. He will see them clambering over the very summit of lofty ridges, through which there is no opening, and again descending on the other side, the sledge often plunging over a precipice, sometimes capsizing and frequently breaking. Again he will see the party baffled in their attempt to cross or find a pass, breaking a track with shovel and handspike; or, again, unable even with these appliances to accomplish their end, they retreat to seek a better track: and they may be lucky enough to find a sort of gap or gateway, upon the winding and uneven surface of which they will make a mile or so with comparative ease. The snow-drifts are sometimes a help and sometimes a hindrance. Their surface is uniformly hard but not always firm to the foot. The crust frequently gives way, and in a most tiresome and provoking manner. It will not quite bear the weight, and the foot sinks at the very moment when the other is lifted. But, worse than this, the chasms between the hummocks are frequently bridged over with snow in such a manner as to leave a considerable space at the bottom quite unfilled; and at the very moment when all looks promising, down sinks one man to his middle, another to the neck, another is buried out of sight; the sledge gives way, and to extricate the whole from this unhappy predicament, is probably the labour of hours. It would be difficult to imagine any kind of labour more disheartening, or which would sooner sap the energies of both men and animals. The strength gave way gradually; and when, as often happened after a long and hard day's work, we could look back from our eminence and almost fire a rifle-ball into our last snow-hut, it was truly discouraging.'

No wonder that after thus toiling on for twenty-five days they had not yet reached half-way across the sound, and that they were all broken down. But their bold leader was fully determined not to abandon his enterprise while still the faintest hope of success remained, and sending the main party back to the schooner, he continued to plunge into the hummocks with three picked companions — Jensen, M'Donald, Knorr—and fourteen dogs. After fourteen days of almost superhuman exertion the sound was at length crossed, and now began a scarcely less harassing journey along the coast. On the fifth day Jensen, the strongest man of the party, completely broke down, and leaving him to the charge of M'Donald, Dr. Hayes now pushed on with Knorr alone, until, on May 18, he reached the border of a deep bay, where further progress to the north was stopped by rotten ice and cracks. Right before him, on the opposite side of the frith, rose Mount Parry, the lofty peak first seen by Morton in 1854 from the shores of Washington Land; and, farther on, a noble headland, Cape Union—the most northern known land upon the globe—stood in faint outline against the dark sky of the open sea. Thus Dr. Hayes divides the honour of extreme northern travel with Parry.

On July 12, the 'United States' was released from her icy trammels, and Dr. Hayes once more attempted to reach the opposite coast and continue his discoveries in Grinnell

Land; but the schooner was in too crippled a state to force her way through the pack-ice which lay in her course, and compelled her commander to return to Boston.

Thus ended this remarkable voyage; but having done so much, Dr. Hayes is eager, and resolved, to do still more. Fully convinced by his own experience that men may subsist in Smith's Sound independent of support from home, he proposes to establish a self-sustaining colony at Port Foulke, which may be made the basis of an extended exploration. Without any second party in the field to co-operate with him, and under the most adverse circumstances, he, by dint of indomitable perseverance, pushed his discoveries a hundred miles farther to the north and west than his predecessors; and it is surely not over sanguine to expect that a party better provided with the means of travel may be able to traverse the 480 miles at least which intervene between Mount Parry and the Pole. The open sea, which both Morton and himself found beyond Kennedy Channel, gives fair promise of success to a strong vessel that may reach it after having forced the ice-blocked passage of Smith's Sound; or should this be impracticable, to a boat transported across the sound and then launched upon its waters.

Captain Sherard Osborne, who is likewise a warm partisan of this route, has been endeavouring to interest Government in its favour; but in the opinion of other scientific authorities an easier passage seems open to the navigator who may attempt to reach the Pole by way of Spitzbergen. To the east of this archipelago the gulf-stream rolls its volume of comparatively warm water far on to the northeast, and possibly sweeps round the Pole itself. It was to the north of Spitzbergen that Parry reached the latitude of 82° 45'; and in 1837 the 'Truelove,' of Hull,* sailed through a perfectly open sea in 82° 30' N. 15° E., and had she continued her course might possibly have reached the Pole as easily as the high latitude which she had already attained.

The distinguished geographer Dr. Augustus Petermann, who warmly advocates the route between Spitzbergen and Greenland, has, by dint of perseverance, succeeded in collect-

---

* 'Athenæum,' Dec. 3, 1853.

ing among his countrymen the necessary funds for a reconnoitring voyage in this direction. Thanks to his exertions, May 24, 1868, witnessed the departure of a small ship of 80 tons, the 'Germania,' Captain Koldewey, from the port of Bergen, for Shannon Island (75° 14′ N. lat.), the highest point on the east coast of Greenland attained by Sabine in 1823. Here the attempt to explore the unknown Arctic Seas beyond was to begin; but, meeting with enormous masses of drift-ice on her repeated endeavours to penetrate to the north-east, the 'Germania' has been obliged to return, after reaching the high latitude of 81° 5′, and accurately surveying a small part of the Greenland coast hitherto but imperfectly explored. An expedition on a more extensive scale is to renew the attempt in 1869.

A third route to the Pole is no less strenuously recommended by M. Gustave Lambert, a French hydrographer, who, having sailed through Behring's Strait in a whaler, in 1865, is persuaded that this is the right way to reach the problematical open North Sea, which, once attained, promises a free passage to the navigator. Liberal subscriptions have been raised in Paris for the accomplishment of his plan, and an expedition, under his command, will most probably set out in 1869.

Thus, after so many illustrious navigators have vainly endeavoured to reach the Pole, sanguine projectors are still as eager as ever to attain the goal; nor is it probable that man will ever rest in his efforts, until every attainable region of the Arctic Ocean shall have been fully explored.

The Racoon.

Icebergs on the Banks of Newfoundland.

# CHAPTER XXXIV.

### NEWFOUNDLAND.

Its desolate Aspect—Forests—Marshes—Barrens—Ponds—Fur-bearing Animals
—Severity of Climate—St. John's—Discovery of Newfoundland by the Scandi-
navians—Sir Humphrey Gilbert—Rivalry of the English and French—Im-
portance of the Fisheries—The Banks of Newfoundland—Mode of Fishing—
Throaters, Headers, Splitters, Salters, and Packers—Fogs and Storms—Seal
Catching.

GENERALLY veiled with mists, Newfoundland appears at
first sight gloomy and repulsive. Abrupt cliffs, showing here and there traces of a scanty vegetation, rise steep
and bare from the sea, and for miles and miles the eye sees
nothing but brown hills or higher mountains, desolate and
wild as they appeared in the eleventh century to the bold
Norwegian navigators who first landed on its desert shores.
The waves of the ocean have everywhere corroded the rocky
coast into fantastic pinnacles, or excavated deep grottoes in
its flanks. In one of these cavities the action of the surge
has produced a remarkable phenomenon, known under the
name of 'The Spout.' In stormy weather the waves penetrate

into the hollow and force their way with a dreadful noise from an aperture in the rock, as a gigantic fountain visible at a distance of several miles.*

The interior of the country corresponds with the forbidding appearance of the coasts, and offers nothing but a succession of forests, marshes, and barrens. The forests, if they may thus be called, generally grow on the declivities of the hills or on the sides of the valleys, where the superfluous waters find a natural drain. The trees consist for the most part of fir, spruce, birch, pine, and juniper or larch; and in certain districts the wych-hazel, the mountain-ash, the elder, the aspen, and some others are found. The character of the timber varies greatly according to the nature of the subsoil and the situation. In some parts, more especially where the woods have been undisturbed by the axe, trees of fair height and girth may be found; but most of the wood is of stunted growth, consisting chiefly of fir trees about twenty or thirty feet high, and not more than three or four inches in diameter. These commonly grow so closely together, that their twigs and branches interlace from top to bottom, while among them may be seen innumerable old and rotten stumps and branches, or newly-fallen trees, which, with the young shoots and brushwood, form a tangled and often impenetrable thicket. The trees are often covered with lichens, and tufts of white dry moss are entangled about the branches. Other green and softer mosses spread over the ground, concealing alike the twisted roots of the standing trees and the pointed stumps of those which have fallen, the sharp edges or slippery surface of the numerous rocks and boulders, and the holes and pitfalls between them. Every step through these woods is consequently a matter of great toil and anxiety. In the heat of summer, while the woods are so thick as to shut out every breath of air, they are at the same time too low and too thinly leaved at top to exclude the rays of the sun, the atmosphere being further rendered close and stifling by the smell of the turpentine which exudes from the trees.

* For an account of the similar phenomena of the 'Buffadero,' on the Mexican coast, and of the 'Souffleur,' Mauritius, see 'The Sea and its Living Wonders,' 3rd ed. p. 52.

Enclosed in these gloomy woods, large open tracts, called marshes, are found covering the valleys and lower lands, and frequently also at a considerable height above the sea, on the undulating backs of the mountains. These tracts are covered to a depth sometimes of several feet with a green, soft, and spongy moss, bound together by straggling grass and various marsh plants. The surface abounds in hillocks and holes, the tops of the hillocks having often dry crisp moss, like that on the trees. A boulder or small crag of rock occasionally protrudes, covered with red or white lichens, and here and there is a bank on which the moss has become dry and yellow. The contrast of these colours with the dark velvety green of the wet moss frequently gives a peculiarly rich appearance to the marshes, so that when seen from a little distance they might easily be mistaken for luxuriant meadow grounds, but a closer inspection soon destroys the illusion, and shows, instead of nutritious grass and aromatic flowers, nothing but a carpet of useless cryptogamic plants. Except in long continued droughts or hard frosts, these marshes are so wet as to be unable to bear the weight of a person walking over them. A march of three miles, sinking at every step into the moss, sometimes knee-deep, and always as far as the ankle, is, it may well be supposed, toilsome and fatiguing, especially when, as must always be the case in attempting to penetrate the country, a heavy load is carried on the shoulders. This thick coating of moss is precisely like a great sponge spread over the country, and becomes at the melting of the snow in the spring thoroughly saturated with water, which it long retains, and which every shower of rain continually renews.

The ' barrens ' of Newfoundland are those districts which occupy the summits of the hills and ridges, and other elevated and exposed tracts. They are covered with a thin and scrubby vegetation, consisting of berry-bearing plants and dwarf bushes of various species, resembling the moorlands of the north of England, and differing only in the kind of vegetation and its scantier quantity. Bare patches of gravel and boulders and crumbling fragments of rock are frequently met with upon the barrens, and they are generally altogether destitute of vegetable soil. But only on the

barrens is it possible to explore the interior of the country
with any kind of ease or expedition. These different tracts
are none of them of any great extent; woods, marshes, and
barrens frequently alternating with each other in the course
of a day's journey.

Another remarkable feature of Newfoundland is the almost
incredible number of lakes of all sizes, all of which are indiscriminately called ponds. They are scattered over the whole
country, not only in the valleys but on the higher lands and
even in the hollows of the summits of the ridges and the very
tops of the hills. They vary in size from pools of fifty yards
in diameter to lakes upwards of thirty miles long and four
or five miles across. The number of those which exceed a
couple of miles in extent must on the whole amount to
several hundreds, while those of a smaller size are absolutely
countless. It is supposed that a full third of the surface of
the island is covered by fresh water, and this reckoning is
rather below than above the mark. In a country so abundantly provided with lakes or ponds, it seems strange to find
no navigable rivers. The undulating surface of the land,
with its abrupt hills and deep gullies, is, without all doubt,
one cause of this absence of larger streams.

Each pond or small set of ponds communicates with a
valley of its own, down which it sends an insignificant brook,
which takes the nearest course to the sea. The chief cause
however both of the vast abundance of ponds and the comparative scantiness of the brooks is to be found in the great
coating of moss which spreads over the country, and retains
the water like a sponge, allowing it to drain off but slowly
and gradually.

The wilds of Newfoundland are tenanted by numerous fur-
bearing animals, affording a great source of gain to some of
the fishermen, who in winter turn furriers. Arctic foxes are
here in all their variety. Beavers, once nearly extirpated, but
now unmolested owing to the low value of their fur, are increasing in numbers. Brown bears are pretty numerous,
and Polar bears sometimes find their way to the northern promontory of the island upon the ice which comes drifting
down in spring from Davis' Straits. By way of contrast, in
hot summers the tropical humming-bird has been known

to visit the southern shores of Newfoundland. Reindeer are abundant, but unfortunately their enemies the wolves have likewise increased in number, since the reward given by the colonial government for their destruction has ceased to be paid.

Although in the same latitude as Central France and the South of Germany, Newfoundland has a long and severe winter, owing to the two vast streams of Arctic water, the Davis' Straits and East Greenland currents, which combine and run by its shores; and the summer, though sometimes intensely hot, is so short and so frequently obscured by fogs, that even were the soil less sterile, agriculture must necessarily be confined to narrow limits. The little wheat and barley, cultivated on the inside lands far above the sea-shore, is often cut green, and carrots, turnips, potatoes, and cabbage are nearly all the esculent vegetables which the land has been proved capable of producing.

Hence we cannot wonder that the whole island, which is considerably larger than Scotland, has only about 90,000 inhabitants, and even these would have had no inducement to settle on so unpromising a soil, if the riches of the sea did not amply compensate for the deficiencies of the land. Fish is the staple produce of Newfoundland, and the bulk of its population consists of poor fishermen, who have established themselves along the deep bays by which the coast is indented, and catch near the coast vast quantities of cod, which they bring in and cure at their leisure, in order to have it ready for the ships when they arrive. With the outer world they have little communication, and a visit to St. John's, the capital of the island, forms an epoch in their solitary lives.

This town lies at the head of a wide and secure bay, and consists of a main street fronting the water, from which narrow, dirty lanes and alleys branch out towards the land. The dingy, unpainted houses are built of wood, the government edifices only being constructed of brick or stone. The long rows of fish-stages along the shore attract the stranger's attention, but he is still more astonished at the countless gin and beer-shops, which at once tell him he is in a place where thirsty sailors and fishermen form the mass of the population. In the winter St. John's is comparatively deserted, as it then has no more than about 10,000 inhabitants, but their number is doubled or trebled during the fishing season.

The island of Newfoundland, first seen and visited in the eleventh century by the Norse colonists of Greenland, and then utterly forgotten, was rediscovered in 1497 or 1498 by John and Sebastian Cabot.

The richness of its cod-fisheries soon attracted attention, and fishermen from Spain, France, Portugal, and England annually visited its banks. The best harbours along the coast were occupied by the first comers in spring, — a circumstance which gave rise to frequent quarrels. To obviate this lawless state of affairs, Sir Humphrey Gilbert was sent out by Queen Elizabeth in 1583 to take possession of the land. He divided the coast about St. John's into districts, and the British settlers willingly agreed to pay a tax to government in the expectation of seeing their interests better protected. The new arrangement had a beneficial effect on the trade of Newfoundland, for in 1615 more than 250 English vessels visited St. John's, and gradually the whole of the eastern coast of the island was occupied by English fishermen.

The French on their part colonised the north and south sides of the island, and founded the town of Placentia, once a very considerable place but now reduced to insignificance. The rivalry of the French was naturally a great source of jealousy to a nation ill-accustomed to brook any foreign intrusion into its commercial interests. Thus, after the war of the Spanish succession, Great Britain demanded and obtained by the Treaty of Utrecht the sole possession of Newfoundland; and Louis XIV., anxious for peace on any terms, willingly acceded to this sacrifice, merely reserving for his subjects the right to dry on the shores of the island the fish they had caught on the banks. By the subsequent treaties of Paris the French were restricted to the small islands of St. Pierre and Miquelon, but not allowed to erect fortifications of any kind.

Besides the English and the French, the Americans also have the right to fish on the banks of Newfoundland, for when England acknowledged the independence of the United States, a formal article of the treaty of peace secured to

the latter the fishing privileges which they had previously
enjoyed as colonies.

The value of the dry cod-fish alone exported every year from
Newfoundland is on an average about 400,000*l.*, while the
total value of the exported productions in fish, oil, and skins,
is upwards of 700,000*l.* This, from a population of 80,000 or
90,000, proves that the people of the island ought to be happy
and prosperous; but unfortunately a system of credit renders
the bulk of the fishermen entirely dependent on the merchants,
and want of education is a further source of evil.

Though vast quantities of cod are taken along the shores
of Newfoundland, yet the most important fishery is carried on
on the banks at some distance from the island.

The great bank lies 20 leagues from the nearest point of
land from latitude 41° to 49°, and extends 300 miles in length
and 75 in breadth. To the east of this lies the False Bank;
the next is styled the Green Bank, about 240 miles long
and 120 broad; then Banquero, about the same size, with
several other shoals of less note, all abounding with fish, but
chiefly with cod, the great magnet which sets whole fleets in
motion. In winter the cod retire to the deeper waters, but
they reappear in March and April, when their pursuers
hasten to the spot, not only from the bays and coves of
Newfoundland but from Great Britain, the United States,
and France.

While fishing, each man has a space three feet and a half
wide allotted to him on deck, so as not to interfere with
his neighbour. The lines are from 30 to 40 fathoms long—
for the cod generally swims at that depth. The chief baits
used are the squid, a species of cuttle-fish, and the capelin,
a small salmon abounding on the North-American coasts.
The herring and the launce, and a shell-fish called clam,
which is found in the belly of the cod, are likewise used.
In spring particularly the cod rushes so eagerly upon the
bait, that in the course of a single day a good fisherman is
able to haul up four hundred one after another. This is no
easy task, considering the size of the fish, which on an average
weighs 14 pounds, but has been taken four feet three inches
long, and 46 pounds in weight. When a large fish, too
heavy for the line, has been caught, the fisherman calls on

his neighbour, who strikes a hook attached to a long pole into the fish, and then safely hauls it on board.

Mindful of the proverb which recommends us all to strike while the iron is hot, the fishermen continue to catch cod for hours, until so many are heaped on the deck, that to make room it becomes necessary to 'dress them down.' This is done on long planks made to rest with both ends on two casks, and thus forming a narrow table. First, each man cuts out the tongues of the fish he has caught, as his wages are reckoned by their number, and then the whole crew divide themselves into *throaters, headers, splitters, salters,* and *packers.* The throater begins the operation of 'dressing' by drawing his knife across the throat of the cod to the bone and ripping open the bowels. He then passes it to the header, who with a strong wrench pulls off the head and tears out the entrails, which he casts overboard, passing the fish at the same time to the splitter, who with one cut lays it open from head to tail, and almost in the twinkling of an eye with another cut takes out the backbone. After separating the sounds, which are placed with the tongues and packed in barrels as a delicacy, the backbone follows the entrails overboard, while the fish at the same moment is passed with the other hand to the salter. Such is the amazing quickness of the operations of heading and splitting, that a good workman will often decapitate and take out the entrails and backbone of six fish in a minute. Every fisherman is supposed to know something of each of these operations, and no rivals at cricket ever entered with more ardour into their work than do some athletic champions for the palm of 'dressing down' after a 'day's catch.'

Generally the fog is so dense, that one ship does not see the other, although both may be so near, that the crews distinctly hear each others' voices. Frequently one is hardly able to see to the distance of a few feet, and the large drops of the condensed mist fall like rain from the yards. During calm weather the aspect of the sea is so dismal, that it requires all the buoyant spirits of a seaman to resist its depressing influence. For days the calm remains unbroken, and no sound is heard but that of a fish darting out of the water, or the screech of a sea-bird flitting over the sea. But sometimes a storm breaks this awful silence of nature. At such times the fishing ships, hidden in mists, run the greatest danger of striking against each other, although signal lanterns and alarm trumpets are used to give warning. A tremendous wave bursting on the deck often strikes them with such force as to sink them or dash them to pieces against the rocky coast. Thus many a widow and orphan has a mournful tale to relate of the dangers of the cod-fishery on the banks of Newfoundland.

In some parts of the coast where the water is sufficiently shallow, the cod-fish are now caught in sieves or nets. This operation requires more capital to commence with than the mere boat and hooks and lines of the common fishermen, and like all improvements met at first with much opposition, on the plea that it must interfere with the interests of the poorer class. It is obvious however that the use of the net is advantageous to the trade at large, for shoals, or as they are termed 'schools,' of fish may sometimes be seen sweeping along shore, which, but for the net, would escape altogether. Besides there seems such an incalculable abundance of the fish, that there will always be enough to hook, enough to jig, enough to net, and more than enough to go away.

'One calm July evening' says Mr. Jukes,* 'I was in a boat just outside St. John's harbour, when the sea was pretty still, and the fish were " breaching," as it is termed. For several miles around us the calm sea was alive with fish. They were sporting on the surface of the water, flirting their tails occasionally into the air, and as far as could be seen the water was rippled and broken by their movements. Looking down into its clear depths, cod-fish under cod-fish of all sizes appeared swimming about as if in sport. Some boats were fishing, but not a bite could they get, the fish being already gorged with food. Had the ground been shallow enough to use nets, the harbour might have been filled with fish.'

Besides the cod-fishery, seal-catching is also carried on with considerable success on the eastern coast, which intercepts many immense fields and islands of ice as they move southwards in the spring from the Arctic Sea. The interior

* 'Excursions in Newfoundland.

parts of these drifting shoals, with the lakes or openings interspersed, remain unbroken, and on them myriads of seals may be found.  In the month of March or April, as soon as the ice-fields descend with the currents from Davis' Straits, many small ships, not only from the harbours of the east coast of Newfoundland but even from the distant Scotch ports, particularly Aberdeen, put out to sea and boldly plunge into all the openings of the ice-fields to make war upon the seals.  Armed with firelocks and heavy bludgeons the crews surprise the animals on the ice.  In this way thousands are killed yearly from the north, but their numbers have latterly decreased, and the seal catchers pay the penalty of their heedless and indiscriminate slaughter.

Red-Breasted Merganser.

Portraits of Greenland Natives.

(From a Photograph by Dr. Rink.)

# CHAPTER XXXV.

## GREENLAND.

A mysterious Region—Ancient Scandinavian Colonists—Their Decline and Fall—
Hans Egede—His Trials and Success—Foundation of Godthaab—Herrenhuth
Missionaries—Lindenow—The Scoresbys—Clavering—The Danish Settlements
in Greenland—The Greenland Esquimaux—Seal Catching—The White Dolphin
—The Narwhal—Shark Fishery—Fiskernasset—Birds—Reindeer Hunting—
Indigenous Plants—Drift-wood—Mineral Kingdom—Mode of Life of the Green-
land Esquimaux—The Danes in Greenland—Beautiful Scenery—Ice Caves.

IN many respects Greenland is one of the most remarkable
countries of the Arctic zone. The whole of the northern
coast of continental America, from Cape Lisburne to Belle
Isle Straits, is known; the borders of Siberia fronting the
icy ocean have been thoroughly explored by water and by
land; the distance of Spitzbergen and Novaya Zemlya from
the Pole has long since been determined; but how far
Greenland may reach to the north, we know not—though
nearly a thousand years have passed since the Icelander
Günnbjorn (970 A.D.) first saw its high mountain coast, and

in spite of all the attempts made since that time to circumnavigate it.   The interior of the island—or continent as it
may perhaps more justly be called, for it has a surface of
at least 750,000 square miles, and is probably larger than
Australia—is also unknown; for of this vast extent of territory only the narrow shores of the coast-line seemed to be
inhabitable, or even accessible to man.   On penetrating into
the deeper fjords, all the valleys are found blocked with
glaciers, which, on climbing the heights, are seen to pass
into a monotonous plateau of ice, or névé, which seems to
cover and conceal the whole interior.   Thus, from its physical configuration, Greenland may well be called a mysterious
region; and, strange to say, the history of the decline and
fall of its first colonists is as little known as its geography.

   We have seen in a previous chapter that Iceland, so peaceful in the present day, was peopled in the ninth century
with a highly turbulent race of jarls and vikings.   One of
these worthies, called Erik Rauda, or the Red, having twice
dyed his hands with blood, was banished by the Althing
(982) for a term of years, and resolved to pass the time of
his compulsory absence in exploring the land discovered
by Günnbjorn.   After spending three years on its western
coasts, he returned to Iceland, and made so favourable a
report of the new country, which—knowing the advantages
of a good name—he called Greenland, that in 986 he induced
a large body of colonists to sail with him and settle there.
Other emigrants followed, and in a few years all the habitable places of southern Greenland were occupied.

   The colony, which soon after its foundation adopted the
Christian religion, was divided into two districts or 'bygds'
(from the Icelandic 'byggia' to inhabit), by an intervening
tract of land named Ubygd, the 'uninhabitable' or 'uninhabited.'   The West Bygd reached from lat. 66° down to
62°, and contained, in its best days, 90 farms and 4 churches.
South of it lay the desert, 'Ubygd,' of 70 geographical
miles, terminated by the East Bygd, consisting of 190 farms,
and having 2 towns, Gardar and Alba, 1 cathedral, and 11
churches.   The whole population may probably have amounted
to 6,000 souls.   The country was governed by Icelandic
laws, and the first of its eighteen bishops, Arnold, was

elected in 1121, the last being Endride Andreason, who was consecrated in 1406. In spite of its poverty and distance, Greenland was obliged to contribute its mite to the revenues of the papal chair, for we read in the ancient annalists, that, in 1326, its tribute, consisting of walrus teeth, was sold by the pope's agent, Bertram of Ortolis, to a merchant of Flanders for the sum of 12 livres and 14 sous.

The time, however, was now fast approaching when the Greenland colony was not only to cease paying tithes and Peter's pence, but to be swept away. During the course of the fourteenth century it was visited by one misfortune after another. The black death, which carried off twenty-five millions of Europeans, did not spare its distant fjords (1348-9); the Esquimaux harassed the survivors with repeated attacks, killing some, and carrying away others captive. A hostile fleet, suspected to be English, laid waste the country in 1418; and finally, the revolutions and wars which broke out in Scandinavia after the death of Queen Margaret of Waldemar, caused Greenland to be entirely neglected and forgotten. The last colonists either retreated to Iceland, or were destroyed by the Esquimaux, and many years elapsed before Greenland was again thought of as a place where Scandinavians had once been living. At length, King Frederic II. of Denmark sent out Mogens Heineson, a famous 'sea-cock' as the chroniclers style him, to the south-eastern coast of Greenland (1581), to see if men of a Norse origin still dwelt along those ice-bound fjords. Heineson reached the coast, but the great transparency of the air, which in the Polar regions frequently causes strange optical delusions, led him into a singular error. After having sailed for many hours in the same direction, and still seeing the mountains which seemed quite near recede as he advanced, he fancied himself fettered by an invisible power, and thus the famous 'sea-cock' returned home with the report that, detained by a magnetic rock, he had not been able to reach the land.

In 1605, King Christian IV. of Denmark sent out a new Greenland expedition, consisting of three ships, under the command of Godske Lindenow, and the guidance of James Hall, an English pilot. This time no magnetic rocks

intervened; but the ships having separated, Hall landed on
the west coast, which had already been rediscovered and
visited by Davis, Hudson, Baffin, and other Arctic navigators; while Lindenow, anchoring off Cape Farewell, kid-
napped two Esquimaux, who afterwards died of nostalgia in
Denmark.  But neither Lindenow, who the year after again
made his appearance on the western coast of Greenland,
nor two later expeditions under Carsten Richardson and
Dannell, were able to effect a landing on any part of the
eastern coast.  It was in sight, but the drift-ice made it
inaccessible.  They were equally unsuccessful in finding any
traces of the lost colony, which came at length to be regarded
as a mere Scandinavian myth.  But while no one else cared
about its existence, the ardent Hans Egede (born in Norway, January 31, 1686), pastor of Vaage, in the Lofoten
Islands, still continued to cherish its memory.  He had
read in the ancient chronicles about the old Christian
communities in Greenland, and could not believe in their
total extinction.  He felt the deepest concern in the fate of
their descendants, and the thought that after so long a
separation from the mother country they must needs be
plunged in barbarism and heathen darkness, left him no rest
by night or day.  At length he resolved to devote his life to
their spiritual welfare, and to become the apostle of rediscovered or regenerated Greenland.  His zeal and perseverance overcame a thousand difficulties.  Neither the public
ridicule, nor the coldness of the authorities to whom he
vainly applied for assistance, nor the exhortations of his
friends, could damp his ardour.  At length, after years of
fruitless endeavours, after having given up his living and
sacrificed his little fortune in the prosecution of his plans, he
succeeded in forming a Greenland Company, with a capital
of 9,000 dollars, and in obtaining an annual stipend from
the Danish Missionary Fund of 300 dollars, to which King
Frederick IV. added a gift of 200 dollars.  With three
ships, the largest of which, 'The Hope,' had forty colonists on
board, Egede, accompanied by his wife and four children, set
sail from the port of Bergen on May 12, 1721, and reached
Greenland on July 3, after a long and tedious passage.  The
winds had driven him to the western coast, in latitude 64°,

and here he resolved at once to begin his evangelical labours with the Esquimaux. A wooden chapel was speedily erected, which formed the first nucleus of the still existing settlement of Godthaab.

But if the life of the worthy Egede had for many a year been full of trouble before he went to Greenland, trials still more severe awaited him during his apostolical career. He had not merely the suspicions of the Esquimaux, the enmity of their medicine-men, the severity of the climate, and not seldom even famine to contend with. His own countrymen, disappointed in their hopes of carrying on a lucrative trade with the Greenlanders, resolved to abandon it altogether, and, after ten laborious years, the Government not only withdrew all further assistance from the mission, but even ordered the colony to be broken up. All his companions, with the exception of a few volunteers who engaged to share his fortunes, now returned to Denmark; but Egede, though his health had been so shattered by almost superhuman exertions, that he had long since been obliged to leave all active duties to his son, resolved, like a faithful soldier, to die at his post. In 1733, his perseverance was at length rewarded by the grateful news that the king, at the entreaty of Count Zinzendorf, the founder of Herrenhuth, had consented to bestow an annual grant of 2,000 dollars on the Greenland mission, and that three Moravian brothers had arrived to assist him in his work. Thus he could at length (1735) return with a quiet heart to his native country, where he died universally regretted in 1758, at the age of seventy-two.

It may easily be supposed, that during his long stay in Greenland he anxiously sought the traces of his lost countrymen, for the desire to help them had first led him to that Arctic country. Nothing in the physiognomy of the Esquimaux, or in their language, pointed in any way to an European origin, and even their traditions said not a word of the old Norse settlers, who had once inhabited the land. The ruins of some churches, and other buildings scattered here and there along the west coast, alone attested their existence, and formed a link between the past and the present. Thus if Greenland still had inhabitants of Scandinavian origin, they must necessarily be confined to the eastern coast, beyond Cape Farewell. But Egede was as little able as his predecessors to penetrate through the ice-belt which, both by land and sea, completely separated it from the rest of the world.

For many years after his death it remained unknown and inaccessible; and Löwenorn, who was sent out in 1786–87 to renew the attempts of Heineson and Lindenow, had no better success. No doubt many a whaler may have admired its distant mountain peaks glowing in the evening sun, or may have been driven by the storm against its shores, but the Scoresbys were the first to determine accurately the position of part of its well-fenced coast. In the year 1817, Captain Scoresby the elder, deviating from the usual course of the whalers, steered through the western ice, and reached the east coast of Greenland, beyond 70°. He could easily have landed; the coast which had so frequently baffled the attempts of previous navigators lay invitingly before him, but he could not sacrifice his duty as the commander of a whaler to curiosity or renown. And thus without having set his foot on shore, he sailed back into the open sea. On a later visit, however, he landed in the sound which bears his name. In the year 1822, Scoresby the younger succeeded in more closely examining the land. Leaving the usual track of the whalers, he had steered to the west, and threaded his way through the drift-ice until between 70° 33′ and 71° 12′ N. lat. the coast of Greenland lay before him. No coast that he had ever seen before had so majestic a character. The mountains, on which he bestowed the name of Roscoe, consisted of numberless jagged stones or pyramids, rising in individual peaks to a height of 3,000 feet, and a chaos of sharp needles covered their rough declivities.

On July 24, he landed on a rocky promontory, which he named Cape Lister (70° 30′), and climbing its summit continued his excursion along its back, which was between three and four hundred feet high. Here and there between the stones, which were either naked or thinly clothed with lichens, bloomed an *Andromeda tetragona*, a *Saxifraga oppositifolia*, a *Papaver nudicanle*, or a *Ranunculus nivalis*. At Cape Swainson he again descended to the shore, which here formed a flat strand, about 600 feet broad. Some deserted

Esquimaux huts soon arrested his attention. Charred drift-wood and a quantity of ashes lay scattered about the hearths, and proved that these dwellings had not been long forsaken. Scarcely a bird was to be seen on land, but countless auks and divers animated the waters. A great number of winged insects—butterflies, bees, musquitoes—flew or buzzed about, particularly on the hillocks between the stones. On July 25, he once more landed on Cape Hope, where he again found traces of inhabitants. Bones of hares and fragments of reindeer-horns lay scattered about on the ground. The skull of a dog was planted on a small mound of earth, for it is a belief of the Greenland Esquimaux that the dog, who finds his way everywhere, must necessarily be the best guide of the innocent children to the land of souls. The heat, which soon put an end to this excursion, was so great, that many of the plants had shed their seeds, and some were already completely dried up and shrivelled.

The part of the coast of East Greenland discovered by Scoresby, and that which was visited the year after by Clavering, lay, however, too far to the north to afford any clue about the extinct Scandinavian settlements, even sup-posing them, as was then still believed, to have been partly situated to the east of Cape Farewell. At length, in the year 1829, Captain Graah, who had been sent out by King Frederick VI. of Denmark, succeeded in exploring the south-eastern coast of Greenland, from its southern extremity to the latitude of 65° 18', beyond which no colony could ever have existed; and as he nowhere found either the most insig-nificant ruins, or the least traces of an ancient Christian settlement in the language and customs of the natives, it was now fully proved that the east bygd of the old chroniclers was, in reality, situated on the south-western coast of Green-land, in the present districts of Julianshaab and Lichtenau; a coast which, in comparison with the more northern colonies of Frederikshaab and Fiskernäs, distinctly trends to the east.

The present Danish settlements, which are confined to the more sheltered fjords of its western coast, are divided into a north and south inspectorate, the former extending from lat. 67° to 72°, and comprising the districts of Upernavik, Omenak, Jakobshavn, Christianshaab, Egedesminde, and

Godhavn on Disco Island; while the latter contains the districts of Holsteensborg, Sukkertoppen, Godthaab, Fiskernässet, Frederikshaab, and Julianshaab.

In the year 1855 the population of the South Inspectorate consisted of 6,128 aboriginal Greenlanders, or Esquimaux, and 120 Europeans; that of the North Inspectorate of 3,516 of the former, and 128 of the latter; a very small number if we consider that it is scattered over a space of 12° of latitude. In a country like this, such *towns* as Godhavn, with 150 inhabitants, or Godthaab, the most populous of all, with 330, pass for considerable cities.

But in spite of its scanty population, Greenland is a valuable possession of the Danish crown, or rather of the Danish company which entirely monopolises the trade, and manages its affairs so well, that the Greenlander receives for his produce only about the sixth part of its price at Copenhagen. According to the average of six years (1850 1855), the total value of the exports from Greenland amounted to 378,588 rix-dollars; that of the importations from Denmark to 164,215, but in the latter sum was included not only the price paid to the Greenlanders for their goods, but all the stores and provisions necessary for the agents and servants of the company, the missionaries, and the administration of the colony. The trifling amount which, after all deductions and charges, the poor Greenlander receives for his seal-skins or his blubber, he generally spends in tobacco, candy-sugar, coffee, and sea-biscuits, for his real wants are amply supplied by his own country, and he has not yet learnt to invest his gains more profitably. Like all other Esquimaux, he depends chiefly upon the sea for his subsistence. Of the various species of Phocæ found in the Greenland waters, the most valuable is the hispid seal (*Phoca hispida*), both from its numbers and from its frequenting the fjords during the whole year; while the larger Greenland seal (*Phoca grœnlandica*) is not stationary like the former, but leaves the coast from March to May, and from July to September. The *Cystophora cristata*, or hooded seal, remarkable for a globular sac, capable of inflation, on the head of the male, appears in the fjords only from April till June. It is the most pugnacious of all the seals. In the southern districts,

THE COLONY OF SUKKERTOPPEN, GREENLAND.

(From a Photograph by Dr. Rink.)

where the seal-hunting must be chiefly carried on in open water, the Greenlander relies upon his boat, the kayak. When the animal is struck, the barbed point of the harpoon detaches itself, by an ingenious mechanism, from the shaft, which otherwise would be broken by its violent contortions, and as the line is attached to a bladder, it can easily be recovered.

Among the cetaceans the white dolphin (*Delphinopterus leucas*) and the narwhal (*Monodon monoceros*) are the most valuable to the Greenlanders of the North Inspectorate, from 500 to 600 of these huge animals being annually caught. The former makes its appearance a short time after the breaking up of the ice, and again in autumn; in summer it seeks the open sea. Sometimes large herds of the white dolphins are cut off from the sea by the closing in of the ice in the neighbourhood of the land, so that several hundred may be killed in the course of a few days. The narwhal is caught only in the Omenak fjord, which it visits regularly in November. As its chase is both difficult and dangerous, the Greenlanders generally hunt it in company, so that after a narwhal has been struck with the first harpoon or lance, others are ready to follow up the advantage. The larger whales are now seldom caught, but the dead body of a fin-back is not seldom cast ashore, and affords a rich harvest to the neighbourhood. Sometimes masses of oil, evidently proceeding from dead whales, are found floating in the fjords. In 1854, 95 tons of this matter were collected near Holsteinburg.

The fishes likewise amply contribute to supply the Greenlander's wants. The shark-fishery (*Scymnus microcephalus*) is of considerable importance. The entrails of seals and other offal are placed in the openings of the ice to attract these sharks to the spot, where they are caught in various ways, particularly by torch-light, which brings them to the surface. The fishermen, watching the moment, strike them with a sharp hook, and then drag them upon the ice. They are also caught with strong iron angles attached to chains. They are captured for the sake of their livers, which yield a good deal of oil. It has very recently been ascertained that a valuable substance resembling spermaceti may be expressed from the carcase which was formerly wasted, and for this purpose powerful screw presses are now employed. About 30,000 of these gluttonous animals are caught every year, and the fishery may be greatly extended, as the bottom of the ice-fjords absolutely swarms with them. Their capture is attended with far less trouble and danger than in Iceland, where they are pursued in boats, and in a capricious and tempestuous sea. Improving upon the old Esquimaux methods of fishing or hunting, the Danish residents set nets for the white whale or the seal; for the former, they are attached to the shore, and extend off at right angles, so as to intercept them in their autumnal southern migration, when they swim close along the rocks to avoid the grampus. When the white whale is stopped by the net, it often appears at first to be unconscious of the fact, and continues to swim against it, and then allows the boat to approach it from behind. If entangled in the net, it is soon drowned, as, like all the whale tribe, it is obliged to come to the surface to breathe.

A large quantity of cod are caught in various parts of the South Inspectorate, particularly at Fiskernasset, which being less subject to fogs and more exposed to the sea-wind offers peculiar advantages for the drying of the fish. The capelin (*Mallotus villosus*), which in May and June visits the coasts of Greenland in great numbers, is eaten both fresh or laid upon the rocks to dry for the winter. The sea-wolf, the lump-fish, the bull-head, the Norway haddock, the salmon-trout, are likewise important articles of food. The halibut grows to a huge size, and a smaller species (*Hippoglossus pinguis*) is fished for at the depth of 180 or even 380 fathoms. The banks frequented by this fish are most valuable to the neighbouring Greenlanders. Many are no doubt still undiscovered, others may be known by the dead fish floating on the surface, or by the seals diving out of the water with a flat fish in their mouth. Long-tailed crabs are easily caught in many parts, and the common mussel may be gathered almost everywhere at ebb tide.

Crowds of birds nestle during the summer on the rocky shores, particularly at Upernavik, where the largest breeding places are found. They are generally killed with small blunted arrows. In the ice-fjord of Jacobshavn, the gulls are caught ingeniously by floating traps on which something brilliant or resembling a fish is fixed. The eggs of the sea-birds are gathered in vast numbers, and the feathers and skins of the eider-duck and auk are both exported and used for the lining of boots.

Compared with the wealth of the seas the land is very poor. The chase of the reindeer is, however, important, as its skin affords both a warmer and a softer clothing than that of the seal, and serves moreover as a bed cover or a sledge carpet. Reindeer hunting is a favourite summer occupation of the Greenlanders, who annually kill from 10,000 to 20,000, and export about one-half of the skins. Only a few cows, sheep, and goats are kept at Julianshaab. For want of hay they are fed with fish during the winter. In south Greenland the potato is cultivated by the European residents as a luxury. The plant never flowers, and even buds are rare. Turnips, cabbages, salad, and spinach likewise grow in South Greenland, but barley sown in the gardens scarcely ever comes to ear. In summer the windows of the houses are gay with geraniums and fuchsias and other flowers of a more temperate zone.

Among the indigenous plants the berries of the *Empetrum nigrum, Vaccinium uliginosum,* and *Vaccinium vitis idæa* furnish the Greenlanders with their only vegetable food. While the coasts exposed to the bleak sea-winds afford scanty traces of vegetation, the valleys and hill slopes of the more sheltered fjords are green during the summer, and justify the name bestowed by Erick on the land of his adoption. Forests are of course out of the question in Greenland, though in some places the birch attains a not inconsiderable size. Thus in a dell at the upper end of Lichtenau Fjord a thicket of these trees, fifteen feet high, surrounds a little lake fed by a waterfall, the largest hitherto known in Greenland. More generally, however, the trees, such as the beech, the willow, the elder, &c., merely creep along the ground, where the dense matting of their roots and branches, mingled with bushes of the empetrum, or with mosses, lichens, and fal'en leaves, forms a kind of turf which is used as fuel by the Danes.

In some measure the sea makes up for the want of timber
by casting on the shore a quantity of drift-wood, the origin of
which is still a matter of doubt, some tracing it to the North
American rivers, others to those of Siberia. It consists
mostly of the uprooted trunks of coniferous trees. Sometimes
also large pieces of bark, such as those of which the Indians
make their canoes, and sewn together with threads of hair,
are drifted into the fjords.

The mineral kingdom, though it has within the last few
years attracted the attention of speculators, will hardly ever
realise their hopes. Several attempts to work the lead and
copper ores at Nanursoak and in the Arksak Fjord have
miserably failed. The cost of transport is immense, and the
difficulty of obtaining the necessary workmen presents an
insuperable obstacle to all mining operations in Greenland.

Though the Greenlanders have now been for more than a
century under the influence of Christian teachers, yet their
mode of life is still much the same as that of their relatives
the wild Esquimaux on the opposite continent of North
America. Like them, they use the 'kayak,' the 'oomiak,'
and the sledge; like them, they live in small winter huts of
stone (the snow-house is unknown to them), or in summer
tents hung with skins, and they are equally improvident in
times of abundance. Their constant intercourse with Europeans has, however, taught them the use of many luxuries
unknown to the wild Esquimaux, and they are now great
consumers of coffee. They are fond of instruction, but the
immense space over which the population is scattered, and
their vagrant life during a great part of the year, are great
hindrances to their improvement. They are also very good-
natured, and live on the best terms with the Danes who reside
among them. The latter, who, with the exception of the
Moravian missionaries, are all in the service of the Company,
soon get attached to the country, and leave it with regret;
sometimes even returning to close their days in Greenland.

The climate, though severe, is very healthy, and the lover
of sport finds ample opportunities for gratifying his favourite passion. In September, or at the beginning of October,
the last ships leave for Europe; and then, till the next April
or May — when the first English whalers appear in the

ports of Godhavn or Upernavik — all communication with the civilised world is totally cut off. Towards the end of January, or the beginning of February, when the days begin rapidly to lengthen, frequent sledge parties keep up a constant interchange of visits between the various settlements. This mode of travelling over the lakes and enclosed fjords is very agreeable in May, as then the sun is pleasantly warm at noon, and though he hardly disappears below the horizon, the nights are sufficiently cold to convert the melted snow into ice hard enough to bear the weight of a sledge. This is the best time for visiting many interesting spots inaccessible at other seasons of the year, and for enjoying many a scene unsurpassed in Switzerland itself. Here, as on the Alps, the glacier and the snow-clad peak appear in all their grandeur; here also, in the valleys, the summer brooks flow between well-clothed banks, and the Helvetian lakes are worthily rivalled by the magnificent fjords of Greenland.

In many parts, the waves beating against the steep coasts of the islands and fjords, render access difficult, if not impossible during the summer; but in winter or spring, they may easily be visited across the ice. The surf has worn many caves in these precipitous rock-walls, which are no less remarkable for their picturesque basaltic forms than for the huge masses of ice on their sides, which, in their tints and grouping, far surpass the stalactites of the most renowned European grottoes.

The Snow Goose.

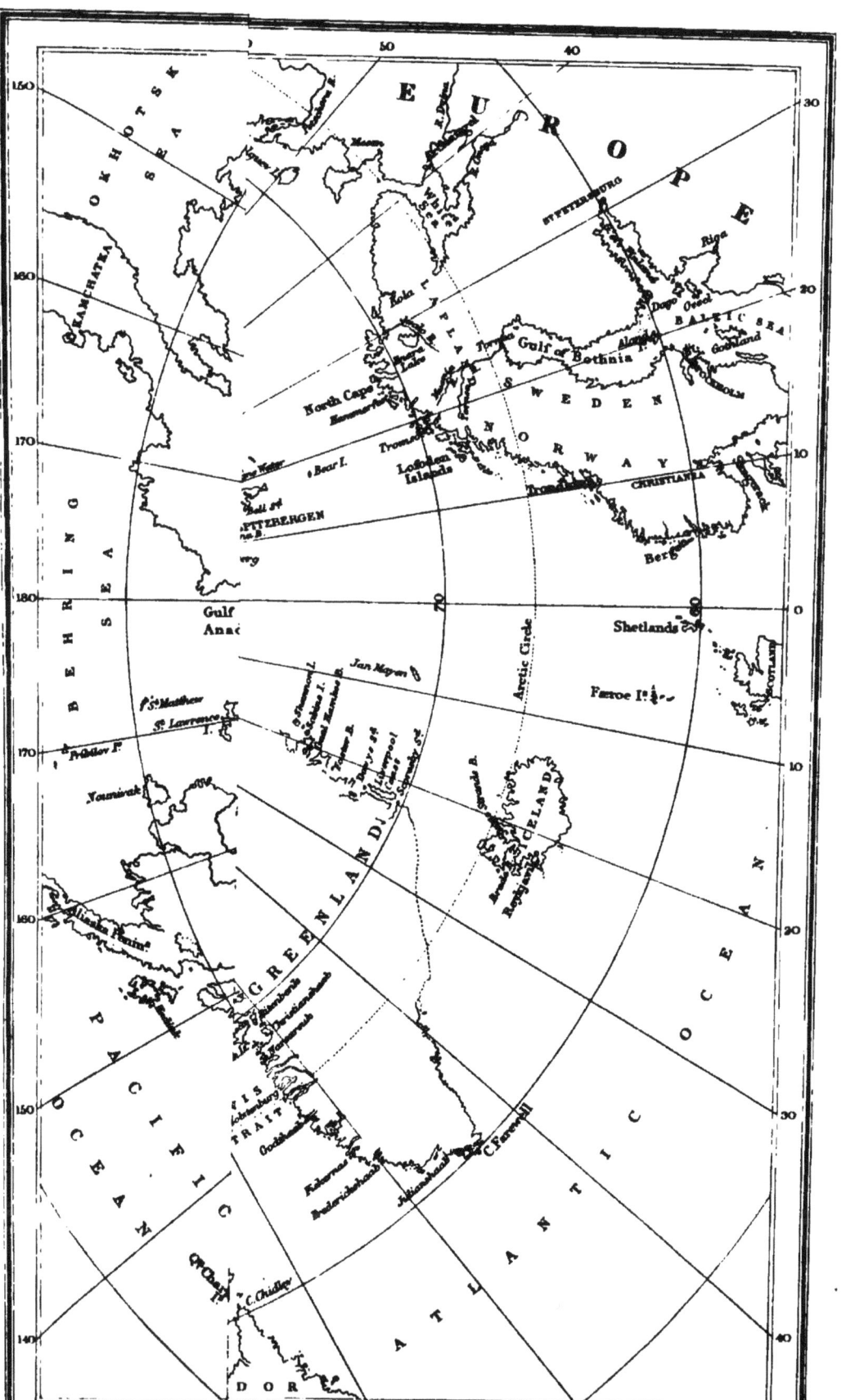

# PART II.

---◆ -

# THE ANTARCTIC REGIONS.

Cape Crozier and Mount Terror.

# CHAPTER XXXVI.

### THE ANTARCTIC OCEAN.

Comparative view of the Antarctic and Arctic Regions—Inferiority of Climate of the former—Its Causes—The New Shetland Islands—South Georgia—The Peruvian Stream—Sea-birds—The Giant Petrel—The Albatross—The Penguin —The Austral Whale—The Hunchback—The Fin-Back—The Grampus— Battle with a Whale—The Sea-Elephant—The Southern Sea-Bear—The Sea-Leopard—Antarctic Fishes.

THE Antarctic regions are far more desolate and barren than the Arctic. Here we have no energetic hunters, like the Esquimaux, chasing the seal or the walrus; no herdsmen following, like the Samoyedes or the Lapps, their reindeer to the brink of the icy ocean; but all is one dreary, uninhabitable waste. While within the Arctic Circle the musk-ox enjoys an abundance of food, and the lemming is still found thriving on the bleakest islands, not a single land quadruped exists beyond 56° of southern latitude.

Summer flowers gladden the sight of the Arctic navigator in the most northern lands yet reached; but no plant of any description—not even a moss or a lichen—has been observed beyond Cockburn Island in 64° 12′ S. lat.; and while even in Spitzbergen vegetation ascends the mountain slopes to a height of 3,000 feet the snow line descends to the water's edge in every land within or near the Antarctic Circle.

An open sea, extending towards the northern pole as far as the eye can reach, points out the path to future discovery; but the Antarctic navigators, with one single exception, have invariably seen their progress arrested by barriers of ice, and none have ever penetrated beyond the comparatively low latitude of 78° 10'.

Even in Spitzbergen and East Greenland, Scoresby sometimes found the heat of summer very great; but the annals of Antarctic navigation invariably speak of a frigid temperature. In 1773, when Captain Phipps visited Spitzbergen, the thermometer once rose to $+58\frac{1}{2}°$; and on July 15, 1820, when the 'Hecla' left her winter-quarters in Melville Island, (74° 47' N.), she enjoyed a warmth of $+56°$. But during the summer months spent by Sir James Ross in the Antarctic Polar area, the temperature of the air never once exceeded $+41° 5'$. In Northumberland Sound (76° 42' N.), probably the coldest spot hitherto visited in the north, the mean of the three summer months was found to be $+30° 8'$, while within the Antarctic Circle it only amounted to $+27° 3'$.

The reader may possibly wonder why the climate of the southern polar regions is so much more severe than that of the high northern latitudes; or why coasts and valleys, at equal distances from the equator, should in one case be found green with vegetation, and in another mere wastes of snow and ice; but the predominance of land in the north, and of sea in the south, fully answers the question. Within the Arctic Circle we see vast continental masses projecting far to the north, so as to form an almost continuous belt round the icy sea; while in the southern hemisphere, the continents taper down in a vast extent of open ocean. In the north, the plains of Siberia and of the Hudson's Bay territories, warmed by the sunbeams of summer, become at that season centres of radiating heat, so that in many parts the growth of forests, or even the culture of the cereals, advances as high as 70° of latitude; while the Antarctic lands are of a comparatively small extent, and isolated in the midst of frigid waters, whose temperature scarcely varies from $+29° 2'$ even in the height of summer. Mostly situated within the Antarctic Circle, and constantly chilled by cold sea-winds, they act at every season as refrigerators of the atmosphere.

In the north, the formation of icebergs is confined to a few mountainous countries, such as the west coast of Greenland or Spitzbergen; but the Antarctic coast-lands generally tower to a considerable height above the level of the sea, and the vast fragments, which are constantly detaching themselves from their glaciers, keep up the low temperature of the seas.

In the north, the cold currents of the Polar Ocean, with their drift-ice and bergs, have but the two wide gates of the Greenland Sea and Davis' Strait through which they can emerge to the south, so that their influence is confined within comparatively narrow limits, while the gelid streams of the Antarctic seas branch out freely on all sides, and convey their floating ice-masses far and wide within the temperate seas. It is only to the west of Newfoundland that single icebergs have ever been known to descend as low as 39° of latitude; but in the southern hemisphere they have been met with in the vicinity of the Cape of Good Hope (35° S. lat.), near Tristan d'Acunha, opposite to the mouth of the Rio de la Plata, and within a hundred leagues of Tasmania. In the north, finally, we find the gulf stream conveying warmth even to the shores of Spitzbergen and Novaya Zemlya; while in the opposite regions of the globe, no traces of warm currents have been observed beyond 55° of latitude.

Thus the predominance of vast tracts of flat land in the boreal hemisphere, and of an immense expanse of ocean in the Antarctic regions, sufficiently accounts for the æstival warmth of the former, and the comparatively low summer temperature of the latter.

It is unnecessary to describe in detail each of the desolate lands which modern navigators have discovered among the Antarctic ice-fields, but it may not be uninteresting to compare one or two of these dreary wastes with the lands of the north, situated in analogous latitudes.

The New Shetland Islands, situated between 61° and 63° of southern latitude, were originally discovered by Dirck Gheritz—a Dutch navigator—who, in attempting to round

Cape Horn, was carried by tempestuous weather within sight of their mountainous coasts. Long forgotten, they were re-discovered in 1819 by Mr. Smith, a master in the royal navy—whom a storm had likewise carried thither—and in the following year more accurately examined by Edward Bransfield, whose name survives in the strait which separates them from D'Urville's Louis Philippe Land.

In 1829, the 'Chanticleer,' Captain Forster, was sent to New Shetland for the purpose of making magnetic and other physical observations, and remained for several months at Deception Island, which was selected as a station from its affording the best harbour in South Shetland.

Though these islands are situated at about the same distance from the pole as the Faroe Islands which boast of numerous flocks of sheep, and where the sea never freezes, yet, when the 'Chanticleer' approached Deception Island, on January 5 (a month corresponding to our July), so many icebergs were scattered about, that Forster counted at one time no fewer than eighty-one. A gale having arisen, accompanied by a thick fog, great care was needed to avoid running foul of these floating cliffs. After entering the harbour, —a work of no slight difficulty, from the violence of the wind —the fogs were so frequent that, for the first ten days, neither sun nor stars were seen; and it was withal so raw and cold, that Lieutenant Kendal, to whom we owe a short narrative of the expedition, did not recollect having suffered more at any time in the Arctic regions, even at the lowest range of the thermometer. In this desolate land, frozen water becomes an integral portion of the soil; for this volcanic island is composed chiefly of alternate layers of ashes and ice, as if the snow of each winter, during a series of years, had been prevented from melting in the following summer, by the ejection of cinders and ashes from some part where volcanic action still goes on. Early in March (the September of the north) the freezing over of the cove, in which the ship was secured, gave warning that it was high time for her to quit this desolate port. With much difficulty and severe labour, from the fury of the gales, they managed to get away, and we may fully credit Lieutenant Kendal's assertion, that it was a day of rejoicing to all on board when the shores of Deception faded from their view.

In 1775, Cook, on his second voyage, discovered the large island of South Georgia, situated in latitude 54° and 55°, a situation corresponding to that of Scarborough or Durham. But what a difference in the climate, for 'we saw not a river or stream of water,' says the great navigator, 'on all the coast of Georgia. The head of the bay, as well as two places on each side, was terminated by perpendicular icebergs of considerable height. Pieces were continually breaking off and floating out to sea, and a great fall happened while we were in the bay, which made a noise like a cannon. The inner parts of the country were not less savage and horrible. The wild rocks raised their lofty summits till they were lost in the clouds, and the valley lay covered with everlasting snow. Not a tree was to be seen, not a shrub even big enough to make a toothpick. The only vegetation was a coarse strong-bladed grass growing in tufts, wild burnet, and a plant like moss, which sprang from the rocks. The lands, or rather rocks, bordering on the sea-coast were not covered with snow like the inland parts, but all the vegetation we could see on the clear places was the grass above mentioned.' To find scenes of a similar wintry desolation, we must travel in the north as far as Novaya Zemlya or Spitzbergen, which are 20° or 24° nearer to the pole!

Thus the influence of the cold Antarctic waters extends far within the temperate zone. We can trace their chilling effects in Kerguelen Land (50° S. lat.), which, when visited by Cook in the height of summer, was found covered with snow, and where only five plants in flower were collected; in Tierra del Fuego (53° S. lat.), where the mean summer temperature is fully $9\frac{1}{2}°$ lower than that of Dublin (53° 21' N. lat.); in the Falkland Islands (51° 30'), which, though flat and low and near Patagonia, have, according to Mr. Darwin, a climate similar to that which is experienced at the height of between one and two thousand feet on the mountains of North Wales, with less sunshine and less frost, but more wind and rain; and finally along the south-west coast of America, where the Peruvian current and the cold sea-winds so considerably depress the snow-line, that while in Europe the most southern glacier which comes down to the sea is met with, according to Von Buch, on the coast of Norway in lat. 67°; the 'Beagle' found a glacier 15 miles long and in one part 7 miles broad descending to the sea-coast, in the gulf of Penas, in a latitude (46° 50') nearly corresponding with that of the Lake of Geneva.

'The position of this glacier,' says Mr. Darwin, 'may be put even in a more striking point of view, for it descends to the sea-coast within less than 9° from where palms grow; within 4½° of a region where the jaguar and puma range over the plains, less than 2½° from arborescent grasses, and (looking to the westward in the same hemisphere) less than 2° from orchideous parasites, and within a single degree of tree-ferns!' As the influence of the tropical gulf stream reaches as far as Spitzbergen, so that of the cold Peruvian stream, which issues from the Antarctic Seas, extends even to the equator, and not seldom reduces the temperature of the waters about the Galapagos to less than + 58½°, so that reef-building corals, which require a minimum warmth of + 60°, are unable to grow near islands situated directly under the line.

Though the Antarctic lands are so bleak and inclement that not a single quadruped is to be found within 60° of latitude, yet they are the resort of innumerable sea-birds which, belonging to the same families as those of the north, generally form distinct genera or species, for with rare exceptions no bird is found to inhabit both the Arctic and the Antarctic regions.

Thus in the petrel family we find the fulmar (*Procellaria glacialis*) and the glacial petrel (*P. gelida*) of the high north represented in the Antarctic Seas by the giant petrel (*Procellaria gigantea*), which extends its flight from Patagonia to the ice-banks of the south, where the Antarctic and the snowy petrels (*P. antarctica et nivea*) first appear, cold-loving birds which never leave those dreary waters, and are often seen in vast flocks floating upon the drift-ice.

The giant petrel, which has received from the Spaniards the significant appellation of '*quebranta huesos*,' or 'break-bones,' is a more powerful bird than the fulmar. It is larger than a goose, with a strong beak 4½ inches long. Its colour is a dirty black, white below, and with white spots on the neck and back. In its habits and manner of flight it closely resembles the albatross, and, as with the albatross, a spectator may watch it for hours together without seeing on what it feeds. Like the fulmar it feasts upon fishes, or the carcases of seals and cetaceans, but it also chases other birds. At Port Saint Antonio it was seen by some of the officers of the 'Beagle' pursuing a diver, which tried to escape by diving and flying, but was continually struck down, and at last killed by a blow on its head. Such is its voracity that it does not even spare its own kind, for a gigantic petrel having been badly wounded by a shot from the 'Terror,' and falling at too great a distance for a boat to be sent after it, was immediately attacked by two others of the same kind, and torn to pieces. It is a common bird both in the open sea and in the inland channels of Tierra del Fuego, and the south-west coast of America.

The wandering albatross (*Diomedea exulans*), closely allied to the petrels and rivalling the condor in size and strength of wing, may truly be ranked among the Antarctic birds, as it is seldom seen in a lower latitude than 36°, and increases in numbers towards the south. Freyssinet saw it most frequently between 55° and 59° S. lat., and it probably knows no other limits than those of the Polar ice. It is found in every meridian of this enormous zone, but the regions of storms—the Cape of Good Hope and Cape Horn—are its favourite resorts. Here it may frequently be seen in the full majesty of its flight.

The auks of the northern hemisphere are represented, in the austral regions, by the penguins, who, as Buffon remarks, are the least bird-like of all birds. Their small wing-stumps, covered with short rigid scale-like feathers, are altogether incapable of raising the body in the air, but serve as admirable paddles in the water, and on land as fore-feet, with whose help they so alertly scale the grassy cliffs, that they might easily be mistaken for quadrupeds. Their feet, like those of the auks, are placed so far back that the body is quite upright when the bird is standing on the ground, a position which renders their gait uncommonly slow and awkward, but greatly facilitates their movements

in the water. When at sea and fishing, the penguin comes
to the surface for the purpose of breathing with such a spring,
and dives again so instantaneously, that at first sight no one
can be sure that it is not a fish leaping for sport. Other sea-
birds generally keep a considerable part of their body out of
the water while swimming, but this is not the case with the
penguin, whose head alone appears above the surface, and
thus rowing at the same time with its wings and feet, it
swims so quickly that many fishes would fail to keep up with
it. Sir James Ross once saw two penguins paddling away
a thousand miles from the nearest land. Protected against
the cold by a thick layer of fat and a warm great-coat of
feathers it remains for months on the high seas, and seeks
land only in the summer for the purpose of breeding. At this
time it is found in vast numbers on the Falkland Islands,
Kerguelen's Land, New Shetland, or wherever in the Antarctic Seas, perhaps even to the Pole itself, a convenient coast
invites its stay. On Possession Island, for instance, a
desolate rock, discovered by Sir James Ross in lat. 71° 56',
myriads of penguins covered the whole surface of the land,
along the ledges of the precipices, and even to the summit
of the hills. Undaunted by the presence of beings whom
they had never seen before, the birds vigorously attacked the British seamen as they waded through their
ranks, and pecked at them with their sharp beaks, a reception which, together with their loud coarse notes, and the
insupportable stench of their guano, made our countrymen
but too happy to depart, after having loaded their boat with
geological specimens and penguins. There are several species
of this singular bird. The largest and rarest (*Aptenodytes
Forsteri*) is generally found singly, while the smaller species
always associate in vast numbers. Several were caught in
lat. 77° by Sir James Ross and brought on board alive ; indeed
it was a very difficult and a cruel operation to kill them,
until hydrocyanic acid was resorted to, of which a table-
spoonful effectually accomplished the purpose in less than
a minute. These enormous birds varied in weight from
sixty to seventy-five pounds. They are remarkably stupid,
and allow a man to approach them so near as to strike them
on the head with a bludgeon, and sometimes, if knocked off

the ice into the water, they will almost immediately leap upon it again as if eager for a fight, though without the smallest means either of offence or defence. They were first discovered during Captain Cook's voyage to the Antarctic regions, but Sir James Ross was fortunate in bringing the first perfect specimens to England, some of which were preserved entire in casks of strong pickle, that the physiologist and comparative anatomist might have an opportunity of thoroughly examining their structure. The principal food of the great penguin consists of various species of crustaceous animals, and in its stomach are frequently found from two to ten pounds' weight of pebbles, swallowed no doubt to promote digestion. 'Its capture,' says Sir James Ross, ' afforded great amusement to our people, for when alarmed and endeavouring to escape, it makes its way over deep snow faster than they could follow it: by lying down on its belly and impelling itself by its powerful feet, it slides along upon the surface of the snow at a great pace, steadying itself by extending its fin-like wings, which alternately touch the ground on the side opposite to the propelling leg.'

Though the Antarctic Seas possess neither the narwhal nor the morse, they abound, perhaps even more than the Arctic waters, in whales, dolphins, and seals, at least in the higher latitudes.

The austral smooth-backed whale (*Balæna australis*) differs from his Greenland relative in many respects: the head is comparatively smaller, being only about one-fourth of the total length, the mouth is broader, the baleen shorter, the pectoral fins are larger and pointed, and the colour is almost totally black, the white on the lower surface being confined to a small part of the abdomen. The skull is also differently formed, and while the Greenland whale has only thirteen pairs of ribs, the austral smooth-back has fifteen.

According to Mr. Bennett the austral smooth-back seldom attains a greater length than fifty feet, but as it yields on an average from eighty to ninety barrels of oil, its capture amply rewards the whaler's trouble. Though met with in the highest latitudes, and roaming over the whole extent of the

Antarctic Seas, it resorts in spring to the sheltered bays of New Zealand, Australia, Kerguelen's Land, Chili, the Falkland Islands, Algoa Bay, &c., for the purpose of bringing forth its young. This of course makes its capture easier, but must at the same time lead to its extirpation, or drive it to the most inaccessible regions of the Polar Ocean. Even now the whale fishery of the southern seas, which twenty or thirty years ago employed hundreds of vessels, has much diminished in importance: it is chiefly carried on by the Americans, the French, and our Australian colonies, which

Christmas Harbour, Kerguelen's Land.

have the advantage of being more conveniently situated than the mother country.

In the higher latitudes of the Antarctic zone the hunch-back and fin-back whales abound; but as the former is meagre and hardly worth the boiling, and the latter, like the rorquals of the north, dives with such rapidity that he snaps the harpoon line or drags the boat along with him into the water, they are seldom hunted. Hence they will most likely continue to prosper in their native seas, unless the improved missiles recently introduced in the whale fishery can be made to conquer them. The hunch-back is distinguished by the great length of his pectoral fins, which extend to full eighteen feet, while these organs are comparatively small in the fin-back. A kind of broad-nosed whale likewise makes its appearance in the Antarctic Seas, but it is not yet determined whether all these fin-backed whales of the south are distinct species from those of the Arctic waters. A circumstance which seems to speak for their identity is that fin-backs are met with in the intervening temperate and tropical seas, so that no limits appear to have been set to their excursions.

The sperm whale or cachalot, though partial to the equinoctial ocean, is also found in the cold Antarctic waters. It was met with by Sir James Ross among the icebergs in 63° 20′ S. lat.; and near Possession Island (71° 50′ S. lat.), where the hunch-backs were so abundant that thirty were counted at one time in various directions, and during the whole day wherever the eyes turned, their blasts were to be seen. A few sperm whales were also distinguished among them by their peculiar manner of blowing or spouting.

Among the dolphins of the Antarctic Ocean we find a species of grampus no less formidable and voracious than that of the northern seas. On January 20, 1840, the American ship ' Peacock,' while cruising in the Antarctic waters, witnessed a conflict between one of them and a whale. The sea was perfectly smooth, so that the whole combat could be distinctly seen. At first the whale was perceived at some distance from the ship lashing the water into foam and apparently making desperate efforts to shake off some invisible enemy. On approaching they found that an enormous grampus had seized it with its jaws. The whale vainly turned and twisted itself in every direction, and its blood tinged the water far around. The grampus had evidently the advantage, and the other whales, of which there were many in sight, instead of assisting their comrade, seemed only intent on their own safety. The grampus had a brown back, a white abdomen, and a large fin on its back. The speed at which the monstrous animals shot through the water prevented the Americans from witnessing the issue of the fight. The classical dolphin of the

ancients has been seen near the Cape of Good Hope, and
most likely wanders far to the south as he is proverbial for
his arrow-like rapidity, and can easily traverse a couple of
hundred miles in a single day.   In the Strait of Magellan
and about Cape Horn are frequently seen the *Delphinus super-
ciliosus*, whose turned-up mouth-corners give his countenance a peculiarly benevolent and friendly expression, belied
by his ravenous propensities, and the *Delphinus leucoramphus*,
who, like the bjeluga of the north, has no dorsal fin, and by
the liveliness of his movements emulates the classical dolphin
of the Mediterranean.

The seal family plays a no less important part in the zoology of the Antarctic Seas than in that of the northern waters.
Here we find the monstrous sea-elephant (*Macrorhinus ele-
phantinus*), so called not only from his size attaining a length
of twenty-five feet, and a girth at the largest part of the
body of from fifteen to eighteen, but also from the singular
structure of his elongated nostrils, which hang down when
he is in a state of repose, but swell out to a proboscis a foot
long when he is enraged.   This gives the animal a very formidable appearance, which along with his bellowing and his
widely-gaping jaws armed with tusk-like canines, might strike
terror into the boldest heart.   But in reality the sea elephant
is a most defenceless creature, for on land it moves its unwieldy carcase with the utmost difficulty, and a single blow
upon the snout with a club suffices to stretch it lifeless on the
ground.   It used to be met with in considerable numbers on all
the flat shores or islands between 35° and 62° S. lat., but as it
yields a large quantity of excellent oil, and as its skin, though
merely covered with thick short bristles, is of some value from
its great strength and thickness, incessant persecution has
greatly thinned its ranks, and in some parts extirpated it.
Thus Sir James Ross relates that the sea-elephant and several
other species of seals, which were formerly in great abundance
at Kerguelen's Land, annually drew a number of fishing-ves-
sels to its shores.   But at the time of his visit (1840), after so
many years of slaughter, they had quite deserted the place.
The flesh of the sea-elephant is black and of an oily taste,
but Anson and his companions, after having been tossed about
for several months on a tempestuous sea and reduced to great

distress by scurvy, relished it at Juan Fernandez. The tongue is said to be a great delicacy.

As the soft jet-black fur of the young southern sea-bear (*Arctocephalus falclandicus*) is no less valuable than that of its northern relative, the eagerness with which it is pursued may easily be imagined. Formerly vast herds of sea-bears used to resort every summer to the New Shetland Islands, but soon after the re-discovery of the group the American and English sealers made their appearance on its desolate shores, and in the short time of four years extirpated the ursine seals, thus destroying by wasteful destruction what might have been a permanent source of profit.

The southern sea-lion (*Otaria jubata*) is a larger animal than his northern namesake, and while the latter is furnished only with an erect and curly hair-tuft at the neck, a complete mane flows round his breast. The remainder of the tawny body is covered with short smooth hairs or bristles. The sea-lioness, who is much smaller than her mate, has no mane, and, as she is of a darker colour and has a differently shaped head, is frequently mistaken for another species, and called wolf or *lobo* by the inhabitants of the south-western coast of America. The fore-flippers of the sea-lion have the appearance of large pieces of black tough leather, showing, instead of nails, slight horny elevations; the hind-fins, which are likewise black, have a closer resemblance to feet, and the five toes are furnished with small nails. It is a formidable looking beast, particularly when full grown to a length of ten feet and more. The sea-leopard (*Leptonyx Weddellii*), which owes its name to its spotted skin, is peculiar to the southern seas. This large seal is from eight to nine feet long, the hind feet have no nails, and greatly resemble the tail of a fish.

The Antarctic seals, dolphins, and petrels chiefly prey upon a genus of fish discovered at Kerguelen's Land, and named Notothenia, by Dr. Richardson. These fish, which are of an elongated eel-like shape, conceal themselves from the persecutions of their enemies in the small cracks and cavities of the pack-ice, and were frequently noticed by Sir James Ross, when driven from shelter by the ship as it struck and passed over their protecting pieces of ice. They, in their turn, live upon the smaller cancri and limacinæ, and these again upon creatures of a still more diminutive size, until finally the chain of created beings terminates in the diatoms,* which are found filling these seas with the minutest forms of organic life.

\* 'The Sea and its Living Wonders,' p. 403.

Sperm Whale.

Mount Minto.

# CHAPTER XXXVII.

### ANTARCTIC VOYAGES OF DISCOVERY.

Cook's Discoveries in the Antarctic Ocean—Bellinghausen—Weddell—Biscoe—
Balleny—Dumont d'Urville—Wilkes—Sir James Ross crosses the Antarctic
Circle on New Year's Day, 1841—Discovers Victoria Land—Dangerous Landing
on Franklin Island—An Eruption of Mount Erebus—The Great Ice Barrier—
Providential Escape—Dreadful Gale—Collision—Hazardous Passage between
Two Icebergs—Termination of the Voyage.

BEFORE Cook, no navigator had left Europe with the
clear design of penetrating into the Antarctic regions.
Dirk Gheritz, indeed, had been driven by a furious storm far
to the south of Cape Horn, and became the involuntary discoverer of the New Shetland Islands in 1600; but his voyage
was soon forgotten, and in an age where the love of gold or
the desire of conquest were the sole promoters of maritime
enterprise, no mariner felt inclined to follow on his track, and
to plunge into a sea where, most probably, he would find
nothing but ice-fields and icebergs to reward his efforts.
Nearly two centuries later, a more scientific age directed its
attention to the unknown regions of the distant south, and

Cook sailed forth to probe the secrets of the Antarctic Seas. This dangerous task he executed with an intrepidity un-paralleled in the annals of navigation. Beyond 60° of southern latitude, he cruised over a space of more than 100° of longitude, and on January 30, 1774, penetrated as far as 71° of southern latitude, where he was stopped by impene-trable masses of ice. Such were the difficulties encountered from dense fogs, snow-storms, intense cold, and everything that can render navigation dangerous, that in his opinion the lands situated to the southward of his discoveries must for ever remain unknown.

Again, for many a year, no one attempted to enter a field where the most celebrated of modern mariners had found but a few desert islands (South Georgia, Sandwich's Land, Southern Thule) until Smith's casual re-discovery of New South Shetland in 1819 once more turned the current of maritime exploration to the Antarctic Seas.

Soon afterwards a Russian expedition under Lazareff and Bellinghausen discovered (January, 1821), in 69° 3′ S. lat., the islands Paul the First and Alexander, the most southern lands that had ever been visited by man.

The year after, Captain Weddell, a sealer, penetrated into the icy ocean as far as 74° 15′ S. lat., 3° nearer to the Pole than had been attained by Cook. The sea lay invitingly open, but as the season was far advanced, and Weddell apprehended the dangers of the return voyage, he steered again to the north.

In 1831 Biscoe discovered Enderby Land, and soon after-wards Graham's Land, to which the gratitude of geographers has since given the discoverer's name. In 1839, Balleny revealed the existence of the group of islands called after him, and of Sabrina Land (69° S. lat.). About the same time, three considerable expeditions fitted out by the govern-ments of France, the United States, and England, made their appearance in the Antarctic Seas.

Dumont d'Urville discovered Terre Louis Philippe (63° 31′ S. lat.) in February, 1838, and Terre Adélie (66° 67′ S. lat.) on January 21, 1840. Almost on the same day, Wilkes, the com-mander of the United States Exploring Expedition, reached an ice-bound coast, which he followed for a length of 1,500

miles, and which has been called Wilkes' Land, to commemorate the discoverer's name.

But of all the explorers of the southern frozen ocean, the
palm unquestionably belongs to Sir James Ross, who penetrated farther towards the Pole than any other navigator
before or after, and made the only discoveries of extensive
land within the area bounded by the Antarctic Circle.

On New Year's Day, 1841, the 'Erebus,' Captain James
Clark Ross, and the 'Terror,' commanded by Francis Crozier,
who died with Franklin in the Arctic Sea, crossed the Antarctic Circle, and after sustaining many severe shocks in
breaking through the pack-ice, emerged, on January 9, into
a clear sea of great extent; but the fog and snow-showers
were so thick, that the navigators could seldom see more
than half a mile before them.  On the following day the fog
began to disperse, and on the 11th, Victoria land, rising in
lofty peaks entirely covered with perennial snow, was seen
at a distance of more than one hundred miles.  On steering
towards Mount Sabine, the highest mountain of the range,
new chains of hills were seen extending to the right and
left.  After sailing for a few days to the south, along the ice-
bound coast, a gale forced the ships to stand out to sea; but
on the morning of January 15, the weather, becoming beautifully clear, allowed a full view of a magnificent chain of
mountains, stretching far away to the southward.  Ross was
most anxious to find a harbour in which to secure the ships,
but every indentation of the coast was found filled with snow
drifted from the mountains, and forming a mass of ice several
hundred feet thick.  It was thus impossible to enter any of
the valleys or breaks in the coast where harbours in other
lands usually occur.  Yet these inhospitable shores (72° 73'
S. lat.) are situated but one or two degrees nearer to the
Pole than Hammerfest, the seat of an active commerce on
the Norwegian coast.

Favoured by northerly winds and an open sea, the ships
reached, on January 22, a higher southern latitude (74° 20' S.)
than that which had been attained by Weddell.  Pursuing
their way to the southward, along the edge of the pack-
ice, which now compelled them to keep at a considerable
distance from the coast, they came, on the 27th, within

two or three miles of a small island, connected by a vast ice-field with the extreme point of the main land. Eager to set his foot on the most southerly soil (76° 8′ S.) he had as yet discovered, Ross left the 'Erebus,' accompanied by several officers, and followed by Crozier and a party from the 'Terror,' pulled towards the shore. A high southerly swell broke so heavily against the cliffs, and on the only piece of beach which they could see as they rowed from one end of the island to the other, as almost to forbid their landing.

By great skill and management Ross succeeded in jumping on to the rocks. By means of a rope some of the officers landed somewhat more easily, but not without getting thoroughly wetted, and one of them nearly lost his life in this difficult affair. The thermometer being at 22°, every part of the rocks washed by the waves was covered with a coating of ice, so that in jumping from the boat he slipped from them into the water between her stern and the almost perpendicular rock on which his companions had landed. But for the promptitude of the men in the boat in instantly pulling off, he must have been crushed between it and the rock. He was taken into the boat without having suffered any other injury than being benumbed by the cold.

The island, which received the name of Franklin, bore not the smallest trace of vegetation, not even a lichen or piece of sea-weed growing on the rocks; but the white petrel and the skua-gull had their nests on the ledges of the cliffs, and seals were seen sporting in the water.

The following day was memorable for the discovery of the southernmost known land of the globe, a magnificent mountain chain, to which the name of Parry was given, in grateful remembrance of the honour which that illustrious navigator had conferred on Ross, by calling the most northern land at that time known by his name. It is not often that men are able to reciprocate such compliments as these! The most conspicuous object of the chain was Mount Erebus (77° 5′ S.), an active volcano, of which Ross had the good fortune to witness a magnificent eruption. The enormous columns of flame and smoke rising two thousand feet above the mouth of the crater, which is elevated

12,400 feet above the level of the sea, combined, with the snow-white mountain-chain and the deep blue ocean, to form a magnificent scene. An extinct volcano to the eastward of Mount Erebus, and little inferior in height, being by measurement 10,900 feet high, was called 'Mount Terror.' A brilliant mantle of snow swept down the sides of both these giants of the south, and projected a perpendicular icy cliff several miles into the sea.

Gladly would Ross have penetrated still further to the south, but all his efforts were baffled by a vast barrier of ice, forming an uninterrupted wall, 450 miles in length, and rising in some parts to a height of 180 feet above the sea-level. While sailing along this barrier, the ships were frequently obliged by the wind and the closely packed ice to keep at a considerable distance; but on February 9, having entered the only indentation which they had perceived throughout its whole extent, they had an excellent opportunity of getting quite close to it, though at no little hazard. This bay was formed by a projecting peninsula of ice, terminated by a cape 170 feet high, but at the narrow isthmus which connected it with the great barrier, it was not more than fifty feet high, affording Ross the only opportunity he had of seeing its upper surface from the masthead. It appeared to be quite smooth, and conveyed to the mind the idea of an immense plain of frosted silver. Gigantic icicles depended from every projecting point of its perpendicular cliffs, proving that it sometimes thawed, which otherwise could not have been believed, for at a season of the year equivalent to August in England, the thermometer at noon did not rise above 14°, and the young ice formed so quickly in the sheltered bay as to warn them of the necessity of a speedy retreat. Favoured by the breeze, and by dint of great exertion, they ultimately emerged from their dangerous position, but scarcely had they escaped when the wind came directly against them, so that had they lingered but half an hour longer near the barrier they would certainly have been frozen up.

On February 13 the approach of winter convinced Ross that it was high time to relinquish the further examination of the barrier to the eastward, and as no place of security

where it was possible to winter could be found upon any
part of the land hitherto discovered, he reluctantly resolved
to recross the Antarctic Circle, and postpone all attempts to
reach the Pole to the next season. The return voyage was
difficult and dangerous. On March 7, the ships, while endeavouring to find a way through the pack-ice in lat. 65°,
had a narrow escape from imminent destruction. The wind
having ceased, they found themselves at the mercy of a
heavy easterly swell, which was driving them down upon
the pack, in which were counted from the masthead eighty-
four large bergs, and some hundreds of smaller size. As
they rapidly approached this formidable chain, no opening
could be discovered through which the ships could pass; the
waves were beating violently against the bergs, and dashing
huge masses of pack-ice against their precipitous faces, now
lifting them nearly to their summit, then forcing them again
far beneath their water line, and sometimes rending them in
a multitude of brilliant fragments against their projecting
points. 'Sublime and magnificent,' says Ross,* 'as such a
scene must have appeared under different circumstances, to
us it was awful, if not appalling. For eight hours we had
been gradually drifting towards what to human eyes appeared inevitable destruction; the high waves and deep rolling of our ships rendered towing with the boats impossible,
and our situation the more painful and embarrassing from
our inability to make any effort to avoid the dreadful cala-
mity that seemed to await us. . . . . . We were now
within half a mile of the range of bergs. The roar of the
surf, which extended each way as far as we could see, and
the crashing of the ice, fell upon the ear with fearful dis-
tinctness, whilst the frequently averted eye as immediately
returned to contemplate the awful destruction that threatened in one short hour to close the world, and all its hopes,
and joys, and sorrows upon us for ever. In this our deep
distress "we called upon the Lord, and He heard our voices
out of His temple, and our cry came before Him." A gentle
air of wind filled our sails; hope again revived, and the
greatest activity prevailed to make the best use of the feeble

* 'Voyage to the Southern Seas,' vol. i. p. 282.

breeze; as it gradually freshened, our heavy ships began to feel its influence, slowly at first, but more rapidly afterwards, and before dark we found ourselves far removed from every danger.'

After passing the winter at Hobarton, the capital of Tasmania, Sir James Ross, in the following year, once more crossed the Antarctic Circle to examine the icy barrier which in his previous voyage had blocked his progress to the south, and to renew his attempts to pass round or through it. But there were new dangers to be encountered. On January 17, 1842, a fearful storm came on as the 'Erebus' and 'Terror' were making their way through the pack-ice, which was this time met with in a more northern latitude than the year before. The sea broke all the hawsers which held them to a large piece of floe, and drove them helplessly along into the heavy pack. They were now involved in an ocean of rolling fragments of ice, which were dashed against them by the waves with so much violence that their masts quivered as if they would fall at every successive blow. The loud crashing noise of the straining and working of the timbers and decks, as they were driven against some of the heavier pieces, might well appal the stoutest heart, and thus hour passed away after hour. During this terrible scene the ships were at one time so close together that, when the 'Terror' rose to the top of one wave, the 'Erebus' was on the top of the wave next to leeward of her, the deep chasm between them being filled with heavy rolling masses; and as the ships descended into the hollow between the waves, the maintopsail-yard of each could be seen, just level with the crest of the intervening wave, from the deck of the other. The night, which now began to draw in, rendered their condition, if possible, more hopeless and helpless than before; but at midnight the snow, which had been falling thickly for several hours, cleared away, as the wind suddenly shifted to the westward; the swell began to subside, and the shocks which the ships still sustained, though strong enough to shatter any vessel less strongly ribbed, were feeble compared with those to which they had been exposed. On the following day, the wind having moderated to a fresh breeze, the crippled ships, whose rudders had been sorely shattered, were securely moored to a large floe-piece in the now almost motionless pack, where, by dint of unceasing labour, the damages were repaired in the course of a week, and the vessels once more fitted to fight their way to the south.

On February 22, the great barrier was seen from the masthead, just before midnight, and the following day, the wind blowing directly on to its cliffs, they approached it within a mile and a half, in lat. 78° 11′, the highest ever attained in the southern hemisphere. From this point, situated about 5° of longitude farther to the east than the indentation where the ships had so narrowly escaped being frozen fast in the preceding year, the barrier trended considerably to the northward of east, so that Ross was obliged to give up all hope of rounding it, and extending his explorations towards the Pole, as the season was already considerably advanced. On his return voyage to the Falklands, where he intended to pass the winter, he had already reached the latitude of 60°, and thought himself out of danger of meeting with bergs, when, in the afternoon of March 12, the southerly wind changed to a strong north-westerly breeze. In the evening the wind increased so much, and the snow-showers became so incessant, that he was obliged to proceed under more moderate sail. Small pieces of ice were also met with, warning him of the presence of bergs, concealed by the thickly falling snow, so that before midnight he directed the topsails of the 'Erebus' to be close-reefed, and every arrangement made for rounding to until daylight, deeming it too hazardous to run any longer. 'Our people,' says the gallant explorer, 'had hardly completed these operations, when a large berg was seen ahead and quite close; the ship was immediately hauled to the wind on the port tack, with the expectation of being able to weather it; but just at this moment the "Terror" was observed running down upon us, under her topsail and foresail; and as it was impossible for her to clear both the berg and the "Erebus," collision was inevitable. We instantly hove all aback to diminish the violence of the shock; but the concussion, when she struck us was such as to throw almost every one off his feet; our bowsprit, foretopmast, and other smaller spars, were carried away, and the ships hanging together entangled by their rigging, and dashing against each other with fearful violence, were falling down upon the weather face of the lofty berg under our lee, against which the waves were breaking and foaming to near the summit of its perpendicular cliffs. Sometimes the "Terror" rose high above us, almost exposing her keel to view, and again descended, as we in our turn rose to the top of the wave, threatening to bury her beneath us, whilst the crashing of the breaking upper-works and boats increased the horror of the scene.  Providentially the ships gradually separated before we drifted down amongst the foaming breakers, and we had the gratification of seeing the "Terror" clear the end of the berg, and of feeling that she was safe.  But she left us completely disabled; the wreck of the spars so encumbered the lower yard, that we were unable to make sail, so as to get headway on the ship; nor had we room to wear round, being by this time so close to the berg that the waves, when they struck against it, threw back their spray into the ship.  The only way left to us to extricate ourselves from this awful and appalling situation, was by resorting to the hazardous expedient of a stern board, which nothing could justify during such a gale but to avert the danger which every moment threatened us of being dashed to pieces.  The heavy rolling of the vessel, and the probability of the masts giving way, each time the lower yard-arms struck against the cliffs, which were towering high above our mast-heads, rendered it a service of extreme danger to loose the mainsail; but no sooner was the order given, than the daring spirit of the British seaman manifested itself—the men ran up the rigging with as much alacrity as on any ordinary occasion; and, although more than once driven off the yard, they after a short time succeeded in loosing the sail. Amidst the roar of the wind and sea, it was difficult both to hear and to execute the orders that were given, so that it was three-quarters of an hour before we could get the yards braced by, and the maintack hauled on board sharp aback —an expedient that perhaps had never before been resorted to by seamen in such weather; but it had the desired effect; the ship gathered sternway, plunging her stern into the sea, and with her lower yard-arms scraping the rugged face of the berg, we in a few minutes reached its western termination; the " under-tow," as it is called, or the reaction of the water from its vertical cliffs, alone preventing us being driven to atoms against it. No sooner had we cleared it than another was seen directly astern of us, against which we were running; and the difficulty now was to get the ship's head turned round and pointed fairly through between the two bergs, the breadth of the intervening space not exceeding three times her own breadth. This, however, we happily accomplished; and in a few minutes, after getting before the wind, she dashed through the narrow channel between two perpendicular walls of ice, and the foaming breakers which stretched across it, and the next moment we were in smooth water, under its lee. The " Terror's " light was immediately seen and answered; she had rounded to waiting for us . . . . , and, as soon as day broke, we had the gratification of learning that she had not suffered any serious damage.'

On December 17, Sir James Ross sailed from the Falkland Islands with the intention of following the track of Weddell, as, from the account of that daring navigator, he had every reason to expect to find a clear sea, which would enable him considerably to extend the limits of geographical knowledge towards the Pole. He was disappointed, for though he discovered some new land (63°—64° 30′ S. lat., 55°—57° W. long.) to the south of D'Urville's Terre Louis Philippe, yet the pack-ice so blocked his progress, that the farthest point he could attain was in lat. 71° 30′ S., long. 14° 51′ W. On March 1 he recrossed the Antarctic Circle, and on the 28th of the same month dropped his anchors at the Cape. Thus ended this most remarkable voyage, so honourable to all engaged in it, for, as Sir John Richardson justly remarks, ' the perseverance, daring, and coolness of the commanding officer, of the other officers, and of the crews of the " Erebus " and " Terror " was never surpassed, and have been rarely, if ever, equalled by seamen of any nation.'

Since then the ' Pagoda,' which had been sent out by the Admiralty for the purpose of observing magnetic phenomena in a quarter of the Antarctic Seas that had not been visited by Sir James Ross, attained the 73rd parallel, but no more recent expedition has been fitted out to prosecute his discoveries, and no man after him has seen Mount Erebus vomiting forth its torrents of flame, or traced the stupendous barrier which stopped his progress to the Pole.

The Sea-Elephant.

Strait of Magellan.
(From an original sketch by Frederick Whymper.)

# CHAPTER XXXVIII.

## THE STRAIT OF MAGELLAN.

Description of the Strait—Western Entrance—Point Dungeness—The Narrows—
Saint Philip's Bay—Cape Froward—Grand Scenery—Port Famine—The Sedger
River—Darwin's Ascent of Mount Tarn — The Bachelor River — English
Reach—Sea Reach—South Desolation—Harbour of Mercy—Williwaws—Dis-
covery of the Strait by Magellan (October 20, 1521)—Drake—Sarmiento—
Cavendish — Schouten and Le Maire — Byron — Bougainville — Wallis and
Carteret—King and Fitzroy—Settlement at Punta Arenas—Increasing Passage
through the Strait—A future Highway of Commerce.

THE celebrated strait which bears the name of Magellan,
is generally pictured as the scene of a wild and dreary
desolation; but though its climate is far from being genial,
and its skies are often veiled with mists and rain, yet nature
can smile even here.

A glance at the map shows us the extreme irregularity
of its formation, as it is constantly changing in width and
direction; now swelling almost to the magnitude of a Medi-

terranean Sea, and then again contracting to a narrow passage; sometimes taking a rapid turn to the north, and at others as suddenly deviating to the south.   Islands and islets of every form—some mere naked rocks, others clothed with umbrageous woods—are scattered over its surface; promontories without number, from the Patagonian mainland or the Fuegian archipelago, protrude their bold fronts into its bosom, as if with the intention of closing it altogether; and countless bays and havens are scooped into its rocky shores, as if the sea in a thousand different places had striven to open a new passage to her waters.

The western entrance of this remarkable strait is formed by Queen Catherine's Foreland (Cape Virgins) and Point Dungeness, the latter having been thus named from its resemblance to the well known Kentish promontory at the eastern mouth of the channel.   Although it rises at most nine feet above low-water mark, the snow-white breakers which the tides are constantly dashing over its sides, render it visible from a great distance.   It is generally the resort of a number of sea-lions.   When the wind comes blowing from the north-east, the passing mariner—who, from the shallow nature of the shore, is obliged to keep at some distance from the Ness—hears their hoarse bellowing, which harmonises well with the wild and desolate character of the scene. Albatrosses and petrels hover about them, while rows of grave-looking penguins seem to contemplate their doings with philosophic indifference.

Beyond these promontories, the strait widens into Possession Bay, which at Punta Delgada and Cape Orange contracts to a narrow passage.   This leads into a wide basin, to which the Spaniards have given the name of Saint Philip's Bay, and which again terminates in a second narrow passage or channel, a formation resembling on a small scale the Sea of Marmora, which, as we all know, has likewise the semblance of a lake, receiving and discharging its waters through the Dardanelles and the Strait of Constantinople. During the rising of the flood, a strong current flows through all these bays and narrows from the west, so as to allow ships an easy passage, even against the wind; but during

ebb tide, the current turns to the east, so that at this time
a vessel, even when favoured by the wind, makes but little
progress, or is even obliged to anchor to avoid losing ground.
When Magellan, after sailing round Cape Virgins, penetrated into the strait, this circumstance at once convinced
that great navigator that he was not in an enclosed bay, but
in an open channel, which would lead him into another
ocean. Thus far the country on both sides of the strait
consists of nearly level plains, like those of Patagonia; but
beyond the second Narrows, the land begins to assume the
more bold and picturesque appearance which is characteristic of Tierra del Fuego. Mountains rise above mountains
with deep intervening valleys, all covered by one thick,
dusky mass of forest; while further to the east, scarcely a
bush clothes the naked soil. The trees reach to an elevation
of between 1,000 and 1,500 feet, and are succeeded by a band
of peat, with minute Alpine plants, and this again is succeeded
by the line of perpetual snow, which, according to Captain
King, descends to between 3,000 and 4,000 feet.

The finest scenery about the Strait of Magellan is undoubtedly to the east of Cape Froward, the most southerly
point of the mainland of South America. This promontory,
which consists of a steep mass of rock about 800 feet high,
abutting from a mountain chain of about 2,000 or 3,000 feet
in height, forms the boundary between two very different
climates, for to the east the weather is finer and more agreeable than to the west, where wind and rain are almost perpetual.

On the Patagonian plains, the drought and the want of
protection against the piercing winds almost entirely impede
vegetation; but the country between Cape Negro—a little
within the second Narrows—and Cape Froward, or the
eastern shore of Brunswick peninsula, is shielded by its situation against the almost perpetual storms from the west, and
enjoys, moreover, a sufficiency of rain, and now and then
serene weather. As, moreover, the soil in this central part
of the strait consists of disintegrated clay-slate, which is
most favourable to the growth of trees, the forests, from all
these causes, are finer here than anywhere else.

The country about Port Famine is particularly distin-

guished for the richness of its vegetation, and both for this
reason, and from its central situation, this harbour has become a kind of chief station for the ships that pass through
the strait. Several unfortunate attempts at colonisation
have been made at Port Famine; here many a naturalist
has tarried, and thus no part of the strait has been oftener
described, or more accurately observed.

'The anchorage,' says Dumont d'Urville, who, in December,
1837, spent several days at Port Famine, 'is excellent, and
landing everywhere easy. A fine rivulet gives us excellent
water, and the neighbouring forests might furnish whole
fleets with the necessary fuel. The cliffs along the shore are
literally covered with mussels, limpets, and whelks, which
afford a delicious variety of fare to a crew tired of salt beef
and peas. Among the plants I noticed with pleasure a species
of celery, which, with another herb resembling our corn flower
in form and taste, gives promise of an excellent salad.

'I made use of my first leisure to visit the romantic banks
of the Sedger River, which discharges its waters on the
western side of the port. At its mouth the swampy strand
is completely covered with enormous trees heaped upon the
ground. These naked giants, stripped of their branches,
afford a remarkable spectacle : they might be taken for huge
bones bleached by time. No doubt they are transported
from the neighbouring forest by the waters of the river,
which, when it overflows its banks, after a deluge of rain,
tears along with it the trees it meets with in its course.
Arrested by the bar at the mouth of the stream, they are
cast out upon its banks, where they remain when the waters
sink to their usual level.

'Having crossed the river, I entered the large and fine
forest with which it is bordered. The chief tree is the
Antarctic beech (*Fagus betuloides*) which is often from 60 to
90 feet high, and about 3 feet in diameter. Along with this
are two other trees, the winter's bark (*Winteria aromatica*)
and a species of berberis, with a very solid wood; but they
are much less abundant, and of a much smaller size. With
the exception of mosses, lichens, and other plants of this
order, these forests afford but little that is interesting to the
naturalist—no quadrupeds, no reptiles, no land-snails; a few

insects and some birds are the only specimens to be gained
after a long search.  After collecting a good supply of mosses
and lichens, I returned to the boat for the purpose of rowing
up the river.  Although the current was tolerably rapid, we
advanced about two miles, admiring the beauty of its umbrageous banks.   On my return I shot two geese that were
crossing the river over our heads, and whose excellent meat
amply supplied my table for several days.  This, together
with the little gobies which were abundantly caught with
hand-lines, the large mussels we detached from the rocks,
and the celery salad, gave me dinners fit for an alderman.
How often since have I regretted the plenty of Port Famine!'

In the month of February (1834), in the height of the
Antarctic summer, Mr. Darwin ascended Mount Tarn, which
is 2,600 feet high, and the most elevated point in the vicinity
of Port Famine.  'The forest,' says our great naturalist,
'commences at the line of high-water mark, and during the
first two hours I gave over all hopes of reaching the summit.
So thick was the wood, that it was necessary to have constant
recourse to the compass, for every landmark, though in a
mountainous country, was completely shut out.   In the deep
ravines, the death-like scene of desolation exceeded all
description; outside it was blowing a gale, but in these
hollows not even a breath of wind stirred the leaves of the
tallest trees.  So gloomy, cold, and wet was every part, that
not even the fungi, mosses, or ferns could flourish.  In the
valleys it was scarcely possible to crawl along, they were
so completely barricaded by great mouldering trunks, which
had fallen down in every direction.  When passing over
these natural bridges, one's course was often arrested by
sinking knee-deep into the rotten wood; at other times,
when attempting to lean against a tree, one was startled
by finding a mass of decayed matter, ready to fall at the
slightest touch.  We at last found ourselves among the
stunted trees, and then soon reached the bare ridge, which
conducted us to the summit.  Here was a view characteristic
of Tierra del Fuego; irregular chains of hills, mottled with
patches of snow, deep yellowish-green valleys, and arms of
the sea, intersecting the land in many directions.  The
strong wind was piercingly cold, and the atmosphere rather

hazy, so that we did not stay long on the top of the mountain. Our descent was not quite so laborious as our ascent; for the weight of the body forced a passage, and all the slips and falls were in the right direction.'

To the west of Cape Froward, the strait extends in a north-westerly, almost rectilinear direction, until it finally opens into the Pacific, between Cape Pillar and Cape Victory. Here a day rarely passes without rain, hail, or snow. Where the dreadful power of the prevailing winds has free play, the mountain sides are naked and bare, but in every sheltered nook the damp climate produces a luxuriant vegetation. The trees, however, do not attain any great height, and at Port Gallant, the beech is already decidedly stunted in its growth. This is no doubt caused by the excessive humidity of the soil, which in all lower situations is converted by the continual rains into a deep morass. The trunks and the branches are covered with a thick layer of moss, and the tree becomes rotten in its youth. But many shrubs, herbs, and mosses thrive under the perpetual deluge; the latter particularly, covering large patches of ground with a spongy carpet. It may easily be imagined how difficult, or rather impossible it must be to penetrate into the interior of such a country. Yet even these wild inhospitable regions can boast of many a romantic scene. Thus the English Reach, which extends from Cape Froward to Carlos Island, is bounded on both sides by lofty mountains, their cones or jagged peaks covered with eternal snow. Its southern bank, formed by Clarence Island, is intersected with bays and channels, two of which, Magdalena Sound and Barbara Channel, lead through a maze of islands into the open sea. Several glaciers descend in a winding course from the upper great expanse of snow to the sea coast, and many a cascade comes dashing down from rock to rock. Skogman * draws an enthusiastic picture of the beauty of York Roads, near the mouth of the small Bachelor River. To the south, behind Carlos Island, mountains rise above mountains, and snow-fields above snow-fields; to the north, lies the jagged colossus, which from its solitary grandeur has been called Bachelor Peak, and at whose foot the crystal river now hides itself beneath a shady

* Voyage of the Swedish ship 'Eugénie.'

-wood, and now rolls its crystal waters through a green lawn, decorated with clumps of fuchsias. But in spite of its romantic beauty, the want of life gives a melancholy character to this solitary vale. Beyond Carlos Island in Long Reach, the banks of the strait become yet more bare and desolate. Vegetation descends lower and lower into the valleys, and even here the trees are misshapen and dwarfish. But the mountain scenery has still all the majesty which snow-fields and glaciers of a beryl-like blue impart to an Alpine landscape. As Sea Reach shows itself, vegetation is almost totally extinct, and on approaching the mouth of the strait, the mountains become lower, their forms are less picturesque, and instead of the stern grandeur which marks the middle part of the strait, low, rounded, barren hills make their appearance, which completely justify the name of South Desolation, which Sir James Narborough gave to this coast, 'because it was so desolate a land to behold.'

It may easily be imagined that the prevailing winds beyond Cape Froward are extremely troublesome to ships sailing to the western mouth of the strait, and that if not entirely beaten back, they can frequently only force the passage after many efforts. Fortunately, the deeply indented coasts possess a number of small havens which may serve the mariner as stations during his gradual advance. Thus, close to the mouth of the strait, where, between Cape Victory and Cape Pillar, the sea during and after storms is so boisterous that even steamers require their utmost strength not to be dashed against the rocks, a secure port, appropriately called 'Harbour of Mercy,' allows the vessels to watch for more tranquil weather, and to seize the first favourable opportunity for emerging into the open sea. But even these harbours and bays are subject to peculiar dangers from sudden gusts of wind that come sweeping down from the mountains, and are known among the seal catchers who frequent these dangerous waters under the name of *williwaws*, or hurricane squalls. For when the wild south-west storms come rushing against the mountain-masses of Tierra del Fuego, the compressed air precipitates itself with redoubled violence over the rock-walls, and then suddenly expanding, flows down the valleys or gullies, tearing up trees by the roots, and hurling rocks into the abyss. Where such a gust of wind touches the surface of the water, the sea surges in mighty waves, and volumes of spray are whirled away to a vast distance. If a ship comes under its influence, its safety depends mainly upon the strength of its anchor ropes.

Some situations are particularly subject to williwaws, and then the total want of vegetation and the evident marks of ruin along the mountain slopes warn the mariner to avoid the neighbourhood. In Gabriel Channel, Captain King saw a spot where the williwaws, bursting over the mountains on the south side, had swept down the declivities, and then rushing against the foot of the opposite hills had again dashed upwards with such fury as to carry away with them everything that could possibly be detached from the bare rock.

It was a memorable day in the annals of maritime discovery (October 20, 1521) when Magellan reached the eastern entrance of the strait that was to lead him, first of all European navigators, from the broad basin of the Atlantic into the still wider expanse of the Pacific Ocean. It was the day dedicated in the Catholic calendar to St. Ursula and her eleven thousand virgins, and he consequently named the promontory which first struck his view, 'Cabo de las Virgines.' The flood-tide streaming violently to the west convinced him that he was at the mouth of an open channel, but he had scarcely provisions for three months—a short allowance for venturing into an unknown world, and thus before he attempted the passage he convoked a council of all his officers. Some were for an immediate return to Europe, but the majority voted for the continuation of the voyage, and Magellan declared that should they even be reduced to eat the leather of their shoes he would persevere to the last, and with God's assistance execute the commands of his imperial master Charles V. He then at once gave orders to enter the strait full sail, and on pain of death forbade any one to say a word more about a return, or the want of provisions.

Fortunately the winds were in his favour, for had the usual inclemencies of this stormy region opposed him, there is no doubt that with such crazy vessels, and such discontented crews, all his heroism would have failed to ensure success. It was the spring of the southern hemisphere, and the strait showed itself in one of its rare aspects of calm. Many fish were caught, and, as Pigafetti, the historian of the voyage, relates, the aromatic winter's bark which served them for fuel 'wonderfully refreshed and invigorated their spirits.'

The fires kindled by the savages on the southern side during the night induced Magellan to give that part of the country the name of Tierra del Fuego, or Fireland; while from their high stature and bulky frames, he called the inhabitants of the opposite mainland, Patagonians (patagon being the Spanish augmentative of pata, foot).

Although several days were lost in exploring some of the numerous passages and bays of the straits, its eastern mouth was reached on November 28, and Magellan saw the wide Pacific expand before him.

In 1525, Charles V. sent out a new expedition of six vessels, under Garcia de Loaisa, to circumnavigate the globe. The vice-admiral of the squadron was Sebastian el Cano, who, after the death of Magellan, had brought the illustrious navigator's ship safely back to Europe, and as a reward had been ennobled with the globe in his coat of arms, and the motto, 'Primus circumdedisti me.'

Loaisa entered the strait on January 26, 1526, but he was beaten back by storms as far as the river Santa Cruz. On April 8, he once more attempted the passage, and emerged into the Pacific on May 25.

Simon de Alcazaba, who in 1534 attempted to pass the Magellans with a number of emigrants for Peru was less successful, but in 1539 Alfonso de Camargo, having lost two vessels in the strait, passed it with the third, and reached the port of Callao.

Until now the Spanish flag had alone been seen in these remote and solitary waters, but the time was come when they were to open a passage to its most inveterate foes. On August 20, 1579, Francis Drake, commissioned by Queen Elizabeth to plunder and destroy the Spanish settlements on the west coast of America, ran into the strait, and on December 6 sallied forth into the Pacific.

To meet this formidable enemy, the Viceroy of Peru sent out in the same year two ships under Pedro Sarmiento de Gamboa. His orders were to intercept Drake's passage through the strait and then to sail on to Spain. Though he failed in the object of his mission, yet Sarmiento displayed in the navigation of the intricate and dangerous passages along the south-west coast of America, the courage and skill of a consummate seaman, and he gave the first exact and detailed account of the land and waters of Fuegia. His voyage, according to the weighty testimony of Captain King, deserves to be noted as one of the most useful of the age in which it was performed.

On his arrival in Spain, Sarmiento strongly pointed out the necessity of establishing a colony and erecting a fort in the strait (at that time the only known passage to the Pacific), so as effectually to prevent the recurrence of a future hostile expedition, like that of Drake. Commissioned by Philip II. to carry his plans into execution, he founded a colony, to which he gave the name of Ciudad de San Felipe, but a series of disasters entirely destroyed it; and when, a few years later, Cavendish, who had fitted out three ships at his own expense to imitate the example of Drake, appeared in the strait, he found but three survivors of many hundreds, and gave the scene of their misery the appropriate name of Port Famine, which it has retained to the present day.

After Cavendish and Hawkins (1594), the Dutch navigators De Cordes (1599), Oliver Van Noort (1599), and Spilberg (1615), attempted, with more or less success, to sail through the strait with the intention of harassing and plundering the Spaniards on the coast of the Pacific.

Strange to say, no attempt had been made since Magellan to discover a passage further to the south, so universal and firmly established was the belief that Fuegia extended without interruption to the regions of eternal ice, until at length, in 1616, the Dutchmen, Schouten and Le Maire, discovered the passage round Cape Horn. Two years later, Garcia de Nodales sailed through the Strait of Le Maire, and returning through the Magellans into the Atlantic was thus the first circumnavigator of Fuegia. In 1669, Sir John Narborough having been sent out by King Charles II. to explore the Magellanic regions, furnished a good general chart of the strait, and many plans of the anchorage within it.

More than sixty years now elapsed before any expedition of historical renown made its appearance in the strait. The dangers and hardships which had assailed the previous navigators, discouraged their successors, who all preferred the circuitous way round Cape Horn to the shorter but, as it was at that time considered, more perilous route through the strait. After this long pause, Byron (December, 1764) and Bougainville (February, 1765) once more attempted the Magellans. The difficulties encountered by them were surpassed by those of Wallis and Carteret. The former spent nearly four months (from December 17, 1766, to April 11, 1767) in a perpetual conflict with stormy weather while slowly creeping through the strait; and the latter required eighty-four days for his passage from Port Famine to Cape Pillar. No wonder that the next circumnavigators, Lütke, Krusenstern, Kotzebue, preferred sailing round Cape Horn, and that adventurous seal hunters became for a long time the sole visitors of these ill-famed waters. At length the British Government came to a resolution worthy of England, and resolved to have the Magellanic regions carefully surveyed, and to conquer them, as it were, anew for geographical science. Under the command of Captain King, the 'Adventure' and the 'Beagle' were engaged in this arduous task from 1826 to 1830; but such were the dangers they had to encounter, that Captain Stokes, the second in command, after contending for four months with the storms and currents which frequently threatened to dash his vessel against the cliffs, became so shattered in mind and body, that after his return to Port Famine he committed suicide in a fit of melancholy.

From 1831 to 1834, Captain Fitzroy was engaged in completing the survey of Patagonia and Tierra del Fuego, and the result of all these labours was a collection of charts and plans which have rendered navigation in those parts as safe as can be expected in the most tempestuous region of the globe.

While formerly the passage round Cape Horn was universally preferred, the more accurate knowledge of the Strait of Magellan, for which navigation is indebted to the labours of King and Fitzroy, has since then turned the scale in favour of the latter.

For a trading-vessel, with only the ordinary number of hands on board, the passage through the strait from east to west is indeed generally very difficult, and even dangerous; but in the opposite direction, the almost constant westerly winds render it commodious and easy, particularly during the summer months, in which they are most prevalent.

For small vessels—clippers, schooners, cutters—the passage in both directions is, according to the excellent authority of Captain King, much to be preferred. Such vessels have far more reason for fearing the heavy seas about Cape Horn; they can more easily cross against the west winds, as their manœuvres are generally very skilful, and they find in the Sound itself a great number of anchoring places, which are inaccessible to larger vessels.

For steamers the advantage is entirely on the side of the strait, and they consequently now invariably prefer this route. Here they find plenty of wood, which enables them to save their coals; and moreover, from Cape Tamar as far as the Gulf of Penas, an easy navigation for about 360 sea miles through the channels along the west coast of America.

As the trade of the Pacific is continually increasing, and the strait of Magellan more frequented from year to year, we cannot wonder that the old project of settling a colony on its shores should have been revived in our days. About the year 1840 the government of Chili established a penal colony at Punta Arenas and Port Famine, which miserably failed in consequence of a mutiny; but in 1853, about 150 German emigrants were settled at Punta Arenas, and when the 'Novara' visited the strait in 1858, they were found in a thriving condition. Should the project of stationing steam-tugs in the strait, and of erecting lighthouses at Cape Virgins and at

the entrance of Smyth Channel,* be executed, the Magellans
would become one of the high-roads of commerce, and the
dangers which proved so dreadful to the navigators of former
days, a mere tale of the past.

* The 'Nassau,' under the command of Captain Richard Mayne, is at present
engaged in completing the survey of the Straits of Magellan and of Smyth
Channel. She arrived in December 1866, and will most probably be employed
three years on a task which proves the increasing importance of the passage.

Wandering Albatross.

Group of Patagonians.

# CHAPTER XXXIX.

## PATAGONIA AND THE PATAGONIANS.

Difference of Climate between East and West Patagonia—Extraordinary Aridity of East Patagonia—Zoology—The Guanaco—The Tucutuco—The Patagonian Agouti—Vultures—The Turkey-Buzzard—The Carrancha—The Chimango—Darwin's Ostrich—The Patagonians—Exaggerated Accounts of their Stature—Their Physiognomy and Dress—Religious Ideas—Superstitions—Astronomical Knowledge—Division into Tribes—The Tent or Toldo—Trading Routes—The Great Cacique—Introduction of the Horse—Industry—Amusements—Character.

PATAGONIA, the southern extremity of the American continent, is divided by the ridge of the Andes into two parts of a totally different character. Its western coast-lands, washed by the cold Antarctic current and exposed to the humid gales of a restless ocean, are almost constantly obscured with clouds and drenched with rain. Dense forests, dripping with moisture, clothe the steep hill sides; and from the coldness of the summer, the snow-line is so low, that for 650 miles northwards of Tierra del Fuego, almost every arm of the sea which penetrates to the interior higher chain is terminated by huge glaciers descending to the water's edge.

East Patagonia, on the contrary, a vast plain rising in successive terraces from the Atlantic to the foot of the Cordillera, is one of the most arid regions of the globe. The extreme dryness of the prevailing westerly winds, which have been totally deprived of their humidity before crossing the Andes, and the well rounded shingles which compose the soil, have entailed the curse of sterility on the land. Monotonous warm tints of brown, yellow, or light red, everywhere fatigue the eye, which vainly seeks for rest in the dark blue sky, and finds refreshing green only on some river banks.

Many broad flat vales transsect the plains, and in these the vegetation is somewhat better. The streams of former ages have no doubt hollowed them out, for the rivers of the present day are utterly inadequate to the task. On account of the dryness of the atmosphere, the traveller may journey for days in these Patagonian plains without finding a drop of water. Springs are rare, and even when found are generally brackish and unrefreshing. While the 'Beagle' was anchoring in the spacious harbour of Port St. Julian, a party one day accompanied Captain Fitzroy on a long walk round the head of the harbour. They were eleven hours without tasting any water, and some of the party were quite exhausted. From the summit of a hill, to which the appropriate name of 'Thirsty Hill' was given, a fine lake was spied, and two of the party proceeded with concerted signals to show whether it was fresh water. The disappointment may be imagined when the supposed lake was found to be a snow-white expanse of salt, crystallised in great cubes.

The extreme dryness of the air, which imparts so sterile a character to the country, favours the formation of guano deposits on the naked islands along the coast, which are frequented by sea-birds. Protracted droughts are essential to the accumulation of this manure, for repeated showers of rain would wash it into the sea, and for this reason no guano deposits are found on the populous bird-mountains of the north. A similar dryness of the atmosphere favours the deposit at Ichaboe on the African coast, at the Kooria Nooria Islands in the Indian Ocean, and at the Chincha Islands on the Peruvian coast; and this kind of climate appears also to be particularly agreeable to the sea-birds.

Considering the excessive aridity of Patagonia, it seems surprising that the country should be traversed from west to east by such considerable rivers as the Rio Negro, the Gallegos, and the Santa Cruz; but all these have their sources in the Andes, and are fed by mountain torrents, which no doubt derive their waters from the atmospherical precipitations of the Pacific.

The zoology of Patagonia is as limited as its flora, and greatly resembles in its character that of the mountain regions of Chili, or of the Puna or high tableland of the tropical Andes of Peru and Bolivia, the height of which varies from 10,000 to 14,000 feet above the level of the sea.

In all these countries, situated in such different latitudes, the explorer is astonished to find not only the same genera, but even animals of the same species. The forest-loving race of monkeys is nowhere to be found in treeless Patagonia. None of the quadrumana ventures farther south than 29° lat., but on the borders of the Rio Negro, the northern boundary of Patagonia, some small bats are seen fluttering about in the twilight.

The dark brown yellow-headed *Galictis vittata*, an animal allied to the Civets and Genets, is likewise found there, but much more frequently its relation the Zorilla, which ranges from 30° lat. to the Strait of Magellan, and like the skunk of the north, has the power of discharging a fluid of an intolerably fetid odour.

The guanaco is the characteristic quadruped of the plains of Patagonia, where it is no less useful to man than the wild reindeer to the savage hunters of the north. It ranges from the Cordillera of Peru as far south as the islands near Cape Horn, but it appears to be more frequent on the plains of South Patagonia than anywhere else. It is of greater size than the llama, and resembles it so much that it was supposed to be the wild variety, until Tschudi, in his 'Fauna Peruana,' pointed out the specific difference between both. The guanaco is a more elegant animal, with a long, slender neck and fine legs; its fleece is shorter and less fine; its colour is brown, the under parts being whitish. It generally lives in small herds of from half a dozen to thirty in each; but on the banks of the Santa Cruz, Mr. Darwin saw one herd which contained at least five hundred. Though extremely shy and wary, it is no match for the cunning of the savage; and, before the horse was introduced into Patagonia, man most probably could not have existed in those arid plains without the guanaco. It easily takes to the water, and this accounts for its presence on the eastern islands of Fuegia, where it has been followed by the puma, or American lion, who likewise pursues it on the plateaus of the Cordillera, 12,000 feet above the level of the sea.

The Brazilian fox (*Canis Azaræ*) is also met with as far as the strait. It is somewhat smaller than our fox, but more robustly built. In Patagonia it preys chiefly upon the small rodents, with which the land, in spite of its sterility, is perhaps more richly stocked than any other country in the world. Among these the tucutuco (*Ctenomys magellanica*), which may briefly be described as a gnawer with the habits of a mole, is one of the most remarkable. It abounds near the strait, where the sandy plain is one vast burrow of these creatures. This curious animal makes, when beneath the ground, a very peculiar noise, consisting of a short nasal grunt, monotonously repeated about four times in quick succession, the name tucutuco being given in imitation of the sound. Where the animal is abundant, it may be heard at all times of the day, and sometimes directly beneath one's feet. The tucutuco is nocturnal in its habits; its food consists chiefly of roots, the search after which seems to be the cause of its burrowing.

Among the indigenous quadrupeds of Patagonia we find, moreover, a species of agouti (*Dasyprocta patagonica*), which in some measure represents our hare, but is about twice the size, and has only three toes on its hind feet; the elegant long-eared mara (*Dolichotis patagonicus*), which, unlike most burrowing animals, wanders, commonly two or three together, for miles from its home; the *Didelphis Azaræ*, a species of opossum; and the pichy (*Dasypus minutus*), a small armadillo, which extends as far south as 50° lat.

It would be vain to seek among the Patagonian birds for

the splendid plumage of the tropical feathered tribes; their colours are simple and monotonous, as those of the naked plains, which are their home. Many birds of prey of the warmer regions of America likewise frequent the arid wastes of Patagonia. When a horse chances to perish from fatigue or thirst, the Turkey-buzzard (*Vultur aura*?) begins to feast upon its carcase, and then the carrancha (*Polyborus brasiliensis*) and the chimango (*Polyborus chimango*) pick its bones clean. Though these birds, which well supply the place of our carrion-crows, magpies, and ravens, generally feed in common, they are by no means on a friendly footing. When the carrancha is quietly seated on the branch of a tree, or on the ground, the chimango often continues for a long time flying backwards and forwards, up and down, in a semicircle, trying each time, at the bottom of the curve, to strike its larger relative, which takes little notice except by bobbing its head. The carrancha, which is common in the dry and open countries, and likewise on the arid shores of the Pacific, is also found inhabiting the forests of West Patagonia and Tierra del Fuego. The chimango is much smaller than the carrancha. Of all the carrion feeders, it is generally the last which leaves the skeleton of a dead animal, and may frequently be seen within the ribs of a horse, like a prisoner behind a grating. It is frequently found on the sea-coast, where it lives on small fishes.

The condor may likewise be reckoned among the Patagonian birds, as it follows its prey, the guanaco, across the Strait of Magellan as far as the eastern lowlands of Tierra del Fuego. In the winter especially, when the cold forces vast numbers of geese and ducks to quit the Antarctic islands in the higher latitudes, all these birds of prey, to which the crowned falcon (*Circœtes coronatus*), the three-coloured buzzard (*Buteo tricolor*), the Aguia eagle (*Haliœtus aguia*), and several others must be added, live in luxury. Most of them are likewise migratory birds, and disappear in summer, with the defenceless tribes on which they prey. The Magellanic thrush (*Turdus magellanicus*) leaves in winter the stormy banks of the strait, and retires to the milder skies of the Rio Negro, where it meets the tuneful Patagonian warbler (*Orpheus patagonicus*), the nimble troglodyte (*Troglo-*

*dytes pallida*), and the inconstant fly-catcher (*Muscicapæ parvulus*).

A peculiar species of ostrich, the nandu (*Rhea Darwini*), roams over the plains of southern Patagonia, as far as the Strait of Magellan. It is smaller than the South American ostrich (*Rhea americana*), which inhabits the country of La Plata, as far as a little south of the Rio Negro; but it is more beautiful, as its white feathers are tipped with black at the extremity, and its black ones in like manner terminate in white.

In the same high latitude one is surprised to meet with a member of the parrot tribe, *Psittacus patagonicus*, feeding on the seeds of the winter's bark, and to see humming-birds (*Trochilus forficatus*) flitting about during the snow-storms in the forests of Tierra del Fuego.

The plains of Patagonia are inhabited by a race of Indians supposed to be gigantic, but the descriptions of modern travellers have dispelled the idea. Thus Pigafetti, the companion of Magellan, relates that the Europeans only reach to the waist of the Patagonians; Simon de Weert tells us that they are from 10 to 11 feet high; Byron, who visited them in the last century, reduces them to 7 feet, and Captain King finally, who accurately measured them, found the medium height of the males about five feet eleven inches. As the Patagonians have most likely not degenerated within the last few centuries, we may infer from these various accounts, that the travellers of the present day are less prone to exaggeration than those of more ancient times. So much is certain, that the Patagonians are a fine athletic race of men, with remarkably broad shoulders and thick muscular limbs. The head is long, broad, and flat, and the forehead low, with the hair growing within an inch of the eyebrows, which are bare; the eyes are often placed obliquely, and have but little expression; the forehead and the large lips are prominent, so that if a perpendicular line were drawn between the two, the thick flat nose would hardly reach it, and but seldom project beyond it. In spite of these coarse features the physiognomy of the young girls is by no means unpleasant, as it has an amiable, lively expression. All of them have small hands and feet, and D'Orbigny says that they have the finest shapes of all the savages he saw. Though they have a wide mouth and thick lips, this fault is redeemed by their beautiful white teeth, which never fall out even in old age.

The colour of the Patagonians is much darker than that of the Pampas Indians, and others further to the north, and most closely resembles that of the mulatto; a fact totally at variance with the common belief that the darkness of the human skin increases on approaching the equator.

The chief garment is the *manuhé*, a wide, square mantle— eight feet long and nearly as broad—which they wear after the fashion of the ancient Greeks and Romans, with one end hanging down to the earth. It generally consists of guanaco skins neatly sewn together with ostrich sinews. In cold weather the manuhé, which serves also as a blanket, is worn with the hair inside; the even surface is therefore orna- mented with red drawings. Sometimes they wear boots of horse-leather, like the Gauchos, from whom they have learnt to make them; formerly sandals of guanaco-skin were alone in use. Their long black hair is tied behind with a thong of leather, or a piece of ribbon; the women plait and adorn it with a number of ornaments of glass and copper. The face is generally painted red, white, and black, and a Patagonian is never seen without the little pouch in which he carries the necessary colours. A remarkable custom, common to all the Indian tribes as far as Bolivia, is that of eradicating the hairs of the beard, and the men may frequently be seen plucking them out with a pair of pincers.

The religious ideas of the Patagonians greatly resemble those of their neighbours the Aucas and the Puelches. The divine Achekenat Kanet is reverenced as the genius both of good and evil; but beside this chief deity they have a number of inferior spirits, generally of a malignant nature, which can be held in check only by the arts of their magicians. Like the shamans, or medicine-men of the north, these im- postors work themselves into an ecstatic state, in which they predict things to come, or announce the will of the unseen gods; but their trade does not seem to be very lucrative if we may judge from the bad condition of their mantles. They also act as physicians, for all diseases are invariably ascribed to the agency of evil spirits.

The Patagonians are quite as superstitious as the Indians of the high northern latitudes. They seldom cut their hair, but when they do, they cast it into the river, or carefully burn it, so that it may not fall into the hands of some malignant magician who might use it ·to the hurt of its quondam owner. When, on journeying along a river, they see some trunks of trees descending with the current, they take them for evil spirits, and address them with a loud voice. If by chance the trees are swept by less rapidly, or are driven round in a whirlpool, they believe that this takes place for the purpose of hearing them. They then make them liberal promises, which they faithfully keep. They cast their weapons, their ornaments, sometimes even their horses with bound feet, into the water, fully persuaded that by this sacrifice they have averted the misfortunes that otherwise would have befallen them. Like many other savage nations, they believe in a future paradise, where they expect to find again all that they prized on earth. For this reason they immolate over the graves of their friends all the animals that belonged to them, and inter with them all they possessed.

The astronomical knowledge of the Patagonians is surprising in a people ranking so low in the scale of civilisation. Continually migrating over their arid land, they soon felt the necessity of directing their movements during the day by the position of the sun, during the night by the stars; and thus they gradually learnt to observe the march of the constellations, and to note the times of their appearance and disappearance, giving them names, so as to be able to communicate their observations to each other. Their lively fancy traces in the starry firmament the picture of the Indian's hunting expedition. The milky way is the path on which he follows the ostrich; the 'Three Kings' are the bolas or balls with which he strikes the bird whose feet form the Southern Cross; and the Magellanic clouds are heaps of its feathers that have been collected by its pursuer.

When the Patagonians speak of the direction they intend to follow, from north to south or from east to west, they always indicate the constellations; so that in these South

American plains, as in those of Chaldea, a similar necessity has led man to lay the first foundations of astronomical knowledge.

The Patagonians are divided into a number of small migratory tribes, each consisting of, at the utmost, thirty or forty families. As they live exclusively by the chase, it is evident that a few days would suffice to destroy or to drive away the game of a great extent of territory were they to assemble in larger numbers. Not to perish of want, they are thus compelled to wander from place to place in small companies, and to carry along with them their leathern toldos or tents. The toldo reposes on a frame of poles stuck into the earth, and is scarcely higher than six feet in its centre, so that one can hardly imagine how a family of tall Patagonians can live in so small a space. The door is invariably to the east, so that early in the morning the chief of the family may sprinkle before it a few drops of water as an offering to the rising sun, for were this sacrifice to be neglected, the evil spirits would infallibly wreak their vengeance upon the inmates of the tent. Horse-hides, or guanaco skins coarsely sewn together, cover the frame, and afford but a scanty protection against the rain and the much more frequent wind. At the top, as in the Laplander's hut, an opening is left to let out the smoke. The hearth is in the middle, and close by lie some earthen vases, and large volute shells which serve as drinking horns. The inmates lie on skins, or sit in a corner cross-legged, after the Oriental fashion. The excessive filth of these wretched tenements makes their poverty appear still more squalid than it really is. Thirty or forty toldos form a migratory village or tolderia. Though the dreadful small-pox epidemic from 1809 to 1812 destroyed whole tribes of Patagonians, their present number may still be estimated at from eight to ten thousand; a small one when compared with the size of the country, yet large enough when we consider the sterile nature of its soil and the vast space of desert needed to feed a sufficient number of guanacos and horses for the wants of even a scanty population. Each tolderia appears to have its territory limited by the hunting-grounds of its neighbours, but commercial transactions take place between the various tribes, and occasion

longer journeys.   One of the chief trading routes runs
along the eastern foot of the Andes, from the Strait of
Magellan to the Rio Negro, as water is here everywhere
found; another, leading parallel with the coast from the
Rio Negro to Port St. Julian and Port Desire, is only
frequented in the rainy season, and even then there are wide
spaces without any sweet water, and where it is necessary to
travel night and day so as to avoid the danger of dying of
thirst.

Every year the various Patagonian tribes wander to the
sources of the Rio Negro, where they provide themselves with
Araucaria seeds, which serve them as food, or with apples,
which have multiplied on the eastern spurs of the Andes in
the same astonishing manner as the peach trees near the
mouths of the La Plata.   The apple tree was introduced by
the first Spaniards who inhabited the Chilian Andes soon
after the conquest; and when later the intruders were expelled
by the victorious Araucanians, the natives found their country
enriched by this valuable acquisition.

One of the chief bartering rendezvous is the island Chole-
chel, which is formed by two arms of the Rio Negro, about
eighty leagues from the mouth of the river.   Here the
Patagonian exchanges his guanaco skins for the articles
which the Puelches, his northern neighbours, either fabricate
themselves or procure in a more easy manner by stealing
them from the white settlers in their neighbourhood.   This
bartering trade is very ancient, and has always existed excepting in times of war.   In this manner the Patagonians
were provided with horses, soon after the introduction of
this valuable animal into the New World; and thus also
articles of Spanish manufacture soon found their way as far
as the Strait of Magellan.

At present there seems to be peace among all the Patagonian tribes, which consider themselves as brothers, though
frequently separated several hundred leagues from each
other.

Their system of government is very simple.   The whole
nation has a chief or great cacique, whom they call carasken,
and whose authority is very limited.   In war, he presides in
the assembly of the minor chiefs, and has the supreme com-

mand in battle. In peace, his sway is confined to his own tribe. He is as poor as his subjects, and far from enjoying a copious civil list, is obliged to hunt for his subsistence like every other Patagonian; the only advantage he owes to his exalted station being a somewhat larger share of the products of the chase; and this he is obliged to distribute among the more needy of his followers, to maintain his influence. The dignity of carasken is not always hereditary. To succeed his father, the son must first prove by his eloquence, his courage, and his liberality, that he is worthy to succeed him; and if he is found wanting, the Indian most distinguished by his moral and intellectual qualities is elected in his place.

The Patagonians are very awkward fishermen; they merely catch what chance throws into their hands, and are unacquainted with nets, or any other piscatorial artifice. In this respect they are totally different from the Fuegians, who derive their chief subsistence from the sea. They have ever been a nation of hunters, and before the introduction of the horse, they pursued their game on foot, using their bolas with great dexterity for the destruction of the guanaco and the ostrich. Their dogs afforded them a valuable assistance, and since they have become accomplished horsemen, their fleet coursers enable them to overtake with ease all the animals of the wilderness. In times of scarcity they dig for a small root, which is either eaten fresh or preserved dry. Horse flesh is their favourite food.

The Patagonian toldos and their weapons are very rudely made, but their skin mantles are not untastefully ornamented with rectilinear figures. In their war dress they have a very hideous appearance, and it would be difficult to imagine a more diabolical figure than that of a tall Patagonian ready for a fight, his broad face painted scarlet, with black or blue stripes under the eyes, and his coarse features distorted with fury. Their arms are bows and arrows, with points of flint loosely attached with sinews, so as to remain sticking in the wound. They are excellent archers, and use with skill the sling, the javelin, and above all their formidable bolas, which serve them both for bringing the guanaco to the ground, or for breaking the skull of an enemy. When not engaged in war or in the chase, the men, like most savages, pass their time in absolute idleness, leaving all the household work to the women. Amusements they have but few. The use of dice they have learnt from the Spaniards. They are said to be a false and deceitful people, but their hospitality and good nature have been frequently extolled by travellers.

The Guanaco.

Staten Island—Cape Horn.
(From an original sketch by Frederick Whymper.)

## CHAPTER XL.

### THE FUEGIANS.

Their miserable Condition—Degradation of Body and Mind—Powers of Mimicry —Notions of Barter—Causes of their low State of Cultivation—Their Food— Limpets—Cyttaria Darwini—Constant Migrations—The Fuegian Wigwam— Weapons—Their probable Origin—Their Number, and various Tribes—Constant Feuds—Cannibalism—Language—Adventures of Fuegia Basket, Jemmy Button, and York Minster—Missionary Labours—Captain Gardiner — His lamentable End.

THE wilds of Tierra del Fuego are inhabited by a race of men generally supposed to occupy the lowest grade in the scale of humanity. In a far more rigorous climate, the Esquimaux, their northern antipodes, exhibit skill in their snow huts, their kayaks, their weapons, and their dress ; but the wretched Fuegians are ignorant of every useful art that could better their condition, and contrive scarcely any defence against either rain or wind.

But even among the Fuegians there are various grades of civilisation—or rather barbarism. The eastern tribes, which inhabit the extensive plains of King Charles' South Land,

seem closely allied to the Patagonians, and are a very different race from the undersized wretches further westward. A
mantle of guanaco skin, with the wool outside—the usual
Patagonian garment—loosely thrown over their shoulders,
and leaving their persons as often exposed as covered,
affords them some protection against the piercing wind.
The condition of the central tribes inhabiting the south-
western bays and inlets of this dreary country, is much
more miserable. Those further to the west possess seal
skins, but here the men are satisfied with an otter skin
or some other covering scarcely larger than a pocket hand-
kerchief. It is laced across the breast by strings, and
according as the wind blows it is shifted from side to side.
But all have not even this wretched garment, for near
Wollaston Island, Mr. Darwin saw a canoe with six Fuegians,
one of whom was a woman, naked. It was raining heavily,
and the fresh water, together with the spray, trickled down
their bodies. In another harbour, not far distant, a woman,
who was suckling a recently-born child, came one day along-
side the vessel, and remained there out of mere curiosity,
whilst the sleet fell and thawed on her naked bosom and on the
skin of her naked baby! These poor wretches were stunted
in their growth, their faces bedaubed with white paint,
their skins filthy, their hair entangled, their voices discordant,
and their gestures violent.

The Fuegians whom Cook met with in Christmas Sound
were equally wretched. Their canoes were made of the bark
of trees stretched over a framework of sticks, and the paddles
which served to propel these miserable boats were small,
and of an equally miserable workmanship. In each canoe
sat from five to eight persons, but instead of greeting the
strangers with the joyful shouts of the South Sea Islanders,
they rowed along in perfect silence; and even when quite
close to the vessel, they only uttered from time to time
the word 'Pescheräh!' After repeated invitations some
of these savages came on board, but without exhibiting the
least sign of astonishment or curiosity. None were above
5 feet 4 inches high; they had large heads, broad faces, with
prominent cheek-bones, flat noses, small and lack-lustre
eyes; and their black hair, smeared with fat, hung in

matted locks over their shoulders. Instead of a beard, their chin exhibited a few straggling bristles, and their whole appearance afforded a striking picture of abject misery. Their shoulders and breast were broad and strongly built, but the extremities of the body so meagre and shrivelled, that one could hardly realize the fact that they belonged to the upper part. The legs were crooked, the knees disproportionately thick. Their sole garment consisted of a small piece of seal skin, attached to the neck by means of a cord, otherwise they were quite naked ; but even these miserable creatures had made an attempt to decorate their olive-brown skin with some stripes of ochre. The women were as ugly as the men. Their food consisted of raw, half-putrid seal's flesh, which made them smell so horribly, that it was impossible to remain long near them. Their intelligence was on a par with the filth of their bodies. The most expressive signs were here of no avail. Gestures which the most dull-headed native of any South Sea island immediately understood, these savages either did not, or would not give themselves the trouble to comprehend. Of the superiority of the Europeans they appeared to have no idea, never expressing by the slightest sign any astonishment at the sight of the ship and the various objects on board. It would however be doing the Fuegians injustice to suppose them all on a level with these wretches. According to Forster, they were most likely outcasts from the neighbouring tribes.

Mr. Darwin, as well as Sir James Ross, describes the Fuegians whom they met with in the Bay of Good Success, and on Hermit Island, as excellent mimics. ' As often as we coughed or yawned,' says the former, ' or made any odd motion, they immediately imitated us. Some of our party began to squint and look awry, but one of the young Fuegians (whose whole face was painted black, excepting a white band across his eyes) succeeded in making far more hideous grimaces. They could repeat with perfect correctness each word in any sentence we addressed them, and they remembered such words for some time. Yet we all know how difficult it is to distinguish apart the sounds in a foreign language.'

Close to the junction of Ponsonby Sound with the Beagle Channel, where Mr. Darwin and his party spent the night, a small family of Fuegians soon joined the strangers round a blazing fire. They seemed well pleased, and all joined in the chorus of the seamen's songs. During the night the news had spread, and early in the morning other Fuegians arrived. Several of these had run so fast that their noses were bleeding, and their mouths frothed from the rapidity with which they talked; and with their naked bodies all bedaubed with black, white, and red, they looked like so many demons.

These people plainly showed that they had a fair notion of barter. Mr. Darwin gave one man a large nail (a most valuable present) without making any signs for a return; but he immediately picked out two fish, and handed them up on the point of his spear. Here at least we see signs of a mental activity, favourably contrasting with the stolid indifference of the Fuegians seen by Forster at Christmas Harbour; and Mr. Darwin is even of opinion, that in general these people rise above the Australians in mental power, although their actual acquirements may be less.

The reason why the Fuegians are so little advanced in the arts of life, are partly to be sought for in the nature of the land, and partly in their political state. The perfect equality among the individuals in each tribe must retard their civilisation; and until some chief shall arise with power sufficient to secure any acquired advantage, such as the domesticated animals, it seems scarcely possible that their condition can improve. But the chief causes of their wretchedness are doubtless the barrenness of their country and their constant forced migrations.

With the exception of the eastern part, the habitable land is reduced to the stones on the beach. In search of food they are compelled to wander from spot to spot; and so steep is the coast, that they can only move about in their canoes. Whenever it is low water, winter or summer, night or day, they must rise to pick limpets from the rock; and the women either dive to collect sea-eggs, or sit patiently in their boats, and with a baited hair-line, without any hook, jerk out little fish. If a seal is killed, or the floating carcase of a putrid whale discovered, it is a feast; and such miserable food is assisted by a few tasteless berries, chiefly of a dwarf arbutus, or by a globular bright yellow fungus (*Cyttaria Darwinii*), which grows in vast numbers on the beech trees. When young, it is elastic, with a smooth surface; but, when mature, it shrinks, becomes tougher, and has its entire surface deeply pitted or honey-combed. In this mature state it is collected in large quantities by the women and children, and is eaten uncooked. It has a mucilaginous, slightly sweet taste, with a faint smell like that of a mushroom.

The necessity of protecting themselves against the extremity of cold, and of obtaining their food from the sea, or by the chase of the reindeer or the white bear, forces the Esquimaux to exert all their faculties, and thus they have raised themselves considerably higher in the scale of civilisation than the Fuegians, whose mode of life requires far less exertion of the mind. To knock a limpet from the rock, or to collect a fungus, does not even call cunning into exercise. Living chiefly upon shell-fish, they are obliged constantly to change their abode, and thus they hardly bestow any thought on their dwellings, which are more like the dens of wild beasts than the habitations of human beings. The Fuegian wigwam consists of a few branches stuck in the ground, and very imperfectly thatched on one side with a few tufts of grass and rushes. The whole cannot be the work of an hour, and it is only used for a few days. At intervals, however, the inhabitants of these wretched huts return to the same spot, as is evident from the piles of old shells, often amounting to several tons in weight. These heaps can be distinguished at a distance by the bright green colour of certain plants, such as the wild celery and scurvy grass, which invariably grow on them.

The only articles in the manufacture of which the Fuegians show some signs of ability are a few ornaments and their weapons, which again are far inferior to those of the Esquimaux. Their bows are small and badly shaped, their arrows, which are between two and three feet long, feathered at one end and blunted at the other. The points are only attached when the arrow is about to be used, and for this purpose the archer carries them about with him in a leathern pouch. The shaft of their larger spears is about ten feet long, and equally thick at both ends. At one of the extremities is a fissure, into which a pointed bone with a barbed hook is inserted and tightly bound with a thread. With this weapon they most probably attack the seals; they also use it to detach the shell fish from the rocks below the surface of the water. A second spear, longer and lighter than the first, with a barbed point, serves most likely as a weapon of war; and a third one, much shorter and comparatively thin, may perhaps be destined for the birds. The females know how to make pretty necklaces of coloured shells and baskets of grass stalks. Here, as with all other races of mankind, we find the germs of improvement, which only require for their development the external impulse of more favourable circumstances.

If it be asked whether they feel themselves as miserable as their wretched appearance would lead us to believe them, it must be replied that most travellers describe them as a cheerful, good-humoured, contented people; and as Mr. Darwin finely remarks, ' Nature, by making habit omnipotent and its effects hereditary, has fitted the Fuegian to the climate and the productions of his country.'

The number of these savages is no doubt very small, as seldom more than thirty or forty individuals are seen together. The interior of the mountainous islands, which is as little known as the interior of Spitzbergen, is no doubt completely uninhabited; as the coasts alone, with the exception of the eastern and more level part of the country, where the guanaco finds pasture, are able to furnish the means of subsistence. The various tribes, separated from each other by a deserted neutral territory, are nevertheless engaged in constant feuds, as quarrels are perpetually arising about the possession of some limpet-bank or fishing-station. When at war they are cannibals; and it is equally certain that when pressed in winter by hunger they kill and devour their old women before they kill their dogs, alleging as an excuse that their dogs catch otters, and old women do not.

It has not been ascertained whether they have any distinct belief in a future life. They sometimes bury their dead in

caves, and sometimes in the mountain forests. Each family
or tribe has a wizard, or conjuring doctor. Their language,
of which there are several distinct dialects, is likewise little
known; it is, however, far inferior to the copious and expressive vocabulary of the Esquimaux.

In 1830, while Captain Fitzroy was surveying the coasts of
Fuegia, he seized on a party of natives as hostages for the loss
of a boat which had been stolen, and some of these natives,
as well as a child belonging to another tribe, whom he bought
for a pearl button, he took with him to England, determining
to educate them at his own expense. One of them afterwards
died of the small-pox; but a young girl, Fuegia Basket, and two
boys, Jemmy Button (thus named from his purchase money)
and York Minster (so called from the great rugged mountain of
York Minster, near Christmas Sound), were placed in a school
at Walthamstow, and moreover had the honour of being presented to King William and Queen Adelaide. Three years
Jemmy and his companions remained in England, at the
end of which time Captain Fitzroy was again sent out to
continue the survey, and took with him these three Fuegians,
intending to return them to the place whence they had come.
In this, however, he was disappointed; but at their own
request York and Fuegia were, with Jemmy, deposited
at Woollya, a pleasant looking spot in Ponsonby Sound,
belonging to Jemmy's tribe. His family, consisting of his
mother and three brothers, was absent at the time, but they
arrived the following morning. Jemmy recognised the sten-
torian voice of one of his brothers at a prodigious distance,
but the meeting, as Mr. Darwin who witnessed the scene
relates, was less interesting than that between a horse turned
out into a field and an old companion. There was no demonstration of affection; they simply stared for a short time
at each other. Three large wigwams were built for them,
gardens planted, and an abundant supply of everything
landed for their use. Jemmy, who had become quite a
favourite on board, was short and fat, but vain of his personal appearance; he used always to wear gloves, his hair
was neatly cut, and he was distressed if his well-polished
shoes were dirtied. York was somewhat coarse and less
intelligent, though in some things he could be quick. He

became attached to Fuegia, and as both were of the same tribe, they became man and wife after their return to Tierra del Fuego. She was the most intelligent of the three, and quick in learning anything, especially languages.

Thus these semi-civilised savages were left among their barbarous countrymen, with the hope that they might become the means of improving their whole tribe; but when Captain Fitzroy returned to the spot twelve months after, he found the wigwams deserted and the gardens trampled under foot. Jemmy came paddling up in his canoe, but the dandy who had been left plump, clean, and well dressed, was now turned into a thin, haggard savage, with long disordered hair, and naked, except a bit of a blanket round his waist. He could still speak English, and said that he had enough to eat, that he was not cold, and that his relations were very good people. He had a wife besides, who was decidedly the best looking female in the company. With his usual good feeling, he brought two beautiful otter-skins for two of his best friends, and some spear heads and arrows made with his own hands for the Captain. He had lost all his property. York Minster had built a large canoe, and with his wife Fuegia had, several months since, gone to his own country, and had taken farewell by an act of consummate villany. He persuaded Jemmy and his mother to come with him, and then on the way deserted them by night, stealing every article of their property. It was the opinion of all on board that the cunning rogue had planned all this long before, and that with this end in view he had desired so earnestly to remain with Jemmy's tribe, rather than be landed on his own country. Eight years after, an English vessel put into a bay in the Magellans for water, and there was found a woman, without doubt Fuegia Basket, who said, 'How do? I have been to Plymouth and London.' York Minster was also seen in 1851. From Captain Snow, commander of the mission yacht, 'Allen Gardiner,' we have the last accounts of Jemmy Button in 1855. Twenty-three years had not obliterated his knowledge of the English language, but he was as wild and shaggy as his untaught countrymen. In spite of his superior knowledge, he was treated as a very inferior personage by the members of his tribe; yet he declared that though he loved England, he loved his country still better; that nothing should induce him to leave it, and that he would never allow any of his children to quit their native soil.

Other efforts have been made to civilise the Fuegians. A Spanish vessel having been shipwrecked on the eastern coast in 1767, its crew was hospitably treated by the natives, who even assisted in saving the cargo. Out of gratitude, the governor of Buenos Ayres sent out some missionaries, who, however, totally failed to make any impression on the savages.

A no less unsuccessful attempt was made about the year 1835 by English missionaries; and the expedition of Captain Gardiner, who, accompanied by a surgeon, a catechist, and four Cornish fishermen, sailed to Fuegia in 1851, with the intention of converting the natives, proved equally fruitless, and had a far more tragic end. His measures for securing the necessary supplies of food were so ill calculated, that the whole party died of hunger in Spaniards' Harbour, on the southern coast. Captain Morshead, of the 'Dido,' had received orders on his way to Valparaiso to visit the scene of the mission, and afford Captain Gardiner any aid he might require, but, on arriving at the cove, he found it deserted. After a few days' search the bodies were discovered, and fragments of a journal written by Captain Gardiner gave proof of the sufferings which they had endured before death relieved them from their misery.

The Penguin.

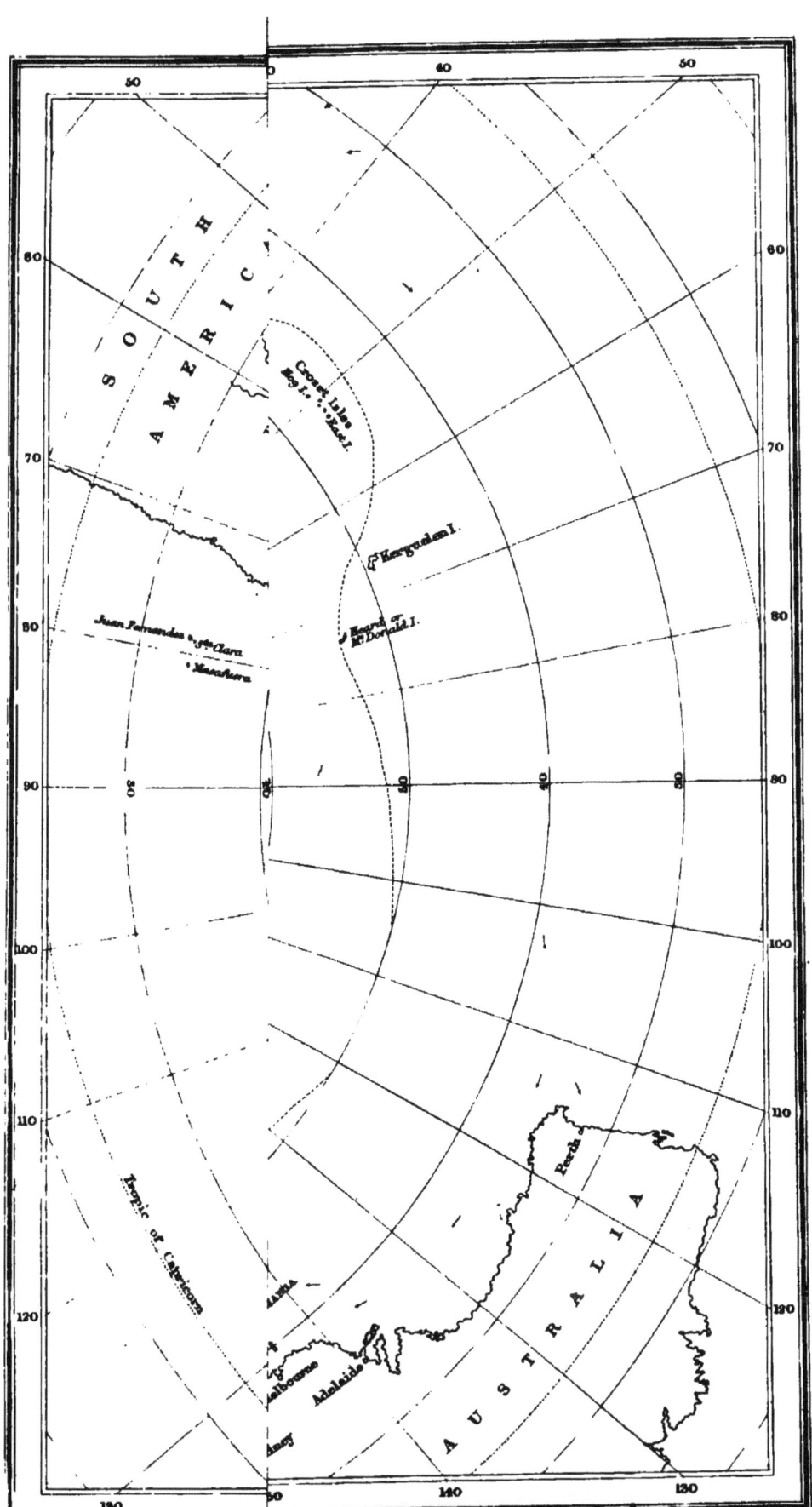

# INDEX.

LONDON: PRINTED BY
SPOTTISWOODE AND CO., NEW-STREET SQUARE
AND PARLIAMENT STREET

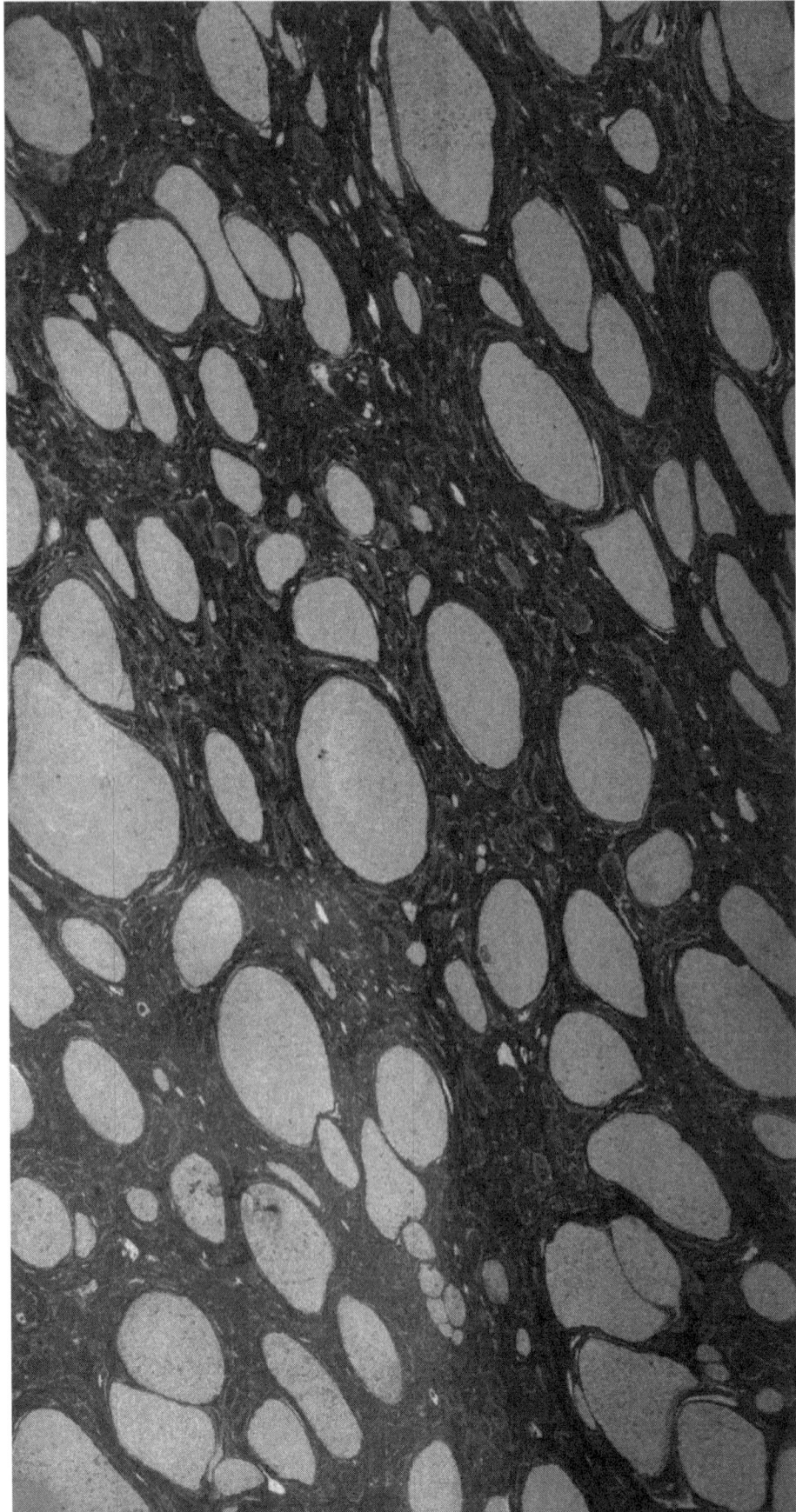

Lightning Source UK Ltd.
Milton Keynes UK
UKHW031331150119
335608UK00005B/312/P